Applied Managerial Statistics

Park J. Ewart

James S. Ford

Chi-Yuan Lin

University of Southern California
Los Angeles, California

PRENTICE-HALL, INC., ENGLEWOOD CLIFFS, NEW JERSEY   07632

Library of Congress Cataloging in Publication Data

Ewart, Park J.
    Applied managerial statistics.

    Includes index.
    1. Management—Statistical methods.   2. Mathe-
matical statistics.   3. Statistical decision.
I. Ford, James S.   II. Lin, Chi-Yuan.
III. Title.
HD30.25.E95   519.5′024658   81-15347
ISBN 0-13-041335-6   AACR2

To **JANET**
     JIM
     MEI-TAI

Editorial/production supervision and interior design by *Barbara Grasso*
Cover design by *Diane Saxe*
Manufacturing buyer: *Edward O'Dougherty*

Printed in the United States of America

10   9   8   7   6   5   4   3   2   1

ISBN 0-13-041335-6

PRENTICE-HALL INTERNATIONAL, INC., *London*
PRENTICE-HALL OF AUSTRALIA PTY. LIMITED, *Sydney*
PRENTICE-HALL OF CANADA, LTD., *Toronto*
PRENTICE-HALL OF INDIA PRIVATE LIMITED, *New Delhi*
PRENTICE-HALL OF JAPAN, INC., *Tokyo*
PRENTICE-HALL OF SOUTHEAST ASIA PTE. LTD., *Singapore*
WHITEHALL BOOKS LIMITED, *Wellington, New Zealand*

Contents

3

Descriptive Measures of
Finite Populations: Parameters   31

4

Introduction to Probability   51

5

Probabilities of Events   66

Contents

8

Sampling Methods and Sample Statistics   143

9

Discrete Sampling Distributions   159

10

The Hypothesis-Testing Approach to Two-Action Decision Problems   183

11

Hypothesis Testing with Discrete Sampling Distributions   200

Contents

Contents

Preface

This book was written in response to a need, repeatedly expressed by students and colleagues over the years, for an introductory statistics text that is conceptually rigorous and, at the same time, easily readable and obviously useful. As such, the book has the following distinguishing features:

- Explains difficult material in a style that can be understood by students and practitioners as well as instructors.
- Presents concepts and theory in a precise and accurate manner which avoids perpetuating common errors and misconceptions that repeatedly appear in introductory statistics texts.
- Discusses diverse topics in an integrated manner that stresses interrelationships and common themes.
- Supplies an abundance of realistic examples and problems that emphasize the application of statistical methods to managerial decisions rather than mere mathematical exercises.
- Treats statistical inference specifically as an approach to solving managerial decision problems.
- Provides extensive discussion and explanation of critical topics that students traditionally find particularly mystifying, such as the *concept* of a sampling distribution and the *rationale* of hypothesis formulation and testing.
- Emphasizes how the choice of statistical procedures depends on the level of the scale of measurement used in making sample observations.
- Distinguishes explicitly among methods based on discrete distributions, continuous distributions, and approximations.
- Employs clear and explicit mathematical notation that is consistent throughout the book.
- Includes extensive appendix tables especially prepared to enhance their readability and usability.

- Contains sufficiently broad coverage so that the instructor can select those topics that meet the needs of a particular course.

The book has been written with the presupposition that the student has had some exposure to elementary calculus, which makes it possible to present the underlying concepts of many statistical procedures in a more insightful way than can be done with algebra alone. The calculus used in the text is limited to simple polynomial functions, and even the student with no calculus background can handle the material with the aid of an appendix that provides a brief tutorial for self-study in the basic rules of integration.

With its balance between theory and application, and with a broad coverage of topics, the text may be used at either the undergraduate or graduate level in a course of one semester, two quarters, or a full year. The text is suitable for either a terminal course or a preparatory course for advanced work. Because of its conceptual rigor, the book abets rather than handicaps those students who wish to pursue higher level courses. The text will especially appeal to professors who are looking for a book that is accurate and avoids common myths, who feel that the use of the simplest calculus is not a serious drawback, who are concerned with stressing applications that are technically sound, and who want a text that presents complicated material in a style that the student can read and understand.

This volume is designed primarily for students in business management, public administration, and economics. It is also suitable as a basic reference or handbook for students, practitioners, and researchers in related disciplines, such as industrial and systems engineering, production and quality control, and the social sciences.

Beginning with a discussion of managerial decision making under uncertainty, Chapter 1 defines statistics as "a branch of scientific methodology dealing with the collection and analysis of numerical evidence for making inferences and decisions in the face of uncertainty." This is followed in Chapter 2 by a discussion of statistical data, including the concepts of observation, variables, and measurement scales, as well as basic methods of organizing and displaying data. Chapter 3 discusses descriptive measures of finite populations. Any discussion of statistics that are used to describe samples and estimate parameters is purposely postponed until Chapter 8, which introduces the concept of sampling.

Chapters 4 through 7 provide a solid foundation in fundamental probability theory necessary for understanding the reasoning underlying the statistical procedures presented later. These chapters are built on basic set theory, give detailed treatment to the concept of a random variable, and clearly distinguish between discrete and continuous probability distributions.

Chapters 8 and 9 introduce the concepts of sampling, sample statistics, and sampling distributions. At this point, descriptive statistics are presented as summary measures to describe characteristics of samples, and the distinction between parameters and descriptive statistics is emphasized. The basic idea of a sampling distribution, which is derived from probability concepts presented in earlier chapters, is illuminated by the development of the hypergeometric, binomial, and Poisson distributions specifically as sampling distributions applicable to particular types of sampling experiments.

In the authors' experience, beginning students find basic hypothesis-testing concepts easier to understand than the theoretically subtler concepts of estimation. Furthermore, they tend to grasp the rationale of hypothesis testing more readily with discrete, rather than continuous, sampling distributions. Thus, Chapter 10 introduces statistical inference with an extended example of a hypothesis-testing problem using a binomial sampling distribution. Treating hypothesis testing as an approach to managerial decision making, this chapter stresses the formulation of hypotheses and the error characteristics of decision rules from the viewpoint of the decision maker. The concepts presented in Chapter 10 are reinforced in Chapter 11, which presents applications of the hypergeometric, binomial, and Poisson distributions to hypothesis-testing problems.

Chapter 12 presents the concept of the sampling distribution of the sample mean, and introduces the normal distribution and central limit theorem in that context. Unlike other books which limit their consideration of the sampling distribution of the mean to the normal distribution, which is continuous, this chapter clearly demonstrates that the sampling distribution of the mean may be either discrete or continuous, depending on the population under investigation.

The concepts of Chapter 12 are applied in Chapter 13, which treats hypothesis tests concerning means of continuous population with known variances. Chapter 14 is devoted entirely to tests using approximations to discrete sampling distributions; these methods are set aside in a separate chapter in order to emphasize that they are indeed approximate procedures.

Chapter 15 is devoted to point and interval estimation of variances, means, and proportions. The t and chi-square distributions are introduced in this context.

Chapter 16, which treats testing of hypotheses concerning normal populations with unknown variances, presents applications of the t, chi-square, and F distributions. An important aspect of this chapter is that these procedures are *not* presented specifically as "small-sample" methods since, strictly speaking, sample size is irrelevant to these applications.

Chapters 17 and 18 are concerned with simple and multiple correlation and regression. The presentation in these chapters stresses practical caveats and the application of computer packages.

Chapters 19 and 20 are concerned with nonparametric methods, including popular applications of multinomial chi-square, Kolmogorov–Smirnov tests, and one- and two-sample tests of location. Considerable effort has been expended to make the presentation of these methods consistent with earlier presentations of parametric techniques.

The last three chapters are devoted to a presentation of decision analysis, which is becoming an increasingly popular topic in business statistics courses. Specifically, Chapter 21 examines various criteria for decision making under conditions of risk and uncertainty. Chapter 22 presents the basic concepts and procedures of decision analysis, including problem formulation, decision trees, value of information, and practical applications. Chapter 23 introduces the concept of utility and discusses the application of utility functions in decision analysis.

During the preparation of this book, we were fortunate to receive valuable assistance from numerous individuals. For reviewing the manuscript and providing helpful suggestions, we wish to extend our gratitude to Professor Austin J. Bonis of the Rochester Institute of Technology, Dr. Janet Fowler of the United States Naval Academy, Professor David K. Hildebrand of the University of Pennsylvania, Professor Arthur Kraft of the University of Nebraska at Lincoln, Professor Kathy Lewis Corriher of Columbia University, and Professor Terry G. Seaks of the University of North Carolina.

Special thanks are due to our colleagues in the Graduate School of Business Administration at the University of Southern California for their intellectual stimulation. Chris DeKlotz typed various versions of the manuscript. Ivy Cherng, Grace Feng, Glen Gomes, Joe Huang, and Andrew Yao performed the tedious tasks of preparing the preliminary art work, proofreading the manuscript, and helping prepare problem solutions. In addition, Beverly Smith read proof with a sharp editorial eye. To all of these, as well as those who remain unnamed, we express our deep appreciation.

We are grateful to the Literary Executor of the late Sir Ronald A. Fisher, F.R.S., to Dr. Frank Yates, F.R.S., and to Longman Group Ltd., London, for permission to reprint Table III from their book *Statistical Tables for Biological, Agricultural and Medical Research* (6th edition, 1974). We also extend our appreciation to Virginia J. Renner, Reader Services Librarian at the Huntington Library, San Marino, California, for providing access to the original printing of Sir John Sinclair's *Statistical Account of Scotland*, from which we quote in our opening chapter.

We will warmly welcome any corrections, comments, and suggestions from readers.

Park J. Ewart
James S. Ford
Chi-Yuan Lin

1

Statistics in Decision Making

The modern leader of a public or private enterprise—the manager—is often characterized as a person harassed by decision problems. Regardless of the size or type of enterprise and the functional area or level of responsibility, the primary role of a manager is to make decisions. This is true whether the manager is the top executive of a multinational corporation or the mayor of a small town. As the organizational and operational problems of business and government have become increasingly technical, and as the art and science of management have grown in complexity and precision, we have witnessed a developing awareness of the practicality of scientifically formal approaches to managerial decision making. Statistics provides one such approach to analyzing and resolving decision problems.

1.1 STATISTICAL DECISION PROBLEMS

The type of managerial decision problem to which the statistical approach is applicable may be conceptualized as follows:

1. There is a perceived need to attain some *goal* or *objective*.
2. There are two or more *alternative courses of action* that might possibly be taken to achieve this goal.
3. Because of *imperfect knowledge* concerning the factors that will determine the *result* or *consequence* of each of the alternative actions, it is not certain which course of action will best lead to satisfaction of the goal.
4. The degree of *uncertainty*, and hence the chances of making a wrong decision, may be reduced by obtaining additional information, usually at some cost.

As an illustration of this type of decision problem, consider the case of the Fairview Development Company, which holds an option to purchase a tract of scenic land on the shores of Green Valley Lake. The company management believes that this tract will be an excellent location for a condominium development *provided* that an initiative measure limiting the density of new housing in designated recreation areas is defeated in an upcoming statewide referendum.

1

The option to buy the land expires in 3 weeks, which is 10 days before the referendum is to be held. Thus, Fairview's decision regarding the purchase must be made before the fate of the initiative measure is known. If the company buys the land and the measure is defeated, management anticipates a handsome profit on the investment; but if the measure is passed, the market value of the land will immediately decline, and the company will suffer a financial loss. If the company decides not to buy the land and the measure is defeated, they will have missed the boat; but if the measure is passed, they will be even with the world—no better or worse than at present.

As a business enterprise, the Fairview Company has the basic goal of making the most profitable use of its resources. In the case of the Green Valley investment, there are two alternative actions available to the company as possible means of achieving this goal. We may denote these alternatives as

a_1: exercise the option
a_2: drop the option

The consequence resulting from either of these courses of action will depend on whether or not the initiative passes. Such conditions, which determine the specific consequences that will result from taking particular courses of action, are referred to by modern decision theorists as *states of nature*. Thus, in deciding between the two alternative courses of action, Fairview must consider two possible states of nature:

θ_1: initiative measure is defeated
θ_2: initiative measure is passed

Hence, as shown in Table 1.1, the consequence of Fairview's decision will depend, not only on which of the two alternative actions is chosen, but also on which of the two states of nature happens to occur. Thus, there are four different possible consequences, each associated with one of the four possible action–state pairs.

Table 1.1 Possible Consequences for Fairview's Decision Problem

| | Alternative Courses of Action | |
State of Nature	a_1: Exercise the Option	a_2: Drop the Option
θ_1: Initiative is defeated	Profit	Miss the boat
θ_2: Initiative is passed	Financial loss	Even

From Table 1.1 it is clear that the correct course of action for Fairview to take depends on the result of the referendum. That is, the act of exercising the option would turn out to be correct if the initiative is defeated, whereas the act of dropping the option would turn out to be correct if the initiative is passed. Thus, in making the decision, Fairview must consider the percentage of voters, out of the total number of people voting, who will cast their ballots against the initiative. Since Fairview must act before this percentage is determined by the referendum, the decision must be made in the face of uncertainty.

To obtain additional information that will reduce the uncertainty concerning the result of the referendum, Fairview decides to allocate a modest budget to hire a local research firm to poll a relatively small group of 400 registered voters throughout the state. If we regard the result of this poll as the number of people out of 400 who respond that they are against the initiative, then the number of such responses may be any integer between 0 and 400 inclusive. Thus, the poll has 401 possible outcomes, but *not all* of these possible outcomes are equally likely. For instance, if 75% of all those who intend to vote in the referendum actually are opposed to the initiative, then the percentage of people in the poll who are opposed to the initiative would more likely be near 75% than, say, 30%.

Although the poll has 401 possible outcomes, only one of these outcomes will actually occur. Now, the real questions are: After the actual outcome of the *poll* of 400 voters has been obtained, how can Fairview use this result to draw a conclusion concerning the percentage of *all* voters who are opposed to the initiative? Once such a conclusion has been drawn, how might Fairview proceed to make their decision regarding the real estate option? To answer these questions, we must appeal to statistical analysis.

1.2 BASIC STATISTICAL CONCEPTS

We have seen that the consequence of whichever course of action Fairview decides to take depends on whether or not the initiative measure is defeated in the referendum. Since the fate of the initiative is to be determined by the people voting at the referendum, Fairview is concerned with how all of these people will vote. This group, consisting of all the people voting in the referendum, is a statistical *population*. In popular usage the term "population" generally refers to the total number of people in some geographical area or political subdivision, such as the population of the United States or the population of Cook County, Illinois. To the statistician, however, "population" is a much broader concept. The term "population" (or *universe*) refers to any *entire* collection of elements under concern in a given situation. Thus, a population may be a group of human beings, as in the popular sense of the term, but it may just as well refer to any other collection of objects or phenomena, such as all of the articles produced by a particular manufacturing process, all of the dwelling units in a particular city, all of the industrial firms belonging to a particular industry, or all of the fatal accidents occurring on a particular stretch of a highway in a given year.

In the Fairview example, the population of persons voting in the referendum might be described in terms of a variety of properties which are *numerical* in nature. For example, this population might be described in terms of the *number* of men and the *number* of women in the population, or the *percentage* of the population who have blue eyes, or the *average weight* of the members of the population. Each of these numerical properties is a *parameter* of the population. Generally speaking, in statistics, a parameter is any *quantity* that describes some property of a population. The particular parameter of the voter population that critically affects the consequence of Fairview's decision is the percentage of the population who will vote against the initiative. Such a parameter, which influences the consequence of a decision, is called a *decision parameter*.

Although the critical parameter for Fairview's decision is the percentage of people voting against the initiative, the actual value of this parameter will not be known until after the time that the decision must be made. Thus, the decision must be made under uncertainty. Theoretically, it would be possible for Fairview essentially to eliminate this uncertainty by interviewing every prospective voter in the state. However, to survey an entire population is usually impractical or economically infeasible unless the population is small and easily accessible. Therefore, as we have seen, Fairview proposes to interview only 400 voters. Of course, the information obtained from interviewing this relatively small group will not eliminate, but will reduce, the uncertainty surrounding the decision. This group, which represents a small portion of the population, is called a *sample*. More generally, a sample is a *subset* of a population. The process of selecting a sample from a population is referred to as *sampling*.

A numerical quantity that is derived from the outcome of a sampling study is called a *statistic*. For example, from Fairview's sample of 400 voters it is possible to count the *number*, or to compute the *percentage*, of persons *in the sample* who are opposed to the initiative. Each of these numerical quantities is a statistic. Thus, more than one statistic may be obtained from a given sample.

The purpose of sampling is to obtain a sample which will yield partial information that can be used to draw conclusions concerning the entire population. This process of making generalizations about a population on the basis of limited evidence obtained from a sample is known as *statistical inference*. For example, suppose that the Fairview survey is conducted and that, out of the sample of 400 voters, 220 persons respond that they are opposed to the initiative. This figure of 220 respondents is a statistic. From this statistic we may compute $220/400 = 55\%$, which is another statistic representing the percentage of the sample who are opposed to the initiative. A common statistical procedure is to use such a sample percentage as an "estimate" of the corresponding population percentage. Thus, Fairview might draw the conclusion (that is, make the statistical inference) that 55% of the people in the entire voting population are opposed to the initiative.

On the basis of the inference that 55% of the voting population will vote against the initiative, Fairview can logically predict that the initiative will be defeated. As we can see from Table 1.1, if this prediction is correct, Fairview will make a profit by deciding to exercise the option to buy the land. However, this decision could result in a financial loss if the prediction should turn out to be wrong. It is entirely possible that the prediction could be wrong, since it is based on an inference that was drawn from the limited evidence obtained from a mere sample.

Even if the results of the poll show that 55% of the people in the *sample* are opposed to the initiative, the percentage of the voting *population* who are opposed to the initiative can still be less than 50%. Thus, if Fairview decides to exercise the option on the basis of the *prediction* that the initiative will be defeated, they still run the risk of suffering a financial loss. To avoid this risk, the company might decide to drop the option. In that case there would be no possibility of suffering an actual loss, but there also would be no possibility of making a profit. This situation places Fairview squarely in a dilemma. The ways and means of resolving such dilemmas are the province of *statistical decision theory*, which extends beyond the procedure of drawing statistical inferences to the process of making rational choices among alternative courses of action.

In modern scientific usage, statistics is regarded as a discipline that is concerned essentially with statistical inference and statistical decision theory. Hence, for the purposes of this book, we shall define *statistics* as a branch of scientific methodology dealing with the collection and analysis of numerical evidence for making inferences and decisions in the face of uncertainty.

The raw material from which evidence is extracted is called *data*. The term "data" is the plural of the Latin word *datum*, meaning "that which is given." In modern English, "data" simply means "facts." When data are *relevant* to a problem at hand, such data may be accepted as *evidence* with respect to that particular problem. Consider, for example, the courtroom attorney's familiar objection that particular testimony should not be allowed on the grounds that it is "irrelevant and immaterial." In other words, to be admissible as evidence, testimony must be relevant. When there is uncertainty regarding a decision parameter, evidence is considered to contain *information* if it leads to a reduction in the amount of uncertainty concerning the parameter.

Historically, the field of statistics evolved as an outgrowth of the body of techniques developed for collecting and compiling census records to meet the informational needs of governmental administrators. Thus, it is understandable that, in common usage, the term "statistics" has come to mean statistical data. However, it is important to distinguish between statistical data and the science of statistics itself. As Kendall has observed: ". . . The science of statistics, as distinct from the raw material with which it works, is an all-embracing branch of scientific method, and in its broadest interpretation is almost scientific method itself. We find statisticians at work in every field where quantitative evidence is available."[1]

1.3 HISTORICAL PERSPECTIVE

From its beginnings in the civilizations of the ancient world, statistics has evolved as a methodology for solving practical problems. Centuries before the word "statistics" was coined, leaders of the ancient civilizations had found the census to be a valuable means of obtaining quantitative information which was useful in solving problems concerning the administration of their domains. Censuses were used in ancient China, Babylonia, and Persia, for determining potential revenues and military strength in various provinces. Accounts of available manpower were used by the builders of the Egyptian pyramids. The Old Testament mentions the counting of military manpower at the Exodus, as well as by Joab under the command of David. Five-year censuses of persons and property were an important administrative procedure of the Roman Empire. As an aid in administering his domain, William the Conqueror had the greatest census of the Middle Ages performed in 1086. The account of this census was the famous *Domesday Book*, so named because it was designed to be as complete and final as the roll call at the Day of Judgment.

The modern word "statistics" is closely related to the word "state." During the Middle Ages, the Latin phrase *ratio status* was used to refer to the study of practical politics or the art of statesmanship. From this term developed the word *statista* to indicate a person skilled in public affairs. It has been claimed that it was from *statista* that the word *statistik* was derived as the German equivalent of *ratio status*.[2] To Achenwall, who is credited with bringing the word into general use during the last half of the eighteenth century, *statistik* encom-

---

[1]M. G. Kendall, "The History and Future of Statistics," in *Statistical Papers in Honor of George W. Snedecor*, ed. T. A. Bancroft (Ames, Iowa: The Iowa State University Press, 1972), p. 193.

[2]See *Encyclopedia of the Social Sciences*, ed. Edwin R. A. Seligman (New York: The Macmillan Company, 1934), Vol. 14, pp. 356–360.

passed *all* knowledge about the state. Gradually, the meaning of statistik evolved to refer only to the numerical characteristics of the state and to include the analysis and interpretation of these characteristics.

The word "statistics" was introduced into the English language by Sir John Sinclair, who used the term as the equivalent of the German "statistik." Late in the eighteenth century Sinclair conducted a census of Scotland that was published in a series of volumes which he entitled *A Statistical Account of Scotland.* In one of these volumes, he explains how he decided to use the new term:

> Many people were at first surprised, at my using the new words, *Statistics* and *Statistical*, as it was supposed, that some term in our own language, might have expressed the same meaning. But in the course of a very extensive tour, through the northern parts of Europe, which I happened to take in 1786, I found, that in Germany they were engaged in a species of political inquiry, to which they had given the name *statistics*; and though I apply a different idea to that word, for by Statistical is meant in Germany, an inquiry for the purpose of ascertaining the political strength of a country, or questions respecting *matters of state*; whereas, the idea I annex to the term, is an inquiry into the state of a country, for the purpose of ascertaining the *quantum of happiness enjoyed by its inhabitants and the means of its future improvement*; yet, as I thought that a new word might attract more public attention, I resolved on adopting it, and I hope that it is now completely naturalized and incorporated with our language.[3]

Sir John's hope has, of course, been more than satisfied. Indeed, his "new word" has become far broader in meaning than he likely ever imagined. Today, the term refers not specifically to a "state" or its inhabitants, but encompasses every facet of scientific inquiry.

The extension of the meaning of "statistics" beyond mere numerical facts concerning the state may be credited largely to Adolphe Quetelet, the great Belgian mathematician, scientist, and public administrator. The particular contribution of Quetelet, who is sometimes identified as the founder of modern statistics, was the incorporation of the mathematics of probability into statistical analysis and the practical application of such analysis to social and administrative problems. The foundations of probability theory had been developed during the seventeenth and eighteenth centuries by such scholars as Blaise Pascal, Jacques Bernoulli, and Abraham de Moivre. Much of this development of probability theory was given patronage by the European nobility, who were concerned with probabilities and strategies in gambling. However, it remained largely for Quetelet, during the middle of the nineteenth century, to apply the mathematical principles of probability to the analysis of political, biological, and social data. Quetelet organized his own country's statistical services as well as acting as statistical consultant to other governments. In this capacity he provided leadership in the development of governmental agencies for enumerating and measuring social conditions and behavior.

Although considerable development of basic statistical techniques occurred during the late 1800s, the field of applied statistics was still in its infancy at the turn of the century. One of the most important breakthroughs contributing to the growth of applied statistics was made by William S. Gossett, a statistician for an Irish brewery. In 1908, under the pen name "Student," Gossett published a paper entitled *The Probable Error of a Mean.* Previous to Gossett, statistical investigations had been carried out with extremely large samples of observations. However, Gossett was among those whose practical problems required them to

---

[3]Sir John Sinclair, *A Statistical Account of Scotland*, Vol. 20, 1798, pp. xiii–xiv.

work with rather small samples. Challenged by the problem of making inferences concerning quantitative characteristics of populations on the basis of small samples taken from those populations, Gossett developed "small sample" theory.

The work of Gossett was extended and popularized by Sir Ronald Fisher, a statistician engaged in applied statistical research at the Rothamsted Experimental Station in England. In 1925, Fisher published a monumental book, *Statistical Methods for Research Workers*, which established statistics as a major tool of experimental science. In 1935, Fisher published *The Design of Experiments*, which today, after nearly half a century, remains an influential authority on scientific inquiry through experimentation. Upon the foundation established by Gossett and Fisher, a large body of techniques of statistical inference has been developed by many other statisticians.

In 1954, Leonard J. Savage published a significant book, *The Foundations of Statistics*, which introduced a new philosophy into the field of statistics. Savage expressed the revolutionary viewpoint that statistical inference is not an end unto itself, but rather a means to the end of selecting and taking decisive actions. This new orientation, which focused on decision-making behavior as a rational process, stimulated the development of a new body of statistical methodology which is known as statistical decision theory. As a practical approach to rational decision making in the face of uncertainty, statistical decision theory emphasizes the economic considerations that influence decision-making behavior.

PROBLEMS

1.1 Explain why there is always some amount of risk involved in acting on a decision that is based on a statistical inference.

1.2 The Tilton Hotel Corporation has obtained an option to purchase a large parcel of hilltop land overlooking Azure Cove. Purchasing this land for building a high-rise hotel should prove to be a profitable investment if a pending statewide referendum limiting building heights in the coastal zone is defeated. However, if the option is exercised and the restrictive legislation is passed, the Corporation will have to dispose of the land at a loss. The referendum is to be held in 60 days, but the option expires in 40 days.

    (a)   In this decision situation, what is Tilton's implicit goal?

    (b)   Prepare a table showing the alternative courses of action, possible states of nature, and possible consequences for Tilton.

    (c)   What is the major source of uncertainty in this decision situation?

    (d)   Describe the population of concern in this decision situation.

    (e)   What is the decision parameter of concern in this problem?

    (f)   How can Tilton obtain additional information to reduce the amount of uncertainty in the decision they must make within the next 40 days?

1.3 The meaning of the word *statistics* depends on whether the word is used in the singular sense or the plural sense. That is, the meaning of the word in the expression "Statistics is . . . " is different from its meaning in the expression "Statistics are . . . ." Explain the difference in meaning between these two usages of *statistics*.

1.4 Distinguish between:

    (a)   Population and sample

    (b)   Parameter and statistic

    (c)   Statistical inference and statistical decision theory

(d)   Data and evidence

(e)   Evidence and information

1.5   Indicate whether each of the following statements describes a population, a sample, a parameter, or a statistic.

(a)   The proportion of defective parts contained in a sample of parts taken from the output of an assembly line.

(b)   All the current subscribers to *The Wall Street Journal*.

(c)   The average age of all the voters who cast their ballot in a particular election.

(d)   A grievance committee selected from all the employees of the Farnsworth Corporation.

(e)   The Dow Jones average computed from 65 stocks selected from all the stocks on the New York Stock Exchange.

1.6   What significant contribution was made by each of the following scholars to the development of statistics?

(a)   Jacques Bernoulli, Abraham de Moivre, and Blaise Pascal

(b)   Sir Ronald Fisher

(c)   William S. Gossett

(d)   Adolphe Quetelet

(e)   Leonard J. Savage

(f)   Sir John Sinclair

2

Organizing and Communicating
Statistical Data

As indicated in Chapter 1, statistics is fundamentally concerned with the collection and analysis of numerical evidence for making inferences and decisions. In this chapter we consider basic methods of obtaining, organizing, and displaying data. This preliminary processing is a first step in extracting numerical evidence from data.

2.1 OBTAINING STATISTICAL DATA

The process of *explicitly formulating* problems in formal statistical terms is an essential first step in applying statistical analysis to decision making. Only after formulating problems in specific terms can decision makers determine whether uncertainty exists and, if so, exactly what data they require to reduce their uncertainty.

2.1.1 Sources of Data

Once a decision maker has formulated a problem and determined that particular data are needed, he or she must determine what sources will provide the data. Frequently, the data will already have been collected for another purpose and are thus available in publications or in some other form, such as punched cards or magnetic tape. Such data, which were not originally collected for the particular problem at hand, are called *secondary data*. Valuable data are often readily available from such secondary sources as the reports and publications of other firms, governmental agencies, privately operated organizations, and research foundations. On occasions when secondary data are unavailable or inadequate, it may be necessary to conduct a special study to collect data specifically for dealing with the present problem. Such data, collected expressly for the particular problem at hand, are called *primary data*.

Whether data are regarded as primary or secondary depends on the purpose for which they were collected and the purpose for which they happen to be used in a given situation. For example, a particular accounting report might be routinely prepared to provide data for the express purpose of determining the firm's quarterly dividend on its common stock, and when used for this purpose the data in the report would be considered primary data. However, if the firm has the problem of deciding whether to make a substantial investment in the development of a new product line, this same accounting report might function as a valuable secondary source of data that would provide information on which to base the decision.

It is fairly obvious that secondary data are usually less expensive to obtain than are primary data. In fact, the cost of obtaining primary data in some situations can be prohibitive. Coupled with the advantage of lower cost, however, is the disadvantage that secondary data frequently are less adequate than primary data. Thus, in deciding whether to use primary or secondary data, considerations of cost must be balanced against considerations of the adequacy of the data.

2.1.2 Observation

Primary data are usually collected through special-purpose studies, which may take the form of either *surveys* or *experiments*. Either of these methods involves the fundamental operation of making *observations* and recording the results of those observations as data. It is through the process of observation—the perception of objects and events by means of our senses—that all scientific knowledge originates. An observation is being made each time a store manager notes the amount of a transaction, or a broker reads the price of a common stock from a ticker tape, or an industrial inspector feels the presence of a surface defect with his finger, or a Gallup Poll interviewer obtains from a housewife the answer to a question.

In collecting primary data, the individual objects of observation are the elements that comprise the population. If we are to obtain the desired information, the observations should focus on particular *characteristics* of the elements being observed. For example, if a housing administrator is making a survey of available housing facilities in a particular city, the elementary objects of observation might be the unoccupied dwelling units in the city. These elements could be described in terms of such characteristics as amount of rental, number of bedrooms, type of heating, type of flooring, or color of walls. However, only some of these characteristics would actually be observed and recorded during the course of the survey. That is, the characteristics to be observed should be selected in such a way that the observations will provide information concerning the decision parameter.

2.1.3 Variables

When we make scientific observations, we usually find differences among the observed elements with respect to the characteristics of observation. If we observe the price of eggs charged by different supermarkets, we note that the markets vary in the price they charge; if we submit a group of flood lamps to life tests, we note that the lamps vary in their number of hours to failure; if we interview a group of credit applicants, we note that the applicants vary with respect to their marital status.

Because of the variability that exists among observations, characteristics of observation are generally referred to as *variables*. In mathematics, the term "variable" is used to denote a *quantity* that may take on any value in a specified set of values. In statistics, however, a variable is defined more broadly as any observable characteristic with respect to which the elements in a population differ and may be described. Since a characteristic of observation may be either a *quantity* (for example, price) or a *quality* (for example, marital status), statistical variables may be either quantitative or qualitative.

Quantitative Variables. When the elements in a group differ in the *magnitude* or *amount* of some characteristic, we refer to that characteristic as a *quantitative variable.* Some examples of quantitative variables are the prices of stocks, test scores of job applicants, time to failure of electronic components, tensile strengths of synthetic fibers, assessed values of parcels of real estate, and diameters of ball bearings. When we observe a group of elements with respect to some quantitative variable, the numerical result obtained from the observation of each element is a *value* of the variable. For instance, suppose that we are conducting a study of the time required by employees in an electronics plant to assemble a particular type of component. In this case the elements of observation are the individual employees in that plant. The characteristic of observation is a quantitative variable—time required to assemble a component. If a particular employee requires 4.10 minutes to assemble a component, this amount of time is a *value* of the variable. Additional examples of quantitative variables are given in Table 2.1.

Table 2.1 Examples of Quantitative Variables

Elements of Observation	Variable	Unit of Measurement	Possible Values
Clerk-typists	Typing speed	Words/minute	57 wpm; 62 wpm
Jockeys	Weight	Pounds	105 lb; 112 lb
Farms	Acreage	Acres	163.8 acres; 206.3 acres
Used cars	Odometer reading	Miles	15,427.3 mi; 29,684.7 mi
Fur coats	Retail price	Dollars	$3,048.16; $4,289.52

In making an observation of a particular element with respect to some quantitative characteristic, the result of the observation is expressed in terms of a number. For instance, suppose that you are in a supermarket and want to determine the weight of a bag of potatoes. You place the bag of potatoes on a scale and observe that the bag weighs 15 pounds. Thus, you are able to describe the bag's weight, a quantitative characteristic, in terms of a number—15 pounds. This process of observing and describing the amount of some quantitative characteristic of an element of observation in numerical terms is called *measurement.* In making and recording quantitative observations, it is essential to define explicitly the *unit of measurement*—that is, to specify what the numbers represent. For example, if you simply announce that the weight of your bag of potatoes is 15, it would not be clear whether it is 15 pounds, 15 ounces, or 15 kilograms.

Qualitative Variables. When the elements in a group differ in *kind,* we refer to the characteristic of observation as a *qualitative variable.* Examples of qualitative variables are the kind of material from which a product is made (such as ceramic, wood, or plastic), colors of bottles in which beverages are marketed, or makes of automobiles. When we observe a group of elements with respect to some qualitative variable, each element is described in terms of an *attribute*. For example, if you are studying organizational behavior of small task groups in a research and development organization, you might focus your attention on each group's type of "leadership climate" (such as democratic, autocratic, or laissez-faire). The individual task groups are the elements of observation; type of leadership climate is the variable. If the leadership climate of a particular task group is democratic, this specific climate would be an attribute of the group. Other examples of qualitative variables are presented in Table 2.2.

Table 2.2   Examples of Qualitative Variables

Elements of Observation	Variable	Possible Attributes
Salesclerks	Sex	Male, female
Business firms	Industry	Construction, retail, financial
U.S. senators	Party	Democrat, Republican
Convertible autos	Color of top	White, tan, black
Crates of eggs	Quality	Grade A, Grade AA

As we have seen, in making observations of a quantitative variable, the process of measurement yields data that are numerical. In making observations of a qualitative variable, however, the "raw" data yielded by the observations are not numerical by nature. In applying statistical analysis to such nonnumerical observations, the data are converted into numerical terms through the process of *enumeration*. To apply this process, the observations are sorted into categories on the basis of the various attributes of the variable, and the number of observations in each category is counted. These *counts* then constitute numerical data. For example, suppose that a financial analyst is performing a study of the 500 largest industrial corporations listed in the *Fortune Directory*. One variable of concern to the analyst might be the industry group to which each firm belongs. The various attributes associated with this variable might include textiles, mining, pharmaceuticals, metal products, and so on. The observational process in this case would be to identify the particular industry group to which each of the 500 corporations belongs. Thus, the raw data would be nonnumerical. To convert these data into numerical form, the analyst would sort the corporations into their respective industry groups, and then count the number of firms in each group.

2.2 SCALES

Regardless of whether numerical data are obtained through measurement or enumeration, some rule or standard must be adopted for the assignment of numerals to the individual observations. Such a rule or standard is called a *scale*. The particular mathematical operations and statistical techniques that may be employed to analyze a set of numerical data depend on the specific nature of the scale on which the data are expressed.

2.2.1 Levels of Scales

The particular mathematical operations that permissibly may be performed on data depend on the *level* of the scale on which the observations are made. In ascending order, there are four levels of scales: nominal, ordinal, interval, and ratio.

The Nominal Scale. The lowest level of scale is the *nominal* scale. The term "nominal" is derived from a Latin word meaning "name." A nominal scale is a naming device by which numbers are assigned to individual observations simply to identify the attribute categories to which they belong. Nominal scales are frequently used to encode qualitative data for computer processing. For instance, an analyst who is studying *Fortune's* 500 largest industrial firms might adopt a coding rule for identifying the industry group of each firm by using the numeral "1" to stand for "textile firm," the numeral "2" to stand for "mining firm," and so on. This coding rule is an example of a nominal scale. The numbers on this scale are used merely to represent various attributes of a qualitative variable, but do not in any way indicate different magnitudes or amounts of the characteristic. Thus, for numbers on a nominal scale, expressions such as "2 > 1" and "6 < 7" are meaningless. As a result, the "higher-level" arithmetic operations such as addition and subtraction are not allowable with numbers on a nominal scale.

The Ordinal Scale. Next in level above the nominal scale is the *ordinal* scale. As the term "ordinal" suggests, there is an "ordered relationship" among the numbers on an ordinal scale. Suppose, for example, that an industrial supervisor is rating the performance of subordinates with a simple numerical scale on which 4 is "excellent," 3 is "good," 2 is "fair," and 1 is "unsatisfactory." The numbers on this scale not only identify different performance categories but also different "amounts" or "levels" of performance. That is, the scale value 2 indicates a higher level of performance than 1, a scale value of 3 indicates a higher level of performance than 2, and so on. Thus, on this ordinal scale, such expressions as "2 > 1" and "3 > 2" are meaningful. However, on scales of this kind, the intervals between the units seldom are equal. That is, the difference in productivity between a "good" employee and a "fair" employee is probably not the same as the difference in productivity between an "excellent" employee and a "good" employee. Thus, if we performed the arithmetic operations $3 - 2 = 1$, and $4 - 3 = 1$, we would have serious difficulty in interpreting these differences. Although both of these differences are numerically the same, they do not necessarily represent the same amount of difference in productivity. Because of this inequality of the intervals between units on an ordinal scale, the basic arithmetic operations of subtraction, addition, multiplication, and division are not permissible. However, since different numbers on an ordinal scale do represent different amounts of the characteristic being measured, this type of scale is highly useful as a ranking device for such purposes as evaluating personnel performance, rating the quality of raw materials, and measuring consumers' brand preferences.

The Interval Scale. In addition to the property of order possessed by the ordinal scale, the interval scale has the "stronger" property of *equal intervals*. That is, equal differences anywhere along the scale represent equal amounts of difference in the characteristic being measured. For example, in measuring temperature changes on the Celsius (centigrade) scale, which is an interval scale, an increase from 50° to 55° represents the same amount of temperature change as an increase from 85° to 90°.

Because of the property of equal intervals, the arithmetic operations of subtraction and addition are both permissible and meaningful with numbers on an interval scale. However, it is not meaningful to compute a ratio between two numbers on an interval scale. For instance, suppose that an observer notes that the temperature on the Celsius scale is 30° in the shop and 10° in the office. She then might compute the ratio 30°/10° = 3 and conclude that it is three times as warm in the shop as it is in the office. Suppose, however, that a second observer uses the Fahrenheit scale to record the same temperatures. As shown in Table 2.3, a Celsius temperature of 30° is equivalent to a Fahrenheit tem-

Table 2.3 Equivalent Values on the Celsius and Fahrenheit Scales for Selected Temperatures

Celsius	0	10	30	50	55	85	90	100
Fahrenheit	32	50	86	122	131	185	194	212

perature of 86°, and a Celsius temperature of 10° is equivalent to a Fahrenheit temperature of 50°. Thus, using the Fahrenheit readings, the second observer might then compute the ratio 86°/50° = 1.72 and conclude that it is less than two times as warm in the shop as it is in the office. Which of these two observers is correct? Neither, since both were using scales without absolute-zero points. That is, on either the Celsius or Fahrenheit scale, the zero point is arbitrary and does not indicate complete absence of temperature. Because of the arbitrary position of the zero point on these two scales, the ratios computed by both observers would be meaningless. More generally, the arithmetic operation of division and the related operation of multiplication are not permissible with numbers on an interval scale.

The Ratio Scale. If an interval scale has an *absolute-zero* point, in the sense that the numeral "0" represents complete absence of the characteristic being measured, the scale is called a ratio scale. Only with this level of scale can a meaningful ratio between two numbers on the scale be computed. In fact, all arithmetic operations are allowable with numbers on a ratio scale.

The most common ratio scale is the scale used in counting or enumerating such things as books, oranges, and chicks. Other examples of ratio scales are the dollar-and-cents scale for measuring monetary value, the centimeter scale for measuring length, the kilogram scale for measuring weight, and the miles-per-hour scale for measuring speed.

In our discussion of interval scales, we observed that, if the temperature on the Celsius scale is 30° in the shop and 10° in the office, it is not meaningful to conclude that it is three times as warm in the shop as it is in the office. However, a meaningful ratio between these two temperatures can be computed by converting the Celsius measures to their equivalent measures on the Kelvin scale, since the Kelvin scale is a ratio scale. A Celsius temperature is converted to a corresponding Kelvin temperature simply by adding 273° to the Celsius temperature. Thus, 30°C is equivalent to 303° on the Kelvin scale and 10°C is equivalent to 283° on the Kelvin scale. Hence, the correct ratio between the temperatures in the shop and the office is

$$\frac{303°}{283°} = 1.07$$

So the temperature is actually only 7% greater in the shop than in the office. This example indicates how seriously conclusions can be in error when ratios are computed between values which are measured on scales that do not have absolute-zero points.

2.2.2 Continuous and Discrete Scales

On many measurement scales, such as scales of time or weight or length, an observation may have any conceivable value within a particular range. A scale of this type is called a *continuous scale*. Characteristics that are measurable on continuous scales are referred to as *continuous variables*.

In contrast to a continuous scale, a *discrete scale* is one on which there are gaps between the possible values that an observation may have. For instance, a family might have 1 child, or 2 children, or 3 children, but it cannot have 2.68 children. A characteristic that is quantified on a discrete scale is called a *discrete variable*. Thus, "number of children" is a discrete variable.

2.2.3 Approximate and Exact Numbers

As we have observed, it is theoretically possible for a continuous measurement to have any conceivable value within a particular range. As a practical matter, however, there is a limit to the precision with which measurements can be obtained on continuous scales. For example, a strand of wire might be exactly 8.4726 centimeters in length, but if you were measuring the wire with an ordinary centimeter scale ruled off in $\frac{1}{10}$-centimeter units, you would not be able to make a reading with the refinement required to give accuracy to the fourth decimal place. You would probably be satisfied to announce your measurement as "approximately" 8.5 centimeters.

Because of the limitation on their precision, all continuous measurements are *approximate numbers*. The accuracy of a continuous measurement depends on the smallest unit to which the measurement is made. For instance, if we are weighing an object to the nearest pound, the figure 1,500 pounds tells us that a particular measurement was 1,500 "pounds." However, if we are weighing to the nearest hundred pounds, the figure 1,500 pounds tells us that the measurement was 15 "hundred pounds." Thus, if the measurement is made to the nearest pound, the number 1,500 is accurate to the fourth digit, and this number is said to have four *significant digits*. However, if the measurement is made to the nearest hundred pounds, the number 1,500 is accurate only to the second digit, and the number contains only two significant digits, with the final two zeros merely "filling in" to indicate the position of the decimal point.

Since the final significant digit of an approximate number is only an approximation, it is convenient to regard approximate numbers as having *boundaries*. When a value is expressed to the nearest unit, the boundaries of that value are $\frac{1}{2}$ unit above and below the value. For example, if a value is expressed as 12 inches to the nearest inch, the true value could lie anywhere between the boundaries of 11.5 inches and 12.5 inches. Similarly, if a measurement is expressed as 12.7 inches to the nearest *tenth* of an inch, the true value could lie between the boundaries of 12.65 inches and 12.75 inches.

Whereas the numbers obtained from continuous measurements are, by their very nature, *approximate* numbers, the numbers that are obtained by enumeration (that is, counting) are *exact* numbers. Except for errors that might occur in counting, an exact number represents a quantity with complete accuracy. If the financial section of your newspaper reports that 524 traded issues on the New York Stock Exchange showed an advance on a particular day, this figure means exactly 524 issues, *not* between 523.5 and 524.5 issues. Because of the complete accuracy which they represent, exact numbers do not have boundaries.

2.3 FREQUENCY DISTRIBUTIONS

In collecting statistical data, the observations are generally recorded in order as they are obtained. This procedure usually results in an accumulation of raw data which are seldom properly organized to make their meaning readily apparent. Thus, in order to extract useful information from original records, the data are usually arranged in a more meaningful form by constructing a *frequency distribution*. To construct a frequency distribution, the observations are grouped into a set of mutually exclusive and collectively exhaustive classes, and then the number of observations in each class is counted. The manner in which this is done depends on two fundamental considerations:

1. Is the characteristic under observation a qualitative or quantitative variable?
2. If the characteristic under observation is quantitative, is it measured on a discrete or a continuous scale?

Taking into account these considerations, our discussion will proceed according to the following diagram:

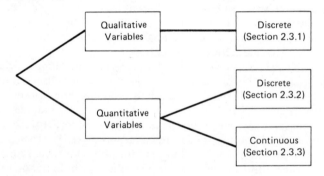

2.3.1 Frequency Distributions for Qualitative Variables

When observations are recorded as attributes of a qualitative variable, they may be regarded essentially as measurements on a nominal scale. As such, all qualitative variables are discrete. To demonstrate the construction of a frequency distribution for a qualitative variable, suppose that a marketing research firm is conducting a taste-testing study with a panel of 50 consumers. Each member of the panel is presented with four brands of diet cola and asked which brand he or she prefers. The resulting raw data are given in Table 2.4. In this raw form, the data are a hodgepodge from which it is difficult to extract meaning. For instance, simply by scanning the data in the table, it is not easy to tell whether any particular brand is preferred by more people than any other brand. However, this information is readily obtained by organizing the data into a frequency distribution.

Table 2.4   Brand-Preference Responses of 50 Consumers

Respondent	Brand Preference	Respondent	Brand Preference
1	A	26	D
2	D	27	B
3	A	28	C
4	C	29	D
5	A	30	C
6	D	31	C
7	C	32	A
8	A	33	C
9	A	34	B
10	C	35	A
11	B	36	A
12	B	37	C
13	C	38	A
14	D	39	D
15	B	40	B
16	B	41	A
17	B	42	D
18	A	43	D
19	C	44	C
20	B	45	B
21	A	46	C
22	A	47	C
23	C	48	B
24	C	49	D
25	A	50	C

Tabulating a Qualitative Distribution. Before constructing the frequency distribution, we should notice that the characteristic of observation—brand preference—is a qualitative variable that has four possible attributes: *A, B, C,* and *D*. These four attributes define four categories, or *classes*, such that each of the 50 responses belongs to one and only one of the classes. Notice that it would be possible to assign a value of "1" to identify a preference for brand *A*, a value of "2" to identify a preference for brand *B*, and so on. These values would simply be numbers on a nominal scale used as substitutes for qualitative descriptors, and would not in any way represent amounts.

The first task in constructing the frequency distribution for the data in Table 2.4 is to list the four classes, as shown in column (1) of Table 2.5. Then, going

Table 2.5   Frequency Distribution of Brand Preferences

(1) Brand Preference	(2) Tally	(3) Frequency
A	⌀⌀ ⌀⌀ ////	14
B	⌀⌀ ⌀⌀ /	11
C	⌀⌀ ⌀⌀ ⌀⌀ /	16
D	⌀⌀ ////	9
Total		50

down the list of brand preferences in Table 2.4, the brand preference of each successive respondent is tallied, as shown in column (2) of Table 2.5. The count associated with each class is called the *frequency* of that class. As the frequencies in column (3) indicate, 14 members of the tasting panel preferred brand A, 11 preferred brand B, 16 preferred brand C, and 9 preferred brand D.

Graphing a Qualitative Distribution. Graphic presentation of a frequency distribution is often a desirable alternative or companion to tabular presentation. Such a graphic presentation is called a *frequency chart*. Two kinds of frequency charts for the distribution in Table 2.5 are shown in Figure 2.1. In both charts, the classes are shown on the horizontal axis and the frequencies are measured by the scale on the vertical axis. Figure 2.1a is called a *vertical line chart* since the frequency in each class is represented by the length of a vertical line; Figure 2.1b is a *vertical bar chart*, since the class frequencies are represented by the lengths of bars rather than lines.

The Relative Frequency Distribution. In interpreting data that have been organized into a frequency distribution, it is often helpful to convert the frequencies to *relative frequencies*. The relative frequency of a class indicates the *proportion* of the number of cases in the class relative to the total number of cases in the distribution. Thus, to obtain the relative frequency for a class, the frequency for that class is divided by the total number of cases in the distribution. For example, as shown in Table 2.6, the relative frequency of those preferring

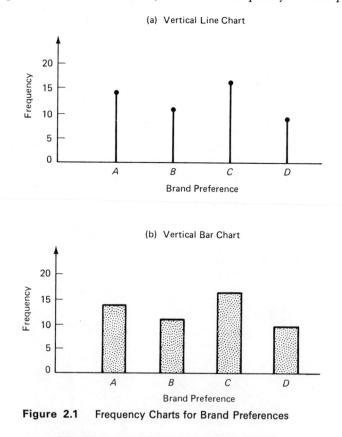

Figure 2.1 Frequency Charts for Brand Preferences

Table 2.6 Relative Frequency Distribution
of Brand Preferences

(1) Brand Preference	(2) Frequency	(3) Relative Frequency
A	14	.28
B	11	.22
C	16	.32
D	9	.18
Total	50	1.00

brand A is $14/50 = .28$, which indicates that 28% of the total members of the panel preferred brand A. It is important to observe that the sum of the relative frequencies is always 1.00.

The chart of a relative frequency distribution is identical to the chart of the frequency distribution itself, except that the "frequency" scale on the vertical axis is replaced by a "relative frequency" scale. This is illustrated by the vertical line chart in Figure 2.2, which may be compared with the vertical line chart in Figure 2.1.

2.3.2 Frequency Distributions
for Discrete Quantitative Variables

The basic procedure for constructing a frequency distribution of a discrete quantitative variable is similar to that for constructing a frequency distribution of a qualitative variable.

Tabulating a Discrete Quantitative Distribution. To illustrate the construction of a frequency distribution for a discrete quantitative variable, consider the raw data in Table 2.7. These data represent the responses of 60 heads of households to the survey question: "How many children under 18 years of age reside in your household?" The first step in preparing a frequency distribution of these data is to list the values of the variable (number of children) in ascending order, as shown in column (1) of Table 2.8. Then the observations are tallied in a manner similar to constructing a qualitative distribution, and the counts of the tally marks are recorded as the frequencies shown in column (2). The corresponding relative frequencies appear in column (3).

Because of the ordered relationship among the classes, it is meaningful to

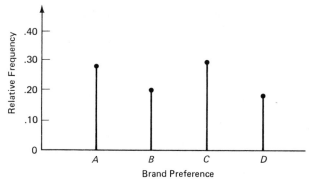

Figure 2.2 Relative Frequency Chart for Brand Preference

Table 2.7 Number of Children in Each of 60 Households

Household	Number of Children	Household	Number of Children	Household	Number of Children
1	1	21	3	41	3
2	2	22	0	42	1
3	2	23	1	43	2
4	1	24	2	44	4
5	4	25	1	45	5
6	2	26	0	46	4
7	1	27	2	47	3
8	5	28	2	48	2
9	1	29	1	49	2
10	3	30	2	50	1
11	4	31	4	51	2
12	2	32	1	52	0
13	4	33	1	53	0
14	3	34	2	54	3
15	3	35	0	55	2
16	1	36	2	56	2
17	2	37	3	57	2
18	3	38	1	58	1
19	3	39	1	59	3
20	3	40	5	60	0

Table 2.8 Frequency Distribution of Number of Children in Households

(1) Number of Children	(2) Frequency	(3) Relative Frequency	(4) Cumulative Frequency	(5) Cumulative Relative Frequency
0	6	.10	6	.10
1	15	.25	21	.35
2	18	.30	39	.65
3	12	.20	51	.85
4	6	.10	57	.95
5	3	.05	60	1.00
Total	60	1.00		

"cumulate" the frequencies. The *cumulative frequency* of a class in a frequency distribution is the total number of cases which have values equal to or less than the value of that class. This value is obtained by adding the frequency for the particular class to the frequencies for all the classes that have smaller values. For example, column (4) in Table 2.8 shows that the cumulative frequency for the class "2 children" is 39, which is obtained by adding $6 + 15 + 18 = 39$. The meaning of the cumulative frequency for this class is that 39 households in the distribution have two children or less.

The *cumulative relative frequency* of a class in a frequency distribution is obtained by dividing the cumulative frequency of that class by the total frequency. For example, in Table 2.8, the cumulative relative frequency for the class "2 children" is $39/60 = .65$, as shown in column (5). This same result may be obtained by adding the relative frequencies in column (3) for those classes with

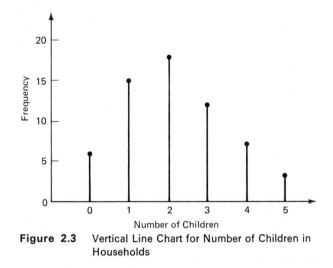

Figure 2.3   Vertical Line Chart for Number of Children in Households

values up to and including 2. That is, .10 + .25 + .30 = .65, which indicates that 65% of the total number of households have two children or less.

Graphing a Discrete Quantitative Distribution.   The frequency distribution for a discrete quantitative variable may be displayed graphically by either a vertical line chart or a vertical bar chart. In either case, the frequency chart for a discrete quantitative variable is similar in appearance to a frequency chart for a qualitative variable, with the classes represented on the horizontal axis and the frequencies measured by the scale on the vertical axis. This may be seen by comparing Figure 2.3 with Figure 2.1a. Although these two graphs look similar, they differ subtly in the way the classes are represented on the horizontal axis. In Figure 2.3, the classes are represented on the axis in ascending numerical order from left to right. This ordering of the classes reflects the ordered relationship among the values of the variable. In Figure 2.1, however, the alphabetical ordering of the classes is purely arbitrary, since no ordered relationship exists among the attributes (brands).

The cumulative frequency distribution may be portrayed graphically by a *step diagram*, in which the classes are displayed in order on the horizontal axis, and the cumulative frequencies are measured by the scale on the vertical axis. The step diagram for the household survey data is presented in Figure 2.4. As this graph illustrates, the cumulative frequencies of the successive classes are represented by horizontal lines that form a sequence of steps. These steps indicate that the cumulative frequency increases by jumps when the variable is discrete. The use of vertical lines to connect the horizontal lines is optional with this type of graph.

2.3.3   Frequency Distributions for Continuous Quantitative Variables

Since a quantitative variable defined on a continuous scale has an infinite number of possible values, it is impossible to define the classes in terms of all the individual values of the variable. Instead, the classes are defined by *intervals* of values. For purposes of analyzing the distribution, it is usually desirable

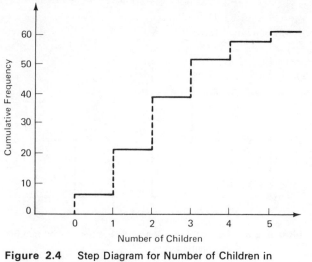

Figure 2.4   Step Diagram for Number of Children in Households

that all classes be defined by intervals that are equal in width. Thus, in a frequency distribution of the weights of airline hostesses in pounds, the classes might be defined by such intervals as "90 up to 95," "95 up to 100," and so on. The exact number of intervals to use is largely a matter of judgment. The main consideration is that the number of intervals be large enough to make the distribution useful, but not so large that the distribution is unwieldy. As a rough rule of thumb, the number of intervals should be about 10. In determining the exact number of intervals to use, a secondary consideration is that the length of the interval be some value that is convenient to manipulate.

Tabulating a Continuous Quantitative Distribution.   To illustrate the construction of a continuous frequency distribution, suppose that an actuary is performing an analysis of 400 applications for group health insurance. One of the items on the application form is "age to nearest birthday." From a quick scan of the applications, the actuary observes that the youngest applicant is 21 years of age and the oldest applicant is 63 years of age. Thus, the total range of ages from 21 to 63, inclusive, is 43 years. Dividing this range by 10, the actuary obtains $43/10 = 4.3$. That is, the total range of ages can be divided into 10 equal intervals of 4.3 years. However, since 4.3 is an awkward value, the actuary decides to adopt a *class interval* of 5 years.

Once the class interval is determined, each class is defined by specifying the *limits* of the class. The limits of a class are the lowest and highest observational values that can be assigned to that class. In specifying class limits, care must be taken to ensure that the classes are defined in such a way that each observation can be assigned unambiguously to one and only one class. To this end, it is important to consider the manner in which the observations have been recorded. In our example, the ages of the applicants were *recorded* to the nearest year. For instance, if an applicant's actual age is approximately 24 years and 2 months, it would be recorded as 24 years. Similarly, the age of an applicant who is approximately 24 years and 8 months would be recorded as 25 years. Because the observations were recorded in integer values, the class limits also are stated in integers. Since the age of the youngest applicant is 21, the lower limit of the class could be specified as 21. However, it is general practice to start the distribution with a lower limit that is a multiple of the class interval. Thus, recalling that the class interval has been specified as 5, the actuary establishes 20 as the lower limit of the first class. Hence, the first class is defined by the interval "20–24," which covers a 5-year span. Having defined the first class, the remaining classes are simply defined as a sequence of 5-year intervals, as shown in column (1) of Table 2.9.

Table 2.9 Frequency Distribution of Ages (to Nearest Birthday) of 400 Applicants for Group Insurance

(1) Class Limits (Age to Nearest Birthday)	(2) Frequency (Number of Applicants)	(3) Relative Frequency	(4) Cumulative Frequency	(5) Cumulative Relative Frequency
20–24	16	.040	16	.040
25–29	48	.120	64	.160
30–34	82	.205	146	.365
35–39	68	.170	214	.535
40–44	56	.140	270	.675
45–49	40	.100	310	.775
50–54	36	.090	346	.865
55–59	30	.075	376	.940
60–64	24	.060	400	1.000
Total	400	1.000		

After the classes have been defined, the observations can be tallied to obtain the class frequencies, which are shown in column (2) of Table 2.9. Corresponding relative frequencies and cumulative frequencies are tabulated in columns (3), (4), and (5).

Graphing a Continuous Quantitative Distribution. One of the commonly used types of charts for graphing a continuous frequency distribution is the *histogram*. To understand how a histogram is drawn, it is helpful to recall that measurements on a continuous scale are *approximate* numbers that have boundaries. Since the limits of a class in a continuous frequency distribution are defined in terms of such numbers, each class may be regarded as having *class boundaries*. The boundaries of a class are the lower boundary of the lower class limit and the upper boundary of the upper class limit. For example, if ages are recorded to the nearest birthday, as in the case of Table 2.9, an observational value of 20 years represents an actual age somewhere between 19.5 years and 20.5 years. Since 19.5 is the lower boundary of 20, which is the lower limit of the first class, 19.5 is the lower boundary of the class. Similarly, since 24.5 is the upper boundary of 24, which is the upper class limit of the first class, 24.5 is the upper boundary of the class. The class boundaries for all of the classes in Table 2.9 are shown in column (2) of Table 2.10. Subtracting the lower boundary of a class from the upper boundary yields the width of the class interval. For instance, for the class "20–24" years, the boundaries are 19.5 and 24.5, and the class interval is $24.5 - 19.5 = 5$.

In our example we have assumed that observations on a continuous scale are recorded to the *nearest* unit of measurement. This is not always the case.

Table 2.10 Class Boundaries and Midpoints for Distribution of Ages to Nearest Birthday

(1) Class Limits	(2) Class Boundaries	(3) Midpoint	(4) Frequency	(5) Cumulative Frequency
20–24	19.5–24.5	22	16	16
25–29	24.5–29.5	27	48	64
30–34	29.5–34.5	32	82	146
35–39	34.5–39.5	37	68	214
40–44	39.5–44.5	42	56	270
45–49	44.5–49.5	47	40	310
50–54	49.5–54.5	52	36	346
55–59	54.5–59.5	57	30	376
60–64	59.5–64.5	62	24	400
			400	

Sometimes observations are recorded to the *next lower* unit of measurement. When you ask a person his age, for example, he usually gives his age at his last birthday. In this case, a recorded age of 20 indicates an age anywhere from exactly 20 up to 21. That is, the value 20 has a lower boundary of exactly 20 and an upper boundary of 20.99 . . . , which may be regarded as 21 for all practical purposes. Similarly, the value 24 has a lower boundary of exactly 24 and an upper boundary of 25. Thus, if the ages in Table 2.9 had been recorded to the last birthday rather than to the nearest birthday, the boundaries of the first class would be 20 and 25 rather than 19.5 and 24.5.

Once the class boundaries have been established, a histogram is constructed in the same way as a vertical bar chart, except that the bars in the histogram are adjoining rather than separated. This is because the classes in a continuous distribution are defined by contiguous intervals on a continuous scale rather

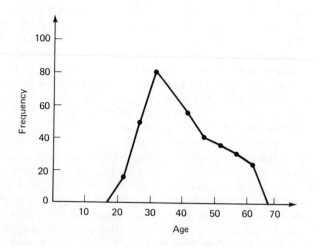

Figure 2.5 Histogram of Age Distribution

than by separate points on a discrete scale. The histogram for the frequency distribution in Table 2.10 is shown in Figure 2.5. Notice that the continuity of the distribution is conveyed by extending the base of each bar all the way from the lower class boundary to the upper class boundary.

An alternative to the histogram for graphing a continuous frequency distribution is the *frequency polygon*. To construct a frequency polygon, it is first necessary to determine the class midpoints. The *midpoint* of a class is the halfway mark between the upper and lower class boundaries.

After the class midpoints have been determined, the next step in constructing the frequency polygon is to locate the midpoint of each class on the horizontal axis. Directly above each class midpoint, a dot is plotted at a height representing the frequency of the class. Then the dots for the adjacent classes are connected by straight lines. Finally, the polygon is "closed" by extending the tails of the graph to the horizontal axis. This is done by bringing the lower end of the polygon to the horizontal axis at a point corresponding to the midpoint of the (nonexistent) class below the lowest class, and bringing the upper end of the polygon to the horizontal axis at a point corresponding to the midpoint of the (nonexistent) class above the highest class. The frequency polygon in Figure 2.6 displays the frequency distribution of ages given in Table 2.10.

As a companion to the frequency polygon, the *ogive* (pronounced oh-jive) is a graph used to depict *cumulative* frequencies in a continuous distribution. The initial step in constructing an ogive is to locate the upper boundary of each class on the horizontal axis. Next, above each of these upper boundaries, a dot is plotted at a height representing the cumulative frequency of the class. Then the dots for the adjacent classes are connected by straight lines. Finally, the graph is completed by bringing the lower end of the figure to the horizontal axis at a point corresponding to the lower boundary of the lowest class. The ogive in Figure 2.7 depicts the cumulative frequencies given in column (5) of Table 2.10. Notice that, unlike the frequency polygon, the ogive is extended to the horizontal axis only at the lower end.

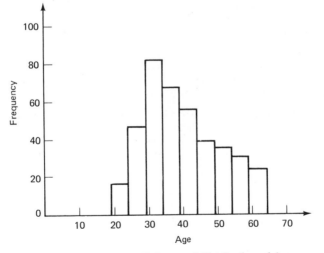

Figure 2.6   Frequency Polygon of Distribution of Ages Recorded to Nearest Birthday

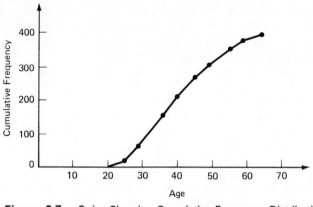

Figure 2.7 Ogive Showing Cumulative Frequency Distribution of Ages Recorded to Nearest Birthday

PROBLEMS

2.1 In applying statistical analysis to decision making, an essential first step is to formulate the problem explicitly in terms of a statistical decision problem.
   (a)   What should be included in such an explicit formulation of the problem?
   (b)   Why is this an essential first step?

2.2 Distinguish between:
   (a)   Primary data and secondary data
   (b)   Quantitative variables and qualitative variables
   (c)   Measurement and enumeration

2.3 Distinguish between:
   (a)   Nominal scale and ordinal scale
   (b)   Ordinal scale and interval scale
   (c)   Interval scale and ratio scale

2.4 Distinguish between:
   (a)   Continuous variables and discrete variables
   (b)   Class limits and class boundaries
   (c)   Approximate and exact numbers

2.5 In each of the following situations, identify the element of observation, the variable being observed, and the unit of measurement.
   (a)   In a marketing survey, an interviewer questions a group of housewives. The interview with each housewife begins with the question: "To the nearest dollar, how much did you spend on your last trip to the supermarket?"
   (b)   A quality control engineer tests a group of photographic flood lamps to determine how many minutes each lamp will operate continuously before burning out.
   (c)   A consumer advocate selects a sample of family-size boxes of Crispo Crunchies from a supermarket shelf and weighs the contents of each box, recording its weight to the nearest ounce.
   (d)   In a study of the acceleration performance of compact cars, a group of cars are started from a standstill, and the speed attained by each car at the end of 30 seconds is recorded in miles per hour.

2.6 A coed who is attempting to reduce on Dr. Slimmo's Nine-Day Fresh Fruit Diet goes to the corner grocery store to purchase her next day's lunch. She selects a peach and a plum. The peach weighs 12 ounces and the plum weighs 4 ounces.

(a) Compute the ratio of the weight of the peach to the weight of the plum.

(b) One ounce is equivalent to 28.35 grams. Convert the weights of the two pieces of fruit to grams.

(c) Using the weights in grams obtained in part (b), compute the ratio of the weight of the peach to the weight of the plum.

(d) Compare the results in parts (a) and (c). Are the two ratios the same or different? Explain.

2.7 The personnel director of a large corporation has developed a mental ability test which is administered to job applicants. A person's score on this test itself is not in IQ units. However, a research study conducted by the personnel director has shown that a person's test score, S, can be converted to IQ units by the formula

$$IQ = .80S + 50$$

(a) Suppose that the mental ability test is administered to two applicants, Alice and Barker. Alice obtains a score of 90 and Barker obtains a score of 80. Compute the ratio of Alice's score to Barker's score.

(b) Convert Alice's and Barker's test scores to their equivalent IQ measures.

(c) Using the IQs obtained in part (b), compute the ratio of Alice's IQ to Barker's IQ.

(d) Compare the results in parts (a) and (c). Are the two ratios the same or different? Explain.

2.8 How many significant digits are contained in each of the following measurements?

(a) Measured to the nearest ounce, the weight of a box of crackers is 17 ounces.

(b) Measured to the nearest 100 miles, the distance between city A and city B is 1,400 miles.

(c) Measured to the nearest inch, the height of a particular skyscraper is 4,000 inches.

(d) Measured to the nearest $\frac{1}{10}$ cubic centimeter, the net contents of a jug of cider is 1,000.2 cubic centimeters.

2.9 The Marco Corporation is a manufacturing firm that employs 12,000 people. The company is divided into 3 divisions. The number of male and female employees in each division is as follows:

	Division			
	I	II	III	Total
Male	2,000	4,000	2,000	8,000
Female	2,000	1,000	1,000	4,000
Total	4,000	5,000	3,000	12,000

(a) In the population of 12,000 employees, what is the number of male employees? female employees? Are these numbers statistics or parameters?

(b) In the population, what percentage of employees are males? females? Should these percentages be regarded as statistics or parameters?

(c) In the population, what percentage of employees belong to Division I? Division II? Division III? Should these percentages be regarded as statistics or parameters?

2.10 The management of the Marco Corporation in Problem 2.9 has been considering an employee stock participation plan. To estimate the potential extent of employee participation in such a plan, the personnel manager decides to poll a sample of 200 employees selected at random from the population of 12,000 employees. After receiving an explanation of the proposed plan, each employee in the sample was asked: "If this plan were made available to you, would you participate?" The number of persons in the sample answering "yes" and "no" is as follows:

	Division						
	I		II		III		
	Yes	No	Yes	No	Yes	No	Total
Male	15	15	40	30	5	15	120
Female	25	5	20	10	5	15	80
Total	40	20	60	40	10	30	200

(a)   In the sample of 200 employees, what percentage of employees are males? females? Should these percentages be regarded as statistics or parameters?

(b)   In the sample, what percentage of employees belong to Division I? Division II? Division III? Should these percentages be regarded as statistics or parameters?

(c)   In the entire sample of 200 employees, what percentage of the employees gave "yes" responses?

(d)   On the basis of the results of the sample poll, what inference might you make about the percentage of "yes" responses that might be obtained if the entire population were polled? Would you have any reservation about your inference?

2.11   Prepare a bar chart for the relative frequencies shown in Table 2.6. Compare your chart with that shown in Figures 2.1b and 2.2.

2.12   Explain why it would not be meaningful to prepare a cumulative relative frequency distribution for the data in Table 2.6.

2.13   Prepare a step diagram for the cumulative relative frequency distribution shown in Table 2.8. Compare your results with Figure 2.4.

2.14   Below is a frequency distribution of ages (at last birthday) of 400 applicants for group insurance.

Class Limits	Frequency	Class Boundaries	Midpoint	Cumulative Frequency
20–24	18			
25–29	46			
30–34	84			
35–39	64			
40–44	60			
45–49	38			
50–54	34			
55–59	30			
60–64	26			

(a)   Complete the missing entries in the frequency table.
(b)   Construct the histogram for this distribution.
(c)   Construct the frequency polygon for this distribution.
(d)   Construct the ogive for this distribution.

2.15 Following is a frequency distribution of scores on a numerical aptitude test administered to 119 employees enrolled in a company's leadership training program.

Class Limits	Frequency	Class Boundaries	Midpoint	Cumulative Frequency
55–59	10			
60–64	19			
65–69	19			
70–74	26			
75–79	11			
80–84	18			
85–89	7			
90–94	6			
95–99	3			

(a) Complete the missing entries in the frequency table.
(b) Construct the histogram for this distribution.
(c) Construct the frequency polygon for this distribution.

2.16 From the frequency table in Problem 2.15, determine:
(a) How many trainees obtained scores no greater than 74.
(b) What proportion of trainees obtained scores of 75 or greater.
(c) How many trainees obtained scores between 70 and 89, inclusive.
(d) What proportion of trainees obtained scores of 69 or lower.

2.17 Following are listed the total dollar amounts of tips earned by the 50 waitresses employed by Joe's 24-Hour Truck Stop during the week of February 20:

$ 78.70	$ 86.96	$106.26	$ 98.12	$105.94
103.00	102.84	99.36	92.11	109.32
91.14	84.62	111.79	85.48	103.87
83.78	92.80	122.86	114.10	117.45
79.66	86.32	105.64	96.04	104.42
86.00	81.38	106.23	96.19	114.35
119.53	113.74	100.13	96.76	93.49
101.92	110.45	97.93	103.32	105.22
101.77	87.91	109.08	75.02	98.07
105.06	121.81	96.90	84.43	105.68

(a) Complete the following frequency table:

Class Limits	Frequency	Relative Frequency	Cumulative Frequency	Cumulative Relative Frequency
$75.00–$79.99				
$80.00–$84.99				
$85.00–$89.99				
$90.00–$94.99				
$95.00–$99.99				
$100.00–$104.99				
$105.00–$109.99				
$110.00–$114.99				
$115.00–$119.99				
$120.00–$124.99				

(b) Construct the histogram for this distribution.
(c) Construct the frequency polygon for this distribution.
(d) Construct the ogive for this distribution.

2.18 You have just been hired as a statistical clerk for Robert Jones, sales manager for Jackrabbit Motors Corporation. For your first assignment, Mr. Jones has asked you to prepare an analysis of the number of cars sold last year by the corporation's 100 dealerships. The data for your analysis are contained in the following list, which gives the number of cars sold by each dealership:

99	48	138	96	98	12	73	41	75	59
20	14	84	89	28	28	35	157	64	71
88	41	28	66	45	33	55	98	53	90
26	75	84	35	67	42	16	89	72	51
72	88	105	132	13	30	141	42	56	64
67	84	149	42	80	164	80	59	61	21
18	85	63	68	72	98	99	23	125	53
39	44	77	81	93	56	26	82	77	63
54	55	38	16	145	90	82	34	63	28
50	24	41	21	23	80	19	17	52	76

To perform your analysis, proceed as follows:
(a) Tally the data to obtain the frequency for each of the following classes: 10–29, 30–49, . . . , 150–169.
(b) Using the results obtained in part (a), prepare a table showing class limits, frequency, relative frequency, cumulative frequency, and cumulative relative frequency.
(c) Construct a vertical bar chart of the frequency distribution.
(d) Construct a step diagram showing the cumulative relative frequency distribution.
(e) Are the data in this problem qualitative or quantitative? Discrete or continuous?

2.19 From the frequency table obtained in Problem 2.18(b), determine:
(a) How many dealers sold 90 or more cars.
(b) What proportion of the dealers sold 90 or more cars.
(c) How many dealers sold from 30 to 69 cars, inclusive.
(d) What proportion of the dealers sold 69 or fewer cars.
(e) How many dealers sold from 50 to 89, inclusive.
(f) What proportion of the dealers sold 109 or fewer cars.

2.20 Using the data in Problem 2.18, prepare a frequency table with the following limits: 10–49, 50–89, 90–129, and 130–169. The distribution you prepared in Problem 2.18 has eight class intervals, whereas the distribution in this problem has only four. Which of the two distributions do you prefer? Explain. Should you present both to the sales manager? Why?

3

Descriptive Measures
of Finite Populations:
Parameters

In studying populations, it is important to distinguish between finite and infinite populations. A *finite population* is one that consists of a fixed, definite number of elements, although the exact number may or may not be known. Examples of finite populations would be all of the legal residents of the state of California, all of the industrial firms incorporated within the state of New Jersey, or all of the refrigerators stored in a particular warehouse. Presumably, if the number of elements in a finite population is not known, it would be theoretically possible to count its elements. In contrast, an *infinite population* has a limitless number of elements, so that it would be impossible to count its elements. Examples of infinite populations would include all of the tourists who might possibly visit Yellowstone National Park, all of the possible flips of a coin, or all of the transistors that could be produced by a particular manufacturing process.

As pointed out in Chapter 1, quantitative properties of a population are called *parameters*. The purpose of the present chapter is to familiarize the reader with the most commonly used parameters. For mathematical simplicity, the present chapter is confined to a discussion of parameters of finite populations. Essentially the same concepts, with mathematical modifications, may be applied to infinite populations. This extension to infinite populations is considered in later chapters.

3.1 FREQUENCIES AND PROPORTIONS

A frequency distribution may be used to describe either a sample or a finite population. When a frequency distribution is used to describe a population, each of the class frequencies may be regarded as a parameter of that population. To illustrate, consider the Bulwark Bank, which has 500 employees, each of whom is assigned to branch 1, branch 2, branch 3, branch 4, or branch 5. The branch in which an employee works is a qualitative variable defined on a nominal scale. Thus, the numbers 1, 2, 3, 4, and 5 are used simply as branch-designation labels that do not possess any ordered relationship. The frequency distribution of the branch assignment is presented in Table 3.1. Each of the

Table 3.1 Frequency Distribution of Branch Assignments of Bulwark Bank Employees

Branch, i	Frequency, f_i	Proportion, π_i
1	70	.14
2	200	.40
3	25	.05
4	150	.30
5	55	.11
Total	500	1.00

frequencies in this table may be regarded as a parameter of this population of 500 employees. Symbolically, if we use f_i to denote the frequency of branch i, we may express these parameters as follows:

$$f_1 = 70 \quad f_2 = 200 \quad f_3 = 25 \quad f_4 = 150 \quad f_5 = 55$$

For a finite population, the *total frequency*, which is the sum of all of the individual class frequencies, is a parameter, which is commonly referred to as the *size* of the population. The population size is usually designated by the symbol N. Thus, for the population of bank employees in Table 3.1, $N = 500$.

As we observed in Chapter 2, dividing a class frequency by the total frequency yields the relative frequency of the class. For a finite population, the relative frequency of a class is the proportion of the number of cases in the class relative to the total number of cases in the population. Using π_i to denote the *proportion* of cases in the ith class, this may be expressed by the formula

$$\pi_i = \frac{f_i}{N} \tag{3.1}$$

Applying this formula to the frequencies in the second column of Table 3.1, we obtain

$$\pi_1 = .14 \quad \pi_2 = .40 \quad \pi_3 = .05 \quad \pi_4 = .30 \quad \pi_5 = .11$$

Each of these proportions, which are also shown in the third column of Table 3.1, is a parameter of the bank employee population.

Since the variable in Table 3.1 is defined on a nominal scale, it would not be meaningful to cumulate the frequencies. However, for population frequency distributions in which the variable is measured on a scale that is at least at the ordinal level, the cumulative frequency and cumulative relative frequency (cumulative proportion) of each class would be meaningful. As an example, consider Table 3.2, which presents a frequency distribution of the scores of a population of 125 middle managers on the Employee Aptitude Survey (EAS)

Table 3.2 Frequency Distribution of Scores of a Population of 125 Middle Managers on EAS Numerical Ability Test

Scores (Class Limits)	Frequency	Relative Frequency	Cumulative Frequency	Cumulative Proportions
5–14	4	.032	4	.032
15–24	13	.104	17	.136
25–34	27	.216	44	.352
35–44	31	.248	75	.600
45–54	23	.184	98	.784
55–64	19	.152	117	.936
65–74	8	.064	125	1.000

Numerical Ability Test, a psychological test used in personnel assessment.[1] Like most psychological measurements, the scores on this test are on an ordinal scale.[2] Thus, in Table 3.2, it is meaningful to present the cumulative frequencies and the cumulative proportions of the classes. Each of these may be regarded as a parameter of the population.

3.2 FRACTILES

From the cumulative proportions in Table 3.2, we can answer such questions as "What proportion of the population have test scores of 14 or less?" or "What proportion of the population have test scores of 44 or less?" However, suppose that we ask such a question as "What is the test score such that the proportion of the population having that score or lower is .20?" The answer to this question is not readily available from inspection of Table 3.2. It is apparent from the table that a proportion of .352 have scores of 34 or less, and a proportion of .136 have scores of 24 or less. Therefore, the score with a cumulative proportion of .20 must lie somewhere between 24 and 34. From the frequency distribution, it is not possible to determine the exact score because the individual scores have been grouped into classes.

To determine the precise score with a cumulative proportion of .20, it is necessary to examine the individual scores from which Table 3.2 was constructed. These 125 individual scores[3] are given in Table 3.3. In this table the scores are *arrayed* in ascending order—listed in order of magnitude from the smallest to the largest. Since the population size is 125, a cumulative proportion of .20 corresponds to a cumulative frequency of $125 \times .20 = 25$. Therefore, the score having a cumulative proportion of .20 is the 25th score in the array. Counting from the lowest score in Table 3.3, we find that the score of the 25th

[1]James S. Ford, Glen Grimsley, Floyd L. Ruch, and Neil D. Warren, *Employee Aptitude Survey* (Los Angeles: Psychological Services, Inc.)

[2]See S. S. Stevens, "Mathematics, Measurement, and Psychophysics," in *Handbook of Experimental Psychology*, ed. S. S. Stevens (New York: John Wiley & Sons, Inc., 1951), pp. 1–49.

[3]These scores were provided by Floyd L. Ruch, president of Psychological Services, Inc., publishers of the *Employee Aptitude Survey*.

Table 3.3 Arrayed Scores of a Population of 125 Middle Managers on EAS Numerical Ability Test

9	21	26	30	34	37	40	43	47	52	55	60	67
12	21	26	31	34	37	41	43	48	52	56	60	68
12	22	27	31	34	38	41	44	48	52	56	61	70
14	22	27	31	34	38	41	44	48	52	57	62	71
16	23	27	32	35	38	41	44	49	53	57	63	72
17	23	28	32	35	38	42	45	50	53	57	63	
18	24	28	32	36	39	42	45	50	54	57	64	
19	25	29	33	36	39	42	45	51	54	58	65	
19	25	29	33	37	39	42	46	51	55	59	66	
20	26	30	33	37	40	43	47	52	55	60	67	

case is 27. We may refer to this test score of 27, which has a cumulative proportion of .20, as the .20 "fractile" of the distribution.

To further illustrate how to obtain a fractile, let us determine the .05 fractile of the scores in Table 3.3. In this case a cumulative proportion of .05 is equivalent to a cumulative frequency of $125 \times .05 = 6.25$. However, it is not meaningful to say that the .05 fractile is the score of the 6.25th case, since no such case exists. Thus, because a cumulative frequency must be an integer that is obtained by counting, the fractional value of 6.25 must be rounded to an integer. If 6.25 is rounded down to 6, the .05 fractile will be the value of the 6th case, which has a cumulative proportion of $6/125 = .048$. If 6.25 is rounded up to 7, the .05 fractile will be the value of the 7th case, which has a cumulative proportion of $7/125 = .056$. Which procedure should we follow? The key to answering this question lies in the definition of a fractile. Using φ (the lowercase Greek letter phi) to denote a cumulative proportion, the φ fractile of a finite population is the lowest observed value such that the cumulative proportion corresponding to that value is *at least* equal to φ. Since .048 is less than .05, whereas .056 is "at least" equal to .05, the .05 fractile must be the value of the seventh case, which is 18. That is, 18 is the lowest score having a cumulative proportion that is at least equal to .05. In other words, any score less than 18 has a cumulative proportion that is less than .05. Of course, any score greater than 18 has a cumulative proportion that is greater than .05.

It will be convenient to adopt a special notation to denote population fractiles. If the population is described in terms of some quantitative variable X, then X_φ will denote the φ fractile of the distribution of X. Thus, if we use X to denote the variable "test score" for the population in Table 3.3, then X_φ represents the lowest test score for which the proportion of managers having that score or lower is at least equal to φ. Since the .20 fractile is 27, we may write $X_{.20} = 27$. Similarly, for the .05 fractile, we have $X_{.05} = 18$.

In defining fractiles, φ is sometimes expressed in terms of a percentage rather than a decimal fraction. When this is done, the fractile is called a *percentile*. For instance, the .20 fractile may be referred to as the 20th percentile. Thus, the 20th percentile of the test scores in Table 3.3 is 27. Similarly, the 5th percentile is 18.

Among the most commonly used fractiles are $X_{.25}$, $X_{.50}$, and $X_{.75}$. Because these three fractiles divide the distribution into four quarters, they are referred to as the "quartiles" of the distribution. Specifically, $X_{.25}$ is called the *first quartile*, $X_{.50}$ the *second quartile*, and $X_{.75}$ the *third quartile*. As the reader may verify, the quartiles for the population in Table 3.3 are $X_{.25} = 31$, $X_{.50} = 41$, and $X_{.75} = 52$. It is important to observe that a quartile is a value at a single point on the scale of measurement, not an interval of values on that scale. Thus, in using quartiles, it is incorrect to say that a particular case falls "in" a particular quartile. For example, if a manager's score lies between $X_{.25}$ and $X_{.50}$, it is improper to say that he is "in the second quartile," but it is proper to say that he is "in the second quarter." Of course, to specify fractiles of a distribution, the variable must be defined on a scale that is at least at the ordinal level. This is because the cumulation of frequencies involved in determining a fractile requires an ordered relationship among the numbers on the scale.

3.3 AVERAGES

To the layperson, an average is usually understood to be a value that is obtained by summing a group of values and then dividing the sum by the number of values in the group. To the statistician, however, the term "average" has a much broader meaning. Depending on the situation, there actually are several different averages from which to choose. The averages that we consider in this section are the mode, the median, and the mean.

3.3.1 The Mode

For a finite population of values, the *mode* is the value that has the greatest frequency. As the value that appears most often, the mode may be considered as the most "typical" or most "popular" value. As such, the mode may be regarded as the "center of concentration" of the population.

The mode is the most "primitive" of the averages in the sense that it is applicable to observations on a scale as low as the nominal level. As an example, consider again the population represented in Table 3.1. As previously noted, the data from which the table was constructed are observations on a nominal scale. Inspection of this table reveals that branch 2 has the highest frequency ($f_2 = 200$). That is, 2 is the scale value that occurs most often. Therefore, the mode of the population is 2.

As another example, consider the frequency distribution presented in Table 3.2. We can see from this table that the most popular class is "35–44," which has a frequency of 31. This class is referred to as the *modal class*, which is simply the class with the greatest frequency. However, because the individual scores have been grouped into classes, it is not possible to determine the specific score that occurs most often. In such a case, it is customary to use the midpoint of the modal class as the mode of the distribution. According to this convention, the mode is 39.5, which is the midpoint of the class "35–44." It should be emphasized that this is only an approximation, which at times can be substantially in error.

To determine the exact mode of the managers' test scores, we must examine the individual scores arrayed in Table 3.3. Inspection of these data indicates that 52 is the mode, which is the value found most often. Notice that this exact value of 52 is substantially different from the approximate value of 39.5 that is obtained by taking the midpoint of the modal class. In fact, the actual mode in this example does not even fall in the modal class.

For the population in Table 3.3, the modal value of 52 occurs five times. However, the values 34, 37, 38, 41, 42, and 57 each occur four times. Since each of these values, scattered over the range from 34 to 57, occurs almost as often as the modal value, the mode in this example is not necessarily typical of the entire population. Thus, unless the modal frequency is substantially greater than the frequencies of other values, use of the mode is somewhat dubious, and its interpretation is rather misty. However, when the distribution does have a definite peak, the mode may have real practical use in terms of providing a measure of the "most typical" or "most popular" value in the population. The mode is also sometimes interpreted as the "most probable" value in a population, in the sense that if a single item is selected from the population "at random," the value of that item is more likely to be the modal value than any other value.

3.3.2 The Median

In our discussion of fractiles, we observed that if the data are on a scale that is at least at the ordinal level, the values may be arrayed in order of magnitude. When this is done, it would seem natural to take the value of the middle case in the array as an average in the sense that it is a central value. This middle value is called the *median*. If a finite population contains an odd number of cases, the middle case can easily be located, and the median is clearly defined as the value of that case. For instance, suppose that a small population consists of five members of a car pool with the following ages: 22, 26, 29, 31, 36. The middle case is the third element in the array. Thus, the median is 29, which is the value of this middle case. Now suppose that the car pool recruits a sixth member who is 27 years old. Then the array of ages will be: 22, 26, 27, 29, 31, 36. Since the car pool now contains an even number of people, the array does not have a single middle case, and the median is no longer clearly defined.

Because a single middle case does not exist when a population contains an even number of elements, the definition of the median as the value of the middle case is inadequate. To resolve this difficulty, the median of a finite population may be more formally defined as the lowest value in the population for which the cumulative relative frequency is at least .50. In other words, the median is the .50 fractile. Thus, when describing a population in terms of some variable X, we may denote the median as $X_{.50}$. That is, Md = $X_{.50}$. Since the second quartile is also equivalent to the .50 fractile, it should be obvious that the median, the second quartile, and the .50 fractile are identical.

Determining the value of a population median is simply a matter of obtaining the .50 fractile. For example, consider once more the data in Table 3.3. Since there are 125 scores, a cumulative relative frequency of .50 is equivalent to a cumulative frequency of $125 \times .50 = 62.5$. Rounding this figure up to 63, the .50 fractile is the value of the 63rd case. From the arrayed scores, the value of the 63rd case is 41. Thus, the median test score of the population is Md = $X_{.50}$ = 41.

Ideally, as a central value, the median should be a value above and below which there are an equal number of cases. However, in a finite population, this ideal may not necessarily be realized. For instance, inspection of Table 3.3 reveals that there are 61 scores below the median value of 41, while there are only 60 scores above the median. Thus, although it is convenient to think of the median as a value that splits the distribution into two equal halves, we should realize that this is only an ideal that may or may not be exactly true in a given distribution.

3.3.3 The Mean

The *arithmetic mean*, often referred to simply as the *mean*, corresponds to the layperson's usual idea of the average. That is, for a finite population, the mean is the sum of the values of all the elements in the population divided by the total number of elements. A population mean is customarily denoted by μ, the lowercase Greek letter mu. In terms of a formula, the mean of a finite population is defined as

$$\mu = \frac{\sum_{i=1}^{N} x_i}{N} \tag{3.2}$$

In this formula, N denotes the total number of elements in the population (size of the population) and x_i denotes the value of the ith element. The symbol $\sum$, which is the capital Greek letter sigma, is used to indicate the operation of summing a set of values. Thus, the numerator in Formula (3.2) simply represents the sum of all values in the population. That is,

$$\sum_{i=1}^{N} x_i = x_1 + x_2 + x_3 + \ldots + x_N$$

This grand total is sometimes referred to as the *aggregate*.[4] Thus, the mean of a finite population is the population aggregate divided by the population size.

To illustrate the use of Formula (3.2), consider a small, finite population consisting of the nine members of the board of directors of the Apollo Motors Company. The individual directors have served on the board for various numbers of years, as follows:

$$11, \quad 12, \quad 12, \quad 13, \quad 13, \quad 13, \quad 14, \quad 14, \quad 15$$

The aggregate for this population of nine elements is

$$\sum_{i=1}^{9} x_i = 11 + 12 + 12 + 13 + 13 + 13 + 14 + 14 + 15 = 117$$

Then, applying Formula (3.2), the population mean is

$$\mu = \frac{117}{9} = 13$$

Since calculation of the mean involves addition, it is legitimate to compute the mean only if the individual observations are measurements on a scale that is at least at the interval level. This requirement is too often violated, as is usually the case in computing a grade-point average, but such common usage does not make the practice legitimate.

As defined by Formula (3.2), the mean is a measure of central value which

---

[4] In most instances when the summation operator $\sum$ is used, the summation includes the entire set of values. When this is true, it is conventional to omit the limits on the summation sign. Thus, the population aggregate is often expressed simply as $\sum x_i$.

is the *centroid* or *center of gravity* of the distribution. To illustrate this concept of center of gravity, consider again the years of service of the members of the board of directors. Suppose that we build a histogram from these data by arranging building blocks on a plank, as shown in Figure 3.1a. In this figure, each block represents an individual element of the population. At equal intervals along the plank, values are marked corresponding to the values of the elements. If we wished to place a fulcrum under the plank so that the plank would balance, the fulcrum would be placed at such a point that the sum of the forces on the left side of the fulcrum is equal to the sum of the forces on the right side of the fulcrum. This point, which is the *center of gravity* of the pile of blocks, corresponds to the mean. Thus, the fulcrum is placed directly beneath the value 13, which is the mean of the distribution.

The distribution illustrated in Figure 3.1a is *symmetrical* around the value 13—the blocks form a symmetrical pattern with the value 13 at the center. In contrast, Figure 3.1b represents an *asymmetrical* pattern, which is formed from the following set of values:

$$\{11, 12, 12, 13, 13, 13, 14, 18, 20\}$$

If the fulcrum were placed under the value 13, the plank would tip to the right. For the plank to balance, the fulcrum must be placed directly beneath the value corresponding to the mean, which, as the reader may verify, is equal to 14.

Inspection of Figure 3.1a reveals that the mean is identical to the mode, so that the mean is not only the center of gravity but also the most typical value. This will always be true when the distribution is symmetrical around

(a) Symmetrical Pattern

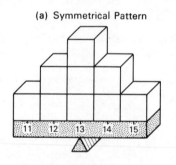

(b) Asymmetrical Pattern

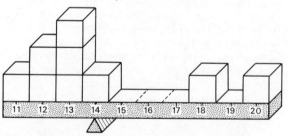

Figure 3.1   Demonstration of the Arithmetic Mean as the Center of Gravity

the mode. In contrast, for the asymmetrical distribution in Figure 3.1b, the mean is not identical with the mode. This is because the values trailing off on the right side of the distribution have "pulled" the center of gravity in their direction away from the mode.

In statistics, an asymmetrical distribution is said to be *skewed*. That is, a skewed distribution is a distribution with an "off-center" mode toward one end and a tail extending in the opposite direction. When the mode is toward the right end, with the long tail extending to the left, the distribution is *negatively* skewed. If the mode is toward the left end, with the long tail extending to the right, the distribution is *positively* skewed. In dealing with socioeconomic phenomena, we often encounter skewed distributions. For instance, personal income data are usually distributed with a mode near the left end of the distribution and a long, thin tail at the right end. This tail reflects the fact that a relatively small number of people have extremely large personal incomes.

When a population is markedly skewed, the mean may give a badly distorted measure of central value. This is because the computation of the mean takes into account the value of every element in the population so that a few extreme values can substantially influence the value of the mean. In contrast, the median is not influenced by extreme values in the population since it is located merely by counting the elements in an array. As such, the determination of the median does not make explicit use of the value of every element in the population. Thus, for a markedly skewed distribution, the median is often the preferred measure of central value. However, as we will see in subsequent chapters, regardless of the shape of the distribution, for many analyses the mean may be the preferred measure of central tendency because of its mathematical properties.

3.4 MEASURES OF VARIABILITY

Although it is convenient to describe a population in terms of an average, we must recognize that it can be misleading to use an average to represent the values of all the individual elements in the population, particularly if these elements differ considerably in their values. Thus, in using an average, we need to ask just how representative that average is. The extent to which an average is representative of an entire population depends on how closely the individual values are concentrated around the average. In other words, the wider the spread of the distribution, the less representative the average becomes. This spread of a distribution is usually referred to as *variability* or *dispersion*. Hence, in using an average to describe a population, it is helpful to accompany that average with some measure of variability.

As we will see, all measures of variability involve the operation of subtraction. Since this operation requires that the numbers be on an interval scale or higher, measures of variability are valid only if the individual observations are measurements on a scale at least at the interval level.

3.4.1 The Range

The simplest measure of variability is the *range*, which is the distance on the scale of measurement between the highest value and the lowest value in the distribution. For a population of values, the range is easily obtained by subtracting the smallest value from the largest value. In terms of a formula,

$$\text{Range} = X_H - X_L \tag{3.3}$$

where X_H = highest value
X_L = lowest value

To illustrate how the range of a population is determined, let us return to our example of the board of directors of Apollo Motors. The years of service of the individual board members are shown in column (1) of Table 3.4. The

Table 3.4 Years of Service of Board Members of Three Companies

(1) Apollo Motors	(2) Bacchus Beverages	(3) Ceres Tractors
11	8	6
12	9	10
12	10	13
13	11	14
13	13	14
13	15	14
14	16	15
14	17	15
15	18	16

highest value in this column is $X_H = 15$ years, and the lowest value is $X_L = 11$ years. Thus, using Formula (3.3), the range of this population is $15 - 11 = 4$ years. That is, with respect to their years of service, the nine members of the board cluster together fairly closely over a 4-year span, as illustrated by the histogram in Figure 3.2a.

Roughly speaking, the greater the amount of dispersion in a population, the larger will be its range. For example, consider the board of directors of another company—Bacchus Beverages. The years of service of the members of this board, given in column (2) of Table 3.4, are presented graphically by the histogram in Figure 3.2b. The range of this population is $18 - 8 = 10$ years. By comparing the histograms in Figure 3.2a and b, we see that the years of service of the Bacchus directors are more "spread out" or "scattered" than the years of service of the Apollo directors. This difference in variability between the two populations results in ranges that are substantially different—4 years for Apollo and 10 years for Bacchus.

Since the range is simply the difference between the highest and lowest values, its magnitude depends solely on these two extreme values, ignoring all other values between these two extremes. Thus, due to its sheer simplicity, the range is a very crude measure of variability that sometimes presents difficulties in its practical application as a descriptive measure. For instance, the presence of a single unusually extreme value can produce a range that may overstate the amount of dispersion among most of the elements in the distribution. To illustrate this point, consider the board of directors of a third company—Ceres Tractors. The years of service of the members of this board, given in

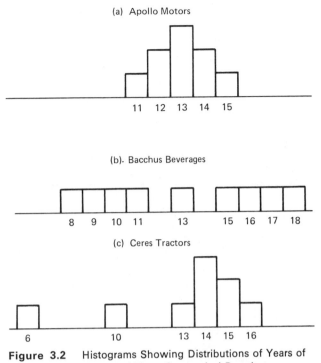

(a) Apollo Motors

11   12   13   14   15

(b). Bacchus Beverages

8   9   10   11   13   15   16   17   18

(c) Ceres Tractors

6   10   13   14   15   16

Figure 3.2   Histograms Showing Distributions of Years of
Service of Three Companies' Boards

column (3) of Table 3.4, are presented graphically by the histogram in Figure 3.2c. As the histogram shows, the years of service of most of the Ceres directors are clustered in the relatively narrow interval from 13 to 16 years. However, the range of this population is $16 - 6 = 10$ years, which is the same as the range of the Bacchus population. The range of 10 years for the Ceres population fails to reflect the fact that most of the elements are fairly closely clustered. In other words, the range of 10 overstates the relatively small variability of most of the elements in the Ceres population. This overstatement is caused by the unusually small value of the element at the lower extreme of the population.

3.4.2   The Interquartile Range

The range is severely limited as a measure of variability because of its sensitivity to any unusually extreme value that may happen to occur at one end or the other of a distribution. This limitation can be mitigated by using the *interquartile range*, which is the distance on the scale of measurement between the third quartile and the first quartile. Thus, if a population is described in terms of some quantitative variable X, the interquartile range is obtained by subtracting the first quartile $(X_{.25})$ from the third quartile $(X_{.75})$. That is,

$$\text{I.R.} = X_{.75} - X_{.25} \tag{3.4}$$

As such, the interquartile range is the scale distance over which approximately the middle 50% of the population values are scattered.

To illustrate the use of the interquartile range as a measure of variability, consider again the three populations in Table 3.4. The calculation of the range and interquartile range of each of these populations is shown in Table 3.5. As

Table 3.5 Determination of Ranges and Interquartile Ranges
of Three Populations

	Apollo Motors	Bacchus Beverages	Ceres Tractors
Highest value	15	18	16
Lowest value	11	8	6
Range	4	10	10
Third quartile	14	16	15
First quartile	12	10	13
Interquartile range	2	6	2

we have already observed, both the Bacchus and Ceres populations have the same range, even though the Bacchus population is actually more scattered than the Ceres population. However, the interquartile range of 6 for the Bacchus population is distinctly greater than the interquartile range of 2 for the Ceres population. Thus, the difference between the variabilities of the two populations is reflected by a difference in their interquartile ranges but not in their ranges.

Compared to the range, the interquartile range is less influenced by outliers[5] in the distribution. This is because the interquartile range is computed from intermediate values in the distribution (first and third quartiles) rather than the two extremes (highest and lowest values). However, like the range, the interquartile range is based on the values of only two elements, ignoring the values of all other elements in the population. Thus, the interquartile range is still a crude measure of variability that does not completely measure the distributional pattern of all the individual values in the population. Consequently, it is possible that two populations with different amounts of scatter may have identical interquartile ranges. For instance, as we can see from Figure 3.2, the Ceres population is slightly more spread out than the Apollo population, but both of these populations have the same interquartile range of 2.

3.4.3 The Mean Absolute Deviation

Because the range and interquartile range are crude measures, their practical applications are limited. The more commonly used measures of dispersion are based on the concept of "deviations" from the mean. For any value in a population, there is a corresponding *deviation*, which is defined as the *algebraic difference* between that value and the mean of the population. If x_i denotes the value of the ith element in a population, and μ denotes the population mean, the deviation of that element may be expressed as $(x_i - \mu)$. Thus, if a value is less than the mean, its deviation is negative, and if the value is greater than the mean, its deviation is positive. Now, the question is: How may deviations be employed to obtain a single measure for representing the variability of the entire population?

---

[5]An outlier is an extreme value that is separated from the main body of the distribution.

An intuitive response to the question just raised is to suggest that we take the mean of all the deviations. That is, we might simply compute

$$\frac{\sum (x_i - \mu)}{N}$$

Unfortunately, this would be futile since, for any population, the mean of the algebraic deviations must be equal to zero. This conforms with the idea that the mean is the center of gravity. That is, the negative forces on one side of the mean counterbalance the positive forces on the other side of the mean.

Since the mean of the algebraic deviations must always be zero, it is useless as a measure of variability. One way to avoid this difficulty is to disregard the algebraic signs of the deviations. In other words, rather than working with *algebraic* deviations, we could work with the *absolute* values of the deviations. This implies that, when measuring dispersion, we are primarily interested in the *magnitudes* of the deviations rather than their *signs*. That is, we are concerned with *how far* the individual values depart from the mean, but not with the *direction* in which they depart. Therefore, we may obtain a meaningful measure of dispersion by averaging the *absolute* deviations instead of the *algebraic* deviations. Specifically, the *mean absolute deviation* (M.A.D.) of a finite population is given by

$$\text{M.A.D.} = \frac{\sum_{i=1}^{N} |x_i - \mu|}{N} \qquad (3.5)$$

To illustrate the application of Formula (3.5), let us return to the Apollo Motors population in Table 3.4. The mean absolute deviation for this population is calculated in Table 3.6. This calculation proceeds as follows:

Table 3.6 Calculation of Mean Absolute Deviation for the Apollo Motors Population

x_i	$x_i - \mu$	$|x_i - \mu|$
11	$11 - 13 = -2$	2
12	$12 - 13 = -1$	1
12	$12 - 13 = -1$	1
13	$13 - 13 = 0$	0
13	$13 - 13 = 0$	0
13	$13 - 13 = 0$	0
14	$14 - 13 = 1$	1
14	$14 - 13 = 1$	1
15	$15 - 13 = 2$	2
Sum 117	0	8

$$\mu = \frac{\sum x_i}{N} = \frac{117}{9} = 13 \qquad \text{M.A.D.} = \frac{\sum |x_i - \mu|}{N} = \frac{8}{9} = .89$$

1. Compute the mean of the population.
2. Calculate the deviations of the elements. As a check, these deviations should sum to zero.

3. Sum the absolute values of the deviations.
4. Divide the sum obtained in step 3 by the population size N.

Table 3.6 shows that the M.A.D. of the Apollo Motors population is .89. As a measure of variability, this figure indicates that, "on the average," the values in this population deviate .89 from the mean. Following the same computational procedure, the reader may verify that the M.A.D. of the Bacchus population is 3.11 and the M.A.D. of the Ceres population is 2.22. Thus, as measured by their mean absolute deviations, the variability of the Bacchus population is greater than the variability of the Ceres population, and the variability of the Ceres population is greater than the variability of the Apollo population. This conforms with our earlier impression obtained from inspection of the histograms in Figure 3.2.

3.4.4 The Variance and Standard Deviation

Although the mean absolute deviation of a distribution is relatively easy to compute and understand, it is not widely employed in statistical practice because its "poor" mathematical properties limit its use for more extensive analysis. Two other measures, which are much more commonly used to describe variability around the mean, are the *variance* and *standard deviation*.

The Variance. Unlike the mean absolute deviation (which is computed from the *absolute* deviations from the mean), the variance is computed by using the *squared* deviations from the mean. Squaring not only makes all deviations positive but also provides mathematical properties that are more desirable for many types of further analysis. For a finite population, the variance is defined by

$$\sigma^2 = \frac{\sum_{i=1}^{N} (x_i - \mu)^2}{N} \tag{3.6}$$

where σ is the lowercase Greek letter sigma.

To illustrate the use of Formula (3.6), the variance of the Apollo population is computed in Table 3.7. As we can see from this table, the computation of the

Table 3.7 Calculation of the Variance for the Apollo Motors Population

x_i	$x_i - \mu$	$(x_i - \mu)^2$
11	$11 - 13 = -2$	4
12	$12 - 13 = -1$	1
12	$12 - 13 = -1$	1
13	$13 - 13 = 0$	0
13	$13 - 13 = 0$	0
13	$13 - 13 = 0$	0
14	$14 - 13 = 1$	1
14	$14 - 13 = 1$	1
15	$15 - 13 = 2$	4
Sum 117	0	12

$$\mu = \frac{\sum x_i}{N} = \frac{117}{9} = 13 \qquad \sigma^2 = \frac{\sum (x_i - \mu)^2}{N} = \frac{12}{9} = 1.33$$

variance proceeds as follows:

1. Compute the mean of the population.
2. Calculate the deviations of the elements. As a check, the sum of these deviations should be zero.
3. Square each of the deviations.
4. Sum the squares of the deviations.
5. Divide the sum obtained in step 4 by the population size N.

Table 3.7 shows that the variance of the years of service of the Apollo Motors population is 1.33. Thus, the average of the squared deviations of the individual values in the population from their mean is 1.33 square years. Notice that the variance is expressed in "square years." This is because, when we square the deviations, we also square the units of measurements in which those deviations are expressed.

Formula (3.6) clearly defines the variance as the average of the squared deviations. However, this formula is cumbersome to use because it requires the squaring of every individual deviation. Fortunately, results identical to those yielded by Formula (3.6) can be obtained from the following alternative formula:[6]

$$\sigma^2 = \frac{\sum\limits_{i=1}^{N} x_i^2}{N} - \mu^2 \tag{3.7}$$

In this formula the first term is the mean of the squared values and the second term is the square of the mean. Thus, the variance is sometimes described as the *mean of the squares* minus the *square of the mean*.

For purposes of computation, Formula (3.7) is generally preferable to (3.6), because it is usually easier to square the individual values than to compute the squared deviations. Using Formula (3.7), the variance of the Apollo Motors population is computed in Table 3.8. This computation proceeds as follows:

1. Compute the mean of the population.
2. Square each value and sum these squares to obtain $\sum x_i^2$.
3. Divide $\sum x_i^2$ by the population size N to obtain the mean of the squares.
4. Square the mean to obtain μ^2.
5. Compute the difference between the mean of the squares and the square of the mean (that is, subtract the result of step 4 from the result of step 3).

Following the foregoing computational steps, Formula (3.7) yields a variance of 1.33 square years, which is the same result obtained previously from Formula (3.6).

The Standard Deviation. Because of its desirable mathematical properties, the variance is used extensively in statistical *analysis*. Difficulty arises, however,

---

[6]The formula generally used in computer computation of the variance is

$$\sigma^2 = \frac{N \sum x_i^2 - (\sum x_i)^2}{N^2}$$

Table 3.8 Alternative Calculation of the Variance for the Apollo Motors Population

x_i	x_i^2
11	121
12	144
12	144
13	169
13	169
13	169
14	196
14	196
15	225
$\sum x_i = \overline{117}$	$\sum x_i^2 = \overline{1,533}$

$$\mu = \frac{\sum x_i}{N} = \frac{117}{9} = 13 \text{ years}$$

$$\sigma^2 = \frac{\sum x_i^2}{N} - \mu^2 = \frac{1,533}{9} - (13)^2$$

$$= 170.33 - 169.00$$

$$= 1.33 \text{ square years}$$

in *interpreting* the variance because it is expressed in squared units of measurement. This difficulty may be resolved by taking the positive square root of the variance. Taking the square root permits us to reconvert the square units of measurement into original units of measurement. The positive square root of the variance is known as the *standard deviation*, which is commonly denoted by σ. That is,

$$\sigma = \sqrt{\sigma^2} \tag{3.8}$$

For our Apollo population, the standard deviation is

$$\sigma = \sqrt{1.33 \text{ square years}} = 1.15 \text{ years}$$

Thus, using the term "average" in the broad sense, we may say that the average deviation of the individual ages from the mean age of the Apollo population is 1.15 years.[7]

As the reader may verify, the standard deviation of the Bacchus population is 3.46 and the standard deviation of the Ceres population is 2.94. This agrees with our previous finding from comparing the mean absolute deviations of the three populations that the variability of the Bacchus population is greater than that of the other two populations, and the variability of the Ceres population is greater than that of the Apollo population.

---

[7]Actually, the standard deviation is the quadratic mean deviation from expectation. As such, it is a type of average.

PROBLEMS

3.1 Consider the data presented in Table 3.1.

(a) Would it be meaningful to compute cumulative relative frequencies for this distribution? Explain.

(b) Would it be meaningful to compute fractiles? Explain.

(c) Would it be meaningful to compute any type of average for this population? Explain.

3.2 Midsouthern University consists of six schools with a total student population of 20,000. The number of students enrolled in each school is as follows:

School of Administration	3,600
School of Education	1,800
School of Engineering	1,200
School of Letters, Arts, and Sciences	12,500
School of Law	500
School of Medicine	400

(a) Of the total student population, what proportion is enrolled in each school?

(b) What is the relative frequency of students enrolled in either the School of Administration or the School of Law?

(c) What proportion of the student population is not enrolled in the School of Education?

3.3 The East Elm Street Investment Club consists of six members. The amounts of money invested by each of the members during the month of January are as follows:

Member	Amount Invested
Alice	$114
Betty	105
Clara	111
Dorothy	107
Emma	108
Fay	115

Determine the mean, variance, and standard deviation of the amounts invested by the members of this small (but exclusive) population.

3.4 The West Oak Street Neighborhood Improvement Society consists of 10 families, all of whom have their homes up for sale. The listed prices (in thousands of dollars) for these homes are as follows:

Family	Listed Price
Aldrich	66.8
Bennett	62.5
Carter	70.2
Dole	73.4
Evans	55.5
Flynn	49.5
Gump	69.3
Hale	68.4
Ives	72.1
Jackson	84.3

Determine the mean and median listed price.

3.5   For the listed prices in Problem 3.4, determine the variance and standard deviation.

3.6   Colonel Culpepper's Mississippi Fried Chicken Company is a take-out food firm with 24 franchises. The gross receipts (in thousands of dollars) for each franchise during the week of September 15 are as follows:

13.8	13.9	14.0	14.0	14.0	14.1
13.7	13.9	14.2	14.2	14.1	14.5
14.6	14.9	13.7	13.9	14.0	14.1
14.9	14.0	14.7	14.3	14.0	14.1

For these receipts of this population of franchises, determine the following:
(a)   Median
(b)   .90 fractile
(c)   .20 fractile
(d)   Mean
(e)   Mode

3.7   For the data in Problem 3.6, determine the following:
(a)   Interquartile range
(b)   Mean absolute deviation
(c)   Variance
(d)   Standard deviation

3.8   Using the data in Table 3.4, verify that the M.A.D. of the Bacchus population is 3.11 and the M.A.D. of the Ceres population is 2.22.

3.9   The Quality Department Store has branches in eight cities. The number of salesclerks employed by each branch is as follows:

Branch	Number of Clerks
A	32
B	41
C	28
D	53
E	46
F	39
G	44
H	49

For these data, calculate the following:
(a)   Mean
(b)   Median
(c)   .25 fractile
(d)   .60 fractile

3.10   For the data in Problem 3.9, calculate the following:
(a)   Mean absolute deviation
(b)   Variance
(c)   Standard deviation

3.11   Using the data for the three populations presented in Table 3.4, complete the following table:

Parameter	Population		
	Apollo	Bacchus	Ceres
Mean			
Median			
Standard deviation			

3.12 The Nonox Treadmill Company is a West Coast firm that employs a total of 25 sales engineers in three field territories. Every 3 months, each sales engineer receives a quarterly performance rating from his or her supervisor. The most recent quarterly ratings are shown below for each employee, together with his or her current age and field territory.

Employee	Territory	Rating	Age
Adams	1	91	42
Babcock	2	89	37
Carlson	2	64	28
Douglas	3	91	32
Earp	2	53	29
Fleming	1	59	29
Gray	3	79	25
Harper	2	69	34
Ives	2	52	25
Jaeger	2	92	43
Kanter	1	82	33
Larsen	1	88	33
Melvan	3	86	28
Nanus	1	59	39
O'Toole	1	51	25
Peterson	3	82	29
Quincy	1	92	27
Rowe	3	53	35
Stevenson	1	82	33
Thrasher	2	69	39
Udall	3	60	40
Vernon	3	71	33
White	2	94	31
Xavier	2	57	31
Yormark	2	56	33

(a) For this population of 25 sales engineers, prepare a table showing the frequency and relative frequency of engineers assigned to each sales territory.

(b) What proportion of the population is assigned to each sales territory?

(c) Determine the median and interquartile range of the performance ratings.

(d) Would it be meaningful to compute the mean of the performance ratings? Discuss.

3.13 For the data in Problem 3.12, do the following:

(a) Determine the median, mean, variance, and standard deviation of the ages of the population.

(b) Compute the mean age of the sales engineers in each of the three territories.

(c) Compute the mean of the three means obtained in part (b). Does your answer agree with the mean of the entire population obtained in part (a)? Why or why not?

3.14 The J. C. Nickell Department Store has two branches—one in Magnolia Falls and the other in the neighboring town of Pine Rapids. As of March 1, the Magnolia Falls branch had 60 delinquent accounts and the Pine Rapids branch had 40 delinquent accounts. The amounts of these accounts (to the nearest dollar) are as follows:

Magnolia Falls Branch						Pine Rapids Branch			
42	12	61	21	84	67	80	149	80	59
68	63	125	53	85	18	99	28	72	23
81	77	77	63	44	39	88	33	93	82
16	38	63	28	55	54	82	42	145	34
21	41	52	76	24	50	19	30	23	132
138	96	59	75	99	48	41	98	164	73
84	89	71	64	20	14	157	28	98	35
28	66	17	53	16	41	98	45	56	55
84	35	51	72	26	75	89	67	90	90
13	26	64	56	72	88	42	105	80	141

(a) Determine the .20, .50, and .80 fractiles of the amounts of the population of Magnolia Falls delinquent accounts.

(b) Repeat part (a) for the population of Pine Rapids delinquent accounts.

(c) From a comparison of the corresponding fractiles for the two branches, what conclusion do you draw?

(d) Compute the mean of each of the two populations. Does a comparison of these two means support your conclusion in part (c)?

(e) Use the two means obtained in part (d) to obtain the grand mean of the two populations combined. (Bear in mind that the sizes of the two populations are different.)

3.15 Show that $\dfrac{\sum (x_i - \mu)}{N} = 0$.

3.16 Show that:

(a) Formulas (3.6) and (3.7) are identical.

(b) $\dfrac{\sum x_i^2}{N} - \mu^2 = \dfrac{N \sum x_i^2 - (\sum x_i)^2}{N^2}$

4

Introduction to Probability

If a population consists of a finite number of elements, and if it is feasible to observe all of these elements, then techniques such as those discussed in Chapter 3 can be applied to determine the values of whatever parameters may be relevant to a particular decision problem. In dealing with a real-world decision problem, however, a total canvass of the population is often impossible or impracticable. In such a case, although *complete* information concerning decision parameters may not be obtainable, it still may be possible to acquire *partial* information by observing a sample. Of course, when a decision must be made on the basis of incomplete information obtained from a sample, some degree of uncertainty will continue to exist. Statistical methods for dealing with uncertainty in decision making are based on the theory of probability, to which we now turn our attention.

4.1 MEANINGS OF PROBABILITY

Even among statisticians, who are greatly concerned with their definitions, there is no single definition of probability that will cover all situations. Before attaching meaning to a probability statement, we must question the *source* of that statement. If a probability is determined by theoretical reasoning, or from actual observation of a sequence of events, we speak of *objective* probability. If an individual states a probability as a measure of the strength of his personal belief in some proposition, we are dealing with *subjective* probability. The distinction between objective and subjective probability involves differences not only in the source of probability statements, but also in the fundamental viewpoint toward the interpretation and application of probability statements.

4.1.1 Objective Probability

A fundamental notion underlying the objectivistic interpretation is the concept of a *random process*. A random process is an operation that is (conceptually, at least) *repetitive*. That is, a random process is conceived as a *sequence of trials* conducted in such a manner that the particular outcome of any given trial is the result of unknown or unassignable causes. In other words, the sequence of outcomes produced by a random process is, as far as we know, solely the result of "chance." A simple example of a random process would be the repeated tossing of a coin. Each toss (trial) has two possible outcomes: heads or tails. The particular sequence of heads and tails obtained through repeated tossings is unpredictable and can be explained only in terms of random effects.

Probabilities Based on Theoretical Reasoning. One source of objective probability statements is the *theoretical analysis* of a random process. As an example, consider the random process of drawing a card from a well-shuffled standard deck of 52 playing cards. We might reason that each card has an *equally likely* opportunity of being drawn, and that the probability of drawing any particular card, say the queen of hearts, is therefore 1/52. Similarly, we know that there are four aces in the deck, and the probability of drawing an ace (without regard to suit) is 4/52. In such cases, wherein each of the possible outcomes is equally likely, we may define the probability of some event E by the ratio

$$P(E) = \frac{n(E)}{n(T)} \tag{4.1}$$

where $n(T)$ = total number of equally likely outcomes
$n(E)$ = number of those outcomes corresponding to event E

For example, we might define an event as drawing a spade from a well-shuffled 52-card deck. Since there are 52 possible cards that might be drawn, the total number of equally likely outcomes is 52—that is, $n(T) = 52$. Also, since there are 13 spades in the deck, 13 of these possible outcomes correspond to "drawing a spade." Therefore, $n(E) = 13$, and the probability of drawing a spade is $13/52 = 1/4 = .25$.

Empirical Probabilities. The term *empirical* (from a Latin word meaning "experiment") is frequently applied to probabilities that are derived from actual experimentation or observation of a random process in operation. Unlike probabilities derived purely through theoretical analysis, empirical probabilities result from "experiencing" the outcomes of random processes. On the basis of pure theoretical analysis we might determine that the probability of obtaining heads when tossing a fair coin is 1/2. That is, we might argue that there are two possible outcomes that are equally likely, and that one of these two outcomes corresponds to the event "heads." Empirically, we would determine the probability of obtaining heads with a particular coin by tossing that coin many times and recording the proportion of times it comes up heads.

Assume that a random process is repeated some number of times, n, and that during these n repetitions some event E occurs with a frequency f (that is, the event E occurs f number of times out of n repetitions). Then the empirical probability of the event E may be defined as the ratio

$$P(E) = \frac{f}{n} \tag{4.2}$$

Suppose, for instance, that a distributor of garden seeds wishes to determine the probability that a particular type of seed will germinate when planted under standard conditions. He might estimate this probability empirically by planting a large number of these seeds and then observing the number of seeds that actually germinate. If he planted 1,000 seeds and if 700 of these seeds germinated, then the empirical probability for this type of seed germinating under the standard conditions would be $700/1,000 = .70$.

If we look at a random process as a repeatable operation, the objective probability of an event is the *relative frequency of occurrence* of that event in the long run. In the example of drawing a spade from a bridge deck, the probability of .25, which was obtained by theoretical analysis, may be interpreted as the relative frequency, in the long run, with which we would expect to draw a spade during an extended series of repeated trials.

In contrast to probabilities obtained by theoretical analysis, probabilities obtained by empirical procedures are usually only *estimates*. To obtain the "true" long-run relative frequency of an event would require an impractically large number of observations.

4.1.2 Subjective Probability

From the subjective viewpoint, a probability is regarded as a measure of an individual's personal confidence in the truth of some proposition, such as the proposition that there will be no business recession within the next two years. The subjectivist maintains that a "reasonable" person who obtains some practice and experience can learn to use the language of probability to describe his or her own attitudes about the degree of certainty or uncertainty in a particular situation.

Consider, for example, a pair of subjectivists, Ann Able and Bob Baker, who are partners in a speculative real estate venture. They have the opportunity to acquire several hundred acres of arid land that could have development potential depending on the outcome of a reclamation proposal currently before the state legislature. Ann feels that the probability is about .70 that the reclamation bill will be passed, whereas Bob judges the probability of the bill's passage to be about .40. In other words, both Ann and Bob feel uncertain about whether the reclamation bill will be passed. Ann has assigned a relative weight of .70 as a measure of her belief that the bill will be passed, and a relative weight of .30 as a measure of her belief that it will not be passed. Similarly, Bob has assigned relative weights of .40 and .60 to indicate the strength of his feelings about these two propositions.

If Ann is a firm subjectivist, she will probably not be distressed by the fact that she and her partner assigned different probabilities to the proposition that the reclamation bill will be passed. The subjectivistic position readily admits— in fact, *assumes*—that two reasonable persons might attach different probabilities to the same event. After all, the beliefs that different people have regarding the likelihood of a particular event are based on their psychological predispositions, which in turn are determined largely by their real-world experiences. If two people with different experiential backgrounds are presented with the same decision problem and are given the same relevant evidence, they may well assign it somewhat different probabilities if their motivational, emotional, and perceptual processes are operating differently at the time.

Because two reasonable individuals may assign different probabilities to the same event, subjective probabilities are frequently described as being *judgmental* or *personalistic*. Nevertheless, a person's subjective probability assessments concerning a particular class of events are usually based on some backlog of experience with similar events, and so usually do not just come from "out of the blue." Indeed, frequently one of the best ways of obtaining information bearing on certain practical decisions is to solicit the personal opinions of individuals who have a great deal of experience with the types of events that concern us. Thus, the personalists may cogently argue that the use of subjective probabilities, obtained from experienced persons, has an important function in the process of making practical decisions.

4.1.3 Comparison of Objective and Subjective Viewpoints

How does the viewpoint of the subjectivist compare with that of the objectivist? To the objectivist, of course, the personalist's probability statements, based on personal feeling, opinion, or attitude, are unacceptable. The objectivistic approach would assume that two reasonable persons who approach the same problem situation with the same set of assumptions and evidence will arrive at the same probability assessments. The personalist, however, would argue that such an approach is narrow and limited; the objectivist is limited to events that can be interpreted in terms of a random process with resultant relative frequencies, whereas the personalist has no such limitation on his or her sphere of operation. The personalist is perfectly willing to apply himself or herself to problems involving the probabilities of events produced by random processes, but is equally willing to work with probabilities of unique events—that is, one-of-a-kind events rather than events that can occur repeatedly. For example, the personalist would feel that the question of the probability that Big Steel will increase its prices during the next 6 months is a perfectly legitimate problem, but the question would be outside the domain of the objectivist since it concerns a unique event rather than a repeatable process.

The objectivistic and personalistic viewpoints arrive at some degree of rapprochement in their treatments of the role of experience in probability assessment. To the extent that an individual's subjective probability assessment for an event is based on his experience with similar past events, he is more or less empirical. If his experience has been relatively informal, and his probability assessment is affected by memory and judgment, then we would consider his probability statements to be essentially personalistic. If, however, his experience has been gained under relatively standardized, formal conditions, and particularly if he has kept careful records of this experience to form the basis of his probability assessment, then his probability statements may closely approach being empirical in the objectivistic sense. Indeed, in actual business applications of some statistical procedures that are associated primarily with the personalistic approach, the appearance of genuine objectivistic probabilities is not at all unheard of.

4.2 PROBABILITY AND ODDS

An individual's subjective appraisal of the likelihood that a particular event will occur is often expressed in terms of *odds* rather than in terms of a probability. The odds in favor of an event relate the chances that the event will occur to the chances that the event will not occur. For example, a football analyst might proclaim that the odds are 3:2 that the Rams will win their next game with the Cowboys. This statement expresses his feeling that the Rams have 3 chances of winning the game compared to 2 chances of not winning.

If the likelihood of an event is expressed in terms of the odds favoring that event, it is a simple matter to convert those odds to the probability that the event will occur. For instance, by announcing that the odds are 3 : 2 that the Rams will beat the Cowboys, the football analyst means that the Rams have 3 chances of winning out of a total of 5 chances. As a general statement, if the odds in favor of an event E are stated $a : b$, then the probability of the event E is

$$P(E) = \frac{a}{a + b} \qquad (4.3)$$

For our example in which the odds are 3 : 2 in favor of the Rams, $a = 3$ and $b = 2$. Applying Formula (4.3), these odds imply that the probability of the Rams' winning is

$$P(E) = \frac{3}{3 + 2} = .60$$

4.3 PROBABILITY AND COUNTING

Many applications of probability theory to decision problems involve random processes that reasonably may be assumed to have a finite number of equally likely outcomes. As an example, consider a manufacturer of electronic equipment who receives transistors from a supplier in lots of 60. Suppose that the manufacturer wishes to test a sample of 10 transistors selected "at random" from each lot. Under these conditions, if a particular lot actually contains three defectives, what is the probability that any two of these three defectives will be included among the 10 transistors that are selected for testing? To answer this question, we can apply Formula (4.1), which is

$$P(E) = \frac{n(E)}{n(T)}$$

In this example, E represents the event that the sample will include any two of the three defectives in the lot, $n(T)$ represents the total number of different groups of 10 transistors that could possibly be drawn at random from the lot of 60 transistors, and $n(E)$ represents the number of possible groups of 10 transistors that contain two defectives.

Applying Formula (4.1) to this problem would be an elementary matter if we could determine the values of $n(E)$ and $n(T)$. One approach might be to identify each transistor by a serial number from 1 to 60. Then we might begin to list all possible groups of 10 different numbers from 1 to 60. If a person had unlimited time, patience, pencils, and paper, he or she eventually could succeed in listing and then counting all the possibilities. This, however, would be an exhausting task, for there are over 75 billion different possible sets of 10 items out of 60 (as you will shortly be able to verify for yourself). Obviously, if we are to approach probability problems in a practical manner, we need methods of counting that are more efficient than the tedious process of listing and enumerating. We would do well to defer answering our transistor problem until the end of this chapter, after we have considered some of these counting methods.

4.3.1 Factorial Notation

In our discussion of "shortcut" counting procedures, it will be helpful to employ *factorial* notation. The expression $n!$ is read "n factorial" and is used to denote the product of all whole numbers from 1 to n. That is,

$$n! = n(n - 1)(n - 2) \ldots (3)\, (2)\, (1)$$

For example,

$$7! = 7 \times 6 \times 5 \times 4 \times 3 \times 2 \times 1 = 5{,}040$$

As a special case, we must define $0! = 1$. In working with factorials, it is also helpful to note that for $n \geq 1$,

$$n! = n(n - 1)!$$

Examples are

$$50! = 50 \times 49!$$
$$100! = 100 \times 99 \times 98!$$

4.3.2 The Fundamental Principle of Counting

Most counting procedures are based on the following fundamental principle:

If a first task can be conducted in n_1 different ways and, after it is done in any one of those ways, a second task can be conducted in n_2 different ways and, after the first two tasks, a third can be conducted in n_3 different ways, and so on for r tasks, then the number of different ways in which the r tasks can be accomplished in the given order is

$$n_1 \times n_2 \times n_3 \times \ldots \times n_r \tag{4.4}$$

Thus, if a first task can be conducted in five different ways, after any one of which a second task can be conducted in six different ways, after any one of which a third task can be conducted in four different ways, then together the three tasks can be accomplished in the stated order in $5 \times 6 \times 4 = 120$ different ways.

Example:

An office manager has four clerks—Alice, Ben, Cora, and Dorothy—to whom she must make work assignments. She needs one clerk to operate the telephone switchboard, one to take dictation, one to type, and one to file. Only Alice and Ben can operate the switchboard, and only Cora and Dorothy can take dictation. All four clerks can type and file. In how many different ways can the tasks be assigned?

There are two ways to fill the switchboard position (either Alice or Ben), and two ways to fill the dictation position (either Cora or Dorothy). After these two positions have been filled, there are two possible ways to fill the typing position; for instance, if Alice is assigned to the switchboard and Cora takes dictation, then either Ben or Dorothy may do the typing. Once the switchboard, dictation, and typing assignments have been made, only one clerk remains to do the filing. Thus, there are $2 \times 2 \times 2 \times 1 = 8$ different possible ways of making the work assignments. The tree diagram in Figure 4.1 illustrates this result.

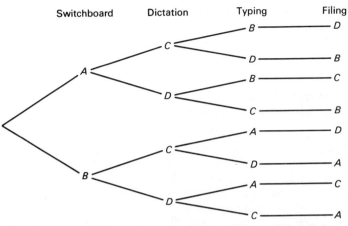

Figure 4.1 Tree Diagram Illustrating Assignment of Office Tasks

4.4 PERMUTATIONS

When we talk about the number of ways in which a set of objects may be *arranged in order*, we are speaking of the number of possible *permutations* of the set. Depending on conditions, there are various permutation formulas, all of which may be derived from the fundamental principle of counting.

4.4.1 Permuting n Distinguishable Objects

Suppose that you are placing 3 books on a shelf. In how many orders, from left to right, could you arrange them on the shelf? Designating the books as *A*, *B*, and *C*, we can list the orders:

$$ABC \quad BAC \quad CAB$$
$$ACB \quad BCA \quad CBA$$

These are the 6 possible permutations of the set of 3 books. We could obtain this same result, without actually listing, by directly applying the fundamental counting principle, reasoning as follows: Any one of the 3 books may be placed in the first position; that is, there are 3 ways in which the first choice may be made. Assuming that the first choice has been made, either of the 2 remaining books may be placed in the second position, so there are two ways in which the second choice may be made. Whichever of the two books is placed in the second position, the one remaining book will go in the third position. Thus, the total number of permutations may be obtained from the calculation $3 \times 2 \times 1 = 6 = 3!$ To generalize, if we have a set consisting of *n* different objects, the *total number of ways in which these n objects, taken all together, may be arranged in order*, is given by the expression

$$_nP_n = n! \tag{4.5}$$

Example:
A door-to-door salesman has 5 different kitchen gadgets that he demonstrates to house-wives. He would like to determine an order of presentation of the 5 gadgets that will

create an optimal "impact" on the housewife. How many different orders of presentation are there?

From Formula (4.5), the total number of permutations of 5 objects, taken all together, is

$$_5P_5 = 5! = 120$$

4.4.2 Permutations Involving Indistinguishable Objects

So far, in discussing the permutations of a set of n objects, we have assumed that all n objects in the set were distinguishably different. Suppose, however, that some of the objects in the set are indistinguishable from others. For instance, we might have a 12-item set composed of three x's, four 0's, and five $+$'s. If all 12 symbols were distinguishably different, we would have $12! = 479,001,600$ possible permutations of the elements of the set. However, since some of the elements are identical to others, not all of these 12! permutations are distinguishably different. For any given permutation of the 12 items, there are 3! ways in which the x's may be permuted among themselves, 4! ways in which the 0's may be permuted among themselves, and 5! ways that the $+$'s may be permuted among themselves. Thus, for every *distinguishably different* permutation of the 12 items, there are 3!4!5! identical permutations that may be obtained by permuting identical items among themselves. Hence, to obtain the number of distinguishably different permutations of the twelve items, we would perform the following division:

$$\frac{12!}{3!\,4!\,5!} = 27,720$$

To generalize this procedure: If we are given a set of n objects, of which n_1 objects of one kind are identical, n_2 objects of a second kind are identical, n_3 objects of a third kind are identical, and so on for k kinds of objects, then *the number of possible distinguishably different permutations of the n objects, taken all together,* is

$$_nP_n(n_1, n_2, \ldots, n_k) = \frac{n!}{n_1!\,n_2!\ldots n_k!} \tag{4.6}$$

where $n = \sum_{i=1}^{k} n_i$.

Example:

A costume jeweler is designing a new necklace. The necklace will consist of a string of 21 beads arranged in a pattern. Of the 21 beads, there are 3 identical red beads, 4 identical blue beads, 6 identical green beads, and 8 identical yellow beads. How many distinguishably different patterns are possible?

From Formula (4.6), the total number of distinguishably different permutations is

$$_{21}P_{21}(3, 4, 6, 8) = \frac{21!}{3!\,4!\,6!\,8!} = 12,221,609,400$$

A special, but important, case of Formula (4.6) is the situation in which there are only two kinds of objects. Suppose that we have a set of just two kinds of objects. If there are r objects of one kind, then there must be $(n - r)$ objects of the other kind. Then Formula (4.6) reduces to

$$_nP_n(r, n - r) = \frac{n!}{r!\,(n - r)!} \tag{4.7}$$

Example:

During the month of June, a space exploration facility conducts 7 successive attempts to launch satellites. Of these attempts, 4 were successes and 3 were failures. In how many different orders might these 4 successes and 3 failures have occurred?

From Formula (4.7)

$$_7P_7(4, 3) = \frac{7!}{4!\,3!} = 35$$

4.4.3 Selecting and Permuting r Objects from n Objects

Formula (4.5) is concerned with the permutations of n objects *taken all together*. Suppose, however, that we have a group of n objects from which we are to select a subgroup of r objects that are to be placed in order. In how many different ways may r objects be selected from n objects and then arranged in order? For example, we might have a group of 5 books from which we are to select 3 books and place them on a shelf in some order. How many different possible arrangements may result?

To obtain the answer, we could designate the 5 books as A, B, C, D, and E and list all the permutations of 3 books: ABC, BAC, ABD, DAB, ECA, and so on. However, with much less effort we can obtain the answer by applying the fundamental counting principle: The first position may be filled by any one of 5 books, after which the second position may be filled by any one of 4 remaining books, after which the third position may be filled by any one of 3 remaining books. Thus, the total number of permutations is $5 \times 4 \times 3 = 60$. Another way of expressing this computation would be

$$\frac{5 \times 4 \times 3 \times 2 \times 1}{2 \times 1} = \frac{5!}{(5 - 3)!}$$

Notice that the numerator of this ratio is the factorial of the total number of books from which the selection of 3 books was made, and the denominator is the factorial of the number of books remaining after the selection. Generalizing this result, we can say that the *total number of possible permutations resulting from selecting and arranging r objects from a group of n objects* is given by the expression

$$_nP_r = \frac{n!}{(n - r)!} \tag{4.8}$$

Example:

A personnel manager has received requisitions for one typist each from the Production Department, Marketing Department, and Research Department. There are 7 applicants available from which these 3 positions may be filled. In how many ways may 3 typists be selected from the 7 applicants and assigned to the 3 different openings?

Applying the fundamental counting principle, there are 7 ways to fill the first position, after which there are 6 ways to fill the second position, after which there are 5 ways to fill the third position. This gives $7 \times 6 \times 5 = 210$ permutations. From Formula (4.8) we obtain the same result.

$$_7P_3 = \frac{7!}{(7 - 3)!} = \frac{7 \times 6 \times 5 \times 4!}{4!} = 7 \times 6 \times 5 = 210$$

4.5 COMBINATIONS

In practical business situations wherein mathematical models involving the counting of possible outcomes are appropriate, the order or arrangement of objects is often inconsequential. For instance, if a quality control inspector randomly selects a sample of 10 items from the output of an automatic production process and finds that 3 of the items are defective, then the particular positions in which the 3 defectives occurred in the sequence of the 10 items is hardly of any consequence (although the fact that there were 3 defectives out of 10 may have an important bearing on a production control decision). In such a case we are interested only in the objects selected and not in their order or position. Such a collection of objects, considered *without regard to order or arrangement,* is called a *combination.*

To see the distinction between combinations and permutations, consider again the illustration presented in Section 4.4.3 to develop Formula (4.8) for calculating the number of *permutations* of r objects selected from n objects. In that illustration it was shown that there are 60 possible ways of selecting 3 books from 5 books and placing them on a shelf *in some order.* However, if we are concerned only with the identities of the 3 books selected, *without regard to the order* in which they are selected or placed on the shelf, how many different 3-book groupings or collections are possible? To answer this question, let us examine the 60 permutations, which are listed in Table 4.1. Careful inspection

Table 4.1   Permutations of Each Combination of 3 Books Selected from 5 Books

Combination	Permutations					
ABC	ABC	ACB	BAC	BCA	CAB	CBA
ABD	ABD	ADB	BAD	BDA	DAB	DBA
ABE	ABE	AEB	BAE	BEA	EAB	EBA
ACD	ACD	ADC	CAD	CDA	DAC	DCA
ACE	ACE	AEC	CAE	CEA	EAC	ECA
ADE	ADE	AED	DAE	DEA	EAD	EDA
BCD	BCD	BDC	CBD	CDB	DBC	DCB
BCE	BCE	BEC	CBE	CEB	EBC	ECB
BDE	BDE	BED	DBE	DEB	EBD	EDB
CDE	CDE	CED	DCE	DEC	ECD	EDC

reveals that certain permutations are merely different arrangements of the same 3 books. For instance, the 6 permutations *ABC, ACB, BAC, BCA, CAB,* and *CBA* are different arrangements of the same 3 books *A, B,* and *C.* If we sort the 60 permutations into groups, such that all the permutations in each group are merely different arrangements of the same 3 books, we obtain the 10 groups shown in the left column of Table 4.1. Each of these groups represents a different *combination* of 3 books selected from 5 books.

As Table 4.1 shows, each combination of 3 books may be arranged in 6 different orders. That is, there are 6 possible permutations associated with each combination of 3 books. This agrees with Formula (4.5), which specifies that for a group of 3 different objects taken all together, there are 3! = 6 permutations. Thus, if we divide the total number of permutations by the total number of permutations per combination, we obtain the total number of combinations. That is,

$$\frac{60 \text{ permutations}}{6 \text{ permutations/combination}} = 10 \text{ combinations}$$

More generally, since there are $r!$ permutations of a group of r objects, the total number of possible combinations of r objects selected from n objects may be obtained by dividing Formula (4.8) by $r!$ Thus, we may obtain *the number of possible combinations of r objects selected from a set of n objects* from

$$_nC_r = \binom{n}{r} = \frac{_nP_r}{r!} = \frac{n!}{(n-r)!\,r!} \qquad (4.9)$$

Notice that the notation $\binom{n}{r}$ is used to denote the combinations of r objects selected from a set of n objects. This notation is more convenient than $_nC_r$ in the more complex formulas to be presented in later chapters.

Example:

A sales manager has 10 field representatives working under him. A local consulting firm, at a fee of $450 per person, is conducting a 5-day sales clinic to which the sales manager would like to send all 10 field representatives. However, the budget will allow him to send only 3 people. How many different ways are there for him to compose this group of 3?

From Formula (4.9) the number of possible combinations of 3 selected from a set of 10 is

$$_{10}C_3 = \binom{10}{3} = \frac{10!}{7!\,3!} = 120$$

A comparison of Formula (4.9) with Formula (4.7) reveals an interesting and important relationship. Specifically,

$$_nP_n(r, n-r) = \frac{n!}{r!(n-r)!} = \binom{n}{r} = {_nC_r}$$

Expressed in words, the number of distinguishable permutations in the special case handled by Formula (4.7) is equal to the number of combinations given by Formula (4.9). We make use of this relationship later during our discussion of the binomial distribution.

4.6 RECAPITULATION

We are now ready to return to the transistor testing problem posed at the outset of Section 4.3. To rephrase the problem: If a lot of 60 transistors contains 3 defectives and a sample of 10 transistors is selected at random from the lot, what is the probability that any 2 of these 3 defectives will be included in the sample? From Formula (4.9), the total number of ways that 2 defectives can be selected from the 3 available is $\binom{3}{2}$. If the sample of 10 contains 2 defectives, then it must contain 8 good transistors. The total number of ways that 8 good transistors can be selected from the 57 good ones in the lot is $\binom{57}{8}$. Applying the fundamental counting principle, the total number of possible groups of 10 transistors that contain 2 defective and 8 good transistors is $\binom{3}{2}\binom{57}{8}$. The total number of different groups of 10 transistors that can possibly be drawn from the lot of 60 transistors is $\binom{60}{10}$. Therefore, applying Formula (4.1), the ratio

$$\frac{\binom{3}{2}\binom{57}{8}}{\binom{60}{10}}$$

specifies the probability that the sample will contain 2 defectives. Evaluating this ratio yields a probability of approximately .066. The objective interpretation of this probability would be that in taking samples of 10 transistors from 60-transistor lots that contain 3 defectives, we would expect to obtain 2 defectives in the sample 6.6% of the time in the long run. The solution to this problem is an example of the application of the hypergeometric probability function, which is considered in detail in Chapter 9.

PROBLEMS

4.1 Nevada gambling casino operators use probabilities to determine the payoffs on various kinds of bets in such games as craps, blackjack, and roulette. Insurance company managements use probabilities to determine the premiums to be charged for different types of life insurance and annuity policies. Contrast these two industries with respect to the source of probabilities that they use.

4.2 The internationally famous Lloyd's of London will insure almost any risk for a fixed premium for a given period of time. Among the unique risks reported to have been insured by Lloyd's are (1) risk of disabling injury to a race horse; (2) risk of disabling injury to legs of a famous dancer; (3) risk of sufficient rain to cause cancellation of a single scheduled sporting event, such as a specific scheduled track meet; and (4) risk of losing a rare collection of jewelry or paintings. What type of probability is likely to dominate the decision-making process as each underwriter of Lloyd's of London decides the premium at which he will insure a given proportion of the risk?

4.3 What is the probability of each of the following outcomes (events) from dealing a single card from a well-shuffled standard deck of 52 cards?
   (a) A king
   (b) A face card
   (c) An ace of clubs
   (d) A diamond
   (e) Either a diamond or a heart
   (f) Either a club, spade, diamond, or heart
   (g) A number less than 10 counting an ace as 1
   (h) A diamond face card
   (i) A red card

4.4 The "defective rate" of a production process may be interpreted as the probability that any randomly selected unit produced by the process will be defective. If a sample of 20 bolts is selected at random from the output of a particular production process, and the sample is found to contain one defective, what would be the empirically estimated defective rate of the process?

4.5 During the year that the total resident population of the United States was approximately 198 million persons, the U.S. Public Health Service reports that there were 20,120 deaths due to accidental falls and 5,724 deaths due to accidental drowning. Based on these data, what is the empirically estimated probability that a person will die from one or the other of these two causes?

4.6 Welton Products Company has four separate sales departments. The ages of outstanding invoices in the different departments are summarized below:

	Sales Department			
Age of Invoice	A	B	C	D
Under 120 days	78	105	86	64
120–180 days	27	36	28	39
Over 180 days	21	9	6	11

(a) If an outstanding invoice is randomly selected from the pooled central files, what is the probability that it is from department B?

(b) What is the probability that a randomly selected invoice from the pooled files is over 180 days old?

(c) If an outstanding invoice is randomly selected from the pooled files, what is the probability that the invoice is over 180 days old and is from department B?

(d) If an outstanding invoice is selected at random from the files of department C, what is the probability that it is not less than 120 days old?

4.7 During a televised interview, a noted economist announced that the odds are 3 : 1 that a strike will occur at United Motors when the current union contract expires. What is the probability that the strike will occur?

4.8 Consolidated Construction Company has been awarded a contract to build a small resort hotel on the tropical island of Motu-Motu. The superintendent of the project feels that the odds are 2 : 3 that the building will be completed before the rainy season begins. What are the respective probabilities that the construction will be completed and will not be completed before the rainy season?

4.9 Three companies have submitted bids for a contract to supply boots to the Army. The president of company A feels that the odds are even (1 : 1) that his company will win the contract. He also feels that the odds are 3 : 7 that company B will win the contract and 1 : 4 that company C will win the contract. Determine the probability that each of the three companies will win the contract, assuming the president's odds assessments are correct.

4.10 In a particular state, auto license plates currently consist of a sequence of 3 digits followed by a sequence of 2 letters. It is predicted that, in a few years, there will be more vehicles than the number of distinguishably different license plates which are possible under this system. If the state adopts a new system of using 3 digits followed by 3 letters, what will be the increase in the number of distinguishably different license plates which are possible?

4.11 A production supervisor has 4 workers—Arthur, Bill, Clara, and Don—to whom she must make work assignments. There are 4 tasks to be performed, but not all workers can perform all tasks. Specifically:

Arthur can perform tasks 1, 3

Bill can perform tasks 1, 2, 4

Clara can perform tasks 1, 2, 3, 4

Don can perform tasks 2, 4

In how many ways can the tasks be assigned if each task is given to a different worker?

4.12 An investment club has 4 candidates for president, 2 candidates for vice-president, and 3 candidates for secretary-treasurer. In how many different ways may a slate of officers be elected?

4.13 In a marketing study, a subject is asked to taste 4 different brands of ginger ale and place them in order of preference. For a given subject, how many different outcomes are possible?

4.14 Seven job applicants in a personnel office are waiting to be interviewed by the personnel manager. If the personnel manager decides to interview them in random order, in how many different orders may the 7 interviews be conducted?

4.15 In a job shop, 6 different operations must be performed on a particular part. These operations may be performed in any sequence. In how many different orders may these operations be performed?

4.16 At a sales clinic, individual presentations are to be given by 3 men (Art, Bob, and Chuck) and 3 women (Dorothy, Eva, and Fanny). In how many different orders might these 6 presentations be arranged if:
  (a)   The order of speakers is completely random?
  (b)   The first speaker must be a man?
  (c)   The first and last speakers must be women?
  (d)   The first speaker must be a man, and the successive presentations must alternate between men and women?
  (e)   The first speaker may be either a man or a woman, but the successive presentations must alternate between men and women?

4.17 Twelve books are scattered on a professor's desk. Among these, there are 2 identical copies of *Wealth of Nations*, 3 identical copies of *Das Kapital*, and 4 identical copies of *The Mentality of Apes*. The remainder of the books are all different. In how many ways may these 12 books be arranged on a shelf in distinguishably different orders?

4.18 A Scrabble player has 8 tiles with the following letters: A, A, B, E, H, S, S, S. In how many distinguishably different ways may these tiles be arranged in a row?

4.19 From a set of nine 1's and five 0's, how many different 14-digit binary numbers can be formed (assuming that the first digit must be 1)?

4.20 A standard deck of cards contains 26 red and 26 black cards. If all 52 cards are dealt in sequence from a well-shuffled deck, how many distinguishably different arrangements of red and black cards may be dealt?

4.21 For a class of 12 students, a professor has a list of 15 topics for class reports. For next week, he plans to assign a different one of these topics to each of the students. The assignments will be made at random, with 3 remaining topics left unassigned. In how many different ways may the assignments be made?

4.22 At a regional track meet, 18 contestants are entered in the mile run. In how many ways may 5 different prizes (first, second, third, fourth, and fifth places) be awarded?

4.23 A television variety show is to consist of 4 different commercial segments and 3 different entertainment segments. The show must begin with a commercial, and each entertainment segment must be followed by a commercial.
  (a)   If the sponsor has already selected the 4 commercials and 3 entertainment segments, in how many different ways may the 7 segments of the show be arranged?
  (b)   Suppose that the producer of the show has 7 different commercials and 5 different entertainment segments from which to choose. In how many different ways may the show's 7 segments be selected and arranged?

4.24 In a job shop, 8 different operations must be performed on a particular part. Operation *A* must be performed first on all parts. After operation *A*, operations *B*, *C*, and *D* may be performed in any sequence, but *A*, *B*, *C*, and *D* must be performed before all other operations.

After A, B, C, and D have been performed, operations E, F, G, and H may be performed in any sequence. In how many different sequences may the operations be performed?

4.25 A real estate developer has just won a contract to build an apartment complex. In order to complete this prime contract, the developer plans to place 6 (distinguishable) subcontracts with one or more of 3 different subcontractors (Allan, Barbara, and Charles). The contracts are labeled 1 through 6 and will be placed with subcontractors in the order 1 through 6.
(a) In how many different ways can the developer place the subcontracts?
(b) In how many distinguishable ways can it place 3 with contractor Allan, 1 with contractor Barbara, and 2 with contractor Charles?

4.26 Three managers of different departments of a large U.S. company are on European vacations. They have made a date to meet at the Tivoli Hotel in Copenhagen, quite unaware that there are 5 hotels in the city with that name. Suppose that each manager independently chooses one of these 5 hotels at random.
(a) What is the probability that all 3 managers choose the same hotel?
(b) What is the probability that all 3 managers choose different hotels?

4.27 A retailing chain has 20 stores. Management decides to try out a new product in a sample of 5 of those stores. How many different possible 5-store samples are there?

4.28 Twelve members of the board of directors of the Homestake Savings and Loan Association attend a board meeting. If each board member shakes hands with each other board member once and only once, how many handshakes will each board member make? What will be the total number of handshakes exchanged?

4.29 A group of 25 nurses are to be assigned to work shifts so that there are 12 on the first shift, 9 on the second shift, and 4 on the third shift. In how many different possible ways might the shift assignments be made?

4.30 A retailer receives a shipment of 20 stereo sets, of which 3 are defective. The retailer plans to select 4 sets from the shipment to place on the showroom floor. In how many ways may this random selection of 4 sets be made such that:
(a) None of the 4 sets is defective?
(b) Exactly 1 of the 4 sets is defective?
(c) Exactly 2 of the 4 sets are defective?
(d) Exactly 3 of the 4 sets are defective?
(e) At least 2 of the 4 sets are defective?
(f) No more than 2 of the 4 sets are defective?

4.31 A bridge hand consists of 13 cards dealt from a deck of 52 cards. How many different possible bridge hands are there?

4.32 Jay Inc. has entered into a contract with television station KTN to purchase 30 seconds of commercial time on the Noontime News 5 days a week for 15 weeks. Each 30-second spot will consist of a cartoon.
(a) Assume that no cartoon may be used more than once during any given week, although any cartoon shown in one week may be shown again in any other week. However, the group of 5 cartoons selected for any week must be different from that for any other week during the 15-week period. What is the minimum number of cartoons required?
(b) Assume that no cartoon can be repeated during the entire 15-week period. What is the minimum number of cartoons needed?

4.33 In how many different possible ways may each of the following types of poker hands be composed from a standard 52-card deck?
(a) One pair (excluding full houses and 2 pairs)
(b) Four of a kind
(c) Full house
(d) Three of a kind (excluding full houses)

5

Probabilities of Events

Until now we have used the term "event" informally. In this chapter we develop the concept of an event more formally and then consider fundamental rules for assigning probabilities to events.

5.1 BASIC SET CONCEPTS

The basic ideas underlying the assignment of probabilities to events originated in the gambling salons of European nobles during the 1600s. In that world of dice and cards, such seventeenth-century philosophers as Bernoulli, Pascal, and de Moivre developed their fundamental insights concerning chance mechanisms. Today, however, the formal approach to analyzing the probabilities of events is based on *set theory*, which was not formally introduced into mathematics until late in the nineteenth century.

5.1.1 Sets

Although the formal development of set theory is both elegant and elaborate, the fundamental idea of a set is simple and intuitive. The term *set* refers in a very general way to any *well-defined collection* of "objects." The objects belonging to a given set are called the *elements* or *members* of that set.

There are two common ways of defining sets: *listing* and *describing*. In either case, the set is defined within braces. By the *listing* method, a set is specified by listing all of its elements. For example, using this method to define a set V of the five English vowels, we would write

$$V = \{a, e, i, o, u\}$$

By the *describing* method, a set is specified by describing the elements of the set in terms of some common property. By this method, the set of English vowels would be denoted as

$$V = \{v \,|\, v \text{ is one of the five English vowels}\}$$

This expression is read "V is the set of elements v such that v is one of the five English vowels." Notice that the symbol "$|$" stands for the phrase "such that." The symbol $\in$ is used to denote that an object "is an element of," "is a member of," or "belongs to" a particular set. In the foregoing example, "$a \in V$" denotes that a is an element of the set V. Similarly, the symbol $\notin$ denotes that an object "is not an element of" or "is not a member of" a particular set. Hence, the expression "$b \notin V$" indicates that b does not belong to the set V.

In the set consisting of the English vowels, it makes no substantive difference whether the set is defined by the listing method or the describing method; either method provides a clear, unambiguous definition of the set. Why, then, should there be two methods? The answer is that, with many important kinds of sets, either one method or the other is not feasible or is impossible. For instance, if a set should contain a very large number of elements, such as the set of all citizens who actually cast their ballots in the last presidential election, it would not be practical to list every member of that set. Thus, the only practical way of defining such a set would be the describing method. In contrast, consider the set consisting of the symbols %, #, k, and 7. For this set, there is no common property that could be used to describe membership in the set unambiguously, and the listing method then would be necessary.

In conceptualizing sets, it is important to distinguish between "finite" and "infinite" sets. A *finite* set is one that consists of a fixed, definite number of elements. For example, the set of all digits from 0 through 9 is a finite set. Using the listing method, this set could be written

$$D = \{0, 1, 2, 3, 4, 5, 6, 7, 8, 9\}$$

or it could be written

$$D = \{0, 1, 2, \ldots, 9\}$$

In the latter expression, the series of three dots (called an *ellipsis*) means "and so on" up to 9. Either of the foregoing expressions denotes a set that contains a definite number of elements—10.

In an *infinite* set, the number of elements is limitless or unspecifiable. For instance, the set of all positive integers is an infinite set that can be written

$$P = \{1, 2, 3, \ldots\}$$

In this case, the ellipsis means "and so on" without end. Thus, the number of elements in the set is limitless. Another example of an infinite set is the set of all real values contained in the interval, say, between 3 and 5 inclusive. This set can be written

$$R = \{r \mid 3 \leq r \leq 5\}$$

This set consists of an infinite number of real values along a continuum between the boundaries of 3 and 5.

5.1.2 Subsets

Consider the following two sets:

$$X = \{r, s, t, u\} \qquad Y = \{r, s, t\}$$

We readily see that every element contained in Y is also contained in X. In this situation, we may say that Y is a "subset" of X. More formally, any set A is a *subset* of set B if each element of A is also an element contained in B. Symbolically, this situation is denoted as $A \subseteq B$, which is read "A is a subset of B." Thus, for the two sets listed above, we may write $Y \subseteq X$.

In set theory, any set is commonly regarded as a subset of itself. Thus, in the example above, X may be considered as a subset of itself, which is denoted as $X \subseteq X$. Similarly, we may write $Y \subseteq Y$.

A set that contains no elements is called the *empty* or *null* set. The empty set is denoted as $\varnothing$. It is customary to regard the empty set as a subset of any set. Therefore, in the example above we have $\varnothing \subseteq X$ and $\varnothing \subseteq Y$.

If A is a subset of B such that A contains at least one element, but not all the elements, contained in B, then A is said to be a *proper subset* of B, which is denoted as $A \subset B$. Thus, although the empty set and the entire set are regarded as subsets of a given set, they are not proper subsets of that set. In our example, expressions such as $Y \subseteq X$ and $Y \subset X$ are both correct. However, $X \subset X$ and $\varnothing \subset X$ are invalid expressions, since the entire set and the empty set are not proper subsets (although they are subsets).

5.1.3 Complementary and Universal Sets

In considering the elements of a set A, we frequently may wish to consider the collection of objects that is not contained in A. This set of objects that is not in A is called the *complement* of A, denoted as A'. For example, suppose we define the set $S = \{s \mid s$ is a utilities issue currently listed on the New York Stock Exchange$\}$. In this case, how do we define the complementary set S'? Our first inclination might be to say that S' is the set of all nonutilities issues currently listed on the New York Stock Exchange. But this would not necessarily be correct, because S' could just as well be the set of all utilities stocks that are not listed on the New York Exchange, the set of all nonutilities stocks that are not listed on the New York Exchange, and so on. It becomes obvious that in order for the complement of a set to be well defined, it is necessary to specify some reference set that limits or bounds the entire collection of elements under consideration in a given situation. This delimiting set is called the *universal* set, denoted as $\mathcal{U}$. Thus, if we define $\mathcal{U}$ as the set of all stock issues currently listed on the New York Stock Exchange, then S' is the set of all nonutilities issues currently listed on the New York Stock Exchange. But if we should define $\mathcal{U}$ as the set of all utilities stocks in the U.S., then S' would be the set of all utilities stocks in the United States that are not currently listed on the New York Exchange.

As we pointed out in Chapter 1, sampling from a population is an important statistical device for *obtaining information to reduce* uncertainty in decision making. We should recognize that a population is simply a universal set. In this context, a sample may be regarded as a subset of the universe.

5.2 DEFINING EVENTS ON SAMPLE SPACES

Let us consider the random process of drawing a card from a well-shuffled bridge deck. In this case, we might regard the deck of cards as a universe, and the card that is drawn from the deck as a sample taken from that universe. Since the deck contains 52 cards, each distinguishably unique, we might say that the process has 52 possible *elementary outcomes*. The set of all possible elementary outcomes of such a random process is called the *sample space*. Each elementary outcome is referred to as a *sample point* or *element* of the sample space. Thus, each element of the sample space represents an elementary outcome of the random process, and each trial of the process must result in an outcome corresponding to exactly one element of the sample space. Diagrammatically, we might represent the sample space of our card-drawing "experiment" as in Figure 5.1.

Having defined a sample space, we may now define an *event* as any subset of a sample space. We use the term *simple event* to designate an event that corresponds to a single sample point. Thus, the event "drawing the queen of spades" is a simple event. A *compound event* is an event that is defined by more than a single sample point. That is, a compound event is composed of two or more simple events. The occurrence of any one of the simple events that comprise a compound event permits us to say that the compound event has occurred. For example, the event "drawing an ace" is a compound event composed of four simple events, represented by the top row of Figure 5.1. If a single draw of a card turns up either the ace of hearts, or ace of diamonds, or ace of clubs, or ace of spades, we may say that the event "drawing an ace" has occurred.

The total number of different events that can be defined on a 52-point sample space is staggering. It can be denonstrated that this total number of events (subsets) is $2^n = 2^{52} = 4,503,599,627,370,496$. Of course, most of these combinations of sample points define only events that are logically possible but would not be of the slightest interest for any practical purpose.

In dealing with probability problems, the critical considerations in defining

	Spades	Hearts	Diamonds	Clubs
Ace	A •	A •	A •	A •
King	K •	K •	K •	K •
Queen	Q •	Q •	Q •	Q •
Jack	J •	J •	J •	J •
10	10 •	10 •	10 •	10 •
9	9 •	9 •	9 •	9 •
8	8 •	8 •	8 •	8 •
7	7 •	7 •	7 •	7 •
6	6 •	6 •	6 •	6 •
5	5 •	5 •	5 •	5 •
4	4 •	4 •	4 •	4 •
3	3 •	3 •	3 •	3 •
2	2 •	2 •	2 •	2 •

Figure 5.1 Sample Space for Drawing a Single Card from a 52-Card Bridge Deck

an event are (1) to define the event such that the definition includes all those sample points, and only those sample points, that represent the elementary outcomes of concern; and (2) to define the event in an unambiguous manner such that each and every point in the sample space may be identified as being included or excluded in the set defining the event. As we will see in later chapters, these considerations are crucial, since whether or not a particular sample point is included in the definition of an event can materially affect the probability assigned to the occurrence of that event.

5.3 INTERSECTIONS OF EVENTS

The *intersection* of two events A and B is the set of all elements that are common to *both* A and B. In set theory, the symbol $\cap$ is used to denote an intersection. The expression $A \cap B$ is read "A cap B," "A intersect B," or "A intersection B."

To illustrate the concept of an intersection, let us define a set V as the set of the five English vowels, and a set W as the set of the first five letters of the English alphabet. Symbolically,

$$V = \{a, e, i, o, u\}$$
$$W = \{a, b, c, d, e\}$$

The elements that are common to these two sets are a and e. Thus, the intersection of the two sets V and W is

$$V \cap W = \{a, e\}$$

Now suppose that the universal set consists of the five vowels and the first five consonants of the English alphabet:

$$\mathcal{U} = \{a, b, c, d, e, f, g, i, o, u\}$$

Recalling that the complement of a given set consists of all elements in the universe that are not contained in that set, the complement of V is

$$V' = \{b, c, d, f, g\}$$

and the complement of W is

$$W' = \{f, g, i, o, u\}$$

Then, out of all of the elements of the universe, those that are contained in V but not in W are those elements that are common to V and W'. This is the intersection of V and W':

$$V \cap W' = \{i, o, u\}$$

Similarly, the elements contained in W but not in V form the intersection of V' and W:

$$V' \cap W = \{b, c, d\}$$

5.4 UNIONS OF EVENTS

We have seen that the intersection of two events A and B, denoted by $A \cap B$, refers to the set of all sample points that are contained in *both* A and B. A related concept is the *union* of two events. The union of A and B is denoted by $A \cup B$, which is read "A cup B" or "A union B." This union is the set of all sample points contained in *either A or B*, where the word "or" is used inclusively to mean "and/or." That is, the union of A and B consists of all the sample points that are contained in both A and B, or in A but not B, or in B but not A. Thus, the set $A \cup B$ consists of all the elements contained in the three sets: $A \cap B$, $A \cap B'$, and $A' \cap B$. Expressed formally,

$$A \cup B = (A \cap B) \cup (A \cap B') \cup (A' \cap B)$$

To illustrate the concept of a union, let us return to our example in which

$$V = \{a, e, i, o, u\}$$
$$W = \{a, b, c, d, e\}$$

The set of all elements that belong to either V or W is the union of V and W:

$$V \cup W = \{a, e, i, o, u, b, c, d\}$$

As the reader may verify, this union may also be obtained by combining the elements of the three sets $V \cap W$, $V \cap W'$, and $V' \cap W$.

5.5 MUTUALLY EXCLUSIVE EVENTS

If two events A and B do not have any sample points in common, A and B are said to be *mutually exclusive*. Because two mutually exclusive events have no sample points in common, their intersection is the empty set. Thus, *if A and B are mutually exclusive events*, we may write

$$A \cap B = \varnothing$$

Consequently, if we wish to know whether two events are mutually exclusive, we need simply to determine whether their intersection is empty. Because two mutually exclusive events have no sample points in common, they cannot occur simultaneously. If two events are mutually exclusive, and if we know that one of these events has occurred, we may definitely conclude that the other event did not occur. However, if we know that one of the two events did not occur, we cannot necessarily conclude that the other event did occur, since it is possible that neither event occurred.

To illustrate the concept of mutually exclusive events, consider three events:

$$V = \{a, e, i, o, u\}$$
$$W = \{a, b, c, d, e\}$$
$$X = \{b, c, d, f, g\}$$

From these three sets we obtain the following intersections:

$$V \cap W = \{a, e\}$$
$$V \cap X = \varnothing$$
$$W \cap X = \{b, c, d\}$$

Since V and X have no elements in common, their intersection is empty, and these two events are therefore mutually exclusive. However, V and W are not mutually exclusive because they have some elements in common. For the same reason, W and X are not mutually exclusive.

5.6 PARTITIONING SAMPLE SPACES

Two or more subsets that are defined on the same universe are said to be *collectively exhaustive* if each and every element of the universe is contained in at least one of the subsets. For example, suppose that the three events V, W, and X in Section 5.5 have all been defined on the same universal set:

$$\mathcal{U} = \{a, b, c, d, e, f, g, i, o, u\}$$

Each of the elements in this universe is contained in at least one of the three events V, W, and X. Therefore, V, W, and X are collectively exhaustive. Careful inspection reveals that just the two events V and X are also collectively exhaustive, since each of the elements in the universe is contained in one or the other of these two events. In addition, as we have already seen, V and X are mutually exclusive. Such a division of a universe into a group of events that are mutually exclusive and collectively exhaustive is called a *partition* of the universe.

Since a sample space is a type of universal set, and since events are subsets defined on a sample space, it is possible to partition a sample space into a group of mutually exclusive and collectively exhaustive events. To illustrate, consider an electronic assembly that requires one each of type A and type B tubes. At a particular point in the assembly process, an assembler reaches with one hand into a bin containing type A tubes, and with the other hand reaches into a bin containing type B tubes. He randomly selects a tube from each bin and inserts them into the assembly. Suppose, at a particular moment when the assembler is going through this operation, there are only 4 tubes remaining in the type A bin (call them A_1, A_2, A_3, and A_4) and 5 tubes remaining in the type B bin (call them B_1, B_2, B_3, B_4, and B_5). If we view this operation of selecting 2 tubes as a random process, with 4 ways of selecting a tube from the type A bin and 5 ways of selecting a tube from the type B bin, there are $4 \times 5 = 20$ elementary outcomes. Thus, we have a 20-element sample space, as shown in Figure 5.2.

Assume that 3 of the 9 tubes—A_4, B_2, and B_5—are defective, whereas the remainder are good. We might then define some events in terms of the total number of defective tubes that the assembler draws from the two bins. Let E_0 be the event that neither of the 2 tubes selected is defective, E_1 be the event that just one of the 2 tubes is defective, and E_2 be the event that both tubes are defective. In terms of the sample points in Figure 5.2:

$$E_0 = \{(A_1B_1), (A_1B_3), (A_1B_4), (A_2B_1), (A_2B_3), (A_2B_4), (A_3B_1), (A_3B_3), (A_3B_4)\}$$
$$E_1 = \{(A_1B_2), (A_1B_5), (A_2B_2), (A_2B_5), (A_3B_2), (A_3B_5), (A_4B_1), (A_4B_3), (A_4B_4)\}$$
$$E_2 = \{(A_4B_2), (A_4B_5)\}$$

Notice that these three events are mutually exclusive and exhaust the sample space. In other words, the three events—E_0, E_1, and E_2—constitute a partition of the sample space.

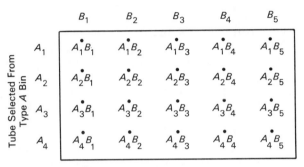

Figure 5.2   Sample Space for Selecting Two Tubes

5.7 DETERMINING PROBABILITIES OF EVENTS

So far in this chapter we have been concerned with how events are defined on sample spaces. We are now ready to begin consideration of how probabilities of such events are determined.

5.7.1 Basic Requirements for Assigning Probabilities

In assigning probabilities to a set of events, regardless of whether the probabilities are objective or subjective, we must satisfy three requirements:

1. The probability of an event must be a number between 0 and 1 inclusive. In other words, an event cannot have a negative probability or a probability greater than 1.
2. The probability of the occurrence of one *or* the other of any two mutually exclusive events must equal the sum of the separate probabilities of these two events.
3. The sum of the probabilities of *all* the separate events comprising a partition must equal 1.

To illustrate these rules, consider a speculator who purchases 1,000 shares of a common stock, which he plans to sell at the end of 10 trading days, hopefully at a profit. He considers three possible events: that the stock will go up in price, that it will decline, and that it will remain unchanged. Viewing the short-term behavior of stock prices as a random process, these three events form a partition of the sample space, since they are mutually exclusive and collectively exhaustive. Indicating the three events by the letters U (price goes up), D (price goes down), and N (price remains unchanged), he assigns the following subjective probabilities: $P(U) = .70$, $P(D) = .10$, and $P(N) = .20$. Notice, first, that none of these probabilities is negative or greater than 1. Second, the probability that the speculator will fail to sell at a profit is given by $P(U') = P(D) + P(N)$ $= .10 + .20 = .30$; that is, the probability that the stock will not go up (that is, either go down or remain unchanged) is the sum of the probabilities of two separate, mutually exclusive events. Finally, we see that $P(U) + P(D) + P(N)$ $= .70 + .10 + .20 = 1.00$, indicating it is certain that one of these three events will occur.

5.7.2 Joint and Marginal Probabilities

To illustrate how to determine the probabilities of events defined on a sample space, let us consider the random process of throwing a pair of dice. To keep the two dice distinct in our thinking, let us identify one as a red die and the other as a green die. For each of the 6 faces that might come up on the red die, any of the 6 faces may come up on the green die when the two dice are thrown. Thus, the random process of rolling a pair of dice has $6 \times 6 = 36$ possible elementary outcomes. This 36-element sample space, S, is represented diagrammatically in Figure 5.3. In this sample space, each sample point is defined as an *ordered pair* of values. If we let r denote the number of dots on the upper face of the red die when it is cast and g denote the number of dots on the face of the green die, we may then represent a sample point by the ordered pair (r, g). For example, $(5, 3)$ indicates the outcome that the red die comes up 5 and the green die comes up 3, whereas $(3, 5)$ indicates that the red die comes up 3 and the green die comes up 5.

When the dice are rolled, the sum of the two uppermost faces may be either odd or even. If we let O denote the event that the sum is odd, then O' denotes the complementary event that the sum is even. Since an event and its comple-

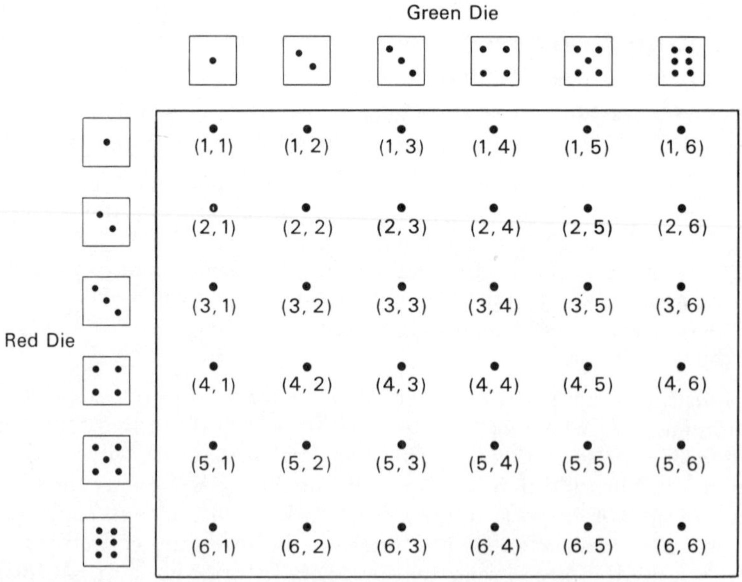

Figure 5.3 Sample Space of Outcomes for Tossing a Pair of Dice

ment are mutually exclusive and collectively exhaustive, the two events O and O' form a partition of the sample space.

Another event that might be defined on the same sample space is the event that the sum is higher than 7. If we denote this event by H, then the complement H' is the event that the sum is 7 or less. The two events H and H' form another partition of the sample space.

The various intersections of O, O', H, and H' form the following four events:

$O \cap H$	an odd number higher than 7
$O \cap H'$	an odd number equal to or less than 7
$O' \cap H$	an even number higher than 7
$O' \cap H'$	an even number equal to or less than 7

From inspection of Figure 5.3 we may list the sample points contained in each of these intersections as follows:

$$O \cap H \ = \{(3, 6), (4, 5), (5, 4), (5, 6), (6, 3), (6, 5)\}$$
$$O \cap H' = \{(1, 2), (1, 4), (1, 6), (2, 1), (2, 3), (2, 5), (3, 2), (3, 4), (4, 1), (4, 3),$$
$$(5, 2), (6, 1)\}$$
$$O' \cap H \ = \{(2, 6), (3, 5), (4, 4), (4, 6), (5, 3), (5, 5), (6, 2), (6, 4), (6, 6)\}$$
$$O' \cap H' = \{(1, 1), (1, 3), (1, 5), (2, 2), (2, 4), (3, 1), (3, 3), (4, 2), (5, 1)\}$$

As the reader may verify, the events defined by these four intersections are mutually exclusive and collectively exhaustive—that is, they form yet another partition of the sample space.

By counting the number of sample points in each of the four intersections listed above, we obtain the results shown in Table 5.1. For instance, the number

Table 5.1 Numbers of Sample Points in Subsets of Partitioned Sample Space

	H	H'	Total
O	$n(O \cap H) \ = 6$	$n(O \cap H') = 12$	$n(O) = 18$
O'	$n(O' \cap H) = 9$	$n(O' \cap H') = 9$	$n(O') = 18$
Total	$n(H) = 15$	$n(H') = 21$	$n(S) = 36$

of sample points contained in $(O \cap H)$ is 6, and the number of sample points contained in $(O' \cap H)$ is 9. Since $(O \cap H)$ and $(O' \cap H)$ are mutually exclusive, and since the union of these two events constitutes the event H, the number of sample points contained in H is obtained by adding the number of points in $(O \cap H)$ and $(O' \cap H)$. That is, $n(H) = n(O \cap H) + n(O' \cap H) = 6 + 9 = 15$. The numbers of sample points contained in the subsets H', O, and O' are obtained according to the same reasoning. The sum of $n(O)$ and $n(O')$ must be equal to the sum of $n(H)$ and $n(H')$, since each of these sums must be equal to $n(S)$, the total number of points in the sample space.

Assuming that the dice are "fair," each of the 36 elements of the sample space is equally likely to occur. Thus, the probabilities of the various events represented in Table 5.1 may be obtained by using Formula (4.1). For instance, the probability of rolling an odd sum higher than 7 is

$$P(O \cap H) = \frac{n(O \cap H)}{n(S)} = \frac{6}{36}$$

The various probabilities shown in Table 5.2 were obtained in the same manner.

Table 5.2 Probability Table for Dice Example

	H	H'	Total
O	$P(O \cap H) = \dfrac{6}{36}$	$P(O \cap H') = \dfrac{12}{36}$	$P(O) = \dfrac{18}{36}$
O'	$P(O' \cap H) = \dfrac{9}{36}$	$P(O' \cap H') = \dfrac{9}{36}$	$P(O') = \dfrac{18}{36}$
Total	$P(H) = \dfrac{15}{36}$	$P(H') = \dfrac{21}{36}$	$P(S) = 1$

Notice that each of the four probabilities shown in the body of Table 5.2 is the probability of an intersection of two events. Since the probability of an intersection of two events is the probability that the two events will occur jointly, such a probability is called a *joint probability*. Probabilities such as $P(H)$ and $P(H')$, which appear in the margins of a probability table such as Table 5.1, are sometimes referred to as *marginal* probabilities. The marginal probability of an event is the probability that the event will occur regardless of any other conditions that might be imposed. For instance, the probability of rolling a sum higher than 7 is 15/36 if we disregard whether the sum is odd or even. Thus, marginal probabilities also are called *unconditional* probabilities.

5.7.3 Conditional Probability

From Table 5.2 you can tell that the probability of rolling a sum higher than 7 with a pair of fair dice is $P(H) = 15/36$. Suppose, however, that your back is turned when a player rolls the dice, so that you do not know the outcome, but you are told that the sum is an odd number. Given this information, what is the probability that the sum rolled by the player is greater than 7? This question may be answered by examining the sample space shown in Figure 5.3. On being informed that the sum was an odd number, you can immediately eliminate 18 of the 36 sample points—that is, those 18 elements corresponding to even-numbered sums. Thus, you may work with a *reduced sample space* consisting of only those 18 elements corresponding to odd-numbered sums. Careful examination of these 18 elements reveals that there are 6 elements corresponding to sums higher than 7 and 12 elements corresponding to sums equal to or less than 7. Since each of these 18 sample points is equally likely, the probability of a sum greater than 7 is 6/18. That is, *given the information* that the sum is odd, the probability that the sum is higher than 7 is $6/18 = 1/3$. Similarly, given the information that the sum is odd, the probability that the sum is not higher than

$$P(C \mid S) = \frac{.05}{.15} = .3333 \qquad \text{Probability of selecting a college graduate if the selection is confined to supervisors}$$

$$P(C' \mid S) = \frac{.10}{.15} = .6667 \qquad \text{Probability of selecting a non-college graduate if the selection is confined to supervisors}$$

$$P(C \mid S') = \frac{.20}{.85} = .2353 \qquad \text{Probability of selecting a college graduate if the selection is confined to nonsupervisors}$$

$$P(C' \mid S') = \frac{.65}{.85} = .7647 \qquad \text{Probability of selecting a non-college graduate if the selection is confined to nonsupervisors}$$

The various joint and conditional probabilities given above may be confirmed by applying formulas (5.1) through (5.4). For example,

$$
\begin{aligned}
P(S' \cap C) &= P(S' \mid C)P(C) = (.8000)(.25) \\
&= P(C \mid S')P(S') = (.2353)(.85) \\
&= .20
\end{aligned}
$$

Readers are left to make formula confirmations of the other probabilities on their own.

5.8 PROBABILITIES OF UNIONS OF EVENTS

In Section 5.4 we observed that the union of two events A and B, denoted by $A \cup B$, is the set of all sample points contained in A or in B or in both A and B. Thus, by the notation $P(A \cup B)$ we mean the probability that either A occurs or B occurs or both A and B occur. The calculation of $P(A \cup B)$ depends on whether or not A and B are mutually exclusive.

5.8.1 Unions of Mutually Exclusive Events

We have mentioned in our discussion of partitioning that if two events defined on the same sample space are mutually exclusive, then the probability of the occurrence of one or the other must equal the sum of the probabilities of the separate events. That is, *if A and B are mutually exclusive events*, then

$$P(A \cup B) = P(A) + P(B) \tag{5.5}$$

Example:

A particular mail-order house usually receives between 2,000 and 4,000 orders per day. Consider the following events:

- A: fewer than 2,000 orders received
- B: at least 2,000 but fewer than 3,000 orders received
- C: at least 3,000 but fewer than 4,000 orders received
- D: 4,000 or more orders received

Obviously, these are mutually exclusive events. From records maintained over a period of years, the following probabilities have been determined for order volume on a randomly selected day:

$$P(A) = .10 \qquad P(B) = .40 \qquad P(C) = .30 \qquad P(D) = .20$$

From these data, we may draw the following conclusions:

Probability of receiving fewer than 3,000 orders	$P(A \cup B)$ $= P(A) + P(B)$ $= .10 + .40 = .50$
Probability of receiving fewer than 4,000 orders	$P(A \cup B \cup C)$ $= P(A) + P(B) + P(C)$ $= .10 + .40 + .30 = .80$
Probability of receiving at least 3,000 orders	$P(C \cup D)$ $= P(C) + P(D)$ $= .30 + .20 = .50$
Probability of receiving at least 2,000 orders	$P(B \cup C \cup D)$ $= P(B) + P(C) + P(D)$ $= .40 + .30 + .20 = .90$

5.8.2 Unions of Non-Mutually Exclusive Events

To illustrate the calculation of the probability of the union of two events that are not mutually exclusive, consider the case of several hundred small business executives who are gathered at a trade show. A drawing is to be held and a door prize awarded. Of the total number of executives present, 40% are under 40 years of age and 80% are college graduates. Of the executives under 40 years of age, 75% are college graduates. What is the probability that the door prize will be won by either a college graduate and/or a person under 40? Let A represent the event that the winner is under 40 and B represent the event that he or she is a college graduate. In this case, A and B are not mutually exclusive. If we were (wrongly) to apply Formula (5.5) to this problem, we would obtain $P(A \cup B) = P(A) + P(B) = .40 + .80 = 1.20$, which is not only incorrect but ridiculous.

To diagnose the error, we might prepare the probability table shown in Table 5.4. From the table it is clear that $P(A \cup B) = P(A \cap B) + P(A \cap B')$

Table 5.4 Probability Table for Small-Business Executives

	B	B'	Total
A	.30	.10	.40
A'	.50	.10	.60
Total	.80	.20	1.00

$+ P(A' \cap B) = .30 + .10 + .50 = .90$. Since $P(A \cap B)$ is included in both $P(A)$ and $P(B)$, the error was one of adding $P(A \cap B)$ to the sum twice instead of only once. To obtain the correct answer, we must amend Formula (5.5) to read

$$P(A \cup B) = P(A) + P(B) - P(A \cap B) \tag{5.6}$$

This is the general formula for the probability of the union of two events. If the two events are mutually exclusive, then $P(A \cap B) = 0$, and Formula (5.6) reduces to Formula (5.5).

Example:

A brewery maintains a large panel of beer tasters. The panel is equally divided among men and women. The panel has just been asked to compare three new brews (call them A, B, C), and of the total panel 50% preferred brew A, 30% preferred brew B, and 20% preferred brew C. Preference for each brew is equally divided between men and women, as shown in Table 5.5. What is the probability that a randomly selected panel member will be either a man and/or a person who prefers brew B?

From the table, the desired probability may be obtained by adding .25 + .15 + .10 + .15 = .65. The same result may be obtained from Formula (5.6) : .50 + .30 − .15 = .65.

Table 5.5   Probability Table for Brewery Panel

	Preference			
	A	*B*	*C*	*Total*
Men	.25	.15	.10	.50
Women	.25	.15	.10	.50
Total	.50	.30	.20	1.00

5.9 INDEPENDENCE

Many statistical decision problems are concerned with establishing the *relevance* of data to a particular decision. Far too often in everyday life—whether the matter be business or personal—we base our decisions on facts that are irrelevant to our problems but that we mistakenly assume to be relevant, in which case we might as well make our decisions by drawing numbers out of a hat.

When knowledge of the occurrence or nonoccurrence of one event has no influence on the probability assessment of the occurrence of another event, the two events are said to be *independent*. Conversely, if the two events are independent, the knowledge that one event has or has not occurred will not influence the probability that the other event will occur. If an event A is independent of another event B, the conditional probability of A, given B, is equal to the marginal (unconditional) probability of A. In terms of a formula, if the event A is independent of the event B, then

$$P(A|B) = P(A) \tag{5.7}$$

Thus, *in the special case in which A and B are independent*, we may revise Formula (5.2) to read

$$P(A \cap B) = P(A)P(B) \tag{5.8}$$

That is, the probability of the joint occurrence of two independent events is equal to the product of the marginal probabilities of those two events.

If Formula (5.7) holds, Formula (5.8) must also hold, and vice versa. If these formulas hold, the two events A and B must be independent. Thus, to determine if two events are independent, we simply check to see if either Formula (5.7) or (5.8) holds.

Example 1 :

For the past several months, a would-be investor has been keeping careful records of the stock-market behavior of a particular issue. His records indicate that, for a randomly selected day, there is a .60 probability that the stock will go up in price. Furthermore, there is a .50 probability that the volume of shares traded on this stock will be high (200,000 shares or more). He also notices that, on those days when the trading volume of the stock is high, the price of the stock goes up 60% of the time.

Let U indicate the event that the price of the stock goes up, and H indicate the event that the trading volume on the stock is high. Then, from the information given above :

$$P(U) = .60$$
$$P(H) = .50$$
$$P(U|H) = .60$$

Since $P(U|H) = P(U)$, Formula (5.7) is satisfied. Thus, the event that the stock will go up in price on a randomly selected trading day is independent of the day's trading volume on that issue. It then follows from Formula (5.8) that $P(H \cap U) = P(H)P(U) = (.60)(.50) = .30$. Then we can construct Table 5.6. Notice that the probability shown

Table 5.6 Probability Table for Stock Behavior

	U	U'	Total
H	.30	.20	.50
H'	.30	.20	.50
Total	.60	.40	1.00

in each of the four cells in the body of the table is equal to the product of the marginal probabilities for the row and column in which the cell resides. Thus, H and H' are both independent of U and U'.

Example 2 :

The reliability of a system or of a component of a system might be regarded as the probability that the system or component will function correctly for a specified period of time. Assume that a particular satellite system is composed of two components, A and B, as shown in Figure 5.4. Each component is composed of two identical parts connected in parallel, and the two components are connected in series. Component A will function properly as long as A_1 and/or A_2 functions properly, and component B will function properly as long as B_1 and/or B_2 functions properly. Parts A_1 and A_2 each has a reliability of .70 ; parts B_1 and B_2 each has a reliability of .80. Assuming that whether a particular part of the system functions is independent of whether any other part functions, what is the reliability of the entire system ?

From Formula (5.8), the probability that both A_1 and A_2 will function properly for the specified length of time is $(.70)(.70) = .49$. From Formula (5.6), the probability that A_1 and/or A_2 will function is $.70 + .70 - .49 = .91$. Thus, the reliability of component A is .91. Similarly, the probability that both B_1 and B_2 will function is $(.80)(.80) = .64$, and the reliability of component B is $.80 + .80 - .64 = .96$. Then, from Formula (5.8), the probability that both components A and B will function properly for the specified time is $(.91)(.96) = .8736$, which is the reliability of the entire system.

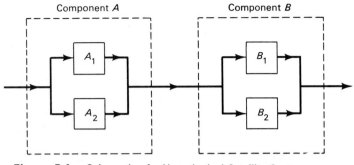

Figure 5.4   Schematic of a Hypothetical Satellite System

It is extremely important to avoid confusing independent events with mutually exclusive events. These two concepts are *not* synonymous. Indeed, they are incompatible in the sense that two possible events cannot be both mutually exclusive and independent. The distinction between independent events and mutually exclusive events can be summarized as follows:

1. If $P(A \cap B) = 0$, then A and B must be dependent. Two mutually exclusive events cannot be independent.
2. If $P(A \cap B) > 0$, then A and B may or may not be independent, depending on whether Formula (5.7) is satisfied. Of course, if Formula (5.7) is satisfied, Formula (5.8) also is necessarily satisfied.
3. If A and B are not independent, $P(A \cap B)$ may or may not be greater than zero.

The foregoing statements are illustrated by the following probability tables:

	B	B'	
A	0	.30	.30
A'	.40	.30	.70
	.40	.60	1.00

A and B are mutually exclusive and therefore dependent.

$P(A \cap B) = 0$; hence, $P(A \cap B) \neq P(A)P(B)$.

	B	B'	
A	.20	.10	.30
A'	.20	.50	.70
	.40	.60	1.00

A and B are neither mutually exclusive nor independent.

$P(A \cap B) > 0$; and $P(A \cap B) \neq P(A)P(B)$.

	B	B'	
A	.12	.18	.30
A'	.28	.42	.70
	.40	.60	1.00

A and B are not mutually exclusive but they are independent.

$P(A \cap B) > 0$; but $P(A \cap B) = P(A)P(B)$.

5.10 BAYES' THEOREM

In his *Essay Towards Solving a Problem in the Doctrine of Chance*, published in 1763, the Reverend Thomas Bayes presented a now well-known formula for computing conditional probabilities that has come to be known as Bayes' theorem. Today this formula occupies such a prominent position in modern statistical decision theory that it demands our particular attention.

To illustrate Bayes' theorem, consider the following random process. There are three urns that contain mixtures of red and green balls as follows:

Urn	Number of Red Balls	Number of Green Balls	Total
A	3	7	10
B	5	15	20
C	6	6	12

Two fair coins are tossed. If they both come up heads (HH), a ball is selected randomly from urn A; if one comes up heads and the other comes up tails (either HT or TH), a ball is selected randomly from urn B; if they both come up tails (TT), a ball is selected randomly from urn C. Thus, there is a .25 probability that the selection will be made from urn A, a .50 probability that the selection will be made from urn B, and a .25 probability that the selection will be made from urn C. If a ball is selected according to this process, and we are told that the ball is red, what is the probability that it was selected from urn A? urn B? urn C? Also, what are the corresponding probabilities if the ball is green?

On the basis of the given information, we may state three marginal probabilities: $P(A) = .25$, $P(B) = .50$, $P(C) = .25$. Also, knowing the particular mixture in each urn, we may state conditional probabilities for drawing a ball of a given color if we know which urn the ball is selected from. Thus, if R denotes the event of drawing a red ball and G denotes the event of drawing a green ball, we have

$$P(R|A) = \frac{3}{10} = .30 \qquad P(G|A) = \frac{7}{10} = .70$$

$$P(R|B) = \frac{5}{20} = .25 \qquad P(G|B) = \frac{15}{20} = .75$$

$$P(R|C) = \frac{6}{12} = .50 \qquad P(G|C) = \frac{6}{12} = .50$$

Applying Formula (5.2) we may compute certain joint probabilities:

$$P(A \cap R) = P(R|A)P(A) = (.30)(.25) = .075$$
$$P(B \cap R) = P(R|B)P(B) = (.25)(.50) = .125$$
$$P(C \cap R) = P(R|C)P(C) = (.50)(.25) = .125$$
$$P(A \cap G) = P(G|A)P(A) = (.70)(.25) = .175$$
$$P(B \cap G) = P(G|B)P(B) = (.75)(.50) = .375$$
$$P(C \cap G) = P(G|C)P(C) = (.50)(.25) = .125$$

From these calculations, we may construct the probability table shown in Table 5.7.

Table 5.7   Probability Table for Urn Experiment

	R	G	Total
A	.075	.175	.25
B	.125	.375	.50
C	.125	.125	.25
Total	.325	.675	1.00

From Table 5.7, we obtain two more marginal probabilities:

$$P(R) = P(A \cap R) + P(B \cap R) + P(C \cap R) = .075 + .125 + .125 = .325$$
$$P(G) = P(A \cap G) + P(B \cap G) + P(C \cap G) = .175 + .375 + .125 = .675$$

Now, by applying Formula (5.1), we may answer the original problem. If we know that a *red* ball was drawn, the probabilities that it was selected from each of the urns are given by the following calculations:

$$P(A \mid R) = \frac{P(A \cap R)}{P(R)} = \frac{.075}{.325} = .230$$

$$P(B \mid R) = \frac{P(B \cap R)}{P(R)} = \frac{.125}{.325} = .385$$

$$P(C \mid R) = \frac{P(C \cap R)}{P(R)} = \frac{.125}{.325} = .385$$

If we know that a *green* ball was drawn, the probabilities that it was selected from each of the urns are calculated as follows:

$$P(A \mid G) = \frac{P(A \cap G)}{P(G)} = \frac{.175}{.675} = .259$$

$$P(B \mid G) = \frac{P(B \cap G)}{P(G)} = \frac{.375}{.675} = .556$$

$$P(C \mid G) = \frac{P(C \cap G)}{P(G)} = \frac{.125}{.675} = .185$$

Thus, if we know that a *red* ball was drawn, there is a .230 probability that it was drawn from urn A, a .385 probability that it was drawn from urn B, and a .385 probability that it was drawn from urn C. Notice that these three probabilities add up to 1, since the ball must have been drawn from one of the three urns. Similarly, if we know that a *green* ball was drawn, the probabilities are .259 that it came from urn A, .556 that it was drawn from urn B, and .185 that it came from urn C.

Notice in this problem that one set of marginal probabilities—$P(A)$, $P(B)$, and $P(C)$—was given at the outset. Such probabilities are sometimes called *prior probabilities*, since they are the probabilities that exist prior to obtaining any information about the outcome of the process. The conditional probabilities that constitute the solution to the problem—$P(A \mid R)$, $P(B \mid R) \ldots$—are called *posterior probabilities,* since they represent probability assessments that have been revised on the basis of later information.

Another method of arriving at the same solution to the problem—a method that is particularly convenient in solving many applied decision problems—is to use a computational table. Such a table is illustrated in Table 5.8 for the condition that a red ball was drawn.

Table 5.8 Computation of Probabilities Posterior to Observing a Red Ball

Urn	(1) Prior Probability	(2) Conditional Probability	(3) Joint Probablity	(4) Posterior Probability
A	$P(A) = .25$	$P(R\mid A) = .30$	$P(A \cap R) = .075$	$P(A\mid R) = .230$
B	$P(B) = .50$	$P(R\mid B) = .25$	$P(B \cap R) = .125$	$P(B\mid R) = .385$
C	$P(C) = .25$	$P(R\mid C) = .50$	$P(C \cap R) = .125$	$P(C\mid R) = .385$
	$\overline{1.00}$		$P(R) = \overline{.325}$	$\overline{1.000}$

In Table 5.8, figures in columns (1) and (2) are given in the statement of the problem. Column (1) contains the prior (marginal) probabilities that each of the three urns will be selected. Column (2) gives the conditional probabilities that a red ball will be drawn if the indicated urn is selected. Column (3) is obtained by multiplying the corresponding values from columns (1) and (2). The resulting figures in column (3) are the joint probabilities that the indicated urn will be selected and a red ball drawn from it. The sum of the values in column (3) is the marginal probability that a red ball will be drawn, regardless of which urn is selected. The figures in column (4) are obtained by dividing the figures in column (3) by their sum. Careful study of this computational table will reveal that the calculations are exactly the same as those that were made in solving the problem by formulas. The solution to the problem under the condition of drawing a green ball is shown in Table 5.9.

Table 5.9 Computation of Probabilities Posterior to Observing a Green Ball

Urn	Prior Probability	Conditional Probability	Joint Probability	Posterior Probability
A	$P(A) = .25$	$P(G\mid A) = .70$	$P(A \cap G) = .175$	$P(A\mid G) = .259$
B	$P(B) = .50$	$P(G\mid B) = .75$	$P(B \cap G) = .375$	$P(B\mid G) = .556$
C	$P(C) = .25$	$P(G\mid C) = .50$	$P(C \cap G) = .125$	$P(C\mid G) = .185$
	$\overline{1.00}$		$P(G) = \overline{.675}$	$\overline{1.000}$

To state Bayes' theorem formally, let $E_1, E_2, \ldots, E_i, \ldots, E_n$ be n mutually exclusive and collectively exhaustive events with known probabilities $P(E_1)$, $P(E_2), \ldots, P(E_i), \ldots, P(E_n)$. Also, let C be an event for which the conditional probabilities $P(C\mid E_i)$, $i = 1, \ldots, n$ are known. Then for any specific event E_j out of the set of n events, the conditional probability $P(E_j\mid C)$ may be computed from the formula

$$P(E_j \mid C) = \frac{P(C \cap E_j)}{P(C)} = \frac{P(C \mid E_j)P(E_j)}{\sum_i [P(C \mid E_i)P(E_i)]} \qquad (5.9)$$

Formula (5.9) is the celebrated Bayes' theorem. Careful examination of the formula will reveal that it specifies exactly the calculations that we have been making in solving the problem of the urns.

PROBLEMS

5.1 Following are four sets that are defined by the describing method.

$S_1 = \{x \mid x$ is one of the first 4 months of the year$\}$

$S_2 = \{x \mid x$ is a prince consort of England since 1800$\}$

$S_3 = \{x \mid x$ is one of the United States' three most populous cities$\}$

$S_4 = \{x \mid x$ is a nonnegative integer$\}$

Define each of these sets by the listing method.

5.2 Following are three sets that are defined by the listing method.

$S_1 = \{$October, November, December$\}$

$S_2 = \{$a, e, i, o, u$\}$

$S_3 = \{2, 4, 6, \ldots\}$

Define each of these sets by the describing method.

5.3 Consider the following two sets:

$$A = \{2, 3, 4\}$$
$$B = \{b \mid 2 \le b \le 4\}$$

(a) Explain how these two sets differ.

(b) Define set A by the describing method.

(c) Explain why it is impossible to define set B by the listing method.

5.4 Without the benefit of set theory, the French mathematician Jean d'Alembert (1717–1783) reasoned that, if two coins are tossed, there are three possible outcomes: (1) two heads, (2) two tails, and (3) one head and one tail. He then concluded that each of these three outcomes is equally likely to occur. Using set theory, evaluate d'Alembert's conclusion.

5.5 A particular sample space is composed of 10 sample points.

(a) How many different events, each encompassing 5 sample points, may be defined on this sample space?

(b) Remembering that the empty set and the universal set are both regarded as events, how many different events of all possible sizes may be defined on this sample space?

5.6 Consider the following sets:

$$S_1 = \{c, r, e, a, m\}$$
$$S_2 = \{c, h, o, r, e\}$$
$$S_3 = \{d, a, m, p\}$$

Using the listing method, define each of the following sets.

(a) $S_1 \cap S_2$

(b) $S_1 \cap S_3$

(c) $S_2 \cap S_3$

(d) $S_1 \cup S_2$

(e) $S_1 \cup S_3$

(f) $S_2 \cup S_3$

5.7 Consider the following sets:

$$A = \{3, 4, 5, 6, 7\}$$
$$B = \{5, 6, 7, 8, 9\}$$
$$C = \{c \mid 3 \leq c \leq 7\}$$
$$D = \{d \mid 5 < d < 9\}$$

Using either the listing or describing method, whichever seems more appropriate in each case, define each of the following sets so that its elements are clearly specified.

$$H = A \cap B \qquad\qquad K = A \cup B$$
$$I = A \cap C \qquad\qquad L = A \cup C$$
$$J = C \cap D \qquad\qquad M = C \cup D$$

5.8 As the president of the XYZ Company, Mr. Anderson must decide whether or not to establish a branch office in a foreign country. This decision depends primarily on the market potential of the company's products in that country. He advised the vice-president, Mr. Baker, to perform an analysis and to submit his recommendation. In addition, he has hired two consultants, Mr. Clark and Mr. Decker, to study the problem separately and make their respective recommendations. Unfortunately, none of the three reports will be perfectly reliable (each has a .10 chance of being wrong). Thus, the president has decided to take the action recommended by a majority of these reports, rather than any single report. He also realizes that such a decision rule does not guarantee that he will make a correct decision.

We may recognize that, under various situations, Mr. Anderson will make a wrong decision. To specify these situations precisely, we let

$$B = \{\text{Baker's report is right}\}$$
$$C = \{\text{Clark's report is right}\}$$
$$D = \{\text{Decker's report is right}\}$$

Use B, C, D, and their complements to express each of the possible events that will lead the president to make a wrong decision.

5.9 An investment club has 100 members, consisting of 50 men between the ages of 25 and 60 inclusive, and 50 women between the ages of 30 and 55 inclusive. At a meeting of the club, the names of the 100 members have been written on separate slips of paper and placed in an urn. These slips have been thoroughly mixed, and one slip is to be drawn from the urn. The person whose name is drawn will win one share of Great Caspian Tea Company stock. Consider the following possible events:

E_1: {the winner is a man}

E_2: {the winner is a woman}

E_3: {the winner is a person less than 57 years old}

E_4: {the winner is a person more than 50 years old}

E_5: {the winner is a woman less than 40 years old}

E_6: {the winner is a woman at least 40 years old}

Which of the following sets of events constitutes partitions of the sample space for the drawing?

(a) E_1 and E_2
(b) E_3 and E_4
(c) E_5 and E_6
(d) E_1, E_5, and E_6

5.10 Suppose that the universal set $\mathcal{U}$ is the set of positive integers : {1, 2, 3, 4, 5, 6, 7, 8, 9}. Consider the following subsets :

$$X = \{x \mid x \text{ is a positive integer in } \mathcal{U} \text{ less than } 4\}$$
$$Y = \{y \mid y \text{ is an even integer in } \mathcal{U}\}$$
$$Z = \{z \mid z \text{ is an integer in } \mathcal{U} \text{ not evenly divisible by } 4\}$$

Using the listing method, define each of the following subsets :
(a) $X \cap Y$
(b) $X' \cap Y'$
(c) $X' \cap Z'$
(d) $X \cap Y \cap Z'$
(e) $(X \cap Y')'$
(f) $(Y \cap Z)'$
(g) $(X \cap Y \cap Z)'$
(h) $(X' \cap Y' \cap Z)'$

5.11 There is a .60 probability that a randomly identified housewife in a supermarket will buy bread. There is a .15 probability that she will buy both bread and cheese. If a housewife buys bread, what is the probability that she will also buy cheese ?

5.12 A job applicant has just taken a vocabulary test and an arithmetic test. He estimates that there is a .60 probability that he obtained a passing score on the vocabulary test, and a .30 probability that he obtained a passing score on both tests. If he learns that he passed the vocabulary test, what is the probability that he passed the arithmetic test ?

5.13 A salesman is demonstrating a vacuum cleaner to Mrs. Smith and Mrs. Jones. The two women have withdrawn to the next room to discuss whether each of them should purchase one of these appliances. The salesman estimates a .60 probability that Mrs. Jones will buy one of his cleaners. He also estimates that if Mrs. Jones buys a vacuum, there is a .40 probability that Mrs. Smith will buy one. What is the probability that both women will buy vacuum cleaners ?

5.14 In a large company, 60% of the employees are males and 25% of the employees are management trainees. Furthermore, 80% of the management trainees are males. Suppose that an employee is to be selected at random from the company's personnel roster. Let M denote the event that the person selected is a male, and T denote the event that the person selected is a management trainee.
(a) Express each of the following probability statements in words :
   (i) $P(T')$
   (ii) $P(M \cap T)$
   (iii) $P(M \cap T')$
   (iv) $P(T \mid M)$
   (v) $P(M' \mid T)$
(b) Compute each of the probabilities in part (a).

5.15 Referring to Problem 5.14, do the following :
(a) Express each of the following probability statements in symbols :
   (i) Probability of selecting a female who is a management trainee.
   (ii) Probability of selecting a female who is not a management trainee.
   (iii) Probability of selecting a male if the person selected is not a management trainee.
   (iv) Probability of selecting a person who is not a management trainee if the person selected is a male.
   (v) Probability of selecting a female if the person selected is not a management trainee.
(b) Compute each of the probabilities in part (a).

5.16 The probability that a customer entering a supermarket buys eggs is .10. If the customer buys eggs, the probability that he will also buy bacon is .40. Whether or not the customer buys eggs, the probability is .50 that he will buy milk.
(a) What is the probability that a customer will buy both eggs and bacon ?
(b) What is the probability that the customer will buy both eggs and milk ?

5.17 Marlo Associates, a marketing research firm, has been retained by the Lipgram Tea Co. to conduct a marketing research study of tea-buying behavior in Greentree County. A randomly selected sample of 200 housewives in Cedar City, the county seat, were asked the question: "The last time you purchased tea, what brand did you buy?" In a discreet manner, each respondent was also queried concerning her age. The frequencies of responses are shown in the following table:

| | Last Brand Purchased | | |
Age	Lipgram	Other	Total
Under 30	10	50	60
30 and over	90	50	140
Total	100	100	200

(a) If a respondent is selected at random from this sample, what is the probability that the last brand of tea she purchased was Lipgram?

(b) If a respondent under 30 is selected at random from this sample, what is the probability that the last brand of tea she purchased was Lipgram?

(c) If a respondent is selected at random from those whose last tea purchase was Lipgram, what is the probability that she is at least 30 years old?

5.18 For two events C and D it is known that $P(C) = .25$ and $P(D) = .35$. It is also known that C and D are mutually exclusive. Determine $P(C \cup D)$.

5.19 Events X, Y, and Z are mutually exclusive and collectively exhaustive. If $P(X') = .60$ and $P(Y) = 2P(Z)$, what is $P(X)$? $P(Y)$? $P(Z)$?

5.20 Of the entrants in a regional contest sponsored by a soap company, 80% were women and 20% were men. Of the total number of entrants, 40% were Californians. Of the Californians, 75% were women.

(a) What percentage of the entrants were either Californians and/or women?

(b) If an entrant was a man, what is the conditional probability that he was *not* a Californian?

5.21 On two successive days, a job seeker is interviewed by Alkol Industries and by Benson Associates. In both cases she is told, "Don't call us, we'll call you." She estimates that the probability of receiving a favorable response from Alkol is .70, that the probability of receiving an unfavorable response from Benson is .50, and that the probability of at least one of the firm's replying unfavorably is .60. What is the probability that she will receive a favorable response from at least 1 of the firms?

5.22 A social-climbing young executive has applied for membership to two exclusive clubs—Les Chevaliers de Vin Aigre and the Sons of the Establishment. He estimates that the probability of being accepted by Les Chevaliers is .40, that he will be accepted by at least 1 of the 2 clubs is .60, but that he has only a .10 probability of being accepted by both clubs. What is the probability that he will be accepted by the Sons of the Establishment?

5.23 In a certain business school, 10% of the senior class were elected to Beta Gamma Sigma, 40% of the class held part-time jobs, and 20% of those holding part-time jobs were elected to Beta Gamma Sigma. What is the probability that a senior chosen at random either held a part-time job and/or was elected to Beta Gamma Sigma?

5.24 Of the 160 supervisors in a company, a total of 100 have college degrees and a total of 55 are veterans of the armed forces. Of the total, 35 of the supervisors are veterans who have college degrees.

(a) If a supervisor is selected at random, what is the probability that he is either a veteran and/or has a college degree?

(b) Suppose that the supervisors who are veterans are separated from the nonveterans and a man is randomly selected from the veteran supervisors. What is the probability that the man has a college degree?

5.25 A political analyst estimated that, in an upcoming statewide election, the probability that Goodheart will be elected governor is .70, and the probability that Morris will be elected Treasurer is .60. The analyst also estimates a .56 probability that both politicians will be elected. Symbolically, these three probabilities may be written

$$P(G) = .70$$
$$P(M) = .60$$
$$P(G \cap M) = .56$$

(a) Express each of the following probability statements in words:
(i) $P(G \cup M)$; (ii) $P(M|G')$; (iii) $P(G|M)$; (iv) $P(G \cap M')$; (v) $P(G \cup M')$; (vi) $P(G'|M)$.

(b) Express each of the following probability statements symbolically:
  (i) Probability that Morris will be elected if Goodheart is elected.
  (ii) Probability that Goodheart will not be elected but Morris will be elected.
  (iii) Probability that either Goodheart and/or Morris will be defeated.
  (iv) Probability that both Goodheart and Morris will be defeated.
  (v) Probability that Morris will be defeated if Goodheart is defeated.
  (vi) Probability that Goodheart will be defeated if Morris is defeated.

(c) Compute each of the probabilities in parts (a) and (b).

5.26 Two events are defined on the same sample space. Let us designate these events A and B. Suppose that $P(B) = .60$, $P(A' \cap B) = .10$, and $P(A \cup B) = .70$. Determine the following:
(a) $P(A \cap B')$; (b) $P(A \cup B')$; (c) $P(A' \cap B')$; (d) $P(A \cap B)$; (e) $P(A|B)$; (f) $P(B|A)$; (g) $P(B'|A')$.

5.27 Consider two *independent* events, G and H, for which $P(G) = .80$ and $P(H) = .40$. Determine each of the following probabilities:
(a) $P(G \cap H)$ (e) $P(G|H)$
(b) $P(G \cap H')$ (f) $P(G|H')$
(c) $P(G' \cap H)$ (g) $P(G'|H)$
(d) $P(G' \cap H')$ (h) $P(G'|H')$

5.28 Of the executives at a convention, 60% attended luncheon and 70% attended dinner. Of the total, 40% attended both luncheon and dinner.
(a) If it is known that an executive attended luncheon, what is the probability that he or she also attended dinner?
(b) Were these two acts—attending luncheon and attending dinner—independent events? Explain.

5.29 The Guessright Employment Agency administers a Verbal Comprehension test and a Verbal Reasoning test to each of its applicants. On the Verbal Comprehension test, a score above 14 is considered passing, and on the Verbal Reasoning test, a score of 19 is considered passing. From the agency's records, it has been determined that 10% of the applicants fail the Verbal Comprehension test, 12% fail the Verbal Reasoning test, and 2% fail both.
(a) What is the probability that a randomly selected applicant passed both tests?
(b) Is the event "pass Verbal Comprehension test" independent of the event "pass Verbal Reasoning test"? Explain.

5.30 Consider two *mutually exclusive* events F and G. It is known that $P(F) = .40$ and $P(G) = .50$.
(a) Compute the following probabilities:
  (i) $P(F \cup G)$
  (ii) $P(F \cup G')$

(iii) $P(F|G')$
(iv) $P(G|F)$
(v) $P(G'|F)$
(b) Are F and G independent events? Explain.

5.31 Two *independent* events, A and B, have the marginal probabilities $P(A) = .30$ and $P(B) = .60$. Determine the following probabilities:
  (a) $P(A \cap B)$; (b) $P(A|B)$; (c) $P(A \cap B')$; (d) $P(A|B')$; (e) $P(A \cup B)$; (f) $P(A' \cup B')$;
  (g) $P(A' \cup B)$; (h) $P(A \cup B')$.

5.32 As manager of the international division of a firm, you must decide whether or not to market your product in a certain foreign country. Your three subordinates—David, Edward, and Frances—have analyzed this matter, and each has prepared a report for you. Experience has shown that each of them is capable of making a faulty analysis and thus might recommend a wrong decision. Furthermore, because of similar backgrounds and experience, the probabilities of their making right recommendations are not necessarily independent.

  Denote D: {David's report is right}
      E: {Edward's report is right}
      F: {Frances's report is right}

The following probabilities have been estimated on the basis of the past performances of these people in similar situations:

$$P(D) = .70 \qquad P(E) = .80 \qquad P(F) = .90$$
$$P(D|E) = .75 \qquad P(F|E) = .90 \qquad P(D \cup F) = .95$$

(a) What is the probability that both Edward's and Frances's reports are wrong?
(b) What is the probability that either David's and/or Frances's reports are wrong?
(c) If we have complete confidence that Edward's report is right, what is the probability that David's report is right?
(d) If David submits a wrong report, what is the probability that Frances will submit a correct report?
(e) What is the probability that both David and Edward will submit correct reports?
(f) What is the probability that either David and/or Edward will submit a correct report?
(g) What is the probability that either Edward or Frances (but not both) will submit a wrong report?

5.33 A group of investors has hatched a plan to organize three different firms, A, B, and C. Before rushing headlong into the project, they pause to consider the circumstances that might confront them during the first year of operation. Let A represent the event that firm A survives its first year (so A' is the event that it fails), B be the event that firm B survives the first year, and C be the event that firm C survives the first year. Upon contemplation, the investors estimate the following probabilities:

$$P(A) = .75 \qquad P(B) = .70 \qquad P(C) = .60 \qquad P(C|B) = .80 \qquad P(A|B) = .75$$

(a) Express in words the event represented by the expression

$$(A \cap B \cap C)'$$

(b) Justify the following expression by stating how the seven terms on the right are related to the meaning of the term on the left:

$$(A \cap B \cap C)' = (A' \cap B \cap C) \cup (A \cap B' \cap C) \cup (A \cap B \cap C') \cup$$
$$(A' \cap B' \cap C) \cup (A' \cap B \cap C') \cup (A \cap B' \cap C') \cup$$
$$(A' \cap B' \cap C')$$

(c) Which of the following is a correct statement? Events B and C are:
  (i) Independent and mutually exclusive
  (ii) Independent but not mutually exclusive

    (iii)   Mutually exclusive but not independent

    (iv)   Neither mutually exclusive nor independent

  (d)   Which of the following is a correct statement? Events A and B are:

    (i)   Mutually exclusive but not independent

    (ii)   Independent but not mutually exclusive

    (iii)   Neither mutually exclusive nor independent

    (iv)   Both mutually exclusive and independent

  (e)   If firm A should fail during the first year, what is the probability that firm B will fail during the first year?

  (f)   What is the probability that both firm A and firm B will fail during the first year?

  (g)   What is the probability that either firm A and/or firm B will survive the first year?

5.34 In its long-range planning, Technox Associates, a major construction engineering firm in the Southwest, is analyzing the prospects for two different large-scale projects—an atomic power plant at Zorro Beach and a dam on the Osoblanco River. Since it is beyond the firm's capacity to undertake both of these projects, the planners must decide which has the greater potential. A study team is sent to the Zorro Beach area and reports that the major concern affecting the possible construction of the atomic plant is whether Juan Muir, an adamant conservationist, becomes the next majority leader in the state legislature. If Muir becomes majority leader, analysts estimate that the probability of state approval for the atomic plant is .20; but if Muir fails to become majority leader, they estimate a .70 probability of approval. Political experts estimate that there is a .40 probability of Muir's becoming the next majority leader. The study group then proceeds to the headquarters of the Osoblanco Water and Power District, where they find considerable uncertainty concerning the dam project. If the Zorro atomic plant is authorized, there appears to be only a .20 chance that the dam construction would be approved; but if the Zorro plant is not authorized, the probability is .90 that the dam project will be approved. From all of these subjective probability assessments, which project has the greater probability of being realized—the atomic plant or the dam?

5.35 An electronic subsystem is composed of three components—A, B, and C—as shown in the diagram. Component A will function only if both parts A_1 and A_2 function. Component B will function as long as either B_1 and/or B_2 functions. Component C will function as long as at least one of its three parts—C_1, C_2, and C_3—functions. The entire subsystem will function only if component C functions, and if either component A and/or component B functions. Components A_1 and A_2 each has a reliability of .90. Components B_1 and B_2 each has a reliability of .80. Components C_1, C_2, and C_3 each has a reliability of .70. Assuming that each individual part operates independently of every other part, what is the reliability of the entire subsystem?

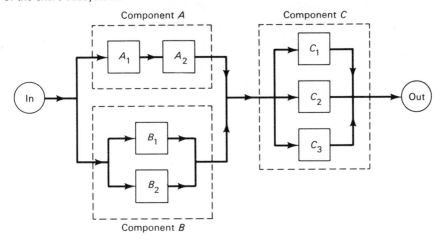

5.36 An electronic subsystem is composed of three components—A, B, and C—as shown in the diagram. Component A will function only if both parts A_1 and A_2 function. Component B will function as long as at least one of its three parts—B_1, B_2, and B_3—functions. Component C will function only if C_1 and C_4 *both* function, *and* if either C_2 and/or C_3 functions. The entire subsystem will function only if component C functions, and if either component A and/or component B functions. The reliabilities of the individual parts are as follows:

Part	Reliability	Part	Reliability	Part	Reliability
A_1	.90	B_2	.40	C_2	.80
A_2	.95	B_3	.40	C_3	.80
B_1	.40	C_1	.90	C_4	.98

Assuming that each individual part operates independently of every other part, what is the reliability of the entire subsystem?

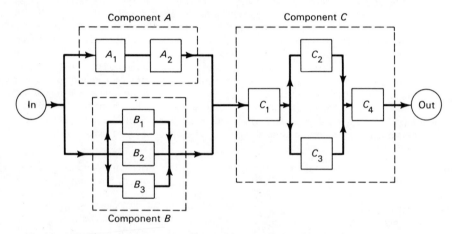

5.37 A selected group of 50 common stocks contains 25 industrials, 10 railroads, and 15 utilities. On a particular day, 20 of the industrials, 7 of the railroads, and 3 of the utilities rose; the rest fell. If a single stock picked at random from the group is discovered to have fallen on that day, what is the probability that it is a railroad issue?

5.38 A medical research group has developed a new diagnostic test for glombitis. The group's research data indicate the following: (1) Of people with glombitis, the test correctly gives a positive result 90% of the time. (2) Of people free of glombitis, the test incorrectly gives a positive result 4% of the time. From a large population of which only 2/10 of 1% have glombitis, 1 person is selected at random, given the test, and the result is positive. What is the probability that the person actually has glombitis?

5.39 Management's prior probability assessment of demand for a newly developed product is as follows:

Demand	Probability
High	.60
Low	.10
Average	.30

A survey, taken to help estimate the true demand level for the product, indicates that demand will be average. The reliability of the survey procedure is such that it will indicate "average" demand 30% of the time when it really will be high, 50% of the time when it really will be low, and 90% of the time when it really will be average. In the light of this information, what would be the revised probabilities of the three possible demand levels?

5.40 A cosmetics firm is considering whether or not to introduce its newly developed "Night in Eden" face cream into a particular marketing area. On the basis of the sales of other of the firm's products in this market, management estimates the following probabilities of demand during the first 6 months:

Demand Level	Probability
High	.30
Moderate	.50
Low	.20

To help reduce the amount of uncertainty in this decision, the firm's marketing research group conducts a survey in the proposed target area. The reliability of the survey procedure is summarized by the following table of conditional probabilities:

If Actual Demand Is:	Probability That Survey Prediction Will Be:		
	High	Moderate	Low
High	.60	.30	.10
Moderate	.10	.70	.20
Low	.10	.10	.80

(a) If the research group's report predicts that demand for "Night in Eden" will be "high," what is the probability that actual demand will be high? moderate? low?

(b) If the research group's report predicts that demand for "Night in Eden" will be "moderate," what is the probability that actual demand will be high? moderate? low?

(c) If the research group's report predicts that demand for "Night in Eden" will be "low," what is the probability that actual demand will be high? moderate? low?

5.41 A marketing research firm is interested in interviewing married couples about certain product preferences. An interviewer from this research firm arrives at a building, which has three apartments. He reads the names on the mailboxes and sees that one of the three apartments is inhabited by two women, another has two men living in it, and the third is occupied by a married couple. Proceeding into the building, the interviewer is surprised to find that there are no names or numbers on the doors of the three apartments. He therefore selects a door at random and rings the bell. A woman answers. Assuming that the woman who answered the bell is an occupant of the apartment, what is the probability that the interviewer has mistakenly chosen the apartment occupied by the two women rather than that of the married couple?

6

Probability Functions
of Random Variables

The application of mathematics, including probability and statistics, to managerial decision problems arises from a need for methods that will enable decision makers to analyze complex relationships among conditions and events in an orderly and precise fashion. The definition and logical manipulation of such relationships is accomplished in mathematics by means of "functions." Indeed, the concept of a function is so pervasive in mathematics that little headway can be made in the application of mathematics to real-world problems without the use of functions.

Throughout this book we make extensive use of various types of mathematical functions. In this chapter we review the basic concept of a function and then consider the following two fundamental types of functions: (1) random variables and (2) probability functions.

6.1 BASIC CONCEPT OF A FUNCTION

Readers may recall from their previous study of mathematics that a *function* is a *rule* that associates with each element of one set, called the *domain*, a unique element of another set, called the *range*. As an illustration, suppose that the total cost of a production run for a particular product consists of a fixed setup cost of $200 plus a cost of $6.00 for each unit produced. If we let c represent this total cost and q represent the number of units produced, we may express c as a function of q as follows:

$$c = 200 + 6q$$

In this function, the value of c depends on the value of q. Thus, we refer to c as the *dependent variable* and q as the *independent variable*. The set of all possible values of the dependent variable is the range of the function, and the set of all possible values of the independent variable is the domain of the function. Suppose, for instance, that a production run can consist of producing any desired number of units between 50 and 100, inclusive. Then the domain of the cost function is the set of all possible values of q:

$$\{50, 51, \ldots, 99, 100\}$$

With each of these values of q, the function associates a particular value of c:

q	50	51	$\cdots$	99	100
c	500	506	$\cdots$	794	800

Thus, the range of the function is the set of all possible values of c:

$$\{500, 506, \ldots, 794, 800\}$$

The function itself is the rule whereby a value of c is assigned to each value of q. As a shorthand notation to indicate that c is a function of q, we may write

$$c = f(q)$$

where $f(q)$ is read "f of q." In this expression, $f(q)$ represents the value of c for any specified value of q. For instance, $c = f(60)$ means that c is equal to the value obtained when the function is evaluated at 60. That is, since $f(q) = 200 + 6q$, we obtain

$$c = f(60) = 200 + 6(60) = 560$$

which means that the total cost of a production run of 60 units is $560.

In the example above, the function took the form of an equation relating two sets of numerical values. However, the general concept of a function is much broader. For instance, the elements of either set may or may not be numbers. As an example, consider the common practice of assigning grades of A, B, C, D, and F in college courses. If students wish to compute their grade-point averages, they must convert their letter grades into numbers. Specifically, they may adopt the following rule (function):

$$g = \begin{cases} 4 & \text{if} \quad A \\ 3 & \text{if} \quad B \\ 2 & \text{if} \quad C \\ 1 & \text{if} \quad D \\ 0 & \text{if} \quad F \end{cases}$$

In this function, the range consists of a set of numerical values, $\{4, 3, 2, 1, 0\}$, but the domain consists of a set of letter grades, $\{A, B, C, D, F\}$.

6.2 DEFINITION OF A RANDOM VARIABLE

When the term "random variable" was introduced into the vocabulary of probability theory, the discipline was limited essentially to the study of *objective* probabilities. Thus, it was only natural that the definition of a random variable was originally formulated in terms of a clearly delineated sample space of a well-defined random process. During recent years, however, the study of *subjective* probability has received increasing attention and recognition, particularly as applied to business decision making. Since subjective probabilities are not necessarily related to well-defined random processes, it has become necessary to extend the traditional definition of a random variable to include situations in which existing uncertainties may not be describable in terms of random processes. In this section we first discuss the concept of a random variable as traditionally defined in terms of a random process, and then consider the more modern extended definition.

6.2.1 Traditional Definition

In Section 5.2, we observed how events may be defined on the sample space of a random process. In analyzing such events, it is generally desirable to redefine the events in numerical terms in order to facilitate mathematical manipulation. For this purpose we may assign a numerical value to each element of the sample space. When this is done, the function that assigns a specific real number to each point in the sample space is called a *random variable*. That is, a random variable is a real-valued function defined on a sample space. More simply, a random variable may be regarded as a quantity that has a set of possible values. Insofar as possible, we will use a capital letter to denote a random variable, and the corresponding lowercase letter to represent any specific value of that random variable. For instance, if X is used to denote a random variable, then x represents any specific value of that random variable. Thus, an expression such as $P(X = x)$ means: probability that the random variable X will have the specific value x.

Example 1 :

Suppose that an automatic machine produces widgets that may be classified as defective or nondefective. Consider the experiment of selecting a sample of two widgets at random from the output of this machine. If we denote a defective item by d and a nondefective item by d', the sample space for this experiment is

$$\{(d', d'), (d', d), (d, d'), (d, d)\}$$

One way of converting these qualitatively described sample points into numerical values is to count the number of defective widgets in the sample. Clearly, this count is a random variable, which assigns a numerical value to each sample point. If we let X denote this random variable, we can express the functional relationship between the count and the sample space as follows :

$$X = \begin{cases} 0 & (d', d') \\ 1 & \text{if} \quad (d', d) \quad \text{or} \quad (d, d') \\ 2 & (d, d) \end{cases}$$

This functional relationship is portrayed graphically in Figure 6.1. Notice that in this

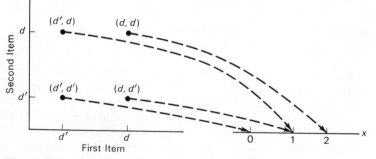

Figure 6.1 Mapping a Sample Space into a Random Variable

function the range (that is, the set of all possible values of the random variable X) is {0, 1, 2}. It is important to observe that the function assigns one and only one value to each sample point, although the same value may be assigned to more than one sample point.

Example 2:

Let us consider again the sample space for the random process of rolling a pair of dice. Recall that each point in this sample space, which was presented in Figure 5.3, was defined in terms of an ordered pair of values. For instance, the ordered pair (1, 3) was used to denote the outcome that the red die comes up 1 and the green die comes up 3. However, if a craps player's point is 4, he would not be particularly interested in which ordered pair he tosses, as long as the sum of the two values that constitute the pair is equal to 4. Thus, he adopts the rule of describing the outcome of a roll by adding the numbers of spots appearing on the upper faces of the two dice. If we let X represent the quantity defined by this rule, then X is a random variable. All possible values of X, together with the sample points associated with each of these values, are shown in Table 6.1. Inspection of Table 6.1 indicates that each sample point is assigned a single value, although the same value may be assigned to several sample points. For instance, the sample point (1, 3) is assigned a single value of 4, although the same value of 4 is also assigned to sample points (3, 1) and (2, 2).

Table 6.1 Defining a Random Variable on a Sample Space

X: Sum of Spots	Corresponding Sample Points	Number of Sample Points
2	(1, 1)	1
3	(1, 2), (2, 1)	2
4	(1, 3), (2, 2), (3, 1)	3
5	(1, 4), (2, 3), (3, 2), (4, 1)	4
6	(1, 5), (2, 4), (3, 3), (4, 2), (5, 1)	5
7	(1, 6), (2, 5), (3, 4), (4, 3), (5, 2), (6, 1)	6
8	(2, 6), (3, 5), (4, 4), (5, 3), (6, 2)	5
9	(3, 6), (4, 5), (5, 4), (6, 3)	4
10	(4, 6), (5, 5), (6, 4)	3
11	(5, 6), (6, 5)	2
12	(6, 6)	1
		36

6.2.2 Extended Definition

In the *extended sense*, a random variable is simply defined as *a quantity whose value is not known with certainty*. We can see that this definition applies to a random variable as traditionally defined as well as to any "uncertain quantity." For instance:

1. A crap shooter is about to roll the dice. He is uncertain about the sum that he will roll. Therefore, the sum is a random variable, which in this case fits the traditional definition as well as the extended definition.

2. An investor is considering buying some stock that he plans to sell in 3 months. Because of various unpredictable factors, he is uncertain about what the price of the stock will be 3 months from now. Thus, this price can be regarded as a random variable in the extended sense.

6.3 DISCRETE AND CONTINUOUS RANDOM VARIABLES

In working with random variables, it is important to distinguish between discrete and continuous variables. A random variable is said to be *discrete* if it can take on a finite or countably infinite number of values. Thus, the set of all possible values of a discrete random variable can be described by the listing method explained in Section 5.1. For instance, in our dice example, the set of all possible values of the random variable X can be listed as follows:

$$\{x \mid x = 2, 3, 4, 5, 6, 7, 8, 9, 10, 11, 12\}$$

Since this set of possible values of X is finite, X must be a discrete random variable. As another example of a discrete random variable, consider the number of bad checks that will be accepted by the Emporium Department Store next week. This number is an uncertain quantity, and thus may be regarded as a random variable in the extended sense. Although the number of bad checks accepted by the store can be counted after the week's receipts have been processed, it is not possible beforehand to specify any precise upper limit on what that count might be. Thus, if we use Y to denote this random variable, the set of all possible values of Y is said to be countably infinite, and would be listed as

$$\{y \mid y = 0, 1, 2, \ldots\}$$

Although a discrete random variable can take on only a countable number of isolated values, a *continuous* random variable can take on any of an infinite number of values along a continuum between specific limits. As such, a continuous random variable has an infinite number of possible values. Therefore, the set of all possible values of a continuous random variable can be defined by the describing method but not by the listing method. For instance, a customer in a self-service supermarket fills a paper bag with a dozen oranges. Although he does not know the exact weight of the bag of oranges, he feels sure that it weighs at least 4 pounds but no more than 7 pounds. Thus, the weight of the bag of oranges is a random variable that may take on any real value between the limits of 4 and 7. If we denote this random variable by W, we may express the possible values of W in set notation as follows:

$$\{w \mid 4 \leq w \leq 7\}$$

Example:

In an assembly plant, a particular quality control procedure requires that an inspector select and test a sample of 10 items from each lot of steel springs received from a supplier. We might define the random variable D as the number of defectives obtained when a sample of 10 items is inspected from a lot; this would be a discrete random variable that can assume only the isolated values 0, 1, . . . , 10. We might, however, define another random variable W as the combined weight in ounces of the 10 items in the sample; this would be a continuous random variable, since the combined weight of the 10 items could assume any of an infinite number of values along a continuous scale.

6.4 DEFINING EVENTS IN TERMS OF RANDOM VARIABLES

In Section 5.2 we defined an event as any subset of a sample space. That is, an event corresponds to one or more sample points. In this chapter we have seen how the concept of a random variable enables us to assign numerical values to sample points. Thus, we now are able to describe an event in terms of the numerical values assigned to the sample points of that event. In other words, events may be described as subsets of all possible values of a random variable.

Example 1 :

In Section 6.2 we used the example of selecting a sample of two widgets from the output of an automatic machine. The sample space for this example is

$$\{(d', d'), (d', d), (d, d'), (d, d)\}$$

It can be demonstrated that it is possible to define $2^4 = 16$ different events on this sample space. Some of these events are

$$E_1 = \{(d', d')\} \qquad E_4 = \{(d', d), (d, d'), (d, d)\}$$
$$E_2 = \{(d', d), (d, d')\} \qquad E_5 = \{(d', d'), (d', d), (d, d')\}$$
$$E_3 = \{(d, d)\} \qquad E_6 = \{(d', d'), (d', d), (d, d'), (d, d)\}$$

Each of these events is shown graphically in Figure 6.2.

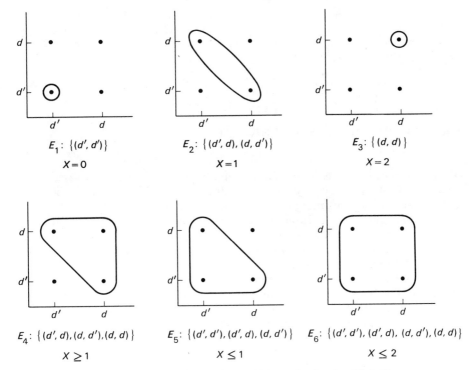

$$E_1 : \{(d', d')\}$$
$$X = 0$$

$$E_2 : \{(d', d), (d, d')\}$$
$$X = 1$$

$$E_3 : \{(d, d)\}$$
$$X = 2$$

$$E_4 : \{(d', d), (d, d'), (d, d)\}$$
$$X \geq 1$$

$$E_5 : \{(d', d'), (d', d), (d, d')\}$$
$$X \leq 1$$

$$E_6 : \{(d', d'), (d', d), (d, d'), (d, d)\}$$
$$X \leq 2$$

Figure 6.2   Sample Points Corresponding to Values of a Random Variable

In this example we defined the random variable X as the number of defective widgets in the sample. The set of possible values of X is $\{0, 1, 2\}$. Since the number of possible values of the random variable is finite, it is obvious that X is discrete. Thus, we may redefine the six events as subsets of the possible values of X. As shown in Figure 6.2, these redefined events are

$$E_1: \ X = 0 \qquad E_4: \ X \geq 1$$
$$E_2: \ X = 1 \qquad E_5: \ X \leq 1$$
$$E_3: \ X = 2 \qquad E_6: \ X \leq 2$$

Example 2:

Let T be a random variable denoting the time (in hours) required to produce a delicate, hand-assembled medical instrument. The profit that the producer makes on a unit depends on the time required to produce it, as follows:

Production Time	Profit
Less than 3 hours	$300
Between 3 and 8 hours	200
Over 8 hours	100

The producer has just received an order for one of these units. He feels sure that it will take at least 1 hour to produce the unit but no more than 12 hours. Therefore, we may describe the set of all possible values of T as follows:

$$\{t \,|\, 1 \leq t \leq 12\}$$

It should be obvious that T is a continuous random variable, since the production time for the unit may be any conceivable value between 1 and 12 hours. Because the profit to be made on the unit will depend on its production time, the producer might be particularly interested in the following three events:

$$E_1 = \{t \,|\, 1 \leq t < 3\}$$
$$E_2 = \{t \,|\, 3 \leq t \leq 8\}$$
$$E_3 = \{t \,|\, 8 < t \leq 12\}$$

6.5 DEFINITION OF A PROBABILITY FUNCTION

To introduce the basic concept of a probability function, we consider again the example of rolling a pair of dice. In our discussion of this example in Section 6.2, we let X denote a random variable representing the sum appearing when the two dice are rolled. In Table 6.1 we saw that each value of the random variable was associated with a specific set of sample points. Each possible value of X, together with the corresponding number of sample points, is shown in the first two columns of Table 6.2.

Each of the 36 sample points represents an equally likely outcome of rolling the dice. Therefore, the probability of any particular value of X may be obtained by applying Formula (4.1). For instance, since there are six sample points associated with $X = 7$, the probability of rolling a sum of 7 is

$$P(X = 7) = \frac{6}{36}$$

Table 6.2   Probability Table for Dice Example

X = x	Number of Sample Points	P(X = x)
2	1	1/36
3	2	2/36
4	3	3/36
5	4	4/36
6	5	5/36
7	6	6/36
8	5	5/36
9	4	4/36
10	3	3/36
11	2	2/36
12	1	1/36
Total	36	36/36

The probabilities of obtaining the various possible values of X are shown in the last column of Table 6.2.

In Table 6.2, we see that for each possible value of X in the first column there is an associated probability value shown in the third column. In other words, the third column can be considered as a function of the first column. Mathematically, this functional relationship may be expressed as follows:

$$f(x) = \begin{cases} \dfrac{x-1}{36} & \text{if } x = 2, 3, 4, 5, 6 \\ \dfrac{13-x}{36} & \text{if } x = 7, 8, 9, 10, 11, 12 \\ 0 & \text{otherwise} \end{cases}$$

Notice that the input of this function is any specific value, x, of the random variable, X, and the output is the probability that the random variable will take on that value. This is an example of one type of probability function.

More generally, consider a function whose domain is the set of all possible values of a random variable and whose range is the set of nonnegative real numbers. If the function permits us to compute the probability for any event that is defined in terms of values of the random variable, then this function is called a *probability function*. Probabilities obtained from such a function must satisfy those requirements specified in Section 5.7.1. A probability function is frequently called a *probability distribution*. Although there is a minor technical difference, we will use these two terms interchangeably.

Just as there are discrete and continuous random variables, so there are discrete and continuous probability functions. Because there are important differences in the mathematical properties and treatment of discrete and continuous probability functions, we must be careful to distinguish between these two types of functions. To emphasize this distinction, our discussion will proceed according to the following diagram.

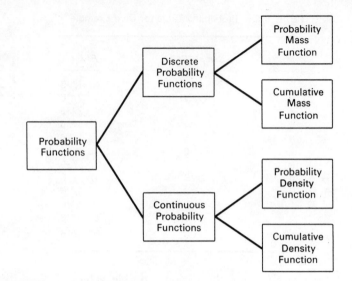

6.6 DISCRETE PROBABILITY FUNCTIONS

A probability function for a discrete random variable is called a *discrete probability function* since the domain of the function is discrete. In the following discussion of discrete probability functions, we distinguish between the "probability mass function" and the "cumulative mass function."

6.6.1 Probability Mass Functions

A probability function that specifies the probability that any single value of a *discrete* random variable will occur is called a *probability mass function* (abbreviated p.m.f.). That is, if $f(x)$ is the probability mass function of the random variable X, then $f(x) = P(X = x)$. As a probability mass function, $f(x)$ has the following properties:

1. $f(x) \geq 0$ for all values of X; that is, $f(x)$ cannot be negative for any value of X.
2. $\sum_{\text{all } x} f(x) = 1$; that is, the sum of the separate values of $f(x)$ over all x-values must equal 1.

To illustrate the concept of a probability mass function, consider a highly fictionalized salesman who schedules four calls a day. He is certain of making at least one sale out of the four, and may make as many as four sales if he is artful and lucky. In fact, the probabilities of making various numbers of sales in a day are specified by the probability mass function:

$$f(x) = \begin{cases} \dfrac{5 - x}{10} & \text{if } x = 1, 2, 3, 4 \\ 0 & \text{otherwise} \end{cases}$$

Notice that the p.m.f. specifies that $f(x) = 0$ for all values of X other than 1, 2, 3, and 4. This specification reflects that (1) this particular salesman cannot make less than one sale in a day, nor can he make more than four sales; (2) the salesman cannot make a fractional number of sales, such as 2.7 sales, in a day.

Using the foregoing probability function, we may obtain the probabilities shown in Table 6.3. In preparing such a probability table, it is customary to

Table 6.3 Probability Mass Function of Salesman's Daily Sales

Number of Sales, x	1	2	3	4
$f(x)$	4/10	3/10	2/10	1/10

show only those x-values for which $f(x) > 0$. From the figures in this table, we see that the sum of the individual probabilities for all the separate values of X is equal to 1.

The probability mass function for our salesman example is shown graphically in Figure 6.3. The possible values of the random variable are represented on the horizontal axis, and the associated probabilities are displayed on the vertical axis. Notice that the graph consists of unconnected straight lines rising from isolated points along the horizontal axis, which emphasizes the discrete nature of the distribution.

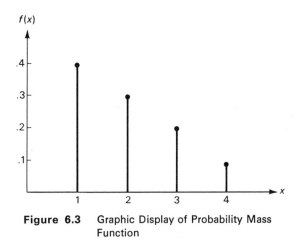

Figure 6.3 Graphic Display of Probability Mass Function

Example:

The credit manager of a large retailing firm has found that, as a long-run figure, 30% of credit applicants are poor risks. Suppose that he selects from his files a random sample of five credit applications. Let R be a random variable denoting the number of poor risks in the sample. The credit manager determines that the probability mass function of R can be expressed as

$$f(r) = \begin{cases} \dfrac{5!}{r!(5-r)!}(.3)^r(.7)^{5-r} & \text{if } r = 0, 1, 2, 3, 4, 5 \\ 0 & \text{otherwise} \end{cases}$$

Probability Functions of Random Variables   **105**

From this function, we obtain the following probabilities:

$$f(0) = \frac{5!}{0!\,(5-0)!}(.3)^0(.7)^5 = .168$$

$$f(1) = \frac{5!}{1!\,(5-1)!}(.3)^1(.7)^4 = .361$$

$$f(2) = \frac{5!}{2!\,(5-2)!}(.3)^2(.7)^3 = .309$$

$$f(3) = \frac{5!}{3!\,(5-3)!}(.3)^3(.7)^2 = .132$$

$$f(4) = \frac{5!}{4!\,(5-4)!}(.3)^4(.7)^1 = .028$$

$$f(5) = \frac{5!}{5!\,(5-5)!}(.3)^5(.7)^0 = \underline{.002}$$

$$\Sigma f(r) = 1.000$$

Thus, the probabilities are .168 that a random sample of five applications will contain no bad risks, .361 that it will contain one bad risk, .309 that it will contain two bad risks, .132 that it will contain three bad risks, .028 that it will contain four bad risks, and .002 that it will contain five bad risks. These six possibilities are mutually exclusive and collectively exhaustive, so that their probabilities add to 1.

6.6.2 Cumulative Mass Functions

If X is a discrete random variable with probability mass function $f(x)$, its *cumulative mass function* (abbreviated c.m.f.), designated by $F(x)$, specifies the probability that an observed value of X will be no greater than x. That is, if $f(x)$ is a probability mass function, $F(x) = P(X \le x)$. Consider again the salesman who makes four calls a day. The probability that he will make no more than one sale is the same as the probability that he will make exactly one sale, since the probability of making no sales is zero. That is,

$$F(1) = f(1) = \frac{4}{10}$$

Also, the probability that he will make no more than two sales is equal to the sum of the probabilities that he will make one sale or two sales:

$$F(2) = f(1) + f(2) = \frac{4}{10} + \frac{3}{10} = \frac{7}{10}$$

Similarly, the probability that the salesman will make at most three sales is given by

$$F(3) = f(1) + f(2) + f(3) = \frac{4}{10} + \frac{3}{10} + \frac{2}{10} = \frac{9}{10}$$

Since the maximum number of sales that this salesman can make in a day is four, it should be obvious that there should be a probability of 1 that his number of sales will be no greater than four. This is verified as follows:

$$F(4) = f(1) + f(2) + f(3) + f(4) = \frac{4}{10} + \frac{3}{10} + \frac{2}{10} + \frac{1}{10} = 1$$

The cumulative probabilities obtained above are presented in Table 6.4, and are displayed graphically in Figure 6.4.

Table 6.4 Cumulative Mass Function of Salesman's Daily Sales

Number of Sales, x	1	2	3	4
F(x)	4/10	7/10	9/10	1

The cumulative probabilities shown in Table 6.4 may be expressed in terms of the following cumulative mass function:

$$F(x) = \begin{cases} 0 & \text{if } x < 1 \\ \sum_{t=1}^{x} \dfrac{5-t}{10} & \text{if } x = 1, 2, 3, 4 \\ 1 & \text{if } x > 4 \end{cases}$$

Since the foregoing expression yields $P(X \leq x)$, which involves a summation of terms, the symbol x is used as the upper limit of the summation. To distinguish between this upper value of the summation and all values of the random variable that are included in the summation, it is necessary in the notation to substitute t for x in the expression for the mass function itself; that is, we write $(5 - t)/10$ rather than $(5 - x)/10$. When used in this manner, t often is called a "dummy variable." (Of course, any letter other than x may be used as a dummy variable for x.) It should be emphasized that the dummy variable t simply is a substitution required for mathematical propriety and does not denote a different variable.

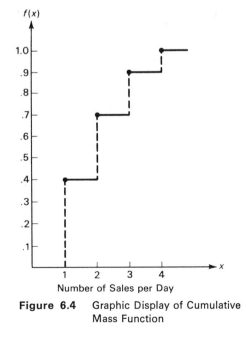

Figure 6.4 Graphic Display of Cumulative Mass Function

Probability Functions of Random Variables

In general, if X is a discrete random variable with probability mass function $f(x)$, then the corresponding cumulative mass function $F(x)$ is given by

$$F(x) = P(X \leq x) = \sum_{t \leq x} f(t) \qquad (6.1)$$

Example:

In a particularly hazardous occupation, nationwide figures gathered over a period of several years indicate that, as a long-run average, there is one fatal accident per month in the occupation. Let X be a random variable representing the number of such fatal accidents in a month. The cumulative mass function for X is shown in Table 6.5.

Table 6.5 Cumulative Probability Distribution of Monthly Number of Fatal Accidents

x	$F(x)$
0	.36788
1	.73576
2	.91970
3	.98101
4	.99634
5	.99941
6	.99992
7	.99999
8	1.00000

From Table 6.5, we may answer the following questions:

1. What is the probability that there will be no more than three fatal accidents in a given month?

$$P(X \leq 3) = F(3) = .98101$$

2. What is the probability that there will be at most two fatal accidents in a given month?

$$P(X \leq 2) = F(2) = .91970$$

3. What is the probability that there will be less than four fatal accidents in a given month?

$$P(X < 4) = P(X \leq 3) = F(3) = .98101$$

4. What is the probability that there will be more than four fatal accidents in a given month?
Since total probability equals 1,

$$P(X > 4) = 1 - P(X \leq 4) = 1 - .99634 = .00366$$

5. What is the probability that there will be no less than two fatal accidents in a given month?

$$P(X \geq 2) = 1 - P(X \leq 1) = 1 - .73576 = .26424$$

6. What is the probability that there will be at least four fatal accidents in a given month?

$$P(X \geq 4) = 1 - P(X \leq 3) = 1 - .98101 = .01899$$

7. What is the probability that in a given month there will be exactly two fatal accidents?

$$P(X = 2) = P(X \leq 2) - P(X < 2) = P(X \leq 2) - P(X \leq 1)$$
$$= .91970 - .73576 = .18394$$

8. What is the probability that in a given month the number of fatal accidents will be between three and five inclusive?

$$P(3 \leq X \leq 5) = P(X \leq 5) - P(X < 3) = P(X \leq 5) - P(X \leq 2)$$
$$= .99941 - .91970 = .07971$$

6.7 CONTINUOUS PROBABILITY FUNCTIONS

A probability function for a continuous random variable is called a *continuous probability function* since the domain of the function is continuous. In discussing continuous probability functions, we will distinguish between the "probability density function" and the "cumulative density function."

6.7.1 Probability Density Functions

As we have seen, the probability mass function $f(x)$ of a discrete random variable X specifies probabilities for specific values of X. For a continuous random variable, the corresponding function $f(x)$ is called a *probability density function* (abbreviated p.d.f.). Unlike a probability mass function, however, a probability density function does not specify probabilities for specific individual values of the random variable.

What, then, is the meaning of the probability function $f(x)$ when X is continuous? To answer this question, we must first observe that it is meaningless to define events in terms of single values of a continuous random variable, because a continuous random variable has an infinite number of possible values. Thus, for a continuous random variable, an event must be defined in terms of an *interval* of values. For example, we might define some event E in terms of a continuous random variable X as follows:

$$E = \{x \mid 3 \leq x \leq 5\}$$

In this expression, the event E is defined as the set of all real values in the interval from 3 to 5 inclusive.

In general, for a continuous random variable X, any event E is defined in terms of the values in an interval between two limits, a and b. Then the probability of the event is the probability that an observed value will fall within the specified interval. Symbolically,

$$P(E) = P(a \leq X \leq b)$$

If $f(x)$ is a probability density function, the probability is obtained by integrating $f(x)$ from a to b. Specifically,

$$P(a \leq X \leq b) = \int_a^b f(x)\, dx \qquad (6.2)$$

Graphically, we may view a p.d.f. as a mathematical function that describes a curve. For any given value x, $f(x)$ is simply the corresponding ordinate (height of the curve above the horizontal axis). That is, $f(x)$ does not represent a probability. Rather, the probability of an event E is represented by the *area* under the curve between the limits that define the event. Furthermore, for a continuous random variable, the probability of any specific single value is mathematically defined as zero. That is, if X is a continuous random variable, it is always true that $P(X = x) = 0$.

As a probability density function, $f(x)$ has the following properties:

1. $f(x) \geq 0$ for all real values; that is, $f(x)$ cannot be negative for any value of X between $-\infty$ and ∞.

2. $\int_{-\infty}^{\infty} f(x)\, dx = 1$; that is, the total area under the curve described by $f(x)$ must equal 1.

Example:

Let X be a continuous random variable with the following probability density function:

$$f(x) = \begin{cases} \dfrac{1}{5} & \text{if } 2 \leq x \leq 7 \\ 0 & \text{otherwise} \end{cases}$$

Graphically, this function describes a rectangle, as shown in Figure 6.5. By inspecting the function, we see that $f(x)$ is not less than zero for any value of X between $-\infty$ and ∞. Also, we may verify that the total area under the curve is equal to 1:

$$\int_{-\infty}^{\infty} f(x)\, dx = \int_{-\infty}^{2} 0\, dx + \int_{2}^{7} \frac{1}{5}\, dx + \int_{7}^{\infty} 0\, dx$$

$$= 0 + \int_{2}^{7} \frac{dx}{5} + 0 = \frac{x}{5}\Big]_{2}^{7} = \frac{7}{5} - \frac{2}{5} = 1$$

Suppose that we define the event E in terms of the interval $(3 \leq X \leq 5)$. Applying Formula (6.2), this probability is given by

$$\int_{3}^{5} f(x)\, dx = \int_{3}^{5} \frac{1}{5}\, dx = \frac{x}{5}\Big]_{3}^{5} = \frac{5}{5} - \frac{3}{5} = .40$$

This probability is represented as an area by the shaded portion of Figure 6.5.

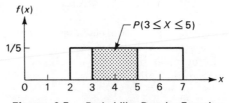

Figure 6.5   Probability Density Function

6.7.2 Cumulative Density Functions

Corresponding to the cumulative mass function of a discrete random variable, the *cumulative density function*[1] (abbreviated c.d.f.) of a continuous random variable specifies the probability that an observed value of X will be no greater than x. In general, if $f(x)$ is the probability density function of the random

---

[1]Collectively, cumulative mass functions and cumulative density functions are referred to as *distribution functions*. The term "cumulative distribution function" is often used to denote a distribution function; however, the word "cumulative" is redundant in this context because a distribution function is cumulative by definition.

variable X, then the corresponding cumulative density function is given by

$$F(x) = P(X \leq x) = \int_{-\infty}^{x} f(t) \, dt \qquad (6.3)$$

In other words, for a continuous probability function, $P(X \leq x)$ is given by the definite integral of the density function evaluated between minus infinity and x. Notice that since x is the upper limit of the integration, the "dummy" expression $f(t) \, dt$ is used in place of $f(x) \, dx$ in the integrand. This procedure is analogous to the use of the dummy variable discussed in connection with the cumulative mass function for a discrete random variable in Section 6.6.2.

For a continuous random variable,

$$P(a \leq X \leq b) = P(X \leq b) - P(X \leq a)$$

since $P(X = a)$ is zero for any specific value a. We now see that $P(X \leq b) = F(b)$, and $P(X \leq a) = F(a)$. Hence, $P(a \leq X \leq b)$ may be expressed as

$$P(a \leq X \leq b) = F(b) - F(a) \qquad (6.4)$$

We have already seen from Formula (6.2) that if $f(x)$ is a p.d.f., then $P(a \leq X \leq b)$ may be computed by integrating the p.d.f. However, if the cumulative density function is known, it is unnecessary to integrate the p.d.f. in order to obtain this probability. Rather, as shown by Formula (6.4), this probability may be obtained simply by subtracting $F(a)$ from $F(b)$. This is the real advantage of using the cumulative density function.

Example 1:

Let us again consider the density function

$$f(x) = \begin{cases} \dfrac{1}{5} & \text{if } 2 \leq x \leq 7 \\ 0 & \text{otherwise} \end{cases}$$

Over the interval $(-\infty < x < 2)$ we have $f(x) = 0$. Since X is continuous, $P(X = 2)$ is zero. Thus, $P(X < 2) = P(X \leq 2)$. Hence, for $x < 2$, the cumulative density function is given by

$$F(x) = \int_{-\infty}^{x} f(t) \, dt = \int_{-\infty}^{x} 0 \, dt = 0$$

Over the interval $(2 \leq x \leq 7)$, we have $f(x) = 1/5$. The cumulative density up to the lower limit of this interval is $F(2)$. Therefore, for any value of X between 2 and 7, $F(x)$ is given by

$$F(x) = F(2) + \int_{2}^{x} f(t) \, dt = 0 + \int_{2}^{x} \frac{1}{5} \, dt = \frac{t}{5} \Big]_{2}^{x} = \frac{x-2}{5}$$

Over the interval $(7 < x < \infty)$, we have $f(x) = 0$. The cumulative density up to the lower limit of this interval is $F(7) = (7 - 2)/5 = 1$. Therefore, for any value of X greater than 7, $F(x)$ is given by

$$F(7) + \int_{7}^{x} f(t) \, dt = 1 + \int_{7}^{x} 0 \, dt = 1 + 0 = 1$$

We now summarize this cumulative density function as follows:

$$F(x) = \begin{cases} 0 & \text{if } x < 2 \\ \dfrac{x-2}{5} & \text{if } 2 \leq x \leq 7 \\ 1 & \text{if } x > 7 \end{cases}$$

Probability Functions of Random Variables   **111**

This cumulative density function is shown graphically in Figure 6.6. For any given x-value, the ordinate of Figure 6.6 is equal to the area to the left of that x-value in Figure 6.5. This is generally true of the relationship between any p.d.f. and its corresponding c.d.f.; that is, for a specified p.d.f., the area under the curve to the left of a given x-value is equal to the corresponding $F(x)$ for that x-value.

Suppose that we wish to determine $P(2.2 \leq X \leq 3.4)$. Using Formula (6.2), we may compute this probability by integration as follows:

$$\int_{2.2}^{3.4} \frac{1}{5} \, dx = \frac{x}{5}\bigg]_{2.2}^{3.4} = \frac{3.4}{5} - \frac{2.2}{5} = .24$$

Alternatively, we may determine this same probability by applying Formula (6.4) as follows:

$$F(2.2) = \frac{2.2 - 2}{5} = .04 \qquad F(3.4) = \frac{3.4 - 2}{5} = .28$$

$$P(2.2 \leq X \leq 3.4) = F(3.4) - F(2.2) = .28 - .04 = .24$$

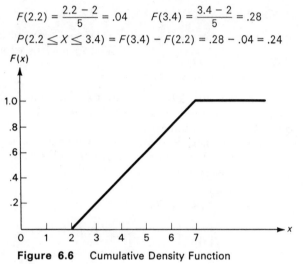

Figure 6.6　Cumulative Density Function

Example 2:

Let Q be a random variable denoting the monthly quantity demanded (in tons) for a particular chemical product. The probability density function for this demand is

$$f(q) = \begin{cases} q - 1 & \text{if } 1 \leq q < 2 \\ 3 - q & \text{if } 2 \leq q \leq 3 \\ 0 & \text{otherwise} \end{cases}$$

This density function, which is illustrated in Figure 6.7a, partitions the domain of the function into four subsets:

$$S_1 = \{q \,|\, q < 1\}$$
$$S_2 = \{q \,|\, 1 \leq q < 2\}$$
$$S_3 = \{q \,|\, 2 \leq q \leq 3\}$$
$$S_4 = \{q \,|\, q > 3\}$$

For any q-value contained in the first interval, $S_1 = \{q \,|\, q < 1\}$, the cumulative density is given by

$$F(q) = \int_{-\infty}^{q} 0 \, dt = 0$$

Over the next interval, $S_2 = \{q \,|\, 1 \leq q < 2\}$, the density function is $f(q) = q - 1$. The cumulative density up to the lower limit of this interval is $F(1) = 0$. Therefore, for any q-value contained in S_2, $F(q)$ is given by

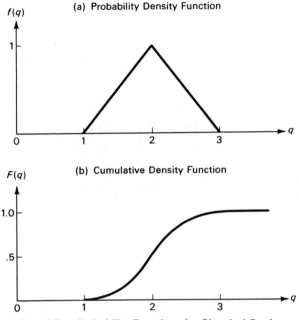

Figure 6.7 Probability Functions for Chemical Product Demand

$$F(q) = F(1) + \int_1^q f(t)\, dt = 0 + \int_1^q (t-1)\, dt$$

$$= \left[\frac{t^2}{2} - t \right]_1^q = \left(\frac{q^2}{2} - q \right) - \left(\frac{1}{2} - 1 \right)$$

$$= \frac{q^2}{2} - q + \frac{1}{2}$$

$$= \frac{q^2 + 1}{2} - q$$

Over the next interval, $S_3 = \{q \mid 2 \le q \le 3\}$, the density function is $f(q) = 3 - q$. The cumulative density up to the lower limit of this interval is

$$F(2) = \frac{(2)^2 + 1}{2} - 2 = \frac{1}{2}$$

Therefore, for any q-value contained in S_3, $F(q)$ is given by

$$F(q) = F(2) + \int_2^q f(t)\, dt = \frac{1}{2} + \int_2^q (3-t)\, dt$$

$$= \frac{1}{2} + \left[3t - \frac{t^2}{2} \right]_2^q = \frac{1}{2} + \left(3q - \frac{q^2}{2} \right) - \left(3(2) - \frac{(2^2)}{2} \right)$$

$$= 3q - \frac{q^2 + 7}{2}$$

Over the final interval, $S_4 = \{q \mid q > 3\}$, the density function is $f(q) = 0$. The cumulative density up to the lower limit of this interval is

$$F(3) = 3(3) - \frac{(3)^2 + 7}{2} = 1$$

Probability Functions of Random Variables   **113**

Therefore, for any q-value contained in S_4, $F(q)$ is given by

$$F(q) = F(3) + \int_3^q f(t)\,dt = 1 + \int_3^q 0\,dt = 1 + 0 = 1$$

The cumulative density function is summarized as follows:

$$F(q) = \begin{cases} 0 & \text{if } q < 1 \\ \dfrac{q^2 + 1}{2} - q & \text{if } 1 \le q < 2 \\ 3q - \dfrac{q^2 + 7}{2} & \text{if } 2 \le q \le 3 \\ 1 & \text{if } q > 3 \end{cases}$$

This function is shown graphically in Figure 6.7b. If we wish to know the probability that demand for this product will be between 1.2 tons and 2.4 tons during a given month, we have

$$P(1.2 \le Q \le 2.4) = \int_{1.2}^{2.4} f(q)\,dq = F(2.4) - F(1.2)$$

$$= \left[3(2.4) - \frac{(2.4)^2 + 7}{2} \right] - \left[\frac{(1.2)^2 + 1}{2} - 1.2 \right]$$

$$= .80$$

PROBLEMS

6.1 An American traveler, arriving at the Manila airport, wishes to exchange some of his U.S. dollars for Philippine pesos. He finds that 1 peso is equivalent to 24 cents in U.S. currency. Write a mathematical statement that expresses y (the number of pesos he receives) as a function of x (the number of dollars he exchanges).

6.2 In retailing, the markup on an item of merchandise is the difference between the cost, c, and the retail selling price, s. Two common methods of determining the amount of markup on an item are (1) to establish markup as a percentage of the cost, and (2) to establish markup as a percentage of selling price.

(a) A particular bookstore computes markup as 25% of cost. Write a mathematical statement expressing selling price as a function of cost.

(b) A particular haberdasher computes markup as 40% of selling price. Write a mathematical statement expressing selling price as a function of cost.

6.3 Consider the function

$$y = f(x) = 1,000 + 10x \qquad x = 1, 2, 3, \ldots, 50$$

(a) Find $f(1)$, $f(5)$, and $f(10)$.
(b) Specify the domain and range of this function.
(c) Identify the dependent and independent variables.

6.4 Consider the function

$$y = f(x) = x^2 - 5x + 10 \qquad x = 0, 1, \ldots, 5$$

(a) What is the value of $f(2)$?
(b) Specify the domain and range of this function.

6.5 The total cost of producing a particular type of hand-assembled device is $20.00 for materials plus $5.00 per hour of labor. Thus, the cost of materials is a fixed cost, and the cost of labor is a variable cost that depends on the amount of labor required to assemble any single device.

(a) Let T be a random variable denoting the total cost of producing one of these devices. Let H be a random variable denoting the amount of labor (in hours) required to produce a device. Write a mathematical equation that expresses T as a function of H.

(b) Suppose that these devices are priced at $50.00 each. Let P be a random variable denoting the manufacturer's profit on a device.

   (i) Write a mathematical equation that expresses P as a function of T.

   (ii) Write a mathematical equation that expresses P as a function of H.

6.6 Consider the experiment of tossing a coin. Let H denote heads and T denote tails.

(a) Suppose that the coin is to be tossed twice. Specify the sample space for this experiment. If X is the random variable denoting the number of heads resulting from this experiment, draw a diagram (such as Figure 6.1) showing the relationship between this random variable and the sample space.

(b) Suppose that the coin is to be tossed three times. Specify the sample space for this experiment. If Y is used to denote the random variable representing the number of heads from this experiment, can you draw a diagram similar to the one you drew for part (a) to show the relationship between this random variable and the sample space? What difficulty do you encounter in this diagramming? Can you resolve it by showing an alternative diagram?

6.7 A discrete random variable X has the probability mass function

$$f(x) = \begin{cases} \dfrac{x+2}{25} & \text{if } x = 1, 2, 3, 4, 5 \\ 0 & \text{otherwise} \end{cases}$$

(a) Present the mass function in the form of a probability table.

(b) Determine the cumulative mass function.

(c) Present the cumulative mass function in the form of a table.

6.8 Using the results obtained in Problem 6.7, determine the following probabilities:

(a) $P(X = 3)$ (d) $P(X > 3)$

(b) $P(X < 3)$ (e) $P(X \geq 3)$

(c) $P(X \leq 3)$

6.9 A discrete random variable X has the probability mass function

$$f(x) = \begin{cases} \dfrac{x+1}{50} & \text{if } x = 2, 3, 4, 5, 6 \\ \dfrac{11-x}{20} & \text{if } x = 7, 8, 9, 10 \\ 0 & \text{otherwise} \end{cases}$$

(a) Present the probability mass function in the form of a table.

(b) Determine the cumulative mass function.

(c) Present the cumulative mass function in the form of a table.

6.10 Using the results obtained in Problem 6.9, determine the following probabilities:

(a) $P(X = 6)$ (c) $P(X < 8)$

(b) $P(X \leq 5)$ (d) $P(X \geq 8)$

6.11 A discrete random variable X has the probability mass function

$$f(x) = \begin{cases} \dfrac{x^2+4}{50} & \text{if } x = 0, 1, 2, 3, 4 \\ 0 & \text{otherwise} \end{cases}$$

Determine the following probabilities:

(a) $P(X = 2)$; (b) $P(X < 2)$; (c) $P(X \leq 2)$; (d) $P(X < 5)$; (e) $P(X \leq 3)$.

6.12 A discrete random variable X has the cumulative mass function shown in the following table:

x	2	3	4	5	6	7	8	9
$F(x)$	.018	.099	.324	.607	.852	.971	.994	1.000

Determine the following probabilities:
(a) $P(X = 5)$
(b) $P(X > 6)$
(c) $P(X \geq 6)$
(d) $P(X < 7)$

(e) $P(X \leq 5)$
(f) $P(4 \leq X \leq 7)$
(g) $P(5 < X \leq 8)$

6.13 From the cumulative mass function in Problem 6.12, determine the following:
(a) Probability that the random variable will have a value equal to or less than 4.
(b) Probability that the random variable will have a value no greater than 4.
(c) Probability that the value of the random variable will be 4 at most.
(d) Probability that the value of the random variable will be less than 5.

6.14 A box of a dozen eggs contains 7 good eggs and 5 bad eggs. A sample of 4 eggs is to be selected at random from the box. Let G be a random variable denoting the number of good eggs in the sample. Under these conditions, the probability mass function of G can be shown to be

$$f(g) = \begin{cases} \dfrac{\binom{7}{g}\binom{5}{4-g}}{\binom{12}{4}} & \text{if } g = 0, 1, 2, 3, 4 \\ 0 & \text{otherwise} \end{cases}$$

What is the probability that the sample will contain:
(a) No good eggs?
(b) Exactly 1 good egg?
(c) Exactly 2 good eggs?
(d) Less than 2 good eggs?
(e) No more than 2 good eggs?
(f) More than 2 good eggs?
(g) No less than 2 good eggs?

6.15 The probability mass function of a discrete random variable R is

$$f(r) = \begin{cases} \binom{4}{r} . 2^r (.8)^{4-r} & \text{if } r = 0, 1, 2, 3, 4 \\ 0 & \text{otherwise} \end{cases}$$

(a) Determine $P(R = 1)$.
(b) Determine $P(R \leq 2)$.

6.16 The probability mass function of a discrete random variable X is

$$f(x) = \begin{cases} kx & \text{if } x = 0, 1, 2, 3, 4 \\ 0 & \text{otherwise} \end{cases}$$

Determine the value of k.

6.17 Let D represent the number of defects produced in an hour's run by a particular automatic machine. The probability mass function of D is given by

$$f(d) = \begin{cases} .10 & \text{if } d = 0 \\ kd & \text{if } d = 1, 2, 3 \\ k(6 - d) & \text{if } d = 4, 5 \\ 0 & \text{otherwise} \end{cases}$$

(a) Determine the value of k.

(b) What is the probability that, in an hour's run, the machine will produce at least four defects, given that it does produce at least one defect?

6.18 Let X represent the demand for a particular product. The *cumulative mass function*, $F(x)$, is given by

$$F(x) = \begin{cases} 0 & \text{if } x < 1 \\ \dfrac{x^2}{25} & \text{if } x = 1, 2, 3, 4, 5 \\ 1 & \text{if } x > 5 \end{cases}$$

Of the four functions that appear below, one and only one is the *probability mass function* corresponding to the above cumulative mass function. Your task is to (1) identify this corresponding probability mass function, and (2) explain why each of the other functions is not the appropriate one.

(a) $f(x) = \begin{cases} \dfrac{2x}{25} & \text{if } 0 \le x \le 5 \\ 0 & \text{otherwise} \end{cases}$

(b) $f(x) = \begin{cases} \dfrac{2x}{25} & \text{if } x = 1, 2, 3, 4, 5 \\ 0 & \text{otherwise} \end{cases}$

(c) $f(x) = \begin{cases} \dfrac{2x - 1}{25} & \text{if } x = 1, 2, 3, 4, 5 \\ 0 & \text{otherwise} \end{cases}$

(d) $f(x) = \begin{cases} \dfrac{11 - 2x}{25} & \text{if } x = 1, 2, 3, 4, 5 \\ 0 & \text{otherwise} \end{cases}$

6.19 Let K be a random variable denoting the number of customers waiting for service in a garden supply shop at any particular moment on a Monday morning. The probability function of K is given by

$$f(k) = \begin{cases} .5^{(k+1)} & \text{if } k = 0, 1, 2, \ldots \\ 0 & \text{otherwise} \end{cases}$$

(a) Is $f(k)$ a p.m.f. or a p.d.f.? Explain.
(b) Determine the cumulative probability function corresponding to $f(k)$.
(c) At exactly 10:15 on a particular Monday morning, what is the probability that:
  (i)   There will be no customers waiting?
  (ii)   There will be exactly 1 customer waiting?
  (iii) There will be exactly 2 customers waiting?
  (iv)   There will be exactly 3 customers waiting?
  (v)   There will be no more than 1 customer waiting?
  (vi)   There will be at most 2 customers waiting?
  (vii) There will be at least 2 customers waiting?
  (viii) There will be more than 2 customers waiting?
  (ix)   There will be at least 1 but no more than 3 customers waiting?
  (x)   There will be at least 1 but less than 3 customers waiting?

6.20 A highly sensitive recording device used in geothermal energy development contains a particularly delicate component that has a life of only a few hours at most. Whenever this component fails it is replaced; if it should last for as long as 6 hours, it is routinely replaced and discarded. Let H denote a random variable denoting the useful life (in hours) of such a component. Experience has shown that H has the probability density function

$$f(h) = \begin{cases} \dfrac{h}{18} & 0 \leq h \leq 6 \\ 0 & \text{otherwise} \end{cases}$$

(a) Determine the cumulative density function of H.
(b) What is the probability that one of these components will last less than 4 hours?
(c) What is the probability that one of these components will last more than 3 hours?

6.21 The probability density function of a continuous random variable Y is

$$f(y) = \begin{cases} 3y^2 & \text{if } 0 \leq y \leq 1 \\ 0 & \text{otherwise} \end{cases}$$

(a) Graph the probability density function of Y.
(b) Determine the corresponding cumulative density function.
(c) Graph the cumulative density function in part (b).
(d) From the graph obtained in part (c), determine the following probabilities:
   (i) $P(Y \leq .60)$
   (ii) $P(Y \leq .80)$
(e) By direct integration, confirm the probabilities obtained in part (d).

6.22 .The probability density function of a continuous random variable W is

$$f(w) = \begin{cases} \dfrac{w}{8} & \text{if } 0 \leq w \leq 4 \\ 0 & \text{otherwise} \end{cases}$$

(a) Determine the corresponding cumulative density function.
(b) From the function obtained in part (a), determine the following probabilities:
   (i) $P(1 < W < 2)$
   (ii) $P(W < 3)$
   (iii) $P(W > 2.5)$
(c) By directly integrating the probability density function of W confirm each of the probabilities obtained in part (b).

6.23 The probability density function of a continuous random variable X is

$$f(x) = \begin{cases} \dfrac{1}{6} & \text{if } 2 \leq x \leq 8 \\ 0 & \text{otherwise} \end{cases}$$

(a) Determine the cumulative density function of X.
(b) Determine the following probabilities:
   (i) $P(2 < X < 5)$
   (ii) $P(5 < X < 6)$

6.24 The probability density function of a continuous random variable H is

$$f(h) = \begin{cases} 6h(1-h) & \text{if } 0 \leq h \leq 1 \\ 0 & \text{otherwise} \end{cases}$$

(a) Verify that $f(h)$ is a p.d.f.
(b) Graph the probability density function of H.
(c) Determine the corresponding cumulative density function.

(d) Determine the following probabilities:
   (i) $P(H \le .20)$
   (ii) $P(H > .85)$
   (iii) $P(.25 \le H \le .75)$

6.25 The probability density function of a continuous random variable X is

$$f(x) = \begin{cases} \dfrac{x^2}{9} & \text{if } 0 \le x \le 3 \\ 0 & \text{otherwise} \end{cases}$$

(a) Graph the probability density function of X.
(b) Determine the corresponding cumulative density function.
(c) Graph the cumulative density function in part (b).
(d) From the graph obtained in part (c), determine the following probabilities:
   (i) $P(X \le 2.0)$
   (ii) $P(X \ge 2.4)$
   (iii) $P(2.0 \le X < 2.4)$

6.26 The probability density function of a continuous random variable S is

$$f(s) = \begin{cases} 2s - 4 & \text{if } 2 \le s \le 3 \\ 0 & \text{otherwise} \end{cases}$$

(a) Graph the probability density function of S.
(b) Determine the corresponding cumulative density function.
(c) Graph the cumulative density function in part (b).
(d) From the graph obtained in part (c), determine the following probabilities:
   (i) $P(S < 2.2)$
   (ii) $P(S > 2.5)$
   (iii) $P(2.4 < S < 2.6)$
(e) By directly integrating the probability density function of S, confirm each of the probabilities obtained in part (d).

6.27 The probability density function of a continuous random variable V is:

$$f(v) = \begin{cases} v - 2 & \text{if } 2 \le v < 3 \\ 4 - v & \text{if } 3 \le v \le 4 \\ 0 & \text{otherwise} \end{cases}$$

(a) Graph the probability density function of V.
(b) Determine the corresponding cumulative density function.
(c) Graph the cumulative density function in part (b).
(d) Determine each of the following probabilities by using the c.d.f. obtained in part (b):
   (i) $P(V \le 2.5)$
   (ii) $P(V \le 3.5)$
   (iii) $P(V > 3.2)$
   (iv) $P(2.4 < V < 3.6)$

6.28 Let X be a random variable denoting the time (in weeks) required to complete a small contract. The probability density function of x is given by

$$f(x) = \begin{cases} \dfrac{x}{16} - \dfrac{1}{8} & \text{for } 2 \le x \le 6 \\ \dfrac{5}{8} - \dfrac{x}{16} & \text{for } 6 < x \le 10 \\ 0 & \text{otherwise} \end{cases}$$

Probability Functions of Random Variables   **119**

(a) Graph the probability density function. Label the axes and the important points.
(b) Determine the corresponding cumulative density function.
(c) The profit of the contract depends on the time required to complete it, as shown by the function

$$\text{profit (in dollars)} = 100 - 10X$$

Determine the probability that the profit will be smaller than \$60.

6.29 Let X be a continuous random variable with the probability density function

$$f(x) = \begin{cases} \dfrac{x}{8} & \text{of } 0 \le x \le 4 \\ 0 & \text{otherwise} \end{cases}$$

Let the events A_1, A_2, and A_3 be defined by

$$\begin{aligned} A_1 &= \{x \mid -\infty < x \le 2\} \\ A_2 &= \{x \mid 1 < x \le 3\} \\ A_3 &= \{x \mid 2 \le x < \infty\} \end{aligned}$$

(a) Determine the cumulative density function corresponding to $f(x)$.
(b) Determine the following probabilities:
   (i) $P(A_1)$
   (ii) $P(A_1 \cap A_2)$
   (iii) $P(A_2 \cap A_3)$
   (iv) $P(A_2 \cup A_3)$
   (v) $P(A_2 \mid A_3)$
(c) Are A_2 and A_3 independent events? Explain.

6.30 Of the four functions that appear below, one and only one meets all the requirements of a probability density function, whereas each of the remaining three functions fails (for one reason or another) to qualify as a probability density function. Your task is to (1) identify the probability density function, and (2) explain why each of the other functions is not a probability density function.

(a)
$$f(x) = \begin{cases} 3x^2 & \text{if } 0 \le x \le 2 \\ 0 & \text{otherwise} \end{cases}$$

(b)
$$f(x) = \begin{cases} \dfrac{4x}{3} - 1 & \text{if } 1 \le x \le 2 \\ 0 & \text{otherwise} \end{cases}$$

(c)
$$f(x) = \begin{cases} \dfrac{3x}{2} - 1 & \text{if } 0 \le x \le 2 \\ 0 & \text{otherwise} \end{cases}$$

(d)
$$f(x) = \begin{cases} \dfrac{x}{10} & \text{if } x = 1, 2, 3, 4 \\ 0 & \text{otherwise} \end{cases}$$

7

Descriptive Measures
of Probability Distributions

Chapter 3 discussed how a finite population may be described by specifying various descriptive measures of the population distribution. In a similar manner, the "behavior" of a random variable can be described by specifying descriptive measures of its probability distribution. That is, just like a population distribution, a probability distribution can be described in terms of such measures as fractiles, mean, variance, and standard deviation. These measures, as applied to the probability distribution of a random variable, are analogous to their counterparts as applied to the distribution of a population variable. However, because the probability distribution of a random variable is conceptually different from the distribution of a finite population, there are important differences in the computation and interpretation of these measures when they are used to describe the behavior of a random variable. Thus, in this chapter we are concerned with descriptive measures specifically as they are applied to probability distributions of random variables.

7.1   FRACTILES

As the reader may recall from Chapter 3, the φ fractile of a finite population is defined as the lowest observed value such that the cumulative relative frequency for that value is at least equal to φ. In a probability distribution, the counterpart of cumulative relative frequency is cumulative probability. Thus, the φ fractile of a probability distribution is defined as the smallest value of the random variable such that the cumulative probability for that value is at least equal to φ. Symbolically, for a random variable X, the φ fractile is the smallest x-value that will satisfy the statement $P(X \leq x) \geq \varphi$. Alternatively, since $P(X \leq x) = F(x)$, the φ fractile may be defined as the smallest x-value for which $F(x) = \varphi$. Then, using x_φ to denote the φ fractile of the probability distribution of the random variable X, it follows that $F(x_\varphi) \geq \varphi$. The way in which x_φ is determined depends on whether X is a discrete or continuous random variable.

7.1.1 Fractiles of a Discrete Distribution

To illustrate the procedure for determining fractiles of a discrete distribution, consider a random variable X that has the following probability mass function:

$$f(x) = \begin{cases} \dfrac{.4 + x}{20} & \text{if } x = 0, 1, 2, 3, 4 \\ \dfrac{7.5 - x}{10} & \text{if } x = 5, 6 \\ 0 & \text{otherwise} \end{cases}$$

To determine fractiles for such a function, we first compute $F(x)$ for each of the possible x-values, as shown in Table 7.1. Suppose that we wish to determine

Table 7.1 Tabulation of a Discrete Probability Distribution

x	f(x)	F(x)
0	.02	.02
1	.07	.09
2	.12	.21
3	.17	.38
4	.22	.60
5	.25	.85
6	.15	1.00

the .60 fractile of the distribution. Scanning down the $F(x)$ column, we find $F(4) = .60$. Thus, 4 is the .60 fractile.

In dealing with a discrete probability distribution, it is not generally true that the cumulative probability of the φ fractile will be exactly equal to φ. For instance, suppose that we wish to obtain the .25 fractile. Scanning down the $F(x)$ column, we cannot find a cumulative probability of exactly .25. However, we see that $F(2) = .21$, and $F(3) = .38$. Thus, since 3 is the smallest x-value for which the cumulative probability is *at least* .25, 3 is the .25 fractile by definition, even though the cumulative probability corresponding to 3 is greater than .25 rather than equal to .25. Most of the time, in obtaining fractiles of a discrete distribution, the actual cumulative probability of the φ fractile will be greater than φ rather than exactly equal to φ. This is because probabilities in a discrete distribution accumulate by "steps" or "jumps" from one value to the next.

7.1.2 Fractiles of a Continuous Distribution

In contrast to a cumulative mass function, which increases by discrete jumps, a cumulative density function increases continuously. Thus, except under rare theoretical circumstances,[1] it is always possible to determine a unique value for

---

[1]For instance, consider the p.d.f.

$$f(x) = \begin{cases} .25(2 - x) & \text{if } 0 \le x \le 2 \\ x - 3 & \text{if } 3 \le x \le 4 \\ 0 & \text{otherwise} \end{cases}$$

As the reader may verify, $F(x) = .50$ for all values in the interval $2 \le x < 3$. Thus, any x-value in this interval will satisfy the definition of the .50 fractile.

any fractile, x_φ, for which the cumulative probability of x_φ will be exactly equal to φ. For a continuous random variable X, the φ fractile may be computed by solving the following equation for the value of x_φ:

$$\int_{-\infty}^{x_\varphi} f(x)\, dx = \varphi \tag{7.1}$$

To illustrate this procedure, consider a highly sensitive recording apparatus employed in medical research. This device contains a particularly delicate component that has a useful life of only a few hours at most. Whenever this component fails, it is replaced; if it should last for as long as 4 hours, it is routinely replaced and discarded. Thus, the maximum possible useful life of one of these components is 4 hours. If we let H designate a random variable representing the useful life (in hours) of such a component, experience has demonstrated that H has the probability density function

$$f(h) = \begin{cases} \dfrac{h}{8} & \text{if } 0 \le h \le 4 \\ 0 & \text{otherwise} \end{cases}$$

Suppose that we wish to determine the .36 fractile of the distribution of H. Applying Formula (7.1), we obtain

$$\int_{-\infty}^{h_{.36}} f(h)\, dh = .36$$

$$\int_{-\infty}^{0} 0\, dh + \int_{0}^{h_{.36}} \frac{h}{8}\, dh = .36$$

$$\frac{h^2}{16}\Bigg]_{0}^{h_{.36}} = .36$$

$$h_{.36}^2 = (.36)(16) = 5.76$$

Taking the positive square root (since $h_{.36}$ must be between 0 and 4), we have

$$h_{.36} = 2.4$$

That is, the .36 fractile is 2.4 hours. Thus, 2.4 hours is the useful life for which the cumulative probability is .36.

7.2 AVERAGES

In our discussion of finite populations in Chapter 3, we examined three different averages: mode, median, and mean. In this section we reexamine these averages as they are applied to probability distributions.

7.2.1 The Mode

We have observed that the mode of a finite population is the value that has the greatest frequency. Similarly, the mode of the probability distribution may be defined as a value of the random variable at which the probability function reaches a *local maximum*. In other words, a mode is an x-value for which $f(x)$ is greater than for any other x-value in its *immediate neighborhood*. Graphically, a mode occurs at any x-value at which the graph of the distribution reaches a peak. For example, the mode of the mass function in Figure 7.1a is 6, which is the x-value for which $f(x)$ reaches a maximum. The mass function in Figure 7.1b has two modes, one at $x = 4$ and one at $x = 10$, since the distribution reaches a local maximum at each of these two x-values. Similarly, the density function[2] in Figure 7.1c has a single mode at $x = 110$, whereas the density function in Figure 7.1d has two modes, one at $x = 90$ and the other at $x = 120$.

A distribution that has a single mode is called *unimodal*, whereas a distribution that has two modes is called *bimodal*. Of course, a distribution may have even more than two modes. Therefore, the use of the mode as a measure of central tendency will be meaningful only if the distribution is unimodal.

7.2.2 The Median

As we observed in Chapter 3, the median of a finite population is the .50 fractile. This definition also holds for the median of a probability distribution. That is, the median of a probability distribution of a random variable X is the smallest x-value for which $F(x)$ is at least .50. It is convenient to regard the median as a value that divides the probability distribution into two equal halves

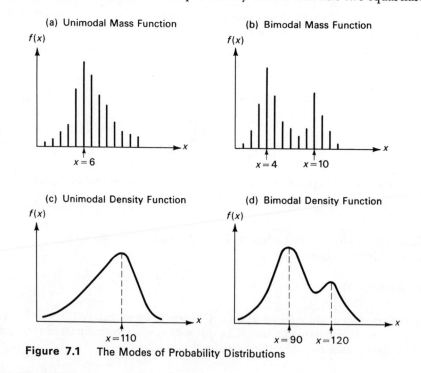

Figure 7.1 The Modes of Probability Distributions

---

[2]Mathematically, if the probability density function $f(x)$ is twice differentiable, a mode is any x-value that satisfies the two expressions

$$\begin{cases} f'(x) = 0 \\ f''(x) < 0 \end{cases}$$

where $f'(x)$ is the first derivative of $f(x)$ and $f''(x)$ is the second derivative of $f(x)$.

in the sense that the chances are 50:50 that the random variable will have a value either above or below the median. However, in the case of a discrete random variable, this is usually only approximately true. To illustrate this point, consider again the distribution in Table 7.1. Scanning down the $F(x)$ column, we find that $F(3) = .38$ and $F(4) = .60$. Thus, the median is $x_{.50} = 4$, since this is the smallest x-value for which the cumulative probability is at least .50. Actually, since $F(4) = .60$, there is a .60 probability that X will have a value of 4 or less, and a .40 probability that X will have a value of 5 or greater. Thus, the median divides the distribution *roughly* in half.

As an example of the median of a continuous probability distribution, consider again the electronic component whose useful life has the density function

$$f(h) = \begin{cases} \dfrac{h}{8} & \text{if } 0 \le h \le 4 \\ 0 & \text{otherwise} \end{cases}$$

To obtain the .50 fractile of this function, we apply Formula (7.1) as follows:

$$\int_{-\infty}^{h_{.50}} f(h)\, dh = .50$$

$$\int_{-\infty}^{0} 0\, dh + \int_{0}^{h_{.50}} \frac{h}{8}\, dh = .50$$

$$\frac{h^2}{16}\bigg]_{0}^{h_{.50}} = .50$$

$$h_{.50}^2 = (.50)(16) = 8$$

Taking the positive square root (since $h_{.50}$ must lie between 0 and 4), we have

$$h_{.50} = 2.828$$

Thus, the median life for this type of component is 2.828 hours. As shown in Figure 7.2, the median divides the distribution exactly in half, in the sense that the area on either side of the median is exactly .50.

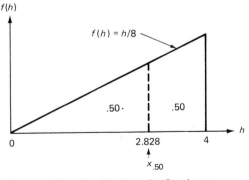

Figure 7.2 The Median of a Continuous Probability Distribution

7.2.3 The Mean or Expected Value

As explained in Chapter 3, the mean of a finite population is the center of gravity of the distribution. This idea applies as well to the mean of a probability distribution. Just as μ is used to denote the mean of the distribution of a population variable, the same symbol is also used to denote the mean of the probability distribution of a random variable. To distinguish the mean of a probability distribution from the mean of a finite population, the mean of a probability distribution is often referred to as the *expected value* (or *expectation*) of the random variable. The expected value of a random variable X is symbolized by $E(X)$, which is an alternative symbol to μ. The computation of $E(X)$ depends on whether X is a discrete or continuous random variable.

The Expected Value of a Discrete Random Variable. For a discrete random variable X with probability mass function $f(x)$, the expected value of X is defined as

$$E(X) = \mu = \sum_{\text{all } x} x f(x) \tag{7.2}$$

In words, the mean of a discrete random variable is computed by multiplying each of the possible values of the random variable by the corresponding probability and summing the products.

Formula (7.2) for the mean of a discrete probability distribution is a direct extension of Formula (3.2) for the mean of a finite population. To understand the relationship between these two formulas, consider a group of applicants for the position of controller of the Confab Corporation. This group consists of eight accountants whose ages are:

$$40, \quad 40, \quad 40, \quad 44, \quad 46, \quad 49, \quad 49, \quad 52$$

The mean of these ages is computed from Formula (3.2) as follows:

$$\frac{40 + 40 + 40 + 44 + 46 + 49 + 49 + 52}{8} = \frac{360}{8} = 45$$

Notice in this example that some of the elements have identical values. Three of the candidates are 40, two are 49, and each of the remaining candidates has a different age. Thus, an alternative way of calculating the mean is

$$\frac{40(3) + 44(1) + 46(1) + 49(2) + 52(1)}{8} = \frac{360}{8} = 45$$

By using simple algebra, we may rewrite the expression above as

$$40\left(\frac{3}{8}\right) + 44\left(\frac{1}{8}\right) + 46\left(\frac{1}{8}\right) + 49\left(\frac{2}{8}\right) + 52\left(\frac{1}{8}\right) = 45$$

In this last expression, each of the fractions contained in parentheses represents the proportion of the number of applicants of a specific age to the total number of applicants of all ages. That is, out of the entire group, there are 3/8 with an age of 40, 1/8 with an age of 44, and so on. Each of these proportions is a relative frequency. Thus, one way to compute the mean is to "weight" each value by the corresponding relative frequency. In a discrete probability distribution, the counterpart of the relative frequency for any x-value is the probability given by $f(x)$. Thus, the expected value of a discrete random variable, as defined by Formula (7.2), can be interpreted as the weighted average of the possible x-values, where each x-value is weighted by its probability.

To illustrate the computation of the expected value of a discrete random variable, consider a random variable X that has the probability mass function given in Table 7.1. Applying Formula (7.2), we may compute the expected value of X as follows:

$$\mu = E(X) = 0(.02) + 1(.07) + 2(.12) + 3(.17) + 4(.22) + 5(.25) + 6(.15)$$
$$= 3.85$$

Using a computation table, these calculations may be performed as shown in Table 7.2.

Table 7.2 Computation of Expected Value of a Discrete Random Variable

x	$f(x)$	$xf(x)$
0	.02	0
1	.07	.07
2	.12	.24
3	.17	.51
4	.22	.88
5	.25	1.25
6	.15	.90
		$\Sigma = \overline{3.85} = \mu = E(X)$

The concept of expected value was first used in connection with games of chance. For example, the type of roulette wheel used in Las Vegas casinos has 38 different "equally likely" values on which a person may bet. Of these values 18 are red, 18 are black, and 2 are green. In one type of play, a person can bet on either red or black or green. If a person bets on red, and the outcome of the spin is either black or green, she loses the amount of her bet; if the outcome is red, she retains the amount of her wager and wins an additional amount equal to her bet. Suppose that a person sits all evening at the table and makes a $1.00 bet on red each time the wheel is spun. On any spin, she has an 18/38 probability of making a $1.00 profit and a 20/38 probability of a $1.00 loss. Then the expectation is

$$\frac{18}{38}(\$1.00) + \frac{20}{38}(-\$1.00) = -\$.053$$

That is, in the long run, the player can expect an average loss close to 5 cents per play. Notice, in our present frame of reference, that we used the word "expect" in a very special sense. The player does not actually expect a $.053 loss *on any given play*; in fact, such a loss is possible only as an average. Thus, in one sense, the expected value is the average value that one would expect to obtain *in the long run*.

On any given play, our roulette player can either win $1.00 or lose $1.00. The random variable in this case has only two possible values ($+$1.00 and $-$1.00). The expected value is computed simply by weighting each of these two values by its corresponding probability. Thus, in another sense, the expected value may be regarded as the weighted average of the two values.

The Expected Value of a Continuous Random Variable. The formula for the expected value of a continuous random variable is analogous to that for a discrete random variable, with the operation of integration replacing the operation of summation. That is, if X is a continuous random variable with probability density function $f(x)$, the expected value of X is given by

$$\mu = E(X) = \int_{-\infty}^{\infty} x f(x)\, dx \tag{7.3}$$

To illustrate the use of Formula (7.3), consider again the example of a component whose useful life (in hours) was described by the probability density function

$$f(h) = \begin{cases} \dfrac{h}{8} & \text{if } 0 \leq h \leq 4 \\ 0 & \text{otherwise} \end{cases}$$

The expected life of this type of component is computed as follows:

$$E(H) = \int_{-\infty}^{\infty} h f(h)\, dh = \int_{-\infty}^{0} h \cdot 0\, dh + \int_{0}^{4} h\left(\frac{h}{8}\right) dh + \int_{4}^{\infty} h \cdot 0\, dh$$

$$= \int_{0}^{4} h\frac{h}{8}\, dh = \int_{0}^{4} \frac{h^2}{8}\, dh$$

$$= \frac{h^3}{24}\Big]_{0}^{4} = \frac{64}{24} - \frac{0}{24} = \frac{8}{3} = 2.67$$

7.2.4 The Expected Value of a Function of a Random Variable

We have seen how to compute the expected value of any random variable X whose probability function $f(x)$ is known. In applying probability theory to decision problems, however, we often encounter a random variable, say Y, whose probability function is not readily available. Nevertheless, if a relationship between Y and X can be specified by a mathematical function, $Y = g(X)$, then it becomes possible to compute the expected value of Y. Specifically, if X is a discrete random variable with mass function $f(x)$, and if $g(X)$ is some other function of X, then the expected value of $g(X)$ is given by

$$E[g(X)] = \sum_{\text{all } x} g(x) f(x) \tag{7.4}$$

If X is a continuous random variable with density function $f(x)$, and if $g(X)$ is some other function of X, then the expected value of $g(X)$ is given by

$$E[g(X)] = \int_{-\infty}^{\infty} g(x) f(x)\, dx \tag{7.5}$$

Example 1 :

Let X be a random variable denoting a job shop's monthly demand for an expensive hand-assembled device. Experience has shown that demand behaves according to the mass function

$$f(x) = \begin{cases} \dfrac{x - 2}{10} & \text{if } x = 3, 4, 5, 6 \\ 0 & \text{otherwise} \end{cases}$$

The shop's monthly profit, as a function of demand, is given by

$$Y = g(X) = \$1{,}000(X^2 - X + 6)$$

For these two functions, we may prepare the following table:

x	$f(x)$	$g(x)$
3	.10	$12,000
4	.20	$18,000
5	.30	$26,000
6	.40	$36,000

Then, applying Formula (7.4) to obtain expected monthly profit, we have

$$E(Y) = E[g(X)]$$
$$= 12{,}000(.10) + 18{,}000(.20) + 26{,}000(.30) + 36{,}000(.40)$$
$$= \$27{,}000$$

Example 2 :

Let X be a random variable denoting the time (in hours) required to produce a hand-assembled article. The probability density function of X is given by

$$f(x) = \begin{cases} .40(x + 1) & \text{if } 1 \le x \le 2 \\ 0 & \text{otherwise} \end{cases}$$

The profit (in dollars) that the producer makes on an article is given by

$$Y = g(X) = 3 - X^2$$

To obtain the expected profit per article, we apply Formula (7.5), which yields

$$E(Y) = E[g(X)] = \int_1^2 (3 - x^2)(.40)(x + 1)\, dx$$
$$= .40 \int_1^2 (3 + 3x - x^2 - x^3)\, dx$$
$$= .40 \left[3x + \frac{3x^2}{2} - \frac{x^3}{3} - \frac{x^4}{4} \right]_1^2$$
$$= .40 \left(5\frac{1}{3} - 3\frac{11}{12} \right)$$
$$= .57 \text{ dollar}$$

7.2.5 *Mathematical Properties of Expectations*

In working with expectations, it is helpful to be aware of certain mathematical properties that may be used to simplify algebraic manipulations. Several of these properties are presented next.

1. For any constant a,

$$E(a) = a \tag{7.6}$$

If a random variable can assume only a single value a, the expected value of this random variable is equal to a. For example, suppose that a magician has a deck of 52 identical cards, each card being the ten of hearts. Then any time a person draws a card at random from this deck, the value of that card must be 10. Obviously then, the expected value must also be 10.

2. For any constant a and any random variable X,

$$E(a + X) = a + E(X) \tag{7.7}$$

This simply says that the expectation of the sum of a constant and a random variable is equal to the sum of the constant and the expected value of the random variable. To illustrate this relationship, consider the random variable X whose probability mass function is shown in Table 7.3.

Table 7.3 Probability Mass Function of X

x	1	4	6
$f(x)$	.3	.2	.5

The expected value of the random variable X is

$$\begin{aligned} E(X) &= 1(.3) + 4(.2) + 6(.5) \\ &= .3 + .8 + 3 \\ &= 4.1 \end{aligned}$$

Suppose that we define a new variable $Y = (5 + X)$. Recognizing that Y is a function of X, we may obtain the expected value of Y by applying Formula (7.4):

$$E(5 + X) = (5 + 1)(.3) + (5 + 4)(.2) + (5 + 6)(.5) = 9.1$$

The same result may be obtained more readily by applying Formula (7.7):

$$E(5 + X) = 5 + E(X) = 5 + 4.1 = 9.1$$

3. For any constant b and any random variable X,

$$E(bX) = bE(X) \tag{7.8}$$

If we multiply a random variable X by a constant b, then the expectation of this product will be equal to the constant b times the expected value of the random variable X. Consider again the random variable X in Table 7.3. If we define a new random variable as $Y = 7X$, the expected value of Y may be computed by applying Formula (7.4),

$$E(7X) = 7(1)(.3) + 7(4)(.2) + 7(6)(.5) = 28.7$$

We may obtain the same answer more easily by applying Formula (7.8):

$$E(7X) = 7E(X) = 7(4.1) = 28.7$$

4. By combining Formulas (7.7) and (7.8), we obtain

$$E(a + bX) = a + bE(X) \tag{7.9}$$

If we multiply X by some constant b and then add another constant a, the expected value of this quantity will be equal to the sum of the constant a and the product of b times $E(X)$. For example, suppose that we wish to find the expected value of the quantity $(5 + 7X)$, using the probability mass function in Table 7.3. This can be done with Formula (7.4), but it is easier to use Formula

(7.9), as follows:

$$E(5 + 7X) = 5 + 7E(X) = 5 + 7(4.1)$$
$$= 5 + 28.7 = 33.7$$

5. If $g_1(X), g_2(X), \ldots, g_n(X)$ are n separate functions of a random variable X, then

$$E[g_1(X) + g_2(X) + \ldots + g_n(X)]$$
$$= E[g_1(X)] + E[g_2(X)] + \ldots + E[g_n(X)] \qquad (7.10)$$

In words, the expected value of a sum of functions of a random variable is equal to the sum of the expected values of the functions. To illustrate this property, suppose that we wish to find the expected value of the quantity $(3X^2 + 5X)$. Using the probability mass function in Table 7.3 and applying Formula (7.4), we compute

$$E(3X^2 + 5X) = \sum_{\text{all } x} (3x^2 + 5x) f(x)$$
$$= [3(1^2) + 5(1)](.3) + [3(4^2) + 5(4)](.2) + [3(6^2) + 5(6)](.5)$$
$$= 85$$

To obtain this same result from Formula (7.10), we first let $g_1(X) = 3X^2$ and $g_2(X) = 5X$. Then

$$E(3X^2 + 5X) = E(3X^2) + E(5X) \qquad \text{by Formula (7.10)}$$
$$= 3E(X^2) + 5E(X) \qquad \text{by Formula (7.8)}$$

Applying Formula (7.4) to the mass function in Table 7.3, we compute

$$E(X^2) = \sum x^2 f(x)$$
$$= (1^2)(.3) + (4^2)(.2) + (6^2)(.5) = 21.5$$

Recalling that $E(X) = 4.1$, we obtain

$$E(3X^2 + 5X) = 3E(X^2) + 5E(X)$$
$$= 3(21.5) + 5(4.1) = 85$$

To simplify our discussion of mathematical properties of expectations, the foregoing demonstrations of Formulas (7.6) through (7.10) were limited to discrete random variables. It should be pointed out, however, that all the five properties shown by these formulas are valid regardless of whether the random variable is discrete or continuous.

7.3 MEASURES OF VARIABILITY

The need for a measure of the variability of a probability distribution is particularly apparent if we realize that two distinctly different probability distributions may have the same mean. One way to distinguish between two such distributions is to compare their variabilities. As an illustration, consider two random variables X and Y whose probability mass functions are, respectively:

$$f(x) = \begin{cases} \dfrac{5 - x}{10} & \text{if } x = 1, 2, 3, 4 \\ 0 & \text{otherwise} \end{cases}$$

$$f(y) = \begin{cases} \dfrac{3}{10} & \text{if } y = 0 \\ \dfrac{y}{10} & \text{if } y = 1, 2, 3 \\ \dfrac{1}{20} & \text{if } y = 5, 7 \\ 0 & \text{otherwise} \end{cases}$$

As the reader may verify by using Formula (7.2), both $E(X)$ and $E(Y)$ are equal to 2. That is, the two random variables have identical means. However, as we can see from Figure 7.3, the distribution of Y has a wider spread than the distribution of X. Thus, if we were to measure the dispersions of these two distributions, the measure for the distribution of Y should be greater than that for the distribution of X.

7.3.1 The Variance and Standard Deviation

In our discussion of the variability of finite populations in Chapter 3, we observed that the variance and standard deviation are the two most commonly used measures of variability because of their desirable mathematical properties. We now reexamine these two measures as they are used to describe the variability of probability distributions.

Just as σ^2 is used to denote the variance of a population distribution, the same symbol can also be used to denote the variance of a probability distribution. For a random variable X, an alternative symbol to σ^2 is $V(X)$. Since the standard deviation is simply the square root of the variance, the symbol σ is used to represent the standard deviation of the probability distribution of a random variable.

Definition of the Variance of a Random Variable. As defined by Formula (3.6), the variance of a finite population is the average of the squared deviations from the mean of the population. Extending this concept to random variables, the variance of the probability distribution of a random variable is the expected value of the squared deviation from the mean of the distribution. In terms of a formula, the variance of the probability distribution of any random variable X is

$$V(X) = \sigma^2 = E[(X - \mu)^2] \tag{7.11}$$

The reader may recognize that the squared deviation $(X - \mu)^2$ is a function of X. Thus, $V(X)$ is the expected value of a function of the random variable X. If we let $g(X)$ represent $(X - \mu)^2$, we may obtain $V(X)$ by using Formula (7.4) or (7.5), depending on whether X is discrete or continuous.

To illustrate the concept of the variance as the expected squared deviation, let us consider again the probability distribution in Figure 7.3a. Since this

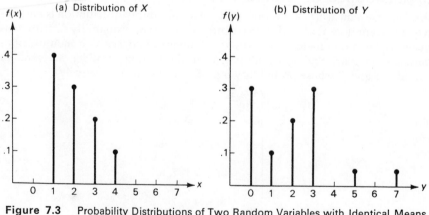

Figure 7.3 Probability Distributions of Two Random Variables with Identical Means but Different Dispersions

distribution is discrete, we may obtain its variance by applying Formula (7.4). Specifically,

$$V(X) = E[(X - \mu)^2] = \sum_{\text{all } x} (x - \mu)^2 f(x)$$

Using this formula, the calculation of the variance is presented in Table 7.4. As shown in this table, the first step is to calculate μ using Formula (7.2), which yields $\mu = 2$. Next, for each x-value, the deviation $(x - \mu)$ is computed. Then each of these deviations is squared and multiplied by the corresponding $f(x)$. Finally, these products are summed to yield the variance. In short, the variance is computed by weighting each possible squared deviation $(x - \mu)^2$ by the corresponding $f(x)$, and then summing the products. In Table 7.4, this sum is equal to 1, which is the variance of X.

Table 7.4   Calculation of the Variance of a Discrete Random Variable

x	$f(x)$	$x - \mu$	$(x - \mu)^2$	$(x - \mu)^2 f(x)$
1	.4	$(1 - 2) = -1$	1	.4
2	.3	$(2 - 2) = 0$	0	0
3	.2	$(3 - 2) = 1$	1	.2
4	.1	$(4 - 2) = 2$	4	.4
Sum	1.0			1.0 = V(X)

Following the same procedure as shown in Table 7.4, we may compute the variance of the random variable Y in Figure 7.3b. As the reader is urged to verify, the variance of Y is equal to 3.3. Thus, for the two distributions in Figure 7.3, the variance of the random variable Y is much larger than the variance of the random variable X. This is in agreement with our intuitive observation that the distribution of Y has a wider spread than the distribution of X.

Computation of the Variance of a Random Variable. We have used Formula (7.11) to compute variances in order to reinforce the meaning of the variance as an expected squared deviation. In practice, however, this formula is seldom used, because it is often cumbersome to work with squared deviations from the mean. Fortunately, this difficulty can be overcome by recalling from Chapter 3 that the variance of a finite population is equal to the mean of the squares minus the square of the mean. Extending this concept to random variables, the variance of a random variable X may be computed by the formula

$$V(X) = \sigma^2 = E(X^2) - \mu^2 \tag{7.12}$$

For purposes of computation, Formula (7.12) is generally preferable to Formula (7.11), since Formula (7.12) requires less computational work. To apply Formula (7.12), we need only compute the quantities $E(X^2)$ and μ^2. We have already seen how to compute μ for either a discrete or continuous random variable, and μ^2 is merely the square of μ. For a discrete random variable, $E(X^2)$ is given by

$$E(X^2) = \sum_{\text{all } x} x^2 f(x) \tag{7.13}$$

Descriptive Measures of Probability Distributions   **133**

For a continuous random variable, $E(X^2)$ is given by

$$E(X^2) = \int_{-\infty}^{\infty} x^2 f(x)\, dx \qquad (7.14)$$

To illustrate the computation of the variance using Formula (7.12) together with Formula (7.13), consider again the distribution shown in Figure 7.3a. Applying these formulas, the variance is computed in Table 7.5. The reader

Table 7.5 Alternative Way of Calculating the Variance of a Discrete Random Variable

x	$f(x)$	$xf(x)$	x^2	$x^2f(x)$
1	.4	.4	1	.4
2	.3	.6	4	1.2
3	.2	.6	9	1.8
4	.1	.4	16	1.6
Sum		$\overline{2.0} = \mu$		$\overline{5.0} = E(X^2)$

$$\mu = E(X) = \Sigma\, xf(x) = 2.0$$
$$E(X^2) = \Sigma\, x^2f(x) = 5.0$$
$$\sigma^2 = V(X) = E(X^2) - \mu^2 = 5 - 2^2 = 1$$

may recall that, with greater computational effort, the same variance was obtained with Formula (7.11), as shown in Table 7.4.

Example 1:

On a particular milk delivery route, the number of quarts of milk consumed daily by a household varies from 1 to 4 quarts. Let Q be a random variable denoting the number of quarts consumed daily by a household. Analysis of the dairy's records shows that the probability mass function of Q is given by

$$f(q) = \begin{cases} \dfrac{q^2}{30} & \text{if } q = 1, 2, 3, 4 \\ 0 & \text{otherwise} \end{cases}$$

From the mass function, we obtain the following probabilities:

q	$f(q)$
1	.033
2	.133
3	.300
4	.533

Applying Formula (7.2), the mean of Q is

$$\mu = E(Q) = .033(1) + .133(2) + .300(3) + .533(4) = 3.33$$

Applying Formula (7.13), we obtain the mean square:

$$E(Q^2) = .033(1^2) + .133(2^2) + .300(3^2) + .533(4^2) = 11.79$$

Finally, using Formula (7.12) to compute the variance, we have

$$\sigma^2 = V(Q) = E(Q^2) - \mu^2 = 11.79 - 3.33^2 = .70$$

Thus, the variance of the milk consumption is .70 square quart.

Example 2:

Consider once more the component whose useful life in hours was described by the density function

$$f(h) = \begin{cases} \dfrac{h}{8} & \text{if } 0 \leq h \leq 4 \\ 0 & \text{otherwise} \end{cases}$$

We found earlier that the mean life was $E(H) = \mu = 2.67$ hours. Applying Formula (7.14), the mean square is

$$E(H^2) = \int_0^4 h^2 f(h)\ dh = \int_0^4 h^2 \frac{h}{8}\ dh$$

$$= \int_0^4 \frac{h^3}{8}\ dh = \frac{h^4}{32}\Bigg]_0^4 = 8$$

Then, from Formula (7.12), the variance of H is

$$\sigma^2 = V(H) = E(H^2) - \mu^2 = 8 - (2.67)^2 = .87$$

Thus, the variance of the lives of this particular type of component is .87 square hour.

The Standard Deviation of a Random Variable. We observed in Chapter 3 that the variance is difficult to interpret because it is expressed in square units of measurement. However, this difficulty can be overcome by using the standard deviation, which is expressed in terms of the original units of measurement. Applying this concept to random variables, the standard deviation of a random variable X is simply the positive square root of the variance of X. In terms of a formula,

$$\sigma = \sqrt{\sigma^2} = \sqrt{V(X)} \tag{7.15}$$

For instance, in Example 1, the variance of the random variable Q is .70 square quart. Thus, the standard deviation is

$$\sigma = \sqrt{.70 \text{ square quart}} = .84 \text{ quart}$$

7.3.2 Mathematical Properties of the Variance

In introducing the concept of the variance, we mentioned that the variance possesses certain mathematical properties that are particularly desirable for further analysis. We now present several of these properties as follows:

1. For any constant a,

$$V(a) = 0 \tag{7.16}$$

This simply says that the variance of any constant is zero. This is reasonable since, if a random variable can take on only a single value, this random variable will have no variability.

2. For any random variable X, the variance is always nonnegative. Algebraically,

$$V(X) \geq 0 \tag{7.17}$$

This property follows from the definition of the variance given in Formula (7.11). Generally, $V(X)$ is greater than zero; $V(X)$ is equal to zero only in the special case in which the random variable can assume only a single value.

3. For any constant a and any random variable X,

$$V(a + X) = V(X) \qquad (7.18)$$

In words, the variance of the sum of a constant and a random variable is simply equal to the variance of the random variable. Adding a constant to every possible value of a random variable shifts the *location* of the distribution but does not change the *dispersion*.

4. For any constant b and any random variable X,

$$V(bX) = b^2 V(X) \qquad (7.19)$$

If we multiply a random variable X by some constant b, then the variance of this product will be equal to b^2 times the variance of X. In other words, multiplying each possible value of a random variable by a constant multiplies the variance by the square of the constant.

5. By combining Formulas (7.18) and (7.19), we obtain

$$V(a + bX) = b^2 V(X) \qquad (7.20)$$

If we multiply X by some constant b and then add another constant a, the variance of this quantity will be merely b^2 times $V(X)$. This reinforces the idea that adding a constant has no effect on the variance.

6. For any constant c and any random variable X whose mean is μ, it is always true that

$$E[(X - \mu)^2] \leq E[(X - c)^2] \qquad (7.21)$$

To clarify this statement, suppose that we choose some constant c and compute the expected squared deviation from c:

$$E[(X - c)^2]$$

Then, it can be shown mathematically that

$$E[(X - c)^2] = E[(X - \mu)^2] + (\mu - c)^2$$

In this expression, the first term on the right is simply the variance. Since the second term is a squared number, it is always nonnegative. Thus, $E[(X - c)^2]$ must be greater than or equal to the variance. It can be equal to the variance only if $c = \mu$. In other words, the expected squared deviation from the mean (that is, the variance) is less than the expected squared deviation from any other value. Hence, the expected squared deviation will have its minimum value when calculated from the mean. This characteristic is known as the "least-squares" property of the mean.

7.4 CHEBYSHEV'S INEQUALITY

Loosely speaking, when the standard deviation is relatively small, the possible values of the random variable are closely concentrated around the mean. When the standard deviation is relatively large, the possible values of the random variable are widely dispersed from the mean. To be more specific, let us refer again to the two random variables X and Y shown in Figure 7.3. From our discussion of measures of dispersion, we have observed that:

1. X and Y have identical means—that is, $E(X) = E(Y) = 2$.
2. X has a smaller dispersion than Y. In terms of the variances, $V(X) = 1$, whereas $V(Y) = 3.3$. Therefore, the standard deviation of X is $\sigma_X = 1$, whereas the standard deviation of Y is $\sigma_Y = 1.8$.

Now suppose that we wish to determine the probability that the random variable X will lie within 1 unit of its mean. Since $E(X)$ is equal to 2, this is equivalent to calculating $P(1 \leq X \leq 3)$. From the probability mass function of X, we obtain

$$P(1 \leq X \leq 3) = \sum_{x=1}^{3} f(x) = .9$$

Similarly, we can determine the probability that the random variable Y will lie within 1 unit of its mean. Since $E(Y)$ also equals 2, this is equivalent to computing $P(1 \leq Y \leq 3)$. From the probability mass function of Y, we have

$$P(1 \leq Y \leq 3) = \sum_{y=1}^{3} f(y) = .6$$

As we should have anticipated, $P(1 \leq X \leq 3)$ is *greater* than $P(1 \leq Y \leq 3)$, since X has a *smaller* standard deviation than Y. In other words, the probability that the random variable will lie *within* the interval between 1 and 3, inclusive, is greater for X than for Y. Therefore, the probability that the random variable will lie *outside* this interval (that is, in the "tails" of the distribution) will be smaller for X than for Y.

In the discussion above, we were able to determine exact probabilities because we knew the probability functions of both X and Y. Suppose, however, that we knew the mean and standard deviation of some random variable but did not know its probability distribution. Then, could we make similar statements regarding the probabilities that a randomly observed value will lie within certain distances from the mean? The answer is that we can set limits on such probabilities with the aid of a mathematical theorem known as *Chebyshev's inequality*. In one of its forms, Chebyshev's inequality may be stated that, for any $k \geq 1$,

$$P(|X - \mu| \leq k\sigma) \geq 1 - \frac{1}{k^2} \tag{7.22}$$

Although this inequality may not look so easy at first glance, it simply says that the probability that a randomly observed value of a random variable will be within $k\sigma$ from the mean is at least $1 - 1/k^2$. In an alternative form, Chebyshev's inequality may be stated as

$$P(|X - \mu| > k\sigma) \leq \frac{1}{k^2} \tag{7.23}$$

In this form the inequality says that the probability that a randomly observed value of a random variable will be more than $k\sigma$ from the mean in either direction can be no greater than $1/k^2$. In other words, the theorem says:

1. The *minimum* probability that the value of a random observation of X will lie *within* the range $\mu \pm k\sigma$ is $1 - 1/k^2$.
2. The *maximum* probability that the value of a random observation of X will lie *outside* the range $\mu \pm k\sigma$ is $1/k^2$.

Example:

A statistical abstract reports that, for the several thousand companies incorporated within a particular state, mean net income in 1971 was $400,000 ,with a standard deviation of $100,000. The abstract fails to indicate, however, how these corporate earnings are distributed. If one of these companies is selected at random, what is the *minimum* probability that its 1971 net earnings were between $200,000 and $600,000? What is the *maximum* probability that its 1971 net earnings were either below $100,000 or above $700,000?

If X represents net earnings of a corporation, $\mu = \$400{,}000$ and $\sigma = \$100{,}000$. Thus, $200,000 is 2σ below μ, and $600,000 is 2σ above μ. From Formula (7.22), the probability that the net earnings of a randomly selected company will lie within this range is at least $(1 - 1/4) = .75$. Similarly, $100,000 is 3σ below μ, and $700,000 is 3σ above μ. From Formula (7.23), the probability that the net earnings of a randomly selected company will lie outside this range is at most $1/9 = .11$.

PROBLEMS

7.1   The probability mass function of a discrete random variable X is

$$f(x) = \begin{cases} \dfrac{x+1}{50} & \text{if } x = 2, 3, 4, 5, 6 \\[2mm] \dfrac{11-x}{20} & \text{if } x = 7, 8, 9, 10 \\[2mm] 0 & \text{otherwise} \end{cases}$$

Determine the following fractiles:
- (a) $x_{.05}$
- (b) $x_{.35}$
- (c) $x_{.50}$
- (d) $x_{.60}$
- (e) $x_{.80}$
- (f) $x_{.95}$

7.2   The probability density function of a random variable W is

$$f(w) = \begin{cases} \dfrac{w}{8} & \text{if } 0 \leq w \leq 4 \\[2mm] 0 & \text{otherwise} \end{cases}$$

Determine the following fractiles:
- (a) $w_{.04}$
- (b) $w_{.25}$
- (c) $w_{.36}$
- (d) $w_{.10}$
- (e) $w_{.50}$
- (f) $w_{.90}$

7.3   The probability mass function of a discrete random variable X is

$$f(x) = \begin{cases} \dfrac{x^2+4}{50} & \text{if } x = 0, 1, 2, 3, 4 \\[2mm] 0 & \text{otherwise} \end{cases}$$

Determine the .10 fractile, mean, median, and mode of X.

7.4   The probability mass function of a discrete random variable X is

$$f(x) = \begin{cases} \dfrac{x+2}{25} & \text{if } x = 1, 2, 3, 4, 5 \\[2mm] 0 & \text{otherwise} \end{cases}$$

Determine the .70 fractile, mean, median, and mode of X.

7.5   According to the *Commissioners 1941 Standard Ordinary Mortality Table*, the probability that a person age 25 will live through the year is .997. An insurance company offers a 1-year term policy at age 25 in an amount of $1,000 for a premium of $8.00. Assuming this mortality experience fits the expected company experience, what should be the expected gain on a $1,000 policy, not considering selling and administrative expenses?

7.6 The probability density function of a continuous random variable X is

$$f(x) = \begin{cases} \dfrac{x}{2} & \text{if } 0 \leq x \leq 2 \\ 0 & \text{otherwise} \end{cases}$$

Determine the .25 fractile, mean, and median of X.

7.7 The probability density function of a continuous random variable X is

$$f(x) = \begin{cases} \dfrac{1}{6} & \text{if } 2 \leq x \leq 8 \\ 0 & \text{otherwise} \end{cases}$$

Determine the mean and median of X.

7.8 The probability density function of a continuous random variable T is

$$f(t) = \begin{cases} 3t(2 - 2t) & \text{if } 0 \leq t \leq 1 \\ 0 & \text{otherwise} \end{cases}$$

Determine the mean of T.

7.9 The probability density function of a continuous random variable G is

$$f(g) = \begin{cases} 10g - 3g^2 - 7 & \text{if } 1 \leq g \leq 2 \\ 0 & \text{otherwise} \end{cases}$$

What is the mean of the distribution of G?

7.10 Let X be a random variable denoting the life span (in months) of a particular mechanical part. The probability density function of X is given by

$$f(x) = \begin{cases} 0.4 & \text{if } 0 \leq x < 2 \\ a + bx & \text{if } 2 \leq x \leq 3 \\ 0 & \text{otherwise} \end{cases}$$

(a) Assuming that $f(3) = 0$, determine the values of a and b in the function.
(b) Determine the probability that the life span of the part is at most 2.5 months.
(c) Determine the expected life span of the part.

7.11 Let X be a random variable denoting the number of automobile accidents on a certain stretch of highway in a 24-hour period. The probability mass function of X is given by

$$f(x) = \begin{cases} .15 & \text{if } x = 0 \\ .05x^2 & \text{if } x = 1, 2 \\ .10(6 - x) & \text{if } x = 3, 4, 5 \\ 0 & \text{otherwise} \end{cases}$$

The daily cost of towing away the wrecks is given by

$$Y = g(X) = \$10(10X - X^2)$$

(a) Find the probability that, during any given 24-hour period, there will be:
   (i) More than 3 accidents on this stretch of highway.
   (ii) At least 1 but less than 4 accidents on this stretch of highway.
(b) What is the expected daily cost of towing away the wrecks?

7.12 Let X represent a retailer's weekly demand for a low-volume, high-quality item. Experience has shown that the demand for this item is a random variable that follows the probability mass function:

$$f(x) = \begin{cases} .10(14 - x) & \text{if } x = 10, 11, 12, 13 \\ 0 & \text{otherwise} \end{cases}$$

The retailer's weekly profit on this item, as a function of demand, is given by

$$Y = g(X) = \$100(X^2 - X)$$

(a) Determine the probability that the weekly demand is at most 11 units.
(b) Determine the expected weekly demand.
(c) Determine the expected weekly profit.

7.13 Let X be a random variable representing a firm's monthly demand for an expensive hand-assembled device. Experience has shown that demand behaves according to the mass function

$$f(x) = \begin{cases} \dfrac{x - 2}{10} & \text{if } x = 3, 4, 5, 6 \\ 0 & \text{otherwise} \end{cases}$$

(a) Determine expected monthly demand.
(b) Determine expected monthly profit if the firm's monthly profit, as a function of demand, is given by

$$Y = g(X) = \$1,000(X^2 - X + 6)$$

7.14 Let X be a random variable denoting monthly demand (in tons) for a chemical product. The probability density function of X is given by

$$f(x) = \begin{cases} .02x & \text{if } 0 \leq x \leq 10 \\ 0 & \text{otherwise} \end{cases}$$

Assume monthly profit (in hundreds of dollars), as a function of demand, is given by

$$Y = g(X) = X^2 + X - 20$$

What is the expected monthly profit?

7.15 Let T be a random variable denoting the time (in hours) required to produce a hand-assembled article. The probability density function of T is given by

$$f(t) = \begin{cases} 2t - 4 & \text{if } 2 \leq t \leq 3 \\ 0 & \text{otherwise} \end{cases}$$

The profit (in dollars) that the manufacturer makes on an article is given by

$$Y = g(T) = 8 - T$$

(a) Determine the expected time to produce an article.
(b) Determine the expected profit per article.
(c) Determine the probability that the profit on an individual article will be greater than $5.50.

7.16 Let X be a random variable denoting the time (in hours) required to produce a delicate device. The probability density function of X is given by

$$f(x) = \begin{cases} \dfrac{x}{50} & \text{if } 0 \leq x \leq 10 \\ 0 & \text{otherwise} \end{cases}$$

The profit that the manufacturer makes on a unit depends on the time required to produce it, as shown by the following table:

Production Time	Profit
Less than 3 hours	$300
Between 3 and 8 hours	200
Over 8 hours	100

(a) What is the expected number of hours required to produce a device?

(b) What is the manufacturer's expected profit per unit?

7.17 Determine the variance and standard deviation of the random variable in Problem 7.3.

7.18 Determine the variance and standard deviation of the random variable described in Problem 7.4.

7.19 Determine the variance and standard deviation of the random variable in Problem 7.1.

7.20 Let X be a random variable representing a worker's production of an expensive hand-assembled device. Experience has shown that X has the following probability mass function:

$$f(x) = \begin{cases} \dfrac{x-2}{15} & \text{if } x = 3, 4, 5, 6, 7 \\ 0 & \text{otherwise} \end{cases}$$

(a) Present the probability mass function and the cumulative mass function in the form of a table.

(b) Calculate the expected production quantity, $E(X)$.

(c) Calculate the variance and standard deviation of X.

7.21 Determine the variance and standard deviation of the random variable in Problem 7.6.

7.22 Determine the variance and standard deviation of the random variable in Problem 7.7.

7.23 Determine the variance and standard deviation of the random variable in Problem 7.8.

7.24 The probability density function of a random variable S is

$$f(s) = \begin{cases} 3s^2 & \text{if } 0 \leq s \leq 1 \\ 0 & \text{otherwise} \end{cases}$$

Determine the mean, variance, and standard deviation of S.

7.25 Let X be a continuous random variable with the probability density function

$$f(x) = \begin{cases} \dfrac{x}{8} & \text{if } 0 \leq x \leq 4 \\ 0 & \text{otherwise} \end{cases}$$

(a) Determine and state completely the corresponding cumulative density function.

(b) Determine the expected value of X.

(c) Determine the variance and standard deviation of X.

(d) Using the cumulative density function, determine $P(2 < X < 3)$.

7.26 A pharmaceutical firm has developed two different processes for extracting gamma globulin from whole blood. Let X be the yield [in cubic centimeters (cc)] of this substance from 1 pint of whole blood. With process A, the probability density function of X is

$$f(x) = \begin{cases} \dfrac{1}{10} & \text{if } 40 \leq x \leq 50 \\ 0 & \text{otherwise} \end{cases}$$

With process B, the probability density function of X is

$$f(x) = \begin{cases} \dfrac{70-x}{400} & \text{if } 40 \leq x \leq 60 \\ 0 & \text{otherwise} \end{cases}$$

Descriptive Measures of Probability Distributions

(a) For which process is mean yield the greater?

(b) Which process has the greater probability of a yield that is less than 45 cc?

(c) In terms of standard deviations, which process is the more variable?

(d) Which process has the greater probability of a yield that is greater than 46 cc?

7.27 An electric utility company has 200,000 domestic subscribers. For the month of October, the mean electric bill for these 200,000 subscribers was μ = $8.50, with a standard deviation σ = $1.25. No additional information is available. What is the minimum number of these 200,000 bills that would lie between $6.00 and $11.00?

7.28 A census of the households in a large city showed that the mean annual household income was μ = $8,500, with a standard deviation of σ = $2,000. No additional information concerning the income distribution is available.

(a) What is the maximum probability that the annual income of a randomly selected household would be either less than $3,500 or greater than $13,500?

(b) Determine a range of household incomes (with μ lying at the center of the range) that will guarantee that at least 75% of the households will have incomes within that range.

8

Sampling Methods and Sample Statistics

As we observed in Chapter 1, a *sample* is a subset of a population, *sampling* is the process of selecting a sample, and a *statistic* is a quantity obtained from the outcome of a sampling study. In this chapter we discuss various methods of sampling and present several statistics that are commonly used to describe or summarize the data obtained from sampling.

8.1 NONPROBABILITY SAMPLING

Methods of sampling may be grouped into two main categories: probability sampling and nonprobability sampling. Probability sampling methods make it possible to apply probability theory to assess or control the amount of uncertainty inherent in conclusions drawn from sample data. In contrast, nonprobability sampling methods do not permit the application of probability theory, although such methods are often used in actual practice because they often can provide a relatively simple means of obtaining information. The most commonly used methods of nonprobability sampling are convenience sampling, judgment sampling, and quota sampling.

In *convenience sampling*, the sample simply consists of some part of the population that happens to be readily or easily available. This type of sampling is also called *chunk sampling*, since some "chunk" of the population is selected because it is conveniently accessible. Examples of studies using convenience sampling are interviewing households all in a handily located neighborhood, or administering a questionnaire to a group of business managers who happen to attend a particular Rotary Club meeting. Attempting to draw generalizations about a population from a convenience sample can be extremely hazardous, and the procedure is best adapted to "pilot" studies which are conducted as preliminary tryouts for questionnaires and other observational procedures.

Judgment sampling, which is somewhat more sophisticated than convenience sampling, depends on the skill of an "expert" who seeks to define a sample which he or she believes to be "typical" or "representative" of the population as a whole. Although peril may lurk in information obtained from judgment samples, the use of judgment sampling is common when probability sampling would be overly costly or time-consuming. Judgment samples are particularly appropriate for studies involving very small samples, such as a mere 5 or 10 observations. As pointed out by W. E. Deming, a prominent authority on sampling methodology: "In such very small samples, the errors of judgment are usually less than the random errors of a probability sample."[1]

Quota sampling is a special type of judgment sampling that is used particularly in public opinion and marketing surveys. In quota sampling, an attempt is made to secure a sample that is a miniature "cross section" of the population with respect to certain characteristics of the population which are known from some source such as a census. For example, "quotas" might be set for the number of males and females to be contained in the sample, for the numbers of persons in different age groups, for the numbers of individuals in different economic classes, and so on. Although this procedure may achieve some "representativeness" with respect to certain demographic characteristics such as sex, age, and income, this does not at all assure that the interview results will accurately reflect the distribution of particular characteristics under investigation such as preference for political candidates or weekly milk consumption.

8.2 PROBABILITY SAMPLING

Probability sampling is an approach whereby, before the sample is selected, each possible sample that might be drawn from a population has a determinable probability of being the sample that actually will be selected. For example, if we were concerned with a population consisting of 500 households, and if we decided to draw a sample of 50 households from this population, there would be a total of $\binom{500}{50}$ different possible samples that might be selected. If we adopt some well-defined sampling procedure that permits us to specify the probability that each of these possible samples actually will be the one selected, then our sample will be a probability sample.

A preliminary task in selecting a probability sample is the construction of the *frame*, which is some device (such as a list or map) for identifying the elements in the population from which the sample is to be drawn. Suppose, for instance, that the management of a manufacturing firm wishes to obtain sample information concerning the attitudes of its hourly paid personnel toward a proposed incentive plan. The population in this case consists of all of the firm's personnel who are paid on an hourly basis. A serial-numbered list of the names of these personnel is a frame from which the sample can be selected.

In the foregoing example, the frame is easily obtainable and "isomorphic" with the population—that is, a one-to-one correspondence exists between the elements of the frame and the elements of the population. Frequently, however, the frame for a statistical study is not so readily available, and its construction may require a great deal of effort and ingenuity. How, for instance, would you propose that a marketing research firm compile a frame for sampling the population of next month's purchasers of Sparkle toothpaste? What approach would you suggest for constructing a frame for sampling the population of traveling

---

[1]W. E. Deming, *Sample Design in Business Research* (New York: John Wiley & Sons, Inc., 1960), p. 31.

salespeople who have college degrees? In such cases, some judgment must be exercised in compiling the frame, and the frame is necessarily incomplete—in the sense that there will be a "gap" between the frame and the population. Strictly speaking, statistical inferences are made with respect to the frame rather than the population. If the frame is complete, such that every element in the population is represented in the frame, then direct inferences concerning the population can be made from the sample evidence. However, if a gap exists between the population and the frame, the decision maker must ask whether the frame includes a sufficient portion of the population to provide adequate information about the population. This question is a judgmental problem of the decision maker and has no statistical answer.

8.2.1 Simple Random Sampling

The most common type of probability sample is a *simple random sample*, which is a sample selected in such a way that each of the possible samples that might be drawn has an equal chance of being the sample that actually is drawn. In practice this is achieved by adopting some sampling procedure such that, at any point in the process of drawing cases from the population into the sample, each element that is available to be drawn has an equal probability of being the next one drawn.

Selecting a simple random sample is similar to conducting a lottery. For example, suppose that the sponsor of a television program decides to promote his product by conducting a lottery in which 10 prize winners will be "randomly selected" to receive free vacation trips to Bora-Bora. To enter the lottery, a viewer simply writes his or her name and address on a post card and sends it to the television station. All cards received before a designated date will be placed in a large drum, which will be rotated until the cards are thoroughly mixed. Then, in front of the television cameras, a movie star will be blindfolded and will draw 10 cards from the drum. If we regard all persons whose postcards are in the drum as a population, then the 10 persons whose cards are selected would be a simple random sample from that population.

The use of a rotating drum is an example of a physical mixing process to achieve randomness. Other examples of physical randomizing procedures are stirring a bowlful of numbered capsules and shuffling a deck of numbered cards. Although such physical mixing processes illustrate the essential notion of randomization, they are seldom used in practical sampling situations. One reason for this is that they require the cumbersome manipulation of special equipment. Furthermore, past experience with these procedures in sweepstakes and lotteries has created considerable doubt that they produce truly random results.[2] Fortunately, the disadvantages of physical mixing devices are easily avoided by the use of tables of random digits generated by computers. The most extensive and best known table of random digits is *A Million Random Digits*, generated by the RAND Corporation. As explained by RAND, the random digits in this table "were produced by rerandomization of a basic table generated by an electronic roulette wheel."[3] A portion of this table is reproduced in Appendix II, Table C.

---

[2]For a technical discussion of randomness, see the RAND Corporation, *A Million Random Digits with 100,000 Normal Deviates* (New York: The Free Press, 1955), pp. xi–xxii.

[3]The RAND Corporation, *A Million Random Digits*, p. ix.

To illustrate the use of a table of random digits, suppose that an auditor has asked us to select a simple random sample of 25 accounts from a ledger containing 5,000 accounts receivable. To do this, we first assign serial numbers from 0001 to 5000 to the accounts in the ledger. This serialized list of the accounts in the ledger is the frame from which the sample is to be drawn.

Next, we enter a random digit table, such as Table C of Appendix II. Notice that the digits in this table are arranged in blocks that are five digits across and five digits down. We may begin reading the table at any point on any page. Also we may read the digits in any direction (such as top to bottom or left to right) as long as we read them in sequence. Arbitrarily, let us start to read numbers from the upper left corner of the second page of Table C. Also arbitrarily, let us read the digits from left to right. Since our serial numbers run from 0001 to 5000, we require four-digit numbers. These can be obtained by reading the first four digits in each five-digit row, ignoring the fifth digit. Following this procedure, we see that the first random number is 1176, which is the serial number of the first account to be drawn into our sample. Moving down to the next row, our second random number is 1020, which is the serial number of the next account to be drawn into our sample. The following random number, 8803, is skipped because it is greater than the largest serial number in our frame. The fourth number in the table is 0148, which becomes the serial number of the third account to be drawn into the sample. This general procedure is followed until 25 account numbers have been selected.

8.2.2   Restricted Random Sampling

In our discussion of various statistical methods throughout the remainder of this book, it will be assumed that the samples under consideration are simple random samples. We will pause at this point, however, to describe briefly some other methods of probability sampling which are of particular importance in marketing and economic survey research. Detailed consideration of these so-called *restricted random sampling* methods is reserved for advanced courses in statistical methodology.

Systematic Sampling. One of the most commonly used forms of restricted random sampling is *systematic sampling*. With this technique, the elements of the frame are arranged in some physical order, such as a list of firms or a card file of customers. The application of systematic sampling involves the concept of the *sampling ratio*, which is the ratio of the size of the frame to the size of the sample. Symbolically, if k is used to denote the sampling ratio, then

$$k = \frac{N_f}{n} \tag{8.1}$$

where N_f = number of elements in the frame

n = number of elements to be selected into the sample

Of course, if there is no gap between the frame and the population, the size of the frame (N_f) will be identical to the size of the population (N).

To obtain a systematic sample, the first item to be included in the sample is selected randomly, and every kth item following in succession through the frame is then taken into the sample. Suppose, for instance, that the frame for a marketing study consists of 20,000 households listed in a city directory, and a systematic sample of 100 households is desired. The first step is to compute the sampling ratio $k = 20,000/100 = 200$. The next step is to obtain a three-digit random number between 001 and 200 inclusive. Suppose that the random number obtained is 078. Then the first household selected into the sample would be the 78th entry in the directory, the second sample household would be the 278th entry, the third sample household would be the 478th entry, and so on.

From a practical standpoint, systematic sampling is easier to apply than simple random sampling, and for this reason is often the preferred procedure. Under certain conditions, systematic random sampling also may be preferred to simple random sampling, for technical reasons that are beyond the scope of this text.[4] The main peril in systematic sampling lies in the possibility of some pattern or *periodicity* in the frame which might happen to coincide with the size of the sampling ratio. For example, if a discount department store is open for business 7 days a week, and if sales are sampled every seventh day, only a single day of the week would be represented in the sample and the results could not be generalized to the entire week.

Stratified Sampling. In using *stratified sampling*, the frame is partitioned into subsets, called *strata*, on the basis of one or more characteristics which are known to be, or logically can be presumed to be, related to the characteristic to be studied. Suppose, for example, that a political pollster wished to conduct a survey to investigate voters' preferences for three competing gubernatorial candidates in an upcoming election in a large state. A roster of the state's registered voters might provide a suitable frame. The pollster might then partition the frame into subsets on the basis of such characteristics as age, economic status, and registered party affiliation—characteristics that are known generally to be related to political preference. Such a partitioning would, presumably, produce subgroups that are relatively *homogeneous*. That is, there would tend to be less variability of opinion within the strata than there would be across the population as a whole. This is the aim of stratification—to obtain a set of subgroups such that there is relatively low variability within strata and relatively large variability between strata. For example, we could reasonably expect that, as a group, upper-income Republicans over 45 years of age would tend, with little variability, to be at the conservative end of the political spectrum. In contrast, lower-income Democrats under 25 years of age would tend to be fairly homogeneously grouped at the liberal end of the political spectrum.

The ability to obtain this goal of homogeneity within groups and variability between groups in stratified sampling depends on two main factors: (1) the extent to which the researcher is successful in selecting variables of classification which are indeed related to the characteristic under investigation; and (2) the availability, prior to sampling, of adequate information concerning the elements in the frame with respect to the variables that are to be used for clas-

---

[4]See Morris H. Hansen, William N. Hurwitz, and William G. Madow, *Sample Survey Methods and Theory*, Vol. 1 (New York: John Wiley & Sons, Inc., 1953), pp. 503–512.

sifying the elements into strata. This second factor, the need for prior information concerning the elements of the frame, can cause serious difficulties in stratified sampling. For example, whereas a roster of voters would probably indicate each voter's party affiliation (if any), it might be more difficult to obtain reliable information on age and economic status. Even when such prior information is available, it can be very costly to obtain.

Once the strata have been defined and each element of the frame has been assigned to its appropriate stratum, the question arises regarding how many elements should be sampled in each stratum. One solution to this question is to use *proportional allocation*, wherein the number of elements selected from each stratum is proportional to the size of the stratum. However, for reasons of cost combined with technical considerations, it may be preferable to use some type of *optimal allocation*, wherein the number of elements selected from each stratum is a function of the amount of variability that the researcher expects to encounter within the stratum. In brief, the question of sample sizes in stratified sampling is a complex problem that is a topic for advanced study.

Cluster Sampling. Stratified sampling is designed to optimize the precision of the information that the sample might yield, but highly precise information has its price. An alternative to stratified sampling is *cluster sampling*, which may be less costly but tends to yield less precise information. In cluster sampling, the frame is partitioned into subsets, called *clusters*, such that the individual elements in each cluster are located close together. For instance, when cluster sampling is used in survey research, the clusters are generally specified in terms of geographical units such as city blocks or census tracts. Once the clusters have been specified, a given number of clusters are randomly selected. One of two procedures may then be followed: (1) all of the elements in each sample cluster may be observed, or (2) a random subsample of elements in each cluster may be observed. Observation of all the elements in each sample cluster is called *single-stage sampling*, whereas observation of a subsample of elements in each sample cluster is called *two-stage sampling*.

Applying this type of sampling to our political poll example, the pollster might begin by obtaining a list of registered voters arranged by precincts. Each precinct would form a natural cluster. He would then select a random sample of precincts. Finally, he might select a random sample of, say, 20% of the voters listed in each of these sample precincts. This would be a two-stage sampling procedure.

In contrast to stratified sampling, the attempt is made in cluster sampling to obtain clusters such that there is relatively high variability within clusters and relatively low variability among clusters. Ideally, the clusters should be as similar as possible and there should be approximately the same amount of variability within each cluster as there is within the population as a whole. In other words, each cluster should be a miniature image of the population. In actual practice, this is only a goal to be pursued; it can seldom be attained. Thus, cluster sampling is seldom as effective as it theoretically might be. The great advantage of this procedure is that surveys based on cluster sampling are generally less expensive to conduct than when other probability sampling methods are employed. This is particularly true when the clusters are specified in geographical units.

8.3 SAMPLE STATISTICS VS. POPULATION PARAMETERS

Chapter 3 discussed various *parameters* that may be used as summary measures to describe finite populations. In a similar manner, various *statistics* may be used as summary measures to describe samples. Many statistics are computed in exactly the same way as the corresponding parameters. However, since statistics are computed from a sample, which is merely a subset of a population, there is a crucial conceptual distinction between statistics and parameters. To preserve this distinction, statistics are denoted by symbols which are different from those used to denote corresponding parameters.

In this section we examine the sample counterparts of some of the parameters discussed in Chapter 3. To do this, let us consider the ages of a population of 100 sales representatives employed by the Blueline Business Forms Company. The ages of these 100 salespersons are listed in array in Table 8.1. Serial

Table 8.1 Ages of a Population of 100 Sales Representatives Employed by the Blueline Business Forms Company

Serial Number	Age	Serial Number	Age	Serial Number	Age	Serial Number	Age
00	22	25	33	50	41	75	51
01	22	26	33	51	41	76	51
02	23	27	33	52	41	77	52
03	23	28	34	53	42	78	52
04	24	29	34	54	42	79	52
05	25	30	34	55	42	80	52
06	25	31	34	56	42	81	52
07	26	32	35	57	43	82	53
08	26	33	35	58	43	83	53
09	26	34	36	59	43	84	54
10	27	35	36	60	44	85	54
11	27	36	37	61	44	86	55
12	28	37	37	62	44	87	55
13	28	38	37	63	45	88	55
14	28	39	37	64	45	89	56
15	29	40	38	65	45	90	56
16	29	41	38	66	46	91	57
17	30	42	38	67	47	92	57
18	30	43	38	68	47	93	57
19	31	44	39	69	48	94	57
20	31	45	39	70	48	95	58
21	31	46	39	71	48	96	59
22	32	47	40	72	49	97	60
23	32	48	40	73	50	98	60
24	32	49	41	74	50	99	60

numbers from 00 through 99 have been assigned to the 100 ages in the list. This serialized list of ages provides a frame suitable for sampling from the population.

Suppose that we decide to select a simple random sample of 10 observations from the frame in Table 8.1. To do this, let us read two-digit random numbers starting at the upper left corner of the first page of Table C in Appendix II. Using the first two digits in each row, we obtain the sample shown in Table 8.2.

Table 8.2 Sample of 10 Ages Selected from Population of 100 Salespersons

Selection Order	Random Number	Age
1	70	48
2	38	37
3	51	41
4	33	35
5	98	60
6	11	27
7	06	25
8	66	46
9	49	41
10	22	32

8.3.1 Sample Proportions vs. Population Proportions

In Section 3.1 the proportion (relative frequency) of cases in the ith class of the frequency distribution of a finite population was defined by Formula (3.1):

$$\pi_i = \frac{f_i}{N}$$

where π_i = proportion of cases in the ith class of the population
  f_i = frequency (number of cases) in the ith class
  N = population size
To apply this formula to the ages of the population in Table 8.1, suppose that we partition the population into the following three classes:

Class	Class Limits
1	Under 30
2	30–40
3	Over 40

A tally of the ages in Table 8.1 shows that $f_1 = 17, f_2 = 32,$ and $f_3 = 51$. Then, using Formula (3.1), we obtain the following proportions for the population of 100 observations:

$$\pi_1 = \frac{17}{100} = .17$$

$$\pi_2 = \frac{32}{100} = .32$$

$$\pi_3 = \frac{51}{100} = .51$$

Corresponding to a population proportion, the proportion of cases in the ith class of a sample is defined by the formula

$$p_i = \frac{n_i}{n} \qquad (8.2)$$

where p_i = proportion of cases in the ith class of the sample
$\quad n_i$ = frequency (number of cases) in the ith class
$\quad n$ = sample size

For the same class limits used in computing the population proportions above, a tally of the ages for the sample in Table 8.2 shows that $n_1 = 2$, $n_2 = 3$, and $n_3 = 5$. Then, applying Formula (8.2), we obtain the following proportions for the sample of 10 observations:

$$p_1 = \frac{2}{10} = .20$$

$$p_2 = \frac{3}{10} = .30$$

$$p_3 = \frac{5}{10} = .50$$

8.3.2 Sample Fractiles vs. Population Fractiles

In Section 3.2 the φ fractile of a finite population, denoted by X_φ, was defined as the lowest observed value in the population such that the cumulative proportion corresponding to that value is at least equal to φ. For example, the .50 fractile (median) of the population arrayed in Table 8.2 is $X_{.50} = 41$.

Similarly, the p fractile of a sample, denoted by x_p, is defined as the lowest observed value in the sample such that the cumulative proportion corresponding to that value is at least equal to p. To apply this definition to the sample data in Table 8.2, we must first array the ages in ascending order, as follows:

$$25, \quad 27, \quad 32, \quad 35, \quad 37, \quad 41, \quad 41, \quad 46, \quad 48, \quad 60$$

Now suppose that we wish to determine the .50 fractile of these ages. Since the size of the sample is $n = 10$, a cumulative proportion of .50 corresponds to a cumulative frequency of 5. Thus, the .50 fractile of the sample is $x_{.50} = 37$, which is the value of the 5th case in the array.

8.3.3 Sample Mean vs. Population Mean

In Section 3.3.3 the mean of a finite population was defined by Formula (3.2):

$$\mu = \frac{\sum\limits_{i=1}^{N} x_i}{N}$$

where μ = population mean
$\quad \sum\limits_{i=1}^{N} x_i$ = sum of all observed values in the population
$\quad N$ = population size

For the population of 100 salespersons in Table 8.1, the sum of all the ages is 4,100. Thus, the population mean is

$$\mu = \frac{4,100}{100} = 41.00$$

Analogous to the population mean, the sample mean is defined by the formula

$$\bar{x} = \frac{\sum\limits_{i=1}^{n} x_i}{n} \tag{8.3}$$

where $\bar{x}$ = sample mean

$\sum\limits_{i=1}^{n} x_i$ = sum of all observed values in the sample

$\quad n$ = sample size

As the reader may verify, the sum of the 10 ages for the sample in Table 8.2 is 392. Thus, the mean of the sample is

$$\bar{x} = \frac{392}{10} = 39.20$$

8.3.4 Sample Variance vs. Population Variance

In Section 3.4.4 the variance of a finite population was defined by Formula (3.6):

$$\sigma^2 = \frac{\sum\limits_{i=1}^{N} (x_i - \mu)^2}{N}$$

where $\qquad \sigma^2$ = population variance

$\sum\limits_{i=1}^{N} (x_i - \mu)^2$ = sum of squared deviations of the observed values from the population mean

$\qquad N$ = population size

For the ages of the 100 salespersons in Table 8.1, the sum of the squared deviations is

$$\sum\limits_{i=1}^{N} (x_i - \mu)^2 = \sum\limits_{i=1}^{100} (x_i - 41)^2 = 11,192$$

Then, from Formula (3.6), the population variance is

$$\sigma^2 = \frac{11,192}{100} = 111.92$$

Thus, the population standard deviation is

$$\sigma = \sqrt{111.92} = 10.58$$

Corresponding to the population variance, the sample variance is defined by the formula

$$s^2 = \frac{\sum_{i=1}^{n} (x_i - \bar{x})^2}{n - 1} \tag{8.4}$$

where

s^2 = sample variance

$\sum_{i=1}^{n} (x_i - \bar{x})^2$ = sum of squared deviations of the observed values from the sample mean

n = sample size

Since the denominator in the formula for the variance of a finite population is N, it might naturally occur to the reader that the denominator in the formula for the sample variance should be n. However, in Formula (8.4) the denominator is $(n - 1)$ rather than n. This is because the sample variance is often used to estimate the population variance and for that purpose, the use of $(n - 1)$ is generally preferred to n. The reason for this will be explained in Chapter 15.

Applying Formula (8.4) to the ages of the sample in Table 8.2, the variance of the sample is calculated in Table 8.3. As this table indicates, the sample

Table 8.3 Calculation of the Variance of the Ages of a Sample of 10 Salespersons

x_i	$x_i - \bar{x}$	$(x_i - \bar{x})^2$
48	48 − 39.2 = 8.8	77.44
37	37 − 39.2 = −2.2	4.84
41	41 − 39.2 = 1.8	3.24
35	35 − 39.2 = −4.2	17.64
60	60 − 39.2 = 20.8	432.64
27	27 − 39.2 = −12.2	148.84
25	25 − 39.2 = −14.2	201.64
46	46 − 39.2 = 6.8	46.24
41	41 − 39.2 = 1.8	3.24
32	32 − 39.2 = −7.2	51.84
Sum 392	0	987.60

$$\bar{x} = \frac{\sum_{i=1}^{n} x_i}{n} = \frac{392}{10} = 39.2 \qquad s^2 = \frac{\sum_{i=1}^{n} (x_i - \bar{x})^2}{9} = \frac{987.6}{9} = 109.73$$

variance is $s^2 = 109.73$. Thus, the sample standard deviation is $s = \sqrt{109.73} = 10.48$.

Formula (8.4) provides a clear definition of the sample variance as the average of the squared deviations of the individual observations from the sample mean. However, as is obvious from Table 8.3, it is cumbersome to use because it requires the squaring of every individual deviation. For computational purposes, a more convenient formula for the sample variance is

$$s^2 = \frac{\sum_{i=1}^{n} x_i^2 - n\bar{x}^2}{n - 1} \tag{8.5}$$

As the reader may verify, application of Formula (8.5) to the sample data in Table 8.3 yields

$$s^2 = \frac{16,354 - 10(39.2)^2}{9} = 109.73$$

This result is the same as that obtained from Formula (8.4), since Formula (8.5) is algebraically identical to Formula (8.4).

8.3.5 Summary Comparison of Parameters and Statistics

In the preceding discussion of parameters vs. statistics, we used the example of drawing a simple random sample of 10 salespersons from a finite population of 100 salespersons. In that example, the age of every person in the population was known, so that it was possible to compute the population parameters as well as the corresponding sample statistics. However, as we have previously observed, the purpose of sampling is usually to obtain partial information concerning a population when it is not possible or feasible to observe all the individual elements of the population with respect to particular characteristics of concern. Naturally, under these circumstances, the exact values of the population parameters cannot be calculated. In such situations, sample statistics are commonly used to estimate corresponding population parameters.

When a statistic obtained from a sample is used to estimate a parameter of a population, such an estimate ordinarily will be more or less in error. This is because the sample is merely a subset of the population, and the value of any statistic depends on the values of the particular elements that happen to be drawn at random into the sample. For our example of salespersons' ages, Table 8.4 shows that every one of the statistics computed from the sample differs

Table 8.4 Population Parameters and Corresponding Sample Statistics

	Parameter	*Statistic*
Proportions	$\pi_1 = .17$	$p_1 = .20$
	$\pi_2 = .32$	$p_2 = .30$
	$\pi_3 = .51$	$p_3 = .50$
Median (.50 fractile)	$X_{.50} = 41$	$x_{.50} = 37$
Mean	$\mu = 41.00$	$\bar{x} = 39.20$
Variance	$\sigma^2 = 111.92$	$s^2 = 109.73$
Standard deviation	$\sigma = 10.58$	$s = 10.48$

somewhat from its corresponding population parameter. For instance, if we did not know that the value of the population mean was 41.00, and if we used the sample mean of 39.20 to estimate the unknown population mean, our estimate would be in error by $39.20 - 41.00 = -1.80$. That is, we would underestimate the population mean by 1.80 years.

In actual situations where a sample statistic is used to estimate a population parameter, the exact value of the parameter is unknown. Thus, the amount of the error of estimation cannot be determined precisely. However, if an estimate is to be used for making practical decisions, it is important to be able to evaluate the possible amount of error of estimation. To do this requires an understanding of how the chance mechanism of random sampling affects the value of a statistic. It is through such understanding of the probabilistic behavior of statistics that we are able to apply the methods of statistical inference to draw conclusions about a population parameter on the basis of partial information obtained from a sample. Chapter 9 provides an introduction to this complex topic.

PROBLEMS

8.1 Distinguish between:
- (a) Probability sampling and nonprobability sampling
- (b) Simple random sampling and restricted random sampling
- (c) Stratified sampling and quota sampling
- (d) Cluster sampling and chunk sampling

8.2 Discuss the procedure you would follow if you wished to select a simple random sample of 50 apartments from the 1,000 apartments in an urban housing project.

8.3 Discuss the procedure you would follow if you wished to take a systematic sample of 100 stock issues from the population of all issues listed on the New York Stock Exchange.

8.4 As a feature of its 2-hour Early Bird News program, which is broadcast between 7 : 00 and 9 : 00 each morning, radio station KXYX asks its listeners to telephone the station and state their opinion on the Burning Question of the Day. After the program ends at 9 : 00, the responses are classified and tabulated so that they can be reported on the following morning's program.
- (a) Identify the population from which this sample was selected. Is this a finite or infinite population?
- (b) Is this a probability sample? Discuss.

8.5 The personnel manager of the Hoople Corporation is undecided whether to hold the company's annual Family Day Picnic at Playland Park or Breakers Beach. To help decide, he surveys a random sample of 80 employees. The results of the survey showed that 48 of the employees preferred Playland Park, 24 preferred Breakers Beach, and 8 had no opinion. What proportion of the sample:
- (a) Preferred Playland Park?
- (b) Preferred Breakers Beach?
- (c) Had no opinion?

8.6 In an investments study, a securities analyst selects a simple random sample of 200 common stocks from the population of all common stocks currently listed by *The Value Line Investment Survey*. Of the stocks in the sample, 13 were bank stocks, 9 were grocery stocks, and 28 were electric utility stocks. What proportion of the sample are bank stocks? Grocery stocks? Electrical utility stocks?

8.7 As part of an ongoing personnel research program, the personnel director of the Steadfast Insurance Company administered the Cronkite Clerical Aptitude test to a sample of 20 clerk typists. The test scores obtained from the sample are as follows:

77	87	51	27	83
41	63	63	64	35
81	59	64	24	15
62	87	50	46	93

Determine the following fractiles for this sample of scores:
- (a) $x_{.25}$
- (b) $x_{.50}$
- (c) $x_{.70}$
- (d) $x_{.90}$

8.8 In a study conducted by the County Housing Authority in the township of Lotus Falls, a sample of 25 dwelling units was observed. The ages of these dwelling units (in years) are as follows:

43	49	71	68	1
18	64	2	52	42
15	53	1	43	43
39	61	70	24	47
71	11	54	31	6

Determine the following fractiles for the sample of ages of dwelling units:

(a) $x_{.20}$ (c) $x_{.05}$ (e) $x_{.95}$

(b) $x_{.50}$ (d) $x_{.01}$ (f) $x_{.99}$

8.9 Consider the brand-preference responses of the population of 50 consumers listed in Table 2.4.

(a) Entering Table C of Appendix II at any randomly chosen point, select a simple random sample of 10 respondents from the population.

(b) From the results of the sample obtained in part (a), prepare a table showing the frequency and relative frequency for each brand preference.

(c) What is the sample proportion preferring brand A? brand B? brand C? brand D?

(d) Compare the relative frequencies obtained in part (b) with the corresponding relative frequencies in Table 2.6. How do you account for the fact that these two relative frequency distributions do not agree exactly?

8.10 Consider the numbers of children in the population of 60 households listed in Table 2.7.

(a) Entering Table C (Appendix II) at any randomly chosen point, select a simple random sample of 20 households from the population.

(b) From the results of the sample obtained in part (a), prepare a table showing the frequency and relative frequency for each number of children.

(c) What is the sample proportion of households with no children? 1 child? 2 children? 3 children? 4 children? 5 children?

(d) Compare the relative frequencies obtained in part (b) with the corresponding relative frequencies in column (4) of Table 2.8. Do these two distributions agree exactly? Explain.

8.11 Table 3.3 presents arrayed aptitude test scores for a population of 125 middle managers.

(a) Convert Table 3.3 into a sampling frame by assigning serial numbers from 001 to 125 to the test scores.

(b) Entering Table C (Appendix II) at any randomly chosen point, select a simple random sample of 20 test scores from the population.

(c) From the results of the sample obtained in part (b), prepare a relative frequency distribution, using the class limits 5–14, 15–24, . . . , 65–74.

(d) Compare the relative frequencies obtained in part (c) with the corresponding relative frequencies in Table 3.2. How do you account for the fact that these two relative frequency distributions do not agree exactly?

8.12 During the month of July, Redwing Airlines had 512 Jumbo Jet flights departing from Los Angeles International Airport. A marketing research analyst selects a random sample of 20 of these flights. The "idle capacity" (number of empty seats) for each of these flights is shown below:

27	14	47	29	62
42	0	26	53	15
16	36	9	22	94
13	81	38	44	12

(a) Compute the mean idle capacity for the sample.

(b) Using Formula (8.4), compute the sample variance.

(c) To confirm your result in part (b), compute the sample variance using Formula (8.5).

(d) Determine the sample standard deviation.

8.13 A quality control engineer selects a sample of 24 cans of Bel Ami cleansing powder as they come off the production line. The net weights (to the nearest $\frac{1}{10}$ ounce) are as follows:

13.8	13.9	14.0	14.0	14.0	14.1
13.7	13.9	14.4	14.2	14.1	14.5
14.6	14.5	14.0	13.9	14.0	14.9
14.9	14.0	14.7	14.3	14.0	14.4

(a) Compute the mean net weight of the cans in the sample.
(b) Using Formula (8.4), compute the sample variance.
(c) To confirm your result in part (b), compute the sample variance using Formula (8.5).
(d) Determine the sample standard deviation.

8.14 In a study of tax-paying behavior, a research analyst for the State Tax Board selects a sample of 10 individual state income tax returns. To the nearest dollar, the final amount on each of these returns is shown as follows (a positive value indicates a tax collectible, and a negative value indicates a refund payable):

$$
\begin{array}{ccccc}
519 & -34 & 13 & -62 & 97 \\
176 & 42 & -197 & -114 & -540
\end{array}
$$

(a) Compute the mean amount due for the sample.
(b) Using Formula (8.4), compute the sample variance.
(c) To confirm your result in part (b), compute the sample variance using Formula (8.5).

8.15 In a pilot study conducted to test a proposed questionnaire for a nationwide consumer survey, the Madison Marketing Research Agency interviewed a sample of 25 female customers shopping in a supermarket. Among the items on the questionnaire were the following questions:

Do you read a daily newspaper regularly?

About how many hours do you watch TV in a typical week?

As a rule, about how many times a month do you attend the movies?

The responses of the women to the questions are as follows:

Respondent Number	Read Newspaper	Hours of TV	Times at Movies
1	Yes	12	1
2	No	15	3
3	No	18	2
4	Yes	10	0
5	Yes	6	5
6	No	20	5
7	No	3	1
8	No	14	4
9	Yes	0	3
10	No	35	1
11	No	24	0
12	Yes	8	2
13	Yes	12	5
14	No	19	3
15	Yes	25	3
16	No	16	3
17	No	0	5
18	No	16	5
19	Yes	28	0
20	No	30	1
21	Yes	12	5
22	Yes	16	4
23	No	20	0
24	No	5	1
25	Yes	18	2

(a) What proportion of the women in the sample read a daily newspaper regularly?

(b) Let X denote the number of times that a respondent in the sample attends the movies in a month. Determine $x_{.25}$, $x_{.50}$, and $x_{.75}$. How do you interpret each of these values?

(c) What is the median number hours per week that the women in the sample watch TV? How do you interpret this figure?

(d) Determine the mean, variance, and standard deviation of the number of times per month that the respondents in the sample attend the movies.

(e) Determine the mean, variance, and standard deviation of the number of hours per week that the women in the sample watch TV.

8.16 Referring to Problem 8.15, answer the following:

(a) Identify the population from which this sample was selected. Is this population finite or infinite?

(b) Is this sample a probability sample? Explain.

8.17 The following table lists the balance (rounded to the nearest dollar) of each of the 100 delinquent accounts of the J. C. Nickle Department Store:

80	12	80	59	42	149	61	21	84	67
99	28	72	23	68	63	125	53	85	18
26	33	93	82	81	77	77	63	44	39
82	42	145	34	16	38	63	28	55	54
19	30	23	17	21	41	52	76	24	50
41	98	164	73	138	96	59	75	99	48
157	28	98	35	84	89	71	64	20	14
98	45	56	55	28	66	90	53	88	41
89	67	90	16	84	35	51	72	26	75
42	13	80	141	105	132	64	56	72	88

(a) Convert the table to a sampling frame by assigning serial numbers from 00 to 99 to the balances listed in the table.

(b) Entering Table C (Appendix II) at any randomly chosen point, select a simple random sample of 10 balances.

(c) From the results of the sample obtained in part (b), compute the following statistics:
  (i) Sample proportion of balances less than $50
  (ii) .50 fractile
  (iii) .80 fractile
  (iv) Sample mean
  (v) Sample variance
  (vi) Sample standard deviation

8.18 In Section 8.3 a simple random sample of 10 ages was selected from the sampling frame in Table 8.2. For that purpose we began reading random numbers at the *upper left* corner of the first page of Table C (Appendix II). To demonstrate how the chance mechanism of random sampling affects the values of statistics, repeat this sampling experiment as follows:

(a) Select a different sample of 10 observations from the frame in Table 8.2 by reading two-digit random numbers starting at the *upper right* corner of the first page of Table C. Read the last two digits at the far right of each row.

(b) From the results of the sample obtained in part (a), compute the following statistics:
  (i) Proportion of the sample with ages under 30, with ages between 30 and 40 inclusive, and with ages over 40
  (ii) Sample median
  (iii) Sample mean
  (iv) Sample variance
  (v) Sample standard deviation

(c) Compare the statistics obtained in part (b) with the corresponding statistics given in Table 8.5 for the previous sample taken from the same population. How do you account for the similarities and differences between these two sets of statistics?

9

Discrete Sampling Distributions

As we observed in Chapter 8, the value of a statistic depends on the particular elements that happen to be drawn into the sample. Thus, the value of a statistic cannot be determined until the sample has actually been selected and observed. Hence, before the sample is observed, a statistic is a random variable. The probability distribution of a statistic when its value is yet to be determined is called the *sampling distribution* of the statistic. A clear comprehension of the concept of a sampling distribution is crucial to understanding the methods of statistical inference and decision making. In this chapter we consider the general concept of a discrete sampling distribution in detail, and then examine some particular discrete sampling distributions that are most commonly used.

9.1 BASIC CONCEPT OF A SAMPLING DISTRIBUTION

To illustrate the basic concept of a sampling distribution, let us consider a box containing 10 transistors, of which four are defective and six are good. We may regard this set of 10 transistors as a finite population. The elements comprising this population are listed in Table 9.1, in which d represents a defective transistor and g denotes a good transistor.

Table 9.1 Finite Population of 10 Transistors

Element	A	B	C	D	E	F	G	H	I	J
Quality	g	d	g	g	d	g	d	d	g	g

Suppose that we plan to take a simple random sample of two elements from the population of 10 elements in Table 9.1. This sampling experiment will be conducted "without replacement" in the sense that once an element has been selected, it is removed from the population so that it will not be available to be selected a second time. Thus, for our proposed sampling experiment, the outcomes $(A, A), (B, B), \ldots, (J, J)$ are impossible. All possible outcomes of the sampling experiment, expressed as ordered pairs, are shown in the sample space presented in Figure 9.1. By counting the ordered pairs in Figure 9.1, we can see that the sample space contains 90 sample points. Using Formula (4.8) to verify this count of the sample points, the total number of possible ways of selecting two elements in order from a set of 10 elements is

$$_{10}P_2 = \frac{10!}{8!} = 90$$

Since the elements B, E, G, and H are defectives, whereas A, C, D, F, I, and J are good, the number of defectives in the sample of two items will depend on the particular pair of elements that happen to be drawn into the sample. In other words, referring to the sample space in Figure 9.1, the particular ordered pair that happens to occur will determine the number of defectives in the sample. For instance, if the ordered pair (A, B) is selected, with the resulting sequence gd (one good item followed by one defective), the sample will contain one defective. Similarly, if the ordered pair (B, G) is selected, with the resulting sequence dd (one defective followed by another defective), the sample will contain two defectives. The number of defectives corresponding to each of the 90 possible ordered pairs is given in Figure 9.2. As shown in this figure, the number of defectives in the sample will be 0, 1, or 2, depending on the particular ordered pair that happens to be drawn at random.

When the sampling experiment is completed, the number of defectives in the sample will be known. That is, once the sample has been drawn and the resulting ordered pair has been observed, the number of defectives can actually be counted. However, until the sample actually has been observed, this number is unknown and hence is a random variable.

As we already have observed, the possible values of the number of defectives

Second Element Selected

	A	B	C	D	E	F	G	H	I	J
A	–	(A, B)	(A, C)	(A, D)	(A, E)	(A, F)	(A, G)	(A, H)	(A, I)	(A, J)
B	(B, A)	–	(B, C)	(B, D)	(B, E)	(B, F)	(B, G)	(B, H)	(B, I)	(B, J)
C	(C, A)	(C, B)	–	(C, D)	(C, E)	(C, F)	(C, G)	(C, H)	(C, I)	(C, J)
D	(D, A)	(D, B)	(D, C)	–	(D, E)	(D, F)	(D, G)	(D, H)	(D, I)	(D, J)
E	(E, A)	(E, B)	(E, C)	(E, D)	–	(E, F)	(E, G)	(E, H)	(E, I)	(E, J)
F	(F, A)	(F, B)	(F, C)	(F, D)	(F, E)	–	(F, G)	(F, H)	(F, I)	(F, J)
G	(G, A)	(G, B)	(G, C)	(G, D)	(G, E)	(G, F)	–	(G, H)	(G, I)	(G, J)
H	(H, A)	(H, B)	(H, C)	(H, D)	(H, E)	(H, F)	(H, G)	–	(H, I)	(H, J)
I	(I, A)	(I, B)	(I, C)	(I, D)	(I, E)	(I, F)	(I, G)	(I, H)	–	(I, J)
J	(J, A)	(J, B)	(J, C)	(J, D)	(J, E)	(J, F)	(J, G)	(J, H)	(J, I)	–

(First Element Selected — row label on left side)

Figure 9.1 Sample Space for Selecting a Sample of Two Elements from a Population of 10 Elements

Discrete Sampling Distributions

	Second Element Selected									
	A	B	C	D	E	F	G	H	I	J
	(g)	(d)	(g)	(g)	(d)	(g)	(d)	(d)	(g)	(g)
A (g)	—	1	0	0	1	0	1	1	0	0
B (d)	1	—	1	1	2	1	2	2	1	1
C (g)	0	1	—	0	1	0	1	1	0	0
D (g)	0	1	0	—	1	0	1	1	0	0
E (d)	1	2	1	1	—	1	2	2	1	1
F (g)	0	1	0	0	1	—	1	1	0	0
G (d)	1	2	1	1	2	1	—	2	1	1
H (d)	1	2	1	1	2	1	2	—	1	1
I (g)	0	1	0	0	1	0	1	1	—	0
J (g)	0	1	0	0	1	0	1	1	0	—

(Row label: First Element Selected)

Figure 9.2 Number of Defectives Corresponding to Each Sample Point

in the sample of two items are 0, 1, and 2. Thus, if we let the random variable R denote the number of defectives in the sample, the possible values of R are 0, 1, 2. A relevant question at this point is: What is the probability of each of these possible values of R? That is, what is the probability distribution of R?

To answer this question, we begin by listing the possible values of R, as shown in column (1) of Table 9.2. The sequences of good and defective items

Table 9.2 Deriving the Probability Distribution of R

(1) Number of Defectives	(2) Corresponding Sequences	(3) Number of Sample Points	(4) Probability
0	gg	30	$\dfrac{30}{90} = \dfrac{5}{15}$
1	dg gd	48	$\dfrac{48}{90} = \dfrac{8}{15}$
2	dd	12	$\dfrac{12}{90} = \dfrac{2}{15}$
		$\overline{90}$	$\overline{1.0}$

resulting in each of these possible values are shown in column (2) of the table. Column (3) shows the number of sample points corresponding to each of the possible values in column (1). These numbers are obtained by tallying the values in Figure 9.2. Notice that the numbers in column (3) add to 90, the total number of points in the sample space. Since we propose to take a simple random sample, each of the sample points is equally likely to occur. Thus, dividing the number of sample points corresponding to any specific value of R by the total number of sample points, we obtain the probability for that value of R. The resulting probabilities are given in column (4). Thus, there is a probability of 5/15 that the sample will contain no defective, a probability of 8/15 that the sample will contain one defective, and a probability of 2/15 that the sample will contain two defectives.

From Table 9.2 we may observe that (1) the three events $R = 0$, $R = 1$, and $R = 2$ are mutually exclusive and collectively exhaustive, and (2) the probabilities of these three events sum to 1. Thus, these three probabilities constitute the probability distribution of R. This discrete probability distribution is shown graphically in Figure 9.3.

In our example, the random variable R was defined as a quantity to be derived from observing a random sample. Stated more formally, R is a numerically defined function of the outcome of a random sampling experiment. As such, R is a statistic. Since R is a statistic, the probability distribution of R is a sampling distribution.

Like other probability distributions, a sampling distribution can be described in terms of the descriptive measures presented in Chapter 7. For instance, applying Formula (7.2) to our example, the expected value of the statistic R is computed from Table 9.2 as follows:

$$E(R) = \mu = \sum_{\text{all } r} rf(r) = 0\left(\frac{5}{15}\right) + 1\left(\frac{8}{15}\right) + 2\left(\frac{2}{15}\right) = \frac{4}{5}$$

To obtain the variance of the statistic R, we first apply Formula (7.13) to compute

$$E(R^2) = \sum_{\text{all } r} r^2 f(r) = 0^2\left(\frac{5}{15}\right) + 1^2\left(\frac{8}{15}\right) + 2^2\left(\frac{2}{15}\right) = \frac{16}{15}$$

Then, from Formula (7.12), the variance of R is

$$V(R) = E(R^2) - \mu^2 = \frac{16}{15} - \left(\frac{4}{5}\right)^2 = \frac{32}{75}$$

In examining the basic concept of a sampling distribution, we have stressed the notion of a statistic as a random variable. However, the term "statistic" does not always connote a random variable. For example, each of the statistics presented in Chapter 8 was computed from a sample that had already been selected and observed. As such, these statistics were not random variables, since their values had already been determined by the actual outcome of the

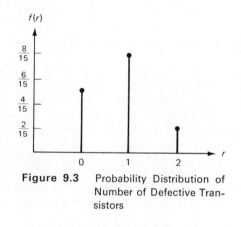

Figure 9.3 Probability Distribution of Number of Defective Transistors

Discrete Sampling Distributions

sampling experiment. Thus, a statistic may or may not be a random variable, depending on whether the sampling outcome actually has been observed. Specifically, before a sample has been observed, a statistic is a random variable, since its value is yet to be determined. Once the sample has been observed, a statistic becomes a known value and is no longer a random variable. In either case, a statistic is a numerically defined function of the outcome of a random sampling experiment. The distinction lies in whether the sampling outcome actually has been observed.

In this section we have used an extremely simple example to illustrate the basic concept of a sampling distribution. Obviously, with larger populations and samples, the derivation of a sampling distribution by constructing a sample space and mapping all its elements into a random variable would be utterly impractical. Fortunately, for many common types of sampling experiments, the desired sampling distributions may be expressed in terms of certain specific mathematical functions. In the remainder of this chapter, we examine some discrete mathematical functions that are frequently used to describe sampling distributions. In Chapter 10 we begin to investigate how the sampling distribution is employed as a key construct in using sample statistics to make inferences about unknown population parameters.

9.2 THE HYPERGEOMETRIC DISTRIBUTION

Many decision problems are concerned with *finite* populations that are *dichotomous*—that is, populations consisting of a definite number of units or elements that may be divided into *two mutually exclusive categories*, such as favorable and unfavorable, defective and nondefective, successes and failures, profits and losses, and so on. Examples of finite dichotomous populations are:

A bin of 1,000 bolts, of which 800 have right-hand threads and 200 have left-hand threads.

A city of 10,000 households, of which 4,000 subscribe to a daily newspaper and 6,000 do not subscribe to a daily newspaper.

A trade association of 600 merchants, of whom 500 favor and 100 do not favor publication of a new trade journal.

In dealing with such populations, we often do not know the actual number of elements in each category. Each of these numbers is a parameter of the population, and we might wish to observe a simple random sample from the population in order to estimate the values of these parameters. If the sampling is conducted without replacement, then the sampling distribution of the number of elements in a given category of the sample is described by the *hypergeometric* distribution.

9.2.1 The Hypergeometric Mass Function

To formalize our presentation of the hypergeometric distribution, consider a sampling situation in which:

1. The population being sampled is:
   a. Finite, in the sense that it consists of a fixed number of elements.
   b. Dichotomous, in the sense that it is composed of two categories, such as "successes" and "failures."
2. A simple random sample is selected without replacement from the population.
3. The random variable of interest is the number of "successes" observed in the sample.

Suppose that we let

$N =$ total number of elements in a finite dichotomous population
$n =$ size of random sample selected from the population
$D =$ number of "successes" in the population
$R =$ number of "successes" that might be observed in the sample

Then the probability mass function of the random variable R is

$$f_h(r \mid N, n, D) = \begin{cases} \dfrac{\dbinom{D}{r}\dbinom{N-D}{n-r}}{\dbinom{N}{n}} & \text{if } r = 0, 1, \ldots, k \\ 0 & \text{otherwise} \end{cases} \qquad (9.1)$$

where k is equal to either n or D, whichever is smaller.

The mathematical function given in Formula (9.1) defines not one, but a family, of hypergeometric distributions, one for each possible combination of values of N, n, and D. Each of these distributions follows the same mathematical rule for assigning probabilities to the possible values of R, but the specific probabilities obtained from the rule depend on the particular values of N, n, and D. Thus, N, n, and D are referred to as the *parameters* of the hypergeometric mass function. It is important to carefully distinguish between the parameters of a function and the parameters of a population. For any given mathematical function that is used to describe a sampling distribution, the parameters of the function may or may not be identical to particular parameters of the population. In the case of the hypergeometric distribution, N and D are parameters of both the function and the population, whereas n is a parameter of the function but not of the population.

In order to apply Formula (9.1) in a specific sampling experiment to determine the probability that the random variable R will have some particular value r, the values of the parameters N, n, and D must be known or somehow specified. In actual sampling experiments that use the hypergeometric distribution, the population size N and the sample size n are usually known. However, the value of D is usually not known and some value must be assumed for it. The basis of specifying this assumed value for D is explained in Chapter 11. Meanwhile, for our present purposes, we assume that the value of D is known.

To illustrate the application of Formula (9.1), let us return to our example of drawing a simple random sample of two transistors from the population of 10 transistors listed in Table 9.1. In this example, we may observe that:

1. The population is finite and dichotomous, since it consists of 10 elements, each of which is classified as either "good" or "defective."
2. A simple random sample is to be drawn without replacement.
3. The random variable of interest is the number of defectives in the sample.

Thus, we have a sampling experiment that satisfies the conditions to which the hypergeometric distribution is applicable. For this experiment, the population size is $N = 10$, the sample size is $n = 2$, and the number of defectives in the population is $D = 4$. Then, using R to denote the number of defectives in the sample, the particular hypergeometric distribution for this situation is:

$$f_h(r \,|\, 10, 2, 4) = \begin{cases} \dfrac{\dbinom{4}{r}\dbinom{10-4}{2-r}}{\dbinom{10}{2}} & \text{if } r = 0, 1, 2 \\[20pt] 0 & \text{otherwise} \end{cases}$$

Applying this formula to obtain the probabilities that $R = 0$, $R = 1$, and $R = 2$, we have

$$P(R = 0) = f_h(0 \,|\, 10, 2, 4) = \frac{\dbinom{4}{0}\dbinom{6}{2}}{\dbinom{10}{2}} = \frac{1 \times 15}{.\ 45} = \frac{5}{15}$$

$$P(R = 1) = f_h(1 \,|\, 10, 2, 4) = \frac{\dbinom{4}{1}\dbinom{6}{1}}{\dbinom{10}{2}} = \frac{4 \times 6}{45} = \frac{8}{15}$$

$$P(R = 2) = f_h(2 \,|\, 10, 2, 4) = \frac{\dbinom{4}{2}\dbinom{6}{0}}{\dbinom{10}{2}} = \frac{6 \times 1}{45} = \frac{2}{15}$$

These probabilities are precisely the same as those obtained in Table 9.2.

Calculation of hypergeometric probabilities can become cumbersome when the values of the parameters of the distribution are large. To relieve the practitioner from the necessity of making any calculations, tabulated values of the hypergeometric function are available.[1] Table D (Appendix II) is abstracted from the hypergeometric tables for $N = 20$.

9.2.2 The Hypergeometric Cumulative Mass Function

The hypergeometric cumulative mass function is given by

$$F_h(r \,|\, N, n, D) = \sum_{t=0}^{r} \frac{\dbinom{D}{t}\dbinom{N-D}{n-t}}{\dbinom{N}{n}} \tag{9.2}$$

Formula (9.2) simply specifies a summation of hypergeometric probabilities. In this formula, t is a dummy variable representing possible values of R, and r represents the upper limit of the summation. Applying this formula to our transistor example, we have

---

[1]G. J. Lieberman and D. B. Owen, *Tables of the Hypergeometric Probability Distribution* (Stanford, Calif.: Stanford University Press, 1961). These tables provide individual and cumulative probabilities for $N = 2, 3, 4, \ldots, 50, 60, 70, 80, 90, 100$, as well as for selected values of N between 100 and 1,000. An appendix provides 15-place logarithms for $1!, 2!, \ldots, 2{,}000!$.

$$P(R \le 0) = F_h(0) = \sum_{t=0}^{0} \frac{\binom{4}{t}\binom{6}{2-t}}{\binom{10}{2}}$$

$$= f_h(0) = \frac{5}{15}$$

$$P(R \le 1) = F_h(1) = \sum_{t=0}^{1} \frac{\binom{4}{t}\binom{6}{2-t}}{\binom{10}{2}}$$

$$= f_h(0) + f_h(1) = \frac{5}{15} + \frac{8}{15} = \frac{13}{15}$$

$$P(R \le 2) = F_h(2) = \sum_{t=0}^{2} \frac{\binom{4}{t}\binom{6}{2-t}}{\binom{10}{2}}$$

$$= f_h(0) + f_h(1) + f_h(2) = \frac{5}{15} + \frac{8}{15} + \frac{2}{15} = 1.0$$

The foregoing cumulative probabilities obtained from Formula (9.2), together with the individual probabilities obtained previously from Formula (9.1), are displayed in Table 9.3.

Table 9.3 Hypergeometric Sampling Distribution
$(N = 10, n = 2, D = 4)$

Number of Defectives in the Sample, r	Individual Probability, $f_h(r)$	Cumulative Probability, $F_h(r)$
0	$\dfrac{5}{15}$	$\dfrac{5}{15}$
1	$\dfrac{8}{15}$	$\dfrac{13}{15}$
2	$\dfrac{2}{15}$	$\dfrac{15}{15}$

9.2.3 Mean and Variance of the Hypergeometric Distribution

In Section 9.1, Formula (7.2) was used to compute the mean of the sampling distribution. By substituting the hypergeometric mass function for the $f(x)$ term in Formula (7.2), it can be shown that the mean of a hypergeometric distribution is

$$\mu = E(R) = n\left(\frac{D}{N}\right) \tag{9.3}$$

This makes it possible to compute the mean of a hypergeometric distribution directly from the parameters of the distribution, without having to make the laborious calculations required when Formula (7.2) is applied directly. Applying Formula (9.3) to the transistor example, we obtain

$$\mu = E(R) = 2\left(\frac{4}{10}\right) = \frac{4}{5}$$

This confirms the result obtained in Section 9.1 through the direct use of Formula (7.2).

Similarly, by using Formula (7.12), the variance of the hypergeometric distribution may be shown to be

$$\sigma^2 = V(R) = n\left(\frac{D}{N}\right)\left(\frac{N-D}{N}\right)\left(\frac{N-n}{N-1}\right) \tag{9.4}$$

For the transistor example, this formula yields

$$\sigma^2 = V(R) = 2\left(\frac{4}{10}\right)\left(\frac{10-4}{10}\right)\left(\frac{10-2}{10-1}\right) = \frac{32}{75}$$

which agrees with the result obtained in Section 9.1 by using Formula (7.12) directly.

9.3 THE BINOMIAL DISTRIBUTION

Our discussion of the hypergeometric distribution was concerned with dichotomous, *finite* populations. Across the spectrum of business activities, however, we encounter types of decision problems that are concerned with dichotomous populations that, rather than being finite, are either *infinite* or so large that they may be considered effectively infinite.

9.3.1 The Bernoulli Process

Consider a dichotomous population composed of elements comprising two mutually exclusive categories that we will identify as "successes" or "failures." Assume that this population is essentially infinite or inexhaustible. Let us propose an experiment in which a random sample of n elements will be drawn from the population, and each element will be observed to determine whether it is a success or a failure. The drawing of each element will be called a "trial" of the experiment. We may refer to the observation resulting from any single trial (that is, whether the observed element is a success or a failure) as the "outcome" of the trial. If we let π represent the probability that an observation on a single trial will be a success, then $(1 - \pi)$ represents the probability that an observation will be a failure. The experiment will be conducted in such a manner that the successive trials are independent, that is, the results of previous trials have no effect on the probability that the next trial will result in a success or a failure. Furthermore, we will require that the value of π remain constant for all trials.

The reader will recognize that our proposed experiment specifies a random process conducted under very particular conditions. A random sampling experiment conducted under such conditions is an example of a *Bernoulli process* (named after Jacques Bernoulli, 1654–1705). A Bernoulli process is a random process in which:

1. Each trial results in one of just two possible outcomes, such as "success" or "failure," "yes" or "no," "good" or "defective," "hit" or "miss," "pass" or "fail," and so on.
2. Each trial is independent of all other trials. That is, on any given trial, the probability of a success is not affected by the outcomes of the previous trials.

3. The probability, π, of the occurrence of an outcome, such as a success, remains constant from trial to trial.

Taking a random sample of n observations from a dichotomous population that is infinite, or effectively infinite, is tantamount to observing n trials of a Bernoulli process. Even if a dichotomous population is finite, the selection of a random sample may be regarded as a Bernoulli process when sampling is conducted with replacement. Under this sampling procedure, after an element has been drawn and observed, it is returned immediately to the population so that it is available to be drawn again. Thus, if sampling is conducted with replacement, the population is inexhaustible and hence may be regarded as infinite from a sampling standpoint.

In practice, many common sampling procedures may be conceptualized essentially as Bernoulli processes. For example, in developing a new missile system, a manufacturer might be interested in test-firing a sample of missiles to estimate the probability that a firing will result in a "hit" on the target under particular conditions. In such a case they would be concerned with an infinite, dichotomous population composed of all possible similar firings, each of which could be classified as either a hit or a miss. If the test firings are conducted in such a way that the probability of a hit is the same for each firing, and if the firings may be considered to represent independent trials, then these trials may be regarded as Bernoulli trials.

As another example, consider a particular state that has several million registered voters. A political analyst might wish, on the basis of interviewing a random sample of 500 of these voters, to estimate the proportions of the total who "favor" or "disfavor" a referendum to be submitted at an upcoming election. In this instance, although the population is technically finite, it is so large (particularly in relation to the sample size) that it may be considered effectively infinite for all practical purposes. We may regard this sampling experiment as a Bernoulli process if we are willing to assume that (1) the survey is conducted in such a manner that the results of the individual interviews are essentially independent, and (2) during the course of conducting the survey, the proportion of voters who favor the referendum remains essentially stable.

9.3.2 The Binomial Mass Function

Suppose that we were to conduct a Bernoulli sampling experiment consisting of n trials. We might then focus our attention on the number, R, of successes that might be observed in the n trials. Then R would be a discrete random variable with the possible values $0, 1, 2, \ldots, n$. For example, suppose that a manufacturer produces items by means of an automatic production process that operates as a Bernoulli process with a .20 defective rate. That is, at any given moment, there is a constant probability of .20 that the next item that is produced will be defective. Furthermore, the defective and good items occur in random sequence such that the probability that the next item will be defective is independent of any preceding sequence of good and defective items. At any given moment we might propose to inspect a sample consisting of the next four items produced by the process, and to count the number of defective items in the sample of four items. In this case, if R represents the number of defective items to be found in the sample, the possible values of R would be 0, 1, 2, 3, 4. Under these conditions we might ask: What is $P(R = 0)$? $P(R = 1)$? $P(R = 2)$? $P(R = 3)$? $P(R = 4)$?

If we let d represent a defective item and g represent a good item, the probability that $R = 0$ is the probability of obtaining the sequence $gggg$. If the probability of obtaining a d at any point in the sequence is .20, then the probability of obtaining a g at any point in the sequence is .80. Furthermore, the successive events in the sequence are independent. Thus, the probability of the sequence $gggg$ is $(.80)(.80)(.80)(.80) = (.80)^4 = .4096$, which is $P(R = 0)$.

The probability that $R = 1$ is the probability of obtaining any of the sequences $dggg, gdgg, ggdg, gggd$. Because of the independence of the elements in the sequence, each of these sequences (composed of one d and three g's in some order) has the same probability; namely $(.20)(.80)^3 = .1024$. Since there are four possible sequences, each with a probability of .1024, we have $4(.1024) = .4096$, which is $P(R = 1)$. Probabilities for the other possible values of R are obtained in a similar manner. The computations are summarized in Table 9.4.

Table 9.4 Probability Distribution of Number of Defectives in a Bernoulli Sample ($n = 4$, $\pi = .20$)

Number of Defectives in the Sample, r	Possible Sequences	Probabilities
0	$gggg$	$(.80)^4 =$ .4096
1	$dggg, gdgg, ggdg, gggd$	$4(.20)(.80)^3 =$ .4096
2	$ddgg, dgdg, dggd, gddg,$ $gdgd, ggdd$	$6(.20)^2(.80)^2 =$ .1536
3	$dddg, ddgd, dgdd, gddd$	$4(.20)^3(.80) =$ .0256
4	$dddd$	$(.20)^4 =$ .0016
		1.0000

By abstracting the procedure employed in Table 9.4, we may arrive at a probability function that will derive the sampling distribution of the number of successes in a given number of Bernoulli trials. For this purpose, let

$\pi =$ probability of a success on a single Bernoulli trial

$n =$ number of Bernoulli trials

$R =$ number of successes in the n trials

Then the probability mass function of the random variable R is

$$f_b(R \mid n, \pi) = \begin{cases} \binom{n}{r} \pi^r (1 - \pi)^{n-r} & \text{if } r = 0, 1, \ldots, n \\ 0 & \text{otherwise} \end{cases} \qquad (9.5)$$

where $0 < \pi < 1$ and $n = 1, 2, \ldots$. The function given in Formula (9.5) is known as the *binomial* distribution, with parameters n and π.

Formula (9.5) gives the probability of obtaining r successes and $(n - r)$ failures in n Bernoulli trials. To understand this formula, we may first observe that the term $\pi^r(1 - \pi)^{n-r}$ represents the probability of any single sequence of r successes and $(n - r)$ failures. Thus, to obtain the total probability of r successes and $(n - r)$ failures for all possible sequences, we must multiply the probability of a single sequence by the total number of equiprobable sequences.

The reader may recognize that the number of possible sequences is equal to the number of distinct permutations of two kinds of objects when there are r objects of one kind and $(n - r)$ objects of the other kind. From Formula (4.7), this number of permutations is equal to $n!/r!(n - r)!$. As pointed out in Section 4.5, this expression is identical to the number of combinations of r objects selected from a set of n objects. Because of this mathematical identity, it is common practice, for notational convenience, to use the term $\binom{n}{r}$ to specify the operation $n!/r!(n - r)!$ in the binomial distribution. The term $\binom{n}{r}$ sometimes is referred to as the *binomial coefficient*. Binomial coefficients for selected values of n and r are tabulated in Table B of Appendix II.

For our production process example, the sample size (number of Bernoulli trials) is $n = 4$, and the defective rate of the process is $\pi = .20$. Then, using R to denote the number of defectives in the sample, the particular binomial distribution for this situation is

$$f_b(r\,|\,4, .20) = \begin{cases} \binom{4}{r}(.20)^r(.80)^{4-r} & \text{if } r = 0, 1, 2, 3, 4 \\ 0 & \text{otherwise} \end{cases}$$

As this function indicates, the possible values of R in this case are 0, 1, 2, 3, 4. The probabilities for these possible values are obtained from the function as follows:

$$P(R = 0) = f_b(0\,|\,4, .20) = \binom{4}{0}(.20)^0(.80)^4 = (1)(1)(.4096) = .4096$$

$$P(R = 1) = f_b(1\,|\,4, .20) = \binom{4}{1}(.20)^1(.80)^3 = (4)(.20)(.512) = .4096$$

$$P(R = 2) = f_b(2\,|\,4, .20) = \binom{4}{2}(.20)^2(.80)^2 = (6)(.04)(.64) = .1536$$

$$P(R = 3) = f_b(3\,|\,4, .20) = \binom{4}{3}(.20)^3(.80)^1 = (4)(.008)(.80) = .0256$$

$$P(R = 4) = f_b(4\,|\,4, .20) = \binom{4}{4}(.20)^4(.80)^0 = (1)(.0016)(1) = .0016$$

These are the same results obtained in Table 9.4.

9.3.3 The Binomial Cumulative Mass Function

The binomial cumulative mass function is given by

$$F_b(r\,|\,n, \pi) = \sum_{t=0}^{r} \binom{n}{t}\pi^t(1 - \pi)^{n-t} \tag{9.6}$$

Formula (9.6) simply specifies a summation of individual binomial probabilities. In this summation, the dummy variable t represents possible values of r, taken in ascending order, and r represents the upper limit of the summation. Applying this formula to our example, we obtain

$$P(R \leq 0) = F_b(0) = \sum_{t=0}^{0} \binom{4}{t}(.20)^t(.80)^{4-t}$$
$$= f_b(0) = .4096$$

$$P(R \leq 1) = F_b(1) = \sum_{t=0}^{1} \binom{4}{t}(.20)^t(.80)^{4-t}$$
$$= f_b(0) + f_o(1) = .4096 + .4096 = .8192$$

$$P(R \leq 2) = F_b(2) = \sum_{t=0}^{2} \binom{4}{t}(.20)^t(.80)^{4-t}$$
$$= f_b(0) + f_b(1) + f_b(2) = .4096 + .4096 + .1536 = .9728$$

$$P(R \leq 3) = F_b(3) = \sum_{t=0}^{3} \binom{4}{t}(.20)^t(.80)^{4-t}$$
$$= f_b(0) + f_b(1) + f_b(2) + f_b(3)$$
$$= .4096 + .4096 + .1536 + .0256 = .9984$$

$$P(R \leq 4) = F_b(4) = \sum_{t=0}^{4} \binom{4}{t}(.20)^t(.80)^{4-t}$$
$$= f_b(0) + f_b(1) + f_b(2) + f_b(3) + f_b(4)$$
$$= .4096 + .4096 + .1536 + .0256 + .0016 = 1.000$$

Table 9.5 summarizes the results obtained from Formulas (9.5) and (9.6).

Table 9.5   Binomial Sampling Distribution ($n = 4$, $\pi = .20$)

Number of Defectives in the Sample, r	Individual Probability, $f_b(r)$	Cumulative Probability, $F_b(r)$
0	.4096	.4096
1	.4096	.8192
2	.1536	.9728
3	.0256	.9984
4	.0016	1.0000

9.3.4   The Use of Binomial Tables

Although Formulas (9.5) and (9.6) provide mathematical definitions of the binomial mass function and binomial cumulative mass function, they are seldom required for actual computational purposes, since binomial tables are readily available.[2] Tables E and F of Appendix II contain individual and cumulative binomial probabilities for selected values of n and π. The following examples illustrate the use of these tables.

---

[2]Two of the most extensive volumes of binomial tables are:

1. National Bureau of Standards, *Tables of the Binomial Probability Distribution* (Washington, D.C.: U.S. Government Printing Office, 1949; corrected reprint, 1952). These tables provide binomial probabilities for $n = 2, 3, \ldots, 49$ and for $p = .01, .02, \ldots, .50$.
2. Harry G. Romig, *50–100 Binomial Tables* (New York: John Wiley & Sons, Inc., 1953). These tables provide binomial probabilities for $n = 50, 51, \ldots, 100$, and for p ranging from .001 to .90.

Example 1 :

Suppose that one month before a senatorial election in a large state, 50% of the voters are still undecided concerning which candidate they favor. From the roster of registered voters, a pollster selects a random sample of 50 voters to be interviewed.

1. What is the probability that, of the 50 voters in the sample, exactly 20 will be undecided? For all practical purposes, we are dealing with an effectively infinite, dichotomous population composed of "decided" and "undecided" voters. Thus, drawing a random sample of 50 cases from this population may be conceived essentially as a Bernoulli process. Therefore, the desired probability, $P(R = 20 | n = 50, \pi = .50)$, is given by the binomial expression

$$f_b(20 | 50, .50) = \binom{50}{20}(.50)^{20}(.50)^{30}$$

Rather than carrying out the computations specified by this expression, we may obtain the desired probability directly from Table E. Entering this table with $n = 50$, $\pi = .50$, and $r = 20$, we find the answer equal to .0419.

2. What is the probability that the sample of 50 voters will contain 20 or less undecided? In this case, the desired probability, $P(R \leq 20 | n = 50, \pi = .50)$, is given by the binomial cumulative expression

$$F_b(20 | 50, .50) = \sum_{t=0}^{20} \binom{50}{t} (.50)^t(.50)^{50-t}$$

We may avoid the computations indicated in this expression by using Table F. Entering this table with $n = 50$, $\pi = .50$, and $R = 20$, we find that $F_b(20) = .1013$.

Example 2 :

Assume that a production line operates as a Bernoulli process with a 10% defective rate.

1. If a sample of 20 items is to be taken from the production output, what is the probability that the sample will contain between three and five defectives inclusive? Symbolically, the probability we desire is given by the expression

$$P(3 \leq R \leq 5 | n = 20, \pi = .10) = F_b(5 | 20, .10) - F_b(2 | 20, .10)$$

With $n = 20$ and $\pi = .10$, Table F indicates that $F_b(5) = .9887$ and $F_b(2) = .6769$. Then our answer is

$$F_b(5) - F_b(2) = .9887 - .6769 = .3118$$

2. If a sample of 15 items is to be taken from the output of the process, what is the probability that it will contain four or more defectives? The probability we wish to find is given by the expression

$$P(R \geq 4 | n = 15, \pi = .10) = 1 - F_b(3 | 15, .10)$$

Table F indicates that $F_b(3) = .9444$, so our answer is $1 - .9444 = .0556$.

9.3.5 The Mean and Variance of the Binomial Distribution

From the individual probabilities in Table 9.5 we may calculate the mean and variance of the binomial distribution with $n = 4$, $\pi = .20$. Applying Formula (7.2) to compute the mean of the distribution, we obtain

$$\mu = E(R) = 0(.4096) + 1(.4096) + 2(.1536) + 3(.0256) + 4(.0016) = .80$$

To obtain the variance of the distribution by using Formula (7.12), we first compute

$$E(R^2) = [.4096(0^2) + .4096(1^2) + .1536(2^2) + .0256(3^2) + .0016(4^2)] = 1.28$$

Then the variance is

$$\sigma^2 = V(R) = E(R^2) - \mu^2 = 1.28 - (.80)^2 = .64$$

By substituting the binomial mass function for the $f(x)$ term in Formula (7.2), it can be shown that the mean of the binomial distribution is

$$\mu = E(R) = n\pi \tag{9.7}$$

For example, for the binomial distribution in Table 9.5, in which $n = 4$ and $\pi = .20$, we obtain

$$E(R) = \mu = 4(.20) = .80$$

which is the same result we obtained previously from applying Formula (7.2).

Similarly, by using Formula (7.12), the variance of a binomially distributed random variable R can be shown to be

$$\sigma^2 = V(R) = n\pi(1 - \pi) \tag{9.8}$$

For the binomial distribution in Table 9.5, Formula (9.8) gives

$$V(R) = 4(.20)(.80) = .64$$

which agrees with the result we obtained from Formula (7.12). In certain applications, we find it useful to recognize that, as the square root of the variance, the standard deviation of a binomially distributed random variable is given by

$$\sigma = \sqrt{n\pi(1 - \pi)} \tag{9.9}$$

Application of this formula yields

$$\sigma = \sqrt{4(.20)(.80)} = \sqrt{.64} = .80$$

9.4 THE POISSON DISTRIBUTION

In our discussion of the binomial distribution, we conceptualized a Bernoulli process as one involving a series of discrete trials, each of which would result in one of the two possible outcomes—success or failure. We consider next a different kind of random process, which differs from a Bernoulli process in two important respects:

1. Rather than consisting of discrete trials, the process operates continuously over some given amount of time, distance, area, or volume.
2. Rather than producing a sequence of successes and failures, the process simply produces successes, which occur at random points in the specified time, distance, area, or volume. These successes are commonly referrred to as "occurrences."

Visualize, for example, a manufacturing process that produces a continuous flow of yard-wide textile. As the yardage flows from the process, burls will occur at random points. Here we can count the number of burls that occur in a given length of the textile, but we cannot count the number of burls that do not occur. As another example, consider the occurrence of machine breakdowns in a manufacturing plant. Over some continuous period of time, such as a week, machine breakdowns may occur at random points in that time interval. For a given week it is possible to count the number of breakdowns that occurred, but it is meaningless to ask how many breakdowns did not occur. To further clarify this type of random process, additional examples are listed below:

1. *Occurrences of an event in a unit of time*
   a. Telephone calls received in an hour at an office switchboard
   b. Articles received in a day at an airline's lost and found office
   c. Auto accidents in a month at a busy intersection
   d. Deaths due to a rare disease in a month
   e. Service calls required in a month for a copying machine
   f. Arrivals of depositors at a bank in an hour on Monday morning

2. *Occurrences of an event in a unit of distance*
   a. Defects occurring in 50 yards of insulated wire
   b. Deaths occurring in 10,000 passenger-miles
   c. Tire repairs for a truck in 1,000 miles traveled on the road

3. *Occurrences of an event in a given area*
   a. Surface blemishes in a square foot of a synthetic wall covering
   b. Burls per square yard of woolen textile
   c. Bacteria on a square centimeter of a culture plate

4. *Occurrences of an event in a given volume*
   a. White cells in a cubic centimeter of blood
   b. Hydrogen atoms in a cubic light-year of intergalactic space
   c. Bacteria in a quart of pasteurized milk

9.4.1 Characteristics of the Poisson Process

Over the years, it has been found that many phenomena, such as those listed above, occur as a *Poisson process*. The Poisson process derives its name from Siméon Denis Poisson (1781–1840), a French mathematician. As a random process that produces successes at random points in some continuous unit of time or space, the Poisson process has the following general characteristics:

1. The number of occurrences of a phenomenon in a unit of any specified size is independent of the number of occurrences in any other unit. Suppose in a large city, for example, that the monthly number of newly detected cases of gout occurs as a Poisson process. Then the probability of the occurrence of any given number of newly detected cases during a particular month would not be affected by the number of newly detected cases in any other month.

2. The mean number of occurrences of the phenomenon in a unit of specified size is proportional to the size of the unit. Suppose that sales of a particular item occur at a mean rate of two sales per day. Then there would be a mean rate of six sales for an interval of 3 days, or a mean rate of ten sales for an interval of 5 days.

3. The probability of two or more occurrences of the phenomenon in an infinitesimal (extremely small) unit is negligible. For example, if incoming calls arrive at a telephone switchboard according to a Poisson process at an average rate of 2 calls per minute, any number of calls may arrive during the course of a 1-minute interval, but it is assumed that there is an essentially zero probability that more than one call would arrive during any given split second.

4. The probability of a single occurrence in an infinitesimal unit remains constant from one such unit to another. For example, if there is a .001 probability that a call will arrive at a switchboard during any given split second, that probability remains constant for every split second.

9.4.2 The Poisson Mass Function

It should be emphasized that the occurrences of a phenomenon in a unit of time or space need not necessarily behave as a Poisson process. However, if such occurrences possess the characteristics listed in the preceding section, then the probabilistic behavior of the number of occurrences in a specified unit of time or space is described by the Poisson distribution. If we let R denote the number of occurrences of a phenomenon that is generated by a Poisson process in a specified number of units of time or space, the probability mass function of R is given by

$$f_P(r \mid \lambda, t) = \begin{cases} \dfrac{(\lambda t)^r e^{-\lambda t}}{r!} & \text{if } r = 0, 1, 2, \dots \\ 0 & \text{otherwise} \end{cases} \qquad (9.10)$$

where e = a constant, the natural logarithm base, approximately equal to 2.7183

λ = average rate of occurrence of the phenomenon in a single unit of time or space

t = number of contiguous units of time or space under consideration

The reader may recognize that λ and t are the parameters of the Poisson distribution. The distribution given in Formula (9.10) can be derived mathematically from the statement of the characteristics of the Poisson process in the preceding section. However, this same function was originally formulated by Poisson as a limiting form of the binomial function as n approaches infinity and π approaches zero. As such, the Poisson distribution has been associated with phenomena that can be described as "rare events." That is, for a given segment of time or space there usually will be few, if any, occurrences of such an event, although there is the possibility, with small probability, that there may be a very large number of occurrences of the event.

As a probability mass function, Formula (9.10) gives the probability of r occurrences of a phenomenon in t units of time or space when the mean number of occurrences in a single unit is λ. To illustrate the use of this formula, consider a manufacturing process that produces steel wire. Flaws occur in this wire as a Poisson process with a mean rate of $\lambda = .2$ flaw per yard. If a 10-yard length of this wire is taken from the output of the process, and the total number of flaws is counted, what is the probability that there will be a total of no flaws, one flaw, two flaws, and so on?

To answer this question, we need simply to apply Formula (9.10), computing $f(r)$ for $r = 0, r = 1, r = 2$, and so on, until we reach a value of R for which $f(r)$ is so negligibly small that it is essentially zero for all practical purposes. We have noted that, for this production process, the mean rate of occurrence is $\lambda = .2$ flaw per yard. However, our sample consists of $t = 10$ yards. Therefore, the mean rate of occurrence in a 10-yard length of wire is $\lambda t = (.2)(10) = 2$ flaws. The calculations to obtain the desired probabilities are shown in Table 9.6.

Table 9.6 Poisson Mass Function for Number of Flaws in 10 Yards of Wire $(\lambda = .2, t = 10)$

Number of Flaws, r					Probability, $f(r)$		
0	$\dfrac{2^0}{0!}e^{-2}$	=		$\dfrac{1}{1}(.135335)$	=	.1353
1	$\dfrac{2^1}{1!}e^{-2}$	=		$\dfrac{2}{1}(.135335)$	=	.2707
2	$\dfrac{2^2}{2!}e^{-2}$	=		$2(.135335)$	=	.2707
3	$\dfrac{2^3}{3!}e^{-2}$	=		$\dfrac{8}{6}(.135335)$	=	.1804
4	$\dfrac{2^4}{4!}e^{-2}$	=		$\dfrac{16}{24}(.135335)$	=	.0902
5	$\dfrac{2^5}{5!}e^{-2}$	=		$\dfrac{32}{120}(.135335)$	=	.0361
6	$\dfrac{2^6}{6!}e^{-2}$	=		$\dfrac{64}{720}(.135335)$	=	.0120
7	$\dfrac{2^7}{7!}e^{-2}$	=		$\dfrac{128}{5,040}(.135335)$	=	.0034
8	$\dfrac{2^8}{8!}e^{-2}$	=		$\dfrac{256}{40,320}(.135335)$	=	.0009
9	$\dfrac{2^9}{9!}e^{-2}$	=		$\dfrac{512}{362,880}(.135335)$	=	.0002
10	$\dfrac{2^{10}}{10!}e^{-2}$	=		$\dfrac{1,024}{3,628,800}(.135335)$	=	.0000+

The probability distribution presented in Table 9.6 is shown graphically in Figure 9.4. This figure indicates that the distribution is positively skewed. Specifically, the distribution comes to a peak near the low end of the scale, with a long thin tail extending to the right. This positive skewness is typical of the Poisson distribution, indicating that, with extremely small probability, there is

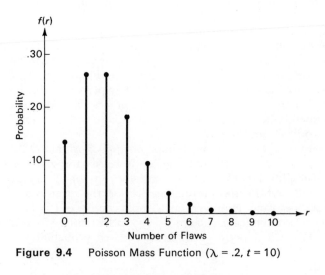

Figure 9.4 Poisson Mass Function $(\lambda = .2, t = 10)$

Discrete Sampling Distributions

the possibility that a Poisson process will produce an indefinitely large number of occurrences in a segment of time or space, even though the mean rate of occurrence may be quite small.

9.4.3 The Poisson Cumulative Mass Function

The Poisson cumulative mass function is given by

$$F_P(r \,|\, \lambda, t) = \sum_{y=0}^{r} \frac{(\lambda t)^y e^{-\lambda t}}{y!} \tag{9.11}$$

As indicated by this formula, the Poisson cumulative mass function is simply a summation of individual terms of the Poisson mass function. This is demonstrated by Table 9.7, which displays the individual terms determined in Table

Table 9.7 Poisson Sampling Distribution ($\lambda = .2$, $t = 10$)

Number of Defects in the Sample, r	Individual Probability, $f(r)$	Cumulative Probability, $F(r)$
0	.1353	.1353
1	.2707	.4060
2	.2707	.6767
3	.1804	.8571
4	.0902	.9473
5	.0361	.9834
6	.0120	.9955
7	.0034	.9989
8	.0009	.9998
9	.0002	1.0000
10	.0000	1.0000

9.6 together with the corresponding cumulative terms. For example, the probability that *exactly* three flaws will be observed in a sample of 10 yards of wire is given by the individual term $f_p(3) = .1804$. Correspondingly, the probability of observing *three flaws or less* is given by the cumulative term

$$
\begin{aligned}
F_P(3 \,|\, .2, 10) &= \sum_{y=0}^{3} \frac{2^y e^{-2}}{y!} \\
&= f_P(0 \,|\, .2, 10) + f_P(1 \,|\, .2, 10) + f_P(2 \,|\, .2, 10) + f_P(3 \,|\, .2, 10) \\
&= .1353 + .2707 + .1804 = .8571
\end{aligned}
$$

9.4.4 The Use of Poisson Tables

Formulas (9.10) and (9.11) are useful for explaining the Poisson distribution and are sometimes necessary for actually calculating Poisson probabilities. For most practical purposes, however, Poisson probabilities are obtained from tables such as Tables G (individual terms) and H (cumulative terms) of Appendix II.[3] The following examples illustrate the use of these tables.

---

[3]For more extensive tables, see E. C. Molina, *Poisson's Exponential Binomial Limit* (Princeton, N.J.: D. Van Nostrand, 1949).

Example 1 :

A manufacturer of vinyl wall covering has found that, with respect to surface blemishes, his manufacturing process operates as a Poisson process with an average of $\lambda = .2$ blemish per square foot of manufactured material. Periodically, a 1-square-yard sample of the material is inspected.

1. What is the probability that a sample will contain exactly two blemishes? Since there are 9 square feet in 1 square yard, $\lambda t = 0.2 \times 9 = 1.8$. Then, from Table G, $P(R = 2 \mid \lambda t = 1.8) = f_P(2) = .2678$.

2. What is the probability that a sample will contain two or less blemishes? From Table H, $P(R \leq 2 \mid \lambda t = 1.8) = F_P(2) = .7306$.

3. What is the probability that a sample will contain at least two blemishes? From Table H, $P(R \leq 1 \mid \lambda t = 1.8) = F_P(1) = .4628$. Thus,

$$P(R \geq 2 \mid \lambda t = 1.8) = 1 - P(R \leq 1 \mid \lambda t = 1.8)$$
$$= 1 - F_P(1) = 1 - .4628 = .5372$$

Example 2 :

During peak hours, calls arrive at a switchboard according to a Poisson process with an average of $\lambda = 90$ calls per hour.

1. During a given 10-minute period during the peak hours, what is the probability of receiving at least 12 calls? Since a 10-minute period is $\frac{1}{6}$ hour, $\lambda t = 90 \times \frac{1}{6} = 15$. Then, using Table H, $P(R \geq 12) \mid \lambda t = 10) = 1 - P(R \leq 11 \mid \lambda t = 15) = 1 - .1848 = .8152$.

2. During a given 5-minute period, what is the probability of receiving at least three but no more than seven calls? Since a 5-minute period is $\frac{1}{12}$ hour, $\lambda t = 90 \times \frac{1}{12} = 7.5$. Then, using Table H, we obtain

$$P(3 \leq R \leq 7 \mid \lambda t = 7.5) = P(R \leq 7 \mid \lambda t = 7.5) - P(R \leq 2 \mid \lambda t = 2.5)$$
$$= F_P(7) - F_P(2)$$
$$= .5246 - .0203$$
$$= .5043$$

9.4.5 The Mean and Variance of the Poisson Distribution

If a random variable R has a Poisson distribution given by Formula (9.10), then the mean can be shown to be

$$\mu = E(R) = \lambda t \qquad (9.12)$$

It can be shown that the variance is

$$\sigma^2 = V(R) = \lambda t \qquad (9.13)$$

It is significant that the mean and the variance are equal. This is a unique feature of the Poisson distribution.

PROBLEMS

9.1 The Franklin Electrical Products Company produces fuses that are packaged in boxes each containing 8 fuses. A housewife purchases a box of these fuses, unaware that the box actually contains 3 defective fuses and only 5 good fuses, as shown below:

Fuse	Quality
A	d
B	g
C	g
D	d
E	g
F	d
G	g
H	g

The housewife has immediate need for only 2 fuses, which she plans to take from the box at random. Considering the housewife's selection of 2 fuses from the box of 8 fuses as a random sampling experiment, determine the sampling distribution of the number of defectives in the sample of 2 fuses by performing the following steps:

(a) Construct a diagram similar to Figure 9.1, showing the sample space of the experiment.

(b) Construct a diagram similar to Figure 9.2, showing the number of defectives corresponding to each sample point in part (a).

(c) Using the results of part (b), derive the sampling distribution of the number of defectives in the sample by constructing a table similar to Table 9.2.

(d) Graph the sampling distribution obtained in part (c).

(e) By direct application of Formula (9.1), confirm the probabilities obtained in part (c).

(f) Explain why it is appropriate to use Formula (9.1) to describe the sampling distribution in this situation.

9.2 Section 9.1 presented a derivation of the sampling distribution for the number of defectives in a simple random sample of 2 transistors selected from a finite population consisting of 4 defective transistors and 6 good transistors. For that particular sampling experiment, it was assumed that sampling would be conducted *without replacement*. Now assume that this sampling experiment is to be conducted *with replacement*.

(a) Construct the sample space of the experiment.

(b) Construct a diagram showing the number of defectives corresponding to each sample point in part (a).

(c) By using the results of part (b), derive the sampling distribution of the number of defectives in the sample by constructing a table similar to Table 9.2.

(d) Graph the sampling distribution obtained in part (c).

(e) By direct application of Formula (9.5), confirm the probabilities obtained in part (c).

(f) Explain why it is appropriate to use Formula (9.5) to describe the sampling distribution in this situation.

(g) Prepare a table showing, for each possible value of the random variable, the difference between the probability obtained in Section 9.1 and that obtained in part (c). Explain why these probabilities differ.

9.3 A box contains 20 bolts with left-hand threads and 30 with right-hand threads. A sample of 10 bolts is drawn at random from the box. What is the probability that the sample will contain at least 2 bolts with left-hand threads if:

(a) Sampling is conducted without replacement?

(b) Sampling is conducted with replacement?

9.4 Certain missile components are shipped in lots of 12. Three components are selected without replacement from each lot, and a particular lot is accepted if none of the 3 components selected is defective.

(a) What is the probability that a lot will be accepted if it contains 5 defectives?

(b) What is the probability that a lot will be rejected if it contains 9 defectives?

(c) Let R be a random variable denoting the number of defectives in a sample of 3 components selected randomly from a lot. If the lot contains 4 defectives, specify the sampling distribution of R (1) as a mathematical expression, and (2) in the form of a table.

(d)   Under the conditions stated in part (c), what is the expected number of defectives in a sample of 3 components?

9.5   An electronics firm purchases a particular component in lots of 50. As a routine acceptance sampling procedure, a random sample of 5 components is selected without replacement, from each lot. After a sample is inspected, the lot is rejected if the sample contains at least 2 defectives.

(a)   If a particular lot contains 4 defectives, what is the probability that exactly 2 defectives will be found in the sample?

(b)   If a lot contains 6 defectives, what is the probability that the sampling and inspection procedure will result in rejection of the lot?

(c)   If R is a random variable denoting the number of defectives in a random sample of 5 items, and if a lot contains 4 defectives, specify the sampling distribution of R (1) as a mathematical expression, and (2) in the form of a table.

(d)   Determine the mean and variance of the random variable R in part (c).

9.6   With respect to quality of output ("defective" vs. "good" items), a particular production process operates as a Bernoulli process, with a long-run defective rate of .10. Suppose that a sample of 5 items is selected from the output of the process, and each of the 5 items is inspected. Let R be a random variable denoting the number of defectives in the sample.

(a)   What is the probability that $R = 3$?
(b)   What is the probability that $R \leq 3$?
(c)   What is the probability that $R < 3$?
(d)   What is the probability that $R \geq 3$?
(e)   What is the probability that $R > 3$?
(f)   What is the probability that $R \neq 3$?

9.7   The Zoomite Corporation has just accepted shipment on a new automatic machine that functions as a Bernoulli process. Anxious to try out the machine, the production manager decides to produce a sample of 10 items. Because the machine has not been adjusted, he does not know the defective rate, π, of the process. What is the probability that there will be 3 or more defectives in the sample if:

(a) $\pi = .05$?
(b) $\pi = .10$?
(c) $\pi = .20$?
(d) $\pi = .25$?

9.8   A personnel manager is in the process of designing a multiple-choice examination as an aid in screening applicants. She plans to use 20 questions, each to contain 1 correct and 3 incorrect answers. She has raised the following questions about the reliability of the examination:

(a)   If an applicant guesses on every question, what is the probability of getting 5 or more answers correct?

(b)   How many right answers should be required to ensure that the chance of an applicant obtaining that score or higher from pure guessing is approximately .10?

(c)   What is the probability of obtaining a score of 8 by pure guessing?

(d)   What is the probability of an applicant obtaining a score of 6 or less on the basis of random guessing?

9.9   If 40% of the voters in a large state favor candidate A, what is the probability that, in a random sample of 20 voters interviewed by a pollster, the majority will favor him?

9.10   In a large metropolitan county, 50% of the registered voters are Democrats, and 40% of the registered voters are men. Assume that political affiliation is independent of sex. If 5 registered voters are selected at random, what is the probability that the group will contain at least 3 Democrats and at least 4 men?

9.11 The Betty Drucker Food Corp. is recruiting housewives for its cake-mix testing panel. For this purpose it has devised the following test of the candidates' ability to discriminate. Each applicant is presented with 4 cakes, 3 of them baked from mix A and one from mix B. The applicant is to identify the cake from mix B. This procedure is repeated 10 times, and the passing score is 7 or more correct choices.

(a) If a housewife cannot discriminate but guesses each time, what is the probability that she will be admitted to the panel?

(b) Let R be a random variable denoting the number of correct choices in the 10 trials. Assuming that a housewife cannot discriminate between the two mixes, specify the sampling distribution of R (1) in terms of a mathematical function, and (2) in the form of a table.

(c) Determine the mean and standard deviation of the random variable R in part (b).

9.12 A study by the Blacksky Oil Company reveals that there is an independent probability of .10 that any given offshore well will develop a leak when it is drilled. It is also determined that, within the drilling regulations, this probability is constant from well to well. If Blacksky is allowed to drill 18 wells:

(a) What is the probability that none of the wells will leak?

(b) What is the probability that between 4 and 6 wells inclusive will develop leaks?

(c) If Blacksky makes a profit of $2 million on each well that does not leak, and loses $5 million on each well that does leak, what is the expected profit from drilling the 18 wells?

9.13 A particular textile is produced in continuous rolls. Burls in the material occur according to a Poisson process at an average rate of 20 burls per 100 linear feet. If a 10-foot length of textile is cut from the roll, what is the probability that it will contain:

(a) Exactly 2 burls?

(b) At least 2 burls?

(c) Less than 2 burls?

(d) More than 2 burls?

(e) No more than 2 burls?

9.14 Industrial accidents commonly occur according to a Poisson process, so that the Poisson distribution is of particular interest to insurance actuaries. Suppose, for instance, that fatal accidents associated with a particular hazardous occupation occur at a rate of .0072 per man-year on the average. If a company insures 1,000 such employees for a given year, what is the probability that it will have to meet at least 10 fatality claims?

9.15 Suppose that the number of calls arriving at a company's switchboard during a 5-minute span has a Poisson distribution with $\lambda = 5.2$.

(a) What is the probability that there will be exactly 4 incoming calls during such a 5-minute span?

(b) What is the probability that there will be at most 4 calls?

(c) What is the probability that there will be at least 4 calls?

(d) Should the sum of the probability in parts (b) and (c) be equal to 1? Explain.

9.16 A telephone switchboard handles 600 calls, on an average, during a rush hour. The board can make a maximum of 20 connections per minute. Use the Poisson distribution to evaluate the probability that the board will be overtaxed during any given minute.

9.17 In a large manufacturing plant, machinists arrive at a tool crib for service at a mean rate of 1.5 arrivals per 5-minute period. It is reasonable to assume that these arrivals occur according to a Poisson process.

(a) What is the probability that exactly 3 machinists will arrive during a specified 5-minute period?

(b) What is the probability that no more than 2 machinists will arrive during a specified 1-minute period?

(c) What is the probability that at least 4 machinists will arrive during a specified 15-minute period?

(d) What is the expected number of arrivals in a 10-minute period?

(e)   In this particular situation, what specific assumptions are made if the occurrence of the arrivals is regarded as a Poisson process?

(f)   If R denotes the number of arrivals in a 20-minute period, write a mathematical expression for the sampling distribution of R.

9.18   Knotholes in a particular kind of pine siding occur according to a Poisson process at a mean rate of 1.4 knotholes per board-foot.

(a)   What is the probability that 2 board-feet of this siding will contain exactly 3 knotholes?

(b)   What is the probability that 10 board-feet of this siding will contain less than 15 knotholes?

(c)   What is the probability that 5 board-feet of this siding will contain at least 8 knotholes?

(d)   What is the expected number of knotholes in 10 board-feet of this siding?

(e)   What is the variance of the number of knotholes in 10 board-feet of this siding? What is the standard deviation?

(f)   If R denotes the number of knotholes in 8 board-feet of this siding, write a mathematical expression for the sampling distribution of R.

9.19   The Kitcheneze Manufacturing Company produces enamel kitchen utensils. One of the best-selling items produced by the firm is a 2-quart enamel-coated sauce pan. With respect to surface blemishes, the manufacturing process may be described by the Poisson model with a mean rate of 3.9 blemishes per pan.

(a)   What is the probability that 1 of these sauce pans will have no more than 5 surface blemishes?

(b)   A customer purchases 6 of these sauce pans. What is the probability that exactly 3 of these pans will each have no more than 5 surface blemishes?

(c)   For the customer in part (b), what is the probability that no more than 3 of the 6 sauce pans will each have no more than 5 surface blemishes?

10

The Hypothesis-Testing Approach
to Two-Action Decision Problems

In Chapter 9 we saw how the logical construct of a sampling distribution can be used to make probabilistic statements about different possible sample results when sampling from a known population. This process of deriving statements about an unknown sample taken from a known population is an example of *deduction*—the logical procedure of reasoning from the general to the particular. From a practical standpoint, however, the purpose of sampling is to use the known results of a particular sample to draw conclusions about the unknown population from which the sample was drawn. As we noted in Chapter 1, this process of making generalizations about an unknown population on the basis of known sample results is called *statistical inference*. The process of statistical inference is an example of *induction*—the logical procedure of reasoning from the particular to the general. In this chapter we begin to study this inductive process.

10.1 TWO-ACTION DECISION PROBLEMS

In Chapter 1 we described a statistical decision problem as one in which there are two or more alternative courses of action whose possible consequences depend upon two or more possible states of nature. Also, we referred to the set of all alternative acts as the *action space*, and the set of all possible states of nature as the *state space*. Many practical decision problems involve a choice between just two alternative courses of action. For example, an industrial buyer might have to decide whether to purchase or not to purchase a batch of assembly parts offered by a producer. Or a marketing manager might have to decide whether to introduce or not to introduce a proposed new product into the market. Or a financial manager might have to decide whether to raise additional funds by issuing stock or issuing bonds.

Although the action space for a two-action decision problem contains only two elements, the number of elements in the state space may be very large or even infinite. In many decision problems, the possible states of nature are expressed in terms of the possible values of a population parameter. When this is the case, the state space is referred to as the *parameter space*.

10.2 FORMULATING HYPOTHESES

One approach to two-action decision problems is a form of statistical inference called *hypothesis testing*. In applying hypothesis testing to a two-action decision problem, the first step is to identify explicitly the action space and the state space. Once this is done, the next step is to partition the state space into two complementary subsets such that one action is preferred if the true state of nature belongs to one subset and the alternative course of action is preferred if the true state of nature belongs to the other subset.

To illustrate the partitioning process, consider the case of George Jones, a successful real estate investor. George holds an option to purchase a large tract of rural land adjacent to a growing town. This land has excellent potential for profitable development if the county will build adequate access roads in the near future. Whether or not such roads will be built depends on the outcome of a countywide bond referendum that will be held in 4 weeks. George's option to buy the land expires in 2 weeks, and he must therefore make his decision regarding the purchase before the outcome of the referendum is known. In this decision situation, George has two alternative courses of action available—either to exercise the option of buying the land or to let the option drop. These alternative actions constitute the action space. The consequence resulting from either of the two actions depends on the proportion of the voters who vote in favor of the bond issue. This proportion is a parameter of the population of persons who will vote in the referendum. Denoting this parameter by π, the parameter space of this decision problem is the set of all possible values between 0 and 1. In set notation, this parameter space may be expressed as $\{\pi \,|\, 0 \leq \pi \leq 1\}$. The bond issue will pass if $\pi > .50$, whereas the bond issue will fail if $\pi \leq .50$. If George exercises the option and the bond issue passes, he anticipates a profit of \$10,000 on his investment; but if the bond issue fails, he will be forced to dispose of the land at a loss of \$4,000. Thus, he should exercise the option if $\pi > .50$, but he should let the option drop if $\pi \leq .50$. George is therefore critically concerned with whether the true value of π (that is, the actual outcome of the referendum) will fall in the subset $\{\pi \,|\, \pi > .50\}$ or in the subset $\{\pi \,|\, \pi \leq .50\}$. These two complementary subsets form a partition of the parameter space.

Since George does not know the actual value of π, he does not know which of the two statements "$\pi > .50$" and "$\pi \leq .50$" is true. Thus, he can only regard these two statements as alternative *propositions* concerning the unknown state of nature. In statistical terminology, such alternative propositions concerning the state of nature are called *hypotheses*. Because George must make his decision before the actual value of π is known, it will be necessary for him to act *as if* one hypothesis or the other is true. Specifically, if he assumes that $\pi > .50$, he will exercise the option; however, if he assumes that $\pi \leq .50$, he will drop the option. Hence, making his decision concerning the option is tantamount to making a choice between the two hypotheses. The hypothesis-testing approach is a procedure whereby the choice between the two hypotheses is made on the basis of evidence obtained by sampling from the population under consideration.

To apply the hypothesis-testing approach, it is necessary to designate one of the two propositions as the *null hypothesis* and the other proposition as the *alternative hypothesis*. This designation is based on the principle that *the decision maker will act as if the null hypothesis is true unless the sample yields overwhelming evidence against the null hypothesis.* If the sample evidence is overwhelmingly against the null hypothesis, the decision maker will act as if the alternative hypothesis is true. Thus, the hypotheses are formulated in such a way that the "burden of proof" is placed upon the alternative hypothesis. The null hypothesis will be rejected in favor of the alternative hypothesis only in the face of convincing evidence favoring the alternative hypothesis. If the null hypothesis is not rejected, the decision maker may either act as if the null hypothesis were true or reserve judgment until additional evidence is obtained.

Because he has limited capital, George is particularly concerned with the risk of suffering the $4,000 loss that he will incur if he exercises the option and the bond issue fails. Therefore, his position is that he will act as if the bond issue will fail ($\pi \leq .50$) unless the sample provides overwhelming evidence against this proposition. Thus, the proposition that $\pi \leq .50$ should be specified as George's null hypothesis, and the complementary proposition that $\pi > .50$ should be specified as his alternative hypothesis. Using H_0 to denote the null hypothesis and H_1 to denote the alternative hypothesis, we may explicitly designate George's hypotheses as follows:

$$H_0: \quad \pi \leq .50$$
$$H_1: \quad \pi > .50$$

Since George is particularly concerned with the risk of losing $4,000 if he exercises the option and the bond issue fails, he feels that he cannot tolerate more than a .10 probability of committing this error. This probability represents the chance of incorrectly rejecting the null hypothesis if actually the null hypothesis happens to be true. In hypothesis testing, the *maximum* tolerable probability of incorrectly rejecting the null hypothesis if actually the null hypothesis is true is called the *level of significance* of the test. The level of significance is denoted by α_{max}. Thus, for George's decision problem, $\alpha_{max} = .10$.

10.3 SPECIFYING THE DECISION RULE

To obtain the evidence on which he will choose between the two hypotheses, George decides to allocate a modest budget to hire a local research firm to poll a random sample of 100 voters from the population of over 1,000,000 registered voters in the county. Each voter in the sample will be contacted at his or her residence and interviewed to determine whether he or she is "in favor" or "not in favor" of the bond issue. The results will then be tallied to determine the value of R, the number of persons in the sample who are in favor of the issue. The reader may recognize that the proposed survey is essentially a Bernoulli sampling experiment since it involves observing a simple random sample taken from a population that (1) is dichotomous if we assume there are no "undecideds" so that each voter in the population is either "in favor" or "not in favor" of the bond issue, and (2) is large enough to be considered effectively infinite. Since the survey may be regarded as a Bernoulli sampling experiment, the sampling distribution of R is a binomial distribution. The domain of this sampling distribution is $\{r \mid r = 0, 1, \ldots, 100\}$, which is the set of all possible values of R.

To determine which possible values of R will constitute overwhelming evidence against the null hypothesis, we begin by recalling that the null hypothesis is H_0: $\pi \leq .50$ and the alternative hypothesis is H_1: $\pi > .50$. Thus, a relatively small proportion of favorable responses in the sample will tend to support H_0, whereas a relatively large proportion of favorable responses in the sample will tend to support H_1. This is equivalent to saying that a relatively small value of R will tend to support H_0, and a relatively large value of R will tend to support H_1. Thus, relatively large values of R—that is, those possible values of R which are so large that they are very unlikely to occur if H_0 actually is true—will constitute overwhelming evidence against H_0. In other words, the null hypothesis will be rejected if the actual value of R obtained from the survey is at least as large as some *critical value* such that, if the null hypothesis should be true, the probability of obtaining such a sample result would be small. More specifically, using c to denote this critical value, the probability

$$P(R \geq c \,|\, H_0 \text{ is true})$$

should be no larger than the level of significance specified by the decision maker. Recalling that George's significance level is $\alpha_{max} = .10$, the desired value of c is that value which satisfies the expression

$$P(R \geq c \,|\, \pi \leq .50) \leq .10$$

In order to use a binomial sampling distribution to solve the foregoing expression for c, we must specify a single value, rather than a range of values, for π. For this purpose, the value selected for π is the *limiting value* in the null hypothesis that $\pi \leq .50$. Using the limiting value of $\pi = .50$ guarantees that the probability of George's incorrectly rejecting the null hypothesis will not exceed .10, regardless of what the specific value of π actually might be. Thus, the sampling distribution for George's decision problems is the binomial distribution with $n = 100$ and $\pi = .50$. Hence, the foregoing expression for obtaining the value of c may be stated more specifically as

$$P(R \geq c \,|\, n = 100, \pi = .50) \leq .10$$

To make use of cumulative binomial tables, this expression may be converted to

$$1 - F_b(c - 1 \,|\, n = 100, \pi = .50) \leq .10$$

It then follows that

$$F_b(c - 1 \,|\, n = 100, \pi = .50) \geq .90$$

Entering Table F of Appendix II for $n = 100$, we search the column under $\pi = .50$, looking for a cumulative probability that is as close as possible to .90 without being less than .90. The tabulated value that meets this specification is $F_b(56) = .9033$. Since $F_b(c - 1) = F_b(56)$, it follows that $(c - 1) = 56$. Consequently, the desired value of c is 57. Thus, the null hypothesis will be rejected if the actual value of R obtained from the survey is equal to or greater than 57. Conversely, the null hypothesis will be accepted if the actual value of R is less than 57.

In effect, the rule to reject H_0 if the obtained value of R is at least 57, and to accept H_0 if the obtained value of R is less than 57, partitions the domain of the sampling distribution of R into two complementary subsets, called the *rejection region* and the *acceptance region*. The null hypothesis will be rejected if the actual sample result happens to be one of the values contained in the rejection region, and the null hypothesis will be accepted if the actual sample result happens to be one of the values contained in the acceptance region. Recalling that the domain of the sampling distribution is the set $\{r \mid r = 0, 1, \ldots, 100\}$, the rejection region is the subset $\{r \mid r = 57, 58, \ldots, 100\}$ and the acceptance region is the subset $\{r \mid r = 0, 1, \ldots, 56\}$. This partition of the sampling distribution of R is illustrated in Figure 10.1.

Having identified the rejection and acceptance regions, we can now examine how George should use the results of the survey to make his decision. If the number of favorable responses in the survey is a value in the rejection region, George should reject H_0 and act as if H_1 is true; that is, he should exercise his option to buy the land. However, if the number of favorable responses in the survey is a value in the acceptance region, he should accept H_0 and act as if H_0 is true; that is, he should let the option drop. Thus, we may state the following rule for George to follow: If the value of R, the number of favorable responses in the sample is equal to or greater than 57, reject H_0 and accordingly exercise the option; otherwise, accept H_0 and accordingly drop the option. Because of the relationship between R and values of the sample proportion P, this rule may alternatively be stated in the following form: If the value of P, the proportion of favorable responses in the sample, is equal to or greater than .57, reject H_0 and accordingly exercise the option; otherwise, accept H_0 and accordingly drop the option.

In hypothesis testing, the rule for choosing between H_0 and H_1 may be regarded as a strategy for testing the validity or tenability of the null hypothesis. Regardless of whether the rule for George's decision is stated in terms of R or P, the essential fact remains that the choice prescribed by the rule depends on the value of a statistic. A statistic such as R or P, which serves as the basis of a rule for choosing between H_0 and H_1, is called a *test statistic*. The rule itself, which indicates, for each possible value of the test statistic, whether to accept or reject the null hypothesis, is referred to as the *decision rule*. The heart of hypothesis testing is in the design of the decision rule.

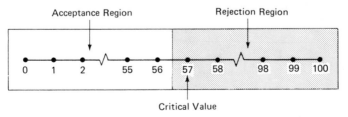

Figure 10.1 Partition of the Domain of the Sampling Distribution of R into Acceptance and Rejection Regions

10.4 EVALUATING THE DECISION RULE

We have seen that George Jones' decision rule is a strategy for choice based on the value of the statistic R. Since a statistic provides only partial information obtained from a mere sample, use of the decision rule does not completely guarantee that George will necessarily make the correct decision. That is, the decision rule can lead George to make either a correct or incorrect decision, since the actual value of R obtained from the sample may fall in either the acceptance or rejection region, regardless of what the true value of π might be. Specifically:

1. If $\pi \leq .50$, and if the survey should yield 56 or fewer favorable responses ($R \leq 56$), the decision rule would lead to acceptance of H_0. This acceptance of H_0, given that H_0 is in fact true, would be a *correct* decision.

2. If $\pi \leq .50$, and if the survey should yield 57 or more favorable responses ($R \geq 57$), the decision rule would lead to rejection of H_0. This rejection of H_0, given that H_0 is in fact true, would be an *incorrect* decision.

3. If $\pi > .50$, and if the survey should yield 56 or fewer responses ($R \leq 56$), the decision rule would lead to acceptance of H_0. This acceptance of H_0, given that H_1 is in fact true (that is, given that H_0 is in fact false), would be an *incorrect* decision.

4. If $\pi > .50$, and if the survey should yield 57 or more favorable responses ($R \geq 57$), the decision rule would lead to rejection of H_0. This rejection of H_0, given that H_1 is in fact true (that is, given that H_0 is in fact false), would be a *correct* decision.

10.4.1 Errors of Inference

As we have just observed, there are two ways that George's decision rule can possibly lead him to make an incorrect decision. One way that an incorrect decision can occur is under the circumstance that the null hypothesis actually is true (that is, $\pi \leq .50$), and that the number of favorable responses in the survey happens to fall in the rejection region (that is, $R \geq 57$). This kind of incorrect decision—rejecting the null hypothesis when, in fact, the null hypothesis is true—is called the *Type I error of inference*. The other way that an incorrect decision can occur is under the circumstance that the alternative hypothesis actually is true (that is, $\pi > .50$), and that the number of favorable responses in the survey happens to fall in the acceptance region (that is, $R \leq 56$). This kind of incorrect decision—accepting the null hypothesis when, in fact, the alternative hypothesis is true—is called the *Type II error of inference*. The conditions under which these two types of errors can occur, as well as the conditions under which a correct decision can occur, are summarized in Table 10.1.

Table 10.1 Possible Results of George Jones' Decision Rule

Possible Values of π	Possible Values of R	
	$R \leq 56$	$R \geq 57$
$\pi \leq .50$	Accept H_0 (correct)	Reject H_0 (Type I error)
$\pi > .50$	Accept H_0 (Type II error)	Reject H_0 (correct)

It is extremely important to recognize that the Type I and Type II errors are *conditional* errors. It is only under the condition that the null hypothesis is true that the Type I error can possibly occur, and it is only under the condition that the alternative hypothesis is true that the Type II error can possibly occur. In other words, it is impossible for the Type I error to occur if the alternative hypothesis is true, and it is impossible for the Type II error to occur if the null hypothesis is true.

10.4.2 Probabilities of the Type I and Type II Errors

Because George's decision rule can possibly lead him to make one or the other of two types of error, it is important to evaluate his rule in terms of the probabilities of committing these errors. Since these errors are conditional errors, their probabilities are conditional probabilities.

Probability of the Type I Error. The probability of the Type I error is the conditional probability of rejecting H_0 given that H_0 is true. Denoting the probability of the Type I error by α (lowercase Greek letter alpha), this probability may be expressed as

$$\alpha = P(\text{reject } H_0 \,|\, H_0 \text{ true}) \tag{10.1}$$

Applying this formula to George's decision rule, which specifies rejection of H_0 if $R \geq 57$, the probability of the Type I error under his rule may be expressed specifically as

$$\alpha = P(R \geq 57 \,|\, H_0 \text{ true})$$

Bearing in mind that George's null hypothesis is $H_0 : \pi \leq .50$, this expression may be rewritten as

$$\alpha = P(R \geq 57 \,|\, \pi \leq .50)$$

Thus, the probability of the Type I error for George's decision rule is defined as the conditional probability that $R \geq 57$, given the condition that $\pi \leq .50$. Since George's null hypothesis is true for any possible value of π in the set $\{\pi \,|\, .00 \leq \pi \leq .50\}$, there is no single value of α that can be specified as *the* probability of the Type I error. However, we can consider what the value of α would be for any selected value of π contained in the null hypothesis. For example, if π is specified as .50, then α is obtained from a binomial distribution, with $n = 100$ and $\pi = .50$; as follows:

$$\begin{aligned} \alpha &= P(R \geq 57 \,|\, n = 100, \pi = .50) \\ &= 1 - F_b(56 \,|\, n = 100, \pi = .50) \\ &= 1 - .9033 = .0967 \end{aligned}$$

Using this same procedure, the value of α may be determined for any other possible value of π contained in the null hypothesis. Table 10.2 shows the value of α for each of the selected values $\pi = .40, .41, \ldots, .50$.

Table 10.2 Type I Error Probabilities for George Jones' Decision Rule Given Selected Values of π

π	$\alpha_\pi = P(R \geq 57 \mid n = 100, \pi)$
.40	.0004
.41	.0009
.42	.0018
.43	.0034
.44	.0061
.45	.0106
.46	.0177
.47	.0286
.48	.0444
.49	.0667
.50	.0967

From Table 10.2 it is clear that the value of α for George's decision rule depends on the specific value of π. For instance, α is equal to .0004 if π is specified as .40, whereas α is equal to .0009 if π is specified as .41. Thus, in using α to denote the probability of the Type I error, it is important to indicate the specific value of π used to obtain that particular value of α. This may be done by designating the specific value of π as a subscript of α. Using this subscript notation, we may write $\alpha_{.40} = .0004$, $\alpha_{.41} = .0009$, and so on. The expression "$\alpha_{.40} = .0004$" means that, if the unknown value of π actually is .40, there is a .0004 probability that George's decision rule will lead him to commit the Type I error of incorrectly rejecting H_0. Similarly, since $\alpha_{.41} = .0009$, there is a .0009 probability that the decision rule will lead him to commit the Type I error if π actually is .41.

By direct reference to Table 10.2, we may obtain the values of $\alpha_{.40}, \alpha_{.41}, \ldots, \alpha_{.50}$. Suppose, however, that we wish to obtain some value not shown in the table, such as $\alpha_{.475}$ or $\alpha_{.495}$. Although we can compute the exact values of these probabilities from the binomial probability function, such calculations would be tedious. However, we can readily obtain the approximate values of these probabilities from a chart like Figure 10.2, in which the horizontal axis represents the set of all possible values of π (the parameter space), and the vertical axis represents corresponding values of α. This chart was constructed by plotting the paired values of π and α given in Table 10.2 as discrete points, and then connecting these points to obtain a smooth curve. Reading from this curve, we see that the value of $\alpha_{.475}$ is approximately .035, and the value of $\alpha_{.495}$ is approximately .078.

As shown in Figure 10.2, the Type I error probability curve for George's decision rule ends at $\pi = .50$, which is the limiting value of π contained in the null hypothesis. The curve does not extend beyond $\pi = .50$ since, as we pointed out earlier, the Type I error can occur only if H_0 is true (that is, only if $\pi \leq .50$). At the limiting value of $\pi = .50$, the curve reaches its maximum. Since this maximum error probability is .0967, it is clear that the use of the limiting value of $\pi = .50$ to determine the critical value for the test resulted in a decision rule for which the probability of incorrectly rejecting H_0 does not exceed the significance level of .10, regardless of what the specific value of π

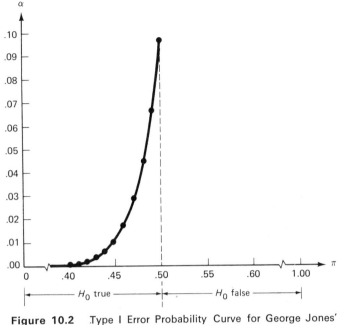

Figure 10.2   Type I Error Probability Curve for George Jones'
Decision Rule

might be. In other words, since the Type I error curve reaches its maximum at the limiting value of the null hypothesis, using this limiting value to determine the decision rule guarantees that the probability of the Type I error will not exceed the level of significance.

Probability of the Type II Error.   Recalling that the Type II error of inference is the error of accepting the null hypothesis when, in fact, the alternative hypothesis is true (that is, the null hypothesis is false), the probability of the Type II error is the conditional probability of accepting H_0 given that H_1 is true (that is, given that H_0 is false). Denoting the probability of the Type II error by β (the lowercase Greek letter beta), this probability may be expressed as

$$\beta = P\,(\text{accept } H_0 \,|\, H_1 \text{ true}) \tag{10.2}$$

Applying this formula to George's decision rule, which specifies acceptance of H_0 if $R \leq 56$, the probability of the Type II error under his rule may be expressed as

$$\beta = P\,(R \leq 56 \,|\, H_1 \text{ true})$$

Bearing in mind that George's alternative hypothesis is $H_1 \colon \ \pi > .50$, this expression may be rewritten as

$$\beta = P\,(R \leq 56 \,|\, \pi > .50)$$

Thus, the probability of the Type II error for George's decision rule is defined as the conditional probability that $R \leq 56$, given the condition that $\pi > .50$.

Since π cannot be greater than 1.00, this condition is satisfied if π is any value in the set $\{\pi \mid .50 < \pi \leq 1.00\}$.

Because George's alternative hypothesis is true for any possible value of π in the set $\{\pi \mid .50 < \pi \leq 1.00\}$, there is no single value of β that can be specified as *the* probability of the Type II error. We can, however, consider what the values of β would be for selected values of π contained in the alternative hypothesis. For instance, if π is specified as .60, then β is obtained from a binomial distribution, with $n = 100$ and $\pi = .60$, as follows:

$$\begin{aligned} \beta &= P(R \leq 56 \mid n = 100, \pi = .60) \\ &= F_b(56 \mid n = 100, \pi = .60) \\ &= .2365 \end{aligned}$$

Using this same procedure, the value of β may be determined for any other possible value of π contained in H_1. Table 10.3 shows the values of β for selected values of π.

Table 10.3 Type II Error Probabilities for George Jones' Decision Rule Given Selected Values of π

π	$\beta_\pi = P(R \leq 56 \mid n = 100, \pi)$	π	$\beta_\pi = P(R \leq 56 \mid n = 100, \pi)$
.50+	.9033−	.60	.2365
.51	.8645	.61	.1778
.52	.8160	.62	.1290
.53	.7580	.63	.0901
.54	.6912	.64	.0605
.55	.6172	.65	.0389
.56	.5385	.66	.0240
.57	.4580	.67	.0141
.58	.3788	.68	.0079
.59	.3041	.69	.0042

Just as the value of α depends on any specific value of π contained in H_0, we see from Table 10.3 that the value of β depends on any specific value of π contained in H_1. Thus, in using β to denote the probability of the Type II error for any specific value of π, we will designate that value of π as a subscript of β. Using this subscript notation, we may write $\beta_{.60} = .2365$, $\beta_{.61} = .1778$, and so on. The expression "$\beta_{.60} = .2365$" means that, if the unknown value of π actually is .60, there is a .2365 probability that George's decision rule will lead him to commit the Type II error of incorrectly accepting H_0.

Using the horizontal axis to represent the possible values of π and the vertical axis to represent the corresponding values of β, we may plot the paired values of π and β given in Table 10.3 to construct the Type II error probability curve shown in Figure 10.3. Such a Type II error probability curve is generally referred to as an *operating characteristic (OC) curve*. The OC curve in Figure 10.3 extends over the domain $\{\pi \mid .50 < \pi \leq 1.00\}$ but does not continue into the domain $\{\pi \mid .00 \leq \pi \leq .50\}$, since the Type II error can possibly occur only if $\pi > .50$ (that is, only if H_1 is true). As the figure shows, the OC curve for George's decision rule rises to its maximum as π approaches the limiting value of .50. For all possible values of π greater than .50, the larger the value of π, the smaller is the value of β.

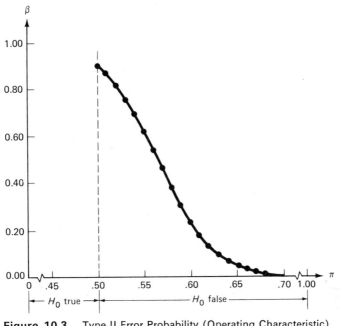

Figure 10.3   Type II Error Probability (Operating Characteristic) Curve for George Jones' Decision Rule

The Error Characteristic Curve.   Since the Type I error is possible only if H_0 is true and the Type II error is possible only if H_1 is true, we may combine the Type I and Type II error probability curves in a single graph, which displays the probabilities of the Type I error for possible values of the parameter contained in H_0 and probabilities of the Type II error for possible values of the parameter contained in H_1. Such a graph is called an *error characteristic curve.* The error characteristic curve for George's decision rule is shown in Figure 10.4.

The error characteristic curve provides a convenient means of comparing the magnitudes of Type I and Type II error probabilities inherent in a given decision rule. From inspection of the error characteristic curve in Figure 10.4, it is clear that the risk of committing the Type I error under George's decision rule is relatively small compared to the risk of committing the Type II error. In other words, the risk of suffering a $4,000 loss by exercising the option when he should let it drop is relatively small compared to the risk of missing the opportunity to make a $10,000 profit by dropping the option when he should pick it up.

10.4.3   The Power Curve

The *power* of a decision rule is defined as the probability that the rule will lead the decision maker to reject the null hypothesis when, in fact, the alternative hypothesis is true (that is, the null hypothesis is false). In terms of a formula

$$\text{Power} = P(\text{reject } H_0 \,|\, H_1 \text{ true}) \tag{10.3}$$

Given the condition that H_1 is true, the probability of rejecting H_0 is the complement of the probability of accepting H_0. Thus,

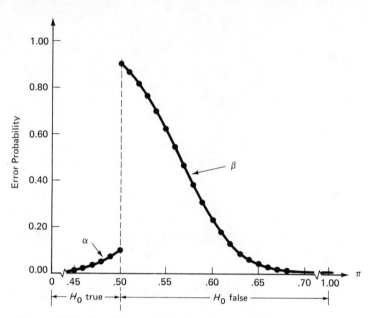

Figure 10.4   Error Characteristic Curve for George Jones' Decision Rule

$$\text{Power} = 1 - P(\text{accept } H_0 \mid H_1 \text{ true})$$

Since $P(\text{accept } H_0 \mid H_1 \text{ true}) = \beta$, it follows that

$$\text{Power} = 1 - \beta \tag{10.4}$$

For George Jones' decision rule, values of β for selected values of π were presented in Table 10.3. Application of Formula (10.4) yields the corresponding power values, which are given in Table 10.4.

Table 10.4   Power of George Jones' Decision Rule for Selected Values of π

π	$1 - \beta_\pi$	π	$1 - \beta_\pi$
.50+	.0967+	.60	.7635
.51	.1355	.61	.8222
.52	.1840	.62	.8710
.53	.2420	.63	.9099
.54	.3088	.64	.9395
.55	.3828	.65	.9611
.56	.4615	.66	.9760
.57	.5420	.67	.9859
.58	.6212	.68	.9921
.59	.6959	.69	.9958

Representing the possible values of π on the horizontal axis, and the corresponding values of $(1 - \beta)$ on the vertical axis, we may plot the values given in Table 10.4 to obtain the curve in Figure 10.5. Such a curve, which shows for

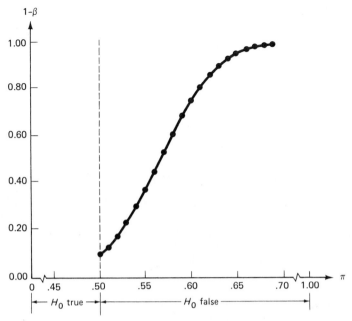

Figure 10.5 Power Curve for George Jones' Decision Rule

every possible value of the parameter contained in H_1 the probability that the rule will lead the decision maker to correctly reject H_0, is called a *power curve*. In contrast to the OC curve, which describes the risk of making a wrong decision if H_1 is true, the power curve describes the probability of making a correct decision if H_1 is true.

10.5 RECAPITULATION

In this chapter we have examined the case of George Jones to introduce and illustrate the basic ingredients of the hypothesis-testing approach to two-action decision problems. Although there are some variations on this approach that will be discussed in later chapters, the general procedure may be summarized in the following 10 steps:

1. *Identify the action space and state space of the decision problem.* This initial step involves explicit identification of the two alternative courses of action and specification of the set of all possible states of nature on which the consequence of the decision will depend.

2. *Partition the state space into two complementary subsets.* This partition is executed in such a way that one of the two available actions is preferred if the true state of nature belongs to one subset, and the other action is preferred if the true state of nature belongs to the complementary subset.

3. *Formulate the null and alternative hypotheses.* The null and alternative hypotheses are complementary propositions concerning the true state of nature. These propositions are expressed in terms of the two complementary subsets obtained in step 2. That is, the null hypothesis is a statement that the true state of nature belongs to one of the subsets of the state space, and the alternative hypothesis is a statement that the true state of nature belongs to the complementary subset. The proposition on which the burden of proof is to be placed is designated as

the alternative hypothesis. This practice is based on the principle that the decision maker will act as if the null hypothesis were true unless the evidence to be obtained from the sample is overwhelmingly against the null hypothesis.

4. *Determine the level of significance for the test.* The level of significance is the maximum probability the decision maker is willing to tolerate that he will be led to incorrectly reject the null hypothesis if actually the null hypothesis is true. Determination of this probability is usually a judgmental task that should be exercised personally by the decision maker.

5. *Specify the sampling experiment.* The decision either to accept or reject the null hypothesis will eventually be made on the basis of evidence obtained from a probability sample. Specification of the exact procedure for obtaining this sample evidence is a necessary step preliminary to determining the appropriate probability distribution that will be used in deriving the decision rule. This step involves a precise specification of the sampling plan and observational procedure to be followed. Usually, the sample size is specified at this step.

6. *Select the test statistic and identify the appropriate sampling distribution.* Since the evidence contained in a sample may be summarized by a variety of statistics, it is necessary to select one particular statistic (the test statistic) in terms of which the decision rule will be formulated. Once the test statistic has been selected, its sampling distribution may be identified by analyzing the specifications of the random sampling experiment determined in step 5.

7. *Partition the domain of the sampling distribution of the test statistic into acceptance and rejection regions.* In this step, the set of all possible values of the test statistic (that is, the domain of the sampling distribution) is partitioned into two complementary subsets. One of these subsets, the rejection region, consists of all those possible values of the test statistic that will lead to rejection of the null hypothesis if any one of them happens to be the value obtained when the sampling experiment is actually conducted. The other subset, the acceptance region, consists of all remaining possible values of the test statistic.

   The rejection region will consist of those values of the test statistic whose probabilities are so small that they are very unlikely to occur if the null hypothesis is true. The rejection region is established in such a way that, under the assumption that the null hypothesis is true, the probability that the actual value of the test statistic will be contained in the rejection region does not exceed the significance level specified by the decision maker. To determine the probability that the actual value of the test statistic will be contained in the rejection region, the parameter(s) of the sampling distribution are established on the assumption that the null hypothesis is true. If the null hypothesis contains a set of values, the limiting value stated in the null hypothesis is used.

8. *State the decision rule explicitly.* Once the acceptance and rejection regions have been established, the decision rule can be stated in straightforward language. This statement of the decision rule clearly indicates, for any possible value of the test statistic, whether the null hypothesis should be accepted or rejected.

9. *Conduct the sampling experiment and compute the value of the test statistic.* The sampling experiment should be conducted strictly according to the specifications established in step 5. The evidence obtained from the sampling experiment is then summarized by computing the test statistic selected in step 6.

10. *Choose a course of action according to the decision rule.* Once the actual value of the test statistic has been computed, direct reference to the decision rule indicates whether the null hypothesis should be accepted or rejected. If the decision rule indicates that the null hypothesis should be accepted, choose that course of action which is preferred if the null hypothesis is true. Otherwise, select that course of action which is preferred if the alternative hypothesis is true.

Using the hypothesis-testing procedure summarized above, it is possible to reduce, but not eliminate, the risk of making a wrong decision. That is, even though additional information is provided by the sampling experiment, the decision still must be made under uncertainty. This is because the sample evidence on which the decision is based provides only partial, rather than complete, information about the unknown state of nature. Hence, before actually following a decision rule, it is prudent to evaluate the decision rule in terms of its error characteristics. The risk of committing the Type I error is measured by α, which is the probability of rejecting the null hypothesis if, in fact, the null hypothesis is true. The risk of committing the Type II error is measured by β, which is the probability of accepting the null hypothesis if, in fact, the alternative hypothesis is true. Of course, $(1 - \alpha)$ is the probability of correctly accepting a true null hypothesis, and $(1 - \beta)$ is the probability of correctly rejecting a false null hypothesis. If any of the error probabilities is greater than the decision maker feels he can tolerate, it may be possible to improve this situation by revising the specifications of the sampling experiment in some manner, such as increasing the sample size. However, the reduction of the risks inherent in a decision rule by increasing the sample size generally will increase the cost of the sampling experiment.

PROBLEMS

10.1 Dingle Bros. Dairy is considering whether or not to offer home delivery service in a newly opened residential community. On the basis of financial analysis, management has determined to offer the service only if a survey of a sample of 50 households in the community provides overwhelming evidence that more than 25% of all households in the community have at least one child under the age of 16.

(a) Identify the action space and state space of this decision problem.
(b) For this decision problem, what is the appropriate partition of the state space?
(c) What are the appropriate null and alternative hypotheses for this decision problem?
(d) What is the appropriate test statistic for this decision problem?
(e) Specify the appropriate sampling distribution for the test.
(f) Specify the domain of the sampling distribution.
(g) For this statistical decision, management has adopted the .05 significance level. Identify the acceptance and rejection regions of the domain of the sampling distribution.
(h) State management's decision rule.

10.2 The Tasty Biscuit Company advertises that at least 95% of their raisin cookies contain two or more raisins. Responding to complaints that this claim is untrue, a county consumer protection agency decides to inspect a sample of 75 cookies. The number of raisins in each cookie in the sample will be counted, and the agency will take action against the bakery only if the results provide overwhelming evidence that the bakery's claim is untrue.

(a) Identify the action space and state space of this decision problem.
(b) For this decision problem, what is the appropriate partition of the state space?
(c) State the consumer protection agency's null and alternative hypotheses.
(d) What is the appropriate test statistic in this situation?
(e) Specify the appropriate sampling distribution for this statistical test.
(f) Specify the domain of the sampling distribution.
(g) For this statistical decision, the consumer protection agency has adopted the .05 level of significance. Identify the acceptance and rejection regions of the domain of the sampling distribution.
(h) State the agency's decision rule.

10.3 The Langston Lighting Corporation is considering whether or not to offer a new stock purchase plan to its more than 100,000 employees. Management has determined that they will offer the plan only if a sample of 100 employees provides overwhelming evidence that more than 50% of all employees would participate in the plan if it were offered.

(a) Identify the action space and state space for management's decision problem.
(b) For this decision problem, what is the appropriate partition of the state space?
(c) State management's null and alternative hypotheses.
(d) What is the appropriate test statistic in this situation?
(e) Specify the appropriate sampling distribution for this statistical test.
(f) Specify the domain of the sampling distribution.
(g) For this statistical decision, management has adopted the .01 significance level. Identify the acceptance and rejection regions of the domain of the sampling distribution.
(h) State management's decision rule.

10.4 The marketing manager of a chain of discount drug stores has determined that it would be profitable to purchase spot commercial time on radio station KZCX if, and only if, more than 25% of the housewives in Central City are regular listeners of that station. To determine whether or not to buy the commercial time, she plans to survey a random sample of 50 housewives in the city, and base her decision on the number of women in the sample who indicate that they are regular listeners to KZCX. In order to determine the precise decision rule, she adopts the hypothesis-testing approach.

(a) Identify the action space and state space of the manager's decision problem.
(b) For this decision problem, what is the appropriate partition of the state space?
(c) The manager has taken the position that she will purchase the time only if the sample provides overwhelming evidence that the proportion of housewives who regularly listen to KZCX is greater than .25. Under this condition, how should the null and alternative hypotheses be formulated?
(d) Identify the test statistic.
(e) Specify the appropriate sampling distribution.
(f) Identify the domain of the sampling distribution.
(g) The manager has adopted the .10 significance level. Identify the acceptance and rejection regions of the domain of the sampling distribution.
(h) State the manager's decision rule.

10.5 Suppose that the manager in Problem 10.4 changes her mind and takes the position that she will purchase the commercial time unless the sample provides overwhelming evidence that the proportion of housewives who regularly listen to KZCX is less than .25. In this case, how should her decision rule be stated?

10.6 Suppose that management in Problem 10.3 changes its mind and takes the position that they will offer the plan unless the sample provides overwhelming evidence that less than 50% of all employees would participate in the stock plan if it were offered. In this case, how should the decision rule be stated?

10.7 An automatic production process stamps out gears for mechanical toys. The process is considered to be operating "under control" if it is producing no more than 10% defectives, and "out of control" if it is producing more than 10% defectives. When the process is operating under control, it should be allowed to continue; when it is out of control, it should be shut down for adjustment. The production manager wishes to devise a plan whereby, at regular intervals, a sample of 20 gears produced by the process is inspected to determine whether to allow the process to continue in operation or shut it down. To develop this plan, he adopts the hypothesis-testing approach.

(a) Identify the action space and state space of the production manager's problem.
(b) For this problem, what is the appropriate partition of the state space?
(c) The manager has taken the position that he will shut down the process only if the sample provides overwhelming evidence that the process is out of control. Under this condition, how should the null and alternative hypotheses be specified?

(d) Identify the test statistic.

(e) Specify the appropriate sampling distribution.

(f) Identify the domain of the sampling distribution.

(g) If the manager adopts the .05 significance level, specify the acceptance and rejection regions of the domain of the sampling distribution.

(h) State the manager's decision rule.

10.8 For the decision rule developed in Problem 10.7, do the following:

(a) Determine the probability of the Type I error for each of the following possible values of π: .10, .05, .03, .01.

(b) Use the results in part (a) to sketch the Type I error probability curve.

10.9 For the decision rule in Problem 10.7, do the following:

(a) Determine the probability of the Type II error for each of the following possible values of π: .20, .25, .50, .60.

(b) Use the results in part (a) to sketch the OC curve.

(c) Sketch the power curve.

10.10 For the decision rule developed in Problem 10.4, determine the following:

(a) Probability of the Type I error if π is actually equal to .25.

(b) Power of the decision rule if π is actually equal to .50.

(c) Probability of the Type II error if π is actually equal to .50.

(d) Probability of the Type I error if π is actually equal to .45.

(e) Probability of the Type II error if π is actually equal to .15.

10.11 For the decision rule developed in Problem 10.4, determine the following:

(a) Probability that the manager will decide to buy the commercial time if π is actually equal to .25.

(b) Probability that the manager will erroneously decide to buy time if π is actually equal to .20.

(c) Probability that the manager will correctly decide to buy time if π is actually equal to .50.

(d) Probability that the manager will erroneously decide not to buy time if π is actually equal to .50.

10.12 For the decision rule developed in Problem 10.5, determine the following:

(a) Probability of the Type I error if π is actually equal to .25.

(b) Probability that the manager will decide not to buy time if π is actually equal to .25.

(c) Probability that the manager will erroneously decide not to buy time if π is actually equal to .50.

(d) Probability of the Type I error if π is actually equal to .20.

(e) Probability of the Type II error if π is actually equal to .20.

(f) Probability of accepting H_0 if π is actually equal to .20.

(g) Power of the decision rule if π is actually equal to .20.

(h) Probability that the manager will erroneously buy time if π is actually equal to .20.

(i) Probability of the Type II error if π is actually equal to .30.

11

Hypothesis Testing with Discrete

Sampling Distributions

Chapter 10 introduced the basic steps of the hypothesis-testing approach to two-action decision problems. For this purpose, the case of George Jones was used to illustrate one specific type of decision situation to which the hypothesis-testing approach is applicable. The sampling experiment employed in testing George's null hypothesis led to the application of a binomial sampling distribution. In the present chapter, with the aid of additional examples, we consider how the various discrete sampling distributions presented in Chapter 9 may be applied to a variety of hypothesis-testing situations.

11.1 SMALL-LOT ACCEPTANCE SAMPLING: HYPOTHESIS TESTING WITH THE HYPERGEOMETRIC DISTRIBUTION

Although the hypergeometric distribution is applicable to testing hypotheses concerning the number of "successes" in any finite dichotomous population, computational considerations usually limit its use in actual practice to situations in which the population size is small. Thus, an area of industrial application in which the hypergeometric distribution has been found particularly useful is *small-lot acceptance sampling*.

Small-lot acceptance sampling is used in situations in which a "consumer" purchases a product from a "producer" in "small lots" such as a dozen or a gross. A lot is considered by the consumer to be of acceptable quality if it contains no more than a specified number of defectives. Since it would be too costly to inspect every item in each lot to determine if the lot is good, the decision to accept or reject a lot is based on inspecting a random sample of items taken from the lot. The consumer will accept a lot only if the sample taken from that lot contains less than some critical number of defectives. The alert reader will recognize that this lot acceptance procedure is an application of the hypothesis-testing approach to a two-action decision problem.

11.1.1 Designing the Decision Rule

To illustrate the formulation of a small-lot acceptance plan, let us consider a purchasing problem confronting Carmel Associates, a commercial display firm specializing in decorating community shopping centers for holidays and special events. Carmel is considering a contract to purchase colored light bulbs from Proton Products, Inc. The bulbs would be packaged in lots of 20 bulbs each. Proton admits that the expected number of defective bulbs per lot is quite high, but it is willing to offer the lots to Carmel at an unusually attractive price. Because of this very low price, Carmel's cost accountant determines that it would be profitable to buy these bulbs as long as there are no more than 4 defective bulbs in each lot. Carmel therefore decides to negotiate the contract with Proton if an appropriate contract provision for lot acceptance sampling can be agreed upon. During negotiations, Proton agrees to include an acceptance sampling plan in the contract, provided that (1) Carmel agree to pay all costs of operating the plan, and (2) under no conditions should the plan result in more than a 10% chance that a lot containing 4 or fewer defectives will be rejected.

The task of arriving at an appropriate small-lot acceptance sampling plan for Carmel is essentially a problem of designing a decision rule to test the hypothesis that a lot is of acceptable quality. This may be accomplished by following the first eight steps of the general hypothesis-testing procedure that was outlined in Section 10.5.

1. *Identify the action space and state space of the decision problem.* Carmel's decision concerning the acceptability of a lot involves a choice between two alternative courses of action: (a) accept the lot, and (b) reject the lot. These two alternatives constitute the action space of the decision problem. The consequence resulting from either of these alternatives will depend on the actual number of defectives in the lot. Regarding each lot of 20 bulbs as a finite population, the number of defective bulbs in the lot is a parameter of that population. Since the number of defectives in a lot can be as low as 0 or as high as 20, the parameter space (state space) is the set of all integers between 0 and 20 inclusive. Using D to denote the number of defective bulbs in a lot, the parameter space may be expressed in set notation as

    $$\{D\,|\,D = 0, 1, \ldots, 20\}$$

2. *Partition the state space into two complementary subsets.* Although the value of the parameter D may be any integer between 0 and 20 inclusive, Carmel is critically concerned with whether $D \leq 4$ or $D > 4$. Since it is to Carmel's advantage to purchase a lot as long as it contains no more than 4 defectives, the preferred action is to accept the lot if $D \leq 4$ and to reject the lot if $D > 4$. Thus, the parameter space should be partitioned into the two complementary subsets $\{D\,|\,D = 0, 1, \ldots, 4\}$ and $\{D\,|\,D = 5, 6, \ldots, 20\}$.

3. *Formulate the null and alternative hypotheses.* Even though the main purpose of small-lot acceptance sampling is to protect the consumer, the usual practice in such situations is to give the "benefit of the doubt" to the producer by placing the burden of proof on the consumer. In other words, an acceptance sampling plan usually requires the consumer to act as if a lot is of acceptable quality unless the sample provides overwhelming evidence to the contrary. Following this practice, Carmel will act as if the number of defectives in a lot is no greater than 4 unless the sample taken from the lot provides overwhelming evidence that the

number of defectives in the lot is greater than 4. Thus, Carmel's null and alternative hypotheses may be stated as

$$H_0: \quad D \leq 4$$

$$H_1: \quad D > 4$$

4. *Determine the level of significance for the test.* By agreement between Carmel and Proton, the acceptance sampling plan should not, under any circumstance, result in more than a 10% chance that a lot containing 4 or fewer defectives will be rejected. In other words, this 10% chance is the maximum tolerable probability of rejecting H_0 if H_0 actually is true. Thus, the level of significance is $\alpha_{max} = .10$.

5. *Specify the sampling experiment.* In order to keep the sampling cost as low as possible and yet keep the size of the sample large enough to provide useful information about the lot, Carmel decides to adopt a sample size of 3 bulbs per lot. The sample from each lot will be obtained by simple random sampling without replacement. Each of the 3 bulbs in the sample will be tested to determine if it is good or defective.

6. *Select the test statistic and identify the appropriate sampling distribution.* Since their basic concern is with the number of defectives in a lot, Carmel chooses to base the decision of whether to accept or reject a lot on the number of defectives in the sample taken from that lot. That is, the number of defectives in a sample is selected as the test statistic, which may be denoted by R. The sampling distribution of R is hypergeometric since the sampling experiment specified in step 5 satisfies the conditions for the hypergeometric distribution stated in Section 9.2.1. Recalling that the sample size is 3, the domain of the sampling distribution of R is the set $\{r \mid r = 0, 1, 2, 3\}$.

7. *Partition the domain of the sampling distribution of the test statistic into acceptance and rejection regions.* To determine which possible values of R belong in the rejection region, we begin by recalling that Carmel's null hypothesis is $H_0: D \leq 4$ and the alternative hypothesis is $H_1: D > 4$. Thus, a relatively small value of R will tend to support H_0, and a relatively large value of R will tend to support H_1. Therefore, the rejection region will contain the relatively large values of R. Specifically, bearing in mind that the level of significance is .10, the rejection region will contain those possible values of R that are at least as great as some critical value c which satisfies the expression

$$P(R \geq c \mid D \leq 4) \leq .10$$

In order to use a hypergeometric sampling distribution to solve the foregoing expression for c, we must specify the parameters of the distribution—N, n, and D. Since there are 20 bulbs in a lot and 3 bulbs in a sample, $N = 20$ and $n = 3$. Also, since 4 is the limiting value in the null hypothesis, the parameter D is set equal to 4. Then, the probability expression for determining the value of c may be stated as

$$P(R \geq c \mid N = 20, n = 3, D = 4) \leq .10$$

Converted to hypergeometric cumulative notation, this expression becomes

$$F_h(c - 1 \mid N = 20, n = 3, D = 4) \geq .90$$

Now the value of c may be obtained from the hypergeometric table for $N = 20$ (Table D of Appendix II). In this table, if $D > n$, probabilities are obtained by interchanging the values of D and n. Thus, since $D = 4$ and $n = 3$ in this example, we locate the tabulated distribution for $n = 4$ and $D = 3$.

Inspecting this distribution, we look for a cumulative probability that is as close as possible to .90 without being less than .90. The tabulated value that meets this specification is $F_h(1) = .9123$. Since $F_h(c - 1) = F_h(1)$, it follows that $(c - 1) = 1$. Consequently, the desired value of c is 2, so that the rejection region is $\{r\,|\,r = 2, 3\}$. Since the acceptance region is the complement of the rejection region, the acceptance region is $\{r\,|\,r = 0, 1\}$.

8. *State the decision rule explicitly.* Having established the rejection and acceptance regions, we now may explicitly state Carmel's decision rule as follows: If the value of R, the number of defectives in the sample, is equal to or greater than 2, reject H_0 and accordingly reject the lot; otherwise accept H_0 and accordingly accept the lot.

11.1.2 Evaluating the Decision Rule

The specification of the decision rule completes the formulation of Carmel's acceptance sampling plan, provided that both Carmel and Proton can tolerate the risks inherent in the decision rule. To determine whether the decision rule is mutually agreeable to both parties requires an examination of the Type I and Type II error probabilities.

As defined by Formula (10.1), the probability of the Type I error is

$$\alpha = P(\text{reject } H_0\,|\,H_0 \text{ true})$$

Since Carmel's decision rule calls for the rejection of a lot if $R \geq 2$, the Type I error probability for any specific value of D contained in the null hypothesis may be written as

$$\alpha_D = P(R \geq 2\,|\,D)$$

Recalling that the sampling distribution of R is hypergeometric with $N = 20$ and $n = 3$, this probability expression becomes

$$\alpha_D = P(R \geq 2\,|\,N = 20, n = 3, D)$$
$$= 1 - F_h(1\,|\,20, 3, D)$$

With the aid of Table D (Appendix II), this last formula yields the specific α_D values shown in Table 11.1. These α_D values are the conditional probabilities of rejecting a lot if, in fact, the lot is of acceptable quality.

Table 11.1 Type I Error Probabilities for Carmel's Decision Rule

Number of Defectives in Lot, D	Type I Error Probability $\alpha_D = P(R \geq 2\,|\,20, 3, D) = 1 - F_h(1\,|\,20, 3, D)$
0	$\alpha_0 = 1 - 1.0000 = .0000$
1	$\alpha_1 = 1 - 1.0000 = .0000$
2	$\alpha_2 = 1 - .9842 = .0158$
3	$\alpha_3 = 1 - .9544 = .0456$
4	$\alpha_4 = 1 - .9123 = .0877$

In general, the probability of the Type I error for a small-lot acceptance sampling plan based on the hypergeometric distribution is given by

$$\alpha_D = P(R \geq c\,|\,N, n, D) \tag{11.1}$$

where $R =$ number of defectives in the sample
$\quad c =$ critical value stated in the decision rule
$\quad N =$ lot size
$\quad n =$ sample size
$\quad D =$ any specific number of defectives in the lot, provided that this number is contained in H_0

As defined by Formula (10.2), the probability of the Type II error is

$$\beta = P(\text{accept } H_0 \,|\, H_1 \text{ true})$$

Since Carmel's decision rule calls for the acceptance of a lot if the sample from that lot contains no more than 1 defective ($R \leq 1$), the Type II error probability for the rule may be stated as

$$\beta_D = P(R \leq 1 \,|\, N = 20, n = 3, D)$$
$$= F_h(1 \,|\, 20, 3, D)$$

For each of the values of D contained in H_1, the corresponding β_D value may be read directly from Table D. These β_D values, shown in Table 11.2, are the

Table 11.2   Type II Error Probabilities for Carmel's Decision Rule

Number of Defectives in Lot, D	Type II Error Probability $\beta_D = P(R < 2 \,|\, 20, 3, D) = F_n(1 \,|\, 20, 3, D)$
5	$\beta_5 = .8596$
6	$\beta_6 = .7982$
7	$\beta_7 = .7298$
8	$\beta_8 = .6561$
9	$\beta_9 = .5789$
10	$\beta_{10} = .5000$
11	$\beta_{11} = .4211$
12	$\beta_{12} = .3439$
13	$\beta_{13} = .2702$
14	$\beta_{14} = .2018$
15	$\beta_{15} = .1404$
16	$\beta_{16} = .0877$
17	$\beta_{17} = .0456$
18	$\beta_{18} = .0156$
19	$\beta_{19} = .0000$
20	$\beta_{20} = .0000$

conditional probabilities of accepting a lot if, in fact, the lot is of unacceptable quality.

In terms of a general formula, the probability of the Type II error for a small-lot acceptance sampling plan based on the hypergeometric distribution is given by

$$\beta_D = P(R < c \,|\, N, n, D) \tag{11.2}$$

where D is any specific number of defectives in the lot, provided that this number is contained in H_1.

The error probabilities in Tables 11.1 and 11.2 are displayed graphically by the error characteristic chart presented in Figure 11.1. This chart clearly

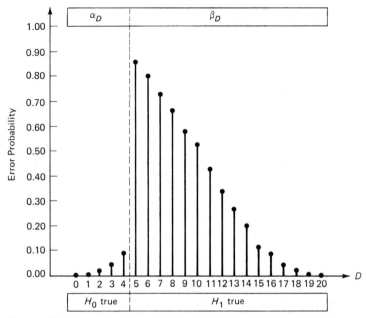

Figure 11.1 Error Characteristic Chart for Carmel's Decision Rule

indicates that, in general, the Type I error probabilities are much smaller than the Type II error probabilities. From Carmel's viewpoint, this means that the chances of missing an opportunity to buy an acceptable lot are much smaller than the chances of buying an unacceptable lot. This would make sense to Carmel if the consequence of missing the opportunity to buy an acceptable lot were more serious than the consequence of buying an unacceptable lot. However, this is not the case. Since buying an unacceptable lot will result in an actual loss, Carmel is far more concerned with the error of buying an unacceptable lot than with the error of merely missing an opportunity to buy an acceptable lot. Thus, because of the relatively high risk of committing a Type II error under the decision rule, it is doubtful that Carmel should agree to including the acceptance plan, as it presently stands, in the contract.

Although a Type II error is a serious concern to Carmel, such an error actually works to the advantage of Proton, since the occurrence of a Type II error means that Proton is able to sell an unacceptable lot to Carmel. Thus, Proton is not vitally concerned with how great the risk of the Type II error might be. However, the occurrence of a Type I error, which is inconsequential to Carmel, is a major concern to Proton. This is because, from Proton's viewpoint, the occurrence of a Type I error will result in losing the sale of an acceptable lot. This is precisely why Proton insisted that the plan should result in no more than a 10% chance of Carmel's rejecting a lot containing no more than four defectives. Under the decision rule as it presently stands, the maximum probability of such an error is only .0877. The rule should therefore be quite agreeable to Proton. Since the rule is agreeable to Proton but unfavorable to Carmel, a conflict exists. The resolution of this conflict will require further negotiation, leading to the development of an alternative plan.

11.2 HYPOTHESIS TESTING WITH THE BINOMIAL DISTRIBUTION

We have already encountered a hypothesis-testing application of the binomial distribution in the case of George Jones, which was introduced in Chapter 10 to illustrate the general hypothesis-testing approach to two-action decision problems. In that case George's predominant concern with the risk of suffering an out-of-pocket loss made it clear that the burden of proof should be placed on the proposition that the bond issue would pass. In this section we consider a different case, in which there are conflicting viewpoints concerning where to place the burden of proof.

Midway Magazine is a monthly publication that goes to the homes of about 300,000 regular subscribers. Because of rising production costs, the publisher is considering increasing the yearly subscription rate from $7.00 to $8.00. In contemplating her decision, the publisher consults the circulation manager, who points out that such a rate hike surely would result in some decrease in the proportion of current subscribers who would renew their subscriptions. The circulation manager therefore requests an analysis by the accounting department, which responds that, for a $1.00 increase in annual rate to be financially sound, the percentage of current subscribers who would renew their subscriptions should exceed 75%. The circulation manager reports this finding to the publisher, who then suggests that additional information be obtained by taking a random sample of 100 current subscribers. All subscribers in the sample will be interviewed to determine whether or not they would renew their subscriptions if the rate were raised to $8.00 per year. The publisher would then base her decision on the results of the interviews.

To determine exactly how the sample results should be used to make the decision, the publisher sets up a meeting with the circulation manager and marketing research director. At the meeting, the marketing research director is briefed on the background of the problem. After some discussion, all three persons agree that the annual subscription rate should be raised to $8.00 if the proportion of current subscribers who would renew their subscriptions exceeds .75 (i.e., if $\pi > .75$), but that the rate should not be raised if this proportion is no greater than .75 (i.e., if $\pi \leq .75$). However, after further discussion, a disagreement arises. Since the circulation manager is particularly concerned with the possible disastrous effect of a rate hike on circulation, he feels that the action of raising the rate should not be taken unless the sample results provide overwhelming evidence that $\pi > .75$. Indeed, the circulation manager proposes, they should not take more than a .05 risk of raising the rate if $\pi \leq .75$. More concerned with the effects of rising costs, the publisher expresses her feeling that the action of raising the rate should be taken unless the sample results provide overwhelming evidence that $\pi < .75$. In fact, the publisher indicates that they should take no more than a .05 risk of failing to raise the rate if $\pi \geq .75$. In other words, while the circulation manager places the burden of proof on the proposition that $\pi > .75$, the publisher places the burden of proof on the proposition that $\pi < .75$.

Warning the publisher that her position is dangerous, the circulation manager suggests that the publisher request the research director to formulate two alternative decision rules, one rule for each of the two conflicting viewpoints. Then the risks inherent in these two rules can be compared before a final selection is made. The publisher agrees to the circulation manager's suggestion.

11.2.1 Designing the Decision Rules

The marketing research director's task of formulating two alternative decision rules is a matter of specifying two hypothesis tests that differ in certain important respects. As we will see, the rule reflecting the circulation manager's viewpoint is an example of an *upper-tail test* because the rejection region is in the upper tail of the sampling distribution, whereas the rule reflecting the publisher's viewpoint is an example of a *lower-tail test* because the rejection region is in the lower tail of the sampling distribution.

Upper-Tail Test. Following the first eight steps of the general hypothesis-testing procedure that was outlined in Section 10.5, the marketing research director proceeds to formulate the decision rule from the circulation manager's viewpoint as follows:

1. The action space of *Midway's* decision problem consists of two alternative courses of action: (a) raise the annual subscription rate to $8.00, and (b) maintain the annual subscription rate at the current level of $7.00. The parameter space (state space) is the set of all possible values of π between 0 and 1, where π denotes the proportion of all current subscribers who will renew their subscriptions if the rate is raised. That is, the parameter space is the set $\{\pi \mid 0 \leq \pi \leq 1\}$.

2. From the statement of the problem, the research director recognizes that it would be undesirable to raise the rate if $\pi \leq .75$; otherwise, it would be desirable to raise the rate. He therefore partitions the parameter space into the two subsets $\{\pi \mid 0 \leq \pi \leq .75\}$ and $\{\pi \mid .75 < \pi \leq 1.00\}$.

3. From the circulation manager's viewpoint, the burden of proof should be placed on the proposition that $\pi > .75$. Thus, the null and alternative hypotheses are stated as

$$H_0: \quad \pi \leq .75$$
$$H_1: \quad \pi > .75$$

4. On the basis of the circulation manager's assertion that they should not take more than a .05 risk of raising the rate if $\pi \leq .75$, the research director sets the level of significance at .05.

5. The research director specifies that a simple random sample of 100 persons will be selected from a frame provided by a computerized list of current subscribers. The people in the sample will be interviewed by telephone to determine whether they would renew their subscriptions to *Midway Magazine* if the annual subscription rate were raised to $8.00.

6. Since it should be an easy matter to record each interviewee's response as "yes" or "no," the research director selects the number of "yes" responses in the sample as the test statistic. Using R to denote this statistic, the sampling distribution of R is binomial, since the sample is to be taken from a dichotomous population that is large enough to be considered effectively infinite. The domain of this sampling distribution is the set $\{r \mid r = 0, 1, \ldots, 100\}$.

7. To determine which possible values of R belong in the rejection region, the research director begins by noting that the alternative hypothesis from the circulation manager's viewpoint is $H_1: \pi > .75$. Thus, a relatively large value of R will be required in order to provide overwhelming evidence in favor of H_1. That is, the rejection region will be located in the *upper tail* of the sampling distribution of R. Specifically, the rejection region will contain those possible values of R that are at least as great as some critical value c that satisfies the expression

$$P(R \geq c \mid \pi \leq .75) \leq .05$$

Recalling that the sample size is $n = 100$, and using the limiting value of π stated in H_0, this expression becomes

$$P(R \geq c \,|\, n = 100, \pi = .75) \leq .05$$

Since the sampling distribution of R is binomial, the preceding expression may be converted to

$$F_b(c - 1 \,|\, n = 100, \pi = .75) \geq .95$$

Entering Table F (Appendix II) for $n = 100$, the research director scans the column under $\pi = .75$, looking for a cumulative probability that is as close as possible to .95 without being less than .95. The tabulated value satisfying this specification is $F_b(82) = .9624$. Since $(c - 1) = 82$, it follows that the desired value of c is 83. Thus, the rejection region is $\{r \,|\, r = 83, 84, \ldots, 100\}$, so that the acceptance region becomes $\{r \,|\, r = 0, 1, \ldots, 82\}$.

8. From the result of step 7, the research director states the decision rule from the circulation manager's viewpoint as follows: If the value of R, the number of "yes" responses in the sample, is equal to or greater than 83, reject H_0 and accordingly raise the annual subscription rate to \$8.00; otherwise, accept H_0 and accordingly maintain the annual subscription rate at the current level of \$7.00.

Lower-Tail Test. Using the same general procedure employed to design the decision rule from the circulation manager's viewpoint, the research director proceeds to formulate the rule from the publisher's viewpoint as follows:

1. Same as before.

2. Same as before.

3. From the publisher's viewpoint, the burden of proof should be placed on the proposition that $\pi < .75$. Hence, the null and alternative hypotheses are[1]

$$H_0: \quad \pi \geq .75$$
$$H_1: \quad \pi < .75$$

4. On the basis of the publisher's feeling that they should not take more than a .05 risk of not raising the rate if $\pi \geq .75$, the research director sets the significance level at .05. It is important to observe that, although the significance levels for both rules are set at .05, they represent distinctly different types of risks.

5. Same as before.

6. Same as before.

7. To determine the possible values of R that belong in the rejection region, the research director begins by observing that the alternative hypothesis from the publisher's viewpoint is $H_1: \pi < .75$. Thus, a relatively small value of R will be required in order to provide overwhelming evidence in favor of H_1. That is, the rejection region will be located in the lower tail of the sampling distribution of R. Specifically, the rejection region will contain those possible values of R that are no greater than some critical value c which satisfies the expression

$$P(R \leq c \,|\, \pi \geq .75) \leq .05$$

Recalling that the sample size is $n = 100$, and using the limiting value of π stated in H_0, this expression becomes

$$P(R \leq c \,|\, n = 100, \pi = .75) \leq .05$$

Since the sampling distribution of R is binomial, the last expression above may be written

$$F_b(c \,|\, n = 100, \pi = .75) \leq .05$$

---

[1]It should be noted that, since the parameter space of π is continuous, it is inconsequential whether the equality sign is included in H_0 or H_1. However, it is customary to include the equality sign in H_0.

Entering Table F for $n = 100$, the research director scans the column under $\pi = .75$, looking for a cumulative probability that is as close as possible to .05 without being greater than .05. The tabulated value satisfying this specification is $F_b(67) = .0446$, and therefore the desired value of c is 67. Thus, the rejection region is $\{r \mid r = 0, 1, \ldots, 67\}$, so that the acceptance region becomes $\{r \mid r = 68, 69, \ldots, 100\}$.

8. From the result of step 7, the research director states the decision rule from the publisher's viewpoint as follows: If the value of R, the number of "yes" responses in the sample, is equal to or less than 67, reject H_0 and accordingly maintain the annual subscription rate at the current level of \$7.00; otherwise, accept H_0 and accordingly raise the annual subscription rate to \$8.00."

11.2.2 Evaluating the Decision Rules

The procedure for determining the Type I and Type II error probabilities for a binomial hypothesis test is fundamentally the same as that followed for a hypergeometric test, except that the probabilities are obtained from a binomial distribution rather than a hypergeometric distribution. For an *upper-tail* binomial test, the decision rule calls for rejection of H_0 if R (the number of "successes" in the sample of n observations) is *equal to or greater than* some critical value c. The Type I error probability for this kind of test is given by

$$\alpha_\pi = P(R \geq c \mid n, \pi) \tag{11.3}$$

which is the binomial probability that R is equal to or greater than c, given that π is any specific value contained in H_0. The Type II error probability for an upper-tail binomial test is given by

$$\beta_\pi = P(R < c \mid n, \pi) \tag{11.4}$$

which is the binomial probability that R is less than c, given that π is any specific value contained in H_1.

For a *lower-tail* binomial test, the decision rule calls for rejection of H_0 if R is equal to or less than some critical value c. The Type I error probability for this kind of test is given by

$$\alpha_\pi = P(R \leq c \mid n, \pi) \tag{11.5}$$

which is the binomial probability that R is equal to or less than c, given that π is any specific value contained in H_0. The Type II error probability for a lower-tail binomial test is given by

$$\beta_\pi = P(R > c \mid n, \pi) \tag{11.6}$$

which is the binomial probability that R is greater than c, given that π is any specific value contained in H_1.

To provide a comparison of the risks inherent in the two alternative decision rules that he has formulated, the marketing research director has prepared the error characteristic curves presented in Figure 11.2. Figure 11.2a shows the

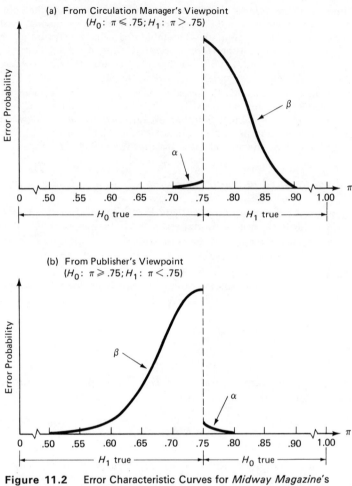

Figure 11.2 Error Characteristic Curves for *Midway Magazine*'s
Decision Rules

Type I and Type II error probabilities for the decision rule reflecting the circulation manager's viewpoint. Since this rule is an upper-tail test, these probabilities were obtained from cumulative binomial tables using Formulas (11.3) and (11.4). Figure 11.2b shows the Type I and Type II error probabilities for the decision rule reflecting the publisher's viewpoint. Since this rule is a lower-tail test, these probabilities were obtained by using Formulas (11.5) and (11.6).

As shown by charts (a) and (b) in Figure 11.2, the α-risk for both decision rules is, in general, much lower than the β-risk. However, since the two decision rules reflect opposite viewpoints concerning where the burden of proof should be placed, α and β have opposite meanings in the two charts. In chart (a), the α curve represents the risk of raising the rate if the raise should not be made, and the β curve represents the risk of not raising the rate if the raise should be made. Conversely, in chart (b), the α curve represents the risk of not raising the rate if the raise should be made, and the β curve represents the risk of raising the rate if the raise should not be made. In other words, the risk of incorrectly raising the rate is represented by the α curve in chart (a) but by the β curve in chart (b), whereas the risk of incorrectly failing to raise the rate is represented by the β curve in chart (a) but by the α curve in chart (b). Thus, by comparing the α curve in chart (a) with the β curve in chart (b), it is clear that risk of incorrectly raising the rate is much smaller for the decision rule based on the circulation manager's viewpoint than for the rule based on the publisher's viewpoint. This reflects the fact that the circulation manager is more concerned than the publisher with the possible disastrous effect of a rate hike on circulation. Similarly, a comparison of the α curve in chart (b) with the β curve in chart (a) shows that the risk of incorrectly failing to raise the rate is much smaller for the decision rule derived from the publisher's viewpoint than for the rule obtained from the circulation manager's viewpoint. This results from the publisher's greater concern with the adverse effect of rising costs on profits if the rate is not increased.

As the person who eventually will make the final decision regarding the rate increase, the publisher will have to select the decision rule that she will follow. In doing this she will need to consider the specific financial consequences of both types of incorrect decisions, and then determine, for each rule, whether the risks of these incorrect decisions can be tolerated in view of their consequences. Presumably, if she feels she can tolerate the risks inherent in the rule designed from her own point of view, that is the rule which the publisher will adopt. Otherwise, she might adopt the rule reflecting the circulation manager's viewpoint. In the event that the publisher feels that she cannot tolerate the risks inherent in either rule, various alternative rules may be designed. For example, if she feels that she might be able to tolerate a higher maximum risk of the Type I error, she could increase the level of significance, which will result in a decision rule having reduced Type II error probabilities. Or, if she is willing to pay for additional sampling costs, she could specify a larger sample size, which would yield a decision rule that will reduce the overall level of both types of risk.

11.3 HYPOTHESIS TESTING WITH THE POISSON DISTRIBUTION

The procedure for testing a hypothesis concerning the parameter λ of a Poisson process is basically the same as that followed for a hypergeometric or binomial test, except that the sampling distribution underlying the decision rule is Poisson rather than hypergeometric or binomial. As an illustration of this procedure, consider the case of Hale's of Hartford, a major insurance firm. Representatives of Hale's have been negotiating with the management of Valence Chemical Products for an industrial accident policy. Although Hale's has agreed to insure Valence's several thousand employees against medical expenses and loss of income from accidents requiring hospitalization, the premium to be charged for this policy has not yet been decided upon. Valence maintains that the mean rate of occurrence of such accidents is under .50 per month. Hale's has agreed to underwrite the policy at a special preferential rate if Valence can provide convincing evidence that this claim is correct; otherwise, Hale's will charge their standard rate for this type of policy. Hale's indicates that the evidence for making the rate decision may be obtained by examining Valence's records for the past 20 months and determining the number of accidents requiring hospitalization during that period.

11.3.1 Designing the Decision Rule

In order to decide whether the preferential or standard rate should be charged on the basis of the evidence obtained from the records search, a decision rule is required. This rule may be formulated as follows:

1. The action space of Hale's decision problem consists of two alternative courses of action: (a) charge the standard rate, and (b) charge the preferential rate. Since the mean monthly accident rate can be as low as zero but has no finite upper limit, the parameter space (state space) is the set of all nonnegative values. Using λ to denote this mean rate, the parameter space is the set $\{\lambda | 0 \leq \lambda < \infty\}$.

2. Hale's position is that the standard rate should be charged if $\lambda \geq .50$, but that the preferential rate should be charged if $\lambda < .50$. Therefore, the parameter space should be partitioned into the two subsets $\{\lambda | .50 \leq \lambda < \infty\}$ and $\{\lambda | 0 \leq \lambda < .50\}$.

3. Since Hale's has agreed to charge the preferential rate only if Valence can provide convincing evidence that the mean monthly accident rate is under .50, the burden of proof should be placed on the proposition that $\lambda < .50$. Thus, the null and alternative hypotheses are

$$H_0: \quad \lambda \geq .50$$
$$H_1: \quad \lambda < .50$$

4. Considering the differential between the standard and preferential rates, Hale's feels that they can tolerate a maximum 10% risk that the evidence will lead them to agree to Valence's claim that $\lambda < .50$ if the claim actually is false. This maximum risk of .10 is the level of significance.

5. As Hale's has specified, the evidence will be obtained by examining Valence's records for the past 20 months. Since industrial accidents typically occur according to a Poisson process, this procedure may be regarded as observing a sample of the output of a Poisson process. In a Poisson sampling experiment, the sample is composed of a continuum of contiguous units rather than a set of discrete elements. Thus, the sample size is the number of these contiguous units over which the observations are made. In the case of Hale's decision problem, λ is expressed as a mean monthly rate and records are to be examined for a 20-month period. Therefore, the sample size is $t = 20$.

6. According to Hale's specification, the sample results will be expressed in terms of the number of accidents requiring hospitalization during the 20-month period under observation. This number of accidents in the sample is the test statistic. Using R to denote this statistic, the sampling distribution of R is a Poisson distribution since the accidents occur according to a Poisson process. The number of accidents in the sample can be as low as zero but has no finite upper limit. Hence, the domain of the sampling distribution of R is the set $\{r | r = 0, 1, 2, \ldots\}$.

7. To determine the possible values of R that belong in the rejection region, we begin by observing that the alternative hypothesis is $H_1: \lambda < .50$. Thus, a relatively small value of R will be required in order to provide overwhelming evidence in favor of H_1. That is, the rejection region will be located in the lower tail of the sampling distribution of R. Specifically, the rejection region will contain those possible values of R that are no greater than some critical value c which satisfies the expression

$$P(R \leq c | \lambda \geq .50) \leq .10$$

Recalling that the sample size is $t = 20$, and using the limiting value of λ stated in H_0, this probability statement may be expressed in terms of the Poisson cumulative distribution as follows:

$$F_P(R \leq c \,|\, \lambda = .50, t = 20) \leq .10$$

Entering Table H (Appendix II) with $\lambda t = .50(20) = 10$, we look for a cumulative probability that is as close as possible to .10 without being greater than .10. The tabulated value satisfying this specification is $F_P(5) = .0671$, so that the desired value of c is 5. Hence, the rejection region is $\{r \,|\, r = 0, 1, \ldots, 5\}$, and the acceptance region becomes $\{r \,|\, r = 6, 7, 8, \ldots\}$.

8. From the result of step 7, Hale's decision rule may be stated as follows: If the value of R, the number of accidents requiring hospitalization during the 20-month period, is equal to or less than 5, reject H_0 and accordingly charge the preferential rate; otherwise, accept H_0 and accordingly charge the standard rate.

11.3.2 Evaluating the Decision Rule

A Poisson decision rule may be evaluated by tabulating and charting its error probabilities in a manner similar to that followed for any hypergeometric or binomial rule. For an *upper-tail* Poisson test, the decision rule calls for rejection of H_0 if R (the number of Poisson occurrences in the sample of t units) is *equal to or greater than* some critical value c. The Type I error probability for this kind of test is given by

$$\alpha_\lambda = P(R \geq c \,|\, \lambda, t) \tag{11.7}$$

which is the Poisson probability that R is equal to or greater than c, given that λ is any specified value contained in H_0. The Type II error probability for an upper-tail Poisson test is given by

$$\beta_\lambda = P(R < c \,|\, \lambda, t) \tag{11.8}$$

which is the Poisson probability that R is less than c, given that λ is any specific value contained in H_1.

For a *lower-tail* Poisson test, the decision rule calls for rejection of H_0 if R is equal to or less than some critical value c. The Type I error probability for this kind of test is given by

$$\alpha_\lambda = P(R \leq c \,|\, \lambda, t) \tag{11.9}$$

which is the Poisson probability that R is equal to or less than c, given that λ is any specific value contained in H_0. The Type II error probability for a lower-tail Poisson test is given by

$$\beta_\lambda = P(R > c \,|\, \lambda, t) \tag{11.10}$$

which is the Poisson probability that R is greater than c, given that λ is any specific value contained in H_1.

Hale's decision rule is based on a lower-tail test, since the rejection region is in the lower tail of the sampling distribution of the test statistic. Therefore, the error probabilities for this rule may be obtained from Table H by using Formulas (11.9) and (11.10). For selected values of λ, the Type I and Type II error probabilities for Hale's rule are presented in Table 11.3. The resulting error characteristic chart is shown in Figure 11.3.

Table 11.3   Type I and Type II Error Probabilities for Hale's Decision Rule

Mean Rate, λ	Type I Error Probability, $\alpha_\lambda = P(R \leq 5 \mid \lambda, t = 20)$	Type II Error Probability, $\beta_\lambda = P(R \geq 6 \mid \lambda, t = 20)$
.10		.0166
.15		.0839
.20		.2149
.25		.3840
.30		.5543
.35		.6993
.40		.8088
.45		.8843
.50	.0671	
.55	.0375	
.60	.0203	
.65	.0107	
.70	.0055	

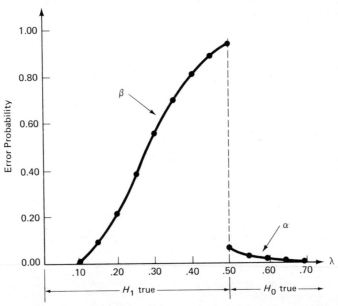

Figure 11.3   Error Characteristic Chart for Hale's Decision Rule
($H_0: \lambda \geq .50$; $H_1: \lambda < .50$)

11.4 RECAPITULATION

In this chapter we have considered examples of hypothesis testing with three commonly used discrete sampling distributions: hypergeometric, binomial, and Poisson. Each of these distributions may be used to conduct either upper-tail or lower-tail tests.[2] This section summarizes the general specifications for

---

[2]Theoretically, these distributions may also be used to perform two-tail tests. However, two-tail tests with these distributions are rarely encountered in practical decision situations.

conducting these tests.

The *hypergeometric* distribution is used to test hypotheses concerning D, the number of "successes" in a finite, dichotomous *population*. The sampling experiment for a hypergeometric test consists of selecting a simple random sample of n elements from the population of N elements (without replacement) and determining the value of the test statistic R, the number of "successes" in the *sample*. The general specifications for formulating the upper-tail and lower-tail decision rules for a hypergeometric test are summarized in Table 11.4.

Table 11.4   General Specifications for Hypergeometric Tests

Test	Hypotheses	Decision Rule	Probability Statement for Determining c
Upper tail	$H_0: \ D \leq D_0$ $H_1: \ D > D_0$	If $R \geq c$, reject H_0; otherwise, accept H_0	$F_h(c - 1 \mid N, n, D_0) \geq 1 - \alpha_{\max}$
Lower tail	$H_0: \ D \geq D_0$ $H_1: \ D < D_0$	If $R \leq c$, reject H_0; otherwise, accept H_0	$F_h(c \mid N, n, D_0) \leq \alpha_{\max}$

In this table, D_0 denotes the limiting value of D stated in the null hypothesis. Since the significance level is the maximum tolerable risk of committing the Type I error, this risk is denoted in the table by $\alpha_{\max}$.

The *binomial* distribution is used to test hypotheses concerning π, the proportion of "successes" in a dichotomous *population* that is either infinite or large enough to be considered effectively infinite. The sampling distribution for a binomial test consists of selecting a simple random sample of n elements from the population and determining the value of the test statistic R, the number of "successes" in the *sample*. The general specifications for upper-tail and lower-tail binomial tests are summarized in Table 11.5. In this table, π_0 denotes the limiting value of π stated in the null hypothesis.

Table 11.5   General Specifications for Binomial Tests

Test	Hypotheses	Decision Rule	Probability Statement for Determining c
Upper tail	$H_0: \ \pi \leq \pi_0$ $H_1: \ \pi > \pi_0$	If $R \geq c$, reject H_0; otherwise, accept H_0	$F_b(c - 1 \mid n, \pi_0) \geq 1 - \alpha_{\max}$
Lower tail	$H_0: \ \pi \geq \pi_0$ $H_1: \ \pi < \pi_0$	If $R \leq c$, reject H_0; otherwise, accept H_0	$F_b(c \mid n, \pi_0) \leq \alpha_{\max}$

The *Poisson* distribution is used to test hypotheses concerning λ, the mean occurrence rate of a Poisson *process*. The sampling experiment for a Poisson test consists of observing the occurrences of a phenomenon generated by a Poisson process over a sample of t contiguous units of time or space. The test statistic is R, the number of occurrences of the phenomenon in the *sample*. The general specifications for upper-tail and lower-tail Poisson tests are summarized in Table 11.6. In this table λ_0 denotes the limiting value of λ stated in the null hypothesis.

Table 11.6 General Specifications for Poisson Tests

Test	Hypotheses	Decision Rule	Probability Statement for Determining c
Upper tail	$H_0: \lambda \leq \lambda_0$ $H_1: \lambda > \lambda_0$	If $R \geq c$, reject H_0; otherwise, accept H_0	$F_P(c - 1 \mid \lambda_0, t) \geq 1 - \alpha_{max}$
Lower tail	$H_0: \lambda \geq \lambda_0$ $H_1: \lambda < \lambda_0$	If $R \leq c$, reject H_0; otherwise, accept H_0	$F_P(c \mid \lambda_0, t) \leq \alpha_{max}$

PROBLEMS

11.1 Nato Electronics purchases a particular type of missile component in lots containing 20 components each. A lot is regarded as "acceptable" if it contains no more than 3 defectives. Because of the high defective rates of some of these lots, management has decided to install a lot acceptance sampling plan. The decision to accept or reject each lot will be based on the number of defectives found in a sample of 5 components taken from the lot. The plan is to be designed in such a way that there will be no greater than a .15 probability of rejecting an acceptable lot.
   (a) Identify the action space and state space for this problem.
   (b) Formulate the null and alternative hypotheses.
   (c) What is the appropriate sampling distribution? Justify your answer.
   (d) Derive and explicitly state the decision rule for the acceptance sampling plan.

11.2 For the acceptance sampling example presented in Section 11.1, suppose that the significance level is changed from .10 to .05.
   (a) Using the revised significance level, derive a new decision rule for Carmel.
   (b) Construct the error characteristic chart for the rule obtained in part (a).

11.3 A supplier provides the Lambert Lawn Mower Company with carburetors that are shipped in lots containing 20 carburetors each. A lot is considered "acceptable" if it contains no more than 4 defectives. Lambert wishes to devise a lot acceptance sampling plan, basing the decision to accept or reject each lot on the number of defectives found in a sample of 8 carburetors taken from the lot. The plan is to be designed so that there will be no more than a .20 probability of rejecting an acceptable lot.
   (a) Identify the action space and state space for this problem.
   (b) Formulate the null and alternative hypotheses.
   (c) What is the appropriate sampling distribution? Explain.
   (d) Derive and explicitly state the decision rule for the acceptance sampling plan.

11.4 Construct an error characteristic chart for the lot acceptance sampling plan described in Problem 11.3.

11.5 For the acceptance sampling plan described in Problem 11.1, suppose that the probability of rejecting an acceptable lot is changed from .15 to .20. Derive and explicitly state the decision rule for the revised plan.

11.6 The Merton Instrumentation Company purchases a particular type of delicate valve in lots containing 20 valves. A lot is considered "acceptable" if it contains no more than 5 defectives. Management wishes to adopt a lot acceptance sampling plan, basing the decision to accept or reject each lot on the number of defectives found in a sample of 6 components taken from the lot. The plan is to be designed in such a way that there will be no greater than a .05 probability of rejecting an acceptable lot.
   (a) Identify the action space and state space for this problem.
   (b) Formulate the null and alternative hypotheses.

(c) What is the appropriate sampling distribution? Explain.
(d) Derive and explicitly state the decision rule for the acceptance sampling plan.

11.7 For the acceptance sampling plan described in Problem 11.6, suppose that the probability of rejecting an acceptable lot is changed from .05 to .20. Derive and explicitly state the decision rule for the revised plan.

11.8 The Specialty Foods Company has developed a new process for producing instant coffee. Management feels that they should convert to this process only if more than 60% of coffee consumers prefer the coffee produced by this new process to the coffee produced by the current process. To determine whether or not to adopt the new process, a taste comparison experiment is proposed. A sample of 100 coffee drinkers will be asked to taste coffee made by each of the two processes and indicate which they prefer. The decision will be based on the number of persons in the sample who prefer the coffee made by the new process.
(a) Identify the action and state spaces for this decision problem.
(b) Specify the null and alternative hypotheses.
(c) What is the appropriate sampling distribution? Justify your answer.
(d) Using the .05 significance level, derive and explicitly state the decision rule.

11.9 For the decision problem described in Problem 11.8, suppose that management decides to reduce the sample size from 100 to 75 consumers. Derive and explicitly state the decision rule for this revised sampling specification.

11.10 For the decision rule derived in Problem 11.8, construct the error characteristic chart.

11.11 The Star Oil Company has received an offer to lease a service station site. Before deciding whether or not to accept the offer, management plans to conduct a sample survey of 75 households within a 5-mile radius of the site. The company will accept the offer unless the sample provides convincing evidence, at the .15 significance level, that less than 10% of the households in the area are Star Oil credit card holders.
(a) Derive and explicitly state the decision rule for Star Oil's decision problem.
(b) If only 5% of the households in the area are Star Oil credit card holders, what is the probability that the decision rule will lead the company to accept the lease offer?
(c) If 20% of the households in the area are Star Oil credit card holders, what is the probability that the decision rule will lead the company to reject the lease offer?

11.12 For the decision problem described in Problem 11.11, suppose that the company takes the position that it will accept the offer only if the sample provides convincing evidence, at the .15 significance level, that more than 10% of the households in the area are Star Oil credit card holders.
(a) Derive and explicitly state the decision rule.
(b) If only 5% of the households in the area are Star Oil credit card holders, what is the probability that the decision rule will lead the company to accept the lease offer?
(c) If 20% of the households in the area are Star Oil credit card holders, what is the probability that the decision rule will lead the company to reject the lease offer?

11.13 The advertising manager of Bart's restaurant chain is considering whether or not the firm should purchase spot commercial time on the Betty Baldwin talk show presented by a metropolitan radio station. To make his decision, the advertising manager plans to have his staff conduct telephone interviews of a sample of 100 households in the area served by the station. He will buy the time unless the number of sample respondents who regularly listen to Betty Baldwin is sufficiently small to conclude, at the .10 significance level, that less than 25% of all households in the area regularly listen to the show.
(a) Identify the action space and state space for this decision problem.
(b) Specify the null and alternative hypotheses.
(c) What is the appropriate sampling distribution? Explain.
(d) Derive and explicitly state the decision rule.

11.14 Consider the decision rule derived in Problem 11.13. If only 20% of all households in the area regularly listen to Betty Baldwin, what is the probability that the decision rule will lead the advertsing manager to buy spot commercial time on the show?

11.15 Madison Marketing Associates has developed a work-sample test for screening keypunch operator applicants. The test consists of presenting an applicant with a standard set of 30 marked survey forms, each of which is to be keypunched on a data processing card. The test is scored by counting the total number of keypunch errors on the 30 cards. The applicant is considered to be "acceptable" unless the test provides convincing evidence, at the .10 significance level, that the applicant's error rate exceeds. .05 error per card.

(a) If a particular applicant takes this test and makes a total of 5 errors, should the applicant be considered acceptable?

(b) What is the maximum number of errors that an applicant may make and still be considered acceptable?

11.16 The Gotham Garment Company is considering installation of a new telephone system, but management is uncertain whether the rate of incoming calls is sufficiently high to justify the expense. Specifically, management feels that the new system should be installed only if the number of calls received during a sample period of 100 minutes provides substantial evidence, at the .05 significance level, that the mean rate of incoming calls exceeds 6 calls per hour.

(a) Identify the action and state spaces of this decision problem.

(b) Specify the null and alternative hypotheses.

(c) Assuming that calls arrive according to a Poisson process, derive and explicitly state the decision rule.

11.17 Construct the OC curve for the decision rule derived in Problem 11.16.

11.18 For the decision problem described in problem 11.16, suppose that the company takes the position that the new system should be installed unless the number of calls received during the 100-minute sample period provides substantial evidence, at the .05 significance level, that the mean rate of incoming calls is less than 6 calls per hour.

(a) Derive and explictly state the decision rule.

(b) If actually the mean rate of incoming calls is 3 calls per hour, what is the probability that the decision rule derived in part (a) will lead the company to install the new system?

11.19 A manufacturer of synthetic wall covering is considering a change in its production process, but feels that the cost of the change can be justified only if the mean number of surface defects in the finished product is less than .20 defect per square yard. The decision as to whether or not to make the change will be based on the total number of surface defects found in a trial production run of 50 square yards of the product using the proposed new process. The decision will be to make the change only if the sample run provides convincing evidence, at the .10 significance level, that the process defective rate is sufficiently low.

(a) Identify the action space and state space of this decision problem.

(b) Specify the null and alternative hypotheses.

(c) Assuming that the surface defects occur according to a Poisson process, derive and explicitly state the decision rule.

11.20 Construct the OC curve for the decision rule derived in Problem 11.19.

12

Sampling Distribution
of the Mean

Our discussion of hypothesis testing in Chapter 11 was limited to particular types of problems in which the test statistic is some number obtained by counting. Specifically, in the case of a hypergeometric or binomial test, the test statistic is the number of "successes" in the sample. Similarly, in the case of a Poisson test, the test statistic is the number of occurrences of some phenomenon in a specified amount of time or space. Since the scale used in counting is a discrete scale, these test statistics are discrete random variables. We now turn our attention to another test statistic, the sample mean, which may be either a discrete or continuous random variable, depending on whether the population being sampled is discrete or continuous.

12.1 SAMPLING DISTRIBUTION OF $\bar{X}$ WHEN POPULATION IS DISCRETE

Regardless of whether the sample mean is a discrete or continuous random variable, it will be denoted by $\bar{X}$. In this section we examine the probability distribution of $\bar{X}$ when the population distribution of the characteristic being observed is discrete.

12.1.1 Deriving the Sampling Distribution of $\bar{X}$ from a Sample Space

To illustrate how the probability distribution of the sample mean can be derived when the population is discrete, consider a population consisting of 5 neckties displayed in a haberdasher's showcase. The prices of these 5 neckties are listed in Table 12.1. A simple random sample of 2 ties is to be taken from this population, and the mean price of the 2 ties in the sample will be computed. Let us derive the sampling distribution of $\bar{X}$ under each of two different conditions: (1) sampling without replacement, and (2) sampling with replacement.

Table 12.1 Prices of a
Population
Consisting of
5 Neckties

Tie	Price
A	$ 3
B	5
C	6
D	9
E	10

Sampling without Replacement. The sample space for our experiment of drawing a random sample of 2 ties from the population of 5 ties *without replacement* is shown in Figure 12.1. The diagonal of this figure is empty since, if sampling is conducted without replacement, the same item cannot be selected on both draws. Thus, the sample space contains 20 sample points. Each of these sample points represents a possible outcome of the random process of selecting a simple random sample of 2 ties which might be selected from the population of 5 ties. Collectively, the 20 sample points represent all possible elementary outcomes of this sampling experiment. For each of the 20 possible samples shown in Figure 12.1, the mean price, $\bar{X}$, is computed in Table 12.2.

Second Item Selected

	A	B	C	D	E
A	—	(A, B)	(A, C)	(A, D)	(A, E)
B	(B, A)	—	(B, C)	(B, D)	(B, E)
C	(C, A)	(C, B)	—	(C, D)	(C, E)
D	(D, A)	(D, B)	(D, C)	—	(D, E)
E	(E, A)	(E, B)	(E, C)	(E, D)	—

First Item Selected

Figure 12.1 Sample Space for Drawing a Sample of 2 Ties from a Population of 5 Ties without Replacement

It is a simple matter to construct the sampling distribution of $\bar{X}$ by grouping the means of the 20 possible samples listed in Table 12.2 into a relative frequency distribution. This relative frequency distribution, shown in Table 12.3, is the sampling distribution of $\bar{X}$ for a random sample of 2 neckties selected without replacement from the population of 5 neckties in Table 12.1. Since the set of possible values of $\bar{X}$ is a discrete set, the sampling distribution of $\bar{X}$ is a discrete distribution.

Sampling with Replacement. If we revise the specifications of our sampling experiment from sampling without replacement to sampling *with replacement*, we obtain the sample space shown in Figure 12.2. This sample space is similar to that shown in Figure 12.1 except that the diagonal is no longer empty. This

Table 12.2 Mean Prices of All Possible Samples of 2 Ties Drawn without Replacement from a Population of 5 Ties

Sample	Sample Values	$\bar{x}$
A, B	$ 3 + $ 5	$4.00
A, C	3 + 6	4.50
A, D	3 + 9	6.00
A, E	3 + 10	6.50
B, A	5 + 3	4.00
B, C	5 + 6	5.50
B, D	5 + 9	7.00
B, E	5 + 10	7.50
C, A	6 + 3	4.50
C, B	6 + 5	5.50
C, D	6 + 9	7.50
C, E	6 + 10	8.00
D, A	9 + 3	6.00
D, B	9 + 5	7.00
D, C	9 + 6	7.50
D, E	9 + 10	9.50
E, A	10 + 3	6.50
E, B	10 + 5	7.50
E, C	10 + 6	8.00
E, D	10 + 9	9.50

Table 12.3 Sampling Distribution of the Mean Price of 2 Ties Selected without Replacement from a Finite Population of 5 Ties

$\bar{x}$	Frequency	Relative Frequency
$4.00	2	.10
4.50	2	.10
5.50	2	.10
6.00	2	.10
6.50	2	.10
7.00	2	.10
7.50	4	.20
8.00	2	.10
9.00	2	.10
	20	1.00

is because, when sampling is conducted with replacement, it is possible for the same article to be selected on both draws. Thus, the number of sample points is 25, rather than 20.

For each of the 25 possible samples shown in Figure 12.2, the mean price, $\bar{x}$, is computed in Table 12.4. When the possible sample means in this table are grouped into a relative frequency distribution, we obtain the sampling distribution of $\bar{X}$ given in Table 12.5. A comparison of Table 12.5 with Table 12.3 indicates that the sampling distribution of $\bar{X}$ is discrete, regardless of whether sampling is conducted with or without replacement.

Second Item Selected

First Item Selected	A	B	C	D	E
A	(A, A)	(A, B)	(A, C)	(A, D)	(A, E)
B	(B, A)	(B, B)	(B, C)	(B, D)	(B, E)
C	(C, A)	(C, B)	(C, C)	(C, D)	(C, E)
D	(D, A)	(D, B)	(D, C)	(D, D)	(D, E)
E	(E, A)	(E, B)	(E, C)	(E, D)	(E, E)

Figure 12.2 Sample Space for Drawing a Sample of 2 Ties from a Population of 5 Ties with Replacement

Table 12.4 Mean Prices of All Possible Samples of 2 Ties Drawn with Replacement from a Population of 5 Ties

Sample	*Sample Values*	$\bar{x}$
A, A	\$ 3 + \$ 3	\$ 3.00
A, B	3 + 5	4.00
A, C	3 + 6	4.50
A, D	3 + 9	6.00
A, E	3 + 10	6.50
B, A	5 + 3	4.00
B, B	5 + 5	5.00
B, C	5 + 6	5.50
B, D	5 + 9	7.00
B, E	5 + 10	7.50
C, A	6 + 3	4.50
C, B	6 + 5	5.50
C, C	6 + 6	6.00
C, D	6 + 9	7.50
C, E	6 + 10	8.00
D, A	9 + 3	6.00
D, B	9 + 5	7.00
D, C	9 + 6	7.50
D, D	9 + 9	9.00
D, E	9 + 10	9.50
E, A	10 + 3	6.50
E, B	10 + 5	7.50
E, C	10 + 6	8.00
E, D	10 + 9	9.50
E, E	10 + 10	10.00

The sampling distributions given in Table 12.3 and 12.5 are presented graphically in Figure 12.3. As this figure demonstrates, the distribution for sampling with replacement has more possible values of $\bar{X}$ than does the distribution for sampling without replacement. This results from the fact that, when sampling

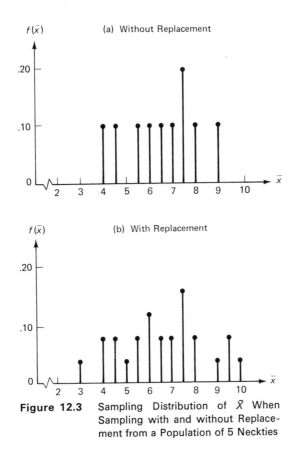

Figure 12.3 Sampling Distribution of $\bar{X}$ When Sampling with and without Replacement from a Population of 5 Neckties

Table 12.5 Sampling Distribution of the Mean Price of 2 Ties Selected with Replacement from a Population of 5 Ties

$\bar{x}$	Frequency	Relative Frequency
$ 3.00	1	.04
4.00	2	.08
4.50	2	.08
5.00	1	.04
5.50	2	.08
6.00	3	.12
6.50	2	.08
7.00	2	.08
7.50	4	.16
8.00	2	.08
9.00	1	.04
9.50	2	.08
10.00	1	.04
	25	1.00

from a specified population of discrete values, sampling with replacement makes it possible to obtain some values of the sample mean that are not possible if sampling is conducted without replacement.

12.1.2 Expected Value of the Random Variable $\bar{X}$

For our example of selecting a sample of 2 ties from a population of 5 ties, Table 12.6 brings together three distributions: (1) the population distribution, (2)

Table 12.6 Demonstration That the Expected Value of $\bar{X}$ Is Equal to the Population Mean

Population		Sampling Distributions of $\bar{X}$					
		Without Replacement			With Replacement		
Item	x_i	$\bar{x}$	$f(\bar{x})$	$\bar{x}f(\bar{x})$	$\bar{x}$	$f(\bar{x})$	$\bar{x}f(\bar{x})$
A	$ 3	$4.00	.10	$0.40	$3.00	.04	$0.12
		4.50	.10	0.45	4.00	.08	0.32
B	5	5.50	.10	0.55	4.50	.08	0.36
		6.00	.10	0.60	5.00	.04	0.20
C	6	6.50	.10	0.65	5.50	.08	0.44
		7.00	.10	0.70	6.00	.12	0.72
D	9	7.50	.20	1.50	6.50	.08	0.52
		8.00	.10	0.80	7.00	.08	0.56
E	10	9.50	.10	0.95	7.50	.16	1.20
$\sum x_i = \$33$			1.00	$6.60	8.00	.08	0.64
					9.00	.04	0.36
					9.50	.08	0.76
					10.00	.04	0.40
						1.00	$6.60

$$\mu = \frac{\sum x_i}{N} = \frac{\$33}{5} = \$6.60 \qquad E(\bar{X}) = \sum \bar{x}f(\bar{x}) = \$6.60 \qquad E(\bar{X}) = \sum \bar{x}f(\bar{x}) = \$6.60$$

the sampling distribution of $\bar{X}$ for sampling without replacement, and (3) the sampling distribution of $\bar{X}$ for sampling with replacement. This table shows the calculation of the mean of the population, as well as the calculation of the expected value of $\bar{X}$ for each of the sampling distributions. The population mean was calculated from Formula (3.2). For each of the two sampling distributions, the expected value of $\bar{X}$ was computed from Formula (7.2).

For each of the two sampling distributions in Table 12.6, we can see that the *expected* value of the sample mean is equal to the population mean of $6.60. This is no mere coincidence, for it is true as a generalization that $E(\bar{X})$, *the expected value of the mean of a simple random sample, is equal to μ, the mean of the population from which the sample was drawn.* For notational convenience, we use $\mu_{\bar{x}}$ interchangeably with $E(\bar{X})$. Using this notation, the generalization above may be expressed in terms of a formula as

$$E(\bar{X}) = \mu_{\bar{x}} = \mu \qquad (12.1)$$

Thus, if the population mean is known or can somehow be specified, the expected value of $\bar{X}$ can be determined directly from Formula (12.1) without actually using the sampling distribution of $\bar{X}$ as was done in Table 12.6.

The statement that the *expected* value of the sample mean is equal to the population mean should *not* be misinterpreted to imply that the mean of any particular sample will necessarily be equal to the population mean. In fact, a sample mean seldom coincides exactly with the mean of the population from which the sample was taken. Indeed, it may even be impossible for the sample mean to coincide with the population mean. This is the case in our particular example summarized in Table 12.6, where we can see that none of the possible values of $\bar{X}$ in either sampling distribution equals the population mean of $6.60.

12.1.3 Variance of the Random Variable $\bar{X}$

In Section 12.1.2 we observed how the *expected value* of the sample mean, $E(\bar{X})$, is related to the population mean, μ. The purpose of this section is to demonstrate how the *variance* of the sample mean, $V(\bar{X})$, is related to the population variance, σ^2. For notational convenience in later applications, we will use $\sigma_{\bar{X}}^2$ interchangeably with $V(\bar{X})$. In the following discussion, the reader should be careful to distinguish between $\sigma_{\bar{X}}^2$ (the variance of the sample mean) and σ^2 (the variance of the population).

Table 12.7 shows the calculation of the variance of (1) the population distribution, (2) the sampling distribution of $\bar{X}$ for sampling without replacement, and (3) the sampling distribution of $\bar{X}$ for sampling with replacement. The population variance was calculated from Formula (3.7). For each of the two sampling distributions, the variance of $\bar{X}$ was computed from Formula (7.12).

As we have already observed in Table 12.6, the *means* of all three distributions are identical. That is, whether sampling is conducted with or without replacement, the expected value of the sampling distribution of $\bar{X}$ is equal to the mean of the population. However, in Table 12.7, we see that the *variances* of the three distributions are all different. The variance of the sampling distribution with replacement is smaller than the variance of the parent population, and the variance of the sampling distribution without replacement is even smaller. In general, when a sample of size n is taken from a population of size N *without replacement*, the variance of $\bar{X}$ is related to the variance of the population according to the formula

$$V(\bar{X}) = \sigma_{\bar{X}}^2 = \frac{\sigma^2}{n}\left(\frac{N - n}{N - 1}\right) \tag{12.2}$$

However, when sampling is conducted *with replacement*, the relationship between $\sigma_{\bar{X}}^2$ and σ^2 is given by

$$V(\bar{X}) = \sigma_{\bar{X}}^2 = \frac{\sigma^2}{n} \tag{12.3}$$

Comparing these two formulas, we see that Formula (12.2) differs from Formula (12.3) by the factor $\left(\dfrac{N - n}{N - 1}\right)$, which is sometimes referred to as the *finite correction factor*. As long as the sample size is greater than 1 but less than the population size, the value of this factor will be less than 1 but greater than 0. Under these conditions, it should be clear that Formula (12.2) will yield a

Table 12.7 Calculation of Variances of Population and Sampling Distributions

Population

Item	x_i	x_i^2
A	$ 3	9
B	5	25
C	6	36
D	9	81
E	10	100
		251

$$\sigma^2 = \frac{\sum x_i^2}{N} - \mu^2$$
$$= \frac{251}{5} - (6.60)^2$$
$$= 6.64$$

Sampling Distribution of $\bar{X}$

Without Replacement

$\bar{x}$	$\bar{x}^2$	$f(\bar{x})$	$\bar{x}^2 f(\bar{x})$
$4.00	16.00	.10	1.600
4.50	20.25	.10	2.025
5.50	30.25	.10	3.025
6.00	36.00	.10	3.600
6.50	42.25	.10	4.225
7.00	49.00	.10	4.900
7.50	56.25	.20	11.250
8.00	64.00	.10	6.400
9.50	90.25	.10	9.025
			46.050

$$\sigma_{\bar{X}}^2 = E(\bar{X}^2) - [E(\bar{X})]^2$$
$$= 46.050 - (6.60)^2$$
$$= 2.49$$

With Replacement

$\bar{x}$	$\bar{x}^2$	$f(\bar{x})$	$\bar{x}^2 f(\bar{x})$
$3.00	9.00	.04	.3600
4.00	16.00	.08	1.2800
4.50	20.25	.08	1.6200
5.00	25.00	.04	1.0000
5.50	30.25	.08	2.4200
6.00	36.00	.12	4.3200
6.50	42.25	.08	3.3800
7.00	49.00	.08	3.9200
7.50	56.25	.16	9.0000
8.00	64.00	.08	5.1200
9.00	81.00	.04	3.2400
9.50	90.25	.08	7.2200
10.00	100.00	.04	4.0000
			46.8800

$$\sigma_{\bar{X}}^2 = E(\bar{X}^2) - [E(\bar{X})]^2$$
$$= 46.8800 - (6.60)^2$$
$$= 3.32$$

smaller value than Formula (12.3). That is, when sampling from a finite population, the variance of $\bar{X}$ for sampling *without* replacement will be smaller than the variance of $\bar{X}$ for sampling *with* replacement. It should also be clear from Formula (12.3) that, as long as the sample size is greater than 1, the variance of $\bar{X}$ for sampling with replacement will be less than the population variance. Since the variance of $\bar{X}$ is less for sampling without replacement than for sampling with replacement, it becomes obvious that, regardless of whether sampling is conducted with or without replacement, the variance of $\bar{X}$ will be less than the population variance.

As the population size becomes relatively large compared to the sample size, the factor $\left(\dfrac{N-n}{N-1}\right)$ in Formula (12.2) approaches a limiting value of 1. When this occurs, the value yielded by Formula (12.2) approaches the value yielded by Formula (12.3). Thus, when a relatively small sample is taken from a very large population, whether sampling is conducted with or without replacement has no material effect on the value of $\sigma_{\bar{X}}^2$. As we observed in Section 9.3, if sampling is conducted with replacement, the population is inexhaustible and hence may be regarded as infinite from a sampling standpoint. Thus, Formula (12.3) is applicable to sampling from an infinite population as well as to sampling from a finite population with replacement.

For our example, we have $N = 5$ and $n = 2$. Thus, the population size is very small, and the sample size is a substantial portion (40%) of the population size. Accordingly, whether sampling is conducted with or without replacement does have a material effect on the value of $\sigma_{\bar{X}}^2$. Recalling that the population variance is $\sigma^2 = 6.64$, the variance of $\bar{X}$ for sampling *without* replacement is obtained from Formula (12.2) as follows:

$$\sigma_{\bar{X}}^2 = \frac{\sigma^2}{n}\left(\frac{N-n}{N-1}\right) = \frac{6.64}{2}\left(\frac{5-2}{5-1}\right) = 2.49$$

Similarly, the variance of $\bar{X}$ for sampling *with* replacement is obtained from Formula (12.3) as follows:

$$\sigma_{\bar{X}}^2 = \frac{\sigma^2}{n} = \frac{6.64}{2} = 3.32$$

These results agree with those obtained earlier in Table 12.7 by using Formula (7.12). Thus, if the population variance is known or can somehow be specified, the variance of $\bar{X}$ may be computed directly from either Formula (12.2) or Formula (12.3) without actually using the sampling distribution of $\bar{X}$ as was done in Table 12.7.

The standard deviation of the sampling distribution of $\bar{X}$ is called the *standard error of the mean*, which is simply the positive square root of $V(\bar{X})$. Thus, when sampling is conducted without replacement, the standard error of the mean is given by

$$\sigma_{\bar{X}} = \frac{\sigma}{\sqrt{n}}\left(\frac{N-n}{N-1}\right) \tag{12.4}$$

When sampling is conducted with replacement, the standard error of the mean is given by

$$\sigma_{\bar{X}} = \frac{\sigma}{\sqrt{n}} \tag{12.5}$$

12.2 THE NORMAL DISTRIBUTION

In Section 12.1 we considered how the sampling distribution of $\bar{X}$ can be derived when $\bar{X}$ is a discrete random variable. The derivation of the discrete sampling distribution was accomplished by a fairly straightforward procedure. However, when $\bar{X}$ is continuous, the derivation of the sampling distribution involves an entirely different approach. To apply this approach, it is first necessary to become familiar with the normal distribution, which is by far the best known and most commonly used of all probability distributions.

12.2.1 Characteristics of the Normal Distribution

The normal distribution is a continuous probability function with two parameters. Denoting these parameters by a and b, the normal density function for a random variable X is given by

$$f_n(x \mid a, b) = \frac{1}{b\sqrt{2\pi}} \exp\left[-\frac{1}{2}\left(\frac{x-a}{b}\right)^2\right] \qquad -\infty < x < \infty \qquad (12.6)$$

where π = the familiar constant, approximately equal to 3.1416

It can be shown mathematically that the mean of the normal distribution is equal to the parameter a and the standard deviation is equal to the parameter b. Therefore, the general normal density function is customarily expressed as

$$f_n(x \mid \mu, \sigma) = \frac{1}{\sigma\sqrt{2\pi}} \exp\left[-\frac{1}{2}\left(\frac{x-\mu}{\sigma}\right)^2\right] \qquad -\infty < x < \infty \qquad (12.7)$$

Because of the considerable importance of the normal distribution in statistical theory and application, it is worthwhile to examine some of the characteristics of the normal density function:

1. The normal density function describes a continuous, bell-shaped curve, as illustrated in Figure 12.4.
2. The normal curve is symmetrical about μ, at which point $f(x)$ reaches its maximum value. Since $f(x)$ reaches its maximum value for $x = \mu$, the mode is equal to the mean. Because of the symmetry, $P(X \le \mu) = P(X \ge \mu) = .50$ for any normal distribution. Thus, the median of any normal distribution also is equal to the mean.

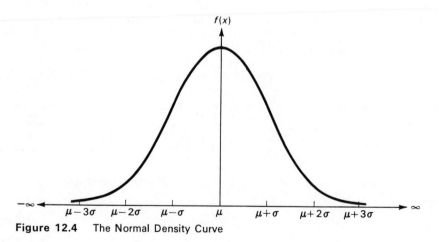

Figure 12.4 The Normal Density Curve

3. In both directions from the mean, the curve is asymptotic to the horizontal axis. That is, as the tails of the distribution extend toward infinity in either direction, they approach the axis more and more closely without ever reaching it.

4. Within the central range of 1 standard deviation on either side of the mean, the curve is concave downward. Beyond that range—that is, for x-values less than $(\mu - \sigma)$ or greater than $(\mu + \sigma)$—the curve is concave upward. In other words, inflection points of the curve lie at a distance of 1 standard deviation above and below the mean.

5. Any normal distribution is determined completely by specifying values for the parameters μ and σ. The spread of the curve—whether it is low and broad, or tall and narrow—is determined by the value of σ. The *location* of the curve with

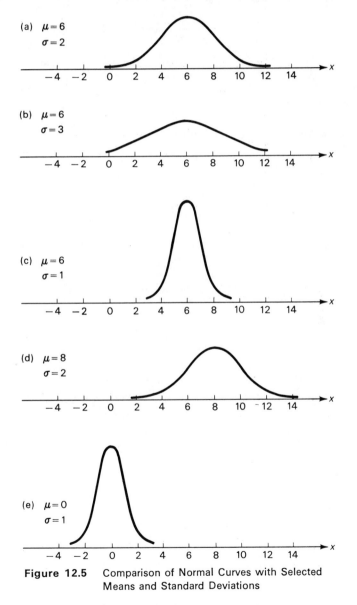

Figure 12.5   Comparison of Normal Curves with Selected Means and Standard Deviations

respect to its position on the x-axis is determined by the value of μ. In Figure 12.5, the distributions (a), (b), and (c) have identical means ($\mu = 6$), so they all are centered at $x = 6$. However, these three distributions differ in spread since they have different standard deviations. Curves (a) and (d) have identical spreads because they have identical standard deviations, but they are located in different positions due to their different means. Similarly, curves (c) and (e) have identical standard deviations (and hence identical spreads) but different means (and hence different locations). The fact that the exact spread of a normal distribution is determined if we know the value of σ, even though the value of μ may be unknown, is extremely important in applying the normal distribution to decision problems.

The normal cumulative density function may be expressed as

$$F_n(x \mid \mu, \sigma) = \int_{-\infty}^{x} \frac{1}{\sigma\sqrt{2\pi}} \exp\left[-\frac{1}{2}\left(\frac{t-\mu}{\sigma}\right)^2\right] dt \qquad (12.8)$$

The cumulative function corresponding to the density function in Figure 12.4 is shown graphically in Figure 12.6. As this figure indicates, the normal cumulative density function describes a smooth sigmoid (S-shaped) curve that is sometimes called the *normal ogive*.

12.2.2 Standard Normal Probability Table

When a random variable has a normal density function with $\mu = 0$ and $\sigma = 1$, Formula (12.7) is reduced to

$$f_n(x \mid \mu = 0, \sigma = 1) = \frac{1}{\sqrt{2\pi}} e^{-(1/2)x^2}$$

This particular density function is called the standard normal density function. To distinguish the standard normal density function from the general normal density function given by Formula (12.7), we adopt the notation $f_N(z)$ in place of $f_n(x \mid \mu, \sigma)$. Using this notation, the standard normal density function is given by

$$f_N(z) = \frac{1}{\sqrt{2\pi}} e^{-(1/2)z^2} \qquad (12.9)$$

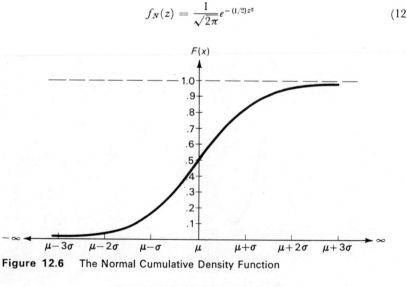

Figure 12.6 The Normal Cumulative Density Function

Sampling Distribution of the Mean

Then the standard normal integral (the standard normal cumulative density function) is

$$F_N(z) = \int_{-\infty}^{z} \frac{1}{\sqrt{2\pi}} e^{-(1/2)t^2} dt \tag{12.10}$$

It is important to observe the following distinctions in notation between the standard normal and the general normal probability distributions.

1. The random variable in the standard normal distribution is symbolized by Z, whereas the random variable in the general normal distribution is denoted by X.
2. The subscript N is used to designate a standard normal function, whereas the subscript n is used to denote a general normal function.
3. The parameters μ and σ are omitted from the standard normal notation since, by definition, μ must be equal to 0 and σ must be equal to 1.

The standard normal integral in Formula (12.10) has been evaluated for selected values of Z. The results are tabulated in Table I of Appendix II. This table gives $F_N(z)$ for selected values of Z. In other words, this table permits us to obtain standard normal probabilities without evaluating the integral in Formula (12.10). Readers should familiarize themselves with Table I by verifying the following probabilities:

$$P(Z < 2.17) = F_N(2.17) = .9850$$
$$P(Z < -1.55) = F_N(-1.55) = .0606$$

The standard normal integral table may be used to obtain probabilities for any normal distribution, regardless of the values of μ and σ. This is because it is possible to convert any normal distribution into the standard normal distribution. Specifically, if X is a normally distributed random variable with mean μ and standard deviation σ, then the quantity $(X - \mu)/\sigma$ is a random variable that has the standard normal distribution. This relationship between the general normal variable X and the standard normal variable Z may be expressed as follows:

$$Z = \frac{X - \mu}{\sigma} \tag{12.11}$$

By means of this formula, values of any normally distributed random variable X may be converted into corresponding values of Z, such that there is a direct linear relationship between the values on the two scales. For instance, suppose that a random variable X is normally distributed with $\mu = 100$ and $\sigma = 10$. Then, applying Formula (12.11) to selected x-values:

$$\text{if } x = 110 \qquad z = \frac{110 - 100}{10} = +1.0$$

$$\text{if } x = 100 \qquad z = \frac{100 - 100}{10} = 0$$

$$\text{if } x = 85 \qquad z = \frac{85 - 100}{10} = -1.5$$

This relationship between corresponding values of X and Z is illustrated in Figure 12.7.

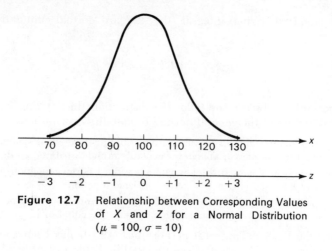

Figure 12.7 Relationship between Corresponding Values of X and Z for a Normal Distribution ($\mu = 100$, $\sigma = 10$)

Because of the direct linear relationship between X and Z, the general normal integral may be converted to the standard normal integral in the following manner:

$$F_n(x \mid \mu, \sigma) = F_N\left(\frac{x - \mu}{\sigma}\right) = F_N(z) \tag{12.12}$$

For instance, let X be a random variable that is normally distributed with $\mu = 100$ and $\sigma = 10$. Then the probability that a value of X will be less than 125 may be computed as follows:

$$P(X < 125) = F_n(125 \mid 100, 10) = F_N\left(\frac{125 - 100}{10}\right) = F_N(2.5)$$

From Table I, we find that $F_N(2.5) = .9938$. Thus, $P(X < 125)$ is equal to .9938.

In a similar manner, the probability that a random variable X will lie in the interval between a and b may be obtained from the standard normal integral table by using the relationship

$$
\begin{aligned}
P(a \leq X \leq b) &= P(X \leq b) - P(X \leq a) \\
&= F_n(b \mid \mu, \sigma) - F_n(a \mid \mu, \sigma) \\
&= F_N\left(\frac{b - \mu}{\sigma}\right) - F_N\left(\frac{a - \mu}{\sigma}\right)
\end{aligned} \tag{12.13}
$$

For example, if X is normally distributed with $\mu = 100$ and $\sigma = 10$, the probability that a value of X will lie between 85 and 110 is obtained as follows:

$$
\begin{aligned}
P(85 \leq X \leq 110) &= F_N\left(\frac{110 - 100}{10}\right) - F_N\left(\frac{85 - 100}{10}\right) \\
&= F_N(1.0) - F_N(-1.5)
\end{aligned}
$$

From Table I, we find $F_N(1) = .8413$ and $F_N(-1.5) = .0668$. Therefore,

$$P(85 \le X \le 110) = .8413 - .0668 = .7745$$

Example 1:

Let X denote the breaking strength of a plastic coat hook produced by an automatic process. Suppose that X is normally distributed with $\mu = 60$ pounds and $\sigma = 4$ pounds.

1. What is the probability that the breaking strength of a randomly selected coat hook will be less than 58? Using Formula (12.7) together with Table I, we may obtain this probability as follows:

$$P(X < 58) = F_n(58 \mid 60,4)$$
$$= F_N\left(\frac{58 - 60}{4}\right) = F_N(-.50) = .3085$$

This probability is shown graphically by the shaded area under the normal curve in Figure 12.8a.

2. What is the probability that the breaking strength of a randomly selected coat hook will be greater than 65? This probability is computed as follows:

$$P(X > 65) = 1 - F_n(65 \mid 60,4)$$
$$= 1 - F_N\left(\frac{65 - 60}{4}\right) = 1 - F_N(1.25)$$
$$= 1 - .8943 = .1057$$

The probability obtained is represented by the shaded area under the normal curve in Figure 12.8b.

3. What is the probability that the breaking strength of a randomly selected coat hook will lie between 59 and 66? Using Formula (12.13) together with Table I, we obtain

$$P(59 \le X \le 66) = F_N\left(\frac{66 - 60}{4}\right) - F_N\left(\frac{59 - 60}{4}\right)$$
$$= F_N(1.50) - F_N(-.25)$$
$$= .9332 - .4013 = .5319$$

This probability is shown by the shaded area under the normal curve in Figure 12.8c.

Example 2:

Assume that the net weights of packages of breakfast cereal produced by an automatic process are normally distributed such that the probability is .33 that the net weight of a package will exceed 16.06 ounces. If the standard deviation of the distribution of weights is .10 ounce, what is the average net weight per package?

Let W be a random variable denoting the net weight of a package. We are told that $P(W > 16.06) = .33$, which implies that $P(W \le 16.06) = .67$. Thus,

$$F_N\left(\frac{16.06 - \mu}{.10}\right) = .67$$

From Table I, we can see that if $F_N(z) = .67$, then $z = .44$. Consequently,

$$\frac{16.06 - \mu}{.10} = .44$$

By simple algebra,

$$\mu = 16.06 - .44(.10) = 16.016$$

Thus, the mean net weight per package produced by the process is 16.016 ounces.

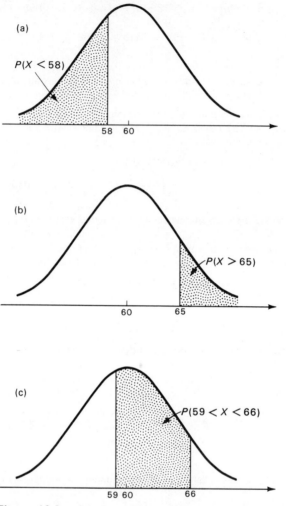

Figure 12.8 Areas under Normal Curve ($\mu = 60$, $\sigma = 4$)

In figure: (a) $P(X < 58)$ with values 58 60; (b) $P(X > 65)$ with values 60 65; (c) $P(59 < X < 66)$ with values 59 60 66

12.2.3 *Fractiles of a Normal Distribution*

We have seen how the standard normal integral table can be used in answering such a question as: If a random variable X is normally distributed with $\mu = 80$ and $\sigma = 12$, what is the probability that a randomly observed value of X will be less than 68? However, with regard to the same random variable, suppose that we ask the question: What is the value of X such that the probability is .40 that a randomly observed value of X will be no greater than this value? This is equivalent to asking: What is $x_{.40}$, the .40 fractile of the distribution of X?

The value of $x_{.40}$ may be obtained with the aid of the standard normal integral table. To do this, we begin by scanning Table I in search of a cumulative probability of .40. Unfortunately, a cumulative probability of exactly .40 does not appear in the table However, the table does show that $F_N(-.25) = .4013$ and $F_N(-.26) = .3974$. By linear interpolation, we obtain $F_N(-.253)$

$= .40$. Thus, $z_{.40} = -.253$, which is the .40 fractile of the standard normal distribution. Next, applying Formula (12.11), we may write

$$z_{.40} = \frac{x_{.40} - \mu}{\sigma}$$

Then, by algebra, we obtain

$$x_{.40} = \mu + z_{.40}\sigma$$

Finally, by substitution,

$$x_{.40} = 80 + (-.253)(12) = 76.964$$

Thus, the .40 fractile of a normal distribution with $\mu = 80$ and $\sigma = 12$ is 76.964.

The approximate value of any desired fractile of the standard normal distribution may be obtained from Table I by linear interpolation. To relieve the reader from this tedious task of interpolation, the most commonly used fractiles of the standard normal distribution are given in Table J (Appendix II). Thus, by direct reference to this table, the reader may immediately verify that $z_{.40}$ is equal to $-.253$.

12.3 SAMPLING DISTRIBUTION OF $\overline{X}$ WHEN POPULATION IS CONTINUOUS

As we observed at the outset of this chapter, when the population being sampled is continuous, the sampling distribution of $\overline{X}$ is also continuous. As given by Formula (12.1), the expected value of $\overline{X}$ is equal to the population mean μ. Since a continuous population is infinite, the standard error of the mean is equal to $\sigma/\sqrt{n}$, as given by Formula (12.5).

12.3.1 Distribution of $\overline{X}$ When Population Is Normal

It may be shown mathematically that if a simple random sample is selected from a normal population, then the sampling distribution of $\overline{X}$ will also be normal. Formally stated as a theorem:

If a simple random sample of size n is to be taken from a normal population with mean μ and standard deviation σ, then the sampling distribution of $\overline{X}$ is also normal, with mean $\mu_{\overline{X}} = \mu$ and standard error $\sigma_{\overline{X}} = \sigma/\sqrt{n}$.

To illustrate the application of this theorem, consider an automatic process that produces vitamin C tablets. Experience has shown that the amount of active ingredient in the tablets produced by this process is normally distributed with $\mu = 50$ milligrams and $\sigma = 6$ milligrams. If a simple random sample of $n = 4$ tablets is to be taken from the output of this process, what is the probability that the sample mean will not differ from the population mean by more than 3 milligrams?

Since the population mean is equal to 50, the above question is equivalent to asking for the probability that the sample mean will lie between 47 and 53 milligrams. To determine the probability $P(47 \leq \overline{X} \leq 53)$, we must first specify the probability distribution of $\overline{X}$. This may be done directly from the theorem. Since the population is normal, the sampling distribution of $\overline{X}$ is also normal. Also, since $\mu = 50$, the mean of the distribution of $\bar{X}$ is $\mu_{\bar{X}} = \mu = 50$. Furthermore, since $\sigma = 6$ and $n = 4$, the standard error of $\bar{X}$ is $\sigma_{\bar{X}} = \sigma/\sqrt{n} = 6/\sqrt{4} = 3$. Then, applying Formula (12.13) and using Table I, we obtain

$$
\begin{aligned}
P(47 \leq \bar{X} \leq 53) &= F_n(53 \mid 50, 3) - F_n(47 \mid 50, 3) \\
&= F_N\left(\frac{53 - 50}{3}\right) - F_N\left(\frac{47 - 50}{3}\right) \\
&= F_N(1.0) - F_N(-1.0) \\
&= .8413 - .1587 \\
&= .6826
\end{aligned}
$$

Thus, there is a .6826 probability that the sample mean will fall between 47 and 53 milligrams. That is, the probability is .6826 that the sample mean will not differ from the population mean by more than 3 milligrams.

From the theorem presented in this section, it should be clear that, for any sample size greater than 1, the standard error of $\bar{X}$ will be smaller than the standard deviation of the population. For instance, in our example, the standard error of $\bar{X}$ is 3, which is smaller than the population standard deviation of 6. Thus, compared to the population distribution, the distribution of $\bar{X}$ is more closely concentrated around the mean. This is clear from inspection of Figure 12.9, which compares the population distribution with the sampling distribution of $\bar{X}$ for $n = 4$.

It should also be clear from the theorem that, the larger the sample size, the smaller will be the value of $\sigma_{\bar{X}}$, since $\sigma_{\bar{X}} = \sigma/\sqrt{n}$. Hence, the larger the sample size, the more closely concentrated the sampling distribution of $\bar{X}$ will be around the mean. This, in turn, implies that, the larger the sample size, the greater will be the probability that the sample mean will lie close to the population mean. To illustrate this point, let us determine the probability that the sample mean in our example will lie between 47 and 53 if the sample size is increased from $n = 4$ to $n = 9$. In this case, the standard error of $\bar{X}$ will be $\sigma_{\bar{X}} = 6/\sqrt{9}$

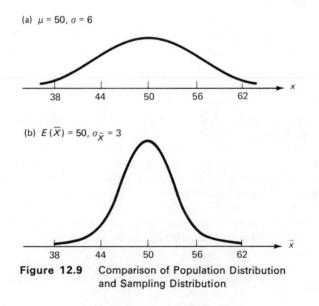

(a) $\mu = 50$, $\sigma = 6$

(b) $E(\bar{X}) = 50$, $\sigma_{\bar{X}} = 3$

Figure 12.9 Comparison of Population Distribution and Sampling Distribution

$= 2$. Then, with this increased sample size, the probability that the sample mean will not differ from the population mean by more than 3 milligrams is

$$P(47 \leq \bar{X} \leq 53) = F_n(53|50, 2) - F_n(47|50, 2)$$
$$= F_N\left(\frac{53 - 50}{2}\right) - F_N\left(\frac{47 - 50}{2}\right)$$
$$= F_N(1.5) - F_N(-1.5)$$
$$= .9332 - .0668$$
$$= .8664$$

Thus, by increasing the sample size from $n = 4$ to $n = 9$, the probability that the sample mean will not differ from the population mean by more than 3 milligrams is increased from .6826 to .8664. Following this procedure, the reader may verify that, if the sample size were increased to $n = 16$, the standard error of $\bar{X}$ would be 1.50, and the probability that the sample mean will not differ from the population mean by more than 3 milligrams would be further increased, to .9544.

The sampling distributions of $\bar{X}$ for the three different sample sizes used in our example are shown in Figure 12.10. Inspection of this figure immediately

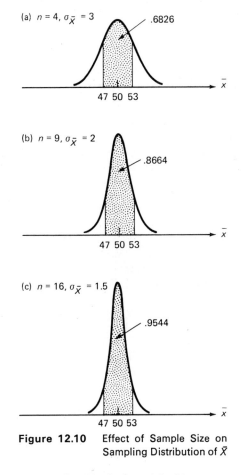

Figure 12.10 Effect of Sample Size on Sampling Distribution of $\bar{X}$

reveals that all three distributions are normal. This reflects the fact that the sampling distribution of $\bar{X}$ for *any* sample size is always normal if the population from which the sample is to be taken is normal. Inspection of Figure 12.10 also confirms our previous observation that the sampling distribution of $\bar{X}$ becomes more closely concentrated around the mean as the sample size increases. Consequently, as the sample size increases, the probability that the sample mean will lie between 47 and 53 grows larger. In other words, as the sample size becomes larger, there is an increasing probability that the sample mean will not differ from the population mean of 50 by more than 3 milligrams. This is equivalent to saying that, as n increases, $P(|\bar{X} - \mu| \leq 3)$ also increases.

Generalizing our observations from Figure 12.10, it is true for any positive value d that $P(|\bar{X} - \mu| \leq d)$ increases as n increases.[1] Indeed, $P(|\bar{X} - \mu| \leq d)$ approaches 1 as n approaches infinity. Expressed more formally,

$$P(|\bar{X} - \mu| \leq d) \longrightarrow 1 \qquad \text{as } n \longrightarrow \infty \qquad (12.14)$$

The expression given in Formula (12.14) is one form of an important probability theorem called the *law of large numbers*. In words, this version of the law of large numbers says that, for any simple random sample selected from a population with mean μ, the probability that the absolute deviation of the sample mean from the population mean will not exceed any arbitrary positive value d, no matter how small, approaches 1 as the sample size approaches infinity. This law applies to sampling from any population—normal or nonnormal, continuous or discrete.

12.3.2 Distribution of $\bar{X}$ When Population Is Not Normal

Although the normal distribution adequately describes many continuous populations, it is important to realize that many other continuous populations are definitely not normal. For example, consider an infinite population of all 9-volt transistor radio batteries that might be manufactured by a particular production process. The operating lives of the batteries produced by this process vary considerably. Of course, the number of hours that any of these batteries will operate cannot be less than zero. Although some batteries may operate for as much as 40 hours or even longer, the typical operating life of these batteries is about 12 hours. Thus, the population distribution of the operating lives is bounded by zero at the lower end, and is skewed in the positive direction. Hence, it would not be reasonable to attempt to describe this population by a normal distribution, since a normal distribution is symmetrical and extends indefinitely in both directions.

When sampling from a continuous population that is not normal, the sampling distribution of $\bar{X}$ is not normal. In such a case, the *exact* shape of the sampling distribution of $\bar{X}$ can be determined only if it is possible to specify the precise form of the population distribution. Unfortunately, in practical situations that require sampling, the precise form of the population distribution is usually unknown and hence the *exact* sampling distribution of $\bar{X}$ cannot be

---

[1]This statement is true without exception for continuous populations. However, the statement is true for discrete populations only as a generalization, since exceptions to the rule can occur.

determined. However, if the sample size is sufficiently large, it is possible to specify the *approximate* sampling distribution of $\bar{X}$ by application of a celebrated statistical law known as the *central limit theorem*.

Mathematically, the central limit theorem is so complex that it not only is difficult to prove but also is difficult to state correctly in a general form. However, as applied to the specific case of the sampling distribution of $\bar{X}$, we may state this theorem as follows:

> If a simple random sample of n observations is to be taken from a population with finite mean and variance, the distribution of the sample mean $\bar{X}$ will approach a normal distribution as n approaches infinity.

The relevant implication of this theorem to our present discussion is that, if the sample size is sufficiently large, the sampling distribution of $\bar{X}$ will be *approximately normal* in shape, regardless of the precise shape of the population distribution. Just *how close* this approximation is to a normal distribution will depend on two interacting factors:

1. *Size of the sample.* The larger the sample size, the closer the sampling distribution of $\bar{X}$ will approximate a normal distribution.

2. *Shape of the population.* For a fixed sample size, the more closely the population approaches the general shape of a normal distribution, the more closely the sampling distribution of $\bar{X}$ will approach normality.

The interactive effects of sample size and shape of the population on the shape of the sampling distribution of $\bar{X}$ is illustrated in Figure 12.11. This figure shows, for selected sample sizes, the sampling distributions of $\bar{X}$ for samples taken from populations having a variety of nonnormal shapes. The most important observation to be made from this figure is that, regardless of the shape of the population distribution, the sampling distribution of $\bar{X}$ approaches the symmetrical, bell-shaped appearance of a normal distribution as the sample size increases. The more closely the population distribution resembles a normal distribution, the smaller is the sample size at which the sampling distribution of $\bar{X}$ begins to resemble a normal distribution.

For each of the population distributions shown in Figure 12.11, the sampling distribution of $\bar{X}$ has an approximately normal appearance at $n = 20$. However, care should be taken to avoid drawing the erroneous conclusion that the sampling distribution of $\bar{X}$ necessarily approximates a normal distribution for a sample size of only 20 observations. Many textbooks suggest the rule of thumb that the sampling distribution of $\bar{X}$ may be assumed to be essentially normal if the sample size is at least 30. However, it has been demonstrated that, if a sample is to be taken from a population that is radically nonnormal, the sampling distribution of $\bar{X}$ may differ markedly from a normal distribution even if the sample contains several hundred observations.[2] Thus, if there is reason to suspect that the population departs radically from normality, we recommend, as a more cautious approach, assuming that the sampling distribution of $\bar{X}$ is essentially normal only if the sample size is at least 50.

If it is reasonable to assume, by virtue of the central limit theorem, that the sampling distribution of $\bar{X}$ is approximately normal, then we may apply the normal distribution to obtain approximate answers to probability questions

---

[2]See James V. Bradley, *Distribution-Free Statistical Tests* (Englewood Cliffs, N.J.: Prentice-Hall, Inc., 1968), pp. 24–32.

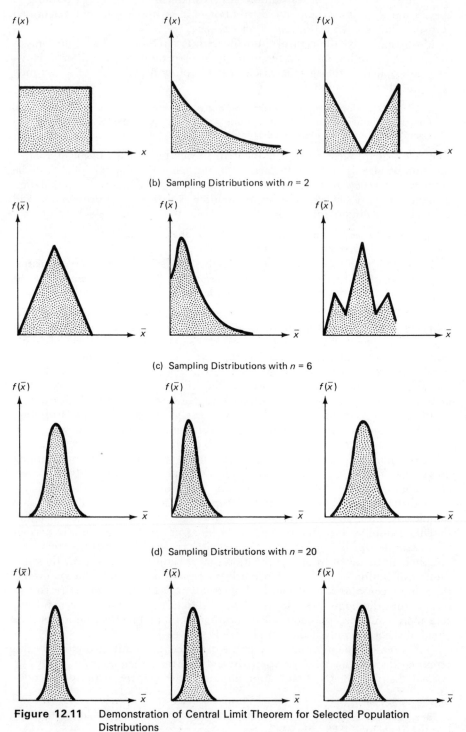

Figure 12.11   Demonstration of Central Limit Theorem for Selected Population Distributions

concerning the sample mean. For example, consider an automatic process that produces lengths of steel wire. The distribution of the breaking strengths of the wires produced by this process has a mean $\mu = 30$ pounds and a standard deviation $\sigma = 12$ pounds. Rather than being normal, this population distribution has a lower bound of zero and is moderately skewed in the upward direction. If a simple random sample of 100 lengths of wire is selected from this population, what is the approximate probability that the mean breaking strength of the wires in the sample will be no greater than 33 pounds?

Using $\bar{X}$ to denote the mean breaking strength of the wires in the sample, the desired probability may be expressed as $P(\bar{X} \leq 33)$. To determine this probability, we must first specify the sampling distribution of $\bar{X}$. By virtue of the central limit theorem, it is reasonable to assume that this sampling distribution is approximately normal. Since the population mean is $\mu = 30$, the mean of the sampling distribution of $\bar{X}$ is $\mu_{\bar{X}} = \mu = 30$. Also, since $\sigma = 12$ and $n = 100$, the standard error of $\bar{X}$ is $\sigma_{\bar{X}} = \sigma/\sqrt{n} = 12/\sqrt{100} = 1.20$. Then, for a normal sampling distribution with $\mu_{\bar{X}} = 30$ and $\sigma_{\bar{X}} = 1.20$, we obtain $P(\bar{X} \leq 33)$ from Table I as follows:

$$
\begin{aligned}
P(\bar{X} \leq 33) &= F_n(33 \mid 30, 1.20) \\
&= F_N\left(\frac{33 - 30}{1.20}\right) \\
&= F_N(2.50) \\
&= .9938
\end{aligned}
$$

Of course, since the sampling distribution of $\bar{X}$ is only *approximately* normal, this probability of .9938 is only an approximate answer. However, inasmuch as the population does not differ radically from normality, and because the sample size of 100 is reasonably large, the amount of error in this approximation should be negligible for most practical purposes.

PROBLEMS

12.1 The population distribution of a random variable X is described by the following mass function:

$$
f(x) = \begin{cases} \dfrac{x + 2}{25} & \text{if } x = 1, 2, 3, 4, 5 \\ 0 & \text{otherwise} \end{cases}
$$

(a) Determine the mean and variance of this infinite population.
(b) Suppose that you wish to select a simple random sample of $n = 20$ observations from the population and compute the sample mean $\bar{X}$. Determine the mean and variance of the sampling distribution of $\bar{X}$.

12.2 Let X be a random variable denoting the life span (in hours) of a very delicate type of laboratory instrument. The population distribution of X is described by the following probability density function:

$$
f(x) = \begin{cases} \dfrac{1}{4} & \text{if } .5 \leq x \leq 4.5 \\ 0 & \text{otherwise} \end{cases}
$$

(a) Graph the density function that describes the population.

(b) Determine the population mean and variance.

(c) Suppose that you wish to select a simple random sample of $n = 4$ observations from this effectively infinite population and compute the sample mean $\bar{X}$. Determine the mean and variance of the sampling distribution of $\bar{X}$.

(d) Repeat part (c) with $n = 36$.

12.3 A particular finite population consists of a box containing 20 numbered tags. Ten of the tags are marked with the value 1, six have the value 2, and the remaining four have the value 3. A sampling experiment is to be conducted in which two tags will be selected from the box at random (without replacement) and the mean of the values on the two tags will be computed.

(a) Derive the sampling distribution of the sample mean for this experiment.

(b) Using the distribution derived in part (a), determine the expected value and variance of the sample mean.

(c) Verify your results in part (b) by applying Formulas (12.1) and (12.2).

12.4 Assume that the experiment described in Problem 12.3 is to be performed with replacement rather than without replacement.

(a) Derive the sampling distribution for the sample mean.

(b) Using the distribution derived in part (a), determine the expected value and variance of the sample mean.

(c) Verify your results in part (b) by applying Formulas (12.1) and (12.3).

12.5 The population distribution of a random variable X is described by the following mass function:

$$f(x) = \begin{cases} .20 & \text{if } x = 1 \\ .40 & \text{if } x = 2, 3 \\ 0 & \text{otherwise} \end{cases}$$

(a) Determine the mean and variance of this infinite population.

(b) A sampling experiment is proposed in which a random sample of 3 observations is to be taken from the population, and the sample mean $\bar{X}$ is to be computed. Determine (1) the sample space for this experiment, and (2) the sampling distribution of $\bar{X}$.

(c) Using the sampling distribution obtained in part (b), determine the mean and variance of $\bar{X}$.

(d) Verify your results in part (c) by applying Formulas (12.1) and (12.3).

12.6 With the aid of Formulas (7.9) and (7.11), show that the expected value of the mean of a simple random sample is equal to the mean of the population from which the sample was drawn. That is, prove that $E(\bar{X}) = \mu$.

12.7 Let $f(z)$ represent the standard normal density function. Using Table I (Appendix II), evaluate each of the following expressions:

(a) $\int_{.60}^{\infty} f(z)\, dz$

(b) $\int_{-\infty}^{-2.06} f(z)\, dz$

(c) $\int_{.20}^{.97} f(z)\, dz$

(d) $\int_{-.20}^{.97} f(z)\, dz$

(e) $\int_{-1.20}^{-1.02} f(z)\, dz$

(f) $\int_{-1.96}^{1.96} f(z)\, dz$

12.8 Let X be a normally distributed random variable with $\mu = 30$ and $\sigma = 2$. Find the following probabilities:

(a) $P(X \leq 34)$

(b) $P(X \leq 26)$

(c) $P(X \geq 31)$

(d) $P(X \geq 33.5)$

(e) $P(29.5 \leq X \leq 33.0)$

12.9 Y is a normally distributed random variable with $\mu = 14$ and $\sigma = 25$. For a single observation, find:

(a) $P(Y < 0)$

(b) $P(Y > 50)$

12.10 Let H be a normally distributed random variable with $\mu = .025$ and $\sigma = .0015$. Find the following probabilities:
  (a) $P(H \le .03)$
  (b) $P(H \le -.022)$
  (c) $P(H \ge .027)$
  (d) $P(.024 \le H \le .026)$

12.11 Assume that the time required for a production crew to produce a custom-made Wombat Special limousine is a normally distributed random variable with a mean of 1,200 man-hours with a standard deviation of 200 man-hours. If a customer orders one of these limousines, what is the probability that its production will require between 1,140 and 1,520 man-hours?

12.12 An electric utility company has 200,000 domestic subscribers. For the month of October, the mean electric bill was $\mu = \$8.50$ and the standard deviation of these bills was $\sigma = \$1.25$.
  (a) If it were reasonable to assume that these bills were normally distributed, how many of these bills would lie between $6.00 and $11.00?
  (b) How reasonable would it be to assume that these bills are normally distributed? Explain.

12.13 A machine produces ball bearings that are considered to meet specification if their diameters are within the limits $12.00 \pm .04$ centimeters. Suppose that the diameters of the bearings produced by the machine are normally distributed with a mean of 11.98 centimeters and a standard deviation of .02 centimeter. What is the probability that a bearing selected randomly from the machine's output will meet the specification?

12.14 A photographic studio purchases a particular type of flood lamp from a distributor, who claims that the lives of these particular lamps are normally distributed with a mean of 80 hours and a standard deviation of 2 hours. If the distributor's claim is correct, what is the probability that a given lamp will last as long as 81 hours?

12.15 A study showed that the lifetimes of a certain kind of automobile battery are normally distributed with a mean of 1,248 days and a standard deviation of 185 days. If the manufacturer wishes to guarantee the battery for 3 years, what percentage of the batteries should be subject to replacement under guarantee?

12.16 Two different processes, A and B, are available for producing a particular type of chain links. The links produced by process A have a mean breaking strength of 50 pounds with a standard deviation of 5 pounds. The links produced by process B have a mean breaking strength of 60 pounds with a standard deviation of 12 pounds. Suppose that the distributions of breaking strength are normal for both processes.
  (a) Which process will yield the greater proportion of links with breaking strengths above 45 pounds?
  (b) Which process will yield the greater proportion of links with breaking strengths less than 40 pounds?

12.17 Let H be a random variable denoting the life (in hours) of a particular type of volume-produced battery designed for transistor radios. Assume that H is normally distributed with $\mu = 26$ and $\sigma = 5$.
  (a) Of this type of battery, 2.5% will have lives less than what value of H?
  (b) Of this type of battery, 67% will have lives greater than what value of H?

12.18 For a normally distributed population, $\mu = 100$ and $\sigma = 12$.
  (a) What is the probability that a single case taken at random from this population will have a value greater than 106?
  (b) What is the probability that a random sample of 36 cases will have a mean less than 102?
  (c) What is the probability that a sample of 16 items will have a mean between 97 and 106?

12.19 The lengths of aluminum ingots produced by a particular mill are normally distributed with $\mu = 30$ centimeters and $\sigma = .50$ centimeter.

(a) What is the probability that a single ingot produced by this process will have a length less than 29.4 centimeters?

(b) What is the probability that a single ingot produced by this process will have a length greater than 30.8 centimeters?

(c) What is the probability that the mean length of a random sample of 4 ingots produced by this process will be less than 29.4 centimeters?

(d) What is the probability that the mean length of a sample of 4 ingots produced by this process will be greater than 30.8 centimeters?

12.20 The breaking strengths of lengths of steel wire produced by a particular automatic process are normally distributed with $\mu = 200$ pounds and $\sigma = 20$ pounds. If a random sample of 64 lengths of this wire are tested, what is the probability that the mean breaking strength of the sample will be:

(a) Greater than 195.5 pounds?

(b) Less than 198.0 pounds?

(c) Between 195.5 and 198.0 pounds?

12.21 In a large metropolitan area, the distribution of annual household income is positively skewed with $\mu = \$12,060$ and $\sigma = \$600$. What is the approximate probability that a random sample of 225 households selected from this population will have a mean annual income:

(a) Less than $12,000?

(b) Greater than $12,150?

(c) Between $12,000 and $12,150?

12.22 If it is known that the mechanical aptitude scores of a particular large population of workers has a mean of 82 and standard deviation of 5, what is the approximate probability that a sample of 400 workers will result in a mean score:

(a) Between 81.5 and 81.95?

(b) Greater than 82.7?

12.23 A certain population is normally distributed with a mean of 400 and a standard deviation of 80. Bill takes a sample of 25 and calculates a sample mean. Mary takes a sample of 64 and calculates a sample mean. What is the probability that at least one of the sample means lies in the interval 410 to 420?

13

Testing Hypotheses Concerning
Means of Continuous Populations
with Known Variances

The examples of hypothesis testing presented in Chapters 10 and 11 followed the general procedure outlined in Section 10.5. In each of those examples, the decision rule was derived from a *discrete* sampling distribution. This chapter demonstrates how the same general procedure may be followed in using a normal sampling distribution to test hypotheses concerning means of continuous populations.

13.1 TESTS CONCERNING THE MEAN OF A SINGLE POPULATION

In testing a hypothesis concerning a population mean μ, the sample mean $\bar{X}$ is a commonly used test statistic. As indicated in Chapter 12, if a continuous population is normally distributed, the sampling distribution of $\bar{X}$ will be normal. Even if a continuous population is not normally distributed, the sampling distribution of $\bar{X}$ will be approximately normal as long as the sample size is large and the population distribution does not differ radically from normality.

13.1.1 Upper-Tail Test

To illustrate the use of a normal sampling distribution in testing a hypothesis concerning a population mean, consider the case of Dave Doolittle, who is the buyer of photographic supplies for a large discount retailing chain. Dave has an opportunity to purchase photographic flood lamps at an attractive price from Fotoline Products. Fotoline claims that, on the average, the burning life of their lamps is over 6 hours. To avoid offering low-quality merchandise to the public, Dave does not want to purchase these lamps unless he feels reasonably confident that the manufacturer's claim is correct. To evaluate the validity of the manufacturer's claim, Dave proposes that a sample of the manufacturer's lamps be submitted to life testing. Dave will then make his decision on the basis of the sample results.

Designing the Decision Rule. Following the first eight steps of the general hypothesis-testing procedure outlined in Section 10.5, Dave's decision rule may be derived as follows:

1. *Identify the action space and state space of the decision problem.* The action space of Dave's decision problem consists of two alternative courses of action: (a) purchase lamps from Fotoline, and (b) do not purchase lamps from Fotoline. The parameter space (state space) is the set of all possible values of μ, where μ denotes the mean burning life (in hours) of the population of lamps produced by Fotoline. Since μ can conceivably have any nonnegative value, this parameter space is the set $\{\mu \,|\, 0 \leq \mu < \infty\}$.

2. *Partition the state space into two complementary subsets.* Dave feels that he should not purchase the lamps unless Fotoline's claim is correct. Thus, the preferred action for Dave is not to purchase Fotoline's lamps if $\mu \leq 6$, but to purchase their lamps if $\mu > 6$. Hence, the parameter space should be partitioned into the two subsets $\{\mu \,|\, 0 \leq \mu \leq 6\}$ and $\{\mu \,|\, 6 < \mu < \infty\}$.

3. *Formulate the null and alternative hypotheses.* Dave does not want to purchase Fotoline's lamps unless he is convinced by the sample results that Fotoline's claim is correct. Thus, the burden of proof should be placed on the manufacturer's claim that $\mu > 6$. Hence, the null and alternative hypotheses are

$$H_0: \quad \mu \leq 6$$
$$H_1: \quad \mu > 6$$

4. *Determine the level of significance for the test.* Since Dave is particularly concerned with the risk of offering low-quality merchandise to the public, he feels that he should not accept more than a .05 risk of purchasing Fotoline's lamps if, in fact, $\mu \leq 6$. Thus, the significance level is specified as .05.

5. *Specify the sampling experiment.* The sampling experiment will be conducted by submitting a random sample of Fotoline's lamps to life testing. Each lamp in the sample will be burned continuously until it fails, and its time to failure will be recorded. Since this type of testing is destructive, the cost of the lamps in the sample becomes an important consideration. To keep this cost reasonably low and yet have a sample large enough to provide reliable information, Dave adopts a sample size of 36 lamps.

6. *Select the test statistic and identify the appropriate sampling distribution.* Since Dave is concerned with the mean burning life of the population of lamps produced by Fotoline, it seems intuitively reasonable to him that he should base his decision on the mean burning life of the lamps in the sample. This sample mean, $\bar{X}$, is therefore the test statistic.

   To identify the sampling distribution of $\bar{X}$, we may first observe that (1) the population of all lamps that might be produced by Fotoline can be regarded as infinite, and (2) the characteristic being observed—time to failure—is measured on a continuous scale. Thus, the sampling distribution of $\bar{X}$ is a continuous distribution. Of course, the exact shape of this sampling distribution depends on the shape of the population distribution and the size of the sample. Since time to failure has a lower bound of zero, the population distribution cannot be exactly normal since a normal distribution is unbounded in both directions. However, there is no cause to suspect that the population distribution deviates radically from normality. Therefore, with a sample size of 36 observations, it is reasonable to assume, on the basis of the central limit theorem, that the sampling distribution of $\bar{X}$ is approximately normal.

   If the sampling distribution of $\bar{X}$ were exactly normal, the domain of the distribution would be the set $\{\bar{x} \,|\, -\infty < \bar{x} < \infty\}$. However, since the population distribution has a lower bound of zero, the domain of the sampling distribution of $\bar{X}$ in this situation is the set $\{\bar{x} \,|\, 0 \leq \bar{x} < \infty\}$.

7. *Partition the domain of the sampling distribution of the test statistic into acceptance and rejection regions.* To determine which possible values of $\bar{X}$ belong in the rejection region, we first recall that the null hypothesis is $H_0: \mu \leq 6$ and the alternative hypothesis is $H_1: \mu > 6$. Thus, a relatively small value of $\bar{X}$ will tend to support H_0, and a relatively large value of $\bar{X}$ will tend to support H_1. Hence, the rejection region will contain the relatively large values of $\bar{X}$ that are located in the *upper tail* of the sampling distribution. Specifically, bearing in mind that the significance level is .05, the rejection region will contain those possible values of $\bar{X}$ that are at least as great as some critical value c which satisfies the expression

$$P(\bar{X} \geq c \,|\, \mu \leq 6) = .05$$

To determine the value of c from this expression, it is necessary to specify a single value, rather than a range of values, for μ. For this purpose, the limiting value of μ stated in the null hypothesis is used, since this guarantees that the probability of incorrectly rejecting H_0 will not exceed the significance level, regardless of what the specific value of μ actually might be. Thus, the foregoing expression becomes

$$P(\bar{X} \geq c \,|\, \mu = 6) = .05$$

In order to use a normal distribution to solve this expression for c, we must specify $\mu_{\bar{X}}$ and $\sigma_{\bar{X}}$, the parameters of the sampling distribution of $\bar{X}$. To specify the value of $\mu_{\bar{X}}$, we need simply recall from Formula (12.1) that $\mu_{\bar{X}} = \mu$. Thus, $\mu_{\bar{X}}$ is specified as 6. To specify the value of $\sigma_{\bar{X}}$, we recall from Formula (12.5) that $\sigma_{\bar{X}} = \sigma/\sqrt{n}$. Making a phone call to Fotoline's quality control engineer, Dave finds that it is reasonable to assume that the standard deviation of the burning lives of the lamps produced by Fotoline is $\sigma = 1.20$ hours. Therefore, since the sample size is 36, the standard error of $\bar{X}$ is specified as $\sigma_{\bar{X}} = 1.20/\sqrt{36} = .20$.

Having specified the mean and standard error of $\bar{X}$, we may restate the expression for determining c as

$$P(\bar{X} \geq c \,|\, \mu_{\bar{X}} = 6, \sigma_{\bar{X}} = .20) = .05$$

It then follows that

$$P(\bar{X} < c \,|\, \mu_{\bar{X}} = 6, \sigma_{\bar{X}} = .20) = .95$$

Assuming that the sampling distribution of $\bar{X}$ is normal, this expression becomes

$$F_n(c \,|\, \mu_{\bar{X}} = 6, \sigma_{\bar{X}} = .20) = .95$$

Converting this expression to standard normal notation, we obtain

$$F_N\left(\frac{c - 6}{.20}\right) = .95$$

From Table J (Appendix II), the .95 fractile of the standard normal distribution is $z_{.95} = 1.645$. Thus,

$$z_{.95} = \frac{c - 6}{.20} = 1.645$$

Then, by simple algebra,

$$c = 6 + 1.645(.20) = 6.329$$

Hence, the rejection region is $\{\bar{x} \,|\, 6.329 \leq \bar{x} < \infty\}$, and the acceptance region is $\{\bar{x} \,|\, 0 \leq \bar{x} < 6.329\}$. This partition of the domain of the sampling distribution of $\bar{X}$ into acceptance and rejection regions is illustrated in Figure 13.1.

8. *State the decision rule explicitly.* Having established the acceptance and rejection regions, we may now explicitly state Dave's decision rule as follows: If the value of $\bar{X}$, the mean burning life of the flood lamps in the sample, is equal to or greater

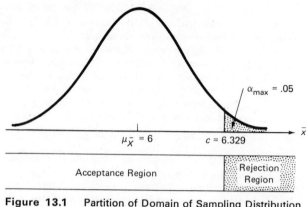

Figure 13.1   Partition of Domain of Sampling Distribution
of $\bar{X}$ into Acceptance and Rejection Regions
for Upper-Tail Test

than 6.329 hours, reject H_0 and accordingly purchase flood lamps from Fotoline; otherwise, accept H_0 and accordingly do not purchase flood lamps from Fotoline.

To generalize from this example of an upper-tail test, suppose that we wish to test the null hypothesis

$$H_0: \quad \mu \leq \mu_0$$

against the alternative hypothesis

$$H_1: \quad \mu > \mu_0$$

where μ is the unknown mean of a continuous population. Suppose further that

1. The population is normal, or the sample size is sufficiently large for the central limit theorem to apply.
2. The population standard deviation σ is known, so that the standard error $\sigma_{\bar{X}}$ can be computed as $\sigma_{\bar{X}} = \sigma/\sqrt{n}$.

Then the decision rule for the test is

If $\bar{X} \geq c$, reject H_0; otherwise, accept H_0

where $c = \mu_0 + z_{1-\alpha}\sigma_{\bar{X}}$.

Evaluating the Decision Rule.   The procedure for determining the Type I and Type II error probabilities for a normal test concerning a population mean is essentially the same as that followed for a binomial test concerning a population proportion. For an upper-tail normal test, the decision rule calls for rejection of H_0 if the sample mean $\bar{X}$ is equal to or greater than some critical value c. The Type I error probability for this kind of test is given by

$$\alpha_\mu = P\left(\bar{X} \geq c \,|\, \mu_{\bar{X}} = \mu, \sigma_{\bar{X}} = \frac{\sigma}{\sqrt{n}}\right) \tag{13.1}$$

which is the probability that $\bar{X}$ is equal to or greater than c, given that μ is any specified value contained in H_0.

To illustrate the application of Formula (13.1), let us first recall that Dave's decision rule partitioned the sampling distribution of $\bar{X}$ at the critical value $c = 6.329$ hours. If the unknown mean life of the *population* of flood lamps produced by Fotoline actually is no greater than 6 hours, and if the test results from the *sample* happen to yield a mean equal to or greater than 6.329 hours, then the decision rule will lead to a Type I error. For example, suppose for the moment that the population mean life is actually $\mu = 5.8$ hours, which is a value contained in H_0. If this is true, what is the probability that $\bar{X}$, the mean life of the sample, will be equal to or greater than 6.329? That is, if $\mu = 5.8$, what is the probability that the decision rule will lead to a Type I error? Applying Formula (13.1) and using Table I (Appendix II), this probability is obtained as follows:

$$\begin{aligned}\alpha_{5.8} &= P(\bar{X} \geq 6.329 \,|\, \mu_{\bar{X}} = 5.8, \sigma_{\bar{X}} = .20) \\ &= 1 - F_n(6.329 \,|\, 5.8, .20) \\ &= 1 - F_N\left(\frac{6.329 - 5.8}{.20}\right) \\ &= 1 - F_N(2.645) \\ &= 1 - .996 \\ &= .004\end{aligned}$$

Thus, if the population mean actually is 5.8 hours, the probability is approximately .004 that the decision rule will result in a Type I error.

Following this same procedure, Type I error probabilities for selected values of μ contained in H_0 are calculated in Table 13.1. These probabilities are illustrated in Figure 13.2.

Table 13.1 Calculation of Type I Error Probabilities for Upper-Tail Test ($H_0: \mu \leq 6$; $H_1: \mu > 6$)

μ	$z = \dfrac{c - \mu}{\sigma_{\bar{X}}}$	$F_N(z)$	$\alpha_\mu = 1 - F_N(z)$
5.8	2.645	.996	$\alpha_{5.8} = .004$
5.9	2.145	.984	$\alpha_{5.9} = .016$
6.0	1.645	.950	$\alpha_{6.0} = .050$

The Type II error probability for an upper-tail normal test concerning a population mean is given by

$$\beta_\mu = P\left(\bar{X} < c \,|\, \mu_{\bar{X}} = \mu, \sigma_{\bar{X}} = \frac{\sigma}{\sqrt{n}}\right) \tag{13.2}$$

which is the probability that $\bar{X}$ is less than c, given that μ is any specified value contained in H_1. To illustrate the use of this formula, suppose momentarily that the mean life of the population of flood lamps produced by Fotoline is actually $\mu = 6.20$ hours, which is a value contained in H_1. If this is true, what is the probability that $\bar{X}$, the mean life of the sample, will be less than 6.329?

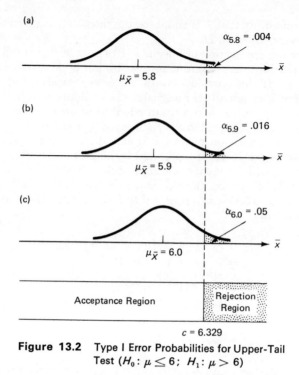

Figure 13.2 Type I Error Probabilities for Upper-Tail
Test ($H_0: \mu \leq 6$; $H_1: \mu > 6$)

That is, if $\mu = 6.20$, what is the probability that the decision rule will lead to a Type II error? Applying Formula (13.2) and using Table I, this probability is obtained as follows:

$$
\begin{aligned}
\beta_{6.20} &= P(\bar{X} < 6.329 \,|\, \mu_{\bar{X}} = 6.20,\ \sigma_{\bar{X}} = .20) \\
&= F_n(6.329 \,|\, 6.20, .20) \\
&= F_N\left(\frac{6.329 - 6.20}{.20}\right) \\
&= F_N(.645) \\
&= .741
\end{aligned}
$$

Following this procedure, Type II error probabilities for various values of μ contained in H_1 are calculated in Table 13.2. The Type II error probabilities for selected values of μ contained in H_1 are shown graphically by the unshaded areas of the curves in Figure 13.3.

The error probabilities given in Tables 13.1 and 13.2 are displayed graphically by the error characteristic curve presented in Figure 13.4. The horizontal axis of this curve represents the parameter space. For those possible values of the parameter contained in H_0, the curve displays probabilities of the Type I error. For those possible values of the parameter contained in H_1, the curve shows probabilities of the Type II error. In this chart, the Type I error probabilities are, generally speaking, much smaller than the Type II error probabilities. This reflects the fact that Dave is more concerned with the risk of

Table 13.2 Calculation of Type II Error Probabilities for Upper-Tail Test ($H_0: \mu \leq 6$; $H_1: \mu > 6$)

μ	$z = \dfrac{c - \mu}{\sigma_{\bar{X}}}$	$\beta_\mu = F_N(z)$
6.00^-	1.645	$\beta_{6.00} = .950^-$
6.10	1.145	$\beta_{6.10} = .874$
6.20	.645	$\beta_{6.20} = .741$
6.30	.145	$\beta_{6.30} = .558$
6.329	0	$\beta_{6.329} = .500$
6.40	$-.355$	$\beta_{6.40} = .361$
6.50	$-.855$	$\beta_{6.50} = .196$
6.60	-1.355	$\beta_{6.60} = .088$
6.70	-1.855	$\beta_{6.70} = .032$
6.80	-2.355	$\beta_{6.80} = .009$

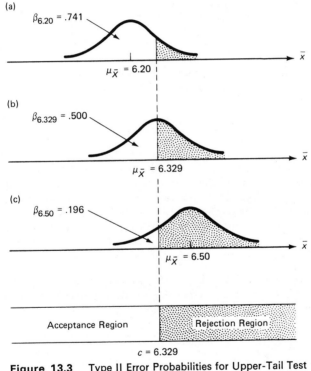

Figure 13.3 Type II Error Probabilities for Upper-Tail Test ($H_0: \mu \leq 6$; $H_1: \mu > 6$)

purchasing low-quality flood lamps than with the risk of missing the opportunity to purchase flood lamps of acceptable quality.

13.1.2 Lower-Tail Test

Suppose that, after inspecting the error characteristic chart in Figure 13.4, Dave wonders whether he might be taking too high a risk of missing the opportunity to buy flood lamps at an attractive price. Thus, he begins to question his

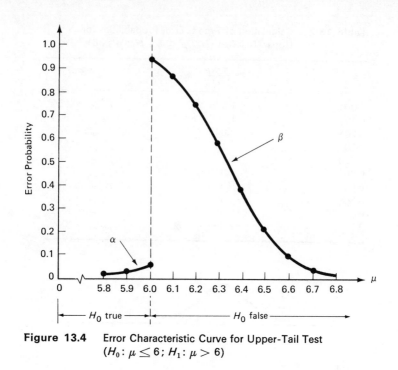

Figure 13.4 Error Characteristic Curve for Upper-Tail Test
$(H_0: \mu \le 6; H_1: \mu > 6)$

own position that he should not purchase flood lamps from Fotoline unless the sample results provide convincing evidence in support of Fotoline's claim. Dave therefore feels that he should investigate what the effect would be on his decision rule if he adopted the position that he should purchase flood lamps from Fotoline unless the sample results provide convincing evidence against Fotoline's claim. To do this, he decides to see how the decision rule will change if he takes the position that he should not accept more than a .05 risk of failing to purchase Fotoline's lamps if, in fact, Fotoline's claim is correct.

Designing the Decision Rule. Using the same general procedure employed in designing Dave's original decision rule, we may proceed to formulate a new rule reflecting his revised position as follows:

1. Same as before.
2. Same as before.
3. Dave's change in position amounts to shifting the burden of proof from the proposition that Fotoline's claim is true to the proposition that Fotoline's claim is false. Hence, the null and alternative hypotheses are

$$H_0: \quad \mu \ge 6$$
$$H_1: \quad \mu < 6$$

4. On the basis of his revised position that he should not accept more than a .05 risk of failing to purchase Fotoline's lamps if Fotoline's claim is correct, the significance level is established as .05. It is important to observe that, although the significance levels for both the original and new rules are specified to be .05, they represent risks of making distinctly different errors.

5. Same as before.

6. Same as before.

7. From inspection of the revised null and alternative hypotheses obtained in step 3, we can see that a relatively large value of $\bar{X}$ will tend to support H_0, and a relatively small value of $\bar{X}$ will tend to support H_1. Thus, the rejection region will contain the relatively small values of $\bar{X}$ that are located in the *lower tail* of the sampling distribution. Specifically, the rejection region will contain those possible values of $\bar{X}$ that are no greater than some critical value c which satisfies the expression

$$P(\bar{X} \le c \,|\, \mu \ge 6) = .05$$

Using the limiting value of μ stated in the null hypothesis, this expression becomes

$$P(\bar{X} \le c \,|\, \mu = 6) = .05$$

Recalling that $\mu_{\bar{X}} = \mu$, and that $\sigma_{\bar{X}} = \sigma/\sqrt{n} = .20$, this expression may be restated as

$$P(\bar{X} \le c \,|\, \mu_{\bar{X}} = 6, \sigma_{\bar{X}} = .20) = .05$$

Assuming that the sampling distribution of $\bar{X}$ is normal, this probability expression becomes

$$F_n(c \,|\, 6, .20) = .05$$

Converting this expression to standard normal notation, we obtain

$$F_N\left(\frac{c - 6}{.20}\right) = .05$$

From Table J (Appendix II), the .05 fractile of the standard normal distribution is $z_{.05} = -1.645$. Thus,

$$z_{.05} = \frac{c - 6}{.20} = -1.645$$

Then, by algebra,

$$c = 6 + (-1.645)(.20) = 5.671$$

Hence, the rejection region is $\{\bar{x} \,|\, 0 \le \bar{x} \le 5.671\}$, and the acceptance region is $\{\bar{x} \,|\, 5.671 < \bar{x} < \infty\}$. This partition of the domain of the sampling distribution of $\bar{X}$ into acceptance and rejection regions is illustrated in Figure 13.5.

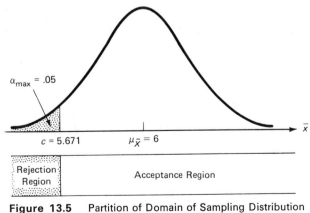

$\alpha_{max} = .05$

$c = 5.671$

$\mu_{\bar{X}} = 6$

$\bar{x}$

Rejection Region

Acceptance Region

Figure 13.5 Partition of Domain of Sampling Distribution of $\bar{X}$ into Acceptance and Rejection Regions for Lower-Tail Test

8. Having established the acceptance and rejection regions, we may now explicitly state Dave's new decision rule reflecting his revised position as follows: If the value of $\bar{X}$, the mean burning life of the flood lamps in the sample, is equal to or less than 5.671 hours, reject H_0 and accordingly do not purchase flood lamps from Fotoline; otherwise, accept H_0 and accordingly purchase flood lamps from Fotoline.

To generalize from this example of a lower-tail test using a normal sampling distribution, suppose that we wish to test the null hypothesis

$$H_0: \quad \mu \geq \mu_0$$

against the alternative hypothesis

$$H_1: \quad \mu < \mu_0$$

The decision rule for this test is

If $\bar{X} \leq c$, reject H_0; otherwise, accept H_0

where $c = \mu_0 + z_\alpha \sigma_{\bar{X}}$.

Evaluating the Decision Rule. For a lower-tail normal test concerning a population mean, the decision rule calls for rejection of H_0 if the sample mean $\bar{X}$ is equal to or less than some critical value c. The Type I error probability for this kind of test is given by

$$\alpha_\mu = P\left(\bar{X} \leq c \mid \mu_{\bar{X}} = \mu, \sigma_{\bar{X}} = \frac{\sigma}{\sqrt{n}}\right) \tag{13.3}$$

which is the probability that $\bar{X}$ is equal to or less than c, given that μ is any specified value contained in H_0. The Type II error probability for a lower-tail normal test concerning μ is given by

$$\beta_\mu = P\left(\bar{X} > c \mid \mu_{\bar{X}} = \mu, \sigma_{\bar{X}} = \frac{\sigma}{\sqrt{n}}\right) \tag{13.4}$$

which is the probability that $\bar{X}$ is greater than c, given that μ is any specified value contained in H_1.

For Dave's revised decision rule, Formulas (13.3) and (13.4) yield the error probabilities shown graphically by the error characteristic curve in Figure 13.6. It is left as an exercise for the reader to verify these probabilities.

A comparison of Figure 13.6 with Figure 13.4 indicates that the risk of the Type I error for both decision rules is, in general, much lower than the risk of the Type II error. However, the curve in Figure 13.6 is a mirror image of the curve in Figure 13.4. This reflects the fact that the two decision rules were based on opposite positions concerning where the burden of proof should be placed, so that α and β have opposite meanings in the two charts.

13.1.3 Two-Tail Test

Each of the decision rules that we have considered so far in our examination of hypothesis testing has been an example of a *one-tail* test in the sense that the rejection region was located entirely in one tail or the other of the sampling distribution. However, there are many practical hypothesis-testing situations in which the rejection region is located partly in the lower tail and partly in the upper tail of the sampling distribution. This type of test is called a *two-tail* test.

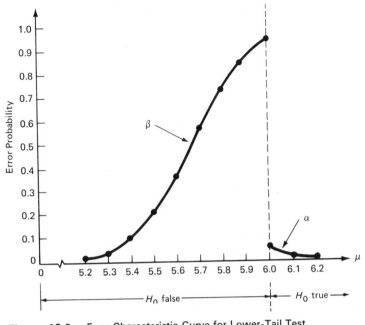

Figure 13.6   Error Characteristic Curve for Lower-Tail Test
$(H_0 : \mu \geq 6; \; H_1 : \mu < 6)$

To illustrate the application of a two-tail test, consider the case of the Kleenum Company, manufacturers of household cleansing products. One of Kleenum's products is a biodegradable detergent that is marketed in boxes which have a specified net weight of 80 ounces. These boxes are filled by an automatic process. Of course, it is unrealistic to expect that this packaging process would be so stable that every box would contain exactly 80 ounces. However, when it is operating "under control," the packaging process produces boxes having a *mean* net contents $\mu = 80$ ounces with a standard deviation $\sigma = 1$ ounce. Unfortunately, from time to time the process goes out of control—that is, the process mean drifts away from 80 ounces in one direction or the other. When this happens, a preponderance of the boxes will be either underfilled or overfilled if the process is not stopped for adjustment. Regardless of whether the process tends to produce a preponderance of underfilled or overfilled boxes, the result of allowing the process to go out of control is undesirable. Although it is desirable to maintain the process under control, it is not economically feasible to stop the process for adjustment unless there is convincing evidence that the process has drifted out of control. Thus, Kleenum desires a quality control plan whereby the output of the process will be sampled periodically to determine whether the process should be allowed to continue in operation or shut down for adjustment.

Designing the Decision Rule.   Applying the first eight steps of the general hypothesis-testing procedure outlined in Section 10.5, we may derive Kleenum's quality control rule as follows:

1. The action space of Kleenum's quality control plan consists of two alternative courses of action: (a) allow the process to continue in operation, and (b) shut

down the process for adjustment. The parameter space is the set of all possible values of μ, where μ denotes the mean net contents (in ounces) of the population of boxes being produced by the process. Since μ can conceivably have any nonnegative value, this parameter space is the set $\{\mu \,|\, 0 \leq \mu < \infty\}$.

2. If the process mean is being maintained at the standard of 80 ounces (i.e., $\mu = 80$), the correct decision is to allow the process to continue in operation. If the process has drifted out of control, so that the process mean is either greater or less than the 80-ounce standard (i.e., $\mu \neq 80$), the correct decision is to stop the process for adjustment. Hence, the parameter space should be partitioned into the two subsets $\{\mu \,|\, \mu = 80\}$ and $\{\mu \,|\, \mu \neq 80\}$.

3. Since it is undesirable to stop the process unless there is convincing evidence that the process has drifted out of control, the burden of proof should be placed on the proposition that $\mu \neq 80$. Thus, the null and alternative hypotheses are

$$H_0: \quad \mu = 80$$
$$H_1: \quad \mu \neq 80$$

4. Kleenum's management determines that they cannot afford to take more than a .10 risk of stopping the process for adjustment if, in fact, the process is under control. Hence, the significance level is specified as .10.

5. To maintain a regular check on the process, sampling will be conducted repeatedly at specified intervals of time. For this purpose, Kleenum specifies that each periodic sample will consist of 25 boxes produced by the process. Each box in the sample will be weighed, and its net contents in ounces will be recorded.

6. The test statistic on which Kleenum will base its decision to stop the process or let it continue is $\bar{X}$, the mean net weight of the boxes in the sample. Since the net weight of a box has a lower bound of zero, the population distribution cannot be exactly normal. However, there is no cause to suspect that the population distribution departs radically from normality. Thus, by virtue of the central limit theorem, it is reasonable to assume that the sampling distribution of $\bar{X}$ for a sample of 25 observations is approximately normal. The domain of this sampling distribution is the set $\{\bar{x} \,|\, 0 \leq \bar{x} < \infty\}$.

7. To partition the set of possible values of $\bar{X}$ into acceptance and rejection regions, we first note that the null hypothesis is $H_0: \mu = 80$ and the alternative hypothesis is $H_1: \mu \neq 80$. Thus, the null hypothesis will tend to be supported if the obtained value of $\bar{X}$ is relatively close to 80, whereas the alternative hypothesis will tend to be supported if the obtained value of $\bar{X}$ is either substantially less than 80 or substantially greater than 80. That is, the null hypothesis will be rejected *either* (a) if $\bar{X}$ is equal to or less than some critical value c_1 *or* (b) if $\bar{X}$ is equal to or greater than some other critical value c_2.

Since the null hypothesis is $H_0: \mu = 80$, a Type I error can occur only if the process mean is exactly 80 ounces. Thus, if the process mean does happen to be exactly 80 ounces, a Type I error can occur either (a) if $\bar{X}$ is equal to or less than c_1 or (b) if $\bar{X}$ is equal to or greater than c_2. Inasmuch as the maximum possible risk of the Type I error has been specified as .10, the values of c_1 and c_2 must be determined in such a way that the following expression will be satisfied:

$$P\{(\bar{X} \leq c_1) \cup (\bar{X} \geq c_2) \,|\, \mu = 80\} = .10$$

Because the two events, $(\bar{X} \leq c_1)$ and $(\bar{X} \geq c_2)$, are mutually exclusive, the above expression may be converted to

$$P(\bar{X} \leq c_1 \,|\, \mu = 80) + P(\bar{X} \geq c_2 \,|\, \mu = 80) = .10$$

In conducting a two-tail test, it is customary to assign equal probabilities to the two ways that the Type I error can occur. This permits us to write

$$P(\bar{X} \leq c_1 \,|\, \mu = 80) = P(\bar{X} \geq c_2 \,|\, \mu = 80)$$

Since these two probabilities are equal, and since their sum is .10, it follows that

$$P(\bar{X} \le c_1 | \mu = 80) = .05$$

and

$$P(\bar{X} \ge c_2 | \mu = 80) = .05$$

In order to use a normal distribution to solve these last two probability expressions for c_1 and c_2, we must first determine the parameters $\mu_{\bar{X}}$ and $\sigma_{\bar{X}}$. Applying Formula (12.1), the value of $\mu_{\bar{X}}$ is

$$\mu_{\bar{X}} = \mu = 80$$

Since the process standard deviation is $\sigma = 1$ and the sample size is $n = 25$, Formula (12.5) yields

$$\sigma_{\bar{X}} = \frac{\sigma}{\sqrt{n}} = \frac{1}{\sqrt{25}} = .20$$

Using a normal sampling distribution with $\mu_{\bar{X}} = 80$ and $\sigma_{\bar{X}} = .20$, the expression for determining c_1 may be written as

$$P(\bar{X} \le c_1 | \mu = 80) = F_n(c_1 | \mu_{\bar{X}} = 80, \sigma_{\bar{X}} = .20) = .05$$

Using standard normal notation, this becomes

$$F_N\left(\frac{c_1 - 80}{.20}\right) = .05$$

From Table J (Appendix II), the .05 fractile of the standard normal distribution is $z_{.05} = -1.645$. Hence,

$$z_{.05} = \frac{c_1 - 80}{.20} = -1.645$$

Then, by algebra,

$$c_1 = 80 + (-1.645)(.20) = 79.671$$

Similarly, the expression for determining c_2 may be written as

$$P(\bar{X} \ge c_2 | \mu = 80) = 1 - F_n(c_2 | \mu_{\bar{X}} = 80, \sigma_{\bar{X}} = .20) = .05$$

In standard normal notation, this becomes

$$1 - F_N\left(\frac{c_2 - 80}{.20}\right) = .05$$

It then follows that

$$F_N\left(\frac{c_2 - 80}{.20}\right) = .95$$

From Table J, the .95 fractile of the standard normal is $z_{.95} = 1.645$. Thus,

$$z_{.95} = \frac{c_2 - 80}{.20} = 1.645$$

Simple algebra then yields

$$c_2 = 80 + 1.645(.20) = 80.329$$

Since $c_1 = 79.671$ and $c_2 = 80.329$, the null hypothesis will be rejected either if $\bar{X} \le 79.671$ or if $\bar{X} \ge 80.329$. Thus, the rejection region is the set

$$\{\bar{x} \,|\, (0 \le \bar{x} \le 79.671) \cup (80.329 \le \bar{x} < \infty)\}$$

and the acceptance region is the set

$$\{\bar{x} \,|\, 79.671 < \bar{x} < 80.329\}$$

This partition of the domain of the sampling distribution of $\bar{X}$ into acceptance and rejection regions is illustrated in Figure 13.7.

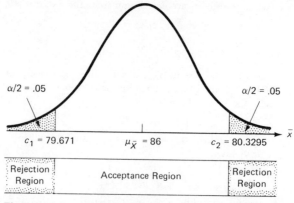

Figure 13.7   Partition of Domain of Sampling Distribution of $\bar{X}$ into Acceptance and Rejection Regions for Two-Tail Test

8. We may now explicitly state Kleenum's decision rule as follows: If the value of $\bar{X}$, the mean net weight of the boxes in the sample, is either (a) equal to or less than 79.671 or (b) equal to or greater than 80.329, then reject H_0 and accordingly shut down the process for adjustment; otherwise, accept H_0 and accordingly allow the process to continue in operation.

To generalize from this example of a two-tail test using a normal sampling distribution, suppose that we wish to test the null hypothesis

$$H_0: \quad \mu = \mu_0$$

against the alternative hypothesis

$$H_1: \quad \mu \neq \mu_0$$

The decision rule for this test is

If $\bar{X} \leq c_1$ or if $\bar{X} \geq c_2$, reject H_0; otherwise, accept H_0

where $c_1 = \mu_0 + z_{\alpha/2}\sigma_{\bar{X}}$
$\quad\quad c_2 = \mu_0 + z_{1-\alpha/2}\sigma_{\bar{X}}$

Evaluating the Decision Rule.   A null hypothesis such as $H_0: \mu = 80$ is called a *point hypothesis*, since it specifies only a single point in the parameter space. The null hypothesis is true only if the value of the parameter corresponds to that single point. When the null hypothesis is a point hypothesis, we cannot generate a Type I error curve, because the "curve" consists of only a single point which represents the significance level of the test. That is, if the null hypothesis is a point hypothesis, there is only a single value of α, and that value is the significance level. In terms of a formula, the probability of the Type I error for a two-tail normal test of a point hypothesis concerning a population mean is given by

$$\alpha_\mu = P\left\{(\bar{X} \leq c_1) \cup (\bar{X} \geq c_2) \,|\, \mu_{\bar{X}} = \mu_0, \sigma_{\bar{X}} = \frac{\sigma}{\sqrt{n}}\right\} \tag{13.5}$$

As we have seen, the value of α for Kleenum's decision rule is .10.

The Type II error probability for a two-tail normal test concerning a population mean is the probability that the sample mean will fall in the acceptance region, given that the alternative hypothesis is true. That is,

$$\beta_\mu = P\left(c_1 < \bar{X} < c_2 \,\middle|\, \mu_{\bar{X}} = \mu, \sigma_{\bar{X}} = \frac{\sigma}{\sqrt{n}}\right) \tag{13.6}$$

which is the probability that $\bar{X}$ will lie in the acceptance region, given that μ is any specified value contained in H_1. To illustrate the use of this formula, suppose that Kleenum's packaging process has drifted out of control and is operating at $\mu = 79.90$ ounces. Under this condition, what is the probability of obtaining a sample mean whose value would lead to the incorrect decision of allowing the process to continue operating? Applying Formula (13.6) and using Table I (Appendix II), this probability is obtained as follows:

$$\begin{aligned}
\beta_{79.90} &= P(79.671 < \bar{X} < 80.329 \,|\, \mu_{\bar{X}} = 79.90, \sigma_{\bar{X}} = .20) \\
&= F_n(80.329 \,|\, 79.90, .20) - F_n(79.671 \,|\, 79.90, .20) \\
&= F_N\left(\frac{80.329 - 79.90}{.20}\right) - F_N\left(\frac{79.671 - 79.90}{.20}\right) \\
&= F_N(2.145) - F_N(-1.145) \\
&= .9840 - .1261 \\
&= .8579
\end{aligned}$$

Following this procedure, Type II error probabilities for various values of μ contained in H_1 are calculated in Table 13.3. These probabilities for selected values of μ are represented by the unshaded areas of the curves in Figure 13.8.

The Type II error probabilities given in Table 13.3 are displayed graphically by the operating characteristic (OC) curve presented in Figure 13.9. Although

Table 13.3 Calculation of Type II Error Probabilities for Two-Tail Test ($H_0: \mu = 80$; $H_1: \mu \neq 80$)

μ	$z_1 = \dfrac{c_1 - \mu}{\sigma_{\bar{X}}}$	$z_2 = \dfrac{c_2 - \mu}{\sigma_{\bar{X}}}$	$F(z_1)$	$F(z_2)$	$\beta_\mu = F(z_2) - F(z_1)$
79.50	.855	4.145	.804	1.000	.196
79.60	.355	3.645	.639	1.000	.361
79.70	-.145	3.145	.442	.999	.557
79.80	-.645	2.645	.259	.996	.737
79.90	-1.145	2.145	.126	.984	.858
79.95	-1.395	1.895	.082	.971	.889
79.99	-1.595	1.695	.055	.955	.900
80.01	-1.695	1.595	.045	.945	.900
80.05	-1.895	1.395	.029	.918	.889
80.10	-2.145	1.145	.016	.874	.858
80.20	-2.645	.645	.004	.741	.737
80.30	-3.145	.145	.001	.558	.557
80.40	-3.645	-.355	.000	.361	.361
80.50	-4.145	-.855	.000	.196	.196

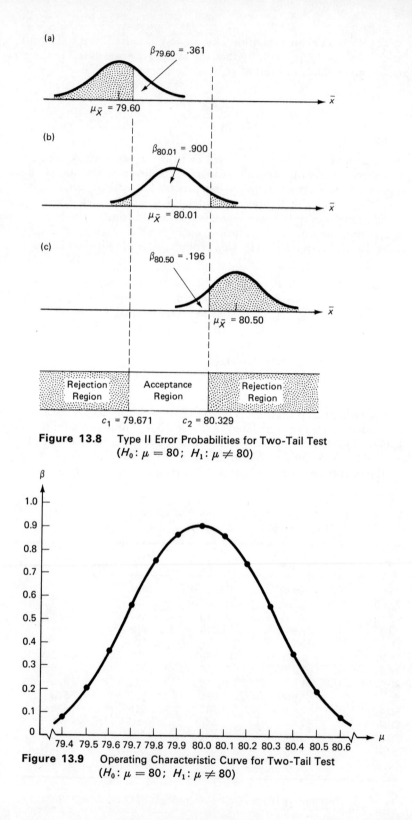

Figure 13.8 Type II Error Probabilities for Two-Tail Test
$(H_0: \mu = 80; \ H_1: \mu \neq 80)$

Figure 13.9 Operating Characteristic Curve for Two-Tail Test
$(H_0: \mu = 80; \ H_1: \mu \neq 80)$

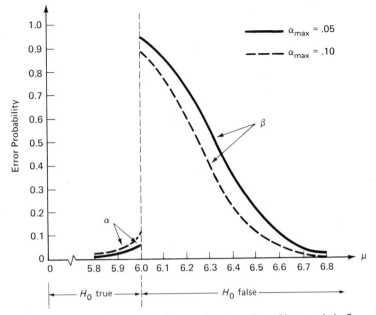

Figure 13.11   Effect of Significance Level on Error Characteristic Curve
$(H_0: \mu \le 6; \ H_1: \mu > 6)$

13.2.2   Effect of the Sample Size

An alternative way of increasing the power of a test is to increase the sample size. To illustrate this point, suppose that the significance level is maintained at .05 but the sample size is increased to $n = 100$. This increase in sample size reduces the standard deviation of the sampling distribution of $\bar{X}$ to

$$\sigma_{\bar{X}} = \frac{\sigma}{\sqrt{n}} = \frac{1.2}{\sqrt{100}} = .12$$

As the reader may verify, the decision rule resulting from this decrease in $\sigma_{\bar{X}}$ will be to reject H_0 if $\bar{X}$ is equal to or greater than 6.197 rather than 6.329. This is illustrated in Figure 13.12.

The change in the rejection region resulting from the increase in sample size produces a change in the error characteristics of the decision rule. This is illustrated by Figure 13.13. As this figure shows, when the sample size is increased from 36 to 100, the risks of both the Type I and Type II errors are reduced for all possible values of μ except the limiting value stated in the null hypothesis. Thus, by increasing the sample size, the power of the test is also increased without changing the significance level.

13.2.3   Interrelations

The preceding examples have demonstrated some relationships among the sample size, risk of the Type I error, and risk of the Type II error. These relationships may be summarized as follows:

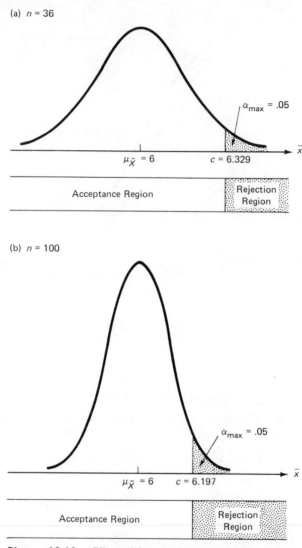

(a) $n = 36$

$\alpha_{max} = .05$

$\mu_{\bar{X}} = 6$ $c = 6.329$ $\bar{x}$

Acceptance Region   Rejection Region

(b) $n = 100$

$\alpha_{max} = .05$

$\mu_{\bar{X}} = 6$ $c = 6.197$ $\bar{x}$

Acceptance Region   Rejection Region

Figure 13.12   Effect of Sample Size on Rejection Region
($H_0 : \mu \leq 6$; $H_1 : \mu > 6$)

1. Holding the sample size constant, the greater the maximum risk of the Type I error, the less will be the risk of the Type II error. Thus, increasing the significance level increases the power of the test.
2. Holding the maximum risk of the Type I error constant, increasing the sample size will reduce the risk of the Type II error, thereby increasing the power of the test.

Because of the relationships among α, β, and n, the specification of any two of these three quantities automatically determines the third. Thus, it is theoretically and mechanically possible to derive the decision rule by specifying either

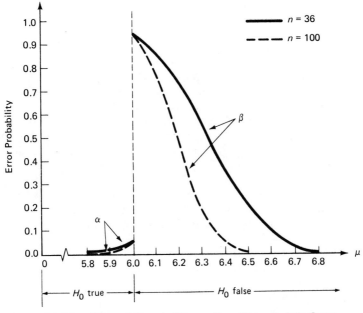

Figure 13.13 Effect of Sample Size on Error Characteristic Curve
$(H_0: \mu \leq 6; \; H_1: \mu > 6)$

(1) the significance level and sample size, or (2) the significance level and power of the test, or (3) the sample size and the power of the test. However, because of practical difficulties in specifying a desired power for the test, only the first of these three possible approaches is used to any great extent in actual practice.

13.3 TESTS CONCERNING THE DIFFERENCE BETWEEN THE MEANS OF TWO POPULATIONS

So far in this chapter we have been concerned with how to test a hypothesis regarding the mean of a single population. In many practical decision situations, however, the crucial decision parameter is the difference between the means of two populations. For example, consider the case of Paul Poulet, who operates a large chicken farm. For several weeks, Paul has been deliberating whether or not to switch from the chicken feed he is presently using to a new feed containing a special dietary supplement. After doing some figuring, Paul has determined that it would be advantageous to switch to the new feed only if, 120 days after hatching, the mean weight of the chickens raised on the new feed would exceed the mean weight of the chickens raised on the present feed by more than four ounces.

Since he is uncertain about how effective the new feed would be, Paul proposes to conduct an experiment, using two separate random samples of newly hatched chicks. The chicks in one sample will be raised on the new feed, and the chicks in the other sample will be raised on the present feed. After a period of 120 days from hatching, the mean weight of the chickens in each sample will be determined. Paul will then base his decision on the amount of the difference between the two sample means.

The crucial parameter on which Paul's decision hinges is the difference between the means of two infinite populations. The first population consists of all chickens that might be raised on the new feed, and the second population consists of all chickens that might be raised on the present feed. If we let μ_1 denote the mean weight of the first population at an age of 120 days, and μ_2 denote the mean weight of the second population at the same age, then the difference between these two population means is $\mu_1 - \mu_2$. We will denote this difference by δ. That is, $\delta = \mu_1 - \mu_2$. Thus, Paul should switch to the new feed only if $\delta > 4$.

Paul's proposed experiment amounts to taking a sample from each of the two populations and determining the mean weight of each sample 120 days after hatching. If $\bar{X}_1$ denotes the mean of the sample to be taken from the first population, and $\bar{X}_2$ denotes the mean of the sample to be taken from the second population, then the difference between the means of the two samples may be denoted by $D = \bar{X}_1 - \bar{X}_2$. Paul's decision will be based on the value of the random variable D. In order to derive the decision rule, we must first investigate the sampling distribution of D.

13.3.1 Sampling Distribution of the Difference between the Means of Two Independent Samples

In the experiment proposed above, a random sample of n_1 observations will be selected from population I, and a random sample of n_2 observations will be selected from population II, and the difference D between the two sample means will be determined. It may be shown mathematically that, if each of the two population distributions is normal, then the sampling distribution of D will be normal. Unless both population distributions are normal, the sampling distribution of D will not be exactly normal. Fortunately, however, the central limit theorem applies to the distribution of the difference between two sample means. Specifically, the sampling distribution of D approaches a normal distribution as the sizes of both samples, n_1 and n_2, approach infinity. Thus, if the sizes of the two samples are sufficiently large, it is reasonable to assume that the sampling distribution of D is approximately normal as long as there is no cause to suspect that either of the population distributions departs radically from normality.

In order to use a normal distribution to derive a decision rule based on D, it is necessary to determine μ_D and σ_D. It can be shown mathematically that the *expected* value of the difference between the means of two *samples* is equal to the *actual* difference between the means of the two *populations* from which the samples are taken. That is,

$$\mu_D = E(D) = \mu_1 - \mu_2 = \delta \qquad (13.7)$$

To determine σ_D, the standard error of D, we assume that the two samples will be selected *independently* in the sense that the particular set of elements that are drawn into one sample will have no effect on which particular set of elements are drawn into the second sample. It may be shown that the variance of the *difference* between the means of two independent samples is equal to the *sum* of the variances of the two sample means. That is,

$$\sigma_D^2 = V(D) = V(\bar{X}_1 - \bar{X}_2)$$
$$= V(\bar{X}_1) + V(\bar{X}_2)$$

If σ_1^2 is the variance of population I and σ_2^2 is the variance of population II, it follows from Formula (12.3) that $V(\bar{X}_1) = \sigma_1^2/n_1$ and $V(\bar{X}_2) = \sigma_2^2/n_2$. Then

$$\sigma_D^2 = \frac{\sigma_1^2}{n_1} + \frac{\sigma_2^2}{n_2}$$

Thus, the standard error of D is

$$\sigma_D = \sqrt{\frac{\sigma_1^2}{n_1} + \frac{\sigma_2^2}{n_2}} \tag{13.8}$$

13.3.2 Designing the Decision Rule

Having developed the sampling distribution of D, we are now ready to develop Paul Poulet's decision rule. To do this, we may proceed according to our general hypothesis-testing approach as follows:

1. The action space of Paul's decision problem consists of two alternative courses of action: (a) continue with the presently used feed, and (b) switch to the new feed. The parameter space is the set of all possible values of δ. Since δ can conceivably have any real value, this parameter space is the set $\{\delta \,|\, -\infty < \delta < \infty\}$.

2. Paul has determined that he should switch feeds only if δ is greater than 4 ounces. Hence, the parameter space should be partitioned into the two subsets:

$$\{\delta \,|\, -\infty < \delta \leq 4\} \quad \text{and} \quad \{\delta \,|\, 4 < \delta < \infty\}$$

3. Paul does not want to switch to the new feed unless the experiment provides convincing evidence that $\delta > 4$. Thus, the null and alternative hypotheses are

$$H_0: \quad \delta \leq 4$$
$$H_1: \quad \delta > 4$$

4. Paul feels that he should not accept more than a .15 risk of switching to the new feed if, in fact, it does not result in the desired increase in weight. Thus, the significance level is specified as .15.

5. The experiment will be conducted by independently selecting two random samples, each containing 50 newly hatched chicks. Each sample will be confined in a separate pen. The chicks in sample I will be raised on the new feed, and the chicks in sample II will be raised on the presently used feed. After 120 days, each sample will be weighed and the mean weight of the sample will be recorded.

6. The test statistic is D, which is the mean weight of sample I minus the mean weight of sample II. That is, $D = \bar{X}_1 - \bar{X}_2$. Since the sizes of the two samples are fairly large, and since there is no cause to suspect that the distribution of weight in either population departs radically from normality, it is reasonable to assume that the sampling distribution of D is approximately normal. Although neither $\bar{X}_1$ nor $\bar{X}_2$ can be negative, the difference D can be any real number. Therefore, the domain of the sampling distribution is the set $\{d \,|\, -\infty < d < \infty\}$.

7. Since the null hypothesis is $H_0: \delta \leq 4$ and the alternative hypothesis is $H_1: \delta > 4$, it follows that a relatively small value of D will tend to support H_0 and a relatively large value of D will tend to support H_1. Hence, the rejection region will contain the relatively large values of D that are located in the upper tail of

the sampling distribution. Since the significance level is .15, the rejection region will contain those possible values of D that are at least as great as some critical value c that satisfies the expression

$$P(D \geq c \,|\, \delta \leq 4) = .15$$

Using the limiting value of δ stated in the null hypothesis, this expression becomes

$$P(D \geq c \,|\, \delta = 4) = .15$$

In order to use a normal distribution to solve this expression for c, we must specify μ_D and σ_D, the parameters of the sampling distribution of D. To specify the value of μ_D, we need simply recall from Formula (13.7) that $\mu_D = \delta$. Thus, μ_D is specified as 4. To specify the value of σ_D, we may apply Formula (13.8). To use this formula, however, we need to know σ_1 and σ_2, the standard deviations of the weight distributions of the two populations. On the basis of his experience with raising chickens on the present feed, Paul feels that it is reasonable to assume that the standard deviation of the weight distribution of that population is $\sigma_2 = 2.5$ ounces. Furthermore, he feels that there is no reason to suspect that the standard deviation of the weight distribution of chickens raised on the new feed would be any different. Therefore, we may assume that $\sigma_1 = \sigma_2 = 2.5$ ounces. Then, since the size of each sample is 50, the value of σ_D is obtained from Formula (13.8) as follows:

$$\sigma_D = \sqrt{\frac{\sigma_1^2}{n_1} + \frac{\sigma_2^2}{n_2}} = \sqrt{\frac{2.5^2}{50} + \frac{2.5^2}{50}} = .50$$

Having specified the mean and standard deviation of D, we may restate the expression for determining c as

$$P(D \geq c \,|\, \mu_D = 4, \sigma_D = .50) = .15$$

It then follows that

$$P(D < c \,|\, \mu_D = 4, \sigma_D = .50) = .85$$

Assuming that the sampling distribution of D is normal, this expression becomes

$$F_n(c \,|\, \mu_D = 4, \sigma_D = .50) = .85$$

Converting this expression to standard normal notation, we obtain

$$F_N\left(\frac{c - 4}{.50}\right) = .85$$

From Table J (Appendix II), the .85 fractile of the standard normal distribution is $z_{.85} = 1.036$. Thus,

$$z_{.85} = \frac{c - 4}{.50} = 1.036$$

Simple algebra yields

$$c = 4 + 1.036(.50) = 4.518$$

Hence, the rejection region is

$$\{d \,|\, 4.518 \leq d < \infty\} \text{ and the acceptance region is } \{d \,|\, -\infty < d < 4.518\}$$

8. We may now explicitly state Paul's decision rule as follows: If the value of D, the mean weight of the sample raised on the new feed less the mean weight of the sample raised on the present feed, is equal to or greater than 4.518 ounces, reject H_0 and accordingly switch to the new feed; otherwise, accept H_0 and accordingly continue with the presently used feed.

13.3.3 Summary of General Specifications

Paul Poulet's decision rule is an example of an upper-tail normal test concerning a difference between the means of two populations. This same general procedure may also be applied to a lower-tail test or a two-tail test. The general specifications for all three types of tests concerning a difference between two population means are summarized in Table 13.5.

Table 13.5 General Specifications for Normal Tests Concerning a Difference Between Means of Two Populations

Test	Hypotheses	Decision Rule	Critical Values
Upper tail	$H_0: \delta \le \delta_0$ $H_1: \delta > \delta_0$	If $D \ge c$, reject H_0; otherwise, accept H_0	$c = \delta_0 + z_{1-\alpha}\sigma_D$
Lower tail	$H_0: \delta \ge \delta_0$ $H_1: \delta < \delta_0$	If $D \le c$, reject H_0; otherwise, accept H_0	$c = \delta_0 + z_\alpha\sigma_D$
Two tail	$H_0: \delta = \delta_0$ $H_1: \delta \ne \delta_0$	If $D \le c_1$ or $D \ge c_2$, reject H_0; otherwise, accept H_0	$c_1 = \delta_0 + z_{\alpha/2}\sigma_D$ $c_2 = \delta_0 + z_{1-\alpha/2}\sigma_D$

PROBLEMS

13.1 Each of the following statements describes a situation in which sample data will be used to perform an hypothesis test concerning a population mean. Using μ to denote the population mean, indicate the appropriate null and alternative hypothesis for each situation.

(a) A dairy is considering whether or not to offer home delivery service in a newly opened residential community. On the basis of financial analysis, management has determined to offer the service only if a sample survey of the households in the new community provides convincing evidence that the mean weekly milk consumption of the community exceeds 10.6 quarts per household.

(b) The manufacturer of a particular type of power cell for hand calculators advertises that the mean operating life of this type of cell is at least 200 hours. Responding to complaints that this claim is untrue, a state consumer protection agency decides to submit a sample of these cells to life test. The agency will take action against the manufacturer only if the sample provides sufficient evidence to support the position that the claim is untrue.

(c) A particular brand of vitamin Q tablets is marketed in 500-tablet bottles that are labeled to contain 100 milligrams of active ingredient per tablet. As part of a program that regularly checks the potency of marketed drugs, the state pharmaceutical commission is about to conduct a routine laboratory test of this particular brand of vitamin Q tablets. The commission will take action against the producer unless the laboratory results provide convincing evidence that the mean active ingredient of this type of tablet exceeds 100 milligrams.

(d) An automatic production process stamps out metal washers for a particular mechanical assembly. When operating "under control," the mean outside diameter of the washer population produced by this process is 14.20 millimeters. If the process mean is either greater or less than 14.20, the process is considered to be "out of control." At regular intervals, a sample of washers produced by the process is examined with respect to their outside diameters. The process will be halted for adjustment if, and only if, the sample evidence is sufficient to conclude that the process is indeed "out of control."

13.2 The Beehive Oil Company holds an option to lease a service station site. To decide whether or not to exercise the option, management plans to survey a sample of 64 households within a 2-mile radius of the site. The company will exercise the option only if the sample provides convincing evidence, at the .10 significance level, that the mean weekly household gasoline consumption in the area exceeds 13.6 gallons. On the basis of past experience with similar surveys, it is reasonable to assume that weekly household gasoline consumption is normally distributed with $\sigma = 3.2$ gallons.

(a) Identify the action and state spaces for this decision problem.

(b) Specify the null and alternative hypotheses.

(c) What is the appropriate sampling distribution? Justify your answer.

(d) Identify the acceptance and rejection regions of the domain of the sampling distribution.

(e) Explicitly state the decision rule.

13.3 For the decision rule developed in Problem 13.2, do the following:

(a) Determine the probability of the Type I error for each of the following possible values of μ: 13.6, 13.4, 13.2, 13.0.

(b) Determine the probability of the Type II error for each of the following possible values of μ: 14.0, 14.4, 14.8, 15.2, 15.6.

(c) Use the results in parts (a) and (b) to sketch the error characteristic chart.

13.4 Using the error characteristic chart obtained in Problem 13.3, determine the following:

(a) Probability that the decision rule will lead to a Type I error if actually $\mu = 13.40$.

(b) Probability that the decision rule will lead to a Type I error if actually $\mu = 13.50$.

(c) Probability that the decision rule will lead to a Type II error if actually $\mu = 14.40$.

(d) Probability that the decision rule will lead to a Type II error if actually $\mu = 14.60$.

(e) Power of the decision rule if actually $\mu = 14.40$.

(f) Power of the decision rule if actually $\mu = 14.60$.

(g) Probability that the decision rule will lead to a Type I error if actually $\mu = 14.60$.

13.5 A manufacturer of dietary supplements advertises that the mean active content of the natural vitamin C tablets that they produce is at least 500 milligrams. A government agency, investigating this claim, decides to conduct a laboratory analysis of a sample of 100 tablets. The agency will take action against the manufacturer only if the sample provides convincing evidence, at the .05 significance level, that the mean active content of the product is less than 500 milligrams per tablet. On the basis of past experience with such investigations, it is reasonable to assume that the active content of such tablets is normally distributed with $\sigma = 12$ milligrams.

(a) Identify the action and state spaces for this decision problem.

(b) State the null and alternative hypotheses.

(c) What is the appropriate sampling distribution? Justify your answer.

(d) Identify the acceptance and rejection regions of the domain of the sampling distribution.

(e) Explicitly state the decision rule.

13.6 For the decision rule developed in Problem 13.5, do the following:

(a) Determine the probability of the Type I error for each of the following possible values of μ: 500.0, 500.6, 501.2, 501.8.

(b) Determine the probability of the Type II error for each of the following possible values of μ: 498.8, 497.6, 496.4, 495.2, 494.0.

(c) Use the results in parts (a) and (b) to sketch the error characteristic chart.

13.7 Using the error characteristic chart obtained in Problem 13.6, determine the following:

(a) Probability that the decision rule will lead the agency to take action against the manufacturer if actually $\mu = 500.60$.

(b) Probability that the decision rule will lead the agency not to take action against the manufacturer if actually $\mu = 497.60$.

(c)   Probability that the decision rule will lead the agency not to take action against the manufacturer if actually $\mu = 498.20$.

(d)   Probability that the decision rule will lead the agency to take action against the manufacturer if actually $\mu = 497.60$.

13.8   When operating under control, the mean fill of an automatic process for filling boxes with cake mix is 12 ounces per box. The process is out of control if the mean fill is either greater or less than 12 ounces. At regular intervals, the contents of a sample of 16 boxes are weighed, and the process is stopped for adjustment if, and only if, the sample evidence is sufficient to conclude, at the .05 significance level, that the process is out of control. Assuming that the contents of the boxes filled by the process are normally distributed with $\sigma = .40$ ounce, derive the decision rule for determining, from the sample results, whether or not to stop the process for adjustment.

13.9   For the decision rule developed in Problem 13.8, do the following:

(a)   Determine the probability of the Type II error for each of the following possible values of μ: 11.5, 11.7, 11.9, 12.1, 12.3, 12.5.

(b)   Use the results in part (a) to sketch the OC curve.

13.10   Using the OC curve obtained in Problem 13.9, determine the following:

(a)   Probability that the decision rule will lead to a Type II error if actually $\mu = 12.20$.

(b)   Power of the decision rule if actually $\mu = 11.60$.

(c)   Probability that, using the decision rule, the manufacturer will fail to stop the process if actually $\mu = 11.80$.

(d)   Probability that the decision rule will lead to the conclusion that the process is under control if actually $\mu = 12.40$.

13.11   A manufacturer of photographic flood lamps advertises that, on the average, the bulbs that they produce have an operating life of at least 40 hours. Responding to complaints that this claim is untrue, a state consumer agency decides to submit a sample of 75 of these bulbs to life test. The agency will take action against the manufacturer only if the sample provides convincing evidence, at the .02 significance level, that the advertising claim is untrue. Assuming that the lives of the bulbs produced by the manufacturer are normally distributed with $\sigma = 3.9$ hours, derive and explicitly state the agency's decision rule.

13.12   For the decision rule developed in Problem 13.11, determine the following:

(a)   Probability that the decision rule will lead to a Type I error if actually $\mu = 40.10$.

(b)   Probability that the decision rule will lead the agency to take action against the manufacturer if $\mu = 40.20$.

(c)   Probability that the decision rule will lead to a Type II error if actually $\mu = 38.90$.

(d)   Probability that, using the decision rule, the agency will take action against the manufacturer if actually $\mu = 38.90$.

13.13   In response to taxpayer complaints, the board of supervisors of a metropolitan county is considering a reduction in the property tax rate on owner-occupied homes. The members of the board are divided on the issue, and the key vote lies with Supervisor Dexter, who is uncertain. Dexter proposes that the board retain a real estate firm to appraise the market value of a sample of 225 owner-occupied homes in the county, and that the tax rate reduction be approved only if the sample provides convincing evidence, at the .01 significance level, that the mean market value of such homes in the county is greater than $55,000.

(a)   Identify the action and state spaces for the decision problem under Dexter's proposal.

(b)   State the null and alternative hypotheses.

(c)   Assuming that the standard deviation of the market values of the homes in the county is $\sigma = \$9,000$, specify the appropriate sampling distribution. Justify your answer.

(d)   Derive and explicitly state the decision rule.

13.14   For the decision rule developed in Problem 13.13, determine the following:

(a)   Power of the decision rule if actually $\mu = \$56,000$.

(b) Probability that the decision rule will lead to a tax-rate reduction if actually $\mu = \$54,500$.

(c) Probability that the decision rule will fail to lead to a tax-rate reduction if actually $\mu = \$57,000$.

(d) Probability that the decision rule will lead to a tax-rate reduction if actually $\mu = \$56,500$.

13.15 Club Pacifico is a travel firm that specializes in providing singles with low-cost tours to romantic locales. As such, the Club caters primarily to the "younger set." The Club's management has recently been approached by the editors of *The National Jester*, a college humor magazine, with an attractive advertising proposal. During a brainstorming session, the executive committee of the club decides that they will accept the proposal only if a sample survey of 400 of the magazine's subscribers provides sufficient evidence, at the .05 level of significance, that the mean age of the subscribers is less than 30 years.

(a) Using μ to denote the mean age of the population of subscribers to *The National Jester*, state the null and alternative hypotheses that the survey is intended to test.

(b) What is meant by the specification that the test will be conducted at the .05 level of significance?

(c) Assuming that the standard deviation of the ages of the magazine's subscribers is $\sigma = 4$ years, specify the appropriate sampling distribution for this test. Justify your answer.

(d) Derive and explicitly state the decision rule.

(e) If the sample yields a mean age of 29.8 years, should the Club accept or reject the magazine's offer?

13.16 For the decision rule developed in Problem 13.15, determine the following:

(a) Probability that the decision rule will incorrectly lead the Club to accept the magazine's offer if actually $\mu = 30.2$ years.

(b) Is the error described in part (a) a Type I or Type II error? Explain.

(c) Probability that the decision rule will lead the Club to reject the magazine's offer if actually $\mu = 29.5$ years.

(d) Probability that the decision rule will lead the Club to reject the magazine's offer if actually $\mu = 30.1$ years.

(e) Probability that the decision rule will lead the Club to accept the magazine's offer if actually $\mu = 29.7$ years.

13.17 For the example described in Section 13.1.2, Dave Doolittle's decision rule was: If the value of $\bar{X}$, the mean burning life of the flood lamps in the sample, is equal to or less than 5.671 hours, reject H_0 and accordingly do not purchase flood lamps from Fotoline; otherwise, accept H_0 and accordingly purchase flood lamps from Fotoline. The error characteristic curve for this decision rule appears in Figure 13.6. Using this chart, determine the following:

(a) Probability that the decision rule will lead to a Type I error if actually $\mu = 6.00$ hours.

(b) Probability that the decision rule will lead to a Type II error if actually $\mu = 5.60$ hours.

(c) Probability that Dave will purchase flood lamps from Fotoline if actually $\mu = 5.80$ hours.

(d) Probability that Dave will not purchase flood lamps from Fotoline if actually $\mu = 5.70$ hours.

13.18 For the decision problem discussed in Section 13.3.2, suppose that Paul Poulet takes the position that he will switch to the new feed unless the experiment provides convincing evidence that $\delta < 4$. Derive and explicitly state the decision rule for Paul.

13.19 A year ago the nationwide securities firm of O'Connell and Jones hired 240 recent M.B.A. graduates as account representatives, half of whom were randomly selected to participate in an experimental training course given at the start of employment. After one year, 104 of those who participated in the training program remain employed by the firm, and 106 of those who did not participate in the training program remain employed. Management must now decide whether to give the training course to all future new employees or drop the program. To make the decision, they will determine the mean first-year commissions for each of the two groups. The training course will be continued only if the sample results make it possible to conclude, at the .05 significance level, that the training produces an increase of more than $2,000 in mean first-year commissions.

(a) Identify the action space for this decision problem.

(b) Let $\delta = \mu_1 - \mu_2$, where μ_1 is the mean first-year commissions of the population of future account representatives who take the course, and μ_2 is the mean commissions of the population who do not take the course. State the appropriate null and alternative hypotheses in terms of δ.

(c) Assume that, regardless of whether the population of future employees does or does not take the course, the standard deviation of first-year commissions is $\sigma = \$2,500$. Derive and explicitly state the decision rule.

(d) Suppose that O'Connell and Jones find that the 104 employees who took the course had mean commissions of $19,780 and the 106 employees who did not take the course had mean commissions of $17,120. Should they retain the training program or drop it?

13.20 Bloomwell Products has developed a new indoor plant food which they plan to sell in supermarkets. Two alternative package designs have been proposed, and management is uncertain which design to select. Design A is less expensive, but there is some feeling that design B may result in sufficiently better sales to justify its greater expense. To make the decision, the sales manager plans to set up displays of the product in 200 supermarkets. In 100 of the sample stores design A will be used, and in the other 100 sample stores design B will be used. The mean sales per store for each design in a 1-week period will be determined. Design A will be adopted unless the sample results provide sufficient evidence to conclude, at the .02 significance level, that design A produces mean weekly sales that are over $20 less than those produced by design B. Assume that the standard deviation of 1 week's sales is $\sigma_A = \$30$ for design A and $\sigma_B = \$32$ for design B. Derive and explicitly state the decision rule.

14

Hypothesis Testing Using Approximations to Discrete Sampling Distributions

Frequently, practical considerations make the use of an *approximate* sampling distribution preferable to the use of an *exact* sampling distribution. For example, suppose that we wish to conduct a sampling experiment consisting of $n = 1,000$ Bernoulli trials to test a hypothesis concerning π, the proportion of "successes" in some dichotomous population. In such a case, the exact sampling distribution is binomial. Unfortunately, however, no available binomial tables contain probabilities for such a large value of n. We could, of course, calculate the necessary binomial probabilities, but this would be a burdensome task, unless a computer program for this purpose is readily available. Thus, from a practical standpoint, we might consider using some alternative sampling distribution that will provide a reasonably accurate approximation to the desired binomial distribution.

Through mathematical derivations that are beyond the scope of this text, it is possible to demonstrate the existence of certain relationships among the hypergeometric, binomial, Poisson, and normal distributions. In this chapter we are particularly concerned with the use of these relationships to obtain approximate solutions to inferential problems for which the exact solutions are overly complex. Specifically, this chapter considers hypothesis-testing procedures based on the following approximations:

1. Binomial approximation to the hypergeometric
2. Poisson approximation to the binomial
3. Normal approximation to the binomial
4. Normal approximation to the discrete sampling distribution of the mean

In many cases, procedures based on approximate distributions are considerably easier to apply than are procedures based on exact distributions. However, an approximate distribution should be used only if it will provide approximate probabilities that are sufficiently accurate for the problem at hand. This proviso concerning the magnitude of error incurred in using an approximation is central to the use of approximation methods in statistical inference. Unfortunately, there are no hard-and-fast rules for deciding whether a particular approximation is adequate in a specific case. In the absence of strict rules for specifying the conditions under which an approximation might be adequate, this chapter presents some general rules of thumb. In the final analysis, however, the decision to employ an approximation procedure must rest on substantive judgment concerning whether it is economically sound to tolerate the inaccuracy introduced by the approximation method.

14.1 BINOMIAL APPROXIMATION TO THE HYPERGEOMETRIC

In our discussion of the hypergeometric and binomial sampling distributions in Chapter 9, we observed that (1) both distributions are applicable to sampling from dichotomous populations, but that (2) the hypergeometric distribution applies to situations involving sampling without replacement from finite populations, whereas the binomial distribution applies to situations involving sampling from infinite populations or sampling with replacement from finite populations. We also noted that, if a finite population were large, and if the sample size were very small relative to the population size, then the population could be considered "effectively infinite" and the binomial distribution would be adequate. Actually, what this means is that, if a random sample of size n is selected from a finite, dichotomous population of size N (where N is large), and if the sampling fraction n/N is quite small (particularly below .10, as a rough rule of thumb), then the binomial distribution will provide reasonably accurate approximations of hypergeometric probabilities.[1]

14.1.1 Mechanics of the Approximation

If the number of observations in the sample is less than the number of successes in the population $(n < D)$, the appropriate binomial approximation to the hypergeometric mass function is given by

$$f_h(r \mid N, n, D) \approx f_b\left(r \mid n, \pi = \frac{D}{N}\right) \tag{14.1}$$

The corresponding binomial approximation to the cumulative hypergeometric function is given by

$$F_h(r \mid N, n, D) \approx F_b\left(r \mid n, \pi = \frac{D}{N}\right) \tag{14.2}$$

For example, suppose that a box contains 100 transistors, of which 15 are defective. If a random sample of 5 transistors are taken without replacement from the box, what is the probability that the sample will contain exactly 2 defectives? In this situation we have a hypergeometric problem with $N = 100$, $n = 5$, $D = 15$, and $r = 2$. The exact hypergeometric solution to the problem is

---

[1] For a discussion of binomial approximations to the hypergeometric with high sampling fractions and success ratios, see G. Lieberman and D. Owen, *Tables of the Hypergeometric Probability Distribution* (Stanford, Calif.: Stanford University Press, 1961): see also H. D. Brunk, J. E. Holstein, and F. Williams, "A Comparison of Binomial Approximations to the Hypergeometric Distribution," *The American Statistician*, February 1968.

$$f_h(2 \mid N = 100, n = 5, D = 15) = \frac{\binom{15}{2}\binom{85}{3}}{\binom{100}{5}} = .1378$$

Notice in this case that the size of the sample ($n = 5$) is less than the number of defectives in the box ($D = 15$). Thus, if we wish to approximate this probability by the binomial mass function, we may apply Formula (14.1), with $n = 5$ and $\pi = 15/100 = .15$. This approximate solution is

$$f_b(2 \mid n = 5, \pi = .15) = \binom{5}{2}(.15)^2(.85)^3 = .1382$$

Thus, in this particular case, the magnitude of error is $.1382 - .1378 = .0004$.

If the number of observations in the sample is greater than the number of successes in the population ($n > D$), the preferred binomial approximation to the hypergeometric is given by

$$f_h(r \mid N, n, D) \approx f_b\left(r \mid D, \pi = \frac{n}{N}\right) \tag{14.3}$$

The corresponding binomial approximation to the cumulative hypergeometric function is given by

$$F_h(r \mid N, n, D) \approx F_b\left(r \mid D, \pi = \frac{n}{N}\right) \tag{14.4}$$

For example, suppose that a box contains 100 transistors, of which 5 are defective. If a random sample of 10 transistors are taken without replacement from the box, what is the probability that the sample will contain exactly 2 defectives? Now we have a hypergeometric problem with $N = 100$, $n = 10$, $D = 5$, and $r = 2$. The exact hypergeometric solution to the problem is

$$f_h(2 \mid N = 100, n = 10, D = 5) = \frac{\binom{5}{2}\binom{95}{8}}{\binom{100}{10}} = .0702$$

In this case, the size of the sample ($n = 10$) is greater than the number of defectives in the box ($D = 5$). Thus, if we wish to solve this problem by the binomial approximation to the hypergeometric, we may use Formula (14.3). Since $D = 5$, and $\pi = n/N = 10/100 = .10$, the approximate binomial solution using this formula is

$$f_b(2 \mid D = 5, \pi = .10) = \binom{5}{2}(.10)^2(.90)^3 = .0729$$

In this instance, the error of approximation is $.0729 - .0702 = .0027$. If we had solved this problem by the "standard" approximation of Formula (14.1), we would have obtained

$$f_b(2 \mid n = 10, \pi = .05) = \binom{10}{2}(.05)^2(.95)^8 = .0746$$

The error of approximation then would have been $.0746 - .0702 = .0044$, which is noticeably greater than the error obtained with the use of Formula (14.3). This observation stresses the fact that when $n > D$, Formula (14.3) tends to yield more accurate approximations of hypergeometric probabilities than the commonly used Formula (14.1). Of course, if $n < D$, Formula (14.1) tends to be more accurate. For the case in which $n = D$, the two approximation formulas will give the same result.

14.1.2 Hypothesis Testing with the Approximation

To illustrate the use of the binomial approximation to the hypergeometric in hypothesis testing, consider the case of Icarus Industries, a large aerospace firm. A subcontractor, Precision Products, supplies Icarus with a particular type of delicate component which is shipped in lots of 200 units each. Icarus considers a lot to be of acceptable quality as long as D, the number of defectives in a lot, is no greater than 10. In recent weeks, several of the lots received by Icarus from Precision Products have contained an excessive number of defective units. To guard against accepting too many of these unacceptable lots, Icarus has decided to establish a lot acceptance plan. For this purpose, a random sample of 5 units from each lot will be inspected, and the decision of whether or not to accept each lot will be based on the number of defectives in the sample taken from that lot. To design the appropriate decision rule for this plan, Icarus has specified a significance level of .30.

The decision rule for Icarus' lot acceptance plan may be derived according to the procedure presented in Section 11.1 for small-lot acceptance sampling. However, since there are no available tables of hypergeometric probabilities for $N = 200$, it is not practical to determine the critical value for the decision rule by using an exact hypergeometric distribution. Fortunately, in this situation, we may use the binomial approximation to the hypergeometric distribution, inasmuch as the lot size is reasonably large ($N = 200$) and the sampling fraction is fairly small ($n/N = 5/200 = .025$).

Following the usual small-lot acceptance sampling practice of placing the burden of proof on the consumer, the null and alternative hypotheses for Icarus' plan are

$$H_0: \quad D \leq 10$$
$$H_1: \quad D > 10$$

Following the specifications for hypergeometric tests given in Table 11.4, the null hypothesis will be rejected if R, the number of defective units in the sample, is equal to or greater than the critical value c. Bearing in mind that the significance level is .30, the expression for determining c is

$$F_h(c - 1 \,|\, N = 200, n = 5, D = 10) \geq .70$$

In order to use the binomial approximation to determine the value of c from this hypergeometric expression, we should first observe that n is less than D. Hence, the approximation to the cumulative hypergeometric function given by Formula (14.2) is preferred over that given by Formula (14.4). Then, since $D/N = 10/200 = .05$, the exact hypergeometric expression for determining c may be approximated by the following binomial expression:

$$F_b(c - 1 \,|\, n = 5, \pi = .05) \geq .70$$

Entering Table F (Appendix II) for $n = 5$ and $\pi = .05$, we look for a cumulative probability that is as close as possible to .70 without being less than .70. The tabulated value satisfying this specification is $F(0) = .7738$. Thus, $c - 1 = 0$, so that the desired value of c is 1. Therefore, Icarus' decision rule may be stated as follows: If the value of R, the number of defective units in the sample, is equal to or greater than 1, reject H_0 and accordingly reject the lot; otherwise, accept H_0 and accordingly accept the lot.

14.2 POISSON APPROXIMATION TO THE BINOMIAL

In our discussion of the binomial distribution in Section 9.3, we observed that the parameter π represents the probability that a Bernoulli trial will result in a success. If π is extremely small, then the occurrence of a success can be regarded as a "rare event," and the binomial distribution is closely approximated by a Poisson distribution.

14.2.1 Mechanics of the Approximation

In Chapter 9 we observed that the parameters of the binomial distribution are n and π, and that the mean of the distribution is given by $n\pi$. Similarly, we noted that the Poisson distribution has the parameters λ and t, and the mean of that distribution is λt. Thus, when π is close to zero,[2] binomial probabilities are approximately the same as the corresponding probabilities given by the Poisson distribution with $\lambda t = n\pi$. In terms of a formula, the Poisson approximation to the binomial mass function is given by

$$f_b(r \,|\, n, \pi) \approx f_P(r \,|\, \lambda t = n\pi) \tag{14.5}$$

The corresponding Poisson approximation to the cumulative binomial function is given by

$$F_b(r \,|\, n, \pi) \approx F_P(r \,|\, \lambda t = n\pi) \tag{14.6}$$

To illustrate the use of Formula (14.5), consider the binomial distribution with $n = 10$ and $\pi = .05$. For this binomial distribution, the mean is

$$n\pi = 10(.05) = .50$$

Thus, the binomial distribution with $n = 10$ and $\pi = .05$ is approximated by a Poisson distribution with $\lambda t = .50$. The close resemblance of these two distributions can be clearly seen in Figure 14.1.[3]

---

[2]The Poisson approximation to the binomial may also be employed when p is close to 1, such that $(1 - p)$ is close to zero. That is, if the probability of a "success" is close to 1, then the probability of a "failure" will be close to zero, and the Poisson approximation may be used by working in terms of "failures" rather than "successes."

[3]For a more detailed technical discussion of the Poisson approximation to the binomial, see T. W. Anderson and S. M. Samuels, "Some Inequalities among Binomial and Poisson Probabilities," *Fifth Berkeley Symposium on Mathematical Statistics and Probability* (Berkeley, Calif.: University of California Press, 1967).

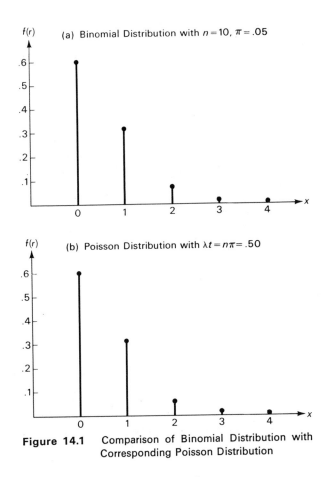

Figure 14.1   Comparison of Binomial Distribution with Corresponding Poisson Distribution

14.2.2 Hypothesis Testing with the Approximation

To illustrate the use of the Poisson approximation to the binomial in hypothesis testing, consider the case of Handy House, a large mail-order firm that is in the process of converting its records of past sales from order forms to punched cards. When completed, this file will contain more than 1 million cards. The actual job of punching the cards is being performed by Sigmaplex Associates, a local computer services firm. Handy House's managers realize that they should expect some keypunch errors to occur in such a large job, but they feel that they can tolerate such errors on no more than 1% of the cards in the file. One way to establish the accuracy of the file, of course, is to verify each and every card. To avoid this expensive task, they have decided to verify the entire file only if a sample of 1,000 cards provides convincing evidence that more than 1% of the cards in the file contain errors. In designing a decision rule for this purpose, management is willing to accept a maximum risk of .05 that the rule will lead to verifying the entire file if in fact no more than 1% of the cards in the file contain errors.

Handy House's decision regarding whether or not to verify the entire file of punched cards will depend on how many cards in the sample contain errors. Deriving the decision rule for this purpose is essentially a matter of designing a test of the hypotheses

$$H_0: \quad \pi \leq .01$$
$$H_1: \quad \pi > .01$$

where π denotes the proportion of cards with errors in the entire file. Since the size of the population (over 1,000,000 cards) is large enough to be considered effectively infinite, the process of selecting a random sample of 1,000 cards and determining the number of those cards containing errors may be regarded as a binomial sampling experiment. Thus, Handy House's decision rule may be derived according to the specifications for binomial tests given in Table 11.5. Following those specifications, Handy House will reject H_0 and accordingly submit the entire file to verification only if R, the number of cards with errors in the sample is equal to or greater than the critical value c. Using a significance level of .05, the expression for determining c is

$$F_b(c - 1 \mid n = 1,000, \pi = .01) \geq .95$$

Lacking tables of cumulative binomial probabilities for $n = 1,000$, the critical value in this binomial expression cannot be readily determined using the exact binomial distribution. However, since the value of π in this expression is very small, we may use the Poisson distribution to approximate the binomial distribution.

In order to use the Poisson approximation to determine the value of c, we first note that $n\pi = 1,000(.01) = 10$. Then, using Formula (14.6), the exact binomial expression for determining c may be approximated by the following Poisson expression:

$$F_P(c - 1 \mid \lambda t = 10) \geq .95$$

Entering Table H (Appendix II) for $\lambda t = 10$, we look for a cumulative probability that is as close as possible to .95 without being less than .95. The tabulated value satisfying this specification is $F(15) = .9513$. Thus, $c - 1 = 15$, so that the desired value of c is 16. Consequently, Handy House's decision rule may be stated as follows: If the value of R, the number of cards with errors in the sample, is equal to or greater than 16, reject H_0 and accordingly submit the entire file to verification; otherwise, accept H_0 and accordingly do not submit the entire file to verification.

14.3 NORMAL APPROXIMATION TO THE BINOMIAL

We have seen that the Poisson distribution provides a reasonably accurate approximation to the binomial distribution when the value of π deviates markedly from .50—that is, when π is close to zero or 1. However, when π does not deviate markedly from .50, the accuracy of the Poisson approximation to the binomial is relatively poor. In such a case, a more accurate approximation to the binomial is provided by the normal distribution.

14.3.1 Effect of the Binomial Parameters on the Shape of the Distribution

To understand how the normal distribution may be used to approximate binomial probabilities, it is helpful to consider how the values of the parameters n and π affect the shape of the binomial distribution. Figure 14.2 presents a comparison of various binomial distributions for selected values of n and π. From careful study of these graphs, we can make the following generalizations:

1. As shown by distributions (c), (f), and (i) in Figure 14.2, when $\pi = .50$ the graph of the binomial is symmetrical regardless of the size of n.
2. If the value of π is not .50, the binomial distribution is skewed. The further π is from .50 in either direction, the greater the skewness. For example, distributions

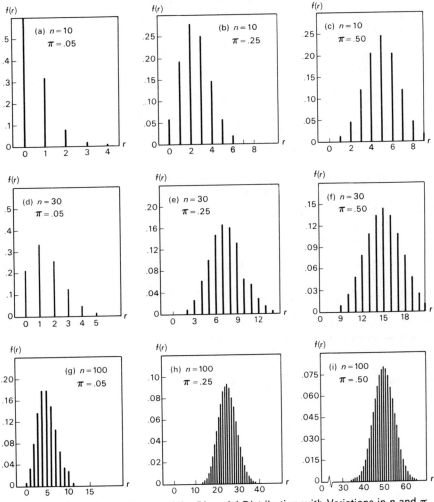

Figure 14.2   Different Shapes of the Binomial Distribution with Variations in n and π

(a), (b), and (c) all represent binomials with $n = 10$ but with different values of π. Distribution (c), with $\pi = .50$. is symmetrical, whereas distribution (b), with $\pi = .25$, is skewed, and distribution (a), with $\pi = .05$. is skewed even more. A similar observation may be made by comparing distributions (d), (e), and (f), or by comparing distributions (g), (h), and (i).

3. If the value of π is not .50, the degree of skewness of the binomial distribution is more pronounced when n is small than when n is large. For example, distributions (a), (d), and (g) all represent binomials with $\pi = .05$ but with different values of n. Distribution (a), with $n = 10$, is markedly skewed, whereas distribution (d), with $n = 30$, is less so, and distribution (g), with $n = 100$, approaches symmetry.

4. As n increases, so that there is an increased number of terms in the binomial, the differences in probability values between successive terms become increasingly small so that, when n is large, the graph approaches the appearance of a continuous curve. This may be seen from Figure 14.2 by comparing the distributions in the bottom row with the corresponding distributions in the top row.

5. Distributions (a) and (i) provide a comparison of extreme conditions. In distribution (a), with small n and π far from .50, we have a markedly skewed, obviously discrete distribution. In distribution (i), with large n and $\pi = .50$, we have a symmetrical distribution that approaches the appearance of a continuous normal curve. This is more than mere coincidence. As early as 1733, Abraham de Moivre demonstrated that the formula for the normal density function is the limit of the binomial distribution as n approaches infinity.

14.3.2 Mechanics and Accuracy of the Approximation

In the case of the Poisson approximation to the binomial, the mechanics of making the approximation were quite simple, since both the Poisson and the binomial are discrete distributions. In the case of the normal approximation to the binomial, however, the mechanics are somewhat more involved since we are using a *continuous* distribution to approximate a *discrete* distribution. To illustrate the procedure for the normal approximation to the binomial, consider a simplified case in which we wish to determine the probability of observing 6 successes in 8 trials of a Bernoulli process with $\pi = .50$. For this particular problem, the normal approximation is not needed, since n is so small that the exact binomial probability may be readily obtained from binomial tables. However, this simple case will be particularly useful for illustrating the approximation procedure and examining its accuracy.

The *first* step in performing the approximation is to determine the mean and standard deviation of the binomial distribution with parameters n and π. Applying Formulas (9.7) and (9.9), we obtain

$$\mu = n\pi = 8(.50) = 4$$
$$\sigma = \sqrt{n\pi(1 - \pi)} = \sqrt{8(.50)(1 - .50)} = 1.414$$

The *second* step is to adopt a normal distribution whose mean is set equal to the binomial mean, and whose standard deviation is set equal to the binomial standard deviation. That is, for our example we use a normal distribution with $\mu = 4$ and $\sigma = 1.414$.

The *third* step is to convert the definition of the event under consideration from discrete terms into continuous terms. This is necessary since we are approximating a discrete distribution by a continuous distribution. The rationale underlying this step is illustrated in Figure 14.3, which shows the normal distribution superimposed on the binomial distribution. The first important point to note in this figure is that the various terms of the binomial have been represented by contiguous bars rather than by separate vertical lines. Each bar extends $\frac{1}{2}$ unit above and $\frac{1}{2}$ unit below the integer value that it represents. That is, each integer value, r, is redefined as an interval extending between the *limits* of $(r - .5)$ and $(r + .5)$. By this redefinition, each of the bars has unit width, so that the area of each bar is equal to the height of the bar. Thus, we are able to represent the various binomial probabilities as areas of rectangles, just as normal probabilities are represented by areas under the curve. As shown in Figure 14.3, the event $(R = 6)$ is redefined as an interval on the horizontal axis from 5.5 to 6.5. By inspection, it may be seen that the shaded area under the normal curve between 5.5 and 6.5 is approximately equal to the area under the bar representing $P(R = 6)$.

The *fourth* step in performing the approximation is to obtain the area under the normal curve over the interval corresponding to the limits of the redefined event. For our example, this step amounts to computing $P(5.5 \leq R \leq 6.5)$, which is represented by the shaded area in Figure 14.3. Bearing in mind that we are dealing with a normal distribution with $\mu = 4$ and $\sigma = 1.414$, we compute this probability as follows:

$$P(5.5 \leq R \leq 6.5) = F_n(6.5 \mid \mu = 4, \sigma = 1.414) - F_n(5.5 \mid \mu = 4, \sigma = 1.414)$$
$$= F_N\left(\frac{6.5 - 4}{1.414}\right) - F_N\left(\frac{5.5 - 4}{1.414}\right)$$
$$= F_N(1.77) - F_N(1.06)$$
$$= .9616 - .8554$$
$$= .1062$$

That is, the normal approximation to the binomial probability $P(R = 6)$ is .1062.

From Table E (Appendix II), we find that the exact binomial probability is

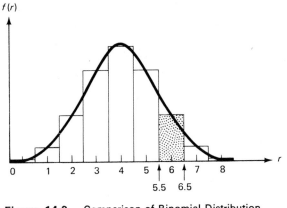

$$ f(r) $$

Figure 14.3   Comparison of Binomial Distribution
($n = 8$, $\pi = .50$) with Corresponding
Normal Distribution ($\mu = 4$, $\sigma = 1.414$)

$$P(R = 6) = f_b(6 \mid n = 8, \pi = .50) = .1094$$

Thus, the error of approximation in this case is $.1062 - .1094 = -.0032$. In cases in which n is much larger, the magnitude of error resulting in such approximations is considerably smaller, and it is only with large values of n that the approximation generally should be applied in actual practice.

Example:

A particular type of component is produced by a new automatic machine that behaves as a Bernoulli process with a defective rate of .20. Suppose that the machine produces a lot of 225 of these components.

(a) What is the probability that there are exactly 40 defectives in the lot?

Step 1: Compute the mean and standard deviation of the binomial distribution

$$\mu = n\pi = 225(.20) = 45$$
$$\sigma = \sqrt{n\pi(1 - \pi)} = \sqrt{225(.20)(.80)} = 6$$

Step 2: Adopt a normal distribution with mean equal to 45 and standard deviation equal to 6.

Step 3: The integer value 40 is redefined as an interval extending between the limits of $(40 - .5)$ and $(40 + .5)$. Thus, for purposes of approximation, $P_b(R = 40) \approx P_n(39.5 \leq R \leq 40.5)$.

Step 4: Since we have adopted a normal distribution with $\mu = 45$ and $\sigma = 6$, we compute

$$P_n(39.5 \leq R \leq 40.5) = F_n(40.5 \mid \mu = 45, \sigma = 6) - F_n(39.5 \mid \mu = 45, \sigma = 6)$$
$$= F_N\left(\frac{40.5 - 45}{6}\right) - F_N\left(\frac{39.5 - 45}{6}\right)$$
$$= F_N(-.750) - F_N(-.917)$$
$$= .2266 - .1796 = .0470$$

(b) What is the probability that there are no more than 40 defectives in the lot?

Steps 1 and 2: Same as above.

Step 3: The event under consideration is $(R \leq 40)$, which includes the value 40. The upper limit of 40 is 40.5, as indicated in part (a). Therefore, $P_b(R \leq 40) \approx P_n(R \leq 40.5)$.

Step 4: For a normal distribution with $\mu = 45$ and $\sigma = 6$, we obtain

$$P_n(R \leq 40.5) = F_n(40.5 \mid \mu = 45, \sigma = 6) = F_N\left(\frac{40.5 - 45}{6}\right)$$
$$= F_N(-.75) = .2266$$

(c) What is the probability that there are fewer than 40 defectives in the lot?

Steps 1 and 2: Same as part (a).

Step 3: The event under consideration is $(R < 40)$, which does not include 40 but does include 39. The upper limit of 39 is 39.5. Therefore, $P_b(R < 40) = P_b(R \leq 39) \approx P_n(R \leq 39.5)$.

Step 4: For the same normal distribution, we compute

$$P_n(R \leq 39.5) = F_n(39.5 \mid \mu = 45, \sigma = 6) = F_N\left(\frac{39.5 - 45}{6}\right)$$
$$= F_N(-.917) = .1796$$

(d) What is the probability that the number of defectives will be between 41 and 49 inclusive?

Steps 1 and 2: same as part (a).

Step 3: The event under consideration is $(41 \leq R \leq 49)$. Thus,

$$P_b(41 \leq R \leq 49) \approx P_n(40.5 \leq R \leq 49.5)$$

Step 4: Using the above normal distribution, we have

$$P(40.5 \leq R \leq 49.5) = F_n(49.5 \,|\, \mu = 45, \sigma = 6) - F_n(40.5 \,|\, \mu = 45, \sigma = 6)$$

$$= F_N\left(\frac{49.5 - 45}{6}\right) - F_N\left(\frac{40.5 - 45}{6}\right)$$

$$= F_N(.75) - F_N(-.75)$$

$$= .7734 - .2266 = .5468$$

Generalizing the procedures employed in this example, we may state the following formulas for obtaining normal approximations to binomial probabilities:

$$f_b(r \,|\, n, \pi) \approx F_N\left(\frac{r + .5 - n\pi}{\sqrt{n\pi(1 - \pi)}}\right) - F_N\left(\frac{r - .5 - n\pi}{\sqrt{n\pi(1 - \pi)}}\right) \quad (14.7)$$

$$F_b(r \,|\, n, \pi) \approx F_N\left(\frac{r + .5 - n\pi}{\sqrt{n\pi(1 - \pi)}}\right) \quad (14.8)$$

The accuracy of the normal approximation to the binomial depends on the values of n and π. As we have seen in Figure 14.2, the binomial distribution becomes closer to a normal distribution in appearance as n increases and π approaches .50. Thus, the larger the value of n, and the closer π is to .50, the more accurate the normal approximation to the binomial will be. As Raff[4] has pointed out, the error incurred in using the normal distribution to approximate *any* binomial probability will always be less than

$$M = \frac{.14}{\sqrt{n\pi(1 - \pi)}} \quad (14.9)$$

Applying this formula to the example above, in which $n = 225$ and $\pi = .20$, we have

$$M = \frac{.14}{\sqrt{225(.20)(.80)}} = .0233$$

Thus, we may conclude that, for any of the approximate probabilities obtained in the example above, the error of approximation is less than .0233. It should be stressed that Formula (14.9) simply yields a theoretical upper bound on the possible error of approximation, and that the actual error of approximation will always be less.

14.3.3 Hypothesis Testing with the Approximation

To illustrate the use of the normal approximation to the binomial in hypothesis testing, let us return to George Jones' decision problem that was discussed in Chapter 10. In that problem, the hypotheses were formulated as

---

[4]Morton S. Raff, "On Approximating the Point Binomial," *Journal of the American Statistical Association*, June 1956.

$$H_0: \quad \pi \leq .50$$
$$H_1: \quad \pi > .50$$

Using an exact binomial sampling distribution, the following expression was derived for determining the critical value for George's decision rule:

$$F_b(c - 1 | n = 100, \pi = .50) \geq .90$$

With the aid of the cumulative binomial table (Table F, Appendix II), the critical value c was found to be 57. The resulting decision rule was: If the value of R, the number of favorable responses in the sample, is equal to or greater than 57, reject H_0 and accordingly exercise the option to purchase the land; otherwise, accept H_0 and accordingly drop the option. Now, suppose that we do not have a binomial cumulative probability table for $n = 100$, and decide to use the normal approximation for determining the critical value c. To do this, we first adopt a normal distribution with

$$\mu = n\pi = 100(.50) = 50$$
$$\sigma = \sqrt{n\pi(1 - \pi)} = \sqrt{100(.50)(1 - .50)} = 5$$

Using Formula (14.8), the exact binomial expression above may be approximated by the following standard normal expression:

$$F_N\left(\frac{(c - 1) + .5 - 50}{5}\right) \geq .90$$

It then follows that

$$\frac{(c - 1) + .5 - 50}{5} \geq z_{.90}$$

From Table J (Appendix II), we find $z_{.90} = 1.282$. Thus,

$$\frac{(c - 1) + .5 - 50}{5} \geq 1.282$$

Then, by algebra,

$$c \geq 50 + 1 - .5 + 1.282(5)$$
$$\geq 56.91$$

Since the number of favorable responses in the sample must be an integer, the value of c is 57. Thus, we see that in this example, the critical value obtained by the normal approximation is identical to that obtained from the exact binomial solution.

The foregoing example illustrates the reasoning underlying hypothesis testing using the normal approximation to the binomial. General specifications for applying this procedure to upper-tail and lower-tail tests are summarized in Table 14.1.

Table 14.1   General Specifications for Normal Approximations to Binomial Tests

Test	Hypothesis	Decision Rule	Critical Value
Upper tail	H_0: $\pi \leq \pi_0$ H_1: $\pi > \pi_0$	If $R \geq c$, reject H_0; otherwise, accept H_0	c is smallest integer satisfying $c \geq \mu + .5 + z_{1-\alpha}\sigma$
Lower tail	H_0: $\pi \geq \pi_0$ H_1: $\pi < \pi_0$	If $R \leq c$, reject H_0; otherwise, accept H_0	c is largest integer satisfying $c \leq \mu - .5 + z_{\alpha}\sigma$

where
$$\mu = n\pi_0$$
$$\sigma = \sqrt{n\pi_0(1 - \pi_0)}$$

14.4 POISSON OR NORMAL APPROXIMATION TO THE BINOMIAL: WHICH?

In situations in which the use of an approximation procedure for the binomial distribution is being considered, the problem may arise whether to select the Poisson approximation or the normal approximation, if either. If our criterion of choice is to adopt the approximation procedure that has the smaller maximum error, we may say that, regardless of sample size, the Poisson approximation is generally preferable to the normal approximation if π is less than about .075 or greater than .925. Also, regardless of sample size, the normal approximation is preferable to the Poisson approximation if π is between .25 and .75. For other values of π, the choice between these two approximations depends on the value of n. A rough guide for the choice between the two approximations is provided by the chart[5] in Figure 14.4. It should not be inferred, however, that either approximation is necesssarily justified under a given set of conditions simply because it is preferable. That is, although one approximation might be preferable to the other for some specific values of n and π, it might be that neither of the two approximations can satisfy the accuracy requirements of a particular problem.

In dealing with the normal approximation to the binomial, statisticians have become increasingly insistent in recent years that the sample size should be substantial in order to obtain acceptable accuracy. If $\pi = .50$, most practitioners prescribe a minimum sample size between 25 and 50. As π departs from .50, the necessary sample size for an adequate approximation may be considerably larger. For example, if π is as small as .10 or as large as .90, a sample size of several hundred cases usually is recommended in order for the normal approximation to provide adequate accuracy.

Because the Poisson approximation to the binomial is suitable only for extreme values of π, and because the normal approximation for moderate values of π requires a substantial value of n, there is a rather wide range of combinations

---

[5]Adapted and abridged from Morton S. Raff, "On Approximating the Point Binomial," *Journal of the American Statistical Association*, June 1956.

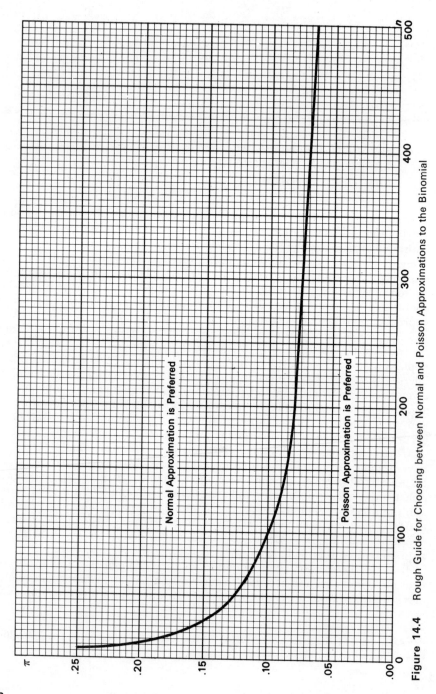

Figure 14.4 Rough Guide for Choosing between Normal and Poisson Approximations to the Binomial

of n and π values for which neither approximation is suitable for many practical situations. For such situations, more accurate approximation methods are available, but they are seldom used because of their mathematical complexity.

14.5 NORMAL APPROXIMATION TO A DISCRETE SAMPLING DISTRIBUTION OF $\overline{X}$

Suppose that a particular population consists of 10,000 circular tags that have been placed in a barrel. Each of these tags is labeled 1, 2, 3, or 4. Specifically, the number of tags bearing each value is as follows:

Value	Number of Tags
1	3,000
2	5,000
3	1,000
4	1,000

Thus, the population may be described by the following probability mass function:

$$f(x) = \begin{cases} .3 & \text{if } x = 1 \\ .5 & \text{if } x = 2 \\ .1 & \text{if } x = 3, 4 \\ 0 & \text{otherwise} \end{cases}$$

This population distribution is shown graphically in Figure 14.5.

Now suppose that a simple random sample of two tags is to be drawn from the population *with replacement*. The values of these two tags, X_1 and X_2, will be recorded, and their mean will be computed. Since each of the two tags may have any of the four possible values in the population, the set of possible outcomes of this experiment consists of $4^2 = 16$ ordered pairs of values. These 16 ordered pairs (possible sample outcomes) are listed in column (1) of Table 14.2. The mean of each of these possible pairs of values is shown in column (2). Because

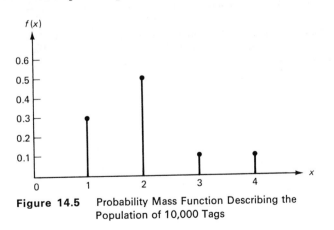

Figure 14.5 Probability Mass Function Describing the Population of 10,000 Tags

sampling is being conducted with replacement, the observations of the two tags are independent events. Thus, the probability of obtaining each of the possible ordered pairs can be computed from Formula (5.8). That is,

$$P[(X_1 = x_1) \cap (X_2 = x_2)] = P(X_1 = x_1)P(X_2 = x_2)$$
$$= f(x_1)f(x_2)$$

Using this formula, the probability of obtaining each of the possible ordered pairs is calculated in column (3) of Table 14.2.

Careful inspection of Table 14.2 reveals that, although there are 16 possible ordered pairs, there are only 7 possible values of $\bar{X}$. These possible values of $\bar{X}$ are listed in column (1) of Table 14.3. Column (2) identifies the ordered pairs

Table 14.2 Means of All Possible Samples of Two Values Drawn with Replacement from the Population of 10,000 Tags

(1) Sample Values, x_1, x_2	(2) Sample Mean, $\bar{x}$	(3) Probability, $f(x_1)f(x_2)$
1, 1	1.0	$(.3)(.3) = .09$
1, 2	1.5	$(.3)(.5) = .15$
1, 3	2.0	$(.3)(.1) = .03$
1, 4	2.5	$(.3)(.1) = .03$
2, 1	1.5	$(.5)(.3) = .15$
2, 2	2.0	$(.5)(.5) = .25$
2, 3	2.5	$(.5)(.1) = .05$
2, 4	3.0	$(.5)(.1) = .05$
3, 1	2.0	$(.1)(.3) = .03$
3, 2	2.5	$(.1)(.5) = .05$
3, 3	3.0	$(.1)(.1) = .01$
3, 4	3.5	$(.1)(.1) = .01$
4, 1	2.5	$(.1)(.3) = .03$
4, 2	3.0	$(.1)(.5) = .05$
4, 3	3.5	$(.1)(.1) = .01$
4, 4	4.0	$(.1)(.1) = .01$

Table 14.3 Sampling Distribution of the Mean of Two Values Drawn with Replacement from the Population of 10,000 Tags

(1) $\bar{x}$	(2) Ordered Pairs	(3) $f(\bar{x})$	
1.0	(1, 1)	.09	= .09
1.5	(1, 2), (2, 1)	.15 + .15	= .30
2.0	(1, 3), (2, 2), (3, 1)	.03 + .25 + .03	= .31
2.5	(1, 4), (2, 3), (3, 2), (4, 1)	.03 + .05 + .05 + .03	= .16
3.0	(2, 4), (3, 3), (4, 2)	.05 + .01 + .05	= .11
3.5	(3, 4), (4, 3)	.01 + .01	= .02
4.0	(4, 4)	.01	= .01
Sum			1.00

having each specific value of $\bar{X}$. Column (3) shows the probability of each of the possible values of $\bar{X}$. Each of these probabilities is simply the sum of the probabilities of the ordered pair having that value of $\bar{X}$. This set of possible values of $\bar{X}$, with their corresponding probabilities, is the sampling distribution of $\bar{X}$.

If we increase the sample size, we increase the number of possible sample outcomes, resulting in an increase in the number of possible values of the sample mean $\bar{X}$. To illustrate this point, the sampling distributions of $\bar{X}$ for $n = 2$, $n = 3$, and $n = 5$ are shown graphically in Figure 14.6. From inspection of this figure, we may make the following observations:

1. None of the sampling distributions of $\bar{X}$ in Figure 14.6 is identical to the population distribution of X shown in Figure 14.5. That is, regardless of sample size, the sample mean $\bar{X}$ has a greater number of possible values than does the population variable X, and the sampling distribution of $\bar{X}$ differs in general shape[6] from the population distribution of X.

2. Each of the sampling distributions of $\bar{X}$ in Figure 14.6 is a discrete distribution, since the population being sampled is discrete.

3. As the sample size increases, the number of possible values of $\bar{X}$ also increases such that the difference between successive values of $\bar{X}$ decreases.

4. As the sample size increases, the sampling distribution of $\bar{X}$ becomes more nearly symmetrical and bell-shaped in appearance.

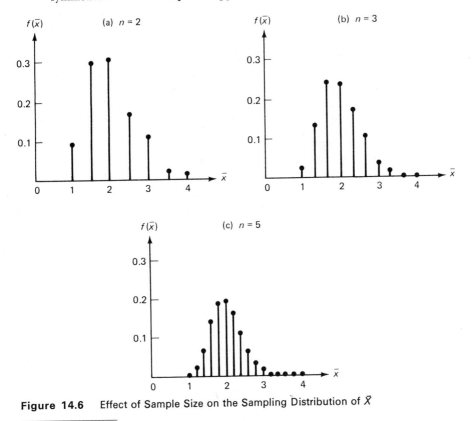

Figure 14.6   Effect of Sample Size on the Sampling Distribution of $\bar{X}$

[6]For the special case in which $n = 1$, the sampling distribution of $\bar{X}$ is identical to the population distribution.

To generalize from the foregoing observations, it is always true that the sampling distribution of $\bar{X}$ for any finite sample size will be discrete if the population being sampled is discrete. However, as the sample size increases, this discrete sampling distribution of $\bar{X}$ approaches a normal distribution[7] which is, of course, continuous. Thus, *the central limit theorem applies to the sampling distribution of $\bar{X}$ regardless of whether the population being sampled is discrete or continuous.* Hence, if the sample size is substantial, the normal distribution may be used as a reasonable approximation to the discrete sampling distribution of $\bar{X}$. The question of how large the sample should be for this approximation to be "reasonable" has no definite answer, since the accuracy of the approximation depends on the shape of the population being sampled. If there is reason to believe that the population distribution departs radically from symmetry, a sample containing at least several hundred observations may be required. Even if available evidence suggests that the population is approximately symmetrical, a sample size of at least 100 is advisable.

14.5.1 Mechanics of the Approximation

To illustrate the mechanics of the normal approximation to the discrete sampling distribution of $\bar{X}$, consider again the population distribution shown in Figure 14.5. Suppose that a sample of 125 tags is to be drawn (with replacement) from this population, and the sample mean $\bar{X}$ is to be computed. We might then ask such a question as: What is the probability that the value of $\bar{X}$ will be no greater than 2.20?

To answer this question, we must first determine the sampling distribution of $\bar{X}$. Although it is theoretically possible to obtain the exact sampling distribution, to do so for a sample of 125 observations would be prohibitively laborious even with the aid of a high-speed computer.[8] However, by virtue of the central limit theorem, it is reasonable to use a normal distribution as an approximation to the sampling distribution of $\bar{X}$.

In order to apply the normal approximation, we must first determine the mean and variance of the sampling distribution of $\bar{X}$. To do this we begin by recalling that the population is described by the following probability mass function:

$$f(x) = \begin{cases} .3 & \text{if } x = 1 \\ .5 & \text{if } x = 2 \\ .1 & \text{if } x = 3, 4 \\ 0 & \text{otherwise} \end{cases}$$

Next, applying Formulas (7.2) and (7.12), the population mean and variance are obtained:

$$\mu = 2.00 \qquad \sigma^2 = .80$$

---

[7]This is essentially the same phenomenon as discussed in Section 14.3, where it was shown that the binomial distribution approaches the normal distribution as the sample size increases.

[8]Since each of the 125 sample observations may have any one of four possible values, there are 4^{125} possible sample points that must be tabulated in order to obtain the exact sampling distribution of $\bar{X}$. The set of possible values of $\bar{X}$ resulting from this tabulation would be

$$\{\bar{x} | \bar{x} = 1.000, 1.008, 1.016, \ldots, 3.992, 4.000\}$$

Then, by virtue of Formula (12.1), the mean of the sampling distribution of $\bar{X}$ is

$$\mu_{\bar{X}} = \mu = 2.00$$

Also, from Formula (12.5), the standard error of $\bar{X}$ is

$$\sigma_{\bar{X}} = \frac{\sigma}{\sqrt{n}} = \frac{\sqrt{.80}}{\sqrt{125}} = .08$$

Thus, the sampling distribution of $\bar{X}$ may be approximated by a normal distribution with mean $\mu_{\bar{X}} = 2.00$ and standard deviation $\sigma_{\bar{X}} = .08$. Using this normal approximation,[9] the approximate probability that the mean of a sample of 125 observations will be no greater than 2.20 is obtained as follows:

$$P(\bar{X} \leq 2.20) \approx F_n(2.20 \mid \mu_{\bar{X}} = 2.00, \sigma_{\bar{X}} = .08)$$
$$F_n(2.20 \mid \mu_{\bar{X}} = 2.00, \sigma_{\bar{X}} = .08) = F_N\left(\frac{2.20 - 2.00}{.08}\right) = F_N(2.50)$$

From Table M (Appendix II), we obtain $F_N(2.50) = .9938$.

14.5.2 Hypothesis Testing with the Approximation

As an example of hypothesis testing using the normal approximation to the discrete sampling distribution of $\bar{X}$, consider the case of the Skinner Pharmaceutical Company. Skinner's principal product is Vim, a dietary supplement which is packaged in bottles that are labeled to contain 500 tablets. Although management realizes that there is some variability in their packaging process, so that not all bottles of Vim contain exactly 500 tablets, they feel that the bottles should contain 500 tablets *on the average*.

Recently, Skinner has been receiving letters from consumers complaining that they have purchased bottles of Vim containing fewer than 500 tablets. Naturally, no complaints were received from consumers who may have purchased bottles containing more than 500 tablets. Actually, management does not really know whether the desired average of 500 tablets per bottle is being achieved. As a result, they have begun to consider whether they should install a quality control program to guard against overfill and underfill. After some thought, management has adopted the position that they should initiate a quality control program if they can obtain convincing evidence that the desired average of 500 tablets per bottle is not being maintained.

To investigate whether the desired average of 500 tablets is being maintained by the packaging process, Skinner retains the services of Dr. Sidney Simplex, a prominent industrial consultant. After some discussion with management,

---

[9]Strictly speaking, the normal approximation to the discrete sampling distribution of $\bar{X}$ involves a continuity correction similar to that used in the normal approximation to the binomial. The correction factor employed in the normal approximation to the binomial distribution of R is always .50 regardless of sample size. However, the correction factor for the normal approximation to the discrete sampling distribution of $\bar{X}$ is $1/2n$. For large sample sizes this correction factor is negligibly small, so that it is rarely used in practice.

Dr. Simplex recognizes that his task is essentially one of testing the hypothesis that the mean fill of Skinner's packing process is 500 tablets per bottle. Specifically, if we let μ denote the mean of this process, the null and alternative hypotheses for Skinner's decision problem are

$$H_0: \quad \mu = 500$$
$$H_1: \quad \mu \neq 500$$

These hypotheses are specified in such a way that Skinner will install the quality control program if there is convincing evidence that the process mean is either above or below 500 tablets per bottle. Further discussion establishes that management is willing to take a 10% risk of installing the quality control program if, in fact, the desired process average of 500 tablets is actually being maintained. Thus, Dr. Simplex specifies a significance level of .10 for the hypothesis test.

To conduct the hypothesis test, Dr. Simplex proposes to take a random sample of 400 bottles produced by the packaging process. The number of tablets in each of these bottles will be carefully counted, and the mean number of tablets per bottle in the sample will be computed. The hypothesis test will then be based on the value of this sample mean, $\bar{X}$. The sampling distribution of $\bar{X}$ is a discrete distribution since $\bar{X}$ is to be computed from counts, which are on a discrete scale. However, because the sample size is substantial ($n = 400$), it is reasonable to approximate this discrete distribution with a normal distribution.

In order to use the normal approximation to the sampling distribution of $\bar{X}$, it is first necessary for Dr. Simplex to determine the parameters $\mu_{\bar{X}}$ and $\sigma_{\bar{X}}$. Since the null hypothesis states that $\mu = 500$, the mean of the sampling distribution is

$$\mu_{\bar{X}} = \mu = 500$$

On the basis of considerable previous experience with similar packaging processes, Dr. Simplex feels that it is reasonable to assume that the standard deviation of Skinner's process is $\sigma = 3$. Thus, the standard error of $\bar{X}$ is specified as

$$\sigma_{\bar{X}} = \frac{\sigma}{\sqrt{n}} = \frac{3}{\sqrt{400}} = .15$$

Since the alternative hypothesis states that $\mu \neq 500$, the hypothesis test will be a two-tail test. Following the specification for normal tests given in Table 13.4, the null hypothesis will be rejected in favor of the alternative hypothesis either (a) if $\bar{X}$ is equal to or less than some critical value c_1 or (b) if $\bar{X}$ is equal to or greater than some other critical value c_2. Bearing in mind that the significance level is .10, the values of c_1 and c_2 are determined as follows:

$$c_1 = \mu_0 + z_{\alpha/2}\sigma_{\bar{X}} = 500 + z_{.05}(.15)$$
$$= 500 + (-1.645)(.15) = 499.75$$
$$c_2 = \mu_0 + z_{1-\alpha/2}\sigma_{\bar{X}} = 500 + z_{.95}(.15)$$
$$= 500 + 1.645(.15) = 500.25$$

From the foregoing calculations, Dr. Simplex is able to state the decision rule for Skinner as follows: If the value of $\bar{X}$, the mean number of tablets per bottle in the sample of 400 bottles, is either (a) equal to or less than 499.75 or (b) equal to or greater than 500.25, then reject H_0 and accordingly install the quality control program; otherwise, accept H_0 and accordingly do not install the quality control program.

PROBLEMS

14.1 Using the binomial approximation, evaluate each of the following hypergeometric expressions:

  (a) $f_h(5 \mid N = 400, n = 20, D = 80)$
  (b) $f_h(3 \mid N = 400, n = 25, D = 60)$
  (c) $f_h(9 \mid N = 400, n = 60, D = 50)$
  (d) $f_h(2 \mid N = 400, n = 40, D = 15)$
  (e) $F_h(5 \mid N = 400, n = 20, D = 80)$
  (f) $F_h(2 \mid N = 400, n = 40, D = 15)$

14.2 The Betatron Electronic Company purchases transistors from the Feedem Corporation in lots of 10,000 units. Upon receipts of a lot, a sample of 100 transistors is selected at random and carefully tested. If a lot actually contains 500 defective transistors, what is the approximate probability that the sample from that lot will contain exactly 4 defective transistors?

14.3 The Bimonthly Book Club, which has a membership of 1 million readers, is considering a new book for an upcoming selection. However, the book will be profitable only if it is accepted by more than one-fourth of the club's members. Unsure of the book's appeal, management decides to survey a sample of 100 members, asking them if they would buy the book if it were offered as a selection. The book will be adopted as a selection only if the sample results provide convincing evidence, at the .05 significance level, that more than a quarter of a million of the club's members would buy the book.

  (a) What is the exact sampling distribution for this hypothesis-testing problem? Explain.

  (b) Using the most appropriate approximation to the exact sampling distribution, derive and explicitly state the book club's decision rule.

14.4 The Softline Corporation produces ball-point pens in production runs of 1,000 pens. A run is considered acceptable if it contains no more than 20 defective pens. Management wishes to devise a quality assurance plan whereby a sample of 10 pens will be selected from each run and carefully inspected. The run will be accepted unless the sample provides sufficient evidence, at the .05 significance level, that it contains more than 20 defectives. Derive and explicitly state the decision rule for this plan.

14.5 Systo Electronics Company purchases a particular component in lots containing 200 components each. A lot is regarded as "acceptable" if it contains no more than 20 defectives. Because of the high defective rates of some of these lots, management has decided to install a lot acceptance sampling plan. The decision to accept or reject each lot will be based on the number of defectives found in a sample of 18 components taken from the lot. The plan is to be designed such that there will be no greater than a .10 probability of rejecting an acceptable lot. Derive and explicitly state the decision rule for this plan.

14.6 Construct the error characteristic chart for the decision rule derived in Problem 14.5.

14.7 The Medex Specialties Company purchases a particular type of surgical clamp in lots containing 300 clamps each. A lot is considered "acceptable" if it contains no more than 15 defectives. Medex wishes to devise a lot acceptance sampling plan, basing the decision to accept or reject each lot on the number of defectives found in a sample of 25 clamps taken from each lot. The plan is to be designed so that there will be no more than .05 probability of rejecting an acceptable lot. Derive and explicitly state the decision rule for this plan.

14.8 Construct the error characteristic chart for the decision rule designed in Problem 14.7.

14.9 Using the Poisson approximation, evaluate each of the following binomial expressions:
  (a) $f_b(4 \mid 200, .003)$
  (b) $f_b(2 \mid 280, .01)$
  (c) $f_b(8 \mid 400, .05)$
  (d) $f_b(5 \mid 10,000, .0002)$
  (e) $F_b(7 \mid 500, .006)$
  (f) $F_b(6 \mid 1200, .004)$

14.10 From records compiled over a period of years, the credit manager of Wood's Department Store has determined that the long-run percentage of accounts receivable that are uncollectible is 1.4%. Currently, the store has 350 accounts receivable. Determine the approximate probability that the number of these accounts that are uncollectible will be:
  (a) 5 or more
  (b) Exactly 5
  (c) 3 or less
  (d) Between 3 and 9 inclusive

14.11 The management of Black Opal Cosmetics Ltd. estimates that 5% of the women who are regular users of hair spray prefer their Lovelox brand to all other brands. In a marketing survey, 400 women indicate that they are regular hair spray users. If Black Opal's estimate is correct, what is the approximate probability that the number of these hair spray users who prefer Lovelox will be:
  (a) More than 29?
  (b) Exactly 20?
  (c) Less than 11?
  (d) More than 14 but less than 26?

14.12 The Heart and Soul Corporation employs an automatic process for manufacturing guitar picks. The process is considered to be out of control if its defective rate exceeds 3%. Management desires a quality control plan whereby, at regular intervals, a sample of 200 picks produced by the process is inspected to determine if the process has gone out of control. The process will be stopped for adjustment only if the sample provides convincing evidence, at the .10 significance level, that the process is out of control.
  (a) What is the exact sampling distribution for deriving this quality control plan? Explain.
  (b) What is the most appropriate approximation to the exact sampling distribution? Justify your answer.
  (c) Using the most appropriate approximation, derive and explicitly state the quality control rule.

14.13 The Dalton Pharmaceutical Company has developed a new oral vaccine against Tibetan flu. However, the company does not wish to announce the availability of the vaccine unless they can provide evidence that the percentage of persons suffering undesirable side effects is very small. For this purpose, they plan to conduct clinical tests with a sample of 1,600 volunteers. They will not announce the vaccine unless the number of those volunteers who suffer undesirable side effects is sufficiently small to conclude, at the .10 significance level, that fewer than one-half of 1% of persons in the population would suffer undesirable side effects. Derive and explicitly state the decision rule for this test.

14.14 For many years, the best-selling product of the Sentinel Corporation has been its Roadrunner battery, which is sold with a 36-month replacement warranty. For promotional purposes, management is considering a new warranty policy under which, if a Roadrunner fails within 36 months, it will be replaced and the purchase price refunded. Of course, the company can afford to institute this policy only if the proportion of Roadrunners that actually fail within the warranty period is very low. To determine if this proportion is sufficiently low, the marketing manager proposes to examine the records of a sample of 2,000 past sales. The new warranty policy will be instituted only if the number of batteries in the sample that had to be replaced during the warranty period is sufficiently small to conclude, at the .05 significance level, that fewer than 1% of all Roadrunners produced by Sentinel fail within 36 months. Derive and explicitly state Sentinel's decision rule.

14.15 Using the normal approximation, evaluate each of the following binomial expressions:

(a) $f_b(100 | 200, .5)$
(b) $f_b(210 | 500, .4)$
(c) $f_b(245 | 300, .8)$
(d) $F_b(125 | 600, .2)$
(e) $F_b(550 | 800, .7)$

14.16 A widely accepted rule of thumb is that the normal model provides satisfactory approximations to binomial probabilities if both $n\pi$ and $n(1 - \pi)$ are 5 or greater. However, unless n is very large, this rule of thumb is not dependable. To demonstrate the unreliability of the rule of thumb, perform the following exercise:

(a) From Table E (Appendix II), find the following exact binomial probabilities:

(i) $F_b(5 | 50, .10)$
(ii) $F_b(10 | 50, .20)$
(iii) $F_b(5 | 100, .05)$
(iv) $F_b(10 | 100, .10)$
(v) $F_b(20 | 100, .20)$

(b) Determine the normal approximation to each of the probabilities found in part (a).
(c) Determine the Poisson approximation to each of the probabilities found in part (a).
(d) Prepare a table as indicated below:

(i) In column (1), enter the exact probabilities obtained in part (a).
(ii) In column (2), enter the corresponding normal approximations obtained in part (b).
(iii) In column (3), subtract the entry in column (1) from the entry in column (2).
(iv) In column (4), divide the entry in column (3) by the entry in column (1).
(v) In column (5), enter the Poisson approximations corresponding to the binomial probabilities in column (1).
(vi) In column (6), subtract the entry in column (1) from the entry in column (5).
(vii) In column (7), divide the entry in column (6) by the entry in column (1).

(e) Explain the meaning of the entries in columns (3), (4), (6), and (7).
(f) Using the evidence contained in the table you have constructed, what conclusions do you draw concerning the rule of thumb stated at the beginning of this exercise?

14.17 Over the years, the best-selling product of Liberated Ladieswear, Inc. has been their Holdtight girdle. Each girdle is inspected, and the defective girdles are marked as irregulars, which wholesale at a lower price. On the average, the irregular girdles account for 12% of the total girdles produced. On a particular production run, 341 of these girdles are produced. What is the probability that there will be 30 irregular girdles at most in this run?

14.18 Suppose that 55% of the registered voters in a large state are planning to vote for Burton House as U.S. senator in an upcoming election.

(a) What is the approximate probability that if a random sample of 582 registered voters is polled, a majority of the sample will indicate that they do *not* intend to vote for Burton House?
(b) Why did you choose the particular approximation procedure that you used?

14.19 Harriet Henderson, advertising manager of the Big Deal Discount Department Store, is considering whether or not the store should purchase spot commercial time on the Lou Martin talk show presented by a local radio station. To make her decision, Harriet plans to have the staff interview a simple random sample of 100 homemakers residing within a 10-mile radius of the store. She will buy the time only if the number of sample respondents who regularly listen to Lou Martin is sufficiently large to conclude, at the .05 significance level, that more than 20% of all homemakers in the area regularly listen to the show.

(a)   State the null and alternative hypotheses for this decision problem.

(b)   Using the exact binomial procedure given in Section 11.2, derive Harriet Henderson's decision rule.

(c)   Derive Harriet Henderson's decision rule using the normal approximation to the binomial.

(d)   Did you obtain the same result in parts (b) and (c) ? Discuss.

14.20   The Longreen Federal Savings and Loan Association is considering opening a branch office in downtown Elysian Hills near the intersection of Pacific Drive and Elysian Boulevard. An economic analysis indicates that an office at this location should be profitable provided that a sufficiently large proportion of households in the community feel that the site would be a convenient place to have a savings account. To make the decision, a sample of 600 households in the community will be surveyed. The branch office will be opened unless the number of sample households considering the site to be convenient is sufficiently small to conclude, at the .10 significance level, that fewer than 40% of all households in the community feel that the site would be convenient. Derive and explicitly state Longreen's decision rule.

14.21   A wholesaling firm that purveys novelty items to several thousand boutiques has an opportunity to purchase a manufacturer's total inventory of simulated diamond dinner rings. To decide whether to purchase the entire inventory, the wholesaler plans to test the sales of these rings in a sample of 225 boutiques. In each of these boutiques, a supply of the rings will be placed on consignment, and the number of rings sold during a 2-week test period will be determined. The wholesaler will purchase the entire inventory only if the mean number of rings sold per boutique in the sample is sufficiently large, at the .02 significance level, to conclude that the mean number of rings that can be sold per boutique in a 2-week period by the client population is greater than 19.50 rings. Assuming that the variance of biweekly sales of this type of ring among the boutiques in the population is $\sigma^2 = 9$, derive and explicitly state the wholesaler's decision rule.

14.22   Refer to Problem 14.21. Suppose that the manufacturer reduces its price to a figure which is so attractive that the wholesaler feels he should purchase the entire inventory unless the sample mean is sufficiently small to conclude, at the .02 significance level, that the population mean is less than 19.50 rings. Under this condition, derive and state the wholesaler's decision rule.

14.23   Recently, the shop employees of the Hercules Machine Works have registered several complaints about the length of the queue of workers waiting for service at the tool crib. To determine whether to install a second tool crib, management plans to observe the length of the queue at 160 points in time selected at random during a 1-week period. The new tool crib will be installed only if the mean number of workers standing in line per sample observation is large enough to conclude, at the .01 significance level, that the mean length of the line over time is greater than 14.30 workers. Assuming that the variance of the number of persons in the queue is $\sigma^2 = 10$, derive and state management's decision rule.

15

Classical Estimation

Up to this point, our consideration of statistical inference has been limited to hypothesis-testing situations in which there are only two alternative courses of action. In many decision situations, however, the number of alternatives is large or even infinite. For example, a construction firm might have to decide how many tons of gravel to order for a particular highway project; the ultimate decision will be to select some tonnage from the set of all possible tonnages. Similarly, an office manager might have to decide how many typists should be assigned to a particular long-term project; the final decision will be to select some number of typists from the set of all possible numbers. Decision problems of this type—in which the action space consists of a large number of alternatives, each of which is quantitatively defined—is the kind of problem to which statistical estimation techniques are applicable.

15.1 POINT ESTIMATION OF μ

The process of employing sample data to obtain a single value as an estimate of a parameter is called *point estimation*. The process of obtaining a point estimate amounts essentially to computing a statistic. As Section 9.1 pointed out, the term "statistic" may be used to connote either (1) a random variable that is defined as a function of the possible outcomes of a random sampling experiment, or (2) a specific value of such a random variable obtained from the actual sample outcome. That is, before the sample has been observed, a statistic is a random variable; but after the sample has been observed, the statistic is merely a numerical value. To distinguish between these two meanings of "statistic," the term *estimator* is used to indicate a random variable employed to estimate a parameter, and the term *estimate* is used to indicate a specific value of the estimator. Thus, following our notational convention for random variables, we will use a capital letter to denote an estimator and the corresponding lowercase letter to denote an estimate.

15.1.1 The Point Estimation Problem

To begin our examination of the point estimation problem, let us consider the case of a subcontractor who manufactures components for space vehicle assemblies. The company has received an invitation to submit a bid on an order for 10,000 units of a particular component. Having made the preliminary decision to submit a bid, the contractor is now confronted with the problem of deciding upon the exact amount of the bid to submit. After analyzing the specifications for the component, determining the cost of raw materials, and assessing the physical and human resources of the plant, the contractor arrives at the following:

1. Undertaking the project would involve a fixed cost of $1,000.
2. Variable costs would be $5.00 per unit for materials, plus $4.00 per hour of production time.

Considering that production time will be variable from unit to unit, the contractor adopts the symbol μ to represent average production time per unit, and obtains the following expression to represent total production cost for the 10,000 units:

$$TC = \$1,000 + 10,000(\$5.00 + \$4.00\mu)$$

Figuring 10% of total production cost as an adequate figure to cover overhead and profit, the amount of his bid may be expressed as

$$B = 1.10[\$1,000 + 10,000(\$5.00 + \$4.00\mu)]$$

Thus, if the contractor knew the value of μ (the mean number of hours of production time per unit), his decision concerning the amount of the bid would essentially be made.

Since the contractor does not know the actual value of μ, he decides to estimate μ from a sample by making a trial run of 25 components and observing the time required to produce each of these components. The question now arises: What procedure should be used to obtain the desired estimate of μ from the sample data? Two obvious possibilities are:

1. Compute the sample mean $\bar{X}$
2. Compute the sample median $X_{.50}$

Thus, a choice must be made between alternative estimators of μ. When alternative estimators of a parameter are available, the choice of which one to use is often based on a comparison of the statistical properties of those estimators.

15.1.2 Properties of Point Estimators

One property which frequently is considered as a criterion of desirability for an estimator is *lack of bias*. An estimator is said to be *unbiased* if the expected value of the estimator is equal to the value of the parameter which is to be estimated. That is, if S is an estimator of some parameter θ, then S is said to be unbiased if $E(S) = \theta$. As we saw in Formula (12.1), $E(\bar{X}) = \mu$, which says that the expected value of the sample mean $\bar{X}$ is equal to the population mean μ. Thus, if $\bar{X}$ is used to estimate μ, it is an unbiased estimator for that purpose. Although the *sample mean* is an unbiased estimator of the *population mean*, it is not generally true that the *sample median* is an unbiased estimator of the *population mean*.

Thus, from the standpoint of lack of bias, the sample mean is preferred to the sample median as an estimator of μ. However, lack of bias is not the only criterion of the "goodness" of an estimator.

Another criterion for comparing alternative estimators is *relative efficiency*. To understand the basic notion of relative efficiency, we must consider the concept of the *mean-square-error* of an estimator. If a sample is drawn from a population with mean μ, and if the sample mean $\bar{X}$ is used as an estimator of μ, then the error of estimation will be $(\bar{X} - \mu)$, and the square of the error will be $(\bar{X} - \mu)^2$. When $\bar{X}$ is used as an estimator of μ, the expected value of the squared error, $E[(\bar{X} - \mu)^2]$, is called the mean-square-error[1] of $\bar{X}$. If the sample median $X_{.50}$ is used as an estimator of the population mean μ, the mean-square-error of $X_{.50}$ is $E[(X_{.50} - \mu)^2]$. It may be demonstrated that, for the purpose of estimating the population mean, the mean-square-error of the sample mean usually is less than the mean-square-error of the sample median.[2] Expressed symbolically, $E[(\bar{X} - \mu)^2] < E[(X_{.50} - \mu)^2]$. If the mean-square-error of one estimator is less than the mean-square-error of another estimator that might be used for estimating the same parameter, the first estimator is said to be *relatively more efficient* than the second estimator. Therefore, for the purpose of estimating a population mean, the sample mean is not only unbiased but also relatively more efficient than the sample median. Thus, the generally preferred estimator of the population mean is the sample mean:

$$\bar{X} = \frac{\sum\limits_{i=1}^{n} X_i}{n} \tag{15.1}$$

For most practical estimation problems, the most pragmatic approach to selecting a "best" estimator is to find that estimator that will minimize the *expected cost* due to the error of estimation. Traditionally, statisticians have implicitly assumed that the loss associated with an error in estimation is a *quadratic* function of the magnitude of the error.[3] For instance, suppose that a decision maker proposed to use a sample mean $\bar{X}$ to estimate a population mean μ, and to determine his course of action under the assumption that μ is equal to the value of $\bar{X}$. Suppose further that the loss associated with any error of this assumption is a quadratic function of the magnitude of that error. Then the loss may be expressed as

$$L = k(\bar{X} - \mu)^2$$

where k is some specified constant. Under these conditions, the expected loss of using $\bar{X}$ as an estimator of μ would be

$$E(L) = k \cdot E[(\bar{X} - \mu)^2]$$

---

[1]Since $\bar{X}$ is an unbiased estimator of μ, the mean-square-error of $\bar{X}$ is identical to the variance of $\bar{X}$.

[2]This statement is generally true except under very rare conditions. See Dudley J. Cowden, *Statistical Methods in Quality Control* (Englewood Cliffs, N.J.: Prentice-Hall, Inc., 1957), pp. 66–67.

[3]The traditional reasons for assuming quadratic loss functions are detailed in H. Chernoff and L. E. Moses, *Elementary Decision Theory* (New York: John Wiley & Sons, Inc., 1959), p. 276.

In this expression, we may recognize $E[(\bar{X} - \mu)^2]$ as the mean-square-error of X. Thus, if the objective in selecting an estimator of μ is to minimize the expected loss due to the error of estimation, and if the loss function is quadratic, then the choice of an estimator would be that estimator which has the minimum mean-square error. However, the assumption of a quadratic loss function is often questionable. As Ackoff[4] indicates, the assumption of a quadratic loss function may be "largely a matter of wishful thinking," and the choice of a "best" estimator depends on the particular function. Thus, in general, there is no simple or single answer to the choice of the preferred estimator of any parameter.

15.1.3 Recapitulation

Having examined the criteria for selecting an estimator, we may now return to the subcontractor's decision problem concerning the amount of his bid for producing space vehicle components. In this problem, the amount of the contractor's bid, as a function of μ, was expressed as

$$B = 1.10[\$1,000 + 10,000(\$5.00 + \$4.00\mu)]$$

We have seen that, for the purpose of estimating μ, the sample mean $\bar{X}$ is unbiased and relatively efficient. Hence, it is reasonable for the contractor to use the sample mean $\bar{X}$ as an estimator of μ. Once the value of the sample mean is determined, that value may be substituted for μ in the foregoing decision function.

Suppose that, when the contractor actually makes his trial run, he finds that the mean time required to produce an item in the sample is $\bar{x} = 30$ minutes $= .5$ hour. Substituting this estimate of μ into the function yields

$$\begin{aligned} B &= 1.10\{\$1,000 + 10,000[\$5.00 + \$4.00(0.5)]\} \\ &= \$78,100 \end{aligned}$$

Thus, according to the decision function, the contractor should submit his bid in the amount of \$78,100.

15.2 POINT ESTIMATION OF σ^2 AND σ

In considering possible statistics for estimating a population variance the sample variance intuitively suggests itself. Indeed, the most commonly used estimator of a population variance is the sample variance

$$S^2 = \frac{\sum_{i=1}^{n}(X_i - \bar{X})^2}{n - 1} \tag{15.2}$$

It may be shown mathematically that S^2 is an *unbiased* estimator of σ^2. That is, $E(S^2) = \sigma^2$. If the denominator in Formula (15.2) were n rather than $(n - 1)$, the estimator would be biased. This is the reason that the sample variance is defined with $(n - 1)$ instead of n in the denominator.

To illustrate the use of S^2 as an estimator of σ^2, consider a drug manufacturer

---

[4]Russel Ackoff, *Scientific Method* (New York: John Wiley & Sons, Inc., 1962), p. 260.

who produces vitamin C tablets which are advertised to contain 50 milligrams of active ingredient. To ensure that most tablets will contain at least the advertised 50 milligrams, the production process is set to produce tablets whose *average* amount of active ingredient is *greater* than 50 milligrams. Even though the manufacturer sets its process average above 50 milligrams, a sizable proportion of the tablets will have an active ingredient content below 50 milligrams unless the variance of the process is maintained at a relatively low level. Suppose that, to estimate the variance of its production process, the manufacturer takes a simple random sample of 10 tablets from the output of the process, and determines the milligrams of active ingredient contained in each of the 10 tablets to be as follows: 55, 49, 57, 55, 56, 52, 59, 57, 58, 52. As the reader may verify from Formula (15.2), the variance of this sample is

$$s^2 = \frac{\Sigma (x - \bar{x})^2}{n - 1} = \frac{88}{9} = 9.78$$

This sample variance of 9.78 square milligrams provides an unbiased estimate of the variance of the manufacturer's process.

Even though the sample variance S^2 is an unbiased estimator of the population variance σ^2, the sample standard deviation S is not an unbiased estimator of the population standard deviation σ. However, if the population is normal, an unbiased estimator of the population standard deviation may be obtained by multiplying the estimator S by a correction factor. The magnitude of this correction factor (called a c-factor) depends on the sample size: the greater the sample size, the less correction for bias is required. Values of the correction factors for different sample sizes are given in Table N (Appendix II). To illustrate the use of this table, recall that the vitamin manufacturer obtained $s^2 = 9.78$ as an unbiased estimate of the variance of its production process. Taking the square root of this figure yields $s = 3.127$. For a sample size $n = 10$, Table N gives $c = 1.028$. Multiplying s by c, we have $(3.127)(1.028) = 3.215$, which is an unbiased estimate of the process standard deviation.

15.3 POINT ESTIMATION OF π

Consider a population containing some unknown proportion, π, of elements having a particular characteristic. A common method for estimating π is to take a simple random sample of n elements from the population and determine R, the number of sample elements that have the particular characteristic. Then the sample proportion having the characteristic is given by

$$P = \frac{R}{n} \tag{15.3}$$

This sample proportion, P, is an unbiased estimator of π since it may be shown that $E(P) = \pi$.

To illustrate the application of P as a point estimator of π, consider the case of Joe Crawford, advertising manager of Thriftland, a large supermarket chain. Joe has been considering the possibility of purchasing 1 minute of weekly "spot" commerical time on a popular television program, *Agony Acres*, which is presented by a local network station every Wednesday evening. In discussion with a representative of the TV station, Joe learns that the price for 1 minute of spot time on the program is determined by the function

$$\text{price} = \$1,000 + \$2,000p$$

where p is an estimate of the proportion of households that watch the program in the two counties which the station reaches. This estimate is provided by a market research firm which conducts a weekly survey of a sample of 200 households in the two counties. When the current week's survey was conducted, 42 households in the sample of 200 were watching *Agony Acres*, which yields an estimated proportion of $p = 42/200 = .21$. Hence, the current week's price for 1 minute of spot commercial time on the program is

$$\text{price} = \$1,000 + \$2,000(.21) = \$1,420.00$$

15.4 INTERVAL ESTIMATION OF μ

In Section 15.1 we observed that point estimation is the process of employing sample data to obtain a single value as an estimate of a parameter. Of course, it is very rare that a point estimate will coincide exactly with the actual value of the parameter. That is, in making a point estimate, it is highly likely that the estimate will differ by some amount from the true value of the parameter being estimated. Thus, in using a point estimate, it is reasonable to want some indication of how much reliance can be placed on the estimate. A useful technique for this purpose is *interval estimation*. The basic task of interval estimation is to determine an interval of values, bounded by upper and lower limits such that it may be stated, with a specified degree of "confidence," that the true value of the parameter is contained in the interval. Such an interval is called a *confidence interval*.

15.4.1 Confidence Intervals for μ with σ^2 Known

The procedure for deriving a confidence interval for a population mean depends on two basic factors: (1) whether or not the population variance is known, and (2) whether or not the population distribution is normal. In this section we consider the situation in which the population variance is known. The situation in which the population variance is unknown is considered in Section 15.4.2.

Derivation of the Confidence Interval. If a population is normally distributed with mean μ and variance σ^2, then the sampling distribution of the estimator $\bar{X}$ is normal with mean $E(\bar{X}) = \mu$ and standard deviation $\sigma_{\bar{X}} = \sigma/\sqrt{n}$. In such a case, the quantity

$$Z = \frac{\bar{X} - \mu}{\sigma_{\bar{X}}}$$

has the standard normal distribution. If we let $z_{\alpha/2}$ and $z_{1-\alpha/2}$, respectively, denote the $\alpha/2$ and $(1 - \alpha/2)$ fractiles of the standard normal random variable Z, we then may write the probability expression

$$P\left(z_{\alpha/2} < \frac{\bar{X} - \mu}{\sigma_{\bar{X}}} < z_{1-\alpha/2}\right) = 1 - \alpha$$

In this expression, the term $(1 - \alpha)$ represents the probability that $(\bar{X} - \mu)/\sigma_{\bar{X}}$ will be contained in the interval bounded by $z_{\alpha/2}$ and $z_{1-\alpha/2}$. By algebra, the foregoing expression may be restated in the form

$$P[(\bar{X} + z_{\alpha/2}\sigma_{\bar{X}}) < \mu < (\bar{X} + z_{1-\alpha/2}\sigma_{\bar{X}})] = 1 - \alpha$$

Stated in this form, $1 - \alpha$ represents the probability that a random sample will yield a value of $\bar{X}$ such that μ will be contained in the interval between the lower limit $(\bar{X} + z_{\alpha/2}\sigma_{\bar{X}})$ and the upper limit $(\bar{X} + z_{1-\alpha/2}\sigma_{\bar{X}})$.

Suppose that a random sample is actually observed, and a specific value, $\bar{x}$, of the sample mean is obtained. It then might be a temptation to make the substitution

$$P[(\bar{x} + z_{\alpha/2}\sigma_{\bar{X}}) < \mu < (\bar{x} + z_{1-\alpha/2}\sigma_{\bar{X}})] = 1 - \alpha$$

Unfortunately, such a probability statement *would not be legitimate*. The reason this is not a probability statement is that none of the terms in the expression is a random variable. That is, μ, $\bar{x}$, $z_{\alpha/2}$, $z_{1-\alpha/2}$, and $\sigma_{\bar{X}}$ are all constants. Therefore, once a specific $\bar{x}$ has been obtained, μ either will or will not be contained in the interval between the limits $(\bar{x} + z_{\alpha/2}\sigma_{\bar{X}})$ and $(\bar{x} + z_{1-\alpha/2}\sigma_{\bar{X}})$.

Since it is illegitimate to write a probability statement concerning μ on the basis of an obtained $\bar{x}$, the eminent statistician Jerzey Neyman[5] originated the concept of *confidence* as an alternative to the concept of probability in dealing with interval estimation. Using the symbol C to denote confidence rather than probability, Neyman's concept of a confidence statement permits us to write

$$C[(\bar{x} + z_{\alpha/2}\sigma_{\bar{X}}) < \mu < (\bar{x} + z_{1-\alpha/2}\sigma_{\bar{X}})] = 1 - \alpha \qquad (15.4)$$

This is the formula for obtaining a confidence interval for the mean of a normally distributed population with known variance σ^2. In case the population is not normal, Formula (15.4) may be used to obtain an approximate confidence interval if σ^2 is known and the sample size is large enough to justify application of the central limit theorem.

Example of a Confidence Interval. Consider again the bidding problem that was discussed in Section 15.1. On the basis of 25 observations, the subcontractor obtained $\bar{x} = 30$ minutes as a point estimate of the population mean production time. For purposes of illustration, suppose that (1) the population distribution is normal, and (2) the population variance is known to be $\sigma^2 = 16$ square minutes. Under these assumptions, the sampling distribution of $\bar{X}$ is normal with standard deviation

$$\sigma_{\bar{X}} = \frac{\sigma}{\sqrt{n}} = \frac{\sqrt{16}}{\sqrt{25}} = .80$$

Now suppose that the contractor wishes to obtain a 90% confidence interval for the population mean μ. To obtain this interval, we first observe that the confi-

---

[5]Jerzey Neyman, "Outline of a Theory of Statistical Estimation Based on the Classical Theory of Probability," *Philosophical Transactions of the Royal Society*, Ser. A, Vol. 236 (1937).

dence coefficient is

$$C = 1 - \alpha = .90$$

It then follows that

$$\alpha = 1 - C = .10$$

$$\frac{\alpha}{2} = .05$$

$$1 - \frac{\alpha}{2} = .95$$

From Table J (Appendix II), we obtain

$$z_{\alpha/2} = z_{.05} = -1.645$$
$$z_{1-\alpha/2} = z_{.95} = +1.645$$

Substituting the values for $\bar{x}$, $\sigma_{\bar{x}}$, $z_{\alpha/2}$, and $z_{1-\alpha/2}$ into Formula (15.4), we have

$$C\{[30 + (-1.645)(.8)] < \mu < [30 + (1.645)(.80)]\} = .90$$

This reduces to

$$C(28.684 < \mu < 31.316) = .90$$

Thus, the subtractor can be 90% "confident" that the actual mean production time per unit is contained in the interval bounded by the limits 28.684 minutes and 31.316 minutes.

Interpretation of a Confidence Interval. As L. J. Savage has pointed out, the probabilistic concept underlying interpretation of interval estimates "is the most disputed technical concept of modern statistics."[6] The classical interpretation of a confidence interval is as follows: If random samples of the same size were repeatedly taken from the same population, and if a confidence interval were computed in the same way for each sample, then "in the long run" the relative frequency of those intervals that contained the parameter would approach C as a limit.

To illustrate the foregoing interpretation of a confidence interval, consider a normal population that has a mean $\mu = 80$ and a standard deviation $\sigma = 20$. Suppose that we intend to observe a simple random sample of $n = 100$ cases selected from this population and compute the sample mean. Then the sampling distribution of $\bar{X}$ will be normal. According to Formula (12.1), the expected value of $\bar{X}$ is $E(\bar{X}) = \mu = 80$. From Formula (12.5), the standard deviation of $\bar{X}$ is

$$\sigma_{\bar{x}} = \frac{\sigma}{\sqrt{n}} = \frac{20}{\sqrt{100}} = 2$$

This sampling distribution of $\bar{X}$ is depicted in the upper part of Figure 15.1.

Suppose that we actually observe a sample of 100 cases and obtain a sample mean $\bar{x} = 78.1$. Suppose further that we wish to use this value to construct a

---

[6] Leonard J. Savage, *The Foundations of Statistics* (New York: John Wiley & Sons, Inc., 1954), p. 262.

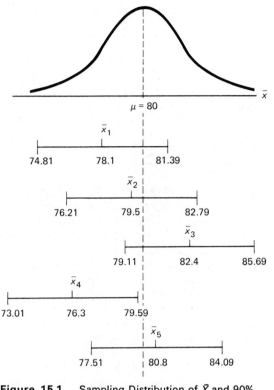

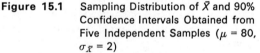

Figure 15.1 Sampling Distribution of $\bar{X}$ and 90% Confidence Intervals Obtained from Five Independent Samples ($\mu = 80$, $\sigma_{\bar{X}} = 2$)

90% confidence interval for μ. Since the confidence coefficient is $C = 1 - \alpha = .90$, we have $\alpha = .10$, $\alpha/2 = .05$, and $1 - \alpha/2 = .95$. From Table J, we obtain $z_{.05} = -1.645$ and $z_{1-.05} = z_{.95} = +1.645$. Formula (15.4) then yields

$$C[(\bar{x} + z_{\alpha/2}\sigma_{\bar{X}}) < \mu < (\bar{x} + z_{1-\alpha/2}\sigma_{\bar{X}})] = 1 - \alpha$$
$$C\{[78.1 + (-1.645)(2)] < \mu < [78.1 + (+1.645)(2)]\} = 1 - .10$$
$$C(74.81 < \mu < 81.39) = .90$$

Thus, the sample mean of $\bar{x} = 78.1$ results in a 90% confidence interval with limits of 74.81 and 81.39.

It is important to observe that the particular limits obtained for a confidence interval depend on the particular value obtained for the sample mean. To illustrate this point, suppose that the sampling experiment described above is repeated four additional times, giving us a total of five independent samples from the same population. Suppose further that each of these samples yields a different sample mean, as shown in column (1) of Table 15.1. Each of these sample means results in a 90% confidence interval bounded by different limits,

Table 15.1 90% Confidence Intervals for μ Obtained from Five Independent Samples ($\sigma_{\bar{x}} = 2$)

(1) Sample Mean, $\bar{x}_i$	(2) Lower Limit, $\bar{x}_i - 1.645(2)$	(3) Upper Limit, $\bar{x}_i + 1.645(2)$
$\bar{x}_1 = 78.1$	74.81	81.39
$\bar{x}_2 = 79.5$	76.21	82.79
$\bar{x}_3 = 82.4$	79.11	85.69
$\bar{x}_4 = 76.3$	73.01	79.59
$\bar{x}_5 = 80.8$	77.51	84.09

as shown in columns (2) and (3) of the table. Notice that these five intervals are all equal in width even though they have different limits.

The five sample means and confidence intervals given in Table 15.1 are shown graphically in the lower part of Figure 15.1. As the figure shows, for any particular interval, the true population mean, μ, is included or not included within the limits of the interval. If this sampling experiment were repeated a very large number of times, we would expect that approximately 90% of the intervals so obtained would include μ.

In this example we assumed, for illustrative purposes, that the true population mean was known to be $\mu = 80$. Of course, in actual practice the reason for constructing a confidence interval for μ is that we do not know the true value of μ. Therefore, we do not know whether or not μ is actually contained in any obtained confidence interval. That is, once a sample mean has been computed and a confidence interval obtained, the true value of μ either is or is not contained in the interval. Thus, from the classical viewpoint, it is not legitimate to attach a probability to the proposition that μ is contained in the interval. As J. W. Pratt has observed:

> What has made the confidence interval popular is "indicating what information is available." . . . a confidence interval probably contains the parameter, and the confidence level measures how probably. But does it? By the formal definition, it no longer does, once we insert the numerical values for the endpoints. Then no probability (except 0 or 1) can be attached to the event that the interval contains the parameter: either it does or it doesn't. Unfortunately we don't know which. We think, and would like to say, it "probably" does; we can invent something else to say, but nothing else to think. . . . The confidence-interval theory dodges the problem of what information is available . . . .[7]

15.4.2 Confidence Intervals for μ with σ² Unknown

In Section 15.4.1 we considered the procedure for constructing a confidence interval for the population mean μ under the condition that the population variance σ^2 is known. In that situation, the confidence interval was derived using a normal sampling distribution. But in actual practice, it is unusual that σ^2 is known if μ is unknown. When σ^2 is unknown, its value can be estimated

---

[7]John W. Pratt, "Review of 'Testing of Statistical Hypotheses' by E. L. Lehman," *Journal of the American Statistical Association*, Vol. 56 (1961), p. 165.

from the sample. In this section we consider procedures for constructing confidence intervals for μ when the sample estimate of σ^2 is used.

Student's t Distribution. If the population variance σ^2 is unknown, and *if the distribution of the population under investigation is normal*, methods for making inferences concerning the population mean μ are based on *Student's t distribution*. "Student" was the pseudonym of an eminent British statistician named William S. Gossett (1876–1947), who was employed by the Guinness brewery. In 1908, Gossett published a paper entitled "The Probable Error of a Mean," in which he introduced the t distribution. Under a ruling of the Guinness firm, Gossett was forbidden to publish under his real name. He therefore signed his paper "Student," and the t distribution became known as Student's t, or simply t.

Student's t distribution is a probability density function that has a single parameter ν (lowercase Greek letter nu), usually referred to as the number of *degrees of freedom*. Like the standard normal distribution, the t distribution is symmetrical around a mean of zero. Unlike the standard normal distribution, however, the variance of the t distribution is greater than 1. Thus, the t distribution is thinner in the center and thicker in the tails than the standard normal distribution. The extent to which the t distribution differs from the standard normal distribution depends on the value of ν. The larger the value of ν, the smaller is the variance of the t distribution and the smaller is the difference between the t distribution and the standard normal distribution. As the number of degrees of freedom approaches infinity, the variance of the t distribution approaches 1 and the t distribution approaches the standard normal distribution. This is illustrated in Figure 15.2, which compares the standard normal distribution to the t distribution for $\nu = 2$, $\nu = 5$, and $\nu = 20$.

Since the shape of Student's t distribution depends on the parameter ν, we will use the symbol t_ν to denote a random variable that has Student's t distribution with ν degrees of freedom.[8] For example, t_9 is a random variable that has Student's t distribution with 9 degrees of freedom. The symbol $t_{\nu;\,\varphi}$ will be used to denote the φ fractile of the t distribution with ν degrees of freedom. That is,

$$P(t_\nu \leq t_{\nu;\,\varphi}) = \varphi$$

Values of $t_{\nu;\,\varphi}$ for selected values of ν and φ are given in Table L (Appendix II). For instance, from this table we find that $t_{9;\,.85} = 1.100$. Thus, if a random variable has Student's t distribution with 9 degrees of freedom, there is a .85 probability that this random variable will have a value no greater than 1.100.

Notice that the bottom row of Table L contains values of $t_{\nu;\,\varphi}$ for $\nu = \infty$. Since the t distribution approaches the standard normal distribution as ν approaches infinity, the t fractiles for $\nu = \infty$ in Table L are identical to the corresponding standard normal fractiles in Table J (Appendix II).

Derivation of the Confidence Interval. The model for obtaining a confidence interval for the mean of a normally distributed population with known variance was given by Formula (15.4). The derivation of this model was based on the fact that, if the population is normal with mean μ and variance σ^2, the quantity

---

[8] In the special case of Student's distribution, it is conventional to use the lowercase t to denote both the random variable and any specific value of the random variable.

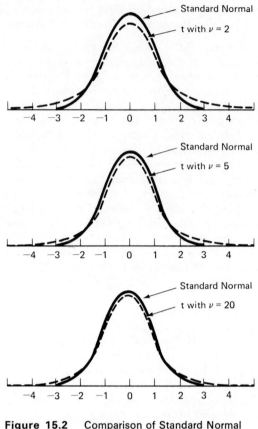

Figure 15.2 Comparison of Standard Normal Distribution with t Distributions for Selected Degrees of Freedom

$$Z = \frac{\bar{X} - \mu}{\sigma_{\bar{X}}}$$

has the standard normal distribution. However, if σ^2 is not known, $\sigma_{\bar{X}}$ cannot be computed. In such a case, it is possible to estimate $\sigma_{\bar{X}}$ from the sample data. For this purpose, the following estimator is used:

$$S_{\bar{X}} = \sqrt{\frac{S^2}{n}} = \frac{S}{\sqrt{n}} \qquad (15.5)$$

where S^2 is the unbiased estimator of the population variance σ^2. When $\sigma_{\bar{X}}$ is replaced by $S_{\bar{X}}$, the quantity

$$t = \frac{\bar{X} - \mu}{S_{\bar{X}}}$$

has Student's t distribution with $(n - 1)$ degrees of freedom. As a result, the formula for obtaining a confidence interval for the mean of a normally distributed population with unknown variance becomes

$$C[(\bar{x} + t_{n-1;\,\alpha/2}s_{\bar{x}}) < \mu < (\bar{x} + t_{n-1;\,1-\alpha/2}s_{\bar{x}})] = 1 - \alpha \qquad (15.6)$$

To illustrate the application of Formula (15.6), consider once more the subcontractor's bidding problem. In Section 15.4.1 a confidence interval for the mean production time per unit was obtained under the assumptions that (1) the population distribution is normal, and (2) the population variance is known to be $\sigma^2 = 16$ square minutes. Now suppose that the population variance is unknown, but can be estimated. Applying Formula (15.2) to the same sample data that were used to estimate the mean, the unbiased estimate $s^2 = 26.8$ is obtained. Recalling that this estimate is based on a sample of $n = 25$ observations, we may then estimate $\sigma_{\bar{x}}$ using Formula (15.5):

$$s_{\bar{x}} = \sqrt{\frac{26.8}{25}} = \frac{5.18}{5} = 1.04$$

Using this result to construct a 90% confidence interval for the process mean, we first observe that the number of degrees of freedom is

$$\nu = n - 1 = 25 - 1 = 24$$

Entering Table L, we find that

$$t_{24;\,.05} = -1.711$$
$$t_{24;\,.95} = +1.711$$

Then, recalling that the sample mean is $\bar{x} = 30$, we obtain the following confidence interval from Formula (15.6):

$$C\{[30 - 1.711(1.04)] < \mu < [30 + 1.711(1.04)]\} = .90$$

This reduces to

$$C(28.221 < \mu < 31.779) = .90$$

Thus, if we are willing to assume that the population of production times is normal, we may say that we are 90% "confident" that the population mean is included in the interval bounded by the limits 28.221 minutes and 31.779 minutes.

Strictly speaking, use of the t distribution in Formula (15.6) requires that the population be normally distributed. In actual practice, however, this condition is seldom satisfied precisely. Fortunately, experience has indicated that moderate departures from normality usually do not materially affect the results obtained from Formula (15.6). Thus, it has become common practice to use the t distribution even when the population being sampled is only approximately normal.

If the population distribution departs markedly from normality, and the population variance is unknown, neither Formula (15.4) nor (15.6) is appropriate for obtaining a confidence interval for μ. The common practice in such a situation is to employ an approximation procedure that requires the use of a large sample. If the sample size is substantial, then the sampling distribution of the estimator $\bar{X}$ will be approximately normal, and s^2 will provide a reasonably reliable estimate of σ^2. In such a case, an approximate confidence interval for μ

may be obtained by substituting $s_{\bar{x}}$ for $\sigma_{\bar{x}}$ in Formula (15.4). This substitution yields

$$C[(\bar{x} + z_{\alpha/2}s_{\bar{x}}) < \mu < (\bar{x} + z_{1-\alpha/2}s_{\bar{x}})] \approx 1 - \alpha \qquad (15.7)$$

To illustrate the application of Formula (15.7), consider a study in which a simple random sample of 225 residential real estate sales is observed to estimate the mean amount of such sales in a large metropolitan area. The study yields a sample mean $\bar{x} = \$55,000$ and a sample standard deviation $s = \$12,000$. Thus, from Formula (15.5), the estimated standard error of the mean is

$$s_{\bar{x}} = \frac{s}{\sqrt{n}} = \frac{\$12,000}{\sqrt{225}} = \$800$$

Then, an approximate 95% confidence interval for the population mean sale may be obtained from Formula (15.7) as follows:

$$C[(12,000 + z_{.025}800) < \mu < (12,000 + z_{.975}800)] = .95$$
$$C\{[12,000 + (-1.96)(800)] < \mu < [12,000 + (1.96)(800)]\} = .95$$
$$C(10,432 < \mu < 13,568) = .95$$

15.5 INTERVAL ESTIMATION OF σ^2

Various procedures have been developed for constructing a confidence interval for a population variance. Since most of these procedures are beyond the scope of this text, we will limit our consideration in this section to a single procedure that is applicable when the population being sampled is normally distributed.

15.5.1 The Chi-Square Distribution

If the population under investigation is normally distributed, methods for making inferences concerning the population variance σ^2 are based on a probability model called the chi-square distribution. Like Student's t distribution, the chi-square distribution is a probability density function with a single parameter ν, called the number of degrees of freedom. As illustrated in Figure 15.3, the exact shape of the distribution depends on the value of ν. Regardless of the value of ν, the distribution approaches zero as a lower limit, with an upper tail extending toward infinity. In other words, unlike Student's t distribution, which is symmetrical around a mean of zero, the chi-square distribution has a lower limit of zero and is skewed to the right.

Since the shape of the chi-square distribution depends on the parameter ν, we will use the symbol χ_ν^2 to denote a random variable that has a chi-square distribution with ν degrees of freedom.[9] For example, χ_6^2 is a random variable which has the chi-square distribution with 6 degrees of freedom. The symbol $\chi_{\nu;\,\varphi}^2$ will be used to denote the φ fractile of the chi-square distribution with ν degrees of freedom. That is,

$$P(\chi_{\nu;\,\varphi}^2 \leq \chi_\nu^2) = \varphi$$

---

[9]In the special case of the chi-square distribution, it is conventional to use the lower-case Greek letter χ to denote both the random variable and any specific value of the random variable.

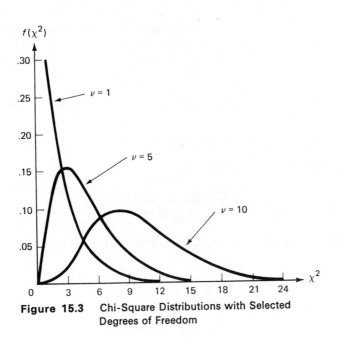

Figure 15.3 Chi-Square Distributions with Selected Degrees of Freedom

Values of $\chi^2_{\nu;\,\varphi}$ for selected values of ν and φ are given in Table K (Appendix II). For instance, from this table we find that $\chi^2_{6;\,.95} = 12.59$. Thus, if a random variable has the chi-square distribution with 6 degrees of freedom, there is a .95 probability that this random variable will have a value less than 12.59.

15.5.2 Derivation of the Confidence Interval

The usual procedure for constructing a confidence interval for the variance of a normal population is based on the use of the unbiased estimator S^2. The sampling distribution of S^2 is not itself a chi-square distribution. However, it may be demonstrated that, if a simple random sample of n observations is taken from a normal population with unknown variance σ^2, then the ratio

$$\frac{(n-1)S^2}{\sigma^2}$$

is a random variable that has a chi-square distribution with $(n-1)$ degrees of freedom. This fundamental fact makes it possible to derive a simple procedure for obtaining a confidence interval for the variance of a normal population.

If we let $\chi^2_{n-1;\,\alpha/2}$ and $\chi^2_{n-1;\,1-\alpha/2}$, respectively, denote the $\alpha/2$ and $(1 - \alpha/2)$ fractiles of the chi-square distribution with $(n-1)$ degrees of freedom, the $(1 - \alpha)$ confidence interval for σ^2 is given by

$$C\left[\frac{(n-1)s^2}{\chi^2_{n-1;\,1-\alpha/2}} < \sigma^2 < \frac{(n-1)s^2}{\chi^2_{n-1;\,\alpha/2}}\right] = 1 - \alpha \tag{15.8}$$

To illustrate the application of Formula (15.8), recall again the case of the drug manufacturer which we considered in Section 15.2. In that section, from a sample of $n = 10$ observations, we obtained $s^2 = 9.78$ as an unbiased estimate of the variance of the active content of the vitamin C tablets produced by their process. Suppose now that the manufacturer wishes to construct a 90% confidence interval for the process variance. We first observe that the number of degrees of freedom is

$$\nu = n - 1 = 10 - 1 = 9$$

Entering Table K, we find that

$$\chi^2_{9;\,.05} = 3.33$$
$$\chi^2_{9;\,.95} = 16.92$$

Then, from Formula (15.8), we obtain the following confidence interval:

$$C\left[\frac{9(9.78)}{16.92} < \sigma^2 < \frac{9(9.78)}{3.33}\right] = .90$$

This reduces to

$$C(5.2 < \sigma^2 < 26.4) = .90$$

15.6 INTERVAL ESTIMATION OF π

An exact confidence interval for a population proportion π can be constructed by the use of a binomial distribution. However, because of the discrete nature of the binomial distribution, this procedure is cumbersome. Therefore, special charts and tables[10] derived from the binomial distribution have been developed to simplify the construction of exact confidence intervals for π. These charts and tables are used primarily when the sample size is small, since a convenient procedure based on the normal approximation to the binomial may be used when the sample size is large.

If the sample size is sufficiently large, the sampling distribution of the sample proportion P is approximately normal. Then an approximate $(1 - \alpha)$ confidence interval for π is given by

$$C[(p + z_{\alpha/2} s_P) < \pi < (p + z_{1-\alpha/2} s_P)] \approx 1 - \alpha \qquad (15.9)$$

where p is the obtained sample proportion and s_P, the estimated standard error of the sample proportion, is given by

$$s_P = \sqrt{\frac{p(1 - p)}{n}} \qquad (15.10)$$

To illustrate the application of Formula (15.9), consider again the *Agony Acres* case, which was introduced in Section 15.3. Recall that the proportion of

---

[10]For example, see Tables A-22, A-23, and A-24 in Mary G. Natrella, *Experimental Statistics*, National Bureau of Standards Handbook 91 (Washington, D.C.: U.S. Government Printing Office, 1963).

households watching *Agony Acres*, out of a sample of 100 households, was $p = .21$. Now suppose that we wish to use this sample result to obtain a 90% confidence interval for π. To do this, we first apply Formula (15.10) to obtain the estimated standard error of P:

$$s_P = \sqrt{\frac{.21(.79)}{200}} = .029$$

Then, from Table J, we find that

$$z_{\alpha/2} = z_{.05} = -1.645$$
$$z_{1-\alpha/2} = z_{.95} = 1.645$$

Finally, substitution into Formula (15.9) yields

$$C\{[.21 - 1.645(.029)] < \pi < [.21 + 1.645(.029)]\} \approx .90$$

which reduces to

$$C(.1623 < \pi < .2577) \approx .90$$

15.7 PRECISION AND SAMPLE SIZE

So far in our discussion of estimation techniques, we have dealt with situations in which the sample size was given. Yet, in planning surveys, one of the most frequently asked questions is: What should the sample size be? This is an important question, since taking a sample that is larger than necessary may be overly costly, whereas taking a sample that is too small may not yield a sufficiently reliable estimate.

The classical approach to determination of optimal sample size is to specify the maximum probability that the estimate will be in error by more than a given amount. Specifically, if some parameter θ is estimated by $\mathcal{S}$, then the absolute error of estimation, either above or below the true value, may be written as $|\mathcal{S} - \theta|$. Of course, before the sample is actually observed, $\mathcal{S}$ is unknown, and the error of estimation is a random variable which may be denoted by $|\mathcal{S} - \theta|$. Then the desired precision of the estimator may be expressed in terms of the maximum probability that the error of estimation will exceed some amount ϵ. If we let α represent this maximum probability, then the precision of the estimator may be expressed in terms of the following probability statement:

$$P(|\mathcal{S} - \theta| > \epsilon) \leq \alpha \tag{15.11}$$

Once the values of α and ϵ are specified by the investigator, the problem of determining the appropriate sample size is one of finding the minimum number of observations such that Formula (15.11) is satisfied. In other words, the optimal sample size is the minimum number of observations such that the probability is no greater than α that the absolute error of estimation will exceed ϵ. The particular procedure for doing this depends on the sampling distribution of the particular estimator being used.

15.7.1 Determination of Sample Size
for Estimating μ

In the case of using the sample mean $\bar{X}$ to estimate the population mean μ, Formula (15.11) may be written

$$P(|\bar{X} - \mu| > \epsilon) \leq \alpha \qquad (15.12)$$

Notice in this expression that the error of estimation is expressed in *absolute* terms: $|\bar{X} - \mu|$. In other words, the statement specifies a maximum risk α that the estimator $\bar{X}$ will differ by more than ϵ either above or below the parameter μ. If $\bar{X}$ is above μ, the *algebraic* difference $(\bar{X} - \mu)$ will be positive; if $\bar{X}$ is below μ, this difference will be negative. Thus, expressing the error of estimation in algebraic rather than absolute terms, we may rewrite Formula (15.12) as

$$P\{[(\bar{X} - \mu) > \epsilon] \cup [(\bar{X} - \mu) < -\epsilon]\} \leq \alpha \qquad (15.13)$$

In determining sample size for a survey, it is customary to split the α-risk equally between making an overestimate and making an underestimate. This permits us to write

$$P[(\bar{X} - \mu) > \epsilon] \leq \frac{\alpha}{2}$$

$$P[(\bar{X} - \mu) < -\epsilon] \leq \frac{\alpha}{2}$$

To obtain a sample size that will satisfy these two probability expressions, it is necessary to specify the sampling distribution of $\bar{X}$. For this purpose, we may assume that the distribution of $\bar{X}$ is normal.[11] Because of the symmetry of the normal distribution, the sample size that satisfies either of the two expressions above will also satisfy the other. Thus, we may proceed to develop a formula for determining sample size on the basis of the single probability requirement

$$P[(\bar{X} - \mu) > \epsilon] \leq \frac{\alpha}{2}$$

which is equivalent to

$$P[(\bar{X} - \mu) \leq \epsilon] \geq 1 - \frac{\alpha}{2}$$

Then, by algebra,

$$P\left(\frac{\bar{X} - \mu}{\sigma_{\bar{X}}} \leq \frac{\epsilon}{\sigma_{\bar{X}}}\right) \geq 1 - \frac{\alpha}{2}$$

Since $\bar{X}$ is assumed to be normally distributed, the quantity $(\bar{X} - \mu)/\sigma_{\bar{X}}$ has the standard normal distribution. Thus,

$$P\left(Z \leq \frac{\epsilon}{\sigma_{\bar{X}}}\right) \geq 1 - \frac{\alpha}{2}$$

---

[11]This assumption is valid if either (1) the population is normal, or (2) the resulting sample is sufficiently large to justify application of the central limit theorem.

This probability statement implies that

$$\frac{\epsilon}{\sigma_{\bar{X}}} \geq z_{1-\alpha/2}$$

where $z_{1-\alpha/2}$ is the $(1 - \alpha/2)$ fractile of the standard normal distribution. Recalling that $\sigma_{\bar{X}} = \sigma/\sqrt{n}$, we may substitute to obtain

$$\frac{\epsilon}{\sigma/\sqrt{n}} \geq z_{1-\alpha/2}$$

Finally, solving for n, we have

$$n \geq \left(\frac{z_{1-\alpha/2}\sigma}{\epsilon}\right)^2 \tag{15.14}$$

The smallest integer value of n that satisfies Formula (15.19) is the desired sample size for estimating μ.

A practical difficulty arises in the application of Formula (15.14), since the formula requires that the population standard deviation σ be known. In actual practice, however, σ is rarely known if μ is unknown. This difficulty is usually overcome in one of the following ways:

1. If previous sample studies have been conducted with similar populations, the results of such studies may be used to arrive at an approximate value for σ.
2. If adequate data from previous studies do not exist, a "pilot" study may be conducted with a small sample from the population under investigation. The standard deviation of this pilot sample may then be used as an approximate value for σ.
3. If data from previous studies are not available, and if a pilot study is not feasible, the value of σ may be approximated by a commonly used rule of thumb sometimes called the empirical rule. This rule of thumb is based on the fact that approximately 99.7% of the area under a normal distribution lies within 3 standard deviations on either side of the mean. Thus, for all practical purposes, if a population is reasonably mound-shaped, the population range is about 6 standard deviations in width. Thus, if it is possible to obtain an informed guess of the population range, then one-sixth of this "guesstimate" may be used as an approximate value for σ.

To illustrate the use of Formula (15.14), let us return to the example of the subcontractor's bidding problem. In that example a sample of size $n = 25$ was specified arbitrarily. Suppose, however, that the subcontractor chooses to base his sample size on the risk specification that there be no greater than a .01 probability that the sample will yield an estimate which will differ from the process mean by more than $\frac{1}{2}$ minute. Suppose further that, on the basis of his experience in producing similar components, he feels that the process standard deviation is approximately 4 minutes. To apply Formula (15.14) to this situation, we first observe that

$$\alpha = .01 \qquad \epsilon = \tfrac{1}{2} \qquad \sigma = 4$$

Then, from Table J,

$$z_{1-\alpha/2} = z_{.995} = 2.576$$

Finally, substituting into Formula (15.14), we obtain

$$n \geq \left[\frac{2.576(4)}{1/2} \right]^2$$
$$\geq 424.77$$

Since the sample size must be an integer, this figure is rounded up to 425, which is the minimum number of observations such that the probability is no greater than .01 that the error of estimation will exceed $\frac{1}{2}$ minute.

15.7.2 Determination of Sample Size for Estimating π

The most common procedure used to determine optimal sample size for estimating a population proportion π from a sample proportion P is based on the normal approximation to the binomial. To derive the sample-size formula, we first note that the standard deviation of the sampling distribution of P is

$$\sigma_P = \sqrt{\frac{\pi(1 - \pi)}{n}} \tag{15.15}$$

Then we follow the same procedure employed to derive Formula (15.14), substituting π for μ, P for $\bar{X}$, and σ_P for $\sigma_{\bar{x}}$. The result is

$$n \geq \frac{z_{1-\alpha/2}^2 \pi(1 - \pi)}{\epsilon^2} \tag{15.16}$$

The smallest integer value of n that satisfies this formula is the minimum number of observations required such that the probability is no greater than α that the absolute error of estimation will exceed ϵ.

In discussing the determination of sample size for estimating a population mean μ, we observed that Formula (15.14) requires knowledge of the population standard deviation σ. A more severe difficulty arises in the determination of sample size for estimating a population proportion π, since Formula (15.16) requires knowledge of π, the very parameter being estimated. One common procedure to overcome this situation is based on the fact that the value of n yielded by Formula (15.16) reaches its maximum when $\pi = .50$. Thus, using .50 as the value of π assures that the resulting value of n will be at least large enough to provide the desired precision. Of course, if the unknown value of π is actually greater or less than .50, this procedure will yield a sample size which is larger than necessary, and hence may result in an unduly high cost of sampling. Therefore, if the investigator is concerned about sampling cost, and if he is reasonably confident that the actual value of π differs from .50, he may prefer to use a guesstimate of π. To arrive at such a guesstimate, the investigator considers the range of reasonably possible values of π, and then selects from that range the value that is closest to .50. For instance, suppose the investigator feels reasonably confident that the actual value of π lies somewhere between .05 and .20. Then he would use .20 as the value of π in Formula (15.16). Similarly, if he feels reasonably confident that the actual value of π lies between .80 and .95, he would select .80 as the value of π. If he feels that the actual value of π lies between .40 and .55, he would use .50 as the value of π.

To illustrate the application of Formula (15.16), suppose that the campaign committee for a gubernatorial candidate in a large state wishes to conduct a sample survey to estimate the proportion of registered voters who favor their candidate. They would like the poll to be conducted with a sample large enough such that there will be no greater than a .10 probability that the sample estimate will deviate more than .03 from the actual proportion in the total voter population. Since this is the first such poll of the campaign, the committee has no strong feeling about what proportion of voters actually favor their candidate. Thus, for the purpose of determining the sample size, they decide to "play it safe" by using .50 as the value of π. Since the specified risk is $\alpha = .10$, it follows that $z_{1-\alpha/2} = z_{.95}$. From Table J, $z_{.95} = 1.645$. Substituting into Formula (15.16), we obtain

$$n \geq \frac{(1.645)^2(.50)(1 - .50)}{(.03)^2}$$

$$\geq 751.67$$

Since the sample size must be an integer, this figure is rounded up to 752.

PROBLEMS

15.1 The lives of electronic components produced by an automatic process are known to be normally distributed with a standard deviation of 250 hours. A random sample of 25 components is drawn and found to have a mean life of 2,000 hours. Construct a 95% confidence interval for the process mean life.

15.2 Axionics, Inc. is a subcontracting firm that manufactures components for TV sets. The company has been asked to submit a bid for 5,000 units of a particular component. To arrive at the amount of the bid, the firm's cost analyst begins by determining the following:
  1. Undertaking the project will involve a fixed setup cost of $8,000.
  2. There will be variable costs of $8.00 per unit for materials, plus $6.00 per hour of production time.
  3. On the basis of past experience, it is reasonable to assume that the production time is normally distributed with $\sigma^2 = .01$ square hour.
  (a) Using μ to denote the mean production time (in hours) per unit, express total cost as a function of μ.
  (b) To estimate μ, the cost analyst requests the production manager to produce a sample of 64 units, carefully recording the amount of time required to produce each unit. From the resulting data, the cost analyst calculates the mean production time to be $\bar{x} = .40$ hour per unit. Determine an unbiased point estimate of mean production time per unit.
  (c) Determine a 95% confidence interval for mean production time.
  (d) Determine an unbiased point estimate of total cost.
  (e) Determine a 95% confidence interval for total cost.

15.3 A firm undertakes a sample study to estimate μ, the average time (in minutes) taken to etch initials on crystal goblets. Observations are to be made of the number of minutes required to etch initials on each of a sample of 25 goblets. The sample mean $\bar{X}$ will be used as a point estimator of μ. From this estimate of μ, the cost of the etching operation for an order of 20,000 goblets will be estimated. On the basis of past experience, it seems reasonable to assume that the etching time is normally distributed with $\sigma^2 = 9$ square minutes.
  (a) What is the approximate probability that the value of $\bar{X}$ will overestimate μ by more than 1.5 minutes?
  (b) What is the approximate probability that the value of $\bar{X}$ will underestimate μ by more than 1.4 minutes?

(c) What is the probability that the error of estimation in either direction will be greater than 1.2 minutes?

15.4 Assume that the sample in Problem 15.3 yields the following results recorded to the nearest $\frac{1}{10}$ minute:

5.7	17.1	15.9	10.5	3.0
11.9	15.2	13.5	4.2	8.3
15.6	17.2	11.6	6.2	16.6
14.9	4.8	9.7	16.8	4.4
17.4	16.8	13.4	19.2	10.9

(a) Compute the value of $\bar{X}$ for this sample.
(b) Determine a 98% confidence interval for μ.

15.5 Assume that the firm's cost function for the etching operation in Problem 15.3 is given by

$$C = \$5,000 + 20,000(\$.05 + \$.15\mu)$$

(a) Determine a point estimate for the cost of this operation.
(b) Determine a 98% confidence interval for the cost of this operation.

15.6 Refer to Problem 15.4. Assume that the population variance σ^2 is unknown. Use the sample data to determine:
(a) An unbiased point estimate of σ^2
(b) An unbiased point estimate of σ

15.7 Refer to Problem 15.4. Suppose that there is no basis in past experience to assume a value for σ^2, so that σ^2 must be estimated from the sample data.
(a) Determine a 98% confidence interval for μ.
(b) Determine a 98% confidence interval for cost.

15.8 An automatic process produces steel shafts whose diameters are normally distributed. Suppose that a random sample of 16 shafts yields a mean of $\bar{x} = 8$ centimeters and a standard deviation of $s = .20$ centimeter. Construct a 95% confidence interval for the process mean diameter.

15.9 The Arnoff Corporation, manufacturer of the Trailmate transistor radio, is considering marketing its product with the newly available Longlast power cell. Before making the decision, Arnoff desires an estimate of the mean life of these power cells. For this purpose, a sample of 121 Longlast cells are tested in Trailmate radios. The sample yields a mean operating life of 160 hours.
  (a) Suppose that it is reasonable to assume that the operating lives of Longlast cells are normally distributed with $\sigma^2 = 144$ square hours. Determine a 95% confidence interval for μ, the mean life of the population of Longlast cells in Trailmate radios.
  (b) Suppose that it is reasonable to assume that $\sigma^2 = 144$, but that it is not reasonable to assume that the lives are normally distributed. Determine the 95% confidence interval for μ.
  (c) Suppose that it is reasonable to assume that the lives are normally distributed but that there is no basis for assuming a value for σ^2. Suppose that the sample data yield $s^2 = 169$ square hours as an unbiased estimate of σ^2. Determine the 95% confidence interval for μ.
  (d) Suppose that it is not reasonable to assume that the lives are normally distributed and that there is no basis for assuming a value for σ^2. If the sample yields a variance estimate of $s^2 = 144$ square hours, what is the 95% confidence interval for μ?

15.10 The Trilby Corporation produces a mechanical product that incorporates aluminum washers, which are received in lots of 10,000 from a supplier. These washers are specified to have an inside diameter of 20 millimeters. If the inside diameter of a washer is less than 19.5 millimeters or greater than 20.5 millimeters, the washer is not usable and must be scrapped. Thus, both the mean and variance of the inside diameters of the washers in a lot are important in determining the acceptability of a lot. Suppose that an inspector selects a random sample of 25 washers from a particular lot and carefully measures their inside diameters. She obtains a sample mean of $\bar{x} = 19.90$ millimeters and an unbiased variance estimate of $s^2 = .04$ square millimeter. Assuming that the diameters of the washers in the lot are approximately normally distributed:

(a) Determine a 99% confidence interval for the mean inside diameter of the washers in the lot.

(b) Determine a 99% confidence interval for the variance of the washers in the lot.

15.11 Refer to Problem 15.4. Suppose that there is no basis in past experience to assume a value for σ^2. Using the sample data, obtain a 98% confidence interval for σ^2.

15.12 Calvin Kindly, credit manager of the Longreen Federal Savings and Loan Association, wishes to have a 95% confidence interval for the proportion of home-loan applicants who are making their first home purchase. He draws a random sample of 400 home applications from the files and computes the proportion of first timers to be .36. Construct the confidence interval of the proportion for Calvin.

15.13 The Food Queen Minimarket chain is considering opening a store in suburban Oakmont near the intersection of Green Street and Elgin Avenue. To determine the desirability of this location, a sample of 625 Oakmont homemakers are interviewed. One of the questions on the survey was: If Food Queen were to open a store near the intersection of Green Street and Elgin Avenue, would you do your incidental grocery shopping there? Of the 625 homemakers interviewed, 125 answered "yes" and 500 answered "no". Determine a 90% confidence interval for the proportion of all Oakmont homemakers who would do their incidental grocery shopping at the proposed Food Queen store.

15.14 The Westside Bugle is a local newspaper that circulates in a large suburban residential area. In preparing a promotional brochure, the advertising manager wishes to obtain an estimate of the mean household income in the area. To obtain this estimate, she plans to survey a sample of households. She would like to conduct her survey in such a way that there will be no greater than a .05 probability that the sample mean will differ from the population mean by more than $50. If the standard deviation of the household incomes in the population is assumed to be $500, what is the minimum sample size that will satisfy the advertising manager's requirements?

15.15 The Ackroyd Corporation has several thousand employees located in six divisions throughout a large state. For upcoming collective bargaining sessions, the firm's chief negotiator wishes to obtain an estimate of the mean medical expenses incurred last year by the families of the firm's employees. To obtain this estimate, he plans to survey a sample of these families. Assuming that the standard deviation of family medical expenses is approximately $400, what is the minimum number of families that should be surveyed if there is to be no more than a .02 probability that the sample mean will differ from the actual population mean by more than $60?

15.16 A survey is being designed to estimate the proportion, π, of registered voters in a large state who favor capital punishment for the crime of kidnapping. Opinion in the state is sharply divided, so that, for the purpose of the study, there is no reason to assume that π differs from .50. If a simple random sample of registered voters is to be selected, what is the minimal sample size that will assure a .90 probability that the unbiased point estimate of π will be within .02 of the true value?

15.17 The research director of a marketing consulting firm wishes to conduct a sample survey to estimate the proportion of households in Winthrop County that subscribe to *House and Flowers* magazine. If he feels confident that this proportion lies somewhere between .10 and .30, what is the minimum number of households he should survey in order that there will be no greater than a .05 probability that the sample proportion will deviate more than .02 from the actual population proportion?

16

Testing Hypotheses Concerning
Normal Populations
with Unknown Variances

In Chapter 13 we considered methods for testing hypotheses concerning the means of populations with known variances. In reality, however, it rarely happens that the population variance is known when the population mean is unknown. In this chapter we consider some procedures for testing hypotheses concerning populations with unknown variances. Most of the tests presented in this chapter are based on the assumption that *the populations under investigation are normally distributed*. To the extent that a population under investigation is nearly normal, the methods of this chapter are generally adequate for most practical purposes. However, if a population under consideration departs markedly from normality, the methods presented in this chapter may be entirely inappropriate.

16.1 TESTS CONCERNING THE MEAN OF A NORMAL POPULATION

In Section 13.1 we developed procedures for testing hypotheses concerning the mean of a population with known variance. The decision rules for testing these hypotheses, as summarized in Table 13.4, were based on the premise that the quantity

$$z = \frac{\bar{X} - \mu}{\sigma_{\bar{X}}}$$

has the standard normal distribution. However, if the population variance σ^2 is unknown, then $\sigma_{\bar{X}}$ also is unknown. Replacing $\sigma_{\bar{X}}$ by its estimator $S_{\bar{X}}$ results in the quantity

$$t = \frac{\bar{X} - \mu}{S_{\bar{X}}}$$

As we observed in Section 15.4.2, this quantity has Student's t distribution with $(n - 1)$ degrees of freedom. Thus, to test a hypothesis concerning the mean of a normal population with unknown variance, the test statistic is

$$t = \frac{\bar{X} - \mu_0}{S_{\bar{X}}} \qquad (16.1)$$

where μ_0 is the limiting value of μ contained in the null hypothesis. Table 16.1

Table 16.1 General Specifications for *t* Tests Concerning the Mean of a Normal Population with Unknown Variance

Test	Hypotheses	Decision Rule
Upper tail	$H_0: \mu \leq \mu_0$ $H_1: \mu > \mu_0$	Reject H_0 if $t \geq t_{n-1;\, 1-\alpha}$; accept H_0 otherwise
Lower tail	$H_0: \mu \geq \mu_0$ $H_1: \mu < \mu_0$	Reject H_0 if $t \leq t_{n-1;\, \alpha}$; accept H_0 otherwise
Two-tail	$H_0: \mu = \mu_0$ $H_1: \mu \neq \mu_0$	Reject H_0 if $t \leq t_{n-1;\, \alpha/2}$ or $t \geq t_{n-1;\, 1-\alpha/2}$; accept H_0 otherwise

$$\text{where} \quad t = \frac{\bar{X} - \mu_0}{S_{\bar{X}}}$$

summarizes the decision rules for applying this statistic to conduct upper-tail, lower-tail, and two-tail tests of hypotheses concerning the mean of a normal population.

Notice that the decision rules summarized in Table 13.4 are expressed in terms of critical values of the sample mean $\bar{X}$, whereas the decision rules in Table 16.1 are expressed in terms of critical values of t. When the population variance is known, the value of $\sigma_{\bar{X}}$ can be calculated prior to observing the sample, and hence the decision rule can be specified in terms of $\bar{X}$. However, when the population variance is unknown, the value of $\sigma_{\bar{X}}$ is estimated from the sample results, so that the critical value of $\bar{X}$ cannot be determined before observing the sample.

To illustrate the use of a t test of a hypothesis concerning a population mean, consider the case of the Product Studies Institute (PSI), a consumer research agency. PSI is currently investigating an advertising claim by the Hermes Motorcar Corporation that the gasoline consumption of its Meadowlark model averages 16 miles per gallon under ordinary driving conditions. PSI has received complaints from consumers that this mileage claim is too high. To determine whether it should formally challenge Hermes' claim, PSI decides to test the claim statistically. For this purpose, PSI is willing to accept the burden of demonstrating that the claim is too high, and hence establishes the following null and alternative hypotheses:

$$H_0: \quad \mu \geq 16.0$$
$$H_1: \quad \mu < 16.0$$

where μ represents the mean number of miles per gallon for *all* Meadowlark cars. As a matter of policy in performing tests of advertising claims, PSI adopts a significance level of $\alpha_{\max} = .10$, which represents the maximum risk of formally challenging Hermes' claim if the claim is actually correct.

To conduct the test, PSI manages to obtain a sample of 26 Meadowlarks recently added to the Atlas Insurance Company's automobile fleet. Each of these cars is to be driven under ordinary conditions for 200 miles, and the gasoline consumption required to travel this distance is to be measured by a specially installed device. The miles per gallon for each car will then be calculated. On the basis of considerable experience in conducting such mileage studies, PSI feels that gasoline consumption is essentially normally distributed in the population of all Meadowlarks produced by Hermes. Since the variance of this population distribution is unknown, the t distribution is appropriate for conducting the hypothesis test. Referring to Table 16.1, the decision rule for a lower-tail test is to reject the null hypothesis if $t \leq t_{n-1;\,\alpha}$. Since the sample size is $n = 26$ and the significance level is .10, the critical value is $t_{25;\,.10} = -1.316$, which is obtained from Table L (Appendix II). Thus, the null hypothesis will be rejected if the t-value computed from the sample data is equal to or less than -1.316.

Having specified the decision rule, PSI proceeds to conduct the mileage experiment, with the results shown in Table 16.2. As the reader may verify from those data, the unbiased estimates of the mean and variance of the Meadowlark population are

Table 16.2 Gasoline Consumption in Miles per Gallon for a Sample of 26 Meadowlark Cars

11.9	12.0	14.3	11.6
14.8	14.7	13.7	14.5
13.2	14.6	14.7	11.8
16.3	12.7	12.7	12.7
14.0	15.8	14.6	14.9
15.3	14.4	16.7	
15.6	12.9	14.2	

$$\bar{x} = \frac{\sum x}{n} = \frac{364.6}{26} = 14.023$$

$$s^2 = \frac{\sum (x - \bar{x})^2}{n-1} = \frac{49.7662}{25} = 1.9906$$

Next, from Formula (15.5), the estimated value of $\sigma_{\bar{x}}$ is

$$s_{\bar{x}} = \sqrt{\frac{s^2}{n}} = \sqrt{\frac{1.9906}{26}} = \sqrt{.07656} = .2767$$

Then, applying Formula 16.1, we obtain

$$t = \frac{\bar{x} - \mu_0}{s_{\bar{x}}} = \frac{14.023 - 16.0}{.2767} = -7.145$$

Since the obtained t-value of -7.145 is less than the critical t-value of -1.316, the null hypothesis is rejected. Consequently, PSI should formally challenge Hermes' advertising claim.

16.2 TESTS CONCERNING THE VARIANCE OF A NORMAL POPULATION

In many types of managerial decision situations, the variance of a population is a critical consideration. For instance, in manufacturing, where uniformity of output affects the reputation and consumer acceptance of the product, it is desirable to maintain variability at a low level. The logic underlying the procedure for testing a hypothesis concerning the variance of a normal population is essentially the same as that involved in testing a hypothesis concerning a population mean. Whether testing a hypothesis concerning a mean or variance, the basic problem is to design a decision rule that partitions the domain of the sampling distribution of a test statistic into acceptance and rejection regions. The principal distinction among different hypothesis-testing procedures lies in the differences among the various sampling distributions on which they are based. In Chapter 13 we used the normal distribution to derive a procedure for testing a hypothesis concerning the mean of a population with known variance, and in Section 16.1 we used the t distribution to design a procedure for testing a hypothesis concerning the mean of a normal population with unknown variance. In this section we present a procedure for using the chi-square distribution to test a hypothesis concerning the variance of a normal population. A commonly used procedure for testing a hypothesis concerning the variance of a normal population is based on the unbiased variance estimator S^2. As we observed in Section 15.5.2, the quantity

$$\chi^2 = \frac{(n-1)S^2}{\sigma^2}$$

has a chi-square distribution with $(n-1)$ degrees of freedom. Thus, to test a hypothesis concerning the variance of a normal population, the test statistic is

$$\chi^2 = \frac{(n-1)S^2}{\sigma_0^2} \qquad (16.2)$$

where σ_0^2 denotes the limiting value of σ^2 stated in the null hypothesis. Table 16.3 summarizes the decision rules for applying this statistic to conduct upper-tail, lower-tail, and two-tail tests.

Table 16.3 General Specifications for χ^2 Tests Concerning the Variance of a Normal Population

Test	Hypotheses	Decision Rule
Upper tail	$H_0: \sigma^2 \leq \sigma_0^2$ $H_1: \sigma > \sigma_0^2$	Reject H_0 if $\chi^2 \geq \chi_{n-1;\,1-\alpha}^2$; accept H_0 otherwise
Lower tail	$H_0: \sigma^2 \geq \sigma_0^2$ $H_1: \sigma^2 < \sigma_0^2$	Reject H_0 if $\chi^2 \leq \chi_{n-1;\,\alpha}^2$; accept H_0 otherwise
Two tail	$H_0: \sigma^2 = \sigma_0^2$ $H_1: \sigma^2 \neq \sigma_0^2$	Reject H_0 if $\chi^2 \leq \chi_{n-1;\,\alpha/2}^2$ or $\chi^2 \geq \chi_{n-1;\,1-\alpha/2}^2$; accept H_0 otherwise

$$\text{where} \quad \chi^2 = \frac{(n-1)S^2}{\sigma_0^2}$$

To illustrate the use of the chi-square to test a hypothesis concerning the variance of a normal population, let us return to the case of the consumer research agency, PSI. In addition to investigating the *mean* mileage of the population of Meadowlarks produced by Hermes, PSI is concerned with the car-to-car *variability* in gasoline consumption. Specifically, PSI feels that, if the consumer is expected to interpret the mean mileage as being a fairly representative figure, the standard deviation should not exceed 1 mile per gallon. Since the variance is simply the square of the standard deviation, this is equivalent to specifying that $\sigma^2 \leq 1$. Willing to accept the burden of proof that the Meadowlark population exceeds this specification, PSI formulates the following hypotheses:

$$H_0: \quad \sigma^2 \leq 1$$
$$H_1: \quad \sigma^2 > 1$$

For this test, PSI adopts its customary significance level of $\alpha_{max} = .10$. Referring to Table 16.3, the appropriate procedure is to conduct an upper-tail test and reject H_0 if $\chi^2 \geq \chi^2_{n-1;\, 1-\alpha}$. This test may be performed using the same data that were employed to test the hypothesis concerning the mean mileage. Recalling that those data were based on a sample of $n = 26$, the critical value is $\chi^2_{25;\, .90} = 34.382$, which is obtained from Table K (Appendix II).

Recalling that the sample yielded an unbiased variance estimate of $s^2 = 1.9906$, the value of chi-square computed from Formula (16.2) is

$$\chi^2 = \frac{(n-1)s^2}{\sigma^2_0} = \frac{25(1.9906)}{1} = 49.77$$

Since the computed chi-square of 49.77 is greater than the critical value of 34.382, PSI should reject the null hypothesis and conclude that the variance in mileage of the population of Meadowlarks exceeds one.

16.3 TESTING HYPOTHESES CONCERNING THE DIFFERENCE BETWEEN THE VARIANCES OF TWO NORMAL POPULATIONS

In the preceding section, we considered the problem of testing a hypothesis concerning the variance of a *single* population that is normally distributed. In this section we examine the procedure for testing a hypothesis concerning the difference between the variances of *two* normal populations. This procedure is based on a probability model called the F distribution.

16.3.1 The F Distribution

The F distribution is a probability density function named in honor of the eminent British statistician, Sir Ronald A. Fisher. Mathematically, the F distribution may be derived as the distribution of the ratio between two independent chi-square-distributed random variables, each of which is divided by its respective number of degrees of freedom. To clarify this definition, consider two independent random variables, W_1 and W_2. If W_1 has a chi-square distribution with ν_1 degrees of freedom, and W_2 has a chi-square distribution with ν_2 degrees of freedom, then the ratio

$$F = \frac{W_1/\nu_1}{W_2/\nu_2} \qquad (16.3)$$

is a random variable that has an F distribution. As a ratio between two independent chi-square variables, the F distribution has two parameters, ν_1 and ν_2, both of which are called degrees of freedom. Specifically, the first parameter, ν_1, denotes the degrees of freedom associated with the chi-square variable in the numerator, and the second parameter, ν_2, denotes the degrees of freedom associated with the chi-square variable in the denominator.

Like chi-square, the F distribution is a positively skewed density function that approaches zero as a lower limit, with an upper-tail extending toward infinity. As illustrated in Figure 16.1, the exact shape of the F distribution depends on the values of ν_1 and ν_2. We will use the symbol F_{ν_1,ν_2} to denote a random variable that has an F distribution with ν_1 degrees of freedom for the numerator and ν_2 degrees of freedom for the denominator.[1] For example, $F_{4,6}$ is a random variable that has the F distribution with 4 degrees of freedom for the numerator and 6 degrees of freedom for the denominator. The symbol $F_{\nu_1,\nu_2;\,\varphi}$ will be used to denote the φ fractile of the F distribution with ν_1 and ν_2 degrees of freedom. That is,

$$P(F_{\nu_1,\nu_2} \leq F_{\nu_1,\nu_2;\,\varphi}) = \varphi$$

Values of $F_{\nu_1,\nu_2;\,\varphi}$ for selected values of ν_1, ν_2, and φ are given in Table M (Appendix II). For instance, from this table we find that $F_{4,6;\,.90} = 3.18$. Thus, if a random variable has the F distribution with 4 degrees of freedom for the

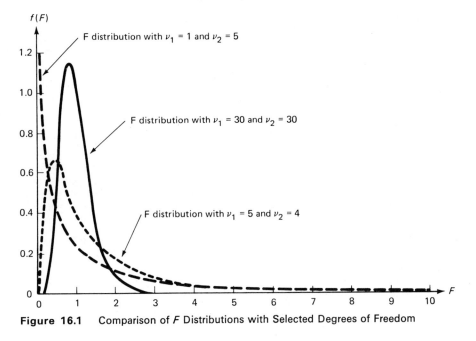

Figure 16.1   Comparison of F Distributions with Selected Degrees of Freedom

---

[1]In the special case of the F distribution, it is conventional to use the capital F to denote both the random variable and any specific value of the random variable.

numerator and 6 degrees of freedom for the denominator, there is a .90 probability that this random variable will have a value less than 3.18.

16.3.2 The Test Procedure

Consider two normal populations with unknown variances σ_1^2 and σ_2^2, respectively. To test a hypothesis concerning the difference between σ_1^2 and σ_2^2, a sample of n_1 observations is taken from population 1 and a sample of n_2 observations is taken from population 2. Then the estimators S_1^2 and S_2^2 may be used to estimate σ_1^2 and σ_2^2. Since both populations are normally distributed, the quantity

$$W_1 = \frac{(n_1 - 1)S_1^2}{\sigma_1^2}$$

has a chi-square distribution with $\nu_1 = (n_1 - 1)$ degrees of freedom, and the quantity

$$W_2 = \frac{(n_2 - 1)S_2^2}{\sigma_2^2}$$

has a chi-square distribution with $\nu_2 = (n_2 - 1)$ degrees of freedom. Then, substituting into Formula (16.3), we obtain

$$F = \frac{W_1/\nu_1}{W_2/\nu_2} = \frac{S_1^2/\sigma_1^2}{S_2^2/\sigma_2^2} \tag{16.4}$$

which has the F distribution with $(n_1 - 1)$ degrees of freedom for the numerator and $(n_2 - 1)$ degrees of freedom for the denominator.

If we assume that there is no difference between the variances of the two populations, so that $\sigma_1^2 = \sigma_2^2$, then Formula (16.4) reduces to

$$F = \frac{S_1^2}{S_2^2} \tag{16.5}$$

Thus, the simple ratio between S_1^2 and S_2^2, which has the F distribution with $(n_1 - 1)$ degrees of freedom for the numerator and $(n_2 - 1)$ degrees of freedom for the denominator, may be used as the statistic to test hypotheses concerning the difference between the variances of two normal populations. Depending on the form in which the null and alternative hypotheses are stated, this statistic may be used to perform an upper-tail, lower-tail, or two-tail test. The decision rules for these tests are summarized in Table 16.4.

To illustrate the use of the F distribution to test a hypothesis concerning the equality of the variances of two normal populations, let us consider again the case of Product Studies Institute, which has been investigating the mileage of Meadowlark cars produced by the Hermes Motorcar Corporation. Hermes also produces a model called the Centennial, to which PSI decides to extend its inquiry. Among the questions that PSI wishes to investigate is whether the variance in the mileage of Centennials differs from the variance in mileage of the Meadowlarks. If we arbitrarily designate the population of Centennials as population 1 and the population of Meadowlarks as population 2, then σ_1^2 represents the mileage variance of the Centennials and σ_2^2 represents the mile-

Table 16.4 General Specifications for F Tests Concerning the Relationship between the Variances of Two Normal Populations

Test	Hypotheses	Decision Rule
Upper tail	$H_0: \sigma_1^2 \leq \sigma_2^2$ $H_1: \sigma_1^2 > \sigma_2^2$	Reject H_0 if $F \geq F_{n_1-1, n_2-1; 1-\alpha}$; accept H_0 otherwise
Lower tail	$H_0: \sigma_1^2 \geq \sigma_2^2$ $H_1: \sigma_1^2 < \sigma_2^2$	Reject H_0 if $F \leq F_{n_1-1, n_2-1, \alpha}$; accept H_0 otherwise
Two tail	$H_0: \sigma_1^2 = \sigma_2^2$ $H_1: \sigma_1^2 \neq \sigma_2^2$	Reject H_0 if $F \leq F_{n_1-1, n_2-1; \alpha/2}$ or $F \geq F_{n_1-1, n_2-1; 1-\alpha/2}$; accept H_0 otherwise

$$\text{where} \quad F = \frac{S_1^2}{S_2^2}$$

age variance of the Meadowlarks. Using this notation, we may express PSI's question concerning the equality of variances in terms of the following hypotheses:

$$H_0: \quad \sigma_1^2 = \sigma_2^2$$
$$H_1: \quad \sigma_1^2 \neq \sigma_2^2$$

To investigate these hypotheses, PSI again secures the cooperation of the Atlas Insurance Company whose fleet of cars contains 21 Centennials in addition to the 26 Meadowlarks. Atlas agrees to gather mileage data on this sample of 21 Centennials under the same conditions as the data on the 26 Meadowlarks were obtained. PSI feels that it is reasonable to assume that the gasoline consumption of the Centennial population, as well as the Meadowlark population, is normally distributed. Thus, the F distribution is appropriate for conducting the hypothesis test in this situation. From the statement of the hypotheses, a two-tail test is indicated. Referring to Table 16.4, the decision rule is to reject H_0 if $F \leq F_{n_1-1, n_2-1; \alpha/2}$ or if $F \geq F_{n_1-1, n_2-1; 1-\alpha/2}$. Since there are 21 cars in the Centennial sample and 26 cars in the Meadowlark sample, $(n_1 - 1) = 20$ and $(n_2 - 1) = 25$. Adopting PSI's usual significance level of .10, the following critical values of F are obtained from Table M (Appendix II):

$$F_{n_1-1, n_2-1; \alpha/2} = F_{20, 25; .05} = .482$$
$$F_{n_1-1, n_2-1; 1-\alpha/2} = F_{20, 25; .95} = 2.01$$

Thus, the decision rule is to reject H_0 if the value of F obtained from the sample data is equal to or less than .482 or is equal to or greater than 2.01.

In order to apply Formula (16.5) to compute the value of F, it is first necessary to obtain the values of S_1^2 and S_2^2. To determine the value of S_1^2, PSI proceeds to collect the Centennial mileage data, which are shown in Table 16.5. As the reader may verify from these data, the unbiased estimates of the mean and variance of the Centennial population are

$$\bar{x}_1 = \frac{291.7}{21} = 13.890$$

$$s_1^2 = \frac{36.2381}{20} = 1.8119$$

Table 16.5 Gasoline Consumption in Miles per Gallon for a Sample of 21 Centennial Cars

13.7	10.2	13.8
12.3	14.2	13.6
14.7	16.7	14.5
13.5	15.1	13.4
14.9	15.2	14.5
14.1	12.8	13.7
14.7	14.2	11.9

As previously determined in Section 16.1, the unbiased estimates of the mean and variance of the Meadowlark population are

$$\bar{x}_2 = 14.023$$
$$s_2^2 = 1.9906$$

Then, using Formula (16.5), we obtain

$$F = \frac{S_1^2}{S_2^2} = \frac{1.8119}{1.9906} = .91$$

Since the obtained F-value lies between .482 and 2.01, the null hypothesis is not rejected. Thus, PSI may conclude that the variance in the mileage of the Centennial population does not differ from the variance in the mileage of the Meadowlark population.

16.4 TESTS CONCERNING THE DIFFERENCE BETWEEN THE MEANS OF TWO NORMAL POPULATIONS

In Section 13.3 we presented a procedure for testing a hypothesis concerning the difference between the means of two populations whose variances are known. The test procedure developed in that section is based on the statistic D, which is the difference between the two *sample* means $\bar{X}_1$ and $\bar{X}_2$. As given in Formula (13.7), the expected value of D is equal to δ, which is the difference between the two *population* means μ_1 and μ_2. Also, as stated in Formula (13.8), the standard error of D is

$$\sigma_D = \sqrt{\frac{\sigma_1^2}{n_1} + \frac{\sigma_2^2}{n_2}}$$

where σ_1^2 and σ_2^2 are the variances of the two populations. Then, if the two populations under investigation are normal, the sampling distribution of D is normal with mean δ and standard deviation σ_D. Thus, the quantity

$$Z = \frac{D - \delta}{\sigma_D} \tag{16.6}$$

has the standard normal distribution. Of course, if the two population variances are unknown, σ_D cannot be computed, since Formula (13.8) requires that σ_1^2 and σ_2^2 be known. As we will see, it is possible to estimate σ_D from the sample data. However, if an estimator S_D is substituted for σ_D in Formula (16.6), the quantity

$$\frac{D - \delta}{S_D}$$

is no longer normally distributed. The particular distribution of this quantity depends on how S_D is obtained. In turn, the particular way that S_D is obtained depends on whether or not the two samples are selected *independently* of each other.

16.4.1 Tests Using Independent Samples

If a first sample is selected from one population and a second sample is selected from a different population, the two samples are said to be independent if they are selected in such a way that the selection of the sample elements from one population has no influence on the selection of the sample elements from the other population. When independent samples are used to test a hypothesis concerning the difference between the means of two normal populations, the choice of the particular test statistic depends on whether or not the two populations have equal variances.

Equal Population Variances. A preliminary step in testing a hypothesis concerning the difference between the means of two normal populations is to determine whether it is reasonable to assume that the two populations have equal variances. This may be accomplished by testing the null hypothesis $H_0 : \sigma_1^2 = \sigma_2^2$, using the F test described in Section 16.3. If this null hypothesis is not rejected, then the assumption of equal population variances is considered to be justified.

Under the assumption of equal variances, we may denote this common variance by σ^2. Then, since $\sigma_1^2 = \sigma_2^2 = \sigma^2$, Formula (13.8) becomes

$$\sigma_D = \sqrt{\frac{\sigma^2}{n_1} + \frac{\sigma^2}{n_2}} = \sigma \sqrt{\frac{1}{n_1} + \frac{1}{n_2}} \tag{16.7}$$

In order to use this formula to compute σ_D, it is necessary to know the value of σ. However, if σ is unknown, it is possible to estimate σ_D by obtaining an appropriate estimate of σ. To obtain this estimate, we first observe that each of the two sample statistics, S_1^2 and S_2^2, is an independent unbiased estimator of the common variance σ^2. This fact allows us to combine S_1^2 and S_2^2 to obtain the following estimator of σ^2.

$$S_p^2 = \frac{(n_1 - 1)\, S_1^2 + (n_2 - 1)S_2^2}{n_1 + n_2 - 2} \tag{16.8}$$

where S_p^2 denotes the *pooled* estimator of the common variance σ^2. It then follows that

$$S_p = \sqrt{\frac{(n_1 - 1)S_1^2 + (n_2 - 1)S_2^2}{n_1 + n_2 - 2}} \tag{16.9}$$

Substituting S_p for σ in Formula (16.7), we obtain the following estimator of σ_D:

$$S_D = S_p\sqrt{\frac{1}{n_1} + \frac{1}{n_2}} \qquad (16.10)$$

It may be demonstrated mathematically that, when s_D is substituted for σ_D in Formula (16.6), the resulting quantity

$$t = \frac{D - \delta}{S_D}$$

has Student's t distribution with $(n_1 + n_2 - 2)$ degrees of freedom. Thus, under the assumption of equal population variances, a hypothesis concerning the difference between the means of two normal populations may be tested by using the t statistic

$$t = \frac{D - \delta_0}{S_D} \qquad (16.11)$$

where δ_0 denotes the limiting value of δ stated in the null hypothesis. Depending on the particular way in which the null and alternative hypotheses are specified, this statistic may be used for an upper-tail, lower-tail, or two-tail test. The decision rules for these tests are summarized in Table 16.6.

Table 16.6 General Specifications for Exact t Tests Concerning the Difference between Means of Two Normal Populations with Equal Variances

Test	Hypotheses	Decision Rule
Upper tail	$H_0: \delta \leq \delta_0$ $H_1: \delta > \delta_0$	Reject H_0 if $t \geq t_{v;\, 1-\alpha}$; accept H_0 otherwise
Lower tail	$H_0: \delta \geq \delta_0$ $H_1: \delta < \delta_0$	Reject H_0 if $t \leq t_{v;\, \alpha}$; accept H_0 otherwise
Two tail	$H_0: \delta = \delta_0$ $H_1: \delta \neq \delta_0$	Reject H_0 if $t \leq t_{v;\, \alpha/2}$ or $t \geq t_{v;\, 1-\alpha/2}$; accept H_0 otherwise

$$\text{where} \quad t = \frac{D - \delta_0}{S_D} \qquad D = \bar{X}_1 - \bar{X}_2 \qquad S_D = S_p\sqrt{\frac{1}{n_1} + \frac{1}{n_2}}$$

$$S_p = \sqrt{\frac{(n_1 - 1)S_1^2 + (n_2 - 1)S_2^2}{n_1 + n_2 - 2}} \qquad v = n_1 + n_2 - 2$$

To illustrate the use of the t distribution for testing a hypothesis concerning the difference between the means of two normal populations with equal variances, let us continue with the case of the PSI investigation of the mileage of Hermes automobiles. Now suppose that PSI wishes to determine whether any difference in mean mileage exists between Centennials and Meadowlarks. Using μ_1 to denote the mean mileage of the Centennial population and μ_2 to denote the mean mileage of the Meadowlark population, the difference between these two means is $\delta = \mu_1 - \mu_2$. Then the null and alternative hypotheses may be specified formally as

$$H_0: \quad \delta = 0$$
$$H_1: \quad \delta \neq 0$$

On the basis of the F test performed in Section 16.3, it is reasonable to assume that the variances of the two populations of cars are equal. Thus the test statistic defined by Formula (16.11) is applicable in this situation. Referring to Table 16.6, the decision rule is to reject H_0 if $t \leq t_{v;\,\alpha/2}$ or if $t \geq t_{v;\,1-\alpha/2}$. Recalling that $n_1 = 21$ and $n_2 = 26$, we obtain $v = n_1 + n_2 - 2 = 45$. Using PSI's usual significance level of .10, the critical values of t are obtained by interpolation from Table L:

$$t_{v,\,\alpha/2} = t_{45;\,.05} = -1.681$$
$$t_{v;\,1-\alpha/2} = t_{45;\,.95} = 1.681$$

Thus, the decision rule is to reject H_0 if the value of t obtained from the sample data is equal to or less than -1.681 or is equal to or greater than 1.681.

In order to apply Formula (16.11) to compute the value of t from the sample data, it is first necessary to recall from Section 16.3 that

$$\bar{x}_1 = 13.890 \qquad \bar{x}_2 = 14.023$$
$$s_1^2 = 1.8119 \qquad s_2^2 = 1.9906$$

Applying Formula (16.9), the pooled estimate of σ is

$$s_p = \sqrt{\frac{(21-1)(1.8119) + (26-1)(1.9906)}{21 + 26 - 2}} = \sqrt{1.9112} = 1.3825$$

Then, from Formula (16.10), the estimate of σ_D is

$$S_D = 1.3825\sqrt{\frac{1}{21} + \frac{1}{26}} = 1.3825(.293) = .405$$

The difference between the two sample means is

$$d = \bar{x}_1 - \bar{x}_2 = 13.890 - 14.023 = -.133$$

Thus, Formula (16.11) yields

$$t = \frac{-1.33 - 0}{.405} = -.328$$

Since this computed t-value lies between -1.681 and 1.681, the null hypothesis is not rejected. Hence, PSI may conclude that the mean mileage of the Centennial population does not differ from the mean mileage of the Meadowlark population.

Unequal Population Variances. If the F test described in Section 16.3 leads to rejection of the null hypothesis H_0: $\sigma_1^2 = \sigma_2^2$, then the assumption of equal population variances is not justified. In such a case, the procedures summarized in Table 16.6 are not applicable.

If the variances of the two populations are unequal, it is possible to estimate σ_D by substituting the unbiased estimators S_1^2 and S_2^2 for σ_1^2 and σ_2^2 in Formula (13.8). Then the estimator of σ_D is

$$S_D = \sqrt{\frac{S_1^2}{n_1} + \frac{S_2^2}{n_2}} \qquad (16.12)$$

If this estimator is used in Formula (16.11), the resulting quantity is distributed *approximately* as Student's t with ν degrees of freedom, where the value of ν must be computed from the sample data according to the formula

$$\nu = \frac{(s_1^2/n_1 + s_2^2/n_2)^2}{\frac{(s_1^2/n_1)^2}{n_1} + \frac{(s_2^2/n_2)^2}{n_2}} \tag{16.13}$$

Usually, the numerical value yielded by Formula (16.13) will not be an integer. In such a case, the practice is to round the obtained value to the nearest integer.

To test a hypothesis concerning the difference between the means of two normal populations with unequal variances, the test statistic is

$$t = \frac{D - \delta_0}{S_D} \tag{16.14}$$

which is distributed approximately as Student's t with ν degrees of freedom as defined by Formula (16.13). Depending on the form in which the null and alternative hypotheses are stated, Formula (16.14) may be used to conduct an upper-tail, lower-tail, or two-tail test. The decision rules for conducting these tests are summarized in Table 16.7.

Table 16.7 General Specifications for Approximate t Tests Concerning the Difference between Means of Two Normal Populations with Unequal Variances

Test	Hypotheses	Decision Rule
Upper tail	$H_0:\ \delta \le \delta_0$ $H_1:\ \delta > \delta_0$	Reject H_0 if $t \ge t_{\nu;\,1-\alpha}$; accept H_0 otherwise
Lower tail	$H_1:\ \delta \ge \delta_0$ $H_0:\ \delta < \delta_0$	Reject H_0 if $t \le t_{\nu;\,\alpha}$; accept H_0 otherwise
Two tail	$H_0:\ \delta = \delta_0$ $H_1:\ \delta \ne \delta_0$	Reject H_0 if $t \le t_{\nu;\,\alpha/2}$ or $t \ge t_{\nu;\,1-\alpha/2}$; accept H_0 otherwise

where $\quad t = \dfrac{D - \delta_0}{S_D} \qquad D = \bar{X}_1 - \bar{X}_2 \qquad S_D = \sqrt{\dfrac{S_1^2}{n_1} + \dfrac{S_2^2}{n_2}}$

$$\nu = \frac{(s_1^2/n_1 + s_2^2/n^2)^2}{\frac{(s_1^2/n_1)^2}{n_1} + \frac{(s_2^2/n_2)^2}{n_2}}$$

16.4.2 Test Using Paired Observations

In Section 16.4.1 we considered methods of testing hypotheses concerning differences between population means using independently selected samples. Many situations arise, however, in which it is experimentally advantageous to *pair* the observations rather than to select the two samples independently. One form of this pairing procedure is the familiar "before and after" type of experiment, in which a single group of cases is observed first under one condition and then under another condition. In other words, the same cases are observed twice, yielding a set of paired observations. Another form of pairing involves the use of two different samples such that each member of one sample is paired with a corresponding member of the other sample on the basis of some characteristic that is related to the characteristic to be observed. For example, suppose that a training director wishes to conduct an experiment to compare two alternative methods of training clerks. He plans to train one sample of 15 clerks using method A and another sample of 15 clerks using method B. Since the amount of previous formal education is likely to affect a trainee's level of achievement, he can remove this effect by pairing the trainees in the two samples on the basis of number of years of prior schooling. That is, for each trainee in sample A, there will be a corresponding trainee in sample B who has the same number of years of previous formal education.

When either of the pairing procedures described above is used, it is possible to apply a more powerful test than the tests that are applied to data obtained from two independent samples. Among its advantages, this pairing approach does *not* require the assumption of equal variances, so that it is unnecessary to conduct the F test for variances preliminary to conducting the test of the difference between means.

To develop the procedure for using paired observations to test a hypothesis concerning the difference between the means of two normal populations, consider a pair of observations, X_{i1} and X_{i2}, where X_{i1} denotes the ith observation in sample 1 and X_{i2} denotes the corresponding (paired) observation in sample 2. Then

$$Y_i = X_{i1} - X_{i2} \qquad (16.15)$$

denotes the difference between the ith pair of observations. For n pairs of sample observations, there will be n differences, and the mean of these differences is given by

$$\bar{D} = \frac{\sum\limits_{i=1}^{n} Y_i}{n} \qquad (16.16)$$

It may be demonstrated that

$$\bar{D} = \bar{X}_1 - \bar{X}_2 \qquad (16.17)$$

where $\bar{X}_1$ = mean of sample 1
$\bar{X}_2$ = mean of sample 2

Expressed in words, the sample mean of the paired differences is equal to the difference between the means of the two samples.

The unbiased estimator of the variance of the population[2] of differences is given by

$$S_Y^2 = \frac{\sum\limits_{i=1}^{n} (Y_i - \bar{D})^2}{n - 1} \qquad (16.18)$$

Then the estimator of the standard deviation of the sampling distribution of the mean difference between paired observations is

$$S_{\bar{D}} = \sqrt{\frac{S_Y^2}{n}} = \frac{S_Y}{\sqrt{n}} \qquad (16.19)$$

---

[2]In this development, it is necessary to conceptualize a single population composed of differences between paired elements, rather than two separate populations.

Using δ to denote the difference between the means of the two populations under investigation (i.e., $\delta = \mu_1 - \mu_2$), it may be demonstrated that $E(\bar{D}) = \delta$. Thus, if the population of paired differences is normal (which will be true if the two populations are normal), the test statistic

$$t = \frac{\bar{D} - \delta_0}{S_{\bar{D}}}$$

(16.20)

will have a t distribution with $(n - 1)$ degrees of freedom, where n denotes the number of pairs of sample observations. Decision rules for conducting upper-tail, lower-tail, and two-tail tests using the statistic defined by Formula (16.20) are summarized in Table 16.8.

Table 16.8 General Specification for t Tests Concerning the Difference between Means of Two Normal Populations Using Paired Observations

Test	Hypotheses	Decision Rule
Upper tail	$H_0: \delta \leq \delta_0$ $H_1: \delta > \delta_0$	Reject H_0 if $t \geq t_{v;\,1-\alpha}$; accept H_0 otherwise
Lower tail	$H_0: \delta \geq \delta_0$ $H_1: \delta < \delta_0$	Reject H_0 if $t \leq t_{v;\,\alpha}$; accept H_0 otherwise
Two tail	$H_0: \delta = \delta_0$ $H_1: \delta \neq \delta_0$	Reject H_0 if $t \leq t_{v;\,\alpha/2}$ or $t \geq t_{v;\,1-\alpha/2}$; accept H_0 otherwise

$$\text{where} \quad t = \frac{\bar{D} - \delta_0}{S_{\bar{D}}} \qquad \bar{D} = \frac{\sum_{i=1}^{n} Y_i}{n} \qquad S_{\bar{D}} = \sqrt{\frac{S_Y^2}{n}}$$

$$S_Y^2 = \frac{\sum_{i=1}^{n} (Y_i - \bar{D})^2}{n - 1} \qquad\qquad \nu = n - 1$$

To illustrate the use of t test with paired observations, we return once more to PSI's investigation of the mileage of Hermes automobiles. One of the items in Hermes' line of accessories is Pow, a gasoline additive that Hermes claims should increase the mileage of Centennials by more than 1.20 miles per gallon on the average. PSI wishes to conduct an experiment to test this claim. Using μ_1 to denote the mean mileage of the Centennial population when Pow is used, and μ_2 to denote the mean mileage of the Centennial population when Pow is not used, the difference between these two means is $\delta = \mu_1 - \mu_2$. Then the null and alternative hypotheses for testing Hermes' claim may be expressed as

$$H_0: \quad \delta \leq 1.20$$
$$H_1: \quad \delta > 1.20$$

Notice that this statement of the hypotheses places the "burden of proof" on Hermes' claim.

To conduct the experiment, PSI arranges to use the same sample of 21 Centennials that were used in their earlier study comparing the mileage of Centennials with the mileage of Meadowlarks. Since the mileage data without Pow have already been obtained for this sample, the only additional sample data required are the corresponding mileages for the same cars with Pow added to their gas tanks. Thus, for each of the 21 cars, there will be a pair of observations—the mileage with Pow (X_{i1}) and the mileage without Pow (X_{i2}). Hence, the test statistic defined by Formula (16.20) is applicable. Referring to Table 16.8, the decision rule is to reject H_0 if $t \geq t_{v;\,1-\alpha}$. Since there will be 21 pairs of observations, the appropriate number of degrees of freedom is $v = n - 1 = 21 - 1 = 20$. Adopting PSI's customary significance level of .10, the critical value of t obtained from Table L is

$$t_{v;\,1-\alpha} = t_{20;\,.90} = 1.325$$

Thus, the decision rule is to reject H_0 if the sample value of t obtained from Formula (16.20) is equal to or greater than 1.325.

Having specified the experimental procedure and decision rule, PSI proceeds to collect and organize the sample data, as shown in Table 16.9. Column (1)

Table 16.9   Calculation of the Unbiased Estimate of the Variance of the Population of Paired Differences

(1) x_{i1} (with Pow)	(2) x_{i2} (without Pow)	(3) y_i $(x_{i1} - x_{i2})$	(4) $(y_i - \bar{d})^2$
15.5	13.7	1.8	.25
13.7	12.3	1.4	.01
17.5	14.7	2.8	2.25
15.8	13.5	2.3	1.00
17.6	14.9	2.7	1.96
16.3	14.1	2.2	.81
17.2	14.7	2.5	1.44
10.0	10.2	−.2	2.25
14.8	14.2	.6	.49
19.4	16.7	2.7	1.96
15.9	15.1	.8	.25
15.1	15.2	−.1	1.96
13.1	12.8	.3	1.00
15.5	14.2	1.3	0.00
15.9	13.8	2.1	.64
13.1	13.6	−.5	3.24
15.7	14.5	1.2	.01
13.4	13.4	0	1.69
16.8	14.5	2.3	1.00
15.3	13.7	1.6	.09
11.4	11.9	−.5	3.24
$\sum x_{i1} = 319.0$	$\sum x_{i2} = 291.7$	$\sum y_i = 27.3$	$\sum (y_i - \bar{d})^2 = 25.54$

$$\bar{x}_1 = \frac{319.0}{21} \qquad \bar{x}_2 = \frac{291.7}{21} \qquad \bar{d} = \frac{27.3}{21} \qquad s_Y^2 = \frac{25.54}{21-1}$$

$$= 15.19 \qquad\qquad = 13.89 \qquad\qquad = 1.30 \qquad\qquad = 1.277$$

of this table gives the mileage of each car with Pow added to the gas tank. Column (2) gives the corresponding mileage of each car without Pow. Notice that the mean mileage of the sample with Pow is $\bar{x}_1 = 15.19$, and the mean mileage without Pow is $\bar{x}_2 = 13.89$. The differences between the paired mileages appear in column (3). Applying Formula (16.16), the mean of these differences is

$$\bar{d} = \frac{\sum\limits_{i=1}^{n} y_i}{n} = \frac{27.3}{21} = 1.30$$

This same result may be obtained from Formula (16.17):

$$\bar{d} = \bar{x}_1 - \bar{x}_2 = 15.19 - 13.89 = 1.30$$

This demonstrates that the mean of the paired differences in the sample is equal to the difference between the two sample means.

In order to apply Formula (16.18) to calculate s_Y^2, the unbiased estimate of the variance of the population of differences, it is first necessary to compute the squared deviation of each paired difference in the sample from the mean of the differences. These squared deviations are shown in column (4) of Table 16.9. As the table shows, the sum of the squared deviations is 25.54. Substituting this sum into Formula (16.18), we obtain

$$s_Y^2 = \frac{\sum\limits_{i=1}^{n} (y_i - \bar{d})^2}{n - 1} = \frac{25.54}{20} = 1.277$$

Then, applying Formula (16.19), the estimate of the standard deviation of the sampling distribution of the mean difference is

$$s_{\bar{D}} = \sqrt{\frac{s_Y^2}{n}} = \sqrt{\frac{1.277}{21}} = \sqrt{.0608} = .2466$$

Finally, applying Formula (16.20), the value of t obtained from the sample is

$$t = \frac{\bar{d} - \delta_0}{s_{\bar{D}}} = \frac{1.30 - 1.20}{.2466} = .406$$

Since this computed t-value of .406 is less than the critical t-value of 1.325, there is not sufficient evidence to reject H_0. In other words, the sample evidence is not sufficient for PSI to accept Hermes' claim.

16.5 INTRODUCTION TO ANALYSIS OF VARIANCE

The procedures summarized in Table 16.6 use the t distribution to test hypotheses concerning the differences between the means of two normal populations with equal variances. Frequently, however, the question arises concerning whether any differences exist among the means of several populations. For instance, an industrial experimenter who is investigating several (say J) populations might wish to test the null hypothesis

$$H_0: \quad \mu_1 = \mu_2 = \cdots = \mu_J$$

against the alternative hypothesis

$$H_1: \quad \mu_1, \mu_2, \ldots, \text{and } \mu_J \text{ are not all equal}$$

That is, the null hypothesis states that the means of the J populations are all equal, whereas the alternative hypothesis states that at least two of the means differ from each other. If all of the populations are *normal with equal variances*, the test of the hypothesis concerning the several means may be performed by a statistical technique called the *analysis of variance* (ANOVA).

It should be emphasized that the application of ANOVA to test the hypothesis of the equality of means of several populations requires the assumption of equal variances. This assumption of *homogeneity of variances* may be checked by testing the null hypothesis

$$H_0: \quad \sigma_1^2 = \sigma_2^2 = \cdots = \sigma_J^2$$

against the alternative hypothesis

$$H_1: \quad \sigma_1^2, \sigma_2^2, \ldots, \text{and } \sigma_J^2 \text{ are not all equal}$$

When there are only two populations under investigation (i.e., when $J = 2$), the test of homogeneity of variances may be performed by the F test described in Section 16.3. When there are more than two populations under investigation (i.e., when $J > 2$), the test of homogeneity of variances may be performed by any one of several statistical procedures, such as Bartlett's test,[3] Cochran's test,[4] or Hartley's test.[5] Because of their complexity, these tests will not be presented here. However, in actual practice, it should be borne in mind that one of these tests should be applied before proceeding with the ANOVA test of the equality of means. If the hypothesis of homogeneity of variances is rejected, the ANOVA test described in this section is not applicable.

To understand the ANOVA procedure, suppose that several populations are under investigation, and the investigator wishes to test the hypothesis that the means of these populations are all equal. For this purpose a random sample of n_1 observations is taken from population 1, a sample of n_2 observations is taken from population 2, and so on. If n_j denotes the size of the sample taken from population j, then the size of all samples combined is

$$n = \sum_{j=1}^{J} n_j \tag{16.21}$$

where J is the total number of populations under investigation.

Using x_{ij} to denote the ith observation in the sample taken from the jth population, the mean of the jth sample is

$$\bar{X}_j = \frac{\sum_{i=1}^{n_j} X_{ij}}{n_j} \tag{16.22}$$

---

[3] M. S. Bartlett, "Some Examples of Statistical Methods of Research in Agriculture and Applied Biology," *Supplement to the Journal of the Royal Statistical Society*, Vol. 4 (1937), pp. 137–183.

[4] W. G. Cochran, "The Distribution of the Largest of a Set of Estimated Variances as a Fraction of Their Total," *Annals of Eugenics*, Vol. 11 (1941), pp. 47–52.

[5] H. O. Hartley, "The Maximum F-ratio as a Short-cut Test for Heterogeneity of Variance," *Biometrika*, Vol. 37 (1950), pp. 308–312.

Then the grand mean, $\overline{\overline{X}}$, of all the observations combined is

$$\overline{\overline{X}} = \frac{\sum\limits_{j=1}^{J} \sum\limits_{i=1}^{n_j} X_{ij}}{n} \tag{16.23}$$

This grand mean can be shown to be the weighted mean of the several sample means, where each sample mean is weighted by its respective sample size. That is,

$$\overline{\overline{X}} = \frac{\sum\limits_{j=1}^{J} n_j \overline{X}_j}{n} \tag{16.24}$$

The total sum of squares of the deviations of all the individual observations in the J samples from their grand mean may be expressed as

$$\text{SST} = \sum\limits_{j=1}^{J} \sum\limits_{i=1}^{n_j} (X_{ij} - \overline{\overline{X}})^2 \tag{16.25}$$

Within any particular sample (say sample j), the sum of squared of the deviations of the individual observations from the mean of that sample is

$$\text{SSW}_j = \sum\limits_{i=1}^{n_j} (X_{ij} - \overline{X}_j)^2 \tag{16.26}$$

Then the pooled sum of squares within samples is given by

$$\text{SSW} = \sum\limits_{j=1}^{J} \text{SSW}_j = \sum\limits_{j=1}^{J} \sum\limits_{i=1}^{n_j} (X_{ij} - \overline{X}_j)^2 \tag{16.27}$$

The square of the difference *between* the mean of the jth sample and the grand mean may be expressed as

$$\text{SB}_j = (\overline{X}_j - \overline{\overline{X}})^2 \tag{16.28}$$

Weighting each of these squared deviations by its corresponding sample size n_j, the sum of squares between means is

$$\text{SSB} = \sum\limits_{j=1}^{J} n_j \, \text{SB}_j = \sum\limits_{j=1}^{J} n_j (\overline{X}_j - \overline{\overline{X}})^2 \tag{16.29}$$

It may be demonstrated that the total sum of squares is equal to the "between" sum of squares plus the "within" sum of squares. That is,

$$\text{SST} = \text{SSB} + \text{SSW} \tag{16.30}$$

Each of the sums of squares in Formula (16.30) is a measure of *variation*. Specifically,

SST measures the variation among the individual observations in all the samples combined.

SSB measures the variation among the means of the several samples.

SSW measures the pooled variation among the individual observations within each of the several samples.

The basic idea underlying the ANOVA procedure is that, if the null hypothesis of equality of population means is true, then the SSB computed from the sample data should be relatively small. Thus, the null hypothesis should be rejected only if SSB is relatively large. To determine if SSB is sufficiently large to reject the null hypothesis, we must examine the sampling distributions of SSB and SSW. It turns out that, if each of the J populations is normal and the assumption of homogeneity of variances is correct, then SSB has a chi-square distribution with $(J - 1)$ degrees of freedom, and SSW has a chi-square distribution with $(n - J)$ degrees of freedom. Therefore, by virtue of Formula (16.3), the ratio

$$F = \frac{SSB/(J - 1)}{SSW/(n - J)} \tag{16.31}$$

is a random variable which has an F distribution with $(J - 1)$ degrees of freedom for the numerator and $(n - J)$ degrees of freedom for the denominator. The numerator in Formula (16.31) is called the *mean square between* (MSB) and the denominator is called the *mean square within* (MSW). Thus, Formula (16.31) may be expressed in the alternative form

$$F = \frac{MSB}{MSW} \tag{16.32}$$

This ratio between MSB and MSW provides the test statistic for testing the hypothesis of equality of two or more means. Using this test statistic, the null hypothesis should be rejected if the F-value computed from the sample data is equal to or greater than the critical value $F_{v_1, v_2; 1-\alpha}$, where $v_1 = J - 1$ and $v_2 = n - J$. The general ANOVA procedure for calculating the F ratio given by Formula (16.32) is summarized in Table 16.10.

Table 16.10 ANOVA Summary Table

Source of Variation	Sum of Squares	Degrees of Freedom	Mean Square	F
Between	SSB	$J - 1$	MSB = SSB/$(J - 1)$	MSB/MSW
Within	SSW	$n - J$	MSW = SSW/$(n - J)$	
Total	SST	$n - 1$		

To illustrate the application of ANOVA for testing the hypothesis of equality of several means, consider a pharmaceutical laboratory that is conducting experiments with three different heart stimulants. The purpose of the experiment is to determine whether these three drugs all produce the same mean amount of increase in pulse rate. Specifically, if μ_i denotes the mean increase produced by the ith drug, the laboratory wishes to test the null hypothesis

$$H_0: \quad \mu_1 = \mu_2 = \mu_3$$

against the alternative hypothesis

$$H_1: \quad \mu_1, \mu_2, \text{ and } \mu_3 \text{ are not all equal}$$

On the basis of past experience in experimenting with such drugs, the laboratory believes that the distributions of pulse rate increases produced by these drugs should be approximately normal. Thus, assuming that the variances of the three distributions are equal,[6] the ANOVA procedure is appropriate for conducting the hypothesis test. To obtain the data for performing the ANOVA, the laboratory administers drug 1 to a sample of 4 patients, drug 2 to a sample of 3 patients, and drug 3 to a sample of 5 patients. Since there are three drugs (populations) under investigation, $J = 3$. Also, since $n_1 = 4$, $n_2 = 3$, and $n_3 = 5$, the total number of sample observations is $n = 12$. Thus, the number of degrees of freedom associated with SSB is $v_1 = J - 1 = 2$, and the number of degrees of freedom associated with SSW is $v_2 = n - J = 9$. Therefore, the test statistic has an F distribution with 2 degrees of freedom for the numerator and 9 degrees of freedom for the denominator. Adopting a significance level of .05, the critical value of F is found from Table M to be

$$F_{v_1, v_2; 1-\alpha} = F_{2,9; .95} = 4.26$$

Hence, the decision rule is to reject H_0 if the value of F obtained from the sample data is equal to or greater than 4.26.

The increases in pulse rate obtained from the individual patients in the three samples are as follows:

Sample 1: 8, 7, 11, 6
Sample 2: 6, 4, 8
Sample 3: 11, 16, 10, 15, 18

Calculations of the mean increase for each of these samples and the mean increase for the three samples combined are shown in Table 16.11. The means

Table 16.11 Calculation of Means

X_{i1}	X_{i2}	X_{i3}
8	6	11
7	4	16
11	8	10
6		15
		18

$$\sum_{i=1}^{n_1} X_{i1} = 32 \qquad \sum_{i=1}^{n_2} X_{i2} = 18 \qquad \sum_{i=1}^{n_3} X_{i3} = 70$$

$$n_1 = 4 \qquad\qquad n_2 = 3 \qquad\qquad n_3 = 5$$

$$\bar{x}_1 = \frac{32}{4} = 8 \qquad \bar{x}_2 = \frac{18}{3} = 6 \qquad \bar{x}_3 = \frac{70}{5} = 14$$

$$n = \sum_{j=1}^{3} n_j = n_1 + n_2 + n_3 = 4 + 3 + 5 = 12$$

$$\bar{\bar{x}} = \frac{\sum_{j=1}^{J} \sum_{i=1}^{n_j} X_{ij}}{n} = \frac{\sum_{i=1}^{n_1} X_{i1} + \sum_{i=1}^{n_2} X_{i2} + \sum_{i=1}^{n_3} X_{i3}}{n} = \frac{32 + 18 + 70}{12} = 10$$

---

[6]Of course, this assumption of homogeneity of variances should be tested once the sample data are obtained.

of the separate samples are computed from Formula (16.22), and the grand mean is computed from Formula (16.23).

For *each* of the separate samples, Table 16.12 shows the calculation of (1)

Table 16.12   Calculation of Sums of Squares for the Three Samples

(a)   For sample 1:

x_{i1}	$(x_{i1} - \bar{x}_1)^2$	$(x_{i1} - \bar{\bar{x}})^2$
8	$(8 - 8)^2 = 0$	$(8 - 10)^2 = 4$
7	$(7 - 8)^2 = 1$	$(7 - 10)^2 = 9$
11	$(11 - 8)^2 = 9$	$(11 - 10)^2 = 1$
6	$(6 - 8)^2 = 4$	$(6 - 10)^2 = 16$
	$\sum_{i=1}^{4}(x_{i1} - \bar{x}_1)^2 = 14$	$\sum_{i=1}^{4}(x_{i1} - \bar{\bar{x}})^2 = 30$

(b)   For sample 2:

x_{i2}	$(x_{i2} - \bar{x}_2)^2$	$(x_{i2} - \bar{\bar{x}})^2$
6	$(6 - 6)^2 = 0$	$(6 - 10)^2 = 16$
4	$(4 - 6)^2 = 4$	$(4 - 10)^2 = 36$
8	$(8 - 6)^2 = 4$	$(8 - 10)^2 = 4$
	$\sum_{i=1}^{3}(x_{i2} - \bar{x}_2)^2 = 8$	$\sum_{i=1}^{3}(x_{i2} - \bar{\bar{x}})^2 = 56$

(c)   For sample 3:

x_{i3}	$(x_{i3} - \bar{x}_3)^2$	$(x_{i3} - \bar{\bar{x}})^2$
11	$(11 - 14)^2 = 9$	$(11 - 10)^2 = 1$
16	$(16 - 14)^2 = 4$	$(16 - 10)^2 = 36$
10	$(10 - 14)^2 = 16$	$(10 - 10)^2 = 0$
15	$(15 - 14)^2 = 1$	$(15 - 10)^2 = 25$
18	$(18 - 14)^2 = 16$	$(18 - 10)^2 = 64$
	$\sum_{i=1}^{5}(x_{i3} - \bar{x}_3)^2 = 46$	$\sum_{i=1}^{5}(x_{i3} - \bar{\bar{x}})^2 = 126$

the sum of squares of the individual observations from the *mean of that sample*, and (2) the sum of squares of the individual observations from the *grand mean* of the three samples combined. Combining the sums of squares obtained in Table 16.12, calculations of SSW, SST, and SSB are presented in Table 16.13.

Using the sums of squares obtained in Table 16.13, calculation of the test statistic defined by Formula (16.32) is shown in Table 16.14. Since the computed F-value of 9.52 is greater than the critical F-value of 4.26, the null hypothesis is rejected. Accordingly, the laboratory may conclude that not all three drugs produce equal mean increases in pulse rate.

The ANOVA procedure presented in this section is limited to experiments in which only a single variable or characteristic is investigated. In our example, this variable was increase in pulse rate. This particular procedure is called *one-way analysis of variance*. There are more complex ANOVA procedures that are used to deal with experimental situations in which two or more variables are investigated simultaneously. For instance, in our example, the pharmaceutical laboratory could have simultaneously observed increases in pulse rate and changes in systolic blood pressure. These more complex ANOVA procedures are topics for advanced texts.

Table 16.13 Calculation of Sums of Squares for the Pooled Samples

From Formula (16.27):

$$SSW = \sum_{j=1}^{J} \sum_{i=1}^{n_j} (x_{ij} - \bar{x}_j)^2$$

$$= \sum_{i=1}^{n_1} (x_{i1} - \bar{x}_1)^2 + \sum_{i=1}^{n_2} (x_{i2} - \bar{x}_2)^2 + \sum_{i=1}^{n_3} (x_{i3} - \bar{x}_3)^2$$

$$= 14 + 8 + 46 = 68$$

From Formula (16.25):

$$SST = \sum_{j=1}^{J} \sum_{i=1}^{n_j} (x_{ij} - \bar{\bar{x}})^2$$

$$= \sum_{i=1}^{n_1} (x_{i1} - \bar{\bar{x}})^2 + \sum_{i=1}^{n_2} (x_{i2} - \bar{\bar{x}})^2 + \sum_{i=1}^{n_3} (x_{i3} - \bar{\bar{x}})^3$$

$$= 30 + 56 + 126 = 212$$

From Formula (16.29):

$$SSB = \sum_{j=1}^{J} n_j (\bar{x}_j - \bar{\bar{x}})^2$$

$$= n_1 (\bar{x}_1 - \bar{\bar{x}})^2 + n_2 (\bar{x}_2 - \bar{\bar{x}})^2 + n_3 (\bar{x}_3 - \bar{\bar{x}})^2$$

$$= 4(8 - 10)^2 + 3(6 - 10)^2 + 5(14 - 10)^2 = 144$$

As a check, using Formula (16.30):

$$SST = SSB + SSW$$
$$212 = 144 + 68$$

Table 16.14 ANOVA Summary Table for Heart Stimulant Experiment

Source of Variation	Sum of Squares	Degrees of Freedom	Mean Square	F
Between	144	2	72.00	9.52
Within	68	9	7.56	
Total	212	11		

16.6 LARGE-SAMPLE TESTS CONCERNING MEANS OF NONNORMAL POPULATIONS

All of the hypothesis-testing procedures presented so far in this chapter may be used with samples of any size—large or small—provided that the assumption of population normality is justified. Because these methods may be used with small samples, they are often referred to as *small-sample statistics*. The reader is cautioned that the term "small-sample statistics" does not imply that these methods are limited to small samples. Furthermore, these methods are not necessarily appropriate simply because a sample is small. Whether the sample is large or small, these methods are appropriate only if the normality assumption is justified.

Since most populations of practical concern are not precisely normal, it is fortunate that small-sample statistics are "robust" in the sense that their validity is not materially affected by moderate departures from the normality requirement. Thus, it is common practice to use these tests whenever it is reasonable to assume that the populations under investigation are essentially bell-shaped. In many practical situations, however, even this relaxed interpretation of the normality assumption is clearly unsupportable. For example, income distributions characteristically are highly skewed; it would be gross abuse to apply the methods discussed so far in this chapter to such distributions.

16.6.1 Test Concerning a Single Mean

The choice of procedures to use for testing a hypothesis concerning the mean of a nonnormal population depends on the sample size and whether or not the population variance σ^2 is known. If σ^2 is known and the sample size is large enough to justify application of the central limit theorem, the normal test described in Section 13.1 is applicable. If the population variance is unknown, but the sample size is substantial, then the following approximate normal test may be used:

$$Z = \frac{\bar{X} - \mu_0}{S_{\bar{X}}} + \frac{\bar{X} - \mu_0}{S/\sqrt{n}} \tag{16.33}$$

To illustrate the application of Formula (16.33), consider a large job shop that produces machinery parts. Management is considering switching to a new kind of bit used in a particular drilling operation, but feels that the change would be desirable only if the mean useful life of the new type of bit exceeds 12 hours. To help make the decision, a sample of 100 bits will be used on an experimental basis, and the useful life of each bit in the sample will be recorded. These sample data will then be used to test

$$H_0: \quad \mu \leq 12 \text{ hours}$$
$$H_1: \quad \mu > 12 \text{ hours}$$

The .05 significance level will be used for the test. On the basis of past experience with the bits used for this operation, it does not seem reasonable to assume that the lives of the bits are normally distributed. Thus, a t test is not applicable but, since the sample size is large, the approximate normal test given by Formula (16.33) can be used. Since this is an upper-tail normal test at the .05 significance level, the decision rule is to reject H_0 if $Z \geq 1.645$. Suppose that the experimental study yields a sample mean $\bar{x} = 12.5$ hours and a sample standard deviation $s = 2.0$ hours. Thus, from Formula (16.33) we obtain

$$z = \frac{12.5 - 12.0}{2.0/\sqrt{100}} = 2.50$$

Since this computed value of Z is greater than the critical value of 1.645, the null hypothesis is rejected and it is concluded that the mean life of the new type of bit exceeds 12 hours.

It is important to appreciate that this test is only an approximation, and that its validity depends on having a sample size which is large enough so that (1) the central limit theorem is applicable, and (2) the estimator $S_{\bar{x}}$ yields a "reliable" estimate of $\sigma_{\bar{x}}$. If the sample size is not substantial, tests concerning the central tendency of nonnormal populations should be performed by "non-parametric" procedures such as those discussed in Chapter 20.

16.6.2 Test Concerning the Difference between Two Means

The choice of procedures for testing a hypothesis concerning the difference between the means of two nonnormal populations also depends on the sample size and whether or not population variances are known. If the sample sizes are substantial, and the variance of the two populations are known, the normal test described in Section 13.3 is applicable. If the sample sizes are substantial, but the population variances are unknown, the following approximate normal test is commonly used:

$$Z = \frac{(\bar{X}_1 - \bar{X}_2) - \delta_0}{\sqrt{S_1^2/n_1 + S_2^2/n_2}} \tag{16.34}$$

This is the two-sample counterpart of Formula (16.33), and the same precautions regarding sample sizes should be observed. Nonparameteric procedures using small samples to test hypotheses concerning the difference between the central tendencies of two nonnormal populations are discussed in Chapter 20.

To illustrate the application of Formula (16.34), suppose that a savings and loan association is considering two alternative sites on which to build a new branch. Since the price of site A is substantially higher than the price of site B, management feels that they should select site A only if it can be demonstrated that the mean household income in the site A trade area exceeds the mean household income in the site B area by more than \$3,200. To aid in the decision, a random sample of 200 households will be selected in each of the two trade areas, and the income of each household determined. The sample data will then be used to test

$$H_0: \quad \mu_A - \mu_B \leq 3,200$$
$$H_1: \quad \mu_A - \mu_B > 3,200$$

Because income distributions are characteristically nonnormal, a t test is not applicable. However, since the sample sizes are large, the approximate normal test given by Formula (16.34) can be used. If the .01 significance level is adopted, the decision rule is to reject H_0 if $Z \geq 2.326$. Suppose that the sample survey yields the following results:

	Trade Area A	Trade Area B
Sample size	$n_A = 200$	$n_B = 200$
Mean	$\bar{x}_A = 24,800$	$\bar{x}_B = 21,200$
Variance	$s_A^2 = 6,210,000$	$s_B^2 = 5,520,000$

Applying Formula (16.34) to these data, we obtain

$$z = \frac{(24,800 - 21,200) - 3,200}{\sqrt{\dfrac{6,210,000}{200} + \dfrac{5,520,000}{200}}} = \frac{400}{24,218} = 1.65$$

Since this computed value of Z is smaller than the critical value of 2.326, the null hypothesis is not rejected. There is insufficient evidence to conclude that the mean household income in the site A trade area exceeds the mean household income in the site B trade area by more than \$3,200.

16.7 SUMMARY

As we have seen in Chapter 13 and in the present chapter, choice of the appropriate statistic for testing a hypothesis concerning a population mean depends on (1) whether or not the population distribution is normal, (2) whether or not the population variance is known, and (3) whether the sample size is large or small. Table 16.15 summarizes the appropriate tests under various sets of conditions.

Table 16.15 Appropriate Tests of Hypotheses Concerning a Population Mean

Population Distribution	Population Variance	Sample	Test Statistic	Remark
Normal	Known	Large	$Z = \dfrac{\bar{X} - \mu_0}{\sigma_{\bar{X}}}$	Exact normal test; see
Normal	Known	Small		Section 13.1
Normal	Unknown	Large	$t = \dfrac{\bar{X} - \mu_0}{S_{\bar{X}}}$	Exact t test; see Section 16.1
Normal	Unknown	Small		
Normal	Known	Large	$Z = \dfrac{\bar{X} - \mu_0}{\sigma_{\bar{X}}}$	Approximate normal test; see Section 13.1
Nonnormal	Known	Small	—	Nonparametric tests; see Chapter 20
Nonnormal	Unknown	Large	$Z = \dfrac{\bar{X} - \mu_0}{S_{\bar{X}}}$	Approximate normal test; see Section 16.6
Nonnormal	Unknown	Small	—	Nonparametric tests; see Chapter 20

When two samples are *selected independently* from two populations to test a hypothesis concerning the difference between the two population means, the choice of the appropriate test statistic depends on (1) whether or not the two populations are normally distributed; (2) whether or not the two population variances are known, and in some cases whether or not the two population variances are equal; and (3) whether the sample sizes are large or small. Table 16.16 summarizes the appropriate tests using independent samples under various sets of conditions. When the two samples are taken in pairs rather than independently, the tests summarized in this table are not applicable. Rather, the usual practice is to use the t test described in Section 16.4.2 or one of the nonparametric tests described in Section 20.2.2.

Table 16.16 Appropriate Tests of Hypotheses Concerning the Difference between Two Population Means

Population Distributions	Population Variances	Sample Sizes	Test Statistic	Remark
Normal	Known	Large	$Z = \dfrac{D - \delta_0}{\sigma_D}$	Exact normal test;
Normal	Known	Small		see Section 13.3
Normal	Unknown (but equal)	Large	$t = \dfrac{D - \delta_0}{S_D}$	Exact t test;
Normal	Unknown (but equal)	Small		see Section 16.4.1
Normal	Unknown (unequal)	Large	$t = \dfrac{D - \delta_0}{S_D}$	Approximate t test;
Normal	Unknown (unequal)	Small		see Section 16.4.1
Nonnormal	Known	Large	$Z = \dfrac{D - \delta_0}{\sigma_D}$	Approximate normal tests; see Section 16.6
Nonnormal	Known	Small	—	Nonparametric test; see Chapter 20
Nonnormal	Unknown	Large	$Z = \dfrac{D - \delta_0}{S_D}$	Approximate normal test; see Section 16.6
Nonnormal	Unknown	Small	—	Nonparametric test; see Chapter 20

PROBLEMS

16.1 The tensile strengths of 1-foot lengths of steel wire produced by a particular process are normally distributed with unknown mean μ and unknown variance σ^2. A laboratory wishes to test hypothesis $H_0: \mu = 100$ pounds against the alternative $H_1: \mu \neq 100$ pounds. For this purpose, the laboratory tests a random sample of 16 lengths of this wire. The sample yields a mean of $\bar{x} = 95.8$ pounds with an unbiased variance estimate $s^2 = 30.25$. Using a .05 significance level, what conclusion should be drawn? Explain fully.

16.2 A manufacturer of indoor gardening accessories advertises that, on the average, their plant lights will burn continuously for at least 1,200 hours. In response to consumer complaints, a state consumer agency decides to investigate the manufacturer's claim by testing a sample of 25 plant lights. The agency plans to take action against the manufacturer only if the sample provides sufficient evidence, at the .05 significance level, to justify the conclusion that the mean burning life of the manufacturer's plant lights is less than 1,200 hours. When the test is conducted, the agency obtains a sample mean burning life of $\bar{x} = 1,170$ hours with a standard deviation of $s = 50$ hours. Assuming that the burning lives of this type of light are approximately normally distributed, do these data justify the agency's taking action?

16.3 The Continental Tobacco Company measures the effectiveness of cigarette filters in terms of a Tar Removal Index (TRI), which is measured in milligrams by a special machine. The company's research and development group has recently developed a new filter production process that is less costly than the present process. The company has therefore made a tentative decision to adopt the new process *unless* laboratory testing provides sufficient evidence, at the .025 level of significance, that the mean TRI of the filters produced by the new process is less than 7 milligrams. To make this determination, the research and development group undertakes a laboratory experiment in which the TRIs of a simple random sample of 9 filters are measured.

(a) Using μ to denote the process mean TRI, state the appropriate null and alternative hypotheses for this laboratory test.

(b) On the basis of previous filtration research, the R&D group feels it is reasonable to assume for all practical purposes that the TRI of the new type of filter is normally distributed. What is the meaning of this assumption?

(c) Making the normality assumption of part (b), what is the appropriate test statistic in this situation? Why?

(d) In terms of the test statistic in part (c), state the decision rule for choosing between H_0 and H_1.

(e) When the experiment is performed, the following TRI measurements are obtained from the sample of 9 filters:

6.85	6.91	6.62
7.22	6.83	6.63
6.92	7.14	6.98

If the company bases its decision on these laboratory results, will the new process be adopted?

16.4 A researcher desires to test the hypothesis H_0: $\mu = 100$ against the alternative H_1: $\mu \neq 100$, where μ represents the unknown mean of a normal population with unknown variance. He adopts a .05 significance level. Using his normal curve tables, he derives the following decision rule: If Z exceeds $+1.645$, reject H_0; otherwise, accept H_0. From a random sample of 16 observations, he obtains $\bar{x} = 104$ and $s^2 = 9$. He makes the following test computation:

$$z = \frac{104 - 100}{9/\sqrt{16}} = 1.78$$

Since his obtained value of Z was greater than $+1.645$, he rejected the null hypothesis. Criticize the researcher's procedure. Indicate and explain his errors.

16.5 Referring to Problem 16.1, suppose that the laboratory wishes to test the hypothesis H_0: $\sigma^2 \leq 22$ against the alternative H_1: $\sigma^2 < 22$. Using a .10 significance level, what conclusion should be drawn? Explain fully.

16.6 The Bixby Pharmaceutical Company has developed a new blood pressure drug, Lexitol. This drug has a high sales potential, and plans are being made to put it into early production. Lexitol will be marketed in capsules containing 5 milligrams of active ingredient. The dosage of Lexitol is critical, so that the variance of the active ingredients of the capsules must be kept below .01 square milligram. Thus, before authorizing the start of production, it is essential to determine whether the newly developed process will meet this low variability requirement. For this purpose a sample run of 81 Lexitol capsules is produced, and the amount of active ingredient in each capsule is carefully measured. This run yields a variance estimate of $s^2 = .008$ square milligram. Does this sample result provide sufficient evidence, at the .005 significance level, that the variance of the process is low enough to start production?

16.7 Consider two normally distributed populations. Population 1 has unknown mean μ_1 and unknown variance σ_1^2. Population 2 has unknown mean μ_2 and unknown variance σ_2^2. A simple random sample of 6 observations from population 1 yields a sample mean of $\bar{x}_1 = 55.8$ and an unbiased variance estimate of $s_1^2 = 10$. A simple random sample of 11 observations from population 2 yields a sample mean of $\bar{x}_2 = 49.2$ and an unbiased variance estimate of $s_2^2 = 40$. Using the .01 significance level, conduct the following hypothesis test.

$$H_0: \mu_1 \leq 50$$
$$H_1: \mu_1 > 50$$

16.8 Use the data in Problem 16.7 to conduct the following hypothesis test at the .01 significance level.

$$H_0: \sigma_2^2 = 50$$
$$H_1: \sigma_2^2 \neq 50$$

16.9 Use the data in Problem 16.7 to conduct the following hypothesis test at the .01 significance level.

$$H_0: \sigma_1^2 = \sigma_2^2$$
$$H_1: \sigma_1^2 \neq \sigma_2^2$$

16.10 The two most popular passenger car models produced by Imperial Motors are the Royale and the Empress. To investigate the gasoline consumption of these two models, a consumer research agency submits a sample of 16 Royales and a sample of 10 Empresses to experimental road tests, measuring the performance of each car in miles per gallon. The following results are obtained:

Model	n	$\bar{x}$	$\sum (x - \bar{x})^2$
Royale	16	21.7	63.0
Empress	10	20.9	34.2

On the basis of previous automobile mileage studies, the laboratory believes it is reasonable to assume that the mileages for the two populations of cars are essentially normally distributed. Using .05 significance level, test the following hypotheses:

(a) $H_0: \mu_r \leq 20$
  $H_1: \mu_r > 20$
  where μ_r is the mean mileage of the Royale population.
(b) $H_0: \mu_e \leq 20$
  $H_1: \mu_e > 20$
  where μ_e is the mean mileage of the Empress population.

16.11 Use the data in Problem 16.10 to conduct the following hypothesis tests at the .05 significance level.

(a) $H_0: \sigma_r^2 \geq 5.0$
  $H_1: \sigma_r^2 < 5.0$
  where σ_r^2 denotes the mileage variance of the Royale population.
(b) $H_0: \sigma_e^2 \leq 5.0$
  $H_1: \sigma_e^2 > 5.0$
  where σ_e^2 denotes the mileage variance of the Empress population.

16.12 Use the data in Problem 16.10 to conduct the following hypothesis tests at the .05 significance level.

(a) $H_0: \sigma_r^2 = \sigma_e^2$
  $H_1: \sigma_r^2 \neq \sigma_e^2$
(b) $H_0: \mu_r = \mu_e$
  $H_1: \mu_r \neq \mu_e$

16.13 The Zeitz Optical Company is preparing to start full-scale production of a new model home movie projector. This projector incorporates a special type of lamp which is available from two different vendors, Kingston Products and Iris Lighting. A tentative decision has been made to procure the lamps from Kingston, since their price is lower. However, before making a final decision, Zeitz wishes to test a sample of each vendor's bulbs. They will purchase the bulbs from Kingston unless the sample provides convincing evidence, at the .05 significance level, that the mean operating life of Iris lamps is greater than that of the Kingston lamps by more than 2 hours. To conduct the test, a sample of 7 lamps produced by Kingston and a sample of 10 lamps produced by Iris are installed in new model projectors and operated continuously to failure. From measurements of the burning lives of the bulbs (in hours), the following results are obtained:

Vendor	n	$\bar{x}$	s^2
Kingston	7	75	20
Iris	10	85	16

From which vendor will Zeitz purchase the lamps?

16.14 Mr. E. G. Blue, procurement officer for a large metropolitan police department, has received bids on two makes of service revolvers—the Keller revolver and the Meisner revolver. Mr. Blue has made a tentative decision to accept the Keller bid, which is lower than the Meisner bid, but before making a final decision he requests a comparative study of the accuracy of the two makes to be performed. For this purpose, fixed-position target firings are conducted with a sample of 25 Keller revolvers and a sample of 25 Meisner revolvers. A single shot is fired from each of these revolvers, and the amount of error of each shot is measured in terms of the distance (in millimeters) of the impact point from the center of the bull's-eye of the target. From these measurements, the following results are obtained:

Make	n	$\bar{x}$	s^2
Keller	25	4.70	20.0
Meisner	25	3.10	8.0

If Mr. Blue has decided to accept the Keller bid unless these results provide convincing evidence, at the .05 significance level, that the mean error of Meisner revolvers is less than that of Keller revolvers, which bid will he accept?

16.15 The Management Science Department of Hercules Industries provides consulting services to the corporation's 17 divisions. Jeff Bannister, Vice President of Management Science Services, is currently in the process of deciding whether or not to replace the department's LTX-30 computer with a new model GTB-6 computer. His analysis indicates that the change would be economically sound only if it would reduce the mean CPU time per job by more than 20 seconds. To aid in his decision, he orders a sample of 15 jobs to be run on each computer and the CPU time for each run be determined. The following results are obtained:

	CPU Time (seconds)	
Job	LTX-30	GTB-6
1	117	84
2	48	32
3	123	97
4	65	43
5	13	11
6	59	42
7	72	49
8	36	26
9	21	19
10	244	207
11	83	65
12	25	20
13	98	59
14	19	23
15	102	78

Testing Hypotheses Concerning Normal Populations

At the .10 significance level, do these results provide convincing evidence to conclude that the mean CPU time per job on the GTB-6 is sufficiently low to justify replacing the LTX-30?

16.16 In a study of managerial achievement, an analyst wishes to determine whether there is a relationship between level of professional achievement and numerical aptitude. To do this he has obtained scores on a numerical aptitude test for a sample of 30 pairs of managers. The two members of each pair are matched for age and amount of education, but one member of each pair has reached the top management level, whereas the other member has reached only the middle management level. For each pair, a difference score is obtained by subtracting the middle manager's aptitude score from the top manager's aptitude score. The results yield a mean difference score of $\bar{d} = 2.4$, with a variance of difference scores $s_Y^2 = 25.50$. Are these results sufficient evidence to conclude, at the .01 level of significance, that the mean numerical aptitude of top managers is higher than the mean numerical aptitude of middle managers, holding age and education constant?

16.17 To investigate the effects of four different production processes on the tensile strength of aluminum chain links, a study was conducted in which 11 links were produced by each of the four processes. The tensile strength of each of the 44 specimens was then determined, and the results submitted to one-way analysis of variance. The sums of squares obtained in this analysis are shown in the following ANOVA table:

Source	Sum of Squares	Degrees of Freedom	Mean Square	F
Between	360			
Within	800			
Total	1,160			

(a) Fill in the appropriate values in the empty cells of the ANOVA table.
(b) Using the .05 significance level, what conclusion do you draw?

16.18 In the late spring, the personnel department of Central City Industries evaluates a large number of recent high school graduates who are applying for clerk-typist positions. Most of these applicants are graduates of Central City's three high schools—Washington High, Adams High, and Jefferson High. As part of the evaluation procedure, each applicant is administered the CCI Clerical Aptitude Test. To investigate whether there are any differences in the mean clerical aptitude of the graduates from the three schools, the personnel manager selects a random sample of six applicants from each school. The clerical aptitude scores of the six applicants are as follows:

Washington	Adams	Jefferson
52	37	67
61	86	96
43	48	78
88	57	43
74	69	79
72	63	57

At the .05 significance level, are these sample data sufficient to justify the conclusion that the applicant populations from the three schools differ in mean clerical aptitude?

16.19 A consumer information agency conducts a study comparing the breaking strengths of three brands of a particular type of mountain-climbing rope. For this purpose, tests are conducted to determine the breaking strengths of a sample of 4 lengths of Everest rope, 5 lengths of Matterhorn rope, and 6 lengths of Olympus rope. The breaking strengths (in pounds) for the lengths of rope in each sample are as follows:

Everest	Matterhorn	Olympus
420	422	410
411	416	424
417	431	416
424	419	429
	417	422
		401

At the .01 significance level, are these sample data sufficient to conclude that any differences exist in the mean breaking strengths of the three brands of rope?

16.20 Midwestern Airlines' telephone reservation center at Metropolitan Airport uses an automatic answering system. When a call is received, a recording asks the caller to wait on the line for the next available operator. During peak hours, the center is staffed by 10 operators, but it is rare that a caller is connected with an operator immediately. In an effort to improve peak-hour service, the reservations manager is considering hiring two additional operators. She feels that the cost of doing this can be justified if the mean waiting time under current conditions is greater than 200 seconds. She therefore decides to monitor a sample of 400 peak-hour calls and record the waiting time for each call. Upon doing this, she obtains a sample mean of $\bar{x} = 215$ seconds and a standard deviation of $s = 60$ seconds.

(a) In this case, is it reasonable to assume that the population of peak-hour waiting times is normally distributed? Explain.

(b) Assuming that the additional operators will be hired only if the sample data provide sufficient evidence that mean waiting time exceeds 200 seconds, state the appropriate null and alternative hypotheses.

(c) What is the appropriate test statistic to use in this situation? Explain.

(d) If the reservations manager adopts the .01 significance level, what decision rule should she follow?

(e) On the basis of the decision rule and the sample results, what is the manager's decision?

16.21 In a study of urban household economics, an investigator interviewed a sample of 121 heads of households. The variables investigated in the study are as follows:

Variable 1: Age of household head at last birthday

Variable 2: Household income (in thousands of dollars before taxes) during the past year

Variable 3: Amount (in thousands of dollars) spent for housing during the past year

Variable 4: Amount (in thousands of dollars) spent for food during the past year

The following means and standard deviations for these variables were obtained from the sample results:

Variable	$\bar{x}$	s
1	33.7	3.2
2	12.7	4.0
3	3.4	0.4
4	2.8	0.9

The investigator feels that it is reasonable to assume that, in the population, the ages of the household heads are essentially normally distributed. However, the population distributions of the other three variables are definitely skewed.

(a) Let μ denote the population mean age of heads of households. At the .05 significance level, test $H_0: \mu \le 30$ versus $H_1: \mu > 30$.

(b) Let μ denote the population mean household income (in thousands of dollars). At the .01 significance level, test $H_0: \mu \ge 15$ versus $H_1: \mu < 15$.

(c) Let μ denote the population mean amount (in thousands of dollars) spent for housing. At the .10 significance level, test $H_0: \mu = 3.5$ versus $H_1: \mu \ne 3.5$.

(d) Let μ denote the population mean amount (in thousands of dollars) spent for food. At the .025 significance level, test $H_0: \mu \ge 3.0$ versus $H_1: \mu < 3.0$.

16.22 For the urban household study described in Problem 16.21, let σ^2 denote the variance of the ages of household heads. At the .05 significance level test $H_0: \sigma^2 = 10$ versus $H_1: \sigma^2 \ne 10$.

16.23 For the urban household study described in Problem 16.21, a breakdown of the housing expenditure data by occupation of head of household yielded the following results:

Housing Expenditures (Thousands of Dollars)

	Occupation Category	
	Professional ($n = 40$)	Nonprofessional ($n = 81$)
$\bar{x}$:	5.90	2.16
s:	2.1	.90

Let μ_1 denote the population mean housing expenditure of professional households and μ_2 denote the mean housing expenditure for nonprofessional households. At the .05 significance level, test the null hypothesis

$$H_0: \quad \mu_1 - \mu_2 \le 3.00$$

versus the alternative hypothesis

$$H_1: \quad \mu_1 - \mu_2 > 3.00$$

16.24 For the urban household study described in Problem 16.21, a breakdown of the age data by occupation yielded the following results:

Ages of Heads of Household

	Occupation Category	
	Professional ($n = 40$)	Nonprofessional ($n = 81$)
$\bar{x}$:	36.2	32.5
s:	3.1	3.4

Assuming that the population age distributions in both occupational categories are essentially normal, do the following:

(a) Let σ_1^2 denote the population variance of the ages of the professionals and σ_2^2 denote the variances of the ages of the nonprofessionals. At the .05 significance level, test $H_0: \sigma_1^2 = \sigma_2^2$ versus $H_1: \sigma_1^2 \ne \sigma_2^2$.

(b) Let μ_1 denote the population mean age of the professionals and μ_2 denote the population mean age of the nonprofessionals. At the .01 significance level, test the null hypothesis

$$H_0: \quad \mu_1 \le \mu_2$$

versus the alternative hypothesis

$$H_1: \quad \mu_1 > \mu_2$$

16.25 During the past year, a large metropolitan gas and electric firm has conducted an extensive public relations program to promote conservation of natural gas. To assess the effectiveness of the program, the gas consumption for January of last year is obtained for a sample of 200 households, and the gas consumption for January of this year is determined for another sample of 300 households. The data yield the following sample results:

**Gas Consumption
(Thousands of Cubic Feet)**

	This Year ($n = 300$)	Last Year ($n = 200$)
$\bar{x}$:	32.7	34.9
s:	2.6	2.8

Bearing in mind that the distribution of household gas consumption is markedly skewed, do the data provide sufficient evidence to conclude, at the .01 significance level, that a drop in mean household gas consumption has occurred?

17

Simple Linear Regression and Correlation Analysis

Up to this point, we have limited our consideration of the methods of statistical inference to the situation in which a *single* characteristic of one or more populations is under investigation. For instance, in Chapter 16 we were concerned with such issues as whether the mean mileage of the Meadowlark population exceeded 16 miles per gallon, or whether there was a difference between the mean mileage of the Meadowlark population and the mean mileage of the Centennial population. In either case, only a single characteristic—mileage—was under consideration. In such situations, when only a single characteristic of one or more populations is under investigation, the populations are called *univariate* (one-variable) populations.

In this chapter we turn our attention to situations in which *two* characteristics of a population are investigated simultaneously. When two characteristics of a population are under simultaneous investigation, the population is called a *bivariate* (two-variable) population. An important objective in studying a bivariate population is to analyze the relationship between the two characteristics (variables) in order to *predict* or *estimate* the value of one variable from knowledge of the value of the other variable. For example, a marketing research analyst might wish to estimate the disposable incomes of families from knowledge of their housing expenditures, or a financial analyst might wish to predict the Dow Jones average from knowledge of projected GNP, or a personnel analyst might wish to predict potential sales of job applicants from knowledge of their scores on an employment test.

In analyzing the relationship between two variables for the purpose of making predictions, two basic questions arise: (1) How can the relationship be expressed in the form of a mathematical function from which predictions can be made? (2) Is the relationship sufficiently strong to make useful predictions possible? The first question can be answered by *simple regression analysis*, which is concerned with determining the *functional form* of the relationship between two variables. The second question can be answered by *simple correlation analysis*, which is concerned with measuring the *strength* or *degree of relationship* between two variables.

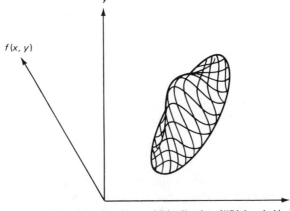

Figure 17.1 Bivariate Normal Distribution ("Bishop's Hat")

17.1 BIVARIATE POPULATIONS

The techniques of simple regression and correlation analysis are concerned with using sample data to draw conclusions concerning some bivariate population. A bivariate population formed by two random variables X and Y may be described mathematically by a bivariate distribution $f(x, y)$. A particularly important bivariate distribution is the *bivariate normal* distribution, illustrated in Figure 17.1. A bivariate normal distribution is sometimes referred to as a "bishop's hat," due to its characteristic shape.

Suppose that we were to slice through the bishop's hat parallel to the y-axis at some particular x-value, say x_j. This would give us the cross-sectional view shown in Figure 17.2. The normal distribution revealed by this cross-sectional cut is the *conditional distribution* of Y given that $X = x_j$. That is, it is the distribution of the y-values for that subset of the population having an x-value equal to x_j.

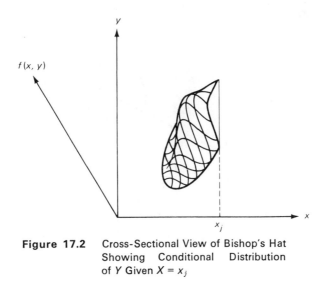

Figure 17.2 Cross-Sectional View of Bishop's Hat Showing Conditional Distribution of Y Given $X = x_j$

Now suppose that we slice through the bishop's hat at several x-values, as shown in Figure 17.3. This series of cross-sectional cuts reveals a series of conditional distributions of Y for different values of X. Notice that, for different values of X, these conditional distributions have different means. That is, the mean value of the conditional distribution of Y depends on the value of X. In Figure 17.3, the means of the conditional distributions lie on a straight line. In other words, the mean of the conditional distribution of Y, given that $X = x$, is a *linear function* of x. This linear function is referred to as the *regression line*, which has the following general form:

$$\mu_{Y|x} = \beta_0 + \beta_1 x \qquad (17.1)$$

where $\mu_{Y|x}$ = mean of the conditional distribution of Y, given that $X = x$
β_0 = a constant, the intercept of the regression line
β_1 = slope of the regression line
In this equation for a straight line, the slope β_1 represents the amount of change in the conditional mean $\mu_{Y|x}$ per unit change in x. When the regression function is linear, as in Figure 17.3, it is said that the *relationship* between the two random variables Y and X is linear. If the slope of the regression line is positive, the linear relationship is said to be positive, and if the slope is negative the linear relationship is said to be negative. If there is a positive relationship between Y and X, there is a tendency for the value of Y to be relatively high when the value of X is relatively high, and for the value of Y to be relatively low when the value of X is relatively low. If there is a negative relationship between Y and X, there is a tendency for the value of Y to be relatively low when the value of X is relatively high, and for the value of Y to be relatively high when the value of X is relatively low. If the slope happens to be zero, $\mu_{Y|x}$ is a constant regardless of the value of X, and hence no linear relationship exists.

The practical importance of a linear regression equation is that it provides a model for predicting the value of a *dependent* variable Y from knowledge of the value of an *independent* variable X. To illustrate the use of the regression line

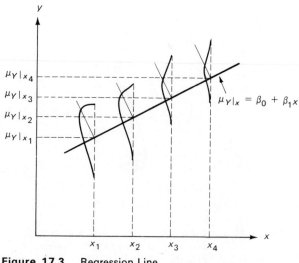

Figure 17.3   Regression Line

Simple Linear Regression and Correlation Analysis

in making predictions, consider a personnel manager who has developed a scoring system for evaluating the responses of industrial salesperson applicants to a standard biodata questionnaire. The ultimate objective of this scoring system is to provide a way of predicting what an applicant's sales would be if he or she were hired. Thus, the dependent variable Y is future sales, and the independent variable X is biodata score. Suppose the personnel manager has determined that, when Y is measured in terms of thousands of dollars of gross sales during the first year of employment, the regression equation relating these two variables is

$$\mu_{Y|x} = 175 + .5x$$

Now suppose that a particular applicant receives a biodata score of 45. Substituting this value of X into the regression equation, we obtain

$$\mu_{Y|45} = 175 + .5(45) = 197.5$$

This result says that the mean amount of first year's gross sales of applicants who obtain a biodata score of 45 is $197,500 (since Y is expressed in thousands of dollars). In other words, if an applicant obtains a biodata score of 45, the *expected* value of his first year's sales would be $197,500. This expected value would constitute the prediction of the applicant's sales.

It is important to bear in mind that predictions obtained from regression equations are merely *expected* values. Thus, in predicting applicants' sales, it is not likely that an applicant's *predicted* sales would agree exactly with his *actual* sales. That is, there probably would be some *error of prediction*, which is the difference between predicted (expected) sales and actual sales. If $\mu_{Y|x}$ denotes predicted (expected) sales of applicants with scores equal to x, and if $Y|x$ denotes the actual sales of such applicants, then the amount of error, ϵ, in predictions can be expressed as the difference between actual and predicted sales. That is,

$$\epsilon = Y|x - \mu_{Y|x} \tag{17.2}$$

In regression analysis, the errors of prediction are often called *residuals*.

The mere existence of a linear relationship between Y and X does not in itself imply that the regression equation will be useful for making predictions in the practical sense. The degree to which the relationship may be useful for making predictions depends on the *strength* of the relationship. To understand how the strength of a linear relationship is measured, we must first clearly distinguish among the following variances:

1. σ_Y^2—the variance of the marginal distribution of Y, that is, the total variance of the dependent variable Y without regard to the values of the independent variable X.

2. σ_ϵ^2—the variance of the distribution of the residuals. Since the residuals are errors of prediction, σ_ϵ^2 represents the expected squared error of prediction. In linear regression, the distribution of the errors of prediction is assumed to have a constant variance regardless of the value of X. This condition that σ_ϵ^2 remains constant for all values of X is called *homoscedasticity*.

3. $\sigma_{\mu_{Y|x}}^2$—the variance of the distribution of conditional means $\mu_{Y|x}$. If a linear relationship exists between Y and X, the value of $\mu_{Y|x}$ will vary as X varies. $\sigma_{\mu_{Y|x}}^2$ represents the expected squared deviation of the conditional mean $\mu_{Y|x}$ from μ_Y, the mean of the marginal distribution of Y.

Under the assumption of homoscedasticity, it may be demonstrated mathematically that

$$\sigma_Y^2 = \sigma_{\mu_{Y1x}}^2 + \sigma_\epsilon^2 \tag{17.3}$$

Thus, the total variance of the dependent variable Y can be partitioned into two components: (1) $\sigma_{\mu_{Y1x}}^2$, the variance of the conditional means, and (2) σ_ϵ^2, the variance of the residuals. In regression analysis, it is common to refer to the variance of the conditional means as the *explained* variance, and the variance of the residuals as the *unexplained* variance. That is, to the extent that knowledge of the value of the independent variable X provides predictive information concerning the value of Y, the variability of Y is partly "explained" by the regression equation; and to the extent that the predictions are in error, the variability of Y is partly "unexplained." Thus, Formula (17.3) may be expressed verbally as

Total Variance of Y = Explained Variance + Unexplained Variance

This partitioning of the total variance of Y enables us to measure the strength of the relationship between Y and X in terms of the proportion of the total variance of Y explained by the linear relationship. This measure, denoted by ρ^2 (rho squared), is called the *coefficient of determination*:

$$\rho^2 = \frac{\text{Explained Variance}}{\text{Total Variance of } Y} = \frac{\sigma_{\mu_{Y1x}}^2}{\sigma_Y^2} \tag{17.4}$$

Since the ratio $\sigma_\epsilon^2/\sigma_Y^2$ represents the proportion of the total variance of Y that is unexplained by the linear relationship, the coefficient of determination may also be expressed as

$$\rho^2 = 1 - \frac{\sigma_\epsilon^2}{\sigma_Y^2} \tag{17.5}$$

Another measure of the strength of linear relationship is the *coefficient of correlation*, ρ, which is equal to either the positive or negative square root of the coefficient of determination, depending on the algebraic sign of the regression coefficient β_1. If there is a positive relationship between Y and X (i.e., if the algebraic sign of β_1 is positive), the algebraic sign of ρ will be positive. If there is a negative relationship between Y and X (i.e., if the algebraic sign of β_1 is negative), the algebraic sign of ρ will be negative. Thus, whereas the coefficient of determination can have any value from 0 to 1, the coefficient of correlation can have any value between -1 and $+1$. The absolute value of the correlation coefficient indicates the *strength* of the relationship, and the algebraic sign of the correlation coefficient indicates the *direction* of the relationship. For instance, a ρ of $+.70$ and a ρ of $-.70$ indicate equally strong relationships, but the ρ of $+.70$ indicates that the relationship is positive, while the ρ of $-.70$ indicates that the relationship is negative. In either case, the coefficient of determination is $\rho^2 = .49$, which indicates that 49% of the total variance of Y is explained by the regression line.

A correlation coefficient of either $+1$ or -1 indicates a *perfect relationship*, which implies that there are no deviations from the regression line. With perfect correlation, predictions can be made completely without error. A correlation coefficient of zero indicates that there is no linear relationship whatsoever, so that the regression equation is totally useless for making predictions. If the regression equation is truly linear, and if homoscedasticity prevails—both of which are true for a bivariate normal population—a zero correlation implies that the two variables are *independent*. If two variables are independent, knowledge of the value of one variable gives no information whatsoever concerning the value of the other variable.

17.2 ESTIMATING THE REGRESSION EQUATION

In the preceding section we considered how the regression equation may be used to predict the value of a dependent variable Y from knowledge of the value of an independent variable X. For this purpose, we assumed that the regression equation was known. In actual practice, however, the regression equation usually is not known, but can be estimated from sample data.

We have denoted the population linear regression equation by

$$\mu_{Y|x} = \beta_0 + \beta_1 x$$

We shall denote the sample estimate of this equation by

$$\bar{y}|x = b_0 + b_1 x \tag{17.6}$$

This estimated regression equation is derived from observations of a sample of n pairs of values randomly selected from the bivariate population under consideration. For example, consider again the personnel manager who has developed a biodata scoring system to predict applicants' first year's sales. Suppose that he does not know the regression equation relating sales to biodata scores, and wishes to estimate it from sample data. To do this, he selects a sample of 20 salespeople who have been with the company between 1 and 2 years. From the firm's personnel files he obtains the biodata forms of these employees and applies his scoring system to their responses. He also obtains the first year's sales for each of these employees. The results are shown in Table 17.1. A graphic plot of the paired values is presented in Figure 17.4. Notice that values of the dependent variable (sales) are represented on the *y*-axis and values of the independent variable (biodata scores) are represented on the *x*-axis. Such a plot of a sample of paired values is called a *scatter diagram*.

Notice that the data points on the scatter diagram in Figure 17.4 appear to exhibit a trend. The task of estimating the regression equation is essentially a matter of finding the straight line that best fits this trend. The method generally used for this purpose is based on the *least-squares criterion*. According to this criterion, the best-fitting straight line is that line which minimizes the sum of the squares of the deviations of the actual *y*-values from the corresponding predicted values on the line. To understand this criterion, suppose that the ith observation on the scatter diagram has an *x*-value equal to x_i. Then $\hat{y}_i$, the predicted *y*-value of that observation (i.e., the *y*-value corresponding to x_i on the estimated regression line), will be

$$\hat{y}_i = b_0 + b_1 x_i \tag{17.7}$$

Table 17.1 Biodata Scores and First Year's Sales of 20 Industrial Salespeople

Salesperson	Biodata Score, x_i	Sales, y_i (thousands of dollars)
A	86	189
B	20	115
C	91	183
D	68	132
E	58	141
F	27	78
G	41	191
H	65	197
I	69	149
J	31	146
K	34	86
L	72	221
M	38	110
N	88	241
O	75	132
P	49	219
Q	83	142
R	52	109
S	40	135
T	78	232

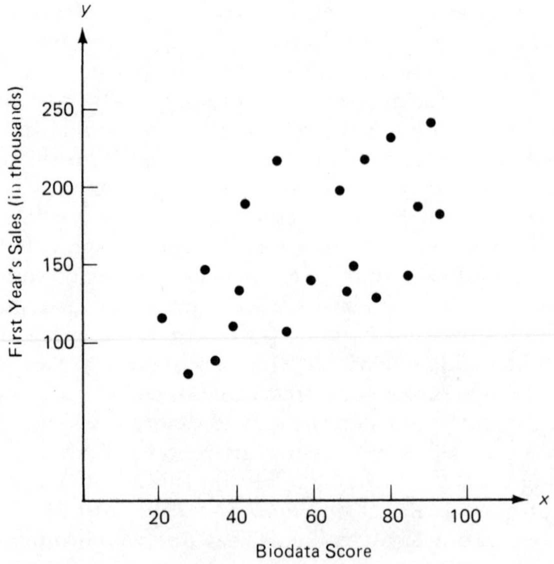

Figure 17.4   Scatter Diagram for Personnel Data

Of course, for any particular case, this predicted y-value will probably be in error by some amount e_i. This amount of error is simply the difference between y_i (the actual y-value) and $\hat{y}_i$ (the predicted y-value). That is,

$$e_i = y_i - \hat{y}_i \tag{17.8}$$

Then, by substitution from Formula (17.7), the error may be written as

$$e_i = y_i - (b_0 + b_1 x_i) \tag{17.9}$$

These relationships are illustrated graphically in Figure 17.5.

According to the least-squares criterion, the straight line which best fits the scatter plot is that line which minimizes the sum of the squares of the e_i's. That is, under the least-squares criterion, the best-fitting straight line is the line that minimizes

$$\sum_{i=1}^{n} e_i^2 = \sum_{i=1}^{n} [y_i - (b_0 + b_1 x_i)]^2 \tag{17.10}$$

To find the values of b_0 and b_1 that will minimize this sum of squared deviations, we take the partial derivatives of the expression in Formula (17.10) with respect to b_0 and b_1. Setting these two partial derivatives equal to zero yields the following pair of equations:

$$\sum y_i = n b_0 + b_1 \sum x_i \tag{17.11}$$

$$\sum x_i y_i = b_0 \sum x_i + b_1 \sum x_i^2 \tag{17.12}$$

These two equations, called the *normal equations*, may be solved simultaneously to give the following direct formulas for calculating b_0 and b_1:

$$b_1 = \frac{n \sum x_i y_i - \sum x_i \sum y_i}{n \sum x_i^2 - (\sum x_i)^2} \tag{17.13}$$

$$b_0 = \frac{\sum y_i - b_1 \sum x_i}{n} \tag{17.14}$$

Since $\sum y / n = \bar{y}$ and $\sum x / n = \bar{x}$, these equations may also be written as

$$b_1 = \frac{\sum x_i y_i - n \bar{x} \bar{y}}{\sum x_i^2 - n \bar{x}^2} \tag{17.15}$$

$$b_0 = \bar{y} - b_1 \bar{x} \tag{17.16}$$

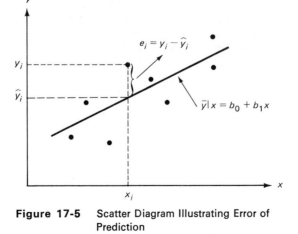

Figure 17-5 Scatter Diagram Illustrating Error of Prediction

Once the values of b_0 and b_1 are determined from the sample data, they may be substituted into the linear model given by Formula (17.6). The result is the estimated regression equation.

To illustrate the procedure for obtaining the least-squares equation for the regression line, let us return to the sample data in Table 17.1. From these data, we may compute the sums shown in Table 17.2. The x's and y's in columns

Table 17.2 Computation of Sums for Simple Linear Regression and Correlation Analysis

(1) x	(2) y	(3) x^2	(4) y^2	(5) xy
86	189	7,396	35,721	16,254
20	115	400	13,225	2,300
91	183	8,281	33,489	16,653
68	132	4,624	17,424	8,976
58	141	3,364	19,881	8,178
27	78	729	6,084	2,106
41	191	1,681	36,481	7,831
65	197	4,225	38,809	12,805
69	149	4,761	22,201	10,281
31	146	961	21,316	4,526
34	86	1,156	7,396	2,924
72	221	5,184	48,841	15,912
38	110	1,444	12,100	4,180
88	241	7,744	58,081	21,208
75	132	5,625	17,424	9,900
49	219	2,401	47,961	10,731
83	142	6,889	20,164	11,786
52	109	2,704	11,881	5,668
40	135	1,600	18,225	5,400
78	232	6,084	53,824	18,096
$\sum x = 1{,}165$	$\sum y = 3{,}148$	$\sum x^2 = 77{,}253$	$\sum y^2 = 540{,}528$	$\sum xy = 195{,}715$

(1) and (2) in this table are taken from Table 17.1. The squares of the values in column (1) are shown in column (3), and the squares of the values in column (2) are shown in column (4). Each value in column (5) is the product of the corresponding values in columns (1) and (2). From the sums of columns (1) and (2) we may compute the two sample means:

$$\bar{x} = \frac{\sum x_i}{n} = \frac{1,165}{20} = 58.25 \qquad \bar{y} = \frac{\sum y_i}{n} = \frac{3,148}{20} = 157.40$$

Applying Formula (17.15), the slope of the regression line is

$$b_1 = \frac{195,715 - 20(58.25)(157.40)}{77,253 - 20(58.25)^2} = 1.314$$

Then, from Formula (17.16), the intercept of the regression line is

$$b_0 = 157.40 - 1.314(58.25) = 80.86$$

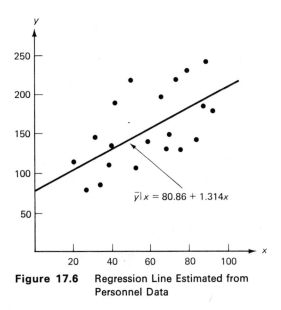

Figure 17.6 Regression Line Estimated from Personnel Data

Thus, the sample regression equation, which is the estimate of the population regression line, is

$$\bar{y}|x = 80.86 + 1.314x$$

This regression line is illustrated in Figure 17.6. As the reader may verify, the same line can be obtained by applying Formulas (17.13) and (17.14).

17.3 ESTIMATING THE POPULATION COEFFICIENT OF DETERMINATION

As expressed by Formula (17.4), the *population* coefficient of determination, denoted by ρ^2, is the ratio of the explained variance to the total variance of the dependent variable. Similarly, the *sample* coefficient of determination denoted by r^2 may be expressed as the ratio of the *explained variation* to the *total variation* of the dependent variable. The total variation of the dependent variable, also referred to as the *total sum of squares*, is the sum of the squares of the deviations of the *actual y*-values of the individual observations from the mean *y*-value of all observations. In terms of a formula, this total sum of squares (denoted by SST) may be expressed as

$$SST = \sum_{i=1}^{n} (y_i - \bar{y})^2 \qquad (17.17)$$

The explained sum of squares, also called the *regression sum of squares*, is the sum of the squares of the deviations of the *predicted y*-values of the individual observations from the mean *y*-value of all the observations. This regression sum of squares (denoted by SSR) may be expressed as

$$\text{SSR} = \sum_{i=1}^{n} (\hat{y}_i - \bar{y})^2 \tag{17.18}$$

The unexplained sum of squares, also called the *error sum of squares*, is the sum of squares of the deviations of the *actual* y-values of the individual observations from the corresponding *predicted* y-values. This error sum of squares may be expressed as

$$\text{SSE} = \sum_{i=1}^{n} e_i^2 = \sum_{i=1}^{n} (y_i - \hat{y}_i)^2 \tag{17.19}$$

It may be shown mathematically that the total sum of squares can be partitioned into the regression sum of squares and the error sum of squares. That is,

$$\text{SST} = \text{SSR} + \text{SSE} \tag{17.20}$$

The sample coefficient of determination is given by

$$r^2 = \frac{\text{SSR}}{\text{SST}} \tag{17.21}$$

This sample coefficient of determination represents the proportion of the total variation of the y-values in the sample that is explained by the sample regression equation. Because of the relationship in Formula (17.20), the sample coefficient of determination may also be expressed as

$$r^2 = 1 - \frac{\text{SSE}}{\text{SST}} \tag{17.22}$$

Stated in this form, the sample coefficient of determination is equal to 1 minus the proportion of the total variation of the y-values in the sample that is unexplained by the sample regression equation.

It can be demonstrated mathematically that r^2, the sample coefficient of determination, is an estimator of ρ^2, the population coefficient of determination. The sample coefficient of correlation is simply r, the square root of the sample coefficient of determination. The algebraic sign of r is the same as the sign of b_1, the slope of the estimated regression line.

Formulas (17.17) through (17.19) are computationally awkward, since they require the tedious squaring of individual deviations. For computational purposes, the following algebraically equivalent formulas are more convenient:

$$\text{SST} = \frac{n \sum y_i^2 - (\sum y_i)^2}{n} \tag{17.23}$$

$$\text{SSR} = b_1^2 \frac{n \sum x_i^2 - (\sum x_i)^2}{n} \tag{17.24}$$

$$\text{SSE} = \text{SST} - \text{SSR} \tag{17.25}$$

Applying these formulas to our personnel data, we obtain

$$\text{SST} = \frac{20(540,528) - (3,148)^2}{20} = 45,032.80$$

$$\text{SSR} = (1.314)^2 \left[\frac{20(77,253) - (1,165)^2}{20} \right] = 16,215.76$$

$$\text{SSE} = 45,032.80 - 16,215.76 = 28,817.04$$

Thus, from Formula (17.21), the sample coefficient of determination is

$$r^2 = \frac{SSR}{SST} = \frac{16,215.76}{45,132.80} = .36$$

As the reader may verify, the same result may also be obtained by using Formula (17.22). From this result we conclude that, in the sample, 36% of the variation of first year's sales is explained by the relationship with biodata scores. This obtained coefficient of .36 is also an estimate of the proportion of the variance of first-year sales in the population that is accounted for by the relationship.

Since the slope of the regression line for our example is positive, the coefficient of correlation is equal to the positive square root of the coefficient of determination. That is,

$$r = +\sqrt{r^2} = +\sqrt{.36} = +.60$$

The correlation coefficient may also be computed from the formula

$$r = \frac{n \sum x_i y_i - \sum x_i \sum y_i}{\sqrt{[n \sum x_i^2 - (\sum x_i)^2][n \sum y_i^2 - (\sum y_i)^2]}} \qquad (17.26)$$

This formula has the advantage that it directly assigns the appropriate algebraic sign to the value of r, without reference to the algebraic sign of the slope of the regression line. As the reader may verify, application of Formula (17.26) to our personnel data yields $r = +.60$.

17.4 ASSUMPTIONS UNDERLYING INFERENCES IN SIMPLE REGRESSION AND CORRELATION ANALYSIS

In previous sections we presented procedures for obtaining point estimates of the population regression equation, coefficient of determination, and coefficient of correlation. To make these point estimates, it was not necessary to make any assumptions regarding the distribution of the bivariate population from which the sample is obtained. However, to construct confidence intervals and test hypotheses concerning the population regression line and population correlation coefficient, certain assumptions are necessary. Throughout the remainder of this chapter we assume that the sample observations are pairs of values selected randomly from a bivariate normal population, such as the one illustrated in Figure 17.2. Mathematically, it may be shown that, if the population is bivariate normal, the following conditions will exist:

1. The regression function relating Y to X will have the linear form

    $$\mu_{Y|x} = \beta_0 + \beta_1 x$$

2. For any given x-value, the error term ϵ, as defined in Formula (17.2), will be normally distributed with mean zero and variance σ_ϵ^2.

3. The variance of the error term, σ_ϵ^2, will be constant for all values of X (i.e., homoscedasticity will prevail).

4. The conditional distribution of Y given $X = x$ will be normal for any x-value. Also, the conditional distribution of X given $Y = y$ will be normal for any y-value.

The customary procedures for making inferences concerning the regression line require that the first three of the above conditions be met. Procedures for making inferences concerning the correlation coefficient require all four of the above conditions.

17.5 CONFIDENCE INTERVALS FOR $\mu_{Y|x}$ AND y_i

At this point it is important to stress the distinction between estimating the mean y-value of a conditional distribution and estimating the y-value of an individual case. We have used $\mu_{Y|x}$ to denote the population mean of the conditional distribution of Y given that $X = x$, and y_i to denote the actual y-value of an individual case. We have also used $\bar{y}|x$ to denote the point estimate of $\mu_{Y|x}$, and $\hat{y}_i$ to denote the point estimate of y_i. Since $\hat{y}_i = \bar{y}|x$ for any specified x-value, the sample regression equation may be used to estimate either $\mu_{Y|x}$ or y_i. To illustrate, let us return to our personnel example, in which we obtained the estimated regression equation

$$\bar{y}|x = 80.86 + 1.314x$$

For $x = 40$, this equation yields the following estimated sales:

$$\hat{y}|40 = 80.86 + 1.314(40) = 133.42$$

or \$133,420 (since Y is expressed in thousands of dollars). This estimate may be interpreted as either (1) the estimated mean sales of all salespeople with biodata scores of 40, or (2) the estimated sales of a particular salesperson who has a biodata score of 40. The formula for determining an interval estimate depends on which of these interpretations is intended.

17.5.1 Confidence Interval for $\mu_{Y|x}$

To obtain a confidence interval for $\mu_{Y|x}$ it is necessary to estimate σ_e^2, the variance of the residuals. The sample estimate of σ_e^2 may be obtained from the formula

$$s_e^2 = \frac{\Sigma(y_i - \hat{y}_i)^2}{n - 2} \tag{17.27}$$

As the reader may observe, the numerator of this formula is the error sum of squares, as defined by Formula (17.19). Thus, the estimated variance of the residuals may also be expressed as

$$s_e^2 = \frac{\text{SSE}}{n - 2} \tag{17.28}$$

The sample estimate of the variance of $\bar{Y}|x$ is obtained from the formula

$$s_{\bar{Y}|x}^2 = s_e^2 \left[\frac{1}{n} + \frac{(x - \bar{x})^2}{\Sigma x_i^2 - n\bar{x}^2} \right] \tag{17.29}$$

The estimated standard error of the conditional mean, denoted by $s_{\bar{Y}|x}$, is simply the square root of $s^2_{\bar{Y}|x}$. If the residuals are normally distributed (which is true for the bivariate normal model), it can be shown that the quantity

$$t = \frac{\bar{Y}|x - \mu_{Y|x}}{s_{\bar{Y}|x}} \tag{17.30}$$

has Student's t distribution with $(n - 2)$ degrees of freedom. Manipulation of Formula (17.30) yields the following expression for a $(1 - \alpha)$ confidence interval for $\mu_{Y|x}$:

$$C[(\bar{y}|x + t_{(n-2;\ \alpha/2)}s_{\bar{Y}|x}) \le \mu_{Y|x} \le (\bar{y}|x + t_{(n-2;\ 1-\alpha/2)}s_{\bar{Y}|x})] = 1 - \alpha \tag{17.31}$$

For our personnel example, we have seen that the point estimate of sales (in thousands of dollars) for salespeople who obtain a biodata score of 40 is $\bar{y}|40 = 133.42$. Suppose that we now want to obtain a 95% confidence interval for the mean of this subpopulation of salespeople. To do this, we go through the following steps:

1. Determine the error sum of squares. In Section 17.3 the error sum of squares for our example was computed to be

$$\text{SSE} = 28{,}817.04$$

2. Determine the estimated variance of the residuals. From Formula (17.28) we obtain

$$s^2_e = \frac{\text{SSE}}{n - 2} = \frac{28{,}817.04}{18} = 1{,}600.95$$

3. Determine the estimated standard error of the conditional mean for the subpopulation under consideration. For our example, this is the subpopulation for which $x = 40$. Using Formula (17.29), the estimated variance of the conditional mean of Y given that $x = 40$ is

$$s^2_{\bar{Y}|40} = s^2_e\left[\frac{1}{n} + \frac{(40 - \bar{x})^2}{\sum x_i^2 - n\bar{x}^2}\right]$$
$$= 1{,}600.95\left[\frac{1}{20} + \frac{(40 - 58.25)^2}{77{,}253 - 20(58.25)^2}\right]$$
$$= 136.82$$

Then the estimated standard error of the conditional mean for the subpopulation is

$$s_{\bar{Y}|40} = \sqrt{136.82} = 11.70$$

4. Determine the appropriate t-values for the confidence interval. For our example we have $(n - 2) = 18$ degrees of freedom and the confidence coefficient is $(1 - \alpha) = .95$. Thus, from Table L (Appendix II), the desired t-values are:

$$t_{18;\ .025} = -2.101 \qquad t_{18;\ .975} = +2.101$$

5. Substitute the appropriate values into Formula (17.31) to obtain the desired confidence interval. For our example

$$C\{[133.42 - 2.101(11.70)] \le \mu_{Y|40} \le [133.42 + 2.101(11.70)]\} = .95$$

which reduces to

$$C(108.8383 \le \mu_{Y|40} \le 158.0017) = .95$$

17.5.2 Prediction Interval for an Individual Case

A confidence interval for the actual y-value of an individual case is commonly called a *prediction interval*. To construct a prediction interval, we first obtain the *standard error of prediction*. Given an individual case for which $X = x$, the standard error of prediction may be obtained from the formula

$$s_{\hat{y}_i} = \sqrt{s^2_{\hat{P}|x} + s^2_e} \tag{17.32}$$

If the residuals are normally distributed, it is possible to demonstrate that the quantity

$$t = \frac{\hat{y}_i - y_i}{s_{\hat{y}_i}} \tag{17.33}$$

has Student's t distribution with $(n - 2)$ degrees of freedom. From this relationship, we can derive the following model for a $(1 - \alpha)$ prediction interval for an individual case:

$$C[(\hat{y}_i + t_{n-2;\ \alpha/2} s_{\hat{y}_i}) \le y_i \le (\hat{y}_i + t_{n-2;\ 1-\alpha/2} s_{\hat{y}_i})] = 1 - \alpha \tag{17.34}$$

To illustrate the procedure for obtaining a prediction interval, suppose that we wish to obtain a 95% confidence interval for a particular salesman who obtains a biodata score of 40. From the estimated regression equation, the prediction of this individual's sales (in thousands of dollars) is $\hat{y}_i = \bar{y}|40 = 133.42$. As we have seen, the estimated variance of the conditional mean of Y given that $X = 40$ is $s^2_{\hat{P}|40} = 136.82$, and the estimated variance of the residuals is $s^2_e = 1{,}600.95$. Therefore, from Formula (17.32), the estimated standard error of prediction is

$$s_{\hat{y}_i} = \sqrt{136.82 + 1{,}600.95} = 41.69$$

For 18 degrees of freedom and a confidence coefficient of .95, the desired t-values are

$$t_{18\ ;.025} = -2.101 \qquad t_{18;\ .975} = +2.101$$

Substitution into Formula (17.34) yields the following 95% prediction interval:

$$C\{[133.42 - 2.101(41.69)] \le y_i \le [133.42 + 2.101(41.69)]\} = .95$$

which reduces to

$$C(45.8293 \le y_i \le 221.0107) = .95$$

17.6 CONFIDENCE INTERVAL FOR A POPULATION CORRELATION COEFFICIENT

Because of the complexity of the sampling distribution of the sample correlation coefficient r, a rather roundabout procedure is required to construct a confidence interval for the population correlation coefficient ρ. This procedure, proposed by R. A. Fisher, involves the transformation of values of r to corresponding values of Z_r according to the function

$$Z_r = \frac{1}{2} \log_e \left(\frac{1 + r}{1 - r} \right) \qquad (17.35)$$

Corresponding values of r and Z_r, obtained from this formula, are listed in Table O (Appendix II). Fisher demonstrated that the sampling distribution of Z_r is approximately normally distributed[1] with an expected value approximately equal to

$$E(Z_r) = Z_\rho = \frac{1}{2} \log_e \left(\frac{1 + \rho}{1 - \rho} \right) \qquad (17.36)$$

and a standard error approximately equal to

$$\sigma_{Z_r} = \sqrt{\frac{1}{n - 3}} \qquad (17.37)$$

Under these conditions, the quantity

$$Z = \frac{Z_r - Z_\rho}{\sigma_{Z_r}} \qquad (17.38)$$

has an approximately standard normal distribution. It is important to notice in Formula (17.38) that Z, Z_r, and Z_ρ represent entirely different quantities: Z denotes the standard normal variable, whereas Z_r and Z_ρ denote the Fisher transformations given by Formulas (17.35) and (17.36).

From Formula (17.38), the following expression for a confidence interval for z_ρ may be derived:

$$C[(Z_r + z_{\alpha/2}\sigma_{Z_r}) \leq z_\rho \leq (Z_r + z_{1-\alpha/2}\sigma_{Z_r})] = 1 - \alpha \qquad (17.39)$$

Once the confidence limits for Z_ρ have been obtained, they may be transformed back to the corresponding values of ρ to obtain the desired confidence limits for ρ.

To illustrate this procedure, suppose that we wish to construct a 95% confidence interval for the value of ρ in our personnel example, for which we obtained the sample correlation coefficient $r = .60$. From Table O, the Fisher transformation of this coefficient is

$$Z_r = \frac{1}{2} \log_e \left(\frac{1 + .60}{1 - .60} \right) = .6931$$

Since the sample size is $n = 20$, the approximate standard error of Z_r is

$$\sigma_{Z_r} = \sqrt{\frac{1}{n - 3}} = \sqrt{\frac{1}{17}} = .2425$$

---

[1]This approximation improves as the absolute value of ρ grows small and the sample size grows large. The example used in this text employs a sample size of 20, which is somewhat smaller than recommended, and should be regarded only as illustrative of the procedure.

For a confidence coefficient of .95, the desired values of the standard normal variable are

$$z_{.025} = -1.96 \qquad z_{.975} = +1.96$$

Substituting into Formula (17.39), we obtain the 95% confidence interval for Z_ρ:

$$C\{[.6931 - 1.96(.2425)] \leq Z_\rho \leq [.6931 + 1.96(.2425)]\} = .95$$

which reduces to

$$C(.2178 \leq Z_\rho \leq 1.1684) = .95$$

From Table O, the values of ρ corresponding to these two values of Z_ρ are .214 and .824. Thus, the 95% confidence interval for ρ is

$$C(.214 \leq \rho \leq .824) = .95$$

17.7 HYPOTHESIS TESTS IN SIMPLE LINEAR REGRESSION

The finding of a relationship between two variables in a sample does not in itself imply that such a relationship exists in the population from which the sample was taken. Inferences concerning the existence of population relationships require the application of hypothesis-testing procedures.

As we have observed, if there is no linear relationship between two random variables, the slope of the linear regression equation will be zero. Conversely, if the slope of the linear regression equation is zero, then no linear relationship exists between the two random variables. Therefore, the hypotheses

H_0: no linear relationship exists between Y and X
H_1: a linear relationship does exist between Y and X

may also be stated in the form

H_0: $\beta_1 = 0$
H_1: $\beta_1 \neq 0$

17.7.1 The t-Test Concerning the Slope β_1

A hypothesis concerning β_1, the slope of the population regression line, may be tested by the statistic

$$t = \frac{b_1 - \beta_1^*}{s_{b_1}} \qquad (17.40)$$

where b_1 = slope of the sample regression line
β_1^* = limiting value of β_1 contained in the null hypothesis
s_{b_1} = estimated standard error of b_1

The estimated standard error of b_1 is given by

$$s_{b_1} = \sqrt{\frac{s_e^2}{\sum x_i^2 - n\bar{x}^2}} \qquad (17.41)$$

where s_e^2 is defined by Formulas (17.27) and (17.28). Under the conditions given in Section 17.4, the test statistic given by Formula (17.40) has Student's t distribution with $(n-2)$ degrees of freedom. Table 17.3 summarizes the deci-

Table 17.3 General Specifications for t Tests Concerning the Slope of a Regression Line

Test	Hypothesis	Decision Rule
Upper tail	H_0: $\beta_1 \leq \beta_1^*$ H_1: $\beta_1 > \beta_1^*$	Reject H_0 if $t \geq t_{n-2;\,1-\alpha}$; accept H_0 otherwise
Lower tail	H_0: $\beta_1 \geq \beta_1^*$ H_1: $\beta_1 < \beta_1^*$	Reject H_0 if $t \leq t_{n-2;\,\alpha}$; accept H_0 otherwise
Two tail	H_0: $\beta_1 = \beta_1^*$ H_1: $\beta_1 \neq \beta_1^*$	Reject H_0 if $t \leq t_{n-2;\,\alpha/2}$ or $t \geq t_{n-2;\,1-\alpha/2}$; accept H_0 otherwise

$$\text{where} \quad t = \frac{b_1 - \beta_1^*}{s_{b_1}}$$

sion rules for applying this statistic to conduct upper-tail, lower-tail, and two-tail tests of hypotheses concerning the slope of the population regression line.

To illustrate the application of Formula (17.40), consider again our example of the personnel manager who has developed a biodata scoring system to predict applicants' first-year sales. In Section 17.2, the following regression equation was obtained from a sample of 20 pairs of observations:

$$\bar{y}\,|\,x = 80.86 + 1.314x$$

Since the slope of this sample regression equation is not zero, we may state that, in the sample, there is a relationship between first-year commissions (y) and biodata scores (x). Now the question is: Does the sample result provide sufficient evidence to conclude that a relationship exists in the population? In other words, is the slope of the population regression line equal to some value other than zero? To answer this question, we may test the following hypotheses:

$$H_0: \quad \beta_1 = 0$$
$$H_1: \quad \beta_1 \neq 0$$

To perform the test, we must first compute the estimated standard error of b_1 using Formula (17.41). To apply this formula, we need the following values previously obtained in Sections 17.2 and 17.5:

$$\sum x_i^2 = 77{,}253 \qquad \bar{x} = 58.25 \qquad s_e^2 = 1{,}600.95$$

Substituting these values into Formula (17.41), we obtain

$$s_{b_1} = \sqrt{\frac{1{,}600.95}{77{,}253 - 20(58.25)^2}} = .4128$$

Then, from Formula (17.40), we obtain the test statistic

$$t = \frac{1.314 - 0}{.4128} = 3.18$$

Simple Linear Regression and Correlation Analysis $\qquad$ 373

Referring to Table 17.3, the decision rule for this two-tail test is to reject the null hypothesis if $t \leq t_{n-2;\,\alpha/2}$ or if $t \geq t_{n-2;\,1-\alpha/2}$. If we adopt the .05 significance level, these critical values are

$$t_{18;\,.025} = -2.101 \qquad t_{18;\,.975} = 2.101$$

Since the computed t of 3.18 exceeds the critical t of 2.101, we reject H_0 and conclude that the slope of the population regression line is not zero. In other words, we conclude that a relationship does exist in the population.

17.7.2 The ANOVA Test

An alternative method for testing whether a linear relationship exists between Y and X is the use of an ANOVA procedure similar to the method described in Section 16.5 for testing a hypothesis concerning the means of several populations. In that section the ANOVA procedure was based on the fact that the total sum of squares (SST) can be partitioned into the between sum of squares (SSB) and the within sum of squares (SSW). Similarly, in linear regression analysis, the total sum of squares (SST) can be partitioned into the regression sum of squares (SSR) and the error sum of squares (SSE), as we have already seen from Formula (17.20).

In simple linear regression analysis there is 1 degree of freedom associated with SSR and $(n - 2)$ degrees of freedom associated with SSE. Thus, the *regression mean square* is

$$\text{MSR} = \frac{\text{SSR}}{1} \tag{17.42}$$

and the *error mean square* is

$$\text{MSE} = \frac{\text{SSE}}{n - 2} \tag{17.43}$$

Then, if the residuals are normally distributed, the ratio

$$F = \frac{\text{MSR}}{\text{MSE}} \tag{17.44}$$

has the F distribution with 1 degree of freedom for the numerator and $(n - 2)$ degrees of freedom for the denominator. The null hypothesis is rejected if the F-value computed from the sample data is equal to or greater than $F_{1,\,(n-2);\,1-\alpha}$. The general ANOVA procedure for calculating the F-ratio given by Formula (17.44) is summarized in Table 17.4.

Table 17.4 ANOVA Summary Table for Simple Linear Regression Analysis

Source of Variation	Sum of Squares	Degrees of Freedom	Mean Square	F
Regression	SSR	1	MSR = SSR/1	MSR/MSE
Error	SSE	$n - 2$	MSE = SSE/$(n - 2)$	
Total	SST	$n - 1$		

To apply this ANOVA procedure to our personnel example, recall that we have already calculated the following sums of squares:

$$SSR = 16,215.75 \qquad SSE = 28,817.04 \qquad SST = 45,032.80$$

There is 1 degree of freedom associated with SSR and $(n - 2) = 18$ degrees of freedom associated with SSE. Thus, from Formulas (17.42) and (17.43), we obtain the following mean squares:

$$MSR = \frac{16,215.76}{1} = 16,215.76$$

$$MSE = \frac{28,817.04}{18} = 1,600.95$$

Then, from Formula (17.44), the calculated F-ratio is

$$F = \frac{MSR}{MSE} = \frac{16,215.76}{1,600.95} = 10.129$$

These calculations are summarized in Table 17.5.

Table 17.5 ANOVA Summary Table for Personnel Data

Source of Variation	Sum of Squares	Degrees of Freedom	Mean Square	F
Regression	16,215.76	1	16,215.76	10.13
Error	28,817.04	18	1,600.95	
Total	45,032.80	19		

If we adopt the .05 significance level, the critical F-value for our hypothesis test is $F_{1, 18; .95}$. From Appendix Table M, this critical value is 4.41. Since the F-value calculated from the sample data exceeds the critical value, the null hypothesis is rejected, and we may conclude that, in the population, a linear relationship does exist between sales and biodata scores.

As we have seen, if there is no linear relationship between Y and X, the slope of the population regression will be zero, and vice versa. Thus, the one-tail F test presented in this section is equivalent to the two-tail t test presented in the preceding section.[2] That is, the F test will always lead to the same conclusion as the t test of the null hypothesis $H_0: \beta_1 = 0$ versus the alternative hypothesis $H_1: \beta_1 \neq 0$. However, the F test cannot be used as a substitute for a one-tail t test in which the alternative hypothesis is either $H_1: \beta_1 > 0$ or $H_1: \beta_1 < 0$. Hence, the F test is a convenient procedure for testing a hypothesis concerning the existence of a relationship, but it cannot be used to test a hypothesis concerning the direction of a relationship.

---

[2]The equivalence of these two tests is expressed by the mathematical relationship $F_{1, v; 1-\alpha} = t^2_{v; 1-\alpha/2}$.

17.8 HYPOTHESIS TESTS IN SIMPLE LINEAR CORRELATION ANALYSIS

If no linear relationship exists between two variables Y and X, such that the slope of the population regression line is zero, the population correlation coefficient ρ also will be zero. However, if a linear relationship does exist, the population correlation coefficient will have some positive or negative value. Thus, it is possible to investigate the existence and strengths of linear relationships by testing hypotheses concerning the value of ρ.

17.8.1 The t Test Concerning the Correlation Coefficient ρ

A simple t test can be used to investigate whether the population correlation coefficient ρ departs from zero. This procedure can be used to test either directional or nondirectional hypotheses, and requires knowledge of only the sample size and the sample correlation coefficient. The formula for this test is

$$t = \frac{r}{\sqrt{(1 - r^2)/(n - 2)}} \tag{17.45}$$

The number of degrees of freedom for this test is $(n - 2)$. Table 17.6 summarizes

Table 17.6 General Specifications for t Tests Concerning the Relationship between Two Random Variables

Test	Hypotheses	Decision Rule
Upper tail	H_0: $\rho \leq 0$ H_1: $\rho > 0$	Reject H_0 if $t \geq t_{n-2;\,1-\alpha}$; accept H_0 otherwise
Lower tail	H_0: $\rho \geq 0$ H_1: $\rho < 0$	Reject H_0 if $t \leq t_{n-2;\,\alpha}$; accept H_0 otherwise
Two tail	H_0: $\rho = 0$ H_1: $\rho \neq 0$	Reject H_0 if $t \leq t_{n-2;\,\alpha/2}$ or if $t \geq t_{n-2;\,1-\alpha/2}$; accept H_0 otherwise

where $t = \dfrac{r}{\sqrt{(1 - r^2)/(n - 2)}}$

the decision rules for applying this statistic to conduct upper-tail, lower-tail, and two-tail tests of hypotheses concerning the relationship between two random variables.

To apply this test to our personnel example, suppose that we wish to determine whether the sample data provide sufficient evidence to conclude that, in the population, a linear relationship exists between sales and biodata scores. That is, we wish to test

$$H_0: \quad \rho = 0$$
$$H_1: \quad \rho \neq 0$$

Referring to Table 17.6, the decision rule for this two-tail test is to reject the null hypothesis if $t \leq t_{n-2;\,\alpha/2}$ or if $t \geq t_{n-2;\,1-\alpha/2}$. If we adopt the .05 significance level, these critical values are

$$t_{18;\,.025} = -2.101 \qquad t_{18;\,.975} = 2.101$$

Recalling that the sample correlation coefficient is $r = +.60$, we obtain the following t-value from Formula (17.45):

$$t = \frac{.60}{\sqrt{(1 - .60^2)/(20 - 2)}} = 3.18$$

Since this calculated t-value exceeds the critical value of 2.101, we reject H_0 and conclude that the population linear correlation coefficient between sales and biodata scores is not zero.

As the reader may observe, the computed and critical t-values in the above test concerning the population correlation coefficient are exactly the same as those obtained in Section 17.7.1 for the t test concerning the slope of the population regression line. Indeed, a t test concerning a departure of the correlation coefficient from zero is equivalent to a t test concerning a departure of the slope from zero, in the sense that the two t tests will yield identical conclusions.

17.8.2 Approximate Normal Test Using the Fisher Transformation

The hypothesis-testing procedures presented in Table 17.6 are concerned with testing whether a population relationship differs from zero in some manner. In some situations, however, it is desired to test whether the population correlation coefficient differs from some value other than zero. For example, an investigator might want to determine if the sample data are sufficient to conclude that ρ is greater than .50, or if the sample data justify the conclusion that ρ is not equal to .80. In such situations, neither the F test nor the t test is appropriate. However, if the sample size is not too small, an approximate standard normal test using the Fisher transformation may be employed.

The test statistic for the approximate normal test is given by

$$Z = \frac{Z_r - Z_{\rho_0}}{\sigma_{Z_r}} \qquad (17.46)$$

where ρ_0 = limiting value of ρ contained in the null hypothesis
Z = standard normal variable
Z_r = Fisher transformation corresponding to the sample correlation coefficient r
Z_{ρ_0} = Fisher transformation corresponding to the hypothesized population correlation coefficient ρ_0
$\sigma_{Z_r} = \sqrt{\dfrac{1}{n - 3}}$

Table 17.7 summarizes the decision rules for applying this statistic.

Applying this test to our personnel example, suppose that we wish to determine whether the evidence is sufficient to infer that the population correlation coefficient is greater than .50. That is, we wish to test

$$H_0: \quad \rho \le .50$$
$$H_1: \quad \rho > .50$$

Table 17.7 General Specifications for the Approximate Normal Test Concerning a Population Correlation Coefficient

Test	Hypotheses	Decision Rule
Upper tail	$H_0: \rho \leq \rho_0$ $H_1: \rho > \rho_0$	Reject H_0 if $Z \geq z_{1-\alpha}$; accept H_0 otherwise
Lower tail	$H_0: \rho \geq \rho_0$ $H_1: \rho < \rho_0$	Reject H_0 if $Z \leq z_\alpha$; accept H_0 otherwise
Two tail	$H_0: \rho = \rho_0$ $H_1: \rho \neq \rho_0$	Reject H_0 if $Z \leq z_{\alpha/2}$ or if $Z \geq z_{1-\alpha/2}$; accept H_0 otherwise

$$\text{where} \quad Z = \frac{Z_r - Z_{\rho_0}}{\sqrt{\dfrac{1}{n-3}}}$$

From Table 17.7 we see that the decision rule for this upper-tail test is to reject the null hypothesis if $Z \geq z_{1-\alpha}$. At the .05 significance level, this critical value is $z_{.95} = 1.645$ (from Table J, Appendix II). For this test, $r = .60$ and $\rho_0 = .50$. From Appendix Table O, the Fisher transformations for these two values are $Z_r = .6931$ and $Z_{\rho_0} = .5493$. Since the sample size is 20, the standard error of Z_r is

$$\sigma_{Z_r} = \sqrt{\frac{1}{17}} = .2425$$

Thus, from Formula (17.46), the obtained value of Z is

$$Z = \frac{.6931 - .5493}{.2425} = .593$$

Since this calculated z-value is less than the critical value, the null hypothesis is not rejected. The sample evidence is insufficient to conclude that the population correlation coefficient exceeds .50.

17.9 COMPUTER-AIDED ANALYSIS

As the reader may have observed, the procedures of correlation and regression analysis involve extensive and tedious calculations. If an investigator's computational resources were limited to a hand calculator, his or her application of these procedures to large-scale practical problems would be severely limited. Indeed, only since the advent of high-speed digital computers have the methods of regression and correlation analysis begun to experience widespread application to the management and planning of business operations. Today, with the ready availability of "canned" programs and statistical "packages," the use of these methods has become quite common.

An example of the kind of printout that commonly available computer packages provide for simple linear regression and correlation analysis is given in Figure 17.7, which shows the output obtained from a canned program using the biodata scores and sales figures given in Table 17.1. Although various packages differ somewhat in their particular output format and the specific results that they present, the printout in Figure 17.7 is representative of the general type of output they provide.

Figure 17.7   Computer Printout for Simple Linear Regression

VARIABLES			MEAN	STD DEV
DEPENDENT	Y — SALES		157.4000	48.6841
INDEPENDENT	X — BIODATA SCORE		58.2500	22.2329

INTERCEPT	80.8595	
SLOPE	1.3143	
STD ERROR OF SLOPE	0.4128	
R SQUARE	0.3593	
R	0.5994	

ANALYSIS OF VARIANCE

SOURCE	SUM OF SQUARES	DF	MEAN SQUARE	F
REGRESSION	16215.7570	1	16215.7570	10.1288
ERROR	28817.0430	18	1600.9468	
TOTAL	45032.8000	19		

Except for minor discrepancies attributable to rounding, the results shown in the computer printout agree with the corresponding calculations made in previous sections of this chapter. The printout begins by identifying the variables, giving the sample mean and standard deviation of each. The printout then indicates that the intercept of the estimated regression line is 80.8595, and the slope is 1.3143, so that the regression equation is

$$\bar{y}|x = 80.8595 + 1.3143x$$

which is essentially the same result as that we obtained earlier from the application of Formulas (17.15) and (17.16). The value of .4128 which the printout gives for the estimated standard error of the estimated slope agrees with our earlier result obtained from Formula (17.41) for computing s_{b_1}. Knowing the values of the estimated slope and the estimated standard error, it is a simple hand-calculation task to apply the t tests summarized in Table 17.3. Following the estimated standard error of the slope, the output prints the values of the sample coefficient of determination and coefficient of correlation, which are essentially the same as the results obtained in Section 17.3. The final portion of the printout is an analysis of variance summary table, which corresponds closely to the ANOVA summary presented in Table 17.5.

PROBLEMS

17.1 Two commonly used tests for evaluating applicants to graduate schools are the Graduate Management Aptitude Test (GMAT) and the Graduate Record Examination (GRE). For a population of applicants to a particular graduate school, scores on these two tests are related according to the linear regression equation

$$\mu_{Y|x} = 300 + 1.5x$$

where X is the GMAT score and Y is the GRE score. The population means and variances of these variables are:

$$\mu_X = 467 \qquad \sigma_X^2 = 2,500$$
$$\mu_Y = 1,000 \qquad \sigma_Y^2 = 8,100$$

The variance of the residuals is $\sigma_e^2 = 2,475$.

(a) A particular applicant obtains a score of 600 on the GMAT. He plans to take the GRE next month. On the basis of the population regression equation, what is his expected score on the GRE?

(b) Calculate the population coefficient of determination.

(c) Interpret the value obtained in part (b).

(d) Calculate the value of the population correlation coefficient.

17.2 For a particular population of discount dry-goods stores, sales are related to density of home ownership according to the linear regression equation

$$\mu_{Y|x} = 21.23 - .15x$$

where Y denotes a store's annual gross sales (in millions of dollars) and X denotes the percentage of owner-occupied households within a 5-mile radius of the store. The population means and variances of these variables are:

$$\mu_X = 61.20 \qquad \sigma_X^2 = 105.74$$
$$\mu_Y = 12.05 \qquad \sigma_Y^2 = 15.27$$

The variance of the residuals is $\sigma_e^2 = 12.89$.

(a) Within a 5-mile radius of a particular store, 72% of the households are owner-occupied. On the basis of the population regression equation, what is the expected annual gross sales of this store?

(b) Calculate the population coefficient of determination.

(c) Interpret the value obtained in part (b).

(d) Calculate the value of the population coefficient of correlation.

17.3 In the Land of Oz, appraised home value is related to household income according to the linear regression equation

$$\mu_{Y|x} = 8.01 + 1.8x$$

where Y denotes the appraised value of the household residence (in thousands of Ozbills) and X denotes the annual household income (in thousands of Ozbills). Of course, population regression equations are seldom known, and this particular equation is known only to the Wizard of Oz, who does not share his special knowledge with the populace. In order to estimate this relationship, Dr. Ormil, a prominent real estate consultant, conducts a sample survey of 100 randomly selected Oz households. From his sample results, Dr. Ormil obtains the following estimated regression equation:

$$\hat{y}_i = 7.49 + 2.47x_i$$

(a) Suppose that a particular household has an annual income of 30 thousand Ozbills. If the Wizard were asked to estimate the appraised value of the residence of that household, what value would he give us as his estimate?

(b) For the household in part (a), what value would Dr. Ormil give as his estimate of the appraised value of the household's residence?

(c) Which of the two estimates would you expect to have the smaller amount of error? Explain.

17.4 Consider a population of married couples, in which both members of each couple have full-time jobs. Let X represent the husband's annual salary in thousands of dollars, and Y represent the wife's salary in thousands of dollars. For a sample of 10 couples taken at random from this population, the following values of X and Y are obtained:

Couple	x	y
1	10	5
2	9	8
3	13	9
4	12	11
5	16	11
6	16	12
7	20	12
8	21	13
9	23	12
10	23	14

(a) Compute the following sums: $\sum x_i, \sum y_i, \sum x_i^2, \sum y_i^2, \sum x_i y_i$.

(b) Determine unbiased estimates of mean husband's income and mean wife's income.

(c) Assuming that Y is the dependent variable and X is the independent variable, compute the estimated regression equation.

(d) A man is selected at random from the population and his annual salary is determined to be $18,000. Using the regression equation obtained in part (c), estimate his wife's annual salary.

17.5 In wage administration, the "point system" of job evaluation is a procedure for assessing the compensatory value of a job by appraising the job with respect to each of several separate factors—such as physical demand, educational demand, and working conditions—and then combining the separate appraisals into a single point score for the job. In a particular job evaluation study conducted in a large metropolitan area, an analyst selects a random sample of 12 jobs. He determines the point value and obtains the prevailing community hourly wage of each job, as follows:

Job Number	Point Value	Prevailing Wage
1	122	$ 5.67
2	220	7.82
3	84	4.00
4	180	6.40
5	314	11.55
6	163	6.20
7	118	5.20
8	270	11.12
9	116	4.20
10	257	10.20
11	135	5.92
12	172	6.35

Determine the estimated linear regression equation for estimating prevailing wage from point value for jobs in the area.

17.6 The personnel manager of the Argo Insurance Company has recently devised an experimental test to aid in the selection of claims adjusters. To obtain a preliminary evaluation of the test, she administers the test to a random sample of 15 claims adjusters who have worked for the company between 1 and 2 years. From the personnel files she obtains the job performance rating of each employee in the sample. The sample data are as follows:

Employee	Test Score	Performance Rating
1	27	52
2	22	57
3	41	32
4	18	19
5	31	89
6	13	17
7	24	74
8	17	33
9	42	34
10	14	12
11	32	93
12	20	35
13	32	66
14	28	54
15	26	61

(a) Prepare a scatter diagram of the data, using performance rating as the dependent variable.

(b) Compute the sample linear regression equation for estimating performance ratings from test scores. Plot the regression line on the scatter diagram obtained in part (a).

(c) Using the equation obtained in part (b), what is the point estimate of the performance rating of a claims adjuster who receives a score of 30 on the test?

17.7 In a study of telephone utilization, a random sample of 10 U.S. cities with populations over 100,000 persons yielded the following data:

City	Number of Phones (hundreds of thousands)	Population (hundreds of thousands)
1	1.3	1.8
2	4.3	4.6
3	1.7	1.1
4	6.6	5.9
5	3.8	2.9
6	2.0	1.1
7	8.0	6.7
8	1.6	1.7
9	8.3	4.9
10	7.6	8.4

(a) Prepare a scatter diagram of the data.

(b) Compute the sample linear regression equation for estimating the number of phones in a city (Y) from the city's population (X). Plot the regression line on the scatter diagram obtained in part (a).

(c) Using the equation obtained in part (b), what is the point estimate of the number of phones in a city with a population of 240,000 persons?

17.8 For the sample data in Problem 17.4, determine the following:
(a) Regression sum of squares.
(b) Error sum of squares.
(c) Total sum of squares.
(d) Coefficient of determination.
(e) Coefficient of correlation.

17.9 For the sample data in Problem 17.6, determine the following:
  (a) Regression sum of squares.
  (b) Error sum of squares.
  (c) Total sum of squares.
  (d) Coefficient of determination.
  (e) Coefficient of correlation.

17.10 For the sample data in Problem 17.7, determine the following:
  (a) Regression sum of squares.
  (b) Error sum of squares.
  (c) Total sum of squares.
  (d) Coefficient of determination.
  (e) Coefficient of correlation.

17.11 In a study of economic behavior of 42 families, the following sample regression equation was obtained:

$$\hat{y}_i = 40 - .2x_i$$

where $\hat{y}_i$ is the estimated percentage of a family's annual income spent on food and x_i is the family's annual income in thousands of dollars. The sample coefficient of determination was $r^2 = .25$.
  (a) If a family has an annual income of $16,000, what would be your estimate of the percentage of income that they spend on food?
  (b) What is the value of the sample correlation coefficient?
  (c) At the .05 significance level, test the null hypothesis $H_0 : \rho = 0$ against the alternative hypothesis $H_1 : \rho \neq 0$.

17.12 From the sample data in Problem 17.6, determine the following:
  (a) A 99% confidence interval for the mean performance rating of claims adjusters who obtain a test score of 30.
  (b) A 99% prediction interval for the performance rating of a particular claims adjuster who obtains a test score of 30.

17.13 For the sample data in Problem 17.7, determine the following:
  (a) A 95% confidence interval for the mean number of telephones for cities with a population of 350,000.
  (b) A 95% prediction interval for the number of telephones in a particular city with a population of 350,000.

17.14 Using the sample data in Problem 17.6, test the null hypothesis $H_0 : \beta_1 = 2$ versus the alternative hypothesis $H_1 : \beta_1 \neq 2$. Use the .02 level of significance.

17.15 Using the sample data in Problem 17.7, test the null hypothesis $H_0 : \beta_1 \leq 1$ versus the alternative hypothesis $H_1 : \beta_1 > 1$. Use the .05 level of significance.

17.16 For the data in Problem 17.6, prepare an ANOVA table in the format of Table 17.4 in the text. Use the .025 significance level. What conclusion do you draw concerning the relationship?

17.17 For the data in Problem 17.7, prepare an ANOVA table in the format of Table 17.4 in the text. Using the .05 significance level, what conclusion do you draw concerning the relationship?

17.18 From the results of Problem 17.9, determine a 99% confidence interval for the coefficient of correlation between test scores and performance ratings.

17.19 From the results of Problem 17.10, determine a 95% confidence interval for the population coefficient of correlation between population and number of telephones.

17.20 From the maintenance records of a metropolitan taxi company, a random sample of 20 cabs is selected, and the sample coefficient of correlation between total miles driven and total maintenance expenditures is determined to be $r = .78$. Determine a 98% confidence interval for the population correlation coefficient.

17.21 For a particular job, a personnel manager decides that he will adopt a given selection test if it can be demonstrated that the correlation between job performance ratings and test scores is greater than .60. For a sample of 25 employees, an estimated correlation of $r = .70$ is obtained. At the .05 significance level, is this sufficient evidence to justify adoption of the test?

17.22 For a sample of 32 middle managers, the coefficient of correlation between salary and pulse rate is determined to be $r = -.24$. At the .05 significance level, does this finding provide sufficient evidence to conclude that, in the managerial population from which the sample was selected, a linear relationship between salary and pulse rate does indeed exist?

17.23 For a random sample of 42 U.S. cities, the coefficient of correlation between per capita retail sales and proportion of the population under 18 years of age is found to be $r = -.34$. Use this result to test the null hypothesis $H_0: \rho \geq 0$ versus the alternative hypothesis $H_1: \rho < 0$. Let $\alpha = .05$.

17.24 Use the results of Problem 17.9 to test the null hypothesis $H_0: \rho \leq .40$ versus the alternative hypothesis $H_1: \rho > .40$. Let $\alpha = .01$.

17.25 Use the data in Problem 17.20 to test the null hypothesis $H_0: \rho = .60$ versus the alternative hypothesis $H_1: \rho \neq .60$. Let $\alpha = .10$.

17.26 Use the data in Problem 17.23 to test the null hypothesis $H_0: \rho \geq .30$ versus the alternative hypothesis $H_1: \rho < .30$. Let $\alpha = .05$.

17.27 At the end of a 2-week leadership training course in a large corporation, a sample of 42 trainees are administered a final course examination as well as an experimental employment test. To investigate the potential usefulness of the employment test to evaluate future applicants for the course, a simple regression analysis is performed with the results shown in the following computer printout:

VARIABLES			MEAN	STD DEV
DEPENDENT	Y — FINAL EXAM SCORE		72.9660	10.5223
INDEPENDENT	X — EMPLOYMENT TEST SCORE		44.2691	11.3010

INTERCEPT	51.6521
SLOPE	0.4815
STD ERROR OF SLOPE	0.1245
R SQUARE	0.2720
R	0.5216

ANALYSIS OF VARIANCE

SOURCE	SUM OF SQUARES	DF	MEAN SQUARE	F
REGRESSION	1234.9084	1	1234.9084	14.9479
ERROR	3304.5735	40	80.6143	
TOTAL	4539.4819	41		

(a) Explicitly state the estimated regression equation for predicting course final exam scores from the experimental employment test scores.

(b) On the basis of the estimated regression equation, what is the estimated final exam score for an applicant who obtains a score of 50 on the employment test?

(c) At the .05 significance level, does a significant relationship exist between employment test scores and final exam scores in the training course? Explain.

(d) What percentage of the sample variation in final exam scores is explained by the regression on employment test scores ?

17.28 In a study of managerial performance, a sample of 31 middle managers were administered a psychological test designed to measure general vitality level. To investigate the relationship between this personality characteristic and present salary, a simple regression analysis is performed, with salary (in tens of thousands of dollars) as the dependent variable and vitality score as the independent variable. The results are shown in the following computer printout:

VARIABLES			MEAN	STD DEV
DEPENDENT	Y — SALARY		4.5161	2.0635
INDEPENDENT	X — VITALITY SCORE		22.0323	3.7012

INTERCEPT	-3.0153
SLOPE	0.3418
STD ERROR OF SLOPE	1.6580
R SQUARE	0.3759
R	0.6131

ANALYSIS OF VARIANCE

SOURCE	SUM OF SQUARES	DF	MEAN SQUARE	F
REGRESSION	48.0225	1	48.0225	17.4697
ERROR	79.7194	29	2.7489	
TOTAL	127.7419	30		

(a) Explicitly state the estimated regression equation for predicting salary from vitality score.

(b) On the basis of the estimated regression equation, what is the estimated salary of a manager who obtains a vitality score of 20?

(c) At the .01 significance level, does a significant relationship exist between salary and vitality score? Explain.

(d) What percentage of the sample variation in salaries is explained by the regression on vitality scores?

17.29 Derive the two normal equations in Formulas (17.11) and (17.12).

18

Multiple Regression and Correlation Analysis

In this chapter we extend the regression and correlation concepts of Chapter 17 to the situation in which there are two or more independent variables. The purpose of using more than a single independent variable is to obtain models that are more explanatory and provide more precise predictions. The equation that relates the dependent variable to a set of two or more independent variables is called a *multiple regression equation,* and the correlation coefficient that measures the strength of the relationship between the dependent variable and the set of independent variables is called a *multiple correlation coefficient.*

18.1 THE MULTIPLE REGRESSION MODEL

In analyzing the relationship between a dependent variable and a set of two or more independent variables, the population under investigation is called a *multivariate* (many-variable) population. In the case of a bivariate population, as we saw in Section 17.1, the population distribution can be represented graphically by a three-dimensional figure. In the case of a multivariate population, however, we cannot draw a graph of the population distribution, since the graph would extend beyond three dimensions. Fortunately, inability to graph the distribution does not prevent us from describing it mathematically.

Suppose that we wish to predict a dependent variable Y from a set of J independent variables $X_1, X_2, \ldots, X_J$. In the multivariate population under investigation, a conditional distribution of y-values exists for each possible combination of values of the independent variables. For example, suppose that there are three independent variables: X_1, X_2, and X_3. Then there will be a distribution of y-values for the subpopulation in which $X_1 = 5$, $X_2 = 7$, and $X_3 = 11$; there will be another subpopulation of y-values for the subpopulation in which $X_1 = 5$, $X_2 = 8$, and $X_3 = 14$, and so on, for each possible set of values of the independent variables.

For a set of J independent variables, let the symbol $\mathbf{x}$ denote a specific set of values assumed by those variables. Then the expression $\mu_{Y|\mathbf{x}}$ denotes the mean of the conditional distribution of y-values given that $X_1 = x_1$, $X_2 = x_2$, and so on for the J independent variables. Using this notation, the multivariate population regression equation relating the dependent variable to the set of independent variables is given by

$$\mu_{Y|\mathbf{x}} = \beta_0 + \beta_1 x_1 + \beta_2 x_2 + \cdots + \beta_j x_j + \cdots + \beta_J x_J \tag{18.1}$$

where β_0 = intercept of the regression function
x_j = value of the jth independent variable
β_j = partial regression coefficient of the jth independent variable

The intercept β_0 represents the mean value of Y when *all* independent variables are equal to zero. The coefficient β_j is called a *partial* regression coefficient since it represents the amount of change in the mean value of Y when the corresponding x_j changes by 1 unit and the values of all other independent variables are held constant.

If the regression equation given by Formula (18.1) is used to estimate y-values, each estimate will be in error by some amount ϵ, which is equal to the difference between the actual y-value and the expected y-value given by the equation. Thus, the multiple regression model for the actual value of an individual observation may be written as

$$y_i = \beta_0 + \beta_1 x_1 + \beta_2 x_2 + \cdots + \beta_j x_j + \cdots + \beta_J x_J + \epsilon_i \tag{18.2}$$

As indicated in Section 17.1, the discrepancies between actual and expected y-values are called "residuals." In multiple regression analysis, as in simple regression analysis, the variance of the residuals, denoted by σ_ϵ^2, represents the expected squared error of prediction. A practical goal of multiple regression analysis is to find a set of independent variables that will yield a regression equation for which σ_ϵ^2 will be as small as possible.

The population multiple coefficient of determination is defined by

$$\rho^2 = 1 - \frac{\sigma_\epsilon^2}{\sigma_Y^2} \tag{18.3}$$

where ρ^2 = population multiple coefficient of determination
σ_ϵ^2 = variance of the residuals
σ_Y^2 = total variance of the dependent variable Y

Similar to the simple coefficient of determination, the multiple coefficient of determination represents the proportion of the total variance of Y that is explained by the set of independent variables in the multiple regression equation. The coefficient of multiple correlation, ρ, is simply the absolute square root of ρ^2. In contrast to simple regression analysis, the coefficient of correlation in multiple regression analysis does not have an algebraic sign. This is because, if there are several independent variables in the regression equation, some of the partial regression coefficients may be positive while others may be negative.

18.2 ESTIMATING THE REGRESSION EQUATION

The sample multiple regression equation, which is used to estimate the population multiple regression equation, is denoted by

$$\bar{y}\,|\,\mathbf{x} = b_0 + b_1 x_1 + b_2 x_2 + \ldots + b_j x_j + \ldots + b_J x_J \qquad (18.4)$$

This estimated regression equation is derived from observations of a sample of n sets of values randomly selected from the multivariate population under consideration. For example, suppose that a department store chain wishes to develop a multiple regression model to evaluate potential sites which are available for opening new branches. For each site under consideration, the firm would like to predict gross annual sales from available census data concerning certain demographic characteristics of the marketing area in which the site is located. For a sample of 20 stores currently in operation, data for the 1980 census year have been collected on the following variables:

Y : gross sales (in millions of dollars)
X_1: population of the marketing area (in hundreds)
X_2: median household size in the marketing area
X_3: median value of residential units (in thousands of dollars)
X_4: percent of households owning their home

The data for the 20-store sample are shown in Table 18.1.

Table 18.1 Data for Department Store Site Evaluation Problem

Store	Sales, y	Population, x_1	Household Size, x_2	Home Value, x_3	Percent of Home Ownership, x_4
1	10	491	4	32	63
2	9	166	4	32	85
3	15	530	4	35	59
4	10	217	4	35	90
5	8	209	4	35	66
6	19	640	3	33	11
7	8	519	4	34	79
8	13	721	3	34	21
9	24	1109	3	37	13
10	7	180	4	38	90
11	7	188	4	30	68
12	5	244	4	28	83
13	15	134	4	52	50
14	16	871	3	35	56
15	13	646	3	26	69
16	15	338	3	49	46
17	13	607	3	33	38
18	9	202	4	37	94
19	11	231	4	35	75
20	11	159	4	41	67

The method generally used to obtain the estimated multiple regression equation is an extension of the least-squares procedure discussed in Section 17.2. To understand how this is done, we begin by observing that, using the regression equation in Formula (18.4), the predicted y-value of the ith sample observation will be

$$\hat{y}_i = b_0 + b_1 x_{i1} + b_2 x_{i2} + \ldots + b_j x_{ij} + \ldots + b_J x_{iJ} \tag{18.5}$$

where $\hat{y}_i$ = predicted y-value for the ith observation
x_{ij} = value of the ith observation on the jth variable

Then e_i, the amount of error in this estimate, is the difference between y_i (the actual y-value of the ith case) and $\hat{y}_i$ (the predicted y-value for that case). Thus,

$$e_i = y_i - \hat{y}_i = y_i - (b_0 + b_1 x_{i1} + b_2 x_{i2} + \ldots + b_J x_{iJ}) \tag{18.6}$$

Under the least-squares criterion, the desired regression equation is the one that minimizes the sum of the squares of the e_i's. That is, the "best" equation is the one that minimizes

$$\sum_{i=1}^{n} e_i^2 = \sum_{i=1}^{n} [y_i - (b_0 + b_1 x_{i1} + b_2 x_{i2} + \ldots + b_J x_{iJ})]^2 \tag{18.7}$$

To find the values of the intercept and partial regression coefficients of the estimated regression equation, we take the partial derivatives of the expression in Formula (18.7) with respect to $b_0, b_1, b_2, \ldots, b_J$. Setting each of these partial derivatives equal to zero yields the following set of simultaneous equations:

$$\left. \begin{array}{l}
\sum y_i = n b_0 + b_1 \sum x_{i1} + b_2 \sum x_{i2} + \ldots + b_J \sum x_{iJ} \\[4pt]
\sum x_{i1} y_i = b_0 \sum x_{i1} + b_1 \sum x_{i1}^2 + b_2 \sum x_{i1} x_{i2} + \ldots + b_J \sum x_{i1} x_{iJ} \\[4pt]
\sum x_{i2} y_i = b_0 \sum x_{i2} + b_1 \sum x_{i2} x_{i1} + b_2 \sum x_{i2}^2 + \ldots + b_J \sum x_{i2} x_{iJ} \\[4pt]
\qquad \vdots \qquad\qquad \vdots \qquad\qquad \vdots \qquad\qquad \vdots \qquad\qquad \vdots \\[4pt]
\sum x_{iJ} y_i = b_0 \sum x_{iJ} + b_1 \sum x_{iJ} x_{i1} + b_2 \sum x_{iJ} x_{i2} + \ldots + b_J \sum x_{iJ}^2
\end{array} \right\} \tag{18.8}$$

Simultaneous solution of this set of equations will yield the estimated parameters of the regression equation.

Obviously, if the sample contains data for a large number of cases on several variables, hand solution of the equations in Formula (18.8) would be an onerous task indeed. Fortunately, computer packages are readily available for performing multiple regression analyses. A typical computer printout of the regression analysis for our department store site evaluation data is presented in Figure 18.1. We refer repeatedly to this printout throughout the remainder of the chapter.

Part 1 of the printout in Figure 18.1 simply identifies the variables, giving the sample mean and standard deviation of each. The second section of the printout displays a *correlation matrix*, which is a table showing the simple correlation coefficient between each pair of variables. For instance, the correlation matrix in this printout shows that the simple correlation coefficient between

1. VARIABLES   MEAN   STD DEV
   DEPENDENT   Y — SALES   11.9350   4.5943
   INDEPENDENT   X1 — POPULATION   420.1000 277.4548
                  X2 — HOUSEHOLD SIZE   3.6250   0.3291
                  X3 — HOME VALUE   35.3750   6.1896
                  X4 — PCT OWNERSHIP   61.1300   25.0250

2. CORRELATION MATRIX

	Y	X1	X2	X3	X4
Y	1.0000	0.7432	-0.7692	0.2873	-0.8281
X1	0.7432	1.0000	-0.7756	-0.2290	-0.6966
X2	-0.7692	-0.7756	1.0000	-0.1645	0.8526
X3	0.2873	-0.2290	-0.1645	1.0000	-0.1779
X4	-0.8281	-0.6966	0.8526	-0.1779	1.0000

3. ESTIMATED REGRESSION COEFFICIENTS

VARIABLE	COEFFICIENT	STD ERROR	T-VALUE
X1	0.01123	0.00337	3.3323
X2	3.32915	3.38440	0.9837
X3	0.29314	0.09650	3.0377
X4	-0.08973	0.03715	-2.4153
INTERCEPT	-9.73534		

4. ANALYSIS OF VARIANCE

SOURCE	SUM OF SQUARES	DF	MEAN SQUARE	F-RATIO
REGRESSION	336.39904	4	84.09976	19.514
ERROR	64.64635	15	4.30976	
TOTAL	401.04539	19		

5. MULTIPLE CORRELATION
   R-SQUARE = 0.83881
   R = 0.91586

population of the marketing area (X_1) and median home value (X_3) is $-.2290$,
and the simple correlation coefficient between median household size (X_2)
and percent of households owning their home (X_4) is .8526. Notice that the
values forming the main diagonal of the correlation matrix are all 1.0000,
since each of these values represents the correlation of a variable with itself.
Notice also that the entries in the correlation matrix are symmetrical around
the main diagonal.

The estimated regression coefficients, obtained from simultaneous solution
of the equations in (18.8), are given in part 3 of the computer printout, from
which we obtain the following estimated regression equation:

$$\bar{y}|\mathbf{x} = -9.73534 + .01123x_1 + 3.32915x_2 + .29314x_3 - .08973x_4$$

Suppose that the marketing area of a potential department store site has the
following characteristics:

Population: 500 (hundreds)
Median household size: 3

Median home value: $30 thousand

Percent of households owning their home: 65%

Using the regression model obtained from the printout, the predicted gross sales for this site is

$$\hat{y} = -9.73534 + .01123(500) + 3.32915(3) + .29314(30) - .08973(65)$$
$$= 8.83 \text{ millions of dollars}$$

The remainder of the printout is discussed in the following section.

18.3 INFERENCES IN MULTIPLE REGRESSION ANALYSIS

The mere fact that an estimated regression equation has been obtained from the *sample* data does not in itself imply that a relationship actually exists in the *population* from which the sample was drawn. Making a statistical inference concerning whether a population relationship does or does not exist is a matter of hypothesis testing. In order to use the customary methods for testing hypotheses concerning the multiple regression model given by Formula (18.2), the following assumptions are required:

1. For each possible combination of values of the independent variables, the population distribution of the residuals is normal with a mean of zero and variance σ_ϵ^2.
2. For all possible combinations of values of the independent variables, σ_ϵ^2 is a constant.
3. The residual components in the y-values are independent from observation to observation.

18.3.1 The Analysis of Variance

The application of analysis of variance to multiple regression analysis is quite similar to its use in simple regression analysis, discussed in Section 17.7.2. Indeed, in multiple regression analysis, the definitions of the total sum of squares (SST), regression sum of squares (SSR), and error sum of squares (SSE) are precisely the same as those given for simple regression analysis in Formulas (17.7) through (17.9). In a multiple regression analysis with J independent variables, there are J degrees of freedom associated with SSR, so that the regression mean square is

$$\text{MSR} = \frac{\text{SSR}}{J} \tag{18.9}$$

The number of degrees of freedom associated with SSE is $(n - J - 1)$, so that the error mean square is

$$\text{MSE} = \frac{\text{SSE}}{n - J - 1} \tag{18.10}$$

The general ANOVA paradigm for multiple regression analysis is summarized in Table 18.2.

In this analysis of variance, the F-ratio is used to determine whether a significant relationship exists between the dependent variable and the set of independent variables. Specifically, the F-ratio is used to test the null hypothesis

Table 18.2   ANOVA Summary Table for Multiple Regression Analysis

Source of Variation	Sum of Squares	Degrees of Freedom	Mean Square	F
Regression	SSR	J	$MSR = SSR/J$	MSR/MSE
Error	SSE	$n - J - 1$	$MSE = SSE/(n - J - 1)$	
Total	SST	$n - 1$		

$$H_0: \quad \beta_1 = \beta_2 = \cdots = \beta_J = 0$$

versus the alternative hypothesis

$$H_1: \quad \text{not all } \beta\text{'s are equal to zero}$$

Literally, the null hypothesis states that the population regression coefficient for each and every independent variable is equal to zero, in which case no relationship, at least of the form given by Formula (18.2), exists between the dependent variable and the set of independent variables. If the null hypothesis is false, then at least one of the population regression coefficients is equal to some value other than zero, in which case some degree of relationship does exist between the dependent variable and the set of independent variables. It is important to observe that this particular F test is an *overall* test in the sense that it considers all independent variables together as a set. Rejection of the null hypothesis in this test does not imply that any particular population regression coefficient is nonzero, nor does it imply that all β's are nonzero—only that at least one of the β's is nonzero.

For our department store site evaluation problem, the ANOVA table is shown in part 4 of the printout in Figure 18.1. Since there are four independent variables in this analysis, the number of degrees of freedom associated with MSR is $J = 4$. Also, since the sample size is $n = 20$, the number of degrees of freedom associated with MSE is $(20 - 4 - 1) = 15$. Thus, if we adopt the .05 significance level, the critical F-value, obtained from Table M (Appendix II), is $F_{4, 15; .95} = 3.06$. The computer printout reports that the F-ratio calculated from the sample data, is 19.514, which exceeds the critical value. Thus, the null hypothesis is rejected and it is concluded that, in the population, some degree of relationship does exist between sales and the set of independent variables.

An estimate of the magnitude of the relationship between sales and the set of independent variables is given by the sample coefficient of multiple correlation, denoted by R. As part 5 of the computer printout indicates, the multiple coefficient of determination for this analysis is $R^2 = .83881$, which means that 83.881% of the total variation of sales in the sample is explained by the regression on the set of independent variables. Since the coefficient of multiple determination is .83881, the coefficient of multiple correlation is $R = \sqrt{.83881} = .91586$, as the computer printout indicates. This sample result is an estimate of the population coefficient of multiple correlation, ρ.

Notice that the sample coefficient of multiple determination is simply the regression sum of squares divided by the total sum of squares. That is,

$$R^2 = \frac{SSR}{SST} \tag{18.11}$$

As the ANOVA section of the printout indicates, the regression sum of squares for our site evaluation data is SSR = 336.39904 and the total sum of squares is SST = 401.04539, so that the coefficient of multiple determination is

$$R^2 = \frac{336.39904}{401.04539} = .83881$$

Thus, even if the printout did not report the value of the coefficient of multiple determination, this value can easily be determined by hand calculation from the values of SSR and SST given in the ANOVA table.

The ANOVA table for our example also reports that the error mean square for the sample data is MSE = 4.30976. This figure represents the variance of the sample discrepancies between actual and predicted y-values—that is, the MSE is the variance of the e_i's. As such, the MSE provides an estimate of the population variance of the residuals, σ_e^2. Thus, the positive square root of MSE, which is called the *standard error of estimate*, is an estimate of the population standard deviation of the residuals. For our example, the standard error of estimate is $\sqrt{4.30976} = 2.076$.

18.3.2 Inferences Concerning the Individual Regression Coefficients

As we have observed, the F test appearing in part 4 of the computer printout is an overall test that considers all independent variables together as a set. Frequently, however, we wish to investigate the separate contributions of the individual independent variables to the explanation of the dependent variable. For this purpose, we may conduct a separate t test for each partial regression coefficient.

The coefficient which the printout reports for each independent variable in the regression equation is an estimate of the corresponding partial regression coefficient in the population regression model. That is, each b_j in the sample regression equation is an estimator of the corresponding β_j in the population regression equation. As such, each of these estimators is a statistic that has a sampling distribution. In part 3 of the printout, a standard error (STD ERROR) is shown for each independent variable. This standard error is the estimated standard deviation of the sampling distribution of the b-coefficient for that variable. Using s_{b_j} to denote the estimated standard deviation of the sampling distribution of the jth b-coefficient, we see from the printout that

$$s_{b_1} = .00337 \qquad s_{b_2} = 3.38440 \qquad s_{b_3} = .09650 \qquad s_{b_4} = .03715$$

Now suppose, for the jth independent variable, we wish to test the null hypothesis

$$H_0: \quad \beta_j = 0$$

versus the alternative hypothesis

$$H_1: \quad \beta_j \neq 0$$

The test statistic for this purpose is

$$t = \frac{b_j}{s_{b_j}} \qquad (18.12)$$

Under the assumptions stated at the outset of Section 18.3, this statistic has Student's t distribution with $(n - J - 1)$ degrees of freedom. For the two-tail test implied by the hypotheses stated above, the decision rule is to reject H_0 if $|t| \geq t_{n-J-1;\, 1-\alpha/2}$. Rejecting the null hypothesis in this particular test is tantamount to concluding that the jth independent variable, operating in the company of the other independent variables, is making a unique contribution, above and beyond that of the other independent variables, in explaining the variance of the dependent variable.

For the independent variables in our department store example, the t-values computed from Formula (18.12) are shown in the last column of part 3 of the computer printout. Notice that the calculated t-value for each independent variable is simply the b-coefficient for that variable divided by the corresponding standard error. These four calculated t-values represent four separate hypothesis tests, each performed with $(20 - 4 - 1) = 15$ degrees of freedom. If we adopt the .05 significance level, the critical t-value for each of these two-tail tests is $t_{15;\, .975} = 2.131$. That is, for each independent variable separately, the decision rule is to reject H_0 if the *absolute* value of the calculated t exceeds 2.131. Applying this decision rule to the calculated t-values in the printout, we reject H_0 for variables X_1 (population), X_3 (median home value), and X_4 (percent home ownership), but we do not reject H_0 for variable X_2 (median household size). Thus, we conclude that, operating in the company of the other independent variables, median household size is not making a unique contribution to the explanation of the variance of sales, whereas each of the other independent variables is making a unique contribution.

18.4 SPECIAL PROBLEMS IN MODEL CONSTRUCTION

Multiple regression analysis is fraught with complexities that can seriously affect its use in drawing theoretical conclusions and making practical predictions. Indeed, the reader who may be tempted to apply the methods described in this chapter to real problems is well advised to undertake more advanced study before attempting to make serious use of multiple regression analysis. In this section we briefly discuss some of the more prominent considerations of which the user of multiple regression studies should be aware.

18.4.1 Multicollinearity

In the preceding section we considered how a t test may be used to investigate whether any particular independent variable is making a unique contribution, above and beyond that of the other independent variables, in explaining the variance of the dependent variable. In interpreting such t tests, it is extremely important to realize that the contribution made by any particular independent variable is relative to the entire set of independent variables included in the model. This becomes a serious problem when the sample correlation coefficients between pairs of independent variables are substantial. The existence of a substantial correlation (either positive or negative) between a pair of independent variables indicates a high degree of redundancy between the variables—that is, the two variables are providing overlapping information concerning the dependent variable. When such redundancy exists, the estimated regression coefficients provide unsatisfactory measures of the separate contributions of the independent variables, and the t tests are inadequate for assessing those contributions.

The existence of substantial sample correlations between pairs of independent variables is called *multicollinearity*. An example of multicollinearity is provided by the computer printout in Figure 18.1. On the basis of the the t-value in part 3 of the printout, we concluded that X_2 is not making a unique contribution to the explanation of sales, whereas the other independent variables are making unique contributions. Does this imply that X_2 is useless as a predictor of sales? Not necessarily! Indeed, an inspection of the simple correlation coefficients in the top row of the second section of the printout reveals that sales are more strongly related to X_2 ($r = -.7692$) than to either X_1 ($r = .7432$) or X_3 ($r = .2873$). However, we also see that X_2 is substantially related to X_1 ($r = -.7756$) and to X_4 ($r = .8526$). As a result of these strong relationships, X_2 is not able to make a unique contribution above and beyond that provided by X_1 and X_4. Notice also that, although the relationship between X_3 and sales is relatively low ($r = .2873$), X_3 is able to make a unique contribution. This is the result of the weak relationships between X_3 and the other independent variables. In other words, X_3 is providing explanatory information not available from the other independent variables, whereas the information provided by X_2 is redundant with the information provided by X_1 and X_4.

The major effects of multicollinearity on the results of a multiple regression analysis may be summarized as follows:

1. The obtained values of the estimated regression coefficients for the separate independent variables are relative, depending on the specific set of independent variables included in the model. In other words, the estimated regression coefficients do not provide a measure of the "absolute" contribution of any particular independent variable to the explanation of the dependent variable.

2. The estimated standard deviations of the regression coefficients (i.e., the standard errors of the b-coefficients) tend to be large, such that (a) the estimates of the regression coefficients may be highly unreliable, and (b) there is a high probability that computed t-values will be insignificantly small, with consequent high risk that the t tests will result in Type II errors.

The upshot of these difficulties created by multicollinearity is that, when multicollinearity exists, assessment of the model should focus on the overall model rather than its separate components. That is, the model should be evaluated on the basis of the overall F-ratio appearing in the ANOVA table rather than on the basis of the unreliable t tests for the individual variables.

18.4.2 Selection of Independent Variables

For both practical and mathematical reasons, the number of independent variables included in a multiple regression model should be relatively small, typically no more than four or five. Thus, if many independent variables are available, the selection of which ones to include in a multiple regression model is a problem of major concern.

As a primary principle, the number of independent variables that possibly can be included in a multiple regression equation is limited by the available sample size. To obtain reliable results, the number of degrees of freedom associated with the error mean square should be as large as possible, but under no circumstances less than 1. Since the number of degrees of freedom associated with MSE is $(n - J - 1)$, it follows that J (the number of independent variables) cannot possibly be more than $(n - 2)$ if any meaningful statistical inferences are to be made from the results of the analysis.

In selecting the relatively few independent variables that are to be included in the model, a key consideration is the purpose of the analysis: Is the analysis being conducted primarily to obtain a model that will provide a theoretical explanation of the factors influencing the dependent variable, or is the analysis being performed primarily to provide a model for obtaining practical predictions?

Variable Selection for Explanatory Models. If the primary purpose of the analysis is one of providing theoretical explanation of the behavior of the dependent variable, the independent variables that are selected should be ones that theoretically have a *causal* relationship with the dependent variable, rather than merely a statistical relationship. Since the assessment of such an explanatory model would presumably focus on the "absolute" contributions of the separate independent variables to the explanation of the dependent variable, multicollinearity should be avoided. One principle to observe in order to avoid multicollinearity is to define the variables in such a way that their measures do not involve any common elements or ingredients. The following examples illustrate ways in which this principle is commonly violated, with consequent difficulties in interpreting the results of the regression analysis:

1. One independent variable may be defined as a function of another independent variable, such as defining one variable X_1 as tons of coal consumption and defining another variable X_2 as the square root of X_1. If one variable is defined as a *linear* function of another, the simultaneous equations defined by Formula (18.8) cannot even be solved to obtain the estimated regression coefficients.

2. Two or more independent variables may be defined as ratios that have a common base, such as per capita gasoline consumption and per capita income, both of which have population as their base.

3. Two or more independent variables may be defined as different functions of the same inputs, such as defining one variable X_1 as the difference between quantity supplied and quantity demanded and defining another variable X_2 as the ratio of quantity supplied to quantity demanded.

Defining two or more independent variables in ways such as those listed above— that is, in ways such that their measures involve common inputs—tends to create so-called "spurious" correlations which are undesirable if the purpose of the analysis is primarily one of theoretical explanation.

Variable Selection for Predictive Models. If the primary purpose of the multiple regression analysis is to obtain a model for making practical predictions, the independent variables need not be presumed necessarily to have any causal relationship with the dependent variable. When mere prediction rather than theoretical explanation is the goal, assessment of the model is focused on the strength of the overall relationship between the dependent variable and the set of independent variables. It may be possible to obtain two or more equally predictive models that involve quite different sets of independent variables.

The decision of whether to include a particular variable in a given set of predictors depends on whether the multiple correlation obtained when that variable is included is "significantly" greater than when it is excluded. In other words, the "goodness" of a predictive model is measured by the multiple correlation coefficient. It is important to recognize that the existence of a "significant" multiple R does not necessarily imply that a causal relationship exists. That is, *correlation does not necessarily imply causation.* However, in the case of a model designed primarily for the purpose of prediction, the important consideration is not whether there is a causal relationship, but merely whether there is a statistical relationship that is sufficiently strong and stable to make reliable predictions.

In actual practice, the decision of which independent variables to include and which to exclude in a predictive regression model is generally made with the assistance of one or more *stepwise* procedures that are available in the most commonly used statistical computer packages. For an explanation of these procedures, the reader is referred to more advanced books on regression analysis.[1]

In addition to the statistical considerations in selecting independent variables to be included in a multiple regression model that is intended for making predictions, there are certain practical considerations. For instance, it would be impractical to include some variables for which it would be unduly difficult, time-consuming, or expensive to obtain measurements. It is also usually advisable to exclude variables that, even though they might be desirable from a strictly statistical standpoint, might not intuitively appear to future users of the model to be reasonable predictors of the dependent variable. Managers are frequently disinclined to accept predictions based on variables that do not seem to be obvious predictors on the basis of their practical experience and practical judgment.

PROBLEMS

18.1 In a study of urban newsprint consumption, data were obtained on a random sample of 52 U.S. cities with populations over 50,000 persons. A multiple regression analysis was performed with the dependent variable

Y: annual newsprint consumption (in tons)

and the independent variables

X_1: number of households in city
X_2: total annual retail sales (in thousands of dollars)
X_3: proportion of population in white-collar occupations

The estimated regression coefficients are shown in the following section of the computer printout:

VARIABLE	COEFFICIENT	STD ERROR	T-VALUE
X1	1.4193	0.3265	4.3470
X2	−0.1461	0.0547	−2.6710
X3	8483.8731	26491.6978	0.3202
INTERCEPT	−3688.0482		

---

[1]See particularly N. Draper and H. Smith, *Applied Regression Analysis* (New York: John Wiley & Sons, Inc., 1966); and J. Neter and W. Wasserman, *Applied Linear Statistical Models* (Homewood, Ill.: Richard D. Irwin, Inc., 1974).

(a) State the estimated regression equation.
(b) Estimate newsprint consumption for a city with the following characteristics:

Number of households	22,000
Total retail sales	$160,586,000
Proportion white collar	.35

(c) At the .05 significance level, which of the independent variables are making unique contributions to the explanation of newsprint consumption? Explain.

18.2 For the newsprint consumption analysis in Problem 18.1, the ANOVA section of the printout reads as follows:

SOURCE	SUM OF SQUARES	DF	MEAN SQUARE	F-RATIO
REGRESSION	20644783923.4532	3	6881594641.1510	52.1809
ERROR	6330216269.2199	48	131879505.6087	
TOTAL	26975000192.6731	51		

(a) Determine the sample coefficient of determination between newsprint consumption and the set of independent variables.
(b) Interpret the result obtained in part (a).
(c) Determine the standard error of estimate.
(d) Interpret the result obtained in part (c).
(e) At the .05 level of significance, what conclusions do you draw from the F-ratio in the ANOVA table?

18.3 A personnel analyst conducts a multiple regression analysis to determine whether the first-year performance of newly hired salespeople can be predicted from psychological ability tests. The dependent variable is

Y: first-year commissions (in thousands of dollars)

The independent variables are

X_1: score on general intelligence test
X_2: score on reading comprehension test
X_3: score on arithmetic aptitude test

From a sample of 124 salespeople, the analyst obtains the following estimated regression equation:

$$\hat{y} = b_0 + .08X_1 + .10X_2 + .04X_3$$

The sample means and standard deviations of the variables in the regression equation are as follows:

Variable	Mean	Standard Deviation
Y	120	10
X_1	50	5
X_2	80	6
X_3	20	2

(a) What is the value of the constant b_0 in the estimated regression equation?
(b) Suppose that a particular salesperson obtains the following test scores:

General intelligence test	56
Reading comprehension test	75
Arithmetic aptitude test	22

Estimate the first-year commission for this salesperson.

18.4 For the multiple regression analysis in Problem 18.3, the following ANOVA table is obtained:

Source	Sum of Squares	Degrees of Freedom	Mean Square	F-Ratio
Regression	431.9	3	143.97	15.86
Error	1,089.6	120	9.08	—
Total	1,521.5	123	—	—

(a) Determine the sample coefficient of determination. Interpret this result.
(b) At the .01 significance level, what conclusion do you draw from the F-ratio in the ANOVA table?
(c) Determine the standard error of estimate. Interpret the result.

18.5 The Bon Ton Department Store chain is attempting to develop a multiple regression model to estimate gross yearly sales of potential store sites from demographic variables relating to the trade areas surrounding the sites. For this purpose, data are gathered on the following variables for a sample of 20 currently operating stores:

Y: 1979 gross sales (in millions of dollars)
X_1: median household income (in thousands of dollars)
X_2: population of trade area (in thousands)
X_3: median home value (in thousands of dollars)
X_4: percent of households owning a car

The estimated regression coefficients are shown in the following section of the computer printout:

VARIABLE	COEFFICIENT	STD ERROR	T-VALUE
X1	−0.9777	0.8168	−1.1970
X2	0.0104	0.0029	3.5862
X3	0.4367	0.1726	2.5301
X4	−0.0182	0.0516	−0.3527
INTERCEPT	8.0804		

(a) State the estimated regression equation.
(b) Suppose that the following data are gathered concerning the trade area surrounding a particular site:

Median household income (thousands of dollars)	15
Population (thousands)	410
Median home value (thousands of dollars)	35
Percent of households owning a car	60

If a store is opened on this site, what is your prediction of its gross sales (in millions of dollars)?

(c) Using the .05 significance level, which variables are making unique contributions to the prediction of sales?

18.6 For the site evaluation analysis in Problem 18.5, the ANOVA section of the printout reads as follows:

SOURCE	SUM OF SQUARES	DF	MEAN SQUARE	F-RATIO
REGRESSION	340.2290	4	85.0523	20.3107
ERROR	62.8163	15	4.1878	
TOTAL	403.0453	19		

(a) Determine the sample coefficient of determination. What is your interpretation of this result?

(b) Using the .05 significance level, what conclusion do you draw from the F-ratio given in the printout?

(c) Determine the standard error of estimate. Interpret the result.

18.7 In a study of managerial achievement, a researcher administers a battery of psychological tests to a sample of systems analysts and then performs a multiple regression analysis in which the dependent variable is:

Y: current annual salary (in tens of thousands of dollars)

and the independent variables are

X_1: score on Vitality test
X_2: score on Numerical Reasoning test
X_3: score on Sociability test
X_4: score on Verbal Reasoning test

The results on the analysis are shown in the accompanying computer printout.

1. VARIABLES

			MEAN	STD DEV
DEPENDENT	Y — SALARY		3.6000	2.0412
INDEPENDENT	X1 — VITALITY		21.3200	3.6597
	X2 — NUMERICAL REASONING		11.8400	4.9471
	X3 — SOCIABILITY		30.5200	8.2316
	X4 — VERBAL REASONING		48.3200	12.6453

2. CORRELATION MATRIX

	Y	X1	X2	X3	X4
Y	1.0000	0.3469	0.2368	-0.2004	0.2665
X1	0.3469	1.0000	-0.1720	0.0606	-0.0406
X2	0.2368	-0.1720	1.0000	0.2907	0.5634
X3	-0.2004	0.0606	0.2907	1.0000	0.4985
X4	0.2665	-0.0406	0.5634	0.4985	1.0000

3. ESTIMATED REGRESSION COEFFICIENTS

VARIABLE	COEFFICIENT	STD ERROR	T-VALUE
X1	0.24117	0.09797	2.4617
X2	0.09430	0.08727	1.0806
X3	-0.12223	0.04938	-2.4753
X4	0.29044	0.16627	1.7468
INTERCEPT	-2.66863		

4. ANALYSIS OF VARIANCE

SOURCE	SUM OF SQUARES	DF	MEAN SQUARE	F-RATIO
REGRESSION	40.97815	4	10.24454	3.4714
ERROR	59.02185	20	2.95109	
TOTAL	100.00000	24		

5. MULTIPLE CORRELATION
R-SQUARE = 0.40978
R   = 0.64014

(a) Explicitly state the estimated regression equation.
(b) Interpret the R-SQUARE given in the printout.
(c) Using the .05 significance level, what conclusion do you draw from the F-RATIO given in the ANOVA section of the printout?
(d) Determine a point estimate of the salary of a systems analyst who obtains the following test scores:

Vitality	23
Numerical Reasoning	10
Sociability	20
Verbal Reasoning	45

18.8 For the analysis in problem 18.7, what interpretation do you give to the t-values which the printout reports for the estimated regression coefficients? Does multicollinearity appear to present a serious problem in your interpretation?

18.9 Pismo Products, Inc., currently uses the Dixie Dexterity Test as an aid in the selection of employees for one of the assembly tasks in the production department. Intrigued with the results of his analysis of the Dixie Dexterity Test, Pismo's personnel manager decided to make a more extensive analysis of other variables that might be related to performance on the assembly job, thereby providing a basis for more precise prediction of an applicant's performance. After consultation with an industrial headshrinking firm, two additional selection intruments which appeared promising were the Victor Vocabulary Test and the Peephole Perceptual Speed Test. These two intruments were administered to the same sample of 20 employees who had taken the Dixie Dexterity Test. Let

Y = average daily output
X_1 = score on Dixie Dexterity Test
X_2 = score on Victor Vocabulary Test
X_3 = score on Peephole Perceptual Speed Test

Following are the personnel manager's data for these variables:

Employee	y	x_1	x_2	x_3
1	117	13	14	92
2	112	14	9	76
3	133	17	12	94
4	119	18	5	87
5	135	20	24	97
6	157	27	21	91
7	174	27	34	112
8	161	27	26	94
9	152	27	23	93

Employee	y	x_1	x_2	x_3
10	154	28	24	91
11	189	31	46	97
12	201	31	83	96
13	193	32	52	97
14	195	32	65	99
15	166	32	11	117
16	208	39	53	108
17	232	41	90	102
18	234	42	79	107
19	230	45	63	103
20	229	48	57	101

Use a canned computer program to perform a simple regression and correlation analysis of Y on X_1 and use the output from the program to answer the following questions:

(a) What is the value of the coefficient of determination? How do you interpret this value?

(b) Is the relationship between Y and X_1 statistically significant at the .05 level?

(c) If an employee's score on the Dixie Dexterity Test is 45, what is your estimate of his score on average daily output?

18.10 Use a canned computer program to perform a multiple regression and correlation analysis of the data in Problem 18.9. Based on the computer output of the analysis, answer the following questions:

(a) What is the value of the coefficient of determination? How do you interpret this value?

(b) Explicitly state the estimate regression equation.

(c) At the .05 significance level, does a relationship exist between the average daily output and the set of scores on the three tests?

18.11 You are employed in the cost-estimating department of the Burbank Aircraft Company, a large aerospace contractor. Your company is in the process of preparing a proposal to be submitted to the government for the FX, an advanced fighter-interceptor. You have been asked to prepare an estimate of the direct labor-hours required to produce the airframe for the first unit of the aircraft.

Aircraft production records on file indicate the following direct labor requirements and associated aricraft characteristics:

Aircraft	Airframe Weight (thousands of pounds)	Maximum Speed (Mach)	Range (thousands of nautical miles)	Maximum Altitude (thousands of feet)	Direct Labor-Hours (thousands of hours)
F1	4.575	.82	1.050	40.0	124.4
F2	6.523	.82	.570	42.1	130.2
F3	6.715	.89	.914	49.5	129.2
F4	8.755	.97	.668	49.6	107.9
F5	18.120	.89	1.000	51.7	273.1
F6	8.110	.89	1.108	52.1	140.0
F7	12.118	1.29	1.216	52.0	200.7
F8	13.398	1.59	1.898	49.5	261.4
F9	12.052	1.23	1.451	53.4	267.9
F10	8.008	2.10	1.376	55.2	145.1
F11	18.896	2.18	1.935	48.1	353.1

You decide that a multiple regression analysis using direct labor hours as a function of aircraft characteristics will yield an initial estimate of direct labor-hours.

(a) Plot the direct labor-hours as a function of each of the independent variables.

(b) From your inspection of the scatter diagrams obtained in part (a), arrange the independent variables in order of decreasing correlation with direct labor-hours (x_1 = highest, x_2 = next highest, etc.) Then, use a canned computer program to perform a multiple regression and correlation analysis.

(c) Examine the correlation matrix of the computer output obtained in part (b) to verify whether or not your arrangement of independent variables based on decreasing correlation with direct labor-hours is consistent with the analytical results. That is, x_1 has the highest correlation, x_2 has the next highest, and so on.

(d) The FX is expected to have the following characteristics:

Airframe weight	10.000 thousand pounds
Maximum speed	Mach 1.0
Range	1.0 thousand nautical miles
Maximum altitude	50.0 thousand feet

What is your estimate of the direct labor-hours required for the FX?

(e) Suppose that the FX has the following characteristics:

Airframe weight	19.000 thousand pounds
Maximum speed	Mach 2.5
Range	2.0 thousand nautical miles
Maximum altitude	60.0 thousand feet

What would your estimate of direct labor-hours be in this case? Would you be more or less confident of this estimate than the estimate in part (d)? Explain!

18.12 In an economic analysis, a researcher gathers data covering the 27-year period from 1950 to 1976. He then performs a multiple regression in which the dependent variable is

Y: U.S. Productivity Index (1967 = 100)

and the independent variables are

X_1: Farm Price Index (1967 = 100)
X_2: Industrial Production Price Index (1967 = 100)
X_3: Energy Commodities Price Index (1967 = 100)
X_4: U.S. population (in millions)

The results of the analysis are shown in the accompanying computer printout.

(a) Explicitly state the estimated regression equation.

(b) Interpret the R-SQUARE given in the printout.

(c) Using the .01 significance level, what conclusion do you draw from the F-RATIO given in the ANOVA section of the printout?

1. VARIABLES			MEAN	STD DEV
DEPENDENT	Y —	PRODUCTIVITY	90.0815	16.7357
INDEPENDENT	X1 —	FARM PRICE INDEX	116.4410	30.4725
	X2 —	INDUSTRIAL PRODUCTION	104.8780	25.8539
	X3 —	ENERGY PRICE INDEX	114.5440	46.8420
	X4 —	POPULATION	186.5890	20.1611

2. CORRELATION MATRIX

	Y	X1	X2	X3	X4
Y	1.0000	0.5721	0.7793	0.6224	0.9937
X1	0.5721	1.0000	0.8905	0.9042	0.5321
X2	0.7793	0.8905	1.0000	0.9724	0.7658
X3	0.6224	0.9042	0.9724	1.0000	0.6051
X4	0.9937	0.5321	0.7658	0.6051	1.0000

3. ESTIMATED REGRESSION COEFFICIENTS

VARIABLE	COEFFICIENT	STD ERROR	T-VALUE
X1	0.07413	0.02929	2.5309
X2	0.01586	0.18287	0.0867
X3	−0.03982	0.07527	−0.5290
X4	0.80550	0.06914	11.6502
INTERCEPT	−65.95026		

4. ANALYSIS OF VARIANCE

SOURCE	SUM OF SQUARES	DF	MEAN SQUARE	F-RATIO
REGRESSION	7216.55000	4	1804.13750	604.7483
ERROR	65.63230	22	2.98329	
TOTAL	7282.18230	26		

5. MULTIPLE CORRELATION

R-SQUARE = 0.9910
R   = 0.9955

18.13 Notice in the printout for the analysis in Problem 18.12 that there are substantial intercorrelations among the independent variables. How does this affect your interpretation of the t-values reported in the printout?

19

Nonparametric Methods: Chi-Square and Kolmogorov-Smirnov Tests

During the first half of the twentieth century, the development of statistical theory and methodology generally assumed that the populations under investigation had known, specified shapes. For example, in Chapter 16 we observed that the t test concerning the mean of a population assumes that the population is normally distributed. Similarly, the chi-square test for a population variance and the F test for homogeneity of variances assume that the populations under investigation are normal. When the mathematical derivation of a statistical method is based on an assumption which specifies a precise population distribution, that assumption becomes a necessary condition for justifiable use of the statistic, and the applicability of the statistic thereby can be seriously limited.

Because of the difficulty, in actual practice, of meeting assumptions that specify the distributions of the populations under investigation, there has been an increasing trend toward the development and use of *distribution-free* methods, which are techniques of statistical inference that may be used without meeting strict conditions regarding the distributions of the populations in question. In common usage, distribution-free methods frequently are referred to as *nonparametric* methods. Although there is a technical difference between the meanings of these two terms, we will follow the popular convention of using them interchangeably.

The fact that distribution-free methods do not make strict assumptions concerning the exact distribution of the population should not be misinterpreted to suggest that such methods may be applied abandonedly without satisfying any assumptions at all. All distribution-free methods do assume, for instance, that the individual observations comprising the sample are made independently and randomly. Most, but not all, of these methods also make the assumption that the population distribution is continuous. Moreover, these methods differ with respect to the *degree* to which they are distribution-free. For example, some methods, although not specifying the exact distribution of the population, do require that the population distribution be symmetrical.

Compared with the "parametric" methods discussed in previous chapters, distribution-free methods are applicable to a much broader range of statistical problems. Because of their less stringent assumptions, distribution-free statistics may be used to make inferences concerning populations having a wide variety of distributions. Moreover, parametric methods usually require the use of observations which have been made on interval scales, whereas many commonly used distribution-free methods are applicable to measurements on ordinal or even nominal scales. Indeed, it is their ability to handle such "weakly scaled" data, in addition to their applicability to more varied population forms, which accounts for the popularity of nonparametric techniques in practical research.

19.1 POWER EFFICIENCY

Suppose that you wish to test some null hypothesis H_0 against some alternative hypothesis H_1 at some specified significance level α_{max}. Suppose further that two testing procedures are available—statistical test A and statistical test B. For a specified value θ contained in H_1, you find that, with a sample of n_a observations, test A has a power of $(1 - \beta_\theta)$. To achieve the same power under the same conditions, you find that test B will require a sample of n_b observations. Then the ratio n_b/n_a represents the *power efficiency* of test A with respect to test B. For example, to obtain a specified power under identical conditions, suppose that test A requires $n_a = 40$ observations, whereas test B requires $n_b = 30$ observations. In this case, test A is less efficient than test B since test A requires a larger sample to obtain the same power. Specifically, the power efficiency of test A with respect to test B is

$$\frac{n_b}{n_a} = \frac{30}{40} = .75$$

Since power efficiency is a relative concept, it provides a convenient way of comparing various nonparametric statistics to their parametric counterparts. Studies of the efficiencies of various nonparametric methods lead to a number of general conclusions which are of considerable importance in the statistical design of applied research:

1. Generally speaking, the power efficiency of distribution-free statistics is greatest when sample size is small. Thus, most distribution-free procedures are particularly applicable (but certainly not limited) to small samples.

2. When corresponding parametric and nonparametric tests are applied under conditions that meet the assumptions of the parametric test, the nonparametric test generally will be less powerful than the parametric test. If the sample size is quite small, however, the nonparametric test will be only slightly less powerful. As the sample size increases, the nonparametric test usually tends to become less and less powerful relative to its parametric counterpart.

3. When corresponding parametric and nonparametric tests are applied under conditions that meet any assumptions required by the nonparametric test but fail to meet the stricter assumptions required by the parametric test, the nonparametric test may or may not be more powerful than the parametric test. Whether the nonparametric test actually will or will not be the more powerful depends on a complex interaction between (a) sample size and (b) the nature and extent of the violation of the parametric test's assumptions.

19.2 CHI-SQUARE TEST OF INDEPENDENCE

In decision making, the question frequently arises whether particular evidence is relevant to the decision under consideration. For example, if a credit manager proposes to consider an applicant's age as a factor in deciding whether to grant credit to that applicant, we might legitimately ask if age is a factor that is actually relevant to the credit decision. In other words, are the two variables age and credit rating independent or dependent? If credit rating is independent of age, then inquiring into an applicant's age is irrelevant to the credit decision. However, if age and credit rating are not independent, then inquiring into an applicant's age may be meaningful to the credit decision.

The chi-square test of independence is one of the most commonly used techniques for investigating whether or not two random variables are independent. This test requires no assumptions regarding the population distributions of the two variables, whereas the methods of correlation analysis presented in Chapter 17 requires the assumption that the two variables are normally distributed. Indeed, the chi-square test may be used even if the variables are qualitative rather than quantitative.

The chi-square test of independence is designed to test the null hypothesis that two variables are independent against the alternative hypothesis that the two variables are related. To perform the test, a random sample is drawn from the bivariate population under investigation, and each element in the sample is observed with respect to each of the two variables. The observations are then *cross-classified* according to the two variables. For instance, suppose that we obtain the age and credit rating of each person in a sample of 1,367 applicants for credit cards. We can then classify the applicants into age groups, such as "under 25," "25–34," "35–49," and "50 and over." For each age group, we can further classify the applicants into credit-rating groups, such as "*A*," "*B*," "*C*," and "*D*."

The customary way of displaying the results of such a cross-classification is to prepare a two-way frequency table such as Table 19.1. In this table, the

Table 19.1 Observed Frequencies of Applicants for Credit Cards Classified by Age and Credit Rating

Age	Rating				Total
	A	*B*	*C*	*D*	*Total*
Under 25	19	45	112	93	269
25–34	52	207	109	84	452
35–49	128	136	75	68	407
50 and over	72	61	59	47	239
Total	271	449	355	292	1,367

row headings designate the categories of one variable and the column headings designate the categories of the other variable. The entries in the table are *observed frequencies*, which are numbers of sample observations falling in various categories. In chi-square analysis, two-way frequency tables such as Table 19.1 are referred to as *contingency tables*.

In a contingency table the observed frequency at the intersection of the ith row and the jth column is denoted by o_{ij}. For instance, o_{24} denotes the observed frequency at the intersection of the second row and the fourth column. Inspection of Table 19.1 reveals that $o_{24} = 84$, which indicates that there are 84 applicants who are between 25 and 34 years of age and who have a credit rating of D. The symbol $o_{i\cdot}$ is used to denote the marginal observed frequency for the ith row of the contingency table. Since this marginal frequency is the sum of the frequencies in that row, we may write

$$o_{i\cdot} = \sum_{j} o_{ij} \qquad (19.1)$$

For example, in Table 19.1, the marginal observed frequency for the second row is

$$o_{2\cdot} = \sum_{j} o_{2j}$$
$$= o_{21} + o_{22} + o_{23} + o_{24}$$
$$= 52 + 207 + 109 + 84$$
$$= 452$$

which indicates that there is a total of 452 applicants in the age group from 25 to 34 years. Similarly, the symbol $o_{\cdot j}$ denotes the marginal observed frequency for the jth column of the contingency table. Since $o_{\cdot j}$ is the sum of the frequencies in the jth column, we have

$$o_{\cdot j} = \sum_{i} o_{ij} \qquad (19.2)$$

For instance, in Table 19.1, the marginal observed frequency for the fourth column is

$$o_{\cdot 4} = \sum_{i} o_{i4}$$
$$= o_{14} + o_{24} + o_{34} + o_{44}$$
$$= 93 + 84 + 68 + 47$$
$$= 292$$

which shows that there is a total of 292 applicants in credit rating group D.

The chi-square test of independence is based on a comparison of the observed frequencies in the contingency tables to the theoretical frequencies that would be expected if the null hypothesis of independence is actually true. To do this, it is necessary to compute *expected frequencies* corresponding to the observed frequencies in the contingency table. Under the null hypothesis of independence, these expected frequencies are computed by the formula

$$e_{ij} = \frac{(o_{i\cdot})(o_{\cdot j})}{n} \qquad (19.3)$$

To understand this formula, we first observe that, if $f(x_i)$ denotes the marginal probability that an observation will fall in the ith category of variable X, then this probability may be obtained by dividing the marginal frequency $o_{i\cdot}$ by n, the total frequency of the sample. That is,

$$f(x_i) = \frac{o_{i\cdot}}{n}$$

Similarly, if $f(y_j)$ denotes the marginal probability that an observation will fall in the jth category of variable Y, then this probability may be obtained by dividing the marginal frequency $o_{.j}$ by n:

$$f(y_j) = \frac{o_{.j}}{n}$$

Assuming that X and Y are independent (as the null hypothesis states), the joint probability that an observation will fall in the ith category of X and in the jth category of Y is given by

$$f(x_i, y_j) = f(x_i) f(y_j)$$
$$= \left(\frac{o_{i.}}{n}\right)\left(\frac{o_{.j}}{n}\right)$$

Finally, the expected frequency for the intersection of the ith category of X and the jth category of Y is obtained by multiplying the joint probability by the total frequency of the sample. That is,

$$e_{ij} = n\left(\frac{o_{i.}}{n}\right)\left(\frac{o_{.j}}{n}\right)$$

By simple algebra, this reduces to Formula (19.3).

According to Formula (19.3), the expected frequency for the intersection of the ith row and the jth column is obtained by multiplying the marginal observed frequency in the ith row by the marginal observed frequency in the jth column and then dividing this product by the sample size. Applying this procedure to the data in Table 19.1, the expected frequency for applicants between 25 and 34 years with a B rating is $(452)(449)/1367 = 148.5$. The remaining expected frequencies shown in Table 19.2 were obtained in a similar manner. The reader is urged to verify these figures.

Table 19.2 Expected Frequencies of Applicants for Credit Cards Classified by Age and Credit Rating

Age	Rating				Total
	A	B	C	D	
Under 25	53.3	88.3	69.9	57.5	269
25–34	89.6	148.5	117.4	96.5	452
35–49	80.7	133.7	105.7	86.9	407
50 and over	47.4	78.5	62.1	51.0	239
Total	271.0	449.0	355.1	291.9	1,367

Comparison of Table 19.1 and 19.2 reveals that their marginal frequencies are identical except for some minor rounding errors. However, discrepancies exist between the observed frequencies and the corresponding expected frequencies in the bodies of the two tables. The question now arises: Are these discrepancies sufficiently large to constitute overwhelming evidence against the null hypothesis of independence? To answer this question, we compute the following test statistic:

$$\chi^2 = \sum_{i=1}^{r} \sum_{j=1}^{c} \frac{(o_{ij} - e_{ij})^2}{e_{ij}} \tag{19.4}$$

where r is the number of rows and c is the number of columns in the body of the contingency table.[1] Applying Formula (19.4) to the observed frequencies in Table 19.1 and the expected frequencies in Table 19.2, the calculation of χ^2 is shown in Table 19.3.

Table 19.3 Calculation of χ^2 for Credit Data

o_i	e_i	$o_i - e_i$	$(o_i - e_i)^2$	$(o_i - e_i)^2/e_i$
19	53.3	−34.3	1,176.49	22.07
45	88.3	−43.3	1,874.89	21.23
112	69.9	42.1	1,772.41	25.36
93	57.5	35.5	1,260.25	21.92
52	89.6	−37.6	1,413.76	15.78
207	148.5	58.5	3,422.25	23.05
109	117.4	− 8.4	70.56	0.60
84	96.5	−12.5	156.25	1.62
128	80.7	47.3	2,237.29	27.72
136	133.7	2.3	5.29	0.04
75	105.7	−30.7	942.49	8.92
68	86.9	−18.9	357.21	4.11
72	47.4	24.6	605.16	12.77
61	78.5	−17.5	306.25	3.90
59	62.1	− 3.1	9.61	0.15
47	51.0	− 4.0	16.00	0.31
				$\chi^2 = 189.55$

The test statistic, defined by Formula (19.4), is distributed approximately as chi-square with $(r - 1)(c - 1)$ degrees of freedom. The decision rule is to reject the null hypothesis if the computed value of χ^2 exceeds $\chi^2_{(r-1)(c-1);\,1-\alpha}$. Since the contingency table in our example has four rows $(r = 4)$ and four columns $(c = 4)$, the number of degrees of freedom is $(4 - 1)(4 - 1) = 9$. Therefore, using the .05 significance level, we will reject the null hypothesis of independence if the computed value of chi-square exceeds $\chi^2_{9;\,.95}$. From Table K (Appendix II), we find that $\chi^2_{9;\,.95} = 16.92$. As Table 19.3 shows, the computed value of chi-square is 189.55, which far exceeds this critical value of 16.92. Thus, the null hypothesis is rejected, and we may conclude that age and credit rating are dependent (related).

We have noted that the test statistic defined by Formula (19.4) is distributed approximately as chi-square. The accuracy of this approximation depends on the magnitudes of the expected frequencies. The larger the expected frequencies, the greater is the accuracy of the approximation. Thus, great care should be

---

[1]In the special case of a 2×2 contingency table $(r = 2, c = 2)$, some authors have recommended that Formula (19.4) be modified by "Yates' correction for continuity." However, this correction will not be discussed in this text since it has been demonstrated to be undesirable for reasons summarized in James E. Grizzle, "Continuity Correction in the χ^2-test for 2×2 Tables," *The American Statistician*, October 1967, pp. 28–32.

exercised to avoid using the test in a situation where any of the e_i values might be "too small." Various authorities have suggested different rules of thumb concerning minimally acceptable values for the e_i's. Some authorities are willing to apply the test as long as none of the e_i's is less than 3, whereas others are squeamish about applying the test unless the minimal expected frequency is at least 10 or even greater. Suffice it to say that the sample size for this test should be as large as practicable so that every e_i will be as large as possible. In this text, we follow the common rule of thumb that no expected frequency should be less than 5.

19.3 CHI-SQUARE TEST OF HOMOGENEITY

As we have seen, the chi-square test of independence is intended to investigate whether or not a relationship exists between two random variables within a given population. For instance, in our credit example, we were concerned with whether or not there was a relationship between age and credit rating within a population of credit card applicants. The experimental procedure for this type of test consists of selecting a simple random sample of specified size from the population, and observing each case in the sample with respect to the two variables under consideration (in our example, age and credit rating). With this experimental procedure, the total number of sample observations is determined before the observations are made, but neither the row nor column totals in the contingency table are known until the observations have been tabulated.

In contrast to the independence test, the chi-square test of *homogeneity* is designed to investigate whether the distribution of a single random variable is homogeneous across two or more populations. For example, we might wish to investigate whether or not the distribution of grades is the same in the business, engineering, and music schools. The experimental procedure for this type of test consists of selecting a simple random sample from each of the populations under consideration, and observing each case in each sample with respect to the particular variable in question. With this experimental procedure, we specify in advance not only the total number of observations but also the number of observations to be taken from each of the populations under investigation. Thus, if the various populations are represented by the columns of a contingency table and the categories of the variable are represented by the rows, the column totals are determined before the observations are made, but the row totals are not known until the observations have been tabulated.

To illustrate the procedure for performing the homogeneity test, suppose that a marketing research firm wishes to investigate whether there are regional differences in the distribution of preferences for different brands of coffee. Specifically, the firm wishes to test the null hypothesis that the distribution of preferences for four different brands of coffee is the same for the coffee-drinking populations of Atlanta, Boston, Chicago, and Denver. The alternative hypothesis is that the distribution of brand preferences is *not* identical in all four populations. To conduct the test, the firm designs a sampling experiment in which taste tests are administered to 200 consumers in Atlanta, 100 consumers in Boston, 220 consumers in Chicago, and 140 consumers in Denver. The observed frequencies of consumers preferring the various brands in each city are shown in the body of Table 19.4.

Table 19.4 Observed Frequencies of Survey Respondents in Various Cities Preferring Indicated Brands of Coffee

Preference	City				Row Total	Relative Frequency
	Atlanta	Boston	Chicago	Denver		
Brand A	60	40	90	60	250	.3788
Brand B	80	20	70	40	210	.3182
Brand C	40	30	40	25	135	.2045
Brand D	20	10	20	15	65	.0985
Column total	200	100	220	140	660	1.0000

To perform the chi-square test of homogeneity, it is necessary to obtain expected frequencies corresponding to the observed frequencies in Table 19.4. The procedure for obtaining these expected frequencies is based on the assumption that the null hypothesis is true. In our example, if the null hypothesis is true, the distribution of brand preferences must be the same for the coffee-drinking populations of the four cities. If this should be the case, the proportion of the coffee-drinking population preferring any particular brand will be the same in each of the four cities. Assuming this to be true, the best "pooled" estimate of the population proportion preferring a particular brand is the relative frequency of respondents preferring that brand in all four samples combined. The relative frequencies preferring the various brands appear in the extreme right margin of Table 19.4. The relative frequency for each brand (each row) is obtained by dividing the marginal frequency for that brand (row) by the total frequency. For instance, the relative frequency for brand A is 250/660 = .3788, which indicates that, out of all the sample respondents in the four cities combined, 37.88% preferred brand A. Altogether, the relative frequencies for the various brands constitute a relative frequency distribution, which is the best estimate of the common distribution of brand preferences that the null hypothesis asserts to exist across the four populations. Using this relative frequency distribution, the expected frequency preferring a particular brand in a particular sample is obtained by multiplying the common relative frequency for that brand by the size of that sample. More formally, the expected frequency preferring the ith brand in the jth sample is given by

$$e_{ij} = \left(\frac{o_{i.}}{n}\right)(o_{.j}) \tag{19.5}$$

where $o_{i.}$ = observed marginal frequency preferring the ith brand
$o_{.j}$ = size of the jth sample
n = total frequency of all samples combined
In this formula, the term $(o_{i.}/n)$ represents the relative frequency for the ith brand. Applying this formula to the observed frequencies in Table 19.4, we obtain the expected frequencies shown in Table 19.5. As an example, the expected frequency of respondents preferring brand A in the Atlanta sample was obtained from Formula (19.4) as follows:

$$e_{11} = \left(\frac{250}{660}\right)(200) = (.3788)(200) = 75.8$$

Table 19.5 Expected Frequencies of Survey Respondents in Various Cities Preferring Indicated Brands of Coffee

Preference	City				Total
	Atlanta	Boston	Chicago	Denver	
Brand A	75.8	37.9	83.3	53.0	250.0
Brand B	63.6	31.8	70.0	44.6	210.0
Brand C	40.9	20.5	45.0	28.6	135.0
Brand D	19.7	9.8	21.7	13.8	65.0
Total	200.0	100.0	220.0	140.0	660.0

The reader is urged to verify the remaining expected frequencies in Table 19.5. By a minor rearrangement of the terms in Formula (19.5), we obtain

$$e_{ij} = \frac{(o_{i.})(o_{.j})}{n}$$

which is identical to Formula (19.3). Thus, from a purely mechanical standpoint, the expected frequencies for the chi-square homogeneity test may be obtained by exactly the same procedure used for the chi-square independence test. However, as we have seen, the rationale underlying this procedure is quite different for the two tests.

The test statistic for the chi-square homogeneity test is the same as that given by Formula (19.4) for the independence test. This statistic is distributed approximately as χ^2 with $(r-1)(c-1)$ degrees of freedom, where r represents the number of categories of the variable of interest and c represents the number of populations under consideration. For our brand preference example, since we have 4 brand preference categories ($r = 4$) and 4 populations ($c = 4$), the number of degrees of freedom is $(4-1)(4-1) = 9$. Thus, if we adopt the .10 significance level, we will reject the null hypothesis of homogeneity if the computed value of the test statistic exceeds $\chi^2_{9;\,.90}$. From Table K we find that $\chi^2_{9;\,.90} = 14.68$. As the reader may verify by applying Formula (19.4) to the observed and expected frequencies in Tables 19.4 and 19.5, the computed value of the test statistic is $\chi^2 = 19.61$. Since this computed value exceeds the critical value of 14.68, the null hypothesis is rejected. Therefore, we may conclude that not all of the four cities have identical brand-preference distributions.

19.4 CHI-SQUARE GOODNESS-OF-FIT TEST

The situation frequently arises in which it is necessary to make an inference concerning the shape of a population distribution. For example, in production planning, it might be important to know whether the daily number of assembly workers who are absent from work has a Poisson distribution, a binomial distribution, or some other distribution. As another example, if a statistician intends to conduct a t test of some hypothesis concerning a population mean, it is important for him to know whether the population is normally distributed, since the validity of a t test depends on the normality assumption. When such a question arises, it is common practice to conduct a *goodness-of-fit test*. For such a test, the null hypothesis states that the population distribution has some particular form, and the alternative hypothesis states that the population distribution is not the specific one stated in the null hypothesis. One of the most commonly used methods for performing such a test is the chi-square goodness-of-fit test.

19.4.1 Goodness-of-Fit Test for Discrete Distributions

To illustrate the application of the chi-square goodness-of-fit test to discrete distributions, we will use an example in which the null hypothesis states that the population distribution is Poisson. The precise procedure for performing the test depends on whether or not it is necessary to use the sample data to estimate any parameters of the hypothesized distribution.

Test for a Poisson Distribution with Mean Specified.   Suppose that an analyst is developing a mathematical model to describe the operations of the emergency facility of a metropolitan hospital. After making extensive informal observations of the facility's operations, and conducting interviews with the facility's personnel, it appears reasonable to the analyst to assume that the number of emergency cases arriving hourly at the facility between midnight and 5:00 A.M. follows a Poisson distribution with a mean of 1.5 arrivals per hour. To verify this assumption the analyst establishes the hypotheses

H_0:   Hourly arrivals occur as a Poisson process with $\mu = 1.5$
H_1:   Hourly arrivals do not occur as a Poisson process with $\mu = 1.5$

Note in this case that the null hypothesis not only specifies that hourly arrivals are Poisson-distributed, but also specifies the value of the mean. If arrivals were Poisson-distributed with a mean of 1.2 arrivals per hour, the null hypothesis would be false. The null hypothesis also would be false if arrivals did not follow a Poisson distribution at all.

To test the hypothesis, the analyst requests that records be kept of the number of emergency patients arriving each hour between midnight and 5:00 A.M. This will continue for 20 days until records have been obtained for 100 one-hour periods. The results of these observations are summarized in Table 19.6.

Table 19.6   Observed Frequencies
of One-Hour Periods
in Which Indicated Number
of Emergency Cases Arrived
($n = 100$ One-Hour Periods)

Number of Arrivals in a 1-Hour Period	Number of 1-Hour Periods
0	20
1	36
2	24
3	9
4	6
5	3
6	2

The chi-square goodness-of-fit test is based on a comparison of the observed frequencies with the corresponding frequencies that would be expected if the null hypothesis were true. To obtain the expected frequencies for this example, we begin by recalling from Chapter 9 that the mean of a Poisson distribution is $\mu = \lambda t$. Since the null hypothesis specifies that $\mu = 1.5$, we enter Table K with $\lambda t = 1.5$ in order to obtain the individual terms of the Poisson distribution when $\mu = 1.5$. For instance, we find in Table K that $P(R = 0 | \lambda t = 1.5) = .2231$. Therefore, if observations are made for 100 one-hour periods, and if arrivals actually follow a Poisson distribution with $\mu = 1.5$, the expected number of 1-hour periods having zero arrivals would be $(100)(.2231) = 22.31$ periods. The same procedure is followed for $r = 1, r = 2$, and so on, until we reach a value of R for which $f(r)$ is so negligibly small that it is essentially zero for all practical purposes. The expected frequencies obtained in this manner are shown in Table 19.7.

Table 19.7 Expected Frequencies for a Poisson Process with $\mu = 1.5$ Arrivals per Hour and $n = 100$ One-Hour Periods

Number of Arrivals in a 1-Hour Period		$P(R = r \mid \mu = 1.5)$	Expected Number of 1-Hour Periods	
	0	.2231	22.31	
	1	.3347	33.47	
	2	.2510	25.10	
	3	.1255	12.55	
	4	.0471	4.71	
	5	.0141	1.41	
4 or more	6	.0035	.35	6.56
	7	.0008	.08	
	8	.0001	.01	

Note that the expected frequencies in the upper tail of the distribution in Table 19.7 are extremely small—in fact, much too small for valid use of the chi-square test. Following the rule of thumb requiring a minimum expected frequency of 5, the small expected frequencies in the tail have been combined into a single class of "4 or more" arrivals.

Once the observed and expected frequencies have been obtained, the test statistic may be computed from the formula

$$\chi^2 = \sum_{i=1}^{k} \frac{(o_i - e_i)^2}{e_i} \qquad (19.6)$$

where k is the number of classes in the frequency distribution after combining the classes with small expected frequencies. Applying Formula (19.6) to the observed frequencies in Table 19.6 and the expected frequencies in Table 19.7, the calculation of χ^2 is shown in Table 19.8.

When the null hypothesis specifies the mean of the Poisson distribution, which is the case in the present example, the test statistic given by Formula (19.6) is distributed approximately as χ^2 with $(k - 1)$ degrees of freedom. Thus, the decision rule in this situation is to reject the null hypothesis if the computed value of χ^2 exceeds $\chi^2_{k-1;\, 1-\alpha}$. Since the frequency distribution in our example

Table 19.8   Computation of Chi-Square for Hospital Arrival Data

r	o_i	e_i	$o_i - e_i$	$(o_i - e_i)^2$	$(o_i - e_i)^2/e_i$
0	20	22.31	-2.31	5.34	0.24
1	36	33.47	2.53	6.40	0.19
2	24	25.10	-1.10	1.21	0.05
3	9	12.55	-3.55	12.60	1.00
4 or more	11	6.56	4.44	19.71	3.00
					$\chi^2 = 4.48$

has 5 classes after combining the classes with small expectations, the number of degrees of freedom is $k - 1 = 4$. Thus, using the .05 level of significance, we will reject the null hypothesis if the computed value of χ^2 exceeds $\chi^2_{4;\ .95}$, which, from Table K, is equal to 9.49. Since the computed value of 4.48 is less than this critical of 9.49, we accept the null hypothesis and conclude that it is not unreasonable to assume that hourly patient arrivals at the emergency facility between midnight and 5:00 A.M. follow a Poisson distribution with a mean arrival rate of 1.5 arrivals per hour.

Test for a Poisson Distribution with Mean Estimated.   In the preceding example, we considered a goodness-of-fit test for a Poisson distribution in which the null hypothesis specifies the value of the mean μ. In many real-world situations, however, experience with a phenomenon may not be sufficient to enable the analyst to make an a priori specification of the value of the mean. In such a case, it is possible to conduct a chi-square test of the null hypothesis which simply states that the phenomenon under investigation has a Poisson distribution without specifying any particular value for the mean of the distribution. Since μ is not specified it is necessary, for the purpose of determining the expected frequencies, to use an estimate $\hat{\mu}$ in place of μ. To obtain a value for $\hat{\mu}$, it is common practice to use the sample mean $\bar{x}$. Because this estimate is obtained from the same sample data that ultimately will be used in computing chi-square, the number of degrees of freedom for the test is $(k - 2)$ rather than $(k - 1)$.

To illustrate this type of test, suppose that an actuary is concerned with whether the weekly number of accidents in a particular industry follows a Poisson distribution. Because of lack of familiarity with the industry, he has no idea what the mean weekly number of fatal accidents in the industry might be. Since he is unable to make an a priori specification of μ, he simply states his hypotheses as follows:

H_0:   Weekly number of fatal accidents is Poisson-distributed
H_1:   Weekly number of fatal accidents is not Poisson-distributed

Note that these hypotheses state the form of the distribution, but do not specify the mean.

To perform the hypothesis test, the actuary inspects industry records for the past 200 weeks and determines the number of fatal accidents that occurred in each week. The resulting observed frequencies (numbers of 1-week periods) for different numbers of fatal accidents are shown in column (2) of Table 19.9. To obtain the sample mean, we first convert the observed frequencies to relative frequencies, as shown in column (3). Each of these relative frequencies is then multiplied by the corresponding value of the variable in column (1). The sum

Table 19.9 Observed Frequencies and Computation of Sample Mean

(1) Number of Fatal Accidents in a 1-Week Period, r	(2) Observed Frequency, o_i	(3) Relative Frequency, p_i	(4) $r_i p_i$
0	31	.155	0
1	53	.265	.265
2	48	.240	.480
3	36	.180	.540
4	21	.105	.420
5	7	.035	.175
6	4	.020	.120
	200	1.000	$2.000 = \bar{x}$

of these products, which are shown in column (4), is the sample mean. The result $\bar{x} = 2$ indicates that, during the 200-week period observed, fatal accidents occurred at a mean rate of 2 per week.

Computation of the expected frequencies when μ is unspecified is performed in the same manner as when μ is specified, except that $\hat{\mu}$ is used in place of μ. Using the sample mean as the value of $\hat{\mu}$, the expected frequencies (expected numbers of 1-week periods) for the different numbers of fatal accidents are calculated in Table 19.10. Notice that, after combining the classes with small

Table 19.10 Expected Frequencies for a Poisson Process with $\hat{\mu} = 2$ Accidents per Week and $n = 200$ One-Week Periods

Number of Fatal Accidents, r	$P(R = r \mid \hat{\mu} = 2)$	Expected Frequency, e_i
0	.1353	27.06
1	.2707	54.14
2	.2707	54.14
3	.1804	36.08
4	.0902	18.04
5 or more { 5	.0361	7.22 ⎫
6	.0120	2.40 ⎪
7	.0034	.68 ⎬ 10.52
8	.0009	.18 ⎪
9	.0002	.04 ⎭

expected frequencies, the number of classes is $k = 6$. Thus, the number of degrees of freedom for the chi-square test is $(6 - 2) = 4$. If we use a .10 significance level, the null hypothesis will be rejected if the computed value of χ^2 exceeds $\chi^2_{4;\,.90}$ which, from Table K, is equal to 7.78. From Table 19.11, which shows the calculation of chi-square, we see that $\chi^2 = 1.78$. Since this computed value is less than the critical value, the null hypothesis is not rejected. Thus, it is reasonable for the actuary to assume that the weekly number of fatal accidents in the industry follows a Poisson distribution.

Table 19.11   Computation of Chi-Square for Industrial Accident Data

r	o_i	e_i	$o_i - e_i$	$(o_i - e_i)^2$	$(o_i - e_i)^2/e_i$
0	31	27.06	3.94	15.52	.57
1	53	54.14	−1.14	1.30	.02
2	48	54.14	−6.14	37.70	.70
3	36	36.08	−.08	.01	.00
4	21	18.04	2.96	8.58	.47
5 or more	11	10.52	.48	.23	.02

$$\chi^2 = 1.78$$

Generalization of the Procedure. The same general procedure that we have used to test goodness of fit to a Poisson distribution may be applied to test goodness of fit to any hypothesized discrete distribution. This procedure may be summarized as follows:

1. Determine the hypothesized probability for each class in the frequency distribution. Depending on the situation, this is done in one of three ways:
   a. The probability for each class may be computed or determined from tables if the null hypothesis completely specifies the distribution, such as "H_0: hourly arrivals occur as a Poisson process with $\mu = 1.5$."
   b. The null hypothesis may not specify the hypothesized distribution completely, such as "H_0: weekly number of fatal accidents is Poisson-distributed." In such a case, the unspecified parameter(s) may be estimated from the sample data. Then the probability for each class is computed as in part (a), using the estimated value(s) in place of the unspecified parameter(s).
   c. No calculation is necessary if the probability for each class is directly given in the null hypothesis, such as "H_0: 50% of the population is in class A, 30% in class B, and 20% in class C."
2. Determine the expected frequency for each class. This is done by multiplying the probability for the class by the total sample size.
3. Determine the number of degrees of freedom, using the formula

$$\nu = k - 1 - a$$

   where k = number of classes in the frequency distribution after combining any classes with small expected frequencies
        a = number of parameters estimated from the sample data
   When no parameters are estimated, a is equal to zero, and ν reduces to $k - 1$.
4. Compute the observed value of chi-square using Formula (19.6).

19.4.2 Chi-Square Test for a Normal Distribution

As we have seen in previous chapters, many statistical procedures are based on the assumption that the population under consideration is normally distributed. One way to investigate the validity of such an assumption is to conduct a chi-square test of the null hypothesis that the population distribution is normal. The precise procedure for performing this test depends on whether or not the null hypothesis specifies the mean and standard deviation of the distribution.

Test for a Normal Distribution with μ and σ Specified. Suppose that a personnel director has developed a tailor-made employment test for screening applicants for a unique type of job. For special purposes in processing and interpreting applicants' scores on the test, he has attempted to construct the employment test so that the scores will be normally distributed with a mean of 100 and a standard deviation of 10. To determine whether his newly constructed employment instrument meets these specifications, the director decides to conduct a sample study to test the null hypothesis

H_0: For the applicant population, scores on this test are normally distributed with a mean of 100 and a standard deviation of 10

versus the alternative hypothesis

H_1: For the applicant population, scores on this test are not normally distributed with a mean of 100 and a standard deviation of 10

For this purpose, he administers the employment test to a sample of 400 job applicants. From the resulting test scores he obtains the frequency distribution shown in Table 19.12, which indicates the observed frequencies (numbers of applicants) in various test score intervals.

Table 19.12   Scores of 400 Job Applicants on Tailor-Made Test

Test Score	Number of Applicants
60–69	3
70–79	18
80–89	39
90–99	142
100–109	139
110–119	30
120–129	21
130–139	8
Total	400

The hypothesis test in this situation is performed using the chi-square statistic given by Formula 19.6. To compute the statistic, it first is necessary to determine the expected frequencies. This is accomplished as shown in Table 19.13. It should be noted that the characteristic being measured by the employ-

Table 19.13   Computation of Expected Frequencies for Normal Distribution with $\mu = 100$ and $\sigma = 10$

(1) Class Limit		(2) Upper Boundary, x_i	(3) $z_i = \dfrac{x_i - \mu_0}{\sigma_0}$	(4) $F_N(z_i)$	(5) p_i	(6) $e_i = np_i$	
Below 80	Below 70	69.5	−3.05	.0011	.0011	.44	8.08
	70–79	79.5	−2.05	.0202	.0191	7.64	
	80–89	89.5	−1.05	.1469	.1267	50.68	
	90–99	99.5	−0.05	.4801	.3332	133.28	
	100–109	109.5	+0.95	.8289	.3488	139.52	
	110–119	119.5	+1.95	.9744	.1455	58.20	
Above 119	120–129	129.5	+2.95	.9984	.0240	9.60	10.24
	130–139	139.5	+3.95	1.0000	.0016	0.64	
						$n = 400.00$	

ment test is a continuous variable, and that scores on the test are approximate numbers with boundaries $\frac{1}{2}$ unit above and below each value. Thus, each class interval in column (1) of Table 19.13 has an upper boundary which is $\frac{1}{2}$ unit greater than the nominal upper limit of the interval. These upper boundaries are shown in column (2) of this table, and the corresponding z-scores are shown in column (3). These z-scores were computed under the assumption that the values of the mean and standard deviation are those stated in the null hypothesis: $\mu_0 = 100$ and $\sigma_0 = 10$.

Once the z-scores are obtained, the next step is to determine, from Table I (Appendix II), the cumulative normal probability corresponding to each z-score, as shown in column (4) of Table 19.13. Column (5) shows the normal probability for each class interval. For the first interval, this probability is the same as the cumulative probability in column (4). For each of the remaining intervals, the probability is equal to the cumulative probability for that interval minus the cumulative probability for the preceding interval. For instance, for the second interval, the probability is

$$F_N(-2.05) - F_N(-3.05) = .0202 - .0011 = .0191$$

Multiplying the probabilities in column (5) by the sample size, we obtain the expected frequencies shown in column (6).

Just as in the case of the goodness-of-fit test for a Poisson distribution with μ specified, the test for a normal distribution with μ and σ specified has $(k - 1)$ degrees of freedom. After combining classes to avoid small expected frequencies in the two tails of the distribution in Table 19.13, there are $k = 6$ classes. Thus, we have a chi-square test with $(6 - 1) = 5$ degrees of freedom. If the personnel director adopts the .005 level of significance, his decision rule is to reject H_0 if $\chi^2 > \chi^2_{5;\ .995}$. From Table K, this critical value is 16.75. As shown in Table 19.14, the computed value of chi-square is 71.95, which exceeds the critical

Table 19.14 Computation of Chi-Square for Employment Test Data

Test Score	o_i	e_i	$o_i - e_i$	$(o_i - e_i)^2$	$(o_i - e_i)^2/e_i$
Below 80	21	8.08	12.92	166.93	20.66
80–89	39	50.68	−11.68	136.42	2.69
90–99	142	133.28	8.72	76.04	.57
100–109	139	139.52	−0.52	.27	.00
110–119	30	58.20	−28.20	795.24	13.66
120 and above	29	10.24	18.76	351.94	34.37
Total	400	400.00	0		$\chi^2 = 71.95$

value. Thus, the null hypothesis is rejected and it is concluded that the employment test does not yield scores that are normally distributed with a mean of 100 and a standard deviation of 10.

Test for a Normal Distribution with μ and σ Estimated. In the preceding section we applied the chi-square test of normality to a situation where the null hypothesis stated values for the mean and standard deviation, thereby completely specifying the distribution. In most practical situations, however, there is no basis for specifying values of μ and σ prior to observing the sample. In such cases, the mean and standard deviation are estimated from the same sample data that are used to conduct the normality test. The test is conducted in the same manner as our previous example, except that the specified values of μ and σ are replaced by the estimated values $\bar{x}$ and s, and the number of degrees of freedom is $(k - 3)$ rather than $(k - 1)$.

To illustrate this procedure, consider the Medar Manufacturing Company, which has retained the services of a consultant to improve the efficiency of their hand assembly operation. Upon preliminary observation of the assembly operation, the consultant finds that the time required to assemble a unit is highly variable. Before commencing any formal analysis of the sources of this variability, he wishes to determine whether it is reasonable to assume that the distribution of assembly times is normal. Specifically, he wishes to test the null hypothesis

H_0: Assembly time is normally distributed

versus the alternative hypothesis

H_1: Assembly time is not normally distributed

For this purpose, he makes careful observations of the amount of time required to assemble each of 200 units. From these observations he obtains the frequency distributions shown in columns (1) and (2) of Table 19.15.

Table 19.15 Frequency Distribution of Assembly Times

(1) Time (minutes)	(2) Observed Frequency, o_i	(3) Midpoint, x_i	(4) $o_i x_i$	(5) $o_i x_i^2$
40–44	12	42.0	504	21,168
45–49	27	47.0	1269	59,643
50–54	41	52.0	2132	110,864
55–59	60	57.0	3420	194,940
60–64	33	62.0	2046	126,852
65–69	16	67.0	1072	71,824
70–74	6	72.0	432	31,104
75–79	4	77.0	308	23,716
80–84	1	82.0	82	6,724
	200		11,265	646,835

Since the hypotheses do not specify the values of μ and σ, the consultant's first task in performing the goodness-of-fit test is to estimate these two parameters. The formulas for estimating these two parameters from the sample frequency distribution are

$$\hat{\mu} = \bar{X} = \frac{\sum o_i x_i}{n} \tag{19.7}$$

$$\hat{\sigma} = S = \sqrt{\frac{\sum o_i x_i^2 - (\sum o_i x_i)^2/n}{n - 1}} \tag{19.8}$$

where x_i = midpoint of the ith class
   o_i = observed frequency in the corresponding class
   n = sample size

Calculation of $\sum o_i x_i$ and $\sum o_i x_i^2$ for the assembly time data is shown in columns (4) and (5) of Table 19.15. Substituting these sums into Formulas (19.7) and (19.8), the estimated mean and standard deviation are as follows:

$$\hat{\mu} = \bar{x} = \frac{11{,}265}{200} = 56.325$$

$$\hat{\sigma} = s = \sqrt{\frac{646{,}835 - (11{,}265)^2/200}{200 - 1}} = 7.87$$

Once the estimated mean and standard deviation have been obtained, the next step is to compute the expected frequencies for the chi-square test. This is done by the same procedure that was followed in Table 19.13, except that μ_0 is replaced by $\hat{\mu}$ and σ_0 is replaced by $\hat{\sigma}$. These calculations for the assembly time data are shown in Table 19.16.

Table 19.16 Computation of Expected Frequencies for Observations from Hypothesized Normal Distribution with $\hat{\mu} = 56.325$ and $\hat{\sigma} = 7.87$ ($n = 200$)

(1) Assembly Time	(2) Upper Boundary, x_i	(3) $z_i = \dfrac{x_i - \hat{\mu}}{\hat{\sigma}}$	(4) $F(z_i)$	(5) p_i	(6) $e_i = np_i$
Below 45	44.5	−1.50	.0668	.0668	13.36
45–49	49.5	−0.87	.1921	.1253	25.06
50–54	54.5	−0.23	.4000	.2079	41.58
55–59	59.5	0.40	.6554	.2554	51.08
60–64	64.5	1.04	.8508	.1954	39.08
65–69	69.5	1.67	.9527	.1019	20.38
70 or more { 70–74	74.5	2.31	.9896	.0369	7.38 }
75–79	79.5	2.94	.9984	.0088	1.76
80–84	84.5	3.58	.9998	.0014	.28 } 9.46
Above 84			1.0000	.0002	.04
					$n = 200.00$

After combining classes with small expected frequencies, there are $k = 7$ classes. Thus, the degrees of freedom for this test is $(k - 3) = 4$. If the consultant adopts the .05 significance level, his decision rule is to reject H_0 if $\chi^2 > \chi^2_{4;\,.95}$. From Table K this critical value is 9.49. As shown in Table 19.17, the computed value of χ^2 is 4.00. Since this computed value of χ^2 is less than the critical value, the consultant may accept the null hypothesis and proceed on the assumption that the universal distribution of assembly times is essentially normal.

Table 19.17 Computation of Chi-Square for Assembly Time Data

Assembly Time	o_i	e_i	$o_i - e_i$	$(o_i - e_i)^2$	$(o_i - e_i)^2/e_i$
Below 45	12	13.36	−1.36	1.85	.14
45–49	27	25.06	1.94	3.76	.15
50–54	41	41.58	−0.58	.34	.01
55–59	60	51.08	8.92	79.57	1.56
60–64	33	39.08	−6.08	36.97	.95
65–69	16	20.38	−4.38	19.18	.94
70 or more	11	9.46	1.54	2.37	.25
Total	200	200.00	0		$\chi^2 = 4.00$

19.5 KOLMOGOROV-SMIRNOV GOODNESS-OF-FIT TEST

While the chi-square goodness-of-fit test is a very popular method for testing hypotheses concerning population shape, it has a serious shortcoming: it cannot be used with small samples. That is, in order for each of the cell frequencies to be adequately large to perform the chi-square test, the total sample size must be substantial. Thus, to perform a goodness-of-fit test with a small sample, an alternative to chi-square is needed. Such an alternative is the Kolmogorov–Smirnov (K-S) test, which may be used to test goodness of fit to any *continuous* distribution. Unfortunately, this test is not applicable to testing hypotheses concerning *discrete* distributions. While the K-S test is applicable to any continuous distribution, we shall limit our discussion to its use in testing goodness of fit to a normal distribution. In the following discussion we consider the use of the K-S normality test under two different conditions: (1) when values of μ and σ are specified in H_0, and (2) when values of μ and σ are estimated from the sample data.[2]

19.5.1 Kolmogorov–Smirnov Test for Normality with μ and σ Specified

In our discussion of the chi-square goodness-of-fit test, we considered the case of the personnel director's attempt to construct an employment test such that the scores for an applicant population would be normally distributed with $\mu = 100$ and $\sigma = 10$. In that example, the director administered the test to a sample of 400 applicants and applied the chi-square test for normality with μ and σ specified.

Suppose, for our present purposes, that the personnel director administered the test to a sample of only 20 applicants. Then the sample would be too small for the chi-square test, but the K-S test would be appropriate. To illustrate the use of the K-S test, assume that the test scores for the sample of 20 applicants are as follows:

$$92, \quad 103, \quad 74, \quad 101, \quad 127, \quad 99, \quad 93, \quad 91, \quad 109, \quad 82,$$
$$62, \quad 79, \quad 114, \quad 97, \quad 84, \quad 104, \quad 81, \quad 94, \quad 96, \quad 102$$

The procedural steps for the K-S test are summarized in Table 19.18. The first step is to arrange the observed sample values in array, as shown in column (1) of the table. The cumulative frequency corresponding to each of these values then is entered in column (2). The cumulative relative frequencies of the observed values, denoted by $F_0(x)$, are tabulated in column (3). Each of these values is obtained by dividing the corresponding value in column (2) by the total sample size, which is 20 in this example.

Each of the standard normal z-values in column (4) is calculated under the assumption that the null hypothesis is true (i.e., X is normally distributed with $\mu = 100$ and $\sigma = 10$). Since it is assumed that the random variable being observed is continuous, the upper boundary of each x-value is used in computing

---

[2]To use the general Kolmogorov–Smirnov tables, the null hypothesis must completely specify the distribution (i.e., state both the distributional form and the values of its parameters). However, for some distributional forms, special-purpose tables exist for performing the test when the parameters are estimated from the data.

Table 19.18   Kolmogorov–Smirnov Test for Employment Test Data

(1) x	(2) cf	(3) $F_o(x)$	(4) z	(5) $F_e(x)$	(6) $\lvert F_o(x) - F_e(x) \rvert$
62	1	.0500	−3.75	.0001	.0499
74	2	.1000	−2.95	.0016	.0984
79	3	.1500	−2.05	.0202	.1298
81	4	.2000	−1.85	.0322	.1678
82	5	.2500	−1.75	.0401	.2099
84	6	.3000	−1.55	.0606	.2394 ⟵ D
91	7	.3500	− .85	.1977	.1523
92	8	.4000	− .75	.2266	.1734
93	9	.4500	− .65	.2578	.1922
94	10	.5000	− .55	.2912	.2088
96	11	.5500	− .35	.3632	.1868
97	12	.6000	− .25	.4013	.1987
99	13	.6500	− .05	.4801	.1699
101	14	.7000	.15	.5596	.1404
102	15	.7500	.25	.5987	.1513
103	16	.8000	.35	.6368	.1632
104	17	.8500	.45	.6736	.1764
109	18	.9000	.95	.8289	.0711
114	19	.9500	1.45	.9265	.0235
127	20	1.0000	2.75	.9970	.0030

z. For example, the first x-value, 62, has an upper boundary of 62.5. Thus, the corresponding z is $(62.5 - 100)/10 = -3.75$. Similarly, the x-value 109 has an upper boundary of 109.5, so that the corresponding z is

$$(109.5 - 100)/10 = .95.$$

The entries in column (5), designated by $F_e(x)$, are the expected cumulative relative frequencies for each x-value under the assumption that the null hypothesis is true. Each of the entries in column (5) is the value found in Table M (Appendix II) for the corresponding z-value in column (4).

Column (6) is obtained by computing the *absolute* differences between the values in column (3) and the corresponding values in column (5). The actual test statistic, D, is the maximum value in column (6). That is,

$$D = \max \lvert F_o(x) - F_e(x) \rvert \tag{19.9}$$

In our example, the observed value of D is .2394, which is the largest value in column (6). For this application of the Kolmogorov-Smirnov statistic,[3] the decision rule is to reject the null hypothesis if $D > D_{n;\,1-\alpha/2}$. If the personnel director adopts the .05 significance level, his decision rule is to reject the null hypothesis if $D > D_{20;\,.975}$. From Table P (Appendix II) this critical value is 2.94. Since the computed value of D is less than this critical value, the evidence is not sufficient to reject the null hypothesis that the sample was drawn from a normal population with $\mu = 100$ and $\sigma = 10$.

---

[3]This application of the K-S statistic is actually a two-tailed test. However, because the statistic is an absolute value, only the upper-tail critical region is considered in performing the test.

19.5.2 Kolmogorov-Smirnov Test for Normality with μ and σ Estimated

A manufacturer of fireworks produces a particular type of rocket for which the specifications require that the average amount of powder per rocket be no less than 1.45 kilograms. A quality control engineer wishes to perform a statistical test with a small sample to determine whether this specification is being met. Specifically, he proposes to perform a t test of the hypothesis

$$H_0: \quad \mu \geq 1.45 \text{ kilograms}$$
$$H_1: \quad \mu < 1.45 \text{ kilograms}$$

He therefore makes a random selection of 16 rockets and weighs their powder content to the nearest $\frac{1}{100}$ kilogram, with the following results:

$$1.47, \quad 1.18, \quad 1.21, \quad 1.04, \quad 1.20, \quad 1.50, \quad 1.19, \quad 1.46,$$
$$1.48, \quad 1.44, \quad 1.01, \quad 1.05, \quad 1.21, \quad 1.02, \quad 1.45, \quad 1.07$$

Before performing the t test, the engineer feels that he should perform a K-S test to determine whether the data support the necessary assumption that the powder content of the rocket population is normally distributed. Since he has no idea what the population mean and standard deviation might be, he must estimate them from the sample values. From the sample data he obtains $\bar{x} = 1.25$ as an estimate of μ, and $s = .187$ as an estimate of σ.

Once the estimates of the mean and standard deviation have been obtained, the calculation of the test statistic proceeds exactly as in the previous section, using $\bar{x}$ in place of μ and s in place of σ. The steps for our rocket data are summarized in Table 19.19. As the table shows, the data yield an observed value of $D = .2003$.

Table 19.19 Kolmogorov–Smirnov Test for Rocket Data

(1) x_i	(2) c_f	(3) $F_o(x)$	(4) z	(5) $F_e(x)$	(6) $\lvert F_o(x) - F_e(x) \rvert$
1.01	1	.0625	−1.26	.1038	.0413
1.02	2	.1250	−1.20	.1151	.0099
1.04	3	.1875	−1.10	.1357	.0518
1.05	4	.2500	−1.04	.1492	.1008
1.07	5	.3125	−.94	.1736	.1389
1.18	6	.3750	−.35	.3632	.0118
1.19	7	.4375	−.29	.3859	.0516
1.20	8	.5000	−.24	.4052	.0948
1.21⎱ 1.21⎰	10	.6250	−.19	.4247	.2003 ⟵ D
1.44	11	.6875	1.04	.8508	.1633
1.45	12	.7500	1.10	.8643	.1143
1.46	13	.8125	1.15	.8749	.0624
1.47	14	.8750	1.20	.8849	.0091
1.48	15	.9375	1.26	.8962	.0413
1.50	16	1.0000	1.36	.9131	.0869

The decision rule for this test is to reject H_0 if the computed value of D exceeds the critical value $D_{n;\,1-\alpha/2}$. However, in this case, the critical value cannot be obtained from Table P, since that table is applicable only when there is no need to estimate any parameters. When it is necessary to estimate parameters, special tables are required. For the particular purpose of performing the K-S normality test when μ and σ are estimated, H. W. Lilliefors has developed a special table which appears as Table Q in Appendix II. If the quality control engineer adopts the .10 significance level, the critical value from this table is $D_{16;\,.95} = .195$. Since the computed value of D exceeds this critical value, H_0 is rejected and the normality assumption is not justified. Because the data fail to support the normality assumption necessary for the t test, the quality control engineer is now forced to adopt some alternative method for testing his hypothesis concerning the powder content of the rockets. Some common nonparametric tests for this purpose are presented in Chapter 20.

PROBLEMS

19.1 An investigator wishes to test the null hypothesis $H_0: \mu \leq 60$ against the alternative hypothesis $H_1: \mu > 60$, with $\alpha_{max} = .05$. For the alternative $\mu = 62$, he wishes the power of the test to be $1 - \beta_{62} = .90$. To achieve the desired power, test A requires a sample size of 80 cases, and test B requires a sample size of 120 cases. What is the power-efficiency of test B with respect to test A?

19.2 Two alternative statistical tests are available to an investigator who wishes to test the null hypothesis $H_0: \mu = 100$ against the alternative hypothesis $H_1: \mu \neq 100$. If the .01 significance level is used, test A requires a sample size of 60 cases to achieve a probability of .95 that the null hypothesis will be rejected if actually $\mu = 105$. What sample size is required for test B to achieve the same power if the power-efficiency of test B with respect to test A is .75?

19.3 The Gourmet's Club is a charge card firm which considers a "good" credit risk to be a person who regularly pays in full within 30 days of the billing date. In a study to determine whether home ownership is a relevant consideration in issuing a charge card to an applicant, a random sample of 500 current card holders is investigated. The numbers of homeowners and nonhomeowners in the sample who were identified as good and poor credit risks are shown in the following contingency table:

| Home | Risk Evaluation | | |
owner	Good	Poor	Total
Yes	79	41	120
No	231	149	380
Total	310	190	500

At the .01 significance level, are these data sufficient to conclude that homeownership and risk evaluation are related?

19.4 To investigate whether there is any relationship between socioeconomic class and newspaper readership, the advertising manager of *The Daily Bugle* conducts a poll of two samples of 50 persons each taken from the residents of an upper socioeconomic neighborhood and the residents of a middle socioeconomic neighborhood. Each person in the poll was asked how often he or she reads a daily newspaper. The results are summarized in the following frequency table:

Readership Level	Socioeconomic Class		Total
	Upper	Middle	
Every day	20	10	30
Occasionally	20	30	50
Rarely, if ever	10	10	20
Total	50	50	100

At the .05 level of significance, test the null hypothesis that readership level is independent of socioeconomic class.

19.5 During a period of 1,000 trading days, the Midsouthern Stock Exchange daily traded 1,000 issues consisting of 700 industrial stocks, 100 transportation stocks, and 200 utilities stocks. For each of these 1,000 days, the average closing price of each of these groups of stocks was classified as being advanced, declined, or unchanged. The numbers of trading days on which the closing averages of each category of stock exhibited advance, decline, or no change are shown in the following contingency table:

Stock Category	Behavior of Average Price			Total
	Advance	Decline	No Change	
Industrial	290	330	80	700
Transportation	30	60	10	100
Utility	80	110	10	200
Total	400	500	100	1,000

If $\alpha_{max} = .10$, do these results provide sufficient evidence to conclude that a relationship exists between average price behavior and category of stock?

19.6 In a study to determine whether newsstand purchase of *Joyboy* magazine is related to educational level, the publishers commissioned a survey to be conducted of gentlemen browsers in metropolitan newsstands. A total of 1,000 browsers were interviewed. Of these 1,000 browsers, 50 purchased a copy of *Joyboy*, and 300 were college graduates. Among the college graduates, 29 purchased a copy of *Joyboy*. If $\alpha_{max} = .025$, do these results provide sufficient evidence to conclude that a significant relationship exists between educational level and purchase of *Joyboy*?

19.7 The marketing department of a brewery maintains a panel of 100 beer testers, of whom 50 are men and 50 are women. The members of the panel have just been asked to compare two new brews—brew X and brew Y. The numbers of men and women on the panel who preferred each brew are shown in the following contingency table:

Preferred Brew	Sex of Taster		Total
	Male	Female	
X	40	20	60
Y	10	30	40
Total	50	50	100

At the .05 level of significance, are these data sufficient to conclude that the male and female populations are not homogeneous with respect to brew preference?

19.8 A large industrial organization that has plants in three different cities is considering three different profit-sharing plans. In each plant a sample of employees is polled to determine which plan they prefer. The number of employees preferring each plan in each plant is as follows:

Plant	Plan 1	Plan 2	Plan 3
A	10	20	20
B	40	50	20
C	40	30	20
Total	90	100	60

At the .05 significance level, are these data sufficient to conclude that the employee populations in the three plants are not homogeneous with respect to their preferences for the three profit-sharing plans?

19.9 During a 100-day observation period in a factory, the number of daily breakdowns of a particular type of machine was distributed as follows:

Number of Breakdowns	Number of Days This Number of Breakdowns Occurred
0	15
1	25
2	30
3	20
4 or more	10

At the .05 significance level, test the null hypothesis that the breakdowns occur according to a Poisson process at a mean rate of 2 breakdowns per day.

19.10 Biomatics, Inc., is a producer of high-precision medical devices. For the past 100 weeks, the weekly number of orders received for a particular type of respirator was distributed as follows:

Number of Orders	Number of Weeks
0	20
1	36
2	25
3	12
4	7

(a) At the .025 significance level, test the null hypothesis that the weekly number of orders for this type of respirator arrive according to a Poisson process.

(b) At the .025 significance level, test the null hypothesis that orders for this type of respirator arrive according to a Poisson process at a mean rate of 1.5 orders per week.

(c) How do the null hypotheses in parts (a) and (b) differ? How does this difference affect the testing procedure? How do you interpret the difference in the conclusions drawn in parts (a) and (b)?

19.11 In evaluating the warranty policy on its DS-402 model, a manufacturer of home-movie projectors estimates that, during the 1-year period following the date of purchase, 20% of the units sold will require no service, 70% will require service costing less than $30, and 10% will require service costing at least $30. From records of sales dating back at least 1 year, a sample of 50 sales is selected at random. For this sample, 15 required no service, 30 required service costing less than $30, and 5 required service costing at least $30.

(a) Do these sample data provide sufficient evidence to gainsay the manufacturer's estimates of the percentages of units in the three service categories? Use χ^2 with $\alpha_{max} = .01$.

(b) What technical difficulty would arise in part (a) if the sample contained only 25 sales? How might you handle this difficulty?

19.12 To test a particular pair of dice for "fairness," the two dice are tossed 360 times with the following results:

Sum of 2 Dice	Number of Occurrences
2	8
3	16
4	36
5	30
6	60
7	60
8	40
9	50
10	25
11	25
12	10

Are these data sufficient evidence to conclude that the dice are loaded? Use $\alpha_{max} = .05$.

19.13 Below is a frequency distribution of the scores of a sample of 125 middle managers on the EAS Numerical Ability Test. Use these data to test the null hypothesis that in the middle-manager population which the sample represents, scores on this test are normally distributed with $\mu = 50$ and $\sigma = 10$. Assume that $\alpha_{max} = .025$.

Scores	Frequency
5–14	4
15–24	13
25–34	27
35–44	31
45–54	23
55–64	19
65–74	8

19.14 Use the data in Problem 19.13 to test

H_0: Scores on this test are normally distributed in the population

H_1: Scores on this test are not normally distributed in the population

Assume that $\alpha_{max} = .025$.

19.15 Below is a frequency distribution of the burning lives (in hours) of a sample of 200 home-movie projector lamps produced by a particular process. Use these data to test the null hypothesis, at the .05 significance level, that the lives of the lamps produced by this process are normally distributed with $\mu = 22$ and $\sigma = 5$.

Hours	Frequency
0–4	13
5–9	15
10–14	30
15–19	60
20–24	50
25–29	15
30–34	10
35–39	5
40–44	2

19.16 Use the data in Problem 19.15 to test

H_0: Process burning lives are normally distributed
H_1: Process burning lives are not normally distributed

19.17 Below are cigarette filter Tar Removal Index (TRI) measurements obtained by a special machine for a sample of 9 cigarettes:

6.85	6.91	6.62
7.22	6.83	6.63
6.92	7.14	6.98

Use these data to test the null hypothesis that, for the population of cigarettes from which the sample was selected, TRI is normally distributed with $\mu = 6.8$ and $\sigma = .10$. Use the .05 significance level.

19.18 Use the data in Problem 19.17 to test

H_0: Population TRI is normally distributed
H_1: Population TRI is not normally distributed

Assume that $\alpha_{max} = .05$.

19.19 Below are the times (in seconds) required to run a sample of 15 jobs on the LTX-30 Computer.

117	59	83
48	72	25
123	36	98
65	21	19
13	244	102

Use these data to test the null hypothesis that, for the population of jobs from which this sample was selected, running time is normally distributed with $\mu = 90$ and $\sigma = 30$. Use the .10 significance level.

19.20 Use the data in Problem 19.19 to test

H_0: Population running time is normally distributed
H_1: Population running time is not normally distributed

Assume that $\alpha_{max} = .10$.

19.21 The personnel manager of Pismo Products, Inc., has been considering the possibility of using the Dixie Dexterity Test as an aid in the selection of assembly employees. To investigate the feasibility of using this selection instrument, he plans to conduct an extensive statistical study, but before deciding which statistical procedures to employ he would like to know whether it is reasonable to assume that scores on the test are normally distributed in the applicant population. For this purpose, he administers the test to a sample of 20 applicants, and obtains the following scores:

47	38	34	65
33	47	40	48
52	31	47	52
51	68	62	61
47	59	37	52

Using the .05 significance level, is it reasonable for the personnel manager to assume that scores on the Dixie Dexterity Test are normally distributed in the applicant population?

20

Nonparametric Methods:
Additional Techniques

In Chapter 3 we discussed how various "averages"—such as the mean, median, and mode—may be used to describe the "central tendency" of a population. In the jargon of nonparametric statistics, such measures of population central tendency are called *location parameters*. Chapters 13 and 16 presented various techniques of testing hypotheses concerning population location when location is described in terms of the population mean. All of the Z tests and t tests presented in those chapters required that (1) the sample observations be measured on at least an interval scale, and (2) either the population be normal or the sample size be large enough to justify use of the central limit theorem. If these requirements cannot be met, hypotheses concerning location can be tested by various nonparametric methods.

20.1 THE ONE-SAMPLE SIGN TEST

In Section 19.5.2 we considered the example of the quality control engineer who wished to conduct a t test of the null hypothesis that the mean powder content in a particular rocket population was at least 1.45 kilograms. Unfortunately, upon performing a K-S test, the engineer found that the normality assumption required for the t test was not justified. Furthermore, since his sample size ($n = 16$) is too small to justify use of the central limit theorem, he is unable to perform an approximate Z test. However, he still can perform a nonparametric test by restating his hypotheses in terms of the population median rather than the population mean. His hypotheses would then read as follows:

$$H_0: \quad \text{Md} \geq 1.45 \text{ kilograms}$$
$$H_1: \quad \text{Md} < 1.45 \text{ kilograms}$$

A commonly used nonparametric procedure for testing hypotheses concerning a population median is the *one-sample sign test*. This test is less powerful than a t test or Z test, but has the following compensating advantages: (1) it may be applied even if the data are measured on an ordinal scale, (2) it requires no assumption concerning the shape of the population distribution, and (3) it is applicable even if the sample is small.

The first step in performing a sign test for a population median is to list each of the observed sample values. Each value is then coded with a "sign" by comparing that value with Md_0, the value of the population median specified in the null hypothesis. If a particular sample value is greater than Md_0, it is marked by a plus sign; if a value is less than Md_0, it is marked by a minus sign. If a sample value should happen to be equal to Md_0, it is marked "0." Any values that are coded "0" are discarded from the analysis and the sample size is reduced accordingly. Applying this coding process to the data previously given in Section 19.5.2, we obtain the results in Table 20.1. Since one of the observations was equal to the hypothesized value of 1.45, that observation was discarded and the sample size was reduced to $n = 15$.

Table 20.1   Sign Test for Rocket Data
(Md_0 = 1.45 kilograms)

Sample Value	Sign	Sample Value	Sign
1.47	+	1.48	+
1.18	−	1.44	−
1.21	−	1.01	−
1.04	−	1.05	−
1.20	−	1.21	−
1.50	+	1.02	−
1.19	−	1.45	0
1.46	+	1.07	−

The statistic for the sign test is designated by R, which represents either the total number of plus signs or the total number of minus signs, depending on the particular form of the hypotheses. Procedures for determining the value of R, and the corresponding decision rules,[1] are summarized in Table 20.2. Selected fractiles of the distribution of R for this test are given in Table R (Appendix II).

Table 20.2   Decision Rules for the One-Sample Sign Test

Test	Hypotheses	Value of R	Decision Rule
Lower tail	H_0: Md $\geq$ Md_0 H_1: Md $<$ Md_0	R = number of +'s	$\begin{cases} \text{If } R \leq r_{n;\,\alpha}, \text{ reject } H_0; \\ \text{otherwise, accept } H_0 \end{cases}$
Upper tail	H_0: Md $\leq$ Md_0 H_1: Md $>$ Md_0	R = number of −'s	$\begin{cases} \text{If } R \leq r_{n;\,\alpha}, \text{ reject } H_0; \\ \text{otherwise, accept } H_0 \end{cases}$
Two tail	H_0: Md $=$ Md_0 H_1: Md $\neq$ Md_0	R = number of +'s or number of −'s, whichever is smaller	$\begin{cases} \text{If } R \leq r_{n;\,\alpha/2}, \text{ reject } H_0; \\ \text{otherwise, accept } H_0 \end{cases}$

---

[1]To simplify the use of tables for this test, all of these decision rules are expressed in terms of lower-tail probabilities. This is accomplished through the special procedures for determining the value of R. This same approach is followed in our subsequent discussions of the Wilcoxon signed-ranks test and the Mann–Whitney–Wilcoxon test.

For our rocket example, the value of R is 4, which is the total number of plus signs in Table 20.1. If the quality control engineer adopts the .05 significance level, her decision rule is to reject the null hypothesis if $R \leq r_{15, .05}$. From Table R, this critical value is 3. Since the computed value of R is greater than the critical value, the evidence is not sufficient to reject the null hypothesis.

20.2 THE WILCOXON SIGNED-RANKS TEST

The sign test discussed in the preceding section requires no assumption whatever concerning the shape of the population from which the sample is drawn. In some situations, although it may not be reasonable to assume that the population is normal, it still may be possible to make the weaker assumption that the population is symmetrical. If this assumption of population symmetry seems reasonable, the Wilcoxon signed-ranks test provides a more powerful procedure than the sign test.

To illustrate the signed-ranks test, suppose that a utility company requires that the median tensile strength of a particular type of electric cable be at least 2,700 psi. To determine whether the cable being received from a supplier is meeting this requirement, the company decides to conduct an experiment to test the following hypotheses:

$$H_0: \quad \text{Md} \geq 2,700 \text{ psi}$$
$$H_1: \quad \text{Md} < 2,700 \text{ psi}$$

On the basis of experience, management feels that it is reasonable to assume that the tensile strength of this type of cable is distributed symmetrically, so that the Wilcoxon signed-ranks may be used.

To conduct the test, the company measures the tensile strengths of a sample of 25 lengths of cable, with the results shown in Table 20.3. After the observations have been obtained, the next step is to discard any observations that happen to have the same value as the hypothesized value of the population median, which is 2,700 in our example. Since one of the observations in Table 20.3 has a value of 2,700, this observation is discarded, reducing the sample size to $n = 24$.

Table 20.3 Tensile Strengths of 25 Lengths of Cable (psi)

2,440	2,200	2,725	3,000	2,840
2,755	2,600	2,220	2,865	2,925
2,610	2,420	2,665	2,865	2,950
3,125	2,790	2,380	2,500	2,400
2,565	2,635	2,845	2,780	2,700

A worksheet for calculating the test statistic W for the signed-ranks test is given in Table 20.4. Column (1) of this table lists values of the observations. Column (2) shows the *algebraic* deviation of each observed value from the hypothesized median, and column (3) shows the corresponding *absolute* deviation. In column (4) ranks are assigned to the absolute deviations in column (3). A rank of 1 is assigned to the absolute deviation with the lowest value, a rank of 2 is assigned to the next lowest absolute deviation, and so on. If two or more absolute deviations have the same value, they are assigned the same rank. This common rank is the average of the ranks that would have been assigned if the tied $|d|$-values had differed slightly. For instance, column (3) shows that two of the observations have the same absolute deviation $|d| = 300$. In terms of rank order, these are the 19th and 20th absolute difference scores. The average of these ranks is $(19 + 20)/2 = 19.5$, which is the value assigned to both of these cases in column (4). As a rule of thumb, this signed-ranks test should not

Table 20.4   Wilcoxon Signed-Ranks Test for Electric Cable Data
($Md_0 = 2,700$ psi)

(1) Observed Value, x	(2) Algebraic Deviation, $d = x - Md_0$	(3) Absolute Deviation, $\lvert d \rvert$	(4) Rank	(5) Signed Rank
2,440	−260	260	17	−17
2,200	−500	500	24	−24
2,725	25	25	1	1
3,000	300	300	19.5	19.5
2,840	140	140	10	10
2,755	55	55	3	3
2,600	−100	100	8	−8
2,220	−480	480	23	−23
2,865	165	165	12.5	12.5
2,925	225	225	15	15
2,610	−90	90	6	−6
2,420	−280	280	18	−18
2,665	−35	35	2	−2
2,865	165	165	12.5	12.5
2,950	250	250	16	16
3,125	425	425	22	22
2,790	90	90	7	7
2,380	−320	320	21	−21
2,500	−200	200	14	−14
2,400	−300	300	19.5	−19.5
2,565	−135	135	9	−9
2,635	−65	65	4	−4
2,845	145	145	11	11
2,780	80	80	5	5

be used if more than 20% of the absolute deviations are ties. The entries in column (5) are simply the corresponding values in column (4) to which the corresponding algebraic signs in column (2) have been affixed.

Depending on the particular form of the hypotheses, the statistic W is either the absolute sum of the positive signed-ranks or the absolute sum of the negative signed-ranks. Procedures for determining the value of W, and the corresponding decision rules, are summarized in Table 20.5. Selected fractiles of the distribution of W are given in Table S (Appendix II).

Table 20.5   Decision Rules for the One-Sample Wilcoxon Signed-Ranks Test

Test	Hypotheses	Value of W	Decision Rule
Lower tail	H_0: Md $\geq$ Md$_0$ H_1: Md $<$ Md$_0$	W = sum of positive signed-ranks	If $W \leq W_{n;\,\alpha}$, reject H_0; otherwise, accept H_0
Upper tail	H_0: Md $\leq$ Md$_0$ H_1: Md $>$ Md$_0$	W = absolute sum of negative signed-ranks	If $W \leq W_{n;\,\alpha}$, reject H_0; otherwise, accept H_0
Two tail	H_0: Md $=$ Md$_0$ H_1: Md $\neq$ Md$_0$	W = sum of positive signed ranks or absolute sum of negative signed-ranks, whichever is smaller	If $W \leq W_{n;\,\alpha/2}$, reject H_0; otherwise, accept H_0

The hypotheses in our electric cable example prescribe a lower-tail test. Thus, as reference to Table 20.5 indicates, the statistic W is the sum of the positive signed-ranks. As the reader may verify, the sum of the positive signed-ranks in column (5) of Table 20.4 is 134.5. If the .025 significance level is used, the decision rule is to reject H_0 if $W \leq W_{24,\,.025}$. From Table S, this critical value is 81. Since the computed value of W is greater than this critical value, the experimental data provide no basis for rejecting the null hypothesis. Thus, it is not unreasonable for the utility company to assume that the median tensile strength of the cable meets the requirement of at least 2,700 psi.

20.3 THE MANN–WHITNEY–WILCOXON TEST USING TWO INDEPENDENT SAMPLES

When two independent samples are employed to test a hypothesis concerning a difference in the locations of two populations, the most commonly used nonparametric procedure is the Mann–Whitney–Wilcoxon rank-sum test. Strictly speaking, this is a test of the hypothesis that the two population distributions are identical, but if it is reasonable to assume that the populations have identical shapes, the procedure then provides a test of difference in location.

To illustrate the use of the Mann–Whitney–Wilcoxon test, consider a large insurance company that maintains a pool of several hundred clerk-typists. There is a high turnover rate among these clerks, so that hiring of replacements is a continual process. The hiring is done by two different interviewers, each of whom evaluates about half of the applicants. The personnel manager wishes to investigate whether the general level of job performance is the same for the clerks hired by the two different interviewers. Using L_1 to denote the performance level of the population of clerks hired by interviewer I, and L_2 to denote the performance level of the population of clerks hired by interviewer II, the hypotheses for this investigation may be stated as

$$H_0:\ L_1 = L_2$$
$$H_1:\ L_1 \neq L_2$$

To test these hypotheses, the personnel manager takes a random sample of performance ratings for 14 clerks hired by interviewer I, and a random sample of ratings for 16 clerks hired by interviewer II. The ratings for the two samples are as follows:

Interviewer I: 76, 73, 55, 70, 64, 84, 77, 60, 61, 65, 74, 78, 71, 68

Interviewer II: 72, 77, 93, 90, 58, 79, 81, 69, 92, 91, 71, 88, 87, 63, 80, 75

On the assumption that the distributions of performance ratings in the two populations have identical shapes, the Mann–Whitney–Wilcoxon procedure may be used to test the hypotheses. To apply this procedure, the first step is to arrange the observations from the two samples into a single array, beginning with the smallest value. In doing this, it is necessary to identify the sample to which each observation belongs. The next step is to assign ranks to the values, giving a rank of 1 to the lowest value, a rank of 2 to the second lowest value, and so on. If two or more values should be "tied," each of the tied values is assigned the average of their ranks, in the same manner as the Wilcoxon signed-ranks test discussed in Section 20.2. The results of these steps for the clerical performance data are shown in Table 20.6.

Table 20.6   Ranking of Observations for the Mann–Whitney–Wilcoxon Test

Observed Value	Interviewer	Rank	Observed Value	Interviewer	Rank
55	I	1	75	II	16
58	II	2	76	I	17
60	I	3	77	I	18.5
61	I	4	77	II	18.5
63	II	5	78	I	20
64	I	6	79	II	21
65	I	7	80	II	22
68	I	8	81	II	23
69	II	9	84	I	24
70	I	10	87	II	25
71	I	11.5	88	II	26
71	II	11.5	90	II	27
72	II	13	91	II	28
73	I	14	92	II	29
74	I	15	93	II	30

For various forms of hypotheses, the procedures for determining the value of the rank-sum statistic T, and the corresponding decision rules, are summarized in Table 20.7. In this table, the following notation is used:

n_1 = number of cases in sample from population I

n_2 = number of cases in sample from population II

$\sum R_1$ = sum of the ranks assigned to the cases in sample from population I

$\sum R_2$ = sum of the ranks assigned to the cases in sample from population II

n_a = size of the smaller sample

n_b = size of the larger sample

$n = n_1 + n_2 = n_a + n_b$

Table 20.7 Decision Rules for the Mann–Whitney–Wilcoxon Test

Test	Hypotheses	Value of T	Decision Rule
Lower tail	$H_0: L_1 \geq L_2$ $H_1: L_1 < L_2$	If $n_1 \leq n_2$, $T = \sum R_1$ If $n_1 > n_2$, $\quad T = n_2(n+1) - \sum R_2$	If $T \leq T_{n_a, n_b;\ \alpha}$, reject H_0; otherwise, accept H_0
Upper tail	$H_0: L_1 \leq L_2$ $H_1: L_1 > L_2$	If $n_1 \geq n_2$, $T = \sum R_2$ If $n_1 < n_2$, $\quad T = n_1(n+1) - \sum R_1$	If $T \leq T_{n_a, n_b;\ \alpha}$, reject H_0; otherwise, accept H_0
Two tail	$H_0: L_1 = L_2$ $H_1: L_1 \neq L_2$	If $n_1 \leq n_2$, $\quad$compute $T' = \sum R_1$ $\quad$and $T'' = n_1(n+1) - \sum R_1$ If $n_1 > n_2$, $\quad$compute $T' = \sum R_2$ $\quad$and $T'' = n_2(n+1) - \sum R_2$ T is equal to T' or T'', $\quad$whichever is smaller	If $T \leq T_{n_a, n_b;\ \alpha/2}$, reject H_0; otherwise, accept H_0

Applying the specifications in Table 20.7 to our example, we first observe from the hypotheses that we have a two-tail test. Since $n_1 = 14$ and $n_2 = 16$, the smaller of the two sample sizes is n_1. Thus, in this case, we compute $T' = \sum R_1$ and $T'' = n_1(n+1) - \sum R_1$. From the data in Table 20.6, the sum of the ranks of the cases hired by interviewer I is $\sum R_1 = 159$. Hence, $T' = 159$. Then $T'' = 14(31) - 159 = 275$. Since T' is smaller than T'', the value of T is 159.

Selected fractiles of the distribution of T for the Mann–Whitney–Wilcoxon test are given in Table T (Appendix II). In this table, n_a refers to the smaller sample size and n_b refers to the larger sample size. For our example $n_a = 14$ and $n_b = 16$. Then, if the .10 significance level is used, the decision rule is to reject H_0 if $T \leq T_{14,16;\ .05}$. From Table T, this critical value is 176. Since the computed value of T is less than this critical value, the null hypothesis is rejected. Thus, it may be concluded that the general level of job performance is not the same for the populations of clerks hired by the two interviewers.

20.4 TESTS USING PAIRED OBSERVATIONS

The Mann–Whitney–Wilcoxon test discussed in the preceding section is designed for testing hypotheses concerning differences in the locations of two populations when the test is based on two samples that have been selected independently. The nonparametric tests in the present section are designed for testing hypotheses concerning location differences between two populations when the observations have been obtained in pairs.

20.4.1 The Two-Sample Sign Test

The two-sample sign test is an extension of the one-sample sign test presented in Section 20.1. To illustrate this test, consider a firm that is in the process of deciding whether to purchase a Sigmatron-6B computer to replace its Dataplex-7C. The Sigmatron sales representative maintains that, for the types of programs which the company customarily runs, the running time generally should be less on the Sigmatron-6B than on the Dataplex-7C. To test this claim, management decides to run a random sample of jobs on both computers, and to purchase the Sigmatron-6B if the sample results provide convincing evidence that the sales representative's claim is correct. Thus, using L_1 to denote the "average" running time per job on the Sigmatron and L_2 to denote the "average" running time per job on the Dataplex, the hypotheses for this test may be stated as

$$H_0: \quad L_1 \geq L_2$$
$$H_1: \quad L_1 < L_2$$

To test the foregoing hypotheses, a sample of 14 jobs are run on each computer, and the running times (in seconds) are recorded in pairs as shown in columns (2) and (3) of Table 20.8. To apply the two-sample sign test to these data, the difference in running times for each pair is computed, as shown in column (4). The algebraic sign of each difference is recorded in column (5). If the difference for any pair happens to be zero, that pair is discarded from the analysis and the sample size is reduced accordingly.

Table 20.8 Sign Test for Computer Comparison Data

(1) Job	(2) Sigmatron, x_1	(3) Dataplex, x_2	(4) Algebraic Difference, $d = x_1 - x_2$	(5) Sign
1	77	82	−5	−
2	134	127	7	+
3	193	189	4	+
4	687	742	−55	−
5	239	241	−2	−
5	146	199	−53	−
7	298	302	−4	−
8	919	901	18	+
9	5,872	5,904	−32	−
10	57	49	8	+
11	178	172	6	+
12	4,906	4,821	85	+
13	598	607	−9	−
14	1,301	1,312	−11	−

After recording the algebraic signs of the paired differences, the value of the test statistic R is determined according to the specifications in Table 20.9. For the lower-tail test in our example, the value of R is 6, which is the number of plus signs in column (5) of Table 20.8. If management adopts the .025 significance level, the decision rule is to reject H_0 if $R \leq r_{14;\ .025}$. From Table R, this critical value is 2. Since the computed value of R is greater than the critical value, the evidence is not sufficient to reject H_0. Accordingly, management will not purchase the Sigmatron-6B.

Table 20.9 Decision Rules for the Two-Sample Sign Test

Test	Hypotheses	Value of R	Decision Rule
Lower tail	$H_0: L_1 \geq L_2$ $H_1: L_1 < L_2$	R = Number of +'s	If $R \leq r_{n;\,\alpha}$, reject H_0; otherwise, accept H_0
Upper tail	$H_0: L_1 \leq L_2$ $H_1: L_1 > L_2$	R = Number of −'s	If $R \leq r_{n;\,\alpha}$, reject H_0; otherwise, accept H_0
Two tail	$H_0: L_1 = L_2$ $H_1: L_1 \neq L_2$	R = Number of +'s or number of −'s, whichever is smaller	If $R \leq r_{n;\,\alpha/2}$, reject H_0; otherwise, accept H_0

20.4.2 The Two-Sample Signed-Ranks Test

If it is reasonable to assume that the population distribution of paired differences is symmetrical, the more powerful two-sample signed-ranks test may be used instead of the two-sample sign test. To illustrate the two-sample signed-ranks test, let us apply this test to the computer comparison data in Table 20.8. A worksheet for calculating the test statistic W is given in Table 20.10. The first four columns of this table are identical to those in Table 20.8 for performing

Table 20-10 Two-Sample Signed-Ranks Test for Computer Comparison Data

(1) Job	(2) Sigmatron, x_1	(3) Dataplex, x_2	(4) Algebraic Difference, $d = x_1 - x_2$	(5) Absolute Difference, $\lvert d \rvert$	(6) Rank	(7) Signed Rank
1	77	82	−5	5	4	−4
2	134	127	7	7	6	+6
3	193	189	4	4	2.5	+2.5
4	687	742	−55	55	12	−12
5	239	241	−2	2	1	−1
6	146	199	−53	53	13	−13
7	298	302	−4	4	2.5	−2.5
8	919	901	18	18	10	+10
9	5,872	5,904	−32	32	11	−11
10	57	49	8	8	7	+7
11	178	172	6	6	5	+5
12	4,906	4,821	85	85	14	+14
13	598	607	−9	9	8	−8
14	1,301	1,312	−11	11	9	−9

the two-sample sign test. To perform the two-sample signed-ranks test, the algebraic differences in column (4) are converted to corresponding absolute differences, as shown in column (5) of Table 20.10. In column (6), ranks are assigned to the absolute differences in column (5). If two or more absolute differences have the same value, they are assigned the same rank, as is done with the one-sample signed-ranks test. The entries in column (7) are simply the ranks in column (6) to which the algebraic signs in column (4) have been affixed.

The value of the test statistic W is determined according to the specifications in Table 20.11. For the lower-tail test in our example, the value of W is 44.5,

Table 20.11 Decision Rule for the Two-Sample Wilcoxon Signed-Ranks Test

Test	Hypotheses	Value of W	Decision Rule
Lower tail	$H_0: L_1 \geq L_2$ $H_1: L_1 < L_2$	W = sum of positive signed-ranks	If $W \leq W_{n;\,\alpha}$, reject H_0; otherwise, accept H_0
Upper tail	$H_0: L_1 \leq L_2$ $H_1: L_1 > L_2$	W = absolute sum of negative signed-ranks	If $W \leq W_{n;\,\alpha}$, reject H_0; otherwise, accept H_0
Two tail	$H_0: L_1 = L_2$ $H_1: L_1 \neq L_2$	W = sum of positive signed ranks or absolute sum of negative signed-ranks, whichever is smaller	If $W \leq W_{n;\,\alpha/2}$, reject H_0; otherwise, accept H_0

which is the sum of the positive signed-ranks. Using the .025 significance level, the decision rule is to reject H_0 if $W \leq W_{14;\,.025}$. From Table S, this critical value is 21. Since the computed value is less than this critical value, the sample evidence is not sufficient to reject H_0.

PROBLEMS

20.1 The manufacturer of a particular type of power cell for hand calculators advertises that the average operating life of this type of cell is at least 200 hours. Responding to complaints that this claim is untrue, a state consumer protection agency decides to test a sample of 12 of these cells. The agency will take action against the manufacturer only if the sample provides sufficient evidence, at the .025 significance level, to support the position that the manufacturer's claim is untrue. The operating lives (in hours) of the power cells in the sample are as follows:

$$192 \quad 212 \quad 183 \quad 197 \quad 231 \quad 161$$
$$184 \quad 204 \quad 196 \quad 199 \quad 188 \quad 190$$

If the distribution of the lives of the cells produced by the manufacturer is totally unknown, are the sample data sufficient to justify taking action against the manufacturer?

20.2 In Problem 20.1, suppose the agency feels that it is reasonable to assume that the operating lives of the manufacturer's power cells are symmetrically distributed. Under this assumption, are the sample data sufficient, at the .025 significance level, to justify taking action against the manufacturer?

20.3 The Catalina Insurance Company routinely administers the Conklin Clerical Aptitude Test to all applicants for positions as file clerks. According to the manual accompanying this test, the median score for the general adult population is 78. For a sample of 15 of Catalina's file clerk applicants, the following scores were obtained:

$$10, \quad 14, \quad 38, \quad 47, \quad 54, \quad 55, \quad 58, \quad 61, \quad 63, \quad 64, \quad 72, \quad 78, \quad 85, \quad 90, \quad 98$$

(a) Using a sign test at the .05 significance level, are these sample results sufficient to conclude that the median score of Catalina's file clerk applicant population differs from the median score of the general adult population?

(b) Answer part (a) using the Wilcoxon signed-ranks test.

(c) Do the conclusions in parts (a) and (b) agree or disagree? Explain.

20.4 When operating "under control," a particular packaging process fills boxes with cornflakes such that the mean net contents of the boxes is $\mu = 14$ ounces. From time to time the process drifts out of control so that μ is either greater or less than 14 ounces. To decide if the process is under control, an inspector periodically selects a sample of 9 boxes from the process output and weighs the contents of each box. For one of these samples, the following net weights (in ounces) are obtained:

$$13.8 \quad 14.0 \quad 14.4 \quad 14.1 \quad 14.3$$
$$14.5 \quad 13.9 \quad 14.0 \quad 14.2$$

The process will be stopped for adjustment if and only if the sample data provide sufficient evidence at the .05 significance level that the process is out of control.

(a) Suppose that the net contents of the boxes filled by the process are known to be normally distributed with a standard deviation $\sigma = .12$ ounce. Do the sample data justify stopping the process for adjustment?

(b) Suppose that the net contents of the boxes filled by the process are known to be normally distributed, but σ is unknown. In this case, do the sample data justify stopping the process?

(c) Suppose that the distribution of the process output is not known to be normal although it is known to be symmetrical. In this case, do the sample data justify stopping the process?

(d) Suppose that the distribution of the process output is totally unknown. In this case, do the sample data justify stopping the process?

20.5 A manufacturer of animal feeds has developed two experimental formulas for chicken mash. To compare these two formulas, a sample of 12 chickens are fed formula A for the first 90 days after hatching, and another sample of 12 chickens are fed formula B for the same period. At the end of this period, the weight (in ounces) of each chicken is determined. The results are as follows:

Formula A: 36, 47, 31, 40, 35, 42, 50, 42, 32, 49, 37, 46
Formula B: 33, 43, 39, 48, 36, 51, 41, 52, 45, 34, 38, 44

At the .05 significance level, do these results provide sufficient evidence to conclude that the average weights of the chickens raised on the two formulas are different?

20.6 In a study to determine whether age is a relevant consideration in evaluating credit risk, the Vista Charge Card firm investigates a random sample of 25 current card holders. Of these 25 accounts, 15 are identified as good credit risks and 10 as poor credit risks. The ages of the card holders in these two groups are as follows:

Good risks: 25, 32, 22, 46, 24, 59, 36, 29, 24, 40, 37, 54, 27, 35, 37
Poor risks: 24, 39, 21, 42, 26, 62, 23, 34, 28, 31

At the .05 significance level, are these sample data sufficient to conclude that the average age of poor risks is lower than the average age of good risks?

20.7 The two most popular passenger car models produced by Aloha Motors are the Wahine and the Tiki. To investigate the gasoline consumption of these two models, a consumer research agency submits a sample of 10 Wahines and 8 Tikis to experimental road tests, measuring the performance of each car in miles per gallon. The results are as follows:

Wahines: 28.1, 26.4, 24.3, 29.2, 27.8, 25.6, 23.9, 22.7, 27.8, 21.6
Tikis: 26.3, 21.4, 21.6, 25.2, 22.3, 23.4, 19.9, 21.5

The agency feels that it is not reasonable to assume that the mileages of the two models are normally distributed, although it is reasonable to assume that the two mileage distributions have essentially identical shapes. Do the sample data provide sufficient evidence to conclude, at the .10 significance level, that the average mileage of the Wahines is greater than the average mileage of the Tikis?

20.8 The manager of a health club has been approached by an overweight client who is requesting his money back on the grounds that he failed to lose weight while participating in the club's Ten-Day Miracle Reducing Plan. The manager replied that, on the average, participation in the plan does result in a weight loss. To support his claim, the manager presented the following before-and-after weights for 12 clients who had recently participated in the plan:

Client	Weight Before	Weight After
1	148	150
2	174	170
3	152	154
4	159	150
5	167	159
6	196	188
7	227	215
8	123	132
9	151	140
10	216	203
11	194	186
12	160	150

Using a sign test at the .025 significance level, are the sample data sufficient to support the manager's claim?

20.9 Answer the question in Problem 20.8 using a signed-ranks test.

20.10 A personnel manager has developed two alternative forms of a quantitative aptitude test which she plans to use in screening applicants for computer programming positions. Before putting the test in use, she would like to determine whether the two forms are of equal difficulty. For this purpose, she administers both forms of the test to each of 15 applicants, and obtains the following scores:

Applicant	Form A Score	Form B Score
1	59	60
2	72	70
3	86	81
4	61	62
5	65	60
6	69	65
7	74	74
8	56	59
9	83	77
10	99	93
11	47	51
12	61	55
13	93	87
14	82	78
15	65	60

Using a sign test at the .01 significance level, are these sample data sufficient to conclude that the two forms of the test are not of equal difficulty?

20.11 Answer the question in Problem 20.10 using the signed-ranks test. Does this conclusion agree or disagree with the conclusion in Problem 20.10? Explain.

21

Decision Analysis:
Criteria for Decision Making

The estimation and hypothesis-testing procedures discussed in previous chapters are commonly referred to as "classical" or "traditional" methods of statistical inference. These methods are *empirical* in the sense that they use *sample evidence* to make inferences concerning *population characteristics*. In making such inferences, these methods employ only *objective* probabilities without making use of any information that may be available in the form of *subjective* probabilities. Furthermore, at best, they give only implicit consideration to the economic consequences of decisions.

In recent years, statistical methodology has been extended to provide methods that (1) employ *subjective* probabilities as well as *objective* probabilities, and (2) give *explicit* consideration to the economic consequences. These extended methods are known as *statistical decision theory* or *Bayesian decision theory*. The latter term reflects the fact that Bayes' theorem is used to combine subjective probabilities with objective probabilities in the analysis of a decision problem.

Decision making is a complex process, which consists of three major aspects: (1) recognition and formulation of a decision problem, (2) analysis and evaluation of alternatives to arrive at a decision, and (3) implementation of the decision. Initially, statistical decision theory concentrated on the analysis and evaluation aspect of the decision process. More recently, however, this theory has been augmented to provide a general framework for dealing with the entire process of decision making. This framework, which makes use of statistical decision theory, modeling techniques, and behavioral theory has become known as *decision analysis*.

We now devote three chapters to decision analysis. Specifically, the present chapter examines various criteria for decision making. Chapter 22 illustrates the general framework of decision analysis and presents some applications to demonstrate the practical use of this approach. Chapter 23 shows how to incorporate the decision maker's attitude toward risk into the analysis of a decision problem by using utility functions.

21.1 DECISION CONDITIONS

As suggested by our introductory discussion of statistical decision problems in Chapter 1, awareness of a decision problem begins with the realization that there are two or more possible alternative courses of action that are available to achieve some goal or objective. In such a situation, the decision maker attempts to choose the best course of action according to some predetermined *criterion* or standard of judgment. This choice is further complicated by the fact that in many decision situations, the decision maker does not know exactly what consequence will result from each of the available courses of action. This is because the consequence of an action may be the result not only of the course of action that is taken, but also of other factors, or *events*, that are not under the control of the decision maker. In other words, if there are two or more possible events, one of which will occur, the particular consequence resulting from any specific course of action depends on which of the two or more possible events actually occurs. As the reader may recall, these possible events or uncontrollable factors are usually called *states of nature*. Depending on the extent and kind of information available about the states of nature, conditions under which decisions are made can be classified into the following categories:

1. Certainty
2. Risk
3. Uncertainty
4. Conflict

21.1.1 Decision Making Under Certainty

The type of decision situation in which the decision maker has *complete information* concerning all relevant factors affecting the consequence is called decision making under certainty. When a decision is made under certainty, several possible alternative courses of action may be available to the decision maker. However, since the decision maker has complete information, he is certain about which particular state of nature is prevailing. Therefore, he is able to determine with certainty the consequence of each of the alternative actions available to him. Then the solution to the decision problem is simply one of computing the consequence of each course of action for the known state of nature and selecting that course of action that would result in the *optimal* (most desirable) consequence.

Consider, for example, the case of Bob Baker, who has an amount of $10,000 to invest for 1 year. Initially, Bob considers two alternatives: either (1) to purchase a particular state bond issue that matures in a year's time, or (2) to open a savings account with a reliable bank. If he buys the bonds at an annual interest rate of 8.5%, he will receive a profit of $850. If he deposits the amount in the savings account at 9% annual interest rate, he will make $900. Clearly, if Bob's objective is maximizing profit, the solution of this decision problem is for him to deposit the money in the savings account, resulting in the optimal consequence.

21.1.2 Decision Making Under Risk

In decision making under risk, the decision maker has only *partial information* concerning the possible state of nature that will affect the consequence of the decision. Specifically, there are two or more possible states of nature associated with each alternative course of action. The decision maker does not know the true state of nature, but he does know the probability distribution of the occurrences of the states of nature. The solution to the decision problem requires, first, the selection of a decision criterion; second, the evaluation of alternative courses of action; and, finally, the identification of the optimal action according to the criterion selected.

As an illustration, let us continue the example of Bob Baker, who has $10,000 to invest for 1 year. Bob has a good friend, John Carter, who is a successful stock-broker. John has advised Bob to purchase the stock of Elden, Inc. This company is developing a new product. According to John, the price of this stock will go up 16% in 1 year if the new product has been successfully developed, and will drop 4% otherwise. After some discussion with Bob, John estimates the odds are 3:1 that the new product will be successfully developed. In other words, the probability is .75 that the product will be successfully developed, and .25 that it will not. Now, although Bob has decided not to invest in bonds, the intervention of the stockbroker confronts him with a new alternative to depositing his money in a savings account. Thus, he again has two possible courses of action available:

1. deposit the money in the bank (denoted as a_1), or
2. purchase the stock (denoted as a_2).

There are two possible states of nature:

1. the new product is successfully developed (denoted as θ_1), or
2. the new product is not successfully developed (denoted as θ_2).

The consequence of Bob's decision depends on which of the alternative courses of action he will choose and on which of the two possible states of nature will occur. The various consequences associated with the four possible action–state pairs are shown in Table 21.1. This table shows, for each available act, the profit or monetary consequence conditional on each possible state of nature prevailing, and thus is a *conditional profit table*. However, this table is often called *a conditional payoff table* or *payoff table*.

Table 21.1   Conditional Payoff (Profit) Table for Bob Baker

States of Nature (Is New Product Developed?)	a_1(To Deposit in the Bank)	a_2(To Purchase the Stock)	Probability of State of Nature
θ_1 (yes)	$900	$1,600	.75
θ_2 (no)	900	−400	.25

In order for Bob to analyze his problem for the purpose of determining the optimal course of action, he first must specify his decision criterion. Suppose, for example, that he would like to be assured of a minimum profit of $900. Then he should choose a_1, since there is a .25 probability that a_2 could result in a $400 loss. Yet if he would like to select the action that could possibly lead to the highest profit, then clearly he should choose a_2. We will discuss various decision criteria shortly.

21.1.3 Decision Making Under Uncertainty

The term *uncertainty*, as used to describe a decision condition, may be interpreted in both a narrow sense and a broad sense. In the *narrow sense*, uncertainty refers to the situation in which the true state of nature is completely unknown to the decision maker. That is, under this interpretation of uncertainty, the decision maker not only does not know which state of nature actually will occur, but he also does not even know the probabilities of occurrences of the various possible states of nature. The case of Bob Baker, described in Section 21.1.2, would fall into this category if the probabilities of the two possible states of nature were unknown.

In the *broad sense*, decision making under uncertainty refers to the situation in which the true state of nature simply is not known with certainty. This can be either a case in which the true state of nature is partially unknown (i.e., decision making under risk), or a case in which the true state of nature is completely unknown (i.e., decision making under uncertainty in the narrow sense as described above).

For most managerial problems, decision makers do have partial information regarding the states of nature, which can be expressed in terms of subjective or objective probabilities. Consequently, the condition of strict uncertainty seldom exists. Therefore, we shall adopt the broad definition of decision making under uncertainty and use this term interchangeably with decision making under risk.

21.1.4 Decision Making Under Conflict

In decision making under *conflict*, the consequence of a specific course of action chosen by the decision maker depends on the reaction or counteraction taken by his opponent. This opponent is an *adverse intellect* rather than nature. Each of the opposing decision makers attempts to optimize his decision at the other's expense. Thus, neither of them knows exactly which consequence will eventually materialize. Situations such as this may arise in business and other competitive situations.

As an example, consider a simplified cola market in which there exist only two competing brands, *A* and *B*. The producers of the two brands have been contacted by a can manufacturer offering a new cola can design. Unfortunately, this new design is more expensive than the present one. The producer of brand *A* figures as follows: "I am making about $10,000 on cola now. It looks to me as if the consumer will like this new design. If I go ahead with it and the competitor doesn't, I stand to make about $11,000. On the other hand, if he does and I don't, I'll probably fall off to $9,500. If both of us use it, we'll all edge our price up a little, which would likely cause some reduction in sales so that we would come out at about $9,800." From this statement we obtain the conditional payoff table presented in Table 21.2. This table clearly shows that the consequence of *A*'s decision not only depends on the specific course of action chosen by *A*, but also depends on the specific counteraction taken by *B*. Similarly, we could construct a conditional payoff table for *B* that would show that the consequence of *B*'s decision depends on both his choice of course of action and his opponent's reaction.

To summarize, we have described various conditions under which decisions are made. The analysis of decision problems under certainty may require mathematical methods such as calculus and linear programming to identify

Table 21.2 Conditional Payoff Table for Brand A

	A's Action	
B's Action	Not to Adopt the New Can	To Adopt the New Can
Not to Adopt the New Can	$10,000	$11,000
To Adopt the New Can	9,500	9,800

optimal solutions. Consequently, decision problems of this type are treated in books on applied calculus and mathematical programming. The body of the techniques used for analysis of decision problems under conflict is known as game theory. The study of decision problems under risk or uncertainty is the subject of decision analysis.

21.2 CRITERIA FOR DECISION MAKING UNDER UNCERTAINTY

When a decision is made under certainty, the actual consequence should be exactly as determined by the analysis on which the decision is based. But when a decision is made under the condition of uncertainty (i.e., *when the true state of nature is not known with certainty*, regardless of whether it is partially unknown or completely unknown), it is impossible for the decision maker to predict exactly the consequence of his decision. Under such conditions, the decision maker is forced to choose a specific course of action from a set of alternatives, hoping that the action chosen will yield the maximum profit but knowing that it may not result in maximum payoff after a particular state of nature has actually occurred. In effect, the decision maker is forced to gamble against nature or his opponent. He is in a position wherein he must place bets, hoping that he will win but knowing that he may lose. Different decision makers may use different criteria for placing the bets (i.e., for selecting a specific course of action), even though they all may have the same ultimate objective of maximizing profits.

To illustrate various criteria used in decision making under uncertainty, we will analyze an inventory-stocking problem. Consider a large newsstand that carries various newspapers and magazines. One of the items that the dealer stocks is the LAX Sunday paper. She pays 30 cents for each copy of the paper, which she prices at 50 cents a copy. Copies remaining unsold at the end of the day are nonreturnable and have no value. To help to decide the number of copies of the newspaper to stock every Sunday, the dealer has examined the sales record for a period of the last 100 weeks. This record, as shown in Table 21.3, indicates that during the period examined, the dealer has never sold more than 24 or less than 16 copies. Since the dealer foresees no substantial changes in demand in the near future, she wishes to limit her future weekly stock to some number of copies between 16 and 24 inclusive.

The adoption of some symbolic notation will aid our analysis of the news dealer's problem. We shall use the symbol defined below:

Table 21.3 Weekly Demand for LAX
Sunday Paper

Number of Copies Demanded per Week	Number of Weeks
16	5
17	10
18	12
19	16
20	10
21	20
22	16
23	6
24	5
	100

a: a particular course of action (a particular number of copies that the dealer may choose to stock). All possible courses of action ($a = 16, 17, \ldots, 24$) constitute the action space.

θ: a general expression for the state of nature. The reader may recognize that θ is a random variable in the extended sense discussed in Chapter 6. This is because, for any given decision problem under uncertainty, the decision maker does not know which one of the two or more possible states of nature will actually occur. Following our notational convention, we shall use the corresponding lowercase θ to denote any particular state of nature or specific value of the random variable Θ. Thus, in our example, the random variable Θ denotes demand for the Sunday paper and θ represents a particular number of copies demanded. Thus, Θ is a random variable whose possible values are $\theta = 16, 17, \ldots, 24$.

Using this notation, the monetary value (consequence) of a given course of action a is a function of the random variable Θ; this *function* will be denoted as $v(a, \Theta)$. We use $v(a, \theta)$ to denote the *particular* monetary value resulting from a *particular* course of action a (number of copies stocked) when a *specific* state of nature θ occurs (number of copies demanded). A positive value of $v(a, \theta)$ represents a gain or profit; a negative value represents a loss or negative profit. For our present example, we may express $v(a, \theta)$ as a function of a and θ in the following form:

$$v(a, \theta) = \begin{cases} .50\theta - .30a & \text{if } \theta \leq a \\ .50a - .30a & \text{if } \theta > a \end{cases}$$

where $a = 16, 17, \ldots, 24$, and $\theta = 16, 17, \ldots, 24$. This equation tells us the following:

1. If the dealer decides to stock a copies, and if the demand θ is no greater than supply a, her profit will be .50 cents for each copy *sold*, less 30 cents for each copy *stocked*.

2. If demand θ exceeds supply a, so that all copies in stock are sold, then $\theta = a$. Thus, the profit will be 50 cents for each copy *stocked* (all of which are sold), less 30 cents for each copy *stocked*.

For any given course of action chosen, the monetary value is conditional on the occurrence of a specific state of nature. Since there are nine possible states of nature ($\theta = 16, 17, \ldots, 24$), by systematically varying values of θ in the foregoing equation we obtain the conditional monetary values (conditional payoffs) for the particular action as shown in the corresponding column of Table 21.4. This procedure is repeated for each of the available courses of action ($a = 16, 17, \ldots, 24$) to obtain entries for each column of the table. The reader is urged to verify each of the entries in the table.

Table 21.4 Conditional Payoff Table for LAX Sunday Paper

State of Nature (Number of Copies Demanded), θ	Action (Number of Copies Stocked)								
	$a = 16$	$a = 17$	$a = 18$	$a = 19$	$a = 20$	$a = 21$	$a = 22$	$a = 23$	$a = 24$
$\theta = 16$	$3.20	$2.90	$2.60	$2.30	$2.00	$1.70	$1.40	$1.10	$0.80
$\theta = 17$	3.20	3.40	3.10	2.80	2.50	2.20	1.90	1.60	1.30
$\theta = 18$	3.20	3.40	3.60	3.30	3.00	2.70	2.40	2.10	1.80
$\theta = 19$	3.20	3.40	3.60	3.80	3.50	3.20	2.90	2.60	2.30
$\theta = 20$	3.20	3.40	3.60	3.80	4.00	3.70	3.40	3.10	2.80
$\theta = 21$	3.20	3.40	3.60	3.80	4.00	4.20	3.90	3.60	3.30
$\theta = 22$	3.20	3.40	3.60	3.80	4.00	4.20	4.40	4.10	3.80
$\theta = 23$	3.20	3.40	3.60	3.80	4.00	4.20	4.40	4.60	4.30
$\theta = 24$	3.20	3.40	3.60	3.80	4.00	4.20	4.40	4.60	4.80

The reader may recall that, when a decision is made under certainty, the true state of nature is known. Under this condition, the decision maker considers only a single consequence for each act and then chooses the act with the most desirable consequence. When a decision is made under uncertainty, however, the true state of nature is not known for sure. Thus, each act may have two or more possible consequences corresponding to the various possible states of nature. For example, Table 21.4 shows that each alternative act has nine possible monetary consequences corresponding to the nine possible states of nature ($\theta = 16, 17, \ldots, 24$). When a decision must be made under such conditions, the problem then arises about how to compare the alternative acts when each act has more than one possible consequence. This is a complex problem that has no single answer. Rather, a number of different criteria have been proposed for choosing among alternative acts when this problem of uncertainty exists. Some of these criteria entail the explicit use of all the possible consequences of each act, without considering how likely each of these consequences is to occur. That is, such criteria disregard the probabilities of the various possible states of nature occurring. In contrast, there are other criteria that make rather limited use of monetary consequences of the acts, but which do stress the probabilities of the various states of nature. There are still other criteria that combine full use of the monetary consequences with the probabilities of the states of nature. Hence, the various criteria for decision making under uncertainty may be classified into the following three categories:[1]

1. Criteria based on monetary consequences alone
2. Criteria based primarily on the probabilities of states of nature
3. Criteria based on monetary consequences combined with probabilities of states of nature

---

[1]The use of utility in place of monetary consequences is discussed in Chapter 23.

21.3 DECISION CRITERIA BASED ON MONETARY CONSEQUENCES ALONE

In this section we discuss four decision criteria that belong to the first category listed above. All of these criteria formally employ the monetary consequences associated with every possible combination of acts and states of nature. However, none of these criteria makes use of any probability information. A decision maker may determine to use one of these criteria either because the necessary probability information is not available or simply because he chooses to ignore such information. For purposes of illustration, let us continue with the LAX Sunday paper example.

21.3.1 Maximin Criterion

A *pessimistic* decision maker might seek the best payoff that he can be *assured* of, regardless of which state of nature *happens to* occur. He can accomplish this by determining the minimum possible payoff for each act and then selecting that act for which this minimum possible payoff is best. For example, considering the conditional payoffs in Table 21.4, the news dealer might reason as follows: "If I stock 24 copies, the worst payoff that can happen (the minimum of the figures in the column for $a = 24$) is 80 cents. If I stock 23 copies, the worst payoff that can happen is $1.10. If I stock 16 copies, the worst payoff that can happen is $3.20. Similarly, I can obtain the minimum payoff for each of the other possible acts as shown in the first row of Table 21.5. Comparing the minimum payoffs in that row, I will, therefore, choose the act of stocking 16 copies, because I am assured of a payoff of at least $3.20."

Table 21.5 Use of Monetary Consequences to Select a Course of Action

	Action (Number of Copies Stocked)								
	$a = 16$	$a = 17$	$a = 18$	$a = 19$	$a = 20$	$a = 21$	$a = 22$	$a = 23$	$a = 24$
(1) Minimum payoff	$3.20	$2.90	$2.60	$2.30	$2.00	$1.70	$1.40	$1.10	$0.80
(2) Maximum payoff	3.20	3.40	3.60	3.80	4.00	4.20	4.40	4.60	4.80
(3) Hurwicz weighted average with $c = .2$	3.20	3.30	3.40	3.50	3.60	3.70	3.80	3.90	4.00
(4) Maximum regret	1.60	1.40	1.20	1.00	1.20	1.50	1.80	2.10	2.40

This *maximin* criterion identifies the act that *maxi*mizes the *mini*mum payoffs. Under this criterion, the decision maker selects the act with the maximum payoff that can be *assured*. The solution of stocking 16 copies guarantees a profit of $3.20 regardless of what happens, and hence is considered to be the least risky or the most conservative action available. This action, however, precludes any profit higher than $3.20.

21.3.2 Maximax Criterion

Compared to the pessimistic decision maker, an *optimistic* decision maker might seek the maximum payoff that can possibly be obtained. He can accomplish this by determining the maximum possible payoff for each act and then selecting that act for which this maximum possible payoff is the greatest. For example, considering the conditional payoffs in Table 21.4, the news dealer might reason as follows: "If I stock 24 copies, the highest payoff that can be obtained (the maximum of the figures in the column for $a = 24$) is $4.80. If I stock 23 copies, the highest payoff that can be obtained is $4.60. Similarly, I can find the maximum payoff for each of the other possible acts as shown in the second row of Table 21.5. Comparing the maximum payoffs in that row, I will, therefore, choose the act of stocking 24 copies, which can possibly yield a maximum payoff of $4.80." This *maximax* criterion selects the act that *maximizes* the *maximum* possible payoffs. The solution of stocking 24 copies makes it possible for the news dealer to enjoy the largest payoff, but it ignores the possible low payoffs. This action is considered to be the most risky alternative in the sense that the possible profits range from 80 cents (when only 16 copies are sold) to $4.80 (when all 24 copies are sold).

21.3.3 Hurwicz Criterion
(Pessimism–Optimism Coefficient)

The maximin criterion is completely pessimistic in that, relative to each act, it concentrates on the state having the worst consequence. The maximax criterion, on the other hand, is entirely optimistic in that, relative to each act, it concentrates on the state having the best consequence. Hurwicz[2] suggests a pessimism–optimism coefficient that emphasizes a weighted combination of the worst and the best. For the ith act, let m_i be the minimum and M_i be the maximum of the monetary consequences. The minimum and maximum payoffs for various possible acts for the news dealer's problem are shown, respectively in, the first and second rows of Table 21.5. Let a coefficient c between 0 and 1, called the pessimism–optimism coefficient, be given. For each possible act, we may compute the Hurwicz weighted average:

$$H_i = cm_i + (1 - c)M_i \qquad (21.1)$$

Suppose that the news dealer adopts .2 for the value of c. Then we can calculate the weighted average for each of the possible acts. For example, the weighted average for the act of stocking 24 copies is

$$H_{24} = .2(\$.80) + (1 - .2)(\$4.80) = \$4.00$$

The weighted averages for all possible acts are similarly calculated and are shown in the third row of Table 21.5. Comparing the figures in that row, we see that the optimal act is to stock 24 copies, because it has the highest weighted average.

Notice that, if $c = 1$, the pessimism–optimism coefficient criterion becomes the maximin criterion, whereas if $c = 0$, it becomes the maximax criterion.

---

[2]Leonid Hurwicz, "Optimality Criteria for Decision Making under Ignorance," Cowless Commission Discussion Paper, *Statistics*, No. 370, 1951 (mimeographed).

Thus, the larger the magnitude of c that the decision maker selects, the more pessimistic he appears to be. In short, c may be considered the coefficient of pessimism, and $(1 - c)$ the coefficient of optimism. It should be stressed that, in applying the Hurwicz criterion, the value of c must be supplied by the decision maker himself as an expression of his personal degree of pessimism. In the example above, the pessimism coefficient of $c = .2$, with the resulting optimism coefficient of $(1 - c) = .8$, implies that the news dealer feels quite optimistic. Since the c value is not zero, we would expect the solution of the pessimism–optimism coefficient criterion to be different from that of the maximax criterion. However, in this example, the optimal act obtained by this criterion turns out to be identical to that determined by the maximax criterion. This is simply a coincidence because of the particular payoff table involved.

21.3.4 Minimax Regret Criterion

For decision making under uncertainty, the decision maker is forced to choose a specific course of action from a set of alternatives before the fact (prior to knowing the true state of nature). However, the action that appears to be optimal before the fact may not necessarily turn out, after the fact, to be the optimal action that should have been taken. For instance, suppose that the news dealer in our example has decided to stock 16 copies, which is the optimal act according to the maximin criterion. Suppose further, however, that the actual demand turns out to be 20 copies. As may be seen from Table 21.4, if she had known that the demand actually would be 20 copies, she could have maximized her profit at $4.00 by stocking 20 copies. However, by stocking 16 instead of 20 copies, she has made a profit of only $3.20 rather than $4.00. Thus, she suffers an opportunity loss of 80 cents, which is the difference between the $4.00 that she could have made and the $3.20 that she actually made. More generally, if the action chosen does not yield the maximum profit that the decision maker could have made if he had known the true state of nature, then he suffers an opportunity loss that represents the difference between (1) the maximum profit he had the opportunity of obtaining, and (2) the profit he has actually obtained.

The concept of opportunity loss (regret) is basic to the *minimax regret* criterion, which was introduced by Leonard Savage. The application of this criterion requires the computation of the opportunity loss for each possible act conditional on each state of nature The conditional opportunity losses for the news dealer problem are shown in Table 21.6. The opportunity losses shown in this table are derived, row by row, from the conditional payoffs given in Table 21.4. For any given row, the opportunity losses are obtained by subtracting each entry in any given row of the payoff table from the largest entry in that row. For example, consider the first row of the payoff table showing the conditional payoffs for the various acts when $\theta = 16$. For this row, the act "$a = 16$" has the highest conditional payoff, namely, $3.20. For all other acts, the conditional payoffs in this row are smaller, ranging from $2.90 to 80 cents. The difference between the maximum conditional payoff of $3.20 and the conditional payoff associated with each of the other acts is the conditional opportunity loss (COL) associated with that act. For example, if $\theta = 16$, the COL for "$a = 17$" is ($3.20 - $2.90) = 30 cents, the COL for "$a = 18$" is ($3.20 - $2.60) = 60 cents, and so on. The conditional opportunity losses for all other rows of Table 21.6 are obtained in a similar manner. The reader is urged to verify these figures.

Table 21.6   Conditional Opportunity-Loss Table for LAX Sunday Paper

State of Nature (Number of Copies Demanded), θ	Action (Number of Copies Stocked)								
	a = 16	a = 17	a = 18	a = 19	a = 20	a = 21	a = 22	a = 23	a = 24
16	$ 0	$ .30	$ .60	$ .90	$1.20	$1.50	$1.80	$2.10	$2.40
17	.20	0	.30	.60	.90	1.20	1.50	1.80	2.10
18	.40	.20	0	.30	.60	.90	1.20	1.50	1.80
19	.60	.40	.20	0	.30	.60	.90	1.20	1.50
20	.80	.60	.40	.20	0	.30	.60	.90	1.20
21	1.00	.80	.60	.40	.20	0	.30	.60	.90
22	1.20	1.00	.80	.60	.40	.20	0	.30	.60
23	1.40	1.20	1.00	.80	.60	.40	.20	0	.30
24	1.60	1.40	1.20	1.00	.80	.60	.40	.20	0

Thus far we have shown how to find conditional opportunity losses associated with possible courses of action given a particular state of nature. In other words, in constructing the conditional opportunity loss table, as shown in Table 21.6, we obtained the entries row by row. Now let us switch our attention to the entries in each column. Since each column represents one of the alternative acts, the entries in a column indicate the opportunity losses associated with that act. For example, the entries in the column for a = 16 indicate that the opportunity losses associated with this act range from $0 to $1.60, depending on the particular state of nature (the specific value of θ). That is, whenever the news dealer stocks 16 copies, her opportunity loss will be $0 if demand is 16 copies, $.20 if demand is 17 copies, and so on. To determine the optimal act under the minimax regret criterion, we first find the maximum opportunity loss (i.e., the maximum regret) for each act by locating the maximum figure in each column of the COL table. The maximum opportunity loss is $1.60 for a = 16, $1.40 for a = 17, and so on. These maximum opportunity losses for the various alternative acts are shown in row (4) of Table 21.5. Then, comparing the maximum opportunity losses in this row, we see that the minimum figure is $1.00 for a = 19. Thus, if the news dealer adopts the minimax regret criterion, she will stock 19 copies, since this is the act for which the maximum possible opportunity loss is the smallest. In short, the *minimax* regret criterion selects the act that *mini*mizes the *max*imum regret.

21.4   DECISION CRITERIA BASED PRIMARILY ON PROBABILITIES

So far we have examined four criteria, all of which belong to one family, in the sense that they all are based on monetary consequences alone. We consider next another family of criteria that devote primary consideration to the probabilities of the various states of nature, giving only limited attention to monetary consequences. We continue with the LAX Sunday paper example to illustrate three decision criteria of this kind.

21.4.1   Maximum Likelihood Criterion

Since she is operating under uncertainty, the news dealer does not know how many copies of the Sunday paper actually will be sold. However, her historical demand record, which was summarized in Table 21.3 indicates that the demand has been between 16 and 24 copies. From this record, the relative frequencies of various demand levels are calculated, with the results shown in the third column of Table 21.7. Since the news dealer anticipates no significant changes in demand in the near future, she is willing to accept the relative frequencies as probabilities for future demand levels.

Table 21.7 Demand Distribution and Expected Demand
for LAX Sunday Paper

(1) Number of Copies Demanded per Week, θ	(2) Number of Weeks	(3) Relative Frequency, $f(\theta)$	(4) Calculation of Expected Demand, $\theta f(\theta)$
16	5	.05	.80
17	10	.10	1.70
18	12	.12	2.16
19	16	.16	3.04
20	10	.10	2.00
21	20	.20	4.20
22	16	.16	3.52
23	6	.06	1.38
24	5	.05	1.20
Sum	100	1.00	20.00 = $E(\theta)$

Column (3) of Table 21.7 shows clearly that some of the demand levels are more likely to occur than others. This column further indicates that the demand level $\theta = 21$ is most likely to occur, since it has the highest relative frequency. In other words, $\theta = 21$ has the maximum likelihood (highest probability) of occurring. To apply the maximum likelihood criterion, the news dealer will consider the monetary consequences associated only with this particular demand level. Referring to Table 21.4, she will limit her consideration of monetary consequences to the conditional payoffs in the row corresponding to $\theta = 21$. Then, comparing the figures in this row, the highest payoff is $4.20. This is the payoff for $a = 21$. Thus, using the maximum likelihood criterion, the news dealer should choose to stock 21 copies. Generally speaking, the *maximum likelihood* criterion advises the decision maker to identify the state of nature that has the *maximum likelihood* of occurring, and then to select the act that has the most desirable monetary consequence for that state of nature.

21.4.2 Expected State of Nature Criterion

Unlike the maximum likelihood criterion, which focuses on the state of nature most likely to occur, the *expected state of nature criterion* focuses on the *mean* state of nature. Using this criterion, the decision maker first computes the mean state of nature and then selects the act that has the most desirable consequence under the assumption that the actual state of nature will be approximately equal to the mean. The computation of the mean state of nature depends on whether the state space is discrete or continuous. If the state of nature θ is a *discrete* random variable, the expected state of nature may be calculated by using Formula (7.2), which is restated in the following form:

$$E(\theta) = \sum_{\text{all } \theta} \theta f(\theta) \tag{21.2}$$

If the state of nature θ is a continuous random variable, the expected state of nature may be obtained from Formula (7.3), which is restated in the following form:

$$E(\theta) = \int_{-\infty}^{\infty} \theta f(\theta) \, d\theta \qquad (21.3)$$

In our Sunday paper example, the set of possible states of nature consists of the discrete demand levels: $\theta = 16, 17, \ldots, 24$. Therefore, to compute the expected state of nature, the news dealer would use Formula (21.2). These calculations are shown in column (4) of Table 21.7. As shown by the sum of this column, the expected demand is $E(\theta) = 20$ copies. The news dealer will then consider the monetary consequences associated only with $\theta = 20$, under the assumption that this is the state of nature that actually will occur. Referring to the row corresponding to $\theta = 20$ in Table 21.4, the highest payoff is \$4.00. This is the payoff for $a = 20$. Hence, if the news dealer uses the expected state of nature criterion, she will choose to stock 20 copies.

In the illustration above, the mean demand is identical to one of the possible demand levels. This is merely a coincidence. However, when the state space is discrete, the mean state of nature more likely will not coincide exactly with any of the possible states of nature. In this case, the mean demand is rounded to the closest value of a state of nature. Of course, when the state space is continuous, this difficulty does not arise.

The mean or expected value of the state of nature can be calculated and used as a decision criterion only if the various states of nature can be described on a meaningful numerical scale such as in this inventory example. There are, however, decision problems in which the states of nature cannot be naturally expressed in numerical terms. Consider, for example, the case of Bob Baker as presented in Table 21.1, in which the state of nature denotes whether or not the new product will be successfully developed. For such a problem, the expected value of the state of nature is meaningless and hence cannot be used as a decision criterion.

21.4.3 Limited Risk Criterion

When the news dealer chooses to stock a specific number of copies, this stock may turn out to be equal to, larger than, or smaller than the actual demand. Therefore, there are two kinds of possible error: one is overstock (the number of copies stocked is larger than the number of copies sold) and the other is understock (the number of copies stocked is smaller than the number of copies that could be sold). Suppose, for example, that the dealer stocks 18 copies. Then the dealer will suffer overstock if the actual demand is 17 copies or less. Thus, the probability of overstock is equal to the cumulative probability of selling 17 copies or less. This probability is equal to .15, which is obtained from the third column of Table 21.7 by summing the probabilities of demand levels being equal to or less than 17 copies. On the other hand, if the actual demand is 19 copies or more, the dealer will suffer understock. Thus, the probability of understock is equal to the cumulative probability of 19 copies or more being demanded. This probability is equal to .73, which is obtained from the same table by summing the probabilities of demand levels being equal to or greater than 19 copies. Similarly, we can obtain the probabilities of overstock and understock for each of the other possible actions, and the results are shown in the first two rows of Table 21.8. The reader is urged to verify these entries in the table.

Table 21.8 Probabilities of Making Errors—Overstock and Understock

Probability of:	Action (Number of Copies Stocked)								
	$a = 16$	$a = 17$	$a = 18$	$a = 19$	$a = 20$	$a = 21$	$a = 22$	$a = 23$	$a = 24$
Overstock	.00	.05	.15	.27	.43	.53	.73	.89	.95
Understock	.95	.85	.73	.57	.47	.27	.11	.05	.00
Making an error	.95	.90	.88	.84	.90	.80	.84	.94	.95

The first two rows of Table 21.8 show that as the dealer increases the number of copies stocked, the probability of overstock increases but the probability of understock decreases. Similarly, if the dealer reduces the number of copies stocked, the probability of overstock decreases but the probability of understock increases. In other words, the dealer can reduce the probability of one kind of error only at the expense of increasing the probability of the other kind of error. Therefore, the dealer's criterion in deciding how many copies to stock may be to limit the probability of making one type of error to a certain level.

If, for example, the dealer wishes to limit the probability of overstock to zero, which means that all copies stocked will be sold, then she should stock 16 copies. If, however, the dealer wishes to limit the probability of overstock to a reasonably small amount, say .05, then she should stock 17 copies.

On the other hand, the dealer may wish to limit the probability of understock to a preassigned level. For example, if the dealer wishes to limit this probability to zero, which means that no customers will be turned away, she should stock 24 copies. As another example, if the dealer wishes to limit the probability of understock to a reasonably small amount, say .05, she should stock 23 copies.

Since the news dealer can reduce the risk of one type of error only at the expense of increasing the risk of the other type of error, she should take into account the relative seriousness of the two kinds of errors.[3] If the loss of overstock is high relative to that of understock, then the news dealer should limit the probability of overstock to a small amount by allowing a larger probability of understock. Similarly, if the loss of overstock is relatively low, then the news dealer should limit the probability of understock to a small amount by permitting a larger probability of overstock.

If the news dealer feels that the two types of errors are equally serious, she may use the total probability of making an error (either overstock or understock) as her criterion of choice. As shown in the third row of Table 21.8, this total error probability is simply the sum of the probabilities of overstock and understock. Inspection of this row indicates that the minimum total probability of making an error is .80 for $a = 21$. Thus, if the news dealer wishes to minimize the total probability of error, she should stock 21 copies.

---

[3]This is analogous to the relationship between the Type I and Type II errors in classical hypothesis testing.

21.5 DECISION CRITERIA BASED ON MONETARY CONSEQUENCES AND PROBABILITIES COMBINED

We have already examined one family of decision criteria based on monetary consequences alone, and another family of criteria that is primarily concerned with the probabilities of the various states of nature. We now consider a third family of decision criteria that *explicitly* take into account *both* monetary consequences *and* probabilities in making decisions. We shall, in particular, discuss two decision criteria of this nature: (1) the expected monetary value (EMV), and (2) the expected opportunity loss (EOL) criteria.

21.5.1 EMV Criterion

Using the EMV criterion, the decision maker computes the expected monetary value (EMV) for each alternative act and then chooses the act that has the largest expected monetary value. The computation required by this decision criterion explicitly considers both the monetary consequences and the probabilities of obtaining these consequences.

Bearing in mind that θ is a random variable denoting the unknown state of nature, the reader may recall that $v(a, \theta)$ represents the monetary value of an act. Since $v(a, \theta)$ is a function of θ, the expected monetary value of an act may be denoted by $E[v(a, \theta)]$. It may be recognized that $E[v(a, \theta)]$ is the expected value of a function of a random variable, as discussed in Chapter 7. Thus, if the random variable θ is discrete, the expected monetary value of an act may be computed by applying Formula (7.4). For our present purposes, this formula may be restated in the following form:

$$E[v(a, \theta)] = \sum_{\text{all } \theta} v(a, \theta) f(\theta) \tag{21.4}$$

This formula says that the expected monetary value of an act is computed by multiplying (1) the monetary value for that act conditional on the occurrence of each state of nature by (2) the probability of that state of nature occurring, and then summing the products.

In Chapter 7, the expected value of a function of a continuous random variable was given by Formula (7.5). A restatement of that formula provides the following formula for computing the EMV of an act when the state of nature is a *continuous* random variable:

$$E[v(a, \theta)] = \int_{-\infty}^{\infty} v(a, \theta) f(\theta) \, d\theta \tag{21.5}$$

To illustrate the EMV criterion, let us return to the LAX Sunday paper problem. Consider, for example, the act of stocking 24 copies weekly. As shown in Table 21.4, the monetary values (conditional payoffs) associated with this action range from 80 cents to $4.80, depending on how many copies actually are sold. The probabilities of possible numbers of copies demanded have been shown in Table 21.7. For convenience, the conditional payoffs for the act of stocking 24 copies, together with the probabilities of the various demand levels, are now exhibited in Table 21.9. The computation of the expected monetary value (the expected payoff) for this act is shown in column (4) of this table.

Using Formula (21.4), this computation is performed by multiplying the payoff conditional on the occurrence of each demand level by the probability of that demand level occurring, and then summing these products. The resulting EMV for $a = 24$ is $2.80.

Table 21.9 Conditional and Expected Payoffs for the Act of Stocking 24 Copies of LAX Sunday Paper

(1) State of Nature (Number of Copies Demanded), θ	(2) Conditional Payoff, $v(24, \theta)$	(3) Probability of State of Nature, $f(\theta)$	(4) Calculation of Expected Payoff, $v(24, \theta)f(\theta)$
16	$0.80	.05	$.040
17	1.30	.10	.130
18	1.80	.12	.216
19	2.30	.16	.368
20	2.80	.10	.280
21	3.30	.20	.660
22	3.80	.16	.608
23	4.30	.06	.258
24	4.80	.05	.240
Sum		1.00	$2.800 = EMV

By repeating the same general procedure shown in Table 21.9, the EMV for each of the other courses of action is obtained. The EMVs for all available courses of action are summarized in Table 21.10. The reader may wish to verify the entries in the table. From this table we see that the act of stocking 19 copies yields the maximum EMV of $3.565. Therefore, using the EMV criterion, the dealer should stock 19 copies. The EMV of this optimal act is called the *EMV of the decision with available information.*

Table 21.10 Expected Monetary Values of Alternative Actions*

	Action (Number of Copies Stocked)								
	$a = 16$	$a = 17$	$a = 18$	$a = 19$	$a = 20$	$a = 21$	$a = 22$	$a = 23$	$a = 24$
EMV:	$3.200	$3.375	$3.500	$3.565	$3.550	$3.485	$3.320	$3.075	$2.800
				↑ maximum EMV					

*As an example, the calculation of the EMV for $a = 24$ is shown in Table 21.9.

Notice that, although the expected monetary value for stocking 19 copies is equal to $3.565, this amount of profit can never occur on any one Sunday. As pointed out in Section 7.2.3, the word "expected" does *not* mean that the decision maker actually expects that amount of profit. For any given Sunday, the actual profit resulting from stocking 19 copies will be one of the monetary values (ranging from $2.30 to $3.80) shown in the column labeled $a = 19$ of Table 21.4. The EMV is simply a weighted average, the weights being the probabilities of the various states of nature. It is the average profit that is to be "expected" in the long run. In other words, it is the average profit that will result if the decision is repeated many times, and each time the decision maker chooses the same alternative. In the news dealer example, if the decision is to be repeated week after week, the act of stocking 19 copies should produce the highest average weekly profit in the long run.

The EMV criterion explicitly considers both the monetary values and the probabilities, and in that sense may be regarded as superior to the previously discussed criteria that emphasize only one or the other of these two factors. The EMV criterion chooses the act that will yield the maximum average payoff in the long run, and hence, has immediate intuitive appeal for business managers.

21.5.2 EOL Criterion

Another criterion that belongs to the same family as EMV is the *expected opportunity loss* (EOL) criterion. Both of these criteria combine the probabilities of the various states of nature with the monetary consequences of the alternative acts to arrive at an optimal decision. In treating monetary consequences, however, the EMV criterion works with the monetary *values* of the acts, whereas the EOL criterion works with *opportunity losses* of the acts. A decision maker who adopts the EOL criterion will compute the expected opportunity loss for each alternative act and then choose the act that has the *smallest* expected opportunity loss.

Just as $v(a, \theta)$ is used to denote the monetary value resulting from a particular course of action a when a specific state of nature θ occurs, so the expression $\ell(a, \theta)$ is used to designate the corresponding opportunity loss. Then $\ell(a, \Theta)$ represents the opportunity loss of an act as a function of the random variable Θ. Thus, the expected opportunity loss of an act, $E[\ell(a, \Theta)]$ is the expectation of a function of the random variable Θ. Hence, this expectation may be computed by the same general procedure employed in calculating the EMV of an act. Specifically, if the state of nature is a *discrete* random variable, the EOL of an act may be obtained from the following restatement of Formula (7.4):

$$E[\ell(a, \Theta)] = \sum_{\text{all } \theta} \ell(a, \theta) f(\theta) \qquad (21.6)$$

In words, the EOL of an act is computed by multiplying (1) the opportunity loss for that act conditional on the occurrence of each state of nature, by (2) the probability of that state of nature occurring, and then summing the products. In an analogous manner, if the state of nature is a continuous random variable, the EOL of an act may be computed from the following restatement of Formula (7.5):

$$E[\ell(a, \Theta)] = \int_{-\infty}^{\infty} \ell(a, \theta) f(\theta) \, d\theta \qquad (21.7)$$

To apply the EOL criterion to the LAX Sunday paper problem, let us begin by referring back to the opportunity losses shown in Table 21.6. Now, using Formula (21.6), we may compute the expected opportunity loss of each act by multiplying each of the conditional opportunity losses in the column representing that act by the probability of the corresponding state of nature occurring, and then summing the products. As an example, the calculation of the EOL for the act of stocking 16 copies ($a = 16$) is shown in Table 21.11. Column (1) contains the possible states of nature. Column (2) simply reproduces the figures

Table 21.11 Conditional and Expected Opportunity Losses for the Act of Stocking 16 Copies of LAX Sunday Paper

(1) State of Nature (Number of Copies Demanded), θ	(2) Conditional Opportunity Loss, $\ell(16, \theta)$	(3) Probability of State of Nature, $f(\theta)$	(4) Calculation of EOL, $\ell(16, \theta)f(\theta)$
16	$0	.05	$0
17	.20	.10	.020
18	.40	.12	.048
19	.60	.16	.096
20	.80	.10	.080
21	1.00	.20	.200
22	1.20	.16	.192
23	1.40	.06	.084
24	1.60	.05	.080
Sum		1.00	$ .800 = EOL

in the column labeled $a = 16$ for Table 21.6. Each of the figures in this column is the opportunity loss for $a = 16$ conditional on a specific state of nature occurring. Column (3) exhibits the probability of the occurrence of each of these possible states of nature. These probabilities were shown previously in Table 21.7. Column (4) is obtained by multiplying each conditional opportunity loss in column (2) by the corresponding probability in column (3). The sum of these products is equal to 80 cents, which is the EOL associated with the act of stocking 16 copies. The EOL for each of the other acts can be computed in the same general manner. The EOLs for all alternative acts are shown in Table 21.12. The reader is urged to verify these figures. As Table 21.12 indicates, the act of stocking 19 copies yields the minimum EOL of 43.5 cents. Thus, if the news dealer accepts the EOL criterion, she should stock 19 copies.

Table 21.12 Expected Opportunity Losses of Alternative Actions*

	Action (Number of Copies Stocked)								
	$a = 16$	$a = 17$	$a = 18$	$a = 19$	$a = 20$	$a = 21$	$a = 22$	$a = 23$	$a = 24$
EOL:	.800	.625	.500	.435	.450	.515	.680	.925	1.200
				↑ minimum EOL					

*As an illustration, the EOL of $.800 for $a = 16$ is calculated in Table 21.11.

21.5.3 Relationship between EMV and EOL

The EMV of an act represents the expected profit of that act based on the information that is currently available. Similarly, the EOL of an act represents the expected opportunity loss associated with that act due to the existence of uncertainty. In other words, the EOL indicates the additional expected profit that the decision maker could realize if he had perfect information to completely eliminate uncertainty. The sum of the EMV and EOL represents the total expected profit for the decision maker if he has perfect information. For instance, we see from Table 21.13 that if the news dealer were to stock 24 copies, her expected profit with available information is $2.800 and the additional expected profit that could be obtained from using perfect information is $1.200. Similarly, if she were to stock 19 copies, her expected profit with available information is $3.565 and the additional expected profit that could be obtained from using perfect information is $.435. Regardless of how many copies the news dealer chooses to stock, the sum of EMV and EOL is $4.000, which represents her total expected profit if she has perfect information. This sum is called the *EMV of the decision with perfect information*. Since this sum is a constant for each and every act, the act that has the maximum EMV must have the minimum EOL. This relationship between the EMV and EOL is *always* true, so that the EMV and EOL criteria always lead to the same decision.

Table 21.13   EMV and EOL for LAX Sunday Paper*

	Action (Number of Copies Stocked)								
	a = 16	a = 17	a = 18	a = 19	a = 20	a = 21	a = 22	a = 23	a = 24
EMV	$3.200	$3.375	$3.500	$3.565	$3.550	$3.485	$3.320	$3.075	$2.800
EOL	.800	.625	.500	.435	.450	.515	.680	.925	1.200
	$4.000	$4.000	$4.000	$4.000	$4.000	$4.000	$4.000	$4.000	$4.000

*The EMV figures in this table are taken from Table 21.11, and the EOL figures are taken from Table 21.12.

To gain further understanding of the meaning of the constant of $4.00, suppose that the news dealer is offered an option of consignment by the publisher. Under this option, the dealer may return all the unsold copies of the Sunday paper to the publisher, and only pay for the copies sold. This situation is equivalent to the case in which perfect prediction of demand is available, and the dealer stocks the exact number of copies to meet demand every Sunday. When the number of copies stocked exactly equals the number of copies demanded, profit is maximized. Returning to Table 21.4, we observe that this maximum profit is $3.20 if demand is 16 copies, $3.40 if demand is 17 copies, and so on. These maximum profits for the various demand levels are reproduced in the first column of Table 21.14. Since the weekly demand varies from 16 to

Table 21.14   Conditional and Expected Payoffs with Perfect Information

(1) State of Nature (Number of Copies Demanded), θ	(2) Maximum Payoff Conditional on θ	(3) Probability of State of Nature, f(θ)	(4) Calculation of Expected Payoff, (2) × (3)
16	$3.20	.05	$ .160
17	3.40	.10	.340
18	3.60	.12	.432
19	3.80	.16	.608
20	4.00	.10	.400
21	4.20	.20	.840
22	4.40	.16	.704
23	4.60	.06	.276
24	4.80	.05	.240
Sum		1.00	$4.000

24 copies, the expected profit is calculated by multiplying the conditional profit of each demand level by the probability of that demand level occurring, and then summing the products. The result is $4.000, which represents the expected profit to the news dealer if the consignment option is available to her. The expected profit of optimal action *without* such an option, as shown in Table 21.10, is $3.565. The difference between the above two figures is $.435, which is the same as the EOL of the optimal action. This amount measures the contribution of the consignment option, and hence the dealer should not pay more than this amount in order to use this option.

To generalize from our example, the difference between (1) the EMV of the decision with *perfect* information and (2) the EMV of the decision with *available* information is called the *Expected Value of Perfect Information* (EVPI). The EVPI is also equal to the EOL of the decision with available information. This is simply because the EVPI and EOL represent the two sides of the same coin: the EVPI represents the additional expected profit that could be obtained from perfect information and the EOL represents the expected opportunity loss of the decision due to lack of perfect information.

The practical significance of EVPI is that it puts an *upper* limit on what a decision maker should pay for additional information, since *any* information, no matter how accurate, would be worth no more than the value of *perfect information*. In real life, of course, the availability of a perfect predictor is rare. However, regardless of whether or not a perfect predictor actually exists, EVPI still puts an upper limit on the worth of additional information. Thus, the usefulness of the concept of EVPI remains undiminished even if a perfect predictor does not actually exist.

21.6 INCREMENTAL ANALYSIS

According to the EMV criterion, the optimal act is the act that has the maximum EMV. As we have seen, one way of finding this optimal act is to compute the EMV of each alternative act and then to compare these EMVs. Although this procedure is straightforward, it is laborious, particularly if there are many alternative acts. The inventory-stocking problem, such as the one presented in this chapter, is a case in point. In a realistic inventory problem, the random variable representing demand usually has numerous possible values (numerous possible demand levels), and hence numerous alternative courses of action (numerous stock levels) are available. For such a case, it is not practical to compute the EMVs for all the alternative acts. Fortunately, a simple analytical method, called *incremental analysis*, has been developed for finding the optimal stock level without having to compute the EMVs.

Since the EMV and EOL are equivalent criteria, the formulas for incremental analysis may be stated in terms of monetary values or opportunity losses. In the following discussion, we present incremental analysis in terms of loss figures. To gain insight into this method, let us return to Table 21.6, which shows the opportunity losses for the LAX Sunday paper example. Inspection of this table indicates that the opportunity loss is zero whenever the number of copies stocked equals the number of copies demanded. In other words, there is no opportunity loss if the stock is exactly equal to the quantity demanded (i.e., if $a = \theta$). An opportunity loss occurs either when stock exceeds demand $(a > \theta)$ or when demand exceeds stock $(\theta > a)$. In the case of overstock $(a > \theta)$, the opportunity loss is 30 cents per copy, which is equal to the purchase cost of a copy. For instance, if the news dealer stocks 22 copies ($a = 22$) but demand is only 18 copies ($\theta = 18$), then there will be an overstock of $(22 - 18) = 4$ copies. The opportunity loss associated with this situation is ($\$.30 \times 4$) $= \$1.20$, which is exactly the same as that shown in Table 21.6 for $a = 22$ and $\theta = 18$. Similarly, in the case of understock ($\theta > a$), the opportunity loss per copy is 20 cents, which represents the additional profit that the news dealer could have made if she had one more copy in stock. For example, if she stocks 22 copies ($a = 22$) but demand is 24 copies ($\theta = 24$), then there will be an understock of $(24 - 22) = 2$ copies, with a resulting opportunity loss of $\$.20 \times 2 = \$.40$. This is precisely what is shown in Table 21.6 for $a = 22$ and $\theta = 24$.

To generalize the foregoing observations, let

$$k_o = \text{opportunity loss per unit of overstock}$$
$$k_u = \text{opportunity loss per unit of understock}$$

Then the possible opportunity losses associated with an inventory-stocking problem can be calculated from the following function:

$$\ell(a, \theta) = \begin{cases} k_o(a - \theta) & \text{if } a > \theta \\ k_u(\theta - a) & \text{if } \theta > a \end{cases} \tag{21.8}$$

In words, if stock exceeds demand, the total opportunity loss of overstock is equal to k_o times the number of units of overstock. However, if demand exceeds stock, the total opportunity loss of understock is equal to k_u times the number of units of understock. From this opportunity-loss function, a simple analytical solution for optimal stock can be obtained. Specifically, if the state of nature θ, denoting the demand for a perishable product, is a discrete random variable, the optimal act (optimal stock level) is the smallest value of a that satisfies the following inequality:

$$P(\theta \leq a) \geq \frac{k_u}{k_u + k_o} \tag{21.9}$$

In this formula, $P(\theta \leq a)$ represents the probability that demand level will be less than or equal to the stock level. Thus, this probability, $P(\theta \leq a)$, can be obtained from the cumulative mass function $F(\theta)$ by setting θ equal to a. That is, since $\theta = a$, we may write $P(\theta \leq a) = P(\theta \leq \theta) = F(\theta)$. If θ is a continuous random variable, the optimal act is the value of a that satisfies the following equality:

$$P(\theta \leq a) = \frac{k_u}{k_u + k_o} \tag{21.10}$$

The reader may recognize that both Formulas (21.9) and (21.10) satisfy the definition of the fractile of a random variable discussed in Chapter 8. Thus, regardless of whether demand is a discrete or continuous random variable, the optimal stock is the k fractile of the probability distribution of demand, where $k = k_u/(k_u + k_o)$.

Example 1:

Since demand for the LAX Sunday paper is a discrete random variable, we can use Formula (21.9) to obtain the optimal stock level. To apply this formula, we proceed as follows:

Step 1: Determine k_o and k_u. In this example, k_o = $.30, which is the cost of an unsold copy; k_u = $.50 − $.30 = $.20, which is the profit that the news dealer forgoes if he fails to stock 1 unit that could have been sold.

Step 2: Calculate the ratio $k = k_u/(k_u + k_o)$. For our example, we obtain

$$k = \frac{k_u}{k_u + k_o} = \frac{.20}{.20 + .30} = .40$$

Step 3: Find the smallest value of a such that $P(\theta \le a) \ge k$. To do this, we prepare Table 21.15. The probability mass function, $f(\theta)$, in column (2), is taken from Table 21.7. The cumulative mass function, $F(\theta)$, in column (3), is obtained by cumulating the terms in column (2). The cumulative function is then

Table 21.15 Cumulative Probabilities for LAX Sunday Paper

(1) θ or a	(2) $f(\theta)$	(3) $F(\theta)$	(4) $P(\theta \le a)$
16	.05	.05	.05
17	.10	.15	.15
18	.12	.27	.27
19	.16	.43	.43
20	.10	.53	.53
21	.20	.73	.73
22	.16	.89	.89
23	.06	.95	.95
24	.05	1.00	1.00
Sum	1.00		

reexpressed in terms of the cumulative probability $P(\theta \le a)$ in column (4). From this column, we see that the smallest cumulative probability greater than .40 is equal to .43. That is, $P(\theta \le 19) = .43 > .40$. Since 19 is the smallest value of a such that $P(\theta \le a) > .40$, the .40 fractile is 19. Thus, the optimal stock is 19 copies, which is identical to the result that was obtained previously by computing and comparing the EMVs (or EOLs) of all alternative acts.

Example 2:

The application of incremental analysis is not limited to inventory stocking problems. For instance, consider the case of Douglas McAndrew, who receives a monthly paycheck of $2,000. Upon the receipt of his check, he splits his pay between his checking account and savings account. The amount he deposits in the savings account will earn interest at an annual rate of 6%. On the other hand, the funds placed in the checking account will earn no interest. Naturally, Doug would like to deposit as large an amount as possible in the savings account. However, if the amount that he deposits in the checking account for a given month is not sufficient to pay his expenditures for that month, the bank will automatically loan funds to cover his checks. The financial charge for such a loan is 2% of the amount advanced. His experience shows that his monthly checking expenditures have varied between $1,200 and $2,000. After some analysis, he has determined that his next month's expenditures can be approximated by the normal distribution with mean μ = $1,500 and standard deviation σ = $160.

To determine how much money Doug McAndrew should deposit in his checking account, we first observe that the amount of his monthly checking expenditures is a continuous random variable, and hence Formula (21.10) is applicable. We then use this formula to obtain the solution as follows:

Step 1: Determine k_o and k_u. In this problem, we have:

$k_o = 6\%/12 = .5\%$ (i.e., $\frac{1}{2}$ cent per dollar of excess funds in the checking account). This amount is the interest per dollar that could be earned from the savings account.

$k_u = 2\% - .5\% = 1.5\%$ (i.e., 1.5 cents per dollar shortage of funds in the checking account). Notice that although Doug would pay a financial charge of 2%, he would earn an interest of .5% from funds deposited in his savings rather than checking account.

Step 2: Calculate the ratio

$$k = \frac{k_u}{k_u + k_o} = \frac{1.5\%}{1.5\% + .5\%} = .75$$

Step 3: Find the value of c such that

$$P(X \leq c) = .75$$

where X = amount of his next month's expenditures
c = optimal amount to be deposited in his checking account
Thus, c is equal to $x_{.75}$, the .75 fractile of the distribution of X. To determine $x_{.75}$, we first find $z_{.75}$, the .75 fractile of the standard normal distribution. From Table J (Appendix II), we obtain $z_{.75} = .675$. Next, applying Formula (12.11), we may write

$$z_{.75} = \frac{x_{.75} - \mu}{\sigma}$$

Then, by simple algebra, we obtain

$$x_{.75} = \mu + z_{.75}\sigma$$
$$= 1,500 + (.675)(160) = 1,608$$

Hence, Doug's optimal action is to place $1,608 in his checking account and the remaining $392 in his savings account.

PROBLEMS

21.1 Suppose that you have a sum of money that you wish to invest for a 1-year period. You have narrowed your choices to three alternatives:

a_1: invest in a construction firm
a_2: deposit the money in a savings and loan association
a_3: invest in an industrial consulting firm

You are concerned with three possible states of nature that might affect the profit you will realize on your investment:

θ_1: housing starts will increase next year
θ_2: housing starts will remain at the same level
θ_3: housing starts will decline next year

You have determined the possible profits (in thousands of dollars) associated with various action–state pairs as shown in the following payoff table:

State of	Action		
Nature	a_1	a_2	a_3
θ_1	9	6	8
θ_2	7	6	7
θ_3	3	6	5

(a) If you adopt the maximin criterion, which course of action should you take?
(b) If you adopt the maximax criterion, which course of action should you take?
(c) If you adopt the Hurwicz criterion with $c = .5$, which course of action should you take?
(d) If you adopt the minimax regret criterion, which course of action should you take?

21.2 Suppose that you have a sum of money which you wish to invest for a 2-year period. You have narrowed your choices to four alternatives:

a_1: Invest in importing silver products from Mexico

a_2: Invest in exporting cotton textiles to Mexico

a_3: Invest in second mortgages

a_4: Invest in exporting pharmaceuticals to Asia

You are concerned with three possible states of nature that might affect the profit that you will realize on your investment:

θ_1: The value of the Mexican peso will fall below 4.3 cents

θ_2: The value of the Mexican peso will remain between 4.3 and 4.5 cents

θ_3: The value of the Mexican peso will rise above 4.5 cents

You have determined the possible profits (in thousands of dollars) as shown in the following payoff table:

State of	Action			
Nature	a_1	a_2	a_3	a_4
θ_1	7	2	3.5	3
θ_2	4	5	3.5	4
θ_3	1	6	3.5	5

According to your subjective judgment, the probabilities of the possible states of nature are

$$P(\theta_1) = .10 \qquad P(\theta_2) = .70 \qquad P(\theta_3) = .20$$

Use each of the following decision criteria to determine your optimal course of action:
(a) Maximax criterion
(b) Maximin criterion
(c) Hurwicz criterion with $c = .60$
(d) Minimax regret criterion
(e) Maximum likelihood criterion
(f) EMV criterion
(g) EOL criterion

21.3 Hi-Test Tool Company, Inc., and Ever-Rite Machinery Company, Inc., are direct competitors in several product lines. Currently, each is considering the feasibility of constructing a newly designed automated Capston lathe-manufacturing plant. Hi-Test reported net earnings of $20 million for the preceding year. Hi-Test's management estimates that if it builds the plant and Ever-Rite does not, the *present value* of the *increase* in net-income flow will be $15 million. However, it has concluded that if Hi-Test does not build the plant but its competitor does, the present value of the *decrease* in net-income flow will be $12 million. If both companies construct new plants, Hi-Test's *decrease* in the present value of net-income flow will be $15 million.

(a) Should Hi-Test construct the new plant if its decision criterion is maximin?
(b) Should Hi-Test build the plant if its decision criterion is maximax?
(c) If Hi-Test uses the Hurwicz criterion with the pessimism–optimism coefficient $c = .9$, should it build the plant?
(d) What should Hi-Test do if it uses the minimax regret criterion?

21.4 The Ever-Rite Company in Problem 21.3 had net income of $30 million in the preceding year. The company has arrived at the following estimates:

If Ever-Rite builds the new plant, but Hi-Test does not, the present value of the *increase* in Ever-Rite's net-income flow will be $27 million. However, if Ever-Rite does not build, but Hi-Test does, the present value of the *decrease* in net-income flow will be $12 million. If both companies build new plants, the present value of the *decrease* in Ever-Rite's net-income flow is estimated to be $15 million.

Find the optimal course of action for Ever-Rite under each of the following decision criteria:

(a) Maximin criterion
(b) Maximax criterion
(c) Hurwicz criterion with $c = .9$
(d) Minimax regret criterion

21.5 A specialty grocer stocks a type of exotic melon that is flown in daily from Pago Pago. From past experience, he has determined the following probabilities for the daily demand for this type of melon.

Daily Demand	Probability
1 melon	.10
2 melons	.40
3 melons	.30
4 melons	.20

The grocer buys melons at $5.00 each, and sells them for $7.00 each. The melon is a highly perishable item. Any melon that is not sold by the end of the day will be spoiled and will have no value on the next day. Thus, the grocer is very much concerned with the number of melons to stock daily.

(a) Construct the conditional profit table for the grocer's stocking problem.
(b) If the grocer adopts the maximum likelihood criterion, how many melons should he stock?
(c) If the grocer adopts the expected state of nature criterion, how many melons should he stock?
(d) If the grocer wishes to limit the probability of overstock to .10, how many melons should he stock?
(e) If the grocer wishes to limit the probability of understock to .25, how many melons should he stock?

21.6 A retailer stocks a perishable product that costs her $3.00 per unit. She buys the product in the morning and sells it at $5.00 per unit during the day. Any unit not sold by the end of the day must be thrown away at a total loss. Let X be the random variable denoting the demand for the fresh product daily. The retailer has found that the probability mass function of X is given by

$$f(x) = \begin{cases} \dfrac{x-4}{10} & \text{if } x = 5, 6, 7, 8 \\ 0 & \text{otherwise} \end{cases}$$

(a) Construct the conditional payoff table for the retailer's stocking problem.

(b) If the retailer wishes to use the maximum likelihood criterion, how many units should she stock?

(c) If the retailer wishes to use the expected state of nature criterion, how many units should she stock?

(d) Compute the expected monetary value of each of the alternative acts. Using the EMV criterion, how many units should she stock?

(e) If the retailer wishes to limit the probability of overstock to .10, how many units should she stock?

(f) If the retailer wishes to limit the probability of understock to .20, how many units should she stock?

21.7 A trading post operator has limited capital and must decide whether he should stock snow shoes or tennis shoes on next month's order. If he stocks snow shoes and it snows, he will make a profit of $100, but if it does not snow he will suffer a $20 loss. If he stocks tennis shoes and it snows he will suffer a $10 loss, but if it does not snow he will make a profit of $90. He estimates a .60 probability that it will snow.

(a) Construct the conditional payoff table for the trading post operator.

(b) If the operator uses the EMV criterion, should he stock snow shoes or tennis shoes?

(c) Construct the conditional opportunity loss table for the operator.

(d) If the operator uses the EOL criterion, should he stock snow shoes or tennis shoes?

(e) Do the EMV and EOL criteria always lead to the same decision? Explain why.

21.8 One of the publications carried by the AXY newsstand is *Nouvelles de Provence*, a French weekly magazine. The dealer pays 70 cents per copy and sells it for $1.00 per copy. Copies that are unsold after a week's time are nonreturnable and have no value. The probability distribution of demand is as follows:

Demand (Number of Magazines per Week)	Probability
10	.05
11	.05
12	.10
13	.15
14	.20
15	.25
16	.15
17	.05

Use each of the following decision criteria to determine the optimal number of magazines to stock:

(a) Maximin criterion

(b) Maximax criterion

(c) Hurwicz criterion with $c = .7$

(d) Minimax regret criterion

(e) Maximum likelihood criterion

(f) Expected state of nature criterion

(g) Limited risk criterion with maximum probability of overstock equal to .05

(h) Limited risk criterion with maximum probability of understock equal to .20

(i) EMV criterion by computing the EMVs of the alternative acts

(j) EOL criterion

(i) by computing the EOLs of the alternative acts

(ii) by using incremental analysis

21.9 The manager of a small department store must place her order for an expensive line of Christmas cards for the Christmas season. Each box of cards costs $3, sells at $5 during the season, and the price will be reduced to $2 after the season. She feels that any boxes of cards remaining at the end of the season can be sold at this reduced price. The demand for boxes of cards during the season has been estimated as follows:

Demand	Probability
25	.10
26	.15
27	.30
28	.20
29	.15
30	.10

Use each of the following decision criteria to determine the optimal number of boxes of cards to stock:

(a) Maximin criterion

(b) Maximax criterion

(c) Hurwicz criterion with $c = .4$

(d) Minimax regret criterion

(e) Maximum likelihood criterion

(f) Expected state of nature criterion

(g) Limited risk criterion with maximum probability of overstock equal to .25

(h) Limited risk criterion with maximum probability of understock equal to .15

(i) EMV criterion by computing the EMVs of the alternative acts

(j) EOL criterion

   (i) by computing the EOLs of the alternative acts

   (ii) by using incremental analysis

21.10 You have received an offer to engage in a speculative real estate venture for an investment of $4,000. If a bond issue passes at the next election, you will receive a net return of $16,000, but if the bond issue fails your investment will be a total loss. What is the minimum probability you would require for the passage of the issue in order for the investment to be a desirable one if you use the EMV criterion?

21.11 The Copycat Corporation is considering installing a Zorex copying machine in its new branch. The Zorex distributor has offered to provide the machine either (1) as an outright sale at a $5,600 price, or (2) on a rental basis. Either alternative would provide Copycat with the same services. If the branch operates successfully, the present worth of future rentals will be $8,000. If the branch fails, the present worth of future rentals will be only $2,000. On the basis of the EMV criterion, what is the minimum probability of success for the new branch that would make purchase of the machine preferable to rental?

21.12 The conditional opportunity loss table for a particular decision problem is given as follows:

State of Nature	COL	
	a_1	a_2
θ_1	$ 0	$100
θ_2	50	0

The expected opportunity loss of a_1 is \$35. The expected payoff (or EMV) of a_1 is \$225, and the conditional payoff of a_1 given θ_1 is \$400.
   (a) According to the minimax regret criterion, which course of action is preferable?
   (b) Find the probabilities for θ_1 and θ_2.
   (c) According to the EOL criterion, which course of action is preferable?
   (d) Find the expected payoff of a_2.
   (e) Construct the conditional payoff table.

21.13 Consider a decision situation in which there are two possible states of nature (θ_1 and θ_2) and two alternative courses of action (a_1 and a_2). The conditional opportunity loss table for this situation is

| State of | COL | |
Nature	a_1	a_2
θ_1	\$20	\$ 0
θ_2	0	50

The EOL of a_2 is \$40. The EMV of a_2 is \$42. The conditional payoff of a_1 if θ_1 occurs is \$70.
   (a) Using the minimax regret criterion, which course of action is preferred?
   (b) Find the probabilities for θ_1 and θ_2.
   (c) Using the EOL criterion, which course of action is preferred?
   (d) Find the EMV of a_1.
   (e) Construct the conditional payoff table.

21.14 For Problem 21.5, do the following:
   (a) Determine the EMV of the grocer's decision with available information.
   (b) Determine the EMV of the grocer's decision with perfect information.
   (c) Find the EVPI by using the results in parts (a) and (b).
   (d) Construct the opportunity loss table for the grocer. According to the EOL criterion, how many melons should he stock?
   (e) Is the EOL associated with the optimal stock in part (d) equal to the EVPI obtained in part (c)? Is this a general phenomenon or a mere coincidence? Why?
   (f) Find the sum of the EMV and the EOL for each alternative act. Is this sum constant for all alternative acts?
   (g) How is the sum in part (f) related to the EMV of the grocer's decision with perfect information obtained in part (b)?

21.15 For Problem 21.6, do the following:
   (a) Determine the EMV of the retailer's decision with perfect information.
   (b) Find the EVPI by comparing (1) the EMV of the retailer's decision with perfect information and (2) the EMV of the decision with available information.
   (c) Construct the conditional opportunity loss table for the retailer. Compute the EOL of each of the alternative acts. Using the EOL criterion, how many units should she stock?
   (d) Is the EOL associated with the optimal act in part (c) equal to the EVPI obtained in part (b)? Is this a mere coincidence? Explain.

21.16 Suppose that the trading post operator in Problem 21.7 has found an extremely capable weather forecaster. This particular forecaster can foretell *for sure* whether or not it is going to snow. What is the EMV for the operator if he decides to purchase the forecaster's perfect prediction? What is the maximum amount that the operator should pay for the perfect prediction?

21.17 Suppose that the AXY newsstand in Problem 21.8 has received an offer to consider an option of consignment by the magazine publisher. The option allows the dealer to return all the unsold copies of *Nouvelles de Provence* to the publisher, and pay only for the copies sold.

(a) Under the consignment option, what is the dealer's EMV?

(b) What is the maximum amount that the dealer should pay the publisher for the right to use the consignment option?

21.18 Suppose that the department store in Problem 21.9 found that the Christmas card printer does sell on consignment, with prices of the consignment option subject to negotiation.

(a) If the store should decide to use the consignment option, what would be its EMV from selling Christmas cards?

(b) What is the maximum amount that the store should pay for the option?

21.19 One of the publications carried by Joe's newsstand is *Crazy*, a monthly humor magazine. The dealer purchases the magazine at a unit cost of 60 cents and sells it at a unit price of 90 cents. Copies that are unsold at the end of the month are returnable for a rebate of 10 cents per copy. From Joe's records, he is able to estimate the following probability distribution for monthly demand:

Number of Copies Demanded per Month	Probability
25	.05
26	.15
27	.25
28	.20
29	.15
30	.10
31	.05
32	.05

Using incremental analysis, determine the number of copies of *Crazy* that Joe should stock each month to maximize the EMV from sales of this magazine.

21.20 A department store buyer for the Magnum Company is planning to stock a specifically dated scenic diary. The diary will sell for $1.75 and cost $1.00. It is believed that, because of the scenic pictures in the dated diary, any stock remaining after January can be sold for 50 cents per copy. The demand distribution is estimated as follows:

Demand for Diaries, θ	$P(\theta)$
50	.10
51	.10
52	.15
53	.25
54	.20
55	.10
56	.05
57	.05

How many diaries should be stocked?

21.21 The manager of a small gift shop has located a wholesale source for a unique type of bracelet which is currently at the peak of faddish popularity. He can buy these bracelets at a unit cost of $12.00 and sell them at a price of $20.00. He feels that any bracelets remaining in stock after the fad has passed (about 1 month) can be sold at half-price. Since the manager is uncertain about how many of these bracelets he can actually sell in a month's time, he must regard demand as a random variable in deciding how many bracelets to buy. For this purpose, suppose he feels that demand has a Poisson distribution with a mean of 20. To maximize expected profit, how many bracelets should he buy?

21.22 Joan Adgel believes she can make some money for Christmas by selling Christmas trees. She has decided to sell on weekends, since she can use a parking lot only during that time period. Thus, she must stock the lot with the optimal number for weekend sales because any trees not sold on a given weekend are worthless. Joan has decided to sell silver-tip trees only, as her profit potential is greater with high-quality than with less expensive trees. After some investigation, Joan concludes that the weekend demand for trees is Poisson with an average of 20. If the cost per tree is $9.00 and the selling price per tree is $15, how many trees should she stock per weekend?

21.23 The Empire Department Store has decided to stock a unique design of next year's calendars during the coming fall. The calendars will cost $1.50 each. The sale of calendars will last for 10 weeks. The store will sell them for $2.50 each during this period. Any calendars that are not sold by the end of this period will have no value. Based on past experience, the marketing manager estimates that the average demand per week is 90 calendars. Furthermore, he indicates that the weekly demand follows a Poisson process. Determine the optimal number of calendars to stock. [*Hint*: Use normal approximation to the Poisson, $F_P(x|\lambda, t) \approx F_n(x + .5 | \mu, \sigma^2)$. The mechanics are analogous to the normal approximation to the binomial.]

21.24 Weekly demand for a particular perishable product is normally distributed with a mean of 500 kilograms and a standard deviation of 100 kilograms. The product costs the retailer $6.70 per kilogram and sells for $10.00 per kilogram. Stock left unsold at the end of the week has no salvage value. Determine the optimal quantity of this product for the retailer to stock each week.

21.25 A flight kitchen manager for Golden Bird Airlines must decide how many meals to prepare for Flight 534. The cost of preparing each meal is $1.50. Any meals that are not used by passengers will be discarded after landing. If there are not enough meals, however, a meal ticket is issued to each passenger who cannot obtain the meal on the flight. A meal ticket, which costs the airline $6.00, entitles the passenger to a free meal in the airport restaurant. The manager feels that the demand for meals on this particular flight can be approximated by a normal distribution, with mean equal to 200 and standard deviation equal to 30.
 (a) What is the optimal number of meals to prepare for Flight 534?
 (b) If the manager orders the number obtained in part (a), what is the most likely number of meals that will be discarded after landing?

21.26 Sisters, Inc., specializes in designing, making, and selling clothing of original styles for young women. The management has just decided to introduce mini-blouses for the coming summer. The question yet to be resolved is the size of the production order. Once the production for this order begins, it will not be feasible to revise the order since the facility has been scheduled for other styles. The marketing manager feels that the demand for mini-blouses during the season can be approximated by a normal probability distribution. The mean and the standard deviation of this distribution have been estimated as $\mu = 1,000$ and $\sigma = 200$. The variable cost per blouse has been estimated as $5.99. The selling price will be $11.99 per blouse during the season, and the price will be reduced to $1.99 after the season. It is felt that any blouses remaining at the end of the season can be sold at this reduced price. The company's policy is to maintain the reputation of carrying new-style clothing. Thus, the company will sell the leftover blouses at a substantial loss rather than store them for next year.
 (a) Determine the optimal number of mini-blouses to schedule for production.
 (b) Suppose that the management feels that the company will suffer a goodwill loss if they run out of stock. If the management estimates that the goodwill loss is $3.33 per stockout, find the optimal number of mini-blouses to schedule for production.

21.27 Every Friday, the bakery department of Adolph's Supermarket chain features a particular type of orange cake made from a secret recipe obtained from Adolph's Great-Aunt Hetty. Experience over a period of several years indicates that Friday demand for this item can be approximated by a normal distribution with a mean of 1,000 and a standard deviation of 50. The cakes are produced at a unit cost of 80 cents and sell for $1.50. It has been found that any cakes remaining unsold on Friday can be sold the next day at a price of 50 cents. How many of these cakes should be produced for each Friday's trade in order to maximize the expected profit?

21.28 The management of Rectangular Stationery Company must decide how many desk calendar refills to order for next year. Past experience indicates that calendars not sold by January 30 are worthless. From past records it has been determined that distribution of the demand for this particular style of refill is approximately normal with a mean of 375 and a standard deviation of 40 refills. The refills sell for $1.25 and cost 60 cents each.

(a) How many calendar refills should be stocked?

(b) Suppose that management wishes to take into account an estimated 35-cents goodwill loss for each request that cannot be met due to stock shortage. In that case, how many refills should be stocked?

21.29 Suppose that you own the Fair-Price Gasoline Station at the corner of Federal Street and State Avenue. You have found that your gasoline sales are fairly constant over time so that you can predict reasonably well when you need the next delivery. Unfortunately, the delivery service is poor and unreliable. Your experience has shown that the lead time (the time between placing a phone order and receiving truck delivery) varies between 2 and 6 hours. If you do not allow enough lead time for delivery, you face the risk of running out of gasoline. When a stockout happens, you will lose your sales and suffer some goodwill loss. On the other hand, if the delivery arrives too early, the truck has to wait until the gasoline in your tank has reached the minimum level, which will cost you a waiting fee. Thus, you are facing the problem of when to place your order. You have quantified your judgment about the uncertain lead time, T (in hours), in terms of the following probability density function:

$$f(t) = \begin{cases} \dfrac{t}{4} - \dfrac{1}{2} & \text{for } 2 \leq t < 4 \\[2mm] \dfrac{3}{2} - \dfrac{t}{4} & \text{for } 4 \leq t \leq 6 \\[2mm] 0 & \text{otherwise} \end{cases}$$

(a) If you place your order at noon, what is your probability that the truck will arrive no later than 3:00 P.M.?

(b) By analyzing the losses due to early and late delivery, you estimate that the loss due to late delivery is 7 times the loss due to early delivery. At what time should you place your phone order if you need your next delivery at 3:00 P.M.?

21.30 The Chemtex Corporation sells chemicals to pharmaceutical manufacturers. One of the chemicals for which Chemtex receives frequent orders is VIP-27, a compound that is highly perishable in its raw form. Because of its limited market, there is only one manufacturer of VIP-27. This manufacturer is an independent producer who makes the compound available only in 300-pound paper bags, at a price of $3.00 per pound. Thus, Chemtex can purchase VIP-27 only in multiples of 300 pounds. Furthermore, since the compound perishes rapidly, Chemtex must purchase VIP-27 weekly. When a fresh supply arrives each week, any remainder from the preceding week's supply must be destroyed at a total loss. Because of the perishability of VIP-27, the customers of Chemtex are willing to buy the compound only in the exact amounts that will meet their immediate needs. Over a period of time, total weekly demand has varied between 200 and 1,000 pounds. From analysis of past sales, Chemtex has determined that this total weekly demand for VIP-27 (in hundreds of pounds) can be approximated by the following probability density function:

$$f(x) = \begin{cases} \dfrac{x}{16} - \dfrac{1}{8} & \text{if } 2 \leq x \leq 6 \\[2ex] \dfrac{5}{8} - \dfrac{x}{16} & \text{if } 6 \leq x \leq 10 \\[2ex] 0 & \text{otherwise} \end{cases}$$

As a result of the perishability of the product and the variability of demand, Chemtex charges its customers $10.00 per pound for VIP-27.

(a) Determine the expected weekly demand for VIP-27 in pounds.

(b) Determine Chemtex's weekly profit function for sales of VIP-27 if the firm stocks:

   (i)   1 bag each week

  (ii)   2 bags each week

 (iii)   3 bags each week

(c) Using the expected state of nature criterion, how many bags of VIP-27 should Chemtex stock each week?

(d) Compute the EMV for each of the alternative weekly stock levels indicated in part (b).

(e) Using the EMV criterion, how many bags of VIP-27 should Chemtex stock each week?

22

Decision Analysis:

Basic Concepts and Procedures

As pointed out in Chapter 21, decision analysis has been developed to provide a systematic approach to the complex process of managerial decision making. The purpose of this chapter is to provide an overview of the decision analysis approach. Specifically, we examine the general framework of decision analysis and present some applications that demonstrate the practical use of this approach.

22.1 FORMULATION OF A DECISION PROBLEM

To illustrate the basic procedure of the decision analysis approach, consider the case of Andy Adams, who has $20,000 to invest for 1 year. As an investor, Andy has a basic goal of making the most profit on the use of his resources.

After a preliminary study of his investment problem, Andy limits his consideration to two alternatives: either to open a certificate account with a savings institution or to purchase the stock of Carter Engineering Company. If Andy deposits the amount in the savings account, he will earn interest at an annual rate of 8%. Andy has a good friend, Bob Burns, who is a successful stockbroker. According to Bob, the Carter Engineering Company is developing a new chemical process. If the new process is successful, Bob predicts that the price of Carter's stock will go up by 20% in 1 year; otherwise, it will drop 5%.

In considering Andy's present investment problem, there are two alternative actions available to him:

a_1: Deposit the money in the savings account

a_2: Purchase the stock of Carter Co.

The consequences resulting from either of these courses of action will depend on whether or not the new chemical process is successfully developed. Thus, in deciding between the two alternative courses of action, Andy must consider two possible states of nature:

θ_1:   New chemical process is successful

θ_2:   New chemical process is not successful

The logical structure of Andy's investment problem can be represented by a *decision diagram*. As shown in Figure 22.1, Andy is at the origin of the diagram (i.e., at the extreme left of the diagram), and must decide whether to proceed along the upper branch (i.e., to choose a_1) or along the lower branch (i.e., to choose a_2). The consequence of his decision will depend upon which of the two possible states of nature, θ_1 or θ_2, happens to prevail. These possible states of nature are represented by the branches at the right of the decision diagram

A decision diagram is often called a *decision tree* because it resembles the branches of a tree. A decision tree shows all alternative courses of action that the decision maker wishes to consider and all possible states of nature that in his or her judgment may possibly affect the choices among those actions. In drawing the decision tree *from left to right*, the actions and states are displayed in the order in which they would be encountered or become known to the decision maker. An action node (or decision node) is usually represented by a small square (■) and a state node (or chance node) is represented by a small circle (●).

22.2   ANALYSIS BASED ON PRIOR INFORMATION

After the decision maker has constructed a decision tree for a problem, he must next consider how to obtain a numerical description of the consequences for each possible action–state sequence that is shown on the tree. The description must reflect the value of that consequence in the decision maker's judgment for the purpose of arriving at a rational decision. Andy Adams considers monetary profit as an adequate measure of the consequence associated with each action–state sequence. If Andy deposits his money in the savings account with an annual interest rate of 8%, his profit will be

$$\$20,000 \times 8\% = \$1,600$$

If he chooses a_1, he will earn this amount of interest regardless of whether the new chemical process is successfully developed. However, if he chooses a_2, he will either make a profit or a loss, depending on whether or not the new process is successfully developed. If the process is successful, his profit will be

$$\$20,000 \times 20\% = \$4,000$$

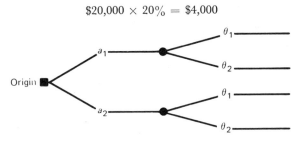

Figure 22.1   Andy Adams' Decision Problem

which represents the amount of price appreciation of the stock. If, however, the process fails, the consequence to Andy will be

$$\$20,000 \times (-5\%) = -\$1,000$$

which represents the loss due to the decrease in stock price. Thus, if Andy chooses a_2, his profit will be either $4,000 or $-\$1,000$, depending upon whether or not the new process is successful.

To determine the likelihood of the success of the process, Andy consults with his friend, Bob Burns. After some discussion with Bob, Andy estimates that the odds are 3:2 that the new process will be successful. Using Formula (4.3), these odds may be converted to probabilities. Specifically, the probability of success is:

$$P(\theta_1) = \frac{3}{3+2} = 0.6$$

whereas the probability of failure is

$$P(\theta_2) = \frac{2}{3+2} = 0.4$$

These subjective probabilities, together with the possible monetary consequences, are shown on the decision tree in Figure 22.2.

As we have seen, construction of a decision tree proceeds from *left to right*. Once the tree is constructed, it may be used for *analysis* of the decision problem by proceeding from *right to left*. When the EMV criterion is used, this analysis consists of two basic operations:

1. At each chance node, the EMV is computed.
2. At each decision node, the act that has the greatest EMV is selected, and the branch(es) not selected are blocked with slashes.

To illustrate this process, the analysis of Andy Adams' decision tree is shown in Figure 22.3. We begin by computing the EMVs at the two chance nodes using the monetary values and corresponding probabilities to the right of these nodes:

At c_1: EMV $= \$1,600(.6) + \$1,600(.4) = \$1,600$
At c_2: EMV $= \$4,000(.6) + (-\$1,000)(.4) = \$2,000$

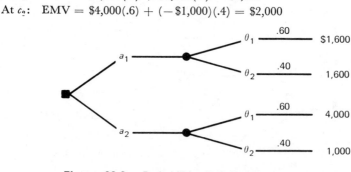

Figure 22.2   Probabilities and Consequences for Andy Adams' Decision Problem

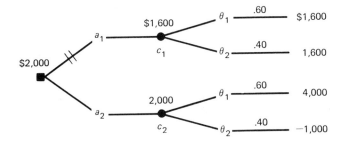

Figure 22.3 Analysis of Andy Adams' Decision Problem Based on Prior Information

The EMV at each chance node is the EMV of the act represented by the branch leading into the node *from the left.* Thus, EMV (a_1) = $1,600 and EMV (a_2) = $2,000. Since the EMV of a_2 is greater than the EMV of a_1, the preferred act is a_2 and hence the branch representing a_1 is blocked with slashes. Thus, according to the EMV criterion, the optimal act is to purchase Carter Company stock. The EMV of this decision is $2,000, which is shown on the decision node at the far left of the tree.

In analyzing a decision problem, an alternative to the decision tree is a payoff table. The payoff table for Andy's decision problem is shown in Table 22.1.

Table 22.1 Payoff Table for Andy Adams' Decision Problem

	Alternative Courses of Action		
State of Nature	a_1: Deposit in Bank	a_2: Buy Stock	Probability
θ_1: successful	$1,600	$4,000	.60
θ_2: unsuccessful	1,600	−1,000	.40
EMV	$1,600	$2,000	

For a simple decision problem such as this one, the table is as effective as the tree diagram. However, when a decision problem involves several sequential decisions, each of which consists of many alternatives and possible states of nature, the tree diagram can show the interrelationship among the alternative actions and possible states of nature much more effectively than the table.

22.3 ANALYSIS USING ADDITIONAL INFORMATION

The analysis of Andy Adams' decision problem shown in Figure 22.3 indicates that the optimal course of action is to purchase the stock. Nevertheless, even though he knows the *expected* monetary value of this action, he is still uncertain about the *actual* monetary value since he does not know for sure which of the two possible states will actually occur. This uncertainty can be reduced or even eliminated by obtaining additional information.

22.3.1 Evaluating Perfect Information

Suppose there exists an expert, Eugene Elliot, who has the uncanny ability to predict the outcome of the new chemical process with 100% accuracy. In other words, if Eugene predicts that the process will be successful, then Andy can be absolutely sure that the process will be successful. Similarly, if Eugene predicts that the process will not be successful, Andy can be absolutely sure that the process will not be successful. Such a *perfect prediction* would totally eliminate Andy's uncertainty if he could obtain the prediction from Eugene.

The structure and analysis of Andy's decision problem with perfect information is shown in Figure 22.4. Under the condition that perfect information will be available, Andy will not decide which of the two alternative courses of action to choose until he has obtained Eugene's prediction. Thus, this figure differs from Figure 22.3 in that it begins with Eugene's two possible predictions —that the process will be successful or that it will be unsuccessful. Furthermore, the availability of perfect information changes the probabilities of the two possible states of nature θ_1 and θ_2.

To understand the changes in probabilities, first recall that Andy initially estimated the probabilities of the possible states of nature as follows:

$$P(\theta_1) = .6$$
$$P(\theta_2) = .4$$

These probabilities are called *prior probabilities* since they reflect the amount of information that is available to Andy *prior to* (before) obtaining any additional information. The effect of the expert's information on the probabilities depends on whether he predicts θ_1 or θ_2.

If Eugene predicts θ_1, then θ_1 will actually occur and θ_2 will not occur. This may be expressed in probability notation as follows:

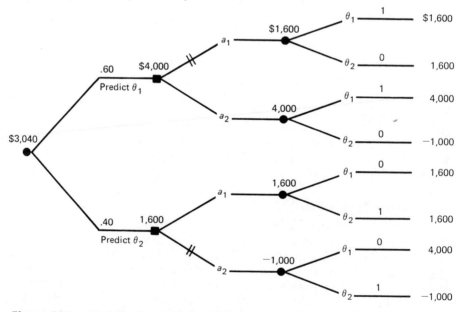

Figure 22.4 Analysis of Andy Adams' Decision Problem Based on Perfect Information (proceed from right to left)

$$P(\theta_1 | \text{Eugene predicts } \theta_1) = 1$$
$$P(\theta_2 | \text{Eugene predicts } \theta_1) = 0$$

These probabilities are called *posterior probabilities* since they represent the probabilities of the possible states of nature occurring *posterior to* (after) receiving additional information (in this case, perfect prediction from Eugene). If, however, Eugene predicts θ_2, then it is certain that θ_1 will not occur and θ_2 will occur. Thus, given this prediction, the posterior probabilities are

$$P(\theta_1 | \text{Eugene predicts } \theta_2) = 0$$
$$P(\theta_2 | \text{Eugene predicts } \theta_2) = 1$$

Since Eugene is a perfect predictor, he will predict θ_1 if and only if θ_1 will actually occur and predict θ_2 if and only if θ_2 will actually occur. Thus, the probability that he will predict θ_1 is identical to the probability that θ_1 will occur, and the probability that he will predict θ_2 is identical to the probability that θ_2 will occur. Since Andy's prior probabilities of θ_1 and θ_2 are .6 and .4, respectively, there is a .6 probability that Eugene will predict θ_1 and .4 probability that Eugene will predict θ_2. Using probability notation:

$$P(\text{Eugene predicts } \theta_1) = P(\theta_1) = .6$$
$$P(\text{Eugene predicts } \theta_2) = P(\theta_2) = .4$$

With the six probabilities just obtained, the analysis of the decision tree in Figure 22.4 proceeds *from right to left* following the same general procedure used to analyze the tree in Figure 22.3. Notice that the EMV on the chance node at the far left of the tree in Figure 22.4 is $3,040, which represents the EMV of Andy's decision if he resolves to act on the basis of additional information that can be obtained from the perfect predictor, Eugene. This value of $3,040 may be compared to the $2,000 that was previously obtained in Figure 22.3 for the EMV of the decision with available information before considering the possibility of a perfect predictor. The difference between these two values is $1,040. This amount is the expected value of perfect information (EVPI). Thus, if Andy can negotiate a fee less than this amount, it would be reasonable for him to purchase the perfect information from the expert.

22.3.2 Evaluating Imperfect Information

Although the EVPI for Andy's decision problem is $1,040, Eugene refuses to provide his perfect information for less than $1,200. Since the cost of information exceeds its value, Andy decides not to purchase Eugene's information. Instead, he approaches another expert, Frances Fair. For a fee of $250, she is willing to investigate the situation and to predict whether or not the Carter Company's new chemical process will be successfully developed. Frances states that her prediction will be quite reliable, but she admits that it will not be a perfect prediction. Specifically, if the process will actually be successful, there is a 70% chance that she will be able to predict this fact. If, however, the process will not be successful, there is an 80% chance that she will be able to predict this fact.

Regardless of whether the additional information is perfect or imperfect, the structure of Andy's decision problem remains the same. However, since the accuracy of the prediction under these two conditions differs, the probabilities are distinctly different. If the information is *perfect*, all the posterior probabilities are *either 0 or 1*. This reflects the fact that uncertainty concerning the consequences of alternatives is completely eliminated by the perfect information. If, however, the information is *imperfect*, the posterior probabilities can be any values *between 0 and 1*, and the derivation of posterior probabilities is more laborious.

To illustrate the calculation of the posterior probabilities, let x_1 and x_2 denote Frances's two possible predictions:

x_1: Frances predicts that the process will be successful

x_2: Frances predicts that the process will be unsuccessful

Then we have the following probabilities:

1. The prior probability that the process will be successful:
$$P(\theta_1) = .6$$

2. The prior probability that the process will not be successful:
$$P(\theta_2) = .4$$

3. The conditional probability that Frances will predict that the process will be successful given that the process will be successful:
$$P(x_1|\theta_1) = .7$$

4. The conditional probability that Frances will predict that the process will be unsuccessful given that the process will be successful:
$$P(x_2|\theta_1) = 1 - P(x_1|\theta_1) = 1 - .7 = .3$$

5. The conditional probability that Frances predicts that the process will be unsuccessful given that the process will not be successful:
$$P(x_2|\theta_2) = .8$$

6. The conditional probability that Frances predicts that the process is successful given that the process is not successful:
$$P(x_1|\theta_2) = 1 - P(x_2|\theta_2) = 1 - .8 = .2$$

From these prior and conditional probabilities, it is possible to compute the posterior probability of each state of nature given each of Frances's possible predictions. This is done by the application of Bayes' theorem, which was presented in Section 5.10. Following the procedure illustrated in Table 5.8, the posterior probabilities for Andy Adams' decision problem are calculated in Tables 22.2 and 22.3.

The posterior probabilities obtained in Table 22.2 indicate that, if Frances predicts Carter's process will be successful, the probabilities are .84 that it actually will be successful and .16 that it will be unsuccessful. The posterior probabilities in Table 22.3 show that, if Frances predicts the process will be unsuccessful, the probabilities are .36 that it actually will be successful and .64 that it will be unsuccessful.

Having obtained the posterior probabilities, the remaining analysis of Andy's decision problem with *imperfect* information can be performed by following the same method used previously to analyze his problem with *perfect* information. The complete analysis is shown in Figure 22.5. This figure indicates that if Andy resolves to act on the basis of Frances's imperfect information, his optimal course of action will depend on her prediction. If Frances predicts that θ_1 will occur, Andy should purchase the stock; otherwise, he should deposit the money in the savings institution. The EMV for this strategy is $2,400, which can be compared to the $2,000 that was previously obtained for the EMV of the decision with prior information. The excess of the EMV with the predictor Frances ($2,400) over the EMV without any predictor ($2,000) is equal to $400, which

Table 22.2 Computation of Probabilities Posterior to Favorable Prediction

State of Nature, θ_i	Prior Probability, $P(\theta_i)$	Conditional Probability, $P(x_1 \mid \theta_i)$	Joint Probability, $P(x_1 \cap \theta_i)$	Posterior Probability, $P(\theta_i \mid x_1)$
θ_1	.6	.7	.42	.84
θ_2	.4	.2	.08	.16
	1.0		.50	1.00

Table 22.3 Computation of Probabilities Posterior to Unfavorable Prediction

State of Nature, θ_i	Prior Probability, $P(\theta_i)$	Conditional Probability, $P(x_2 \mid \theta_i)$	Joint Probability, $P(x_2 \cap \theta_i)$	Posterior Probability, $P(\theta_i \mid x_2)$
θ_1	.6	.3	.18	.36
θ_2	.4	.8	.32	.64
	1.0		.50	1.00

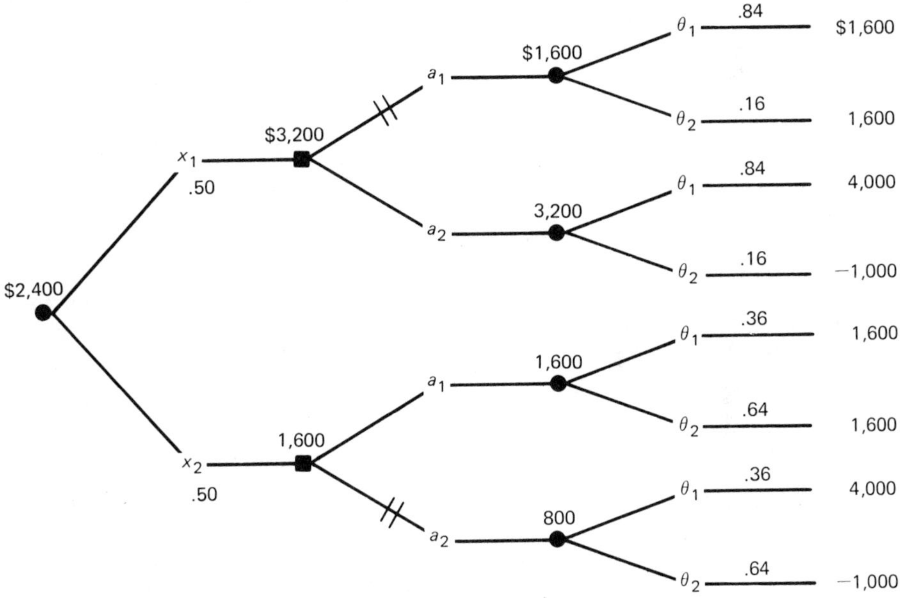

Figure 22.5 Analysis of Andy Adams' Decision Problem Based on Imperfect Information

is the contribution, in expected value, of the predictor. Since the cost of obtaining additional information from Frances ($250) is less than its value ($400), Andy should purchase Frances's information.

22.4 RECAPITULATION

Andy Adams' initial decision problem was to choose between depositing his money in a savings institution and purchasing Carter Company's stock. In the process of analyzing his decision problem, Andy considered three separate conditions under which he might make his decision:

1. To make the decision solely on the basis of prior information, without buying any additional information. Under this condition, Andy's optimal act is to buy the stock. The EMV of this investment decision, shown in Figure 22.3, is $2,000.

2. To buy perfect information from Eugene Elliot at a cost of $1,200. Under this condition, Andy's optimal act is to buy the stock if Eugene's prediction is favorable and to open a certificate account if Eugene's prediction is unfavorable. The EMV of this investment decision, shown in Figure 22.4, is $3,040 before Eugene's fee is deducted. Thus, the net EMV of the decision is $1,840.

3. To buy imperfect information from Frances Fair at a cost of $250. Under this condition, Andy's optimal act is to buy the stock if Frances's prediction is favorable and to open a certificate account if Frances' prediction is unfavorable. The EMV of this investment decision, shown in Figure 22.5 is $2,400 before Frances's fee is deducted. Thus, the net EMV of the decision is $2,150.

The decision diagrams for the three separate analyses summarized above are now combined into a single decision diagram, which is shown in Figure 22.6.

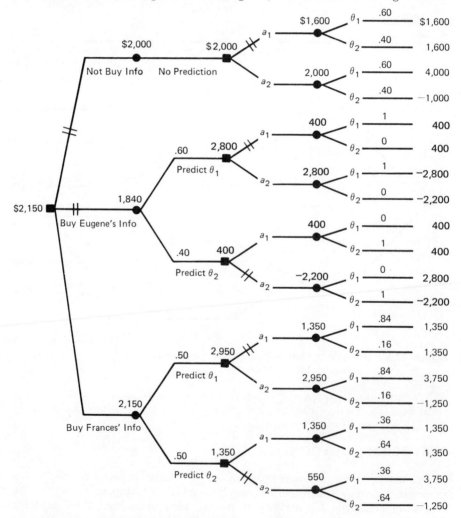

Figure 22.6   Complete Structure and Analysis of Andy Adams' Decision Problem

Whereas Figures 22.4 and 22.5 show monetary values before the cost of additional information is deducted, Figure 22.6 shows the net monetary values after deducting the cost of information. As shown in Figure 22.6, Andy now has a two-stage decision problem. At the first stage, which is concerned with the use of information, Andy must choose one of the three alternative courses of action: not to buy any information, to buy perfect information from Eugene Elliot, or to buy imperfect information from Frances Fair. At the second stage, which is concerned with the investment decision, Andy must decide whether to deposit the money or to purchase the stock. Andy's optimal strategy is to buy Frances's imperfect information. Then, if Frances predicts that Carter Company's new chemical process will be successfully developed, Andy should purchase the Company's stock; otherwise, he should open a certificate account.

22.5 DECISION ANALYSIS CYCLE

The decision analysis approach illustrated by Andy Adams' example discussed in previous sections can be summarized by the decision analysis cycle shown in Figure 22.7. The *first* phase of the cycle is the formulation of a decision problem. Typically, the problem that has been identified by the decision maker is structured in terms of a model. The model can be a decision diagram, a decision table, or a set of mathematical functions. Regardless of the form, the model specifies the alternatives that are under consideration, and describes the uncertain states of nature that will affect the consequence of each of the alternatives. In addition, it indicates the interrelationship among the alternatives and states.

The *second* phase is to obtain *numerical inputs* in order to perform a quantitative analysis of the model. Two types of numerical input are required. One type of input required is the probability distribution of the possible states of nature. This input provides a measure of the amount of uncertainty inherent in the decision problem. The other type of input required is a measure of the decision maker's values of various possible consequences. In dealing with business problems, profit is often used as the measure. However, the *value* of money to a decision maker is not necessarily a linear function of the *amount* of money being considered. When the value of money is not linear, the monetary amounts will not accurately reflect the relative values that the decision maker attaches to various monetary consequences. This difficulty can be resolved by replacing the monetary values by utility measures.[1]

The *third* phase employs *quantitative analysis* to evaluate available alternatives and determine the value of additional information. The analysis will indicate the relative desirability of the alternatives, and identify the optimal course of action (i.e., the most desirable alternative). In addition, the analysis will compare the value of additional information that may be available to reduce uncertainty with the cost of obtaining such potentially available information.

If the quantitative analysis indicates that it is worthwhile to purchase additional information, then the *fourth* phase of the decision analysis cycle is to *obtain the information*, and repeat the three phases described above on the basis of the new information. If, however, the analysis indicates that no additional information is worthwhile, then the *final* phase consists of *making and carrying out the decision*.

---

[1]Decision analysis based on utility measures is discussed in Chapter 23.

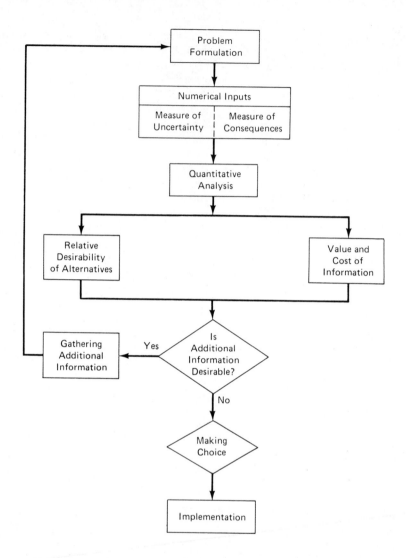

Figure 22.7   Decision Analysis Cycle

When a decision problem is analyzed by the decision analysis approach, all available information is used to deduce which of the alternative courses of action best promotes achievement of the decision maker's objectives. However, selecting the best possible logical decision that is consistent with objectives and information does not guarantee that this particular alternative will turn out, after the fact, to be the most desirable one. In other words, unless the decision maker can obtain perfect information to totally eliminate uncertainty, a good decision will not necessarily lead to a good outcome. Consider the example of betting on coins. Suppose that you have to pay $1.00 to call the toss of a coin. If you call that toss correctly, you win $30.00; if your call is incorrect, you win nothing. Now the problem is whether or not you should participate in this game. Regardless of whether the choice is based on intuition or a careful decision analysis, most people would consider participating as a good decision. Suppose that you decide to participate and pay $1.00. The coin is tossed; you call it and you lose. Now what do we say? You had a bad outcome, even though it was a good decision. Thus, it is obvious that a good decision is no guarantee of a good outcome.

22.6 PRACTICAL APPLICATIONS

Decision analysis was introduced into business education and practice over two decades ago, and during the past decade, it has become increasingly popular. In 1970, Robert Newman, who was then Manager of Planning Services at General Electric, forecast that:

> Within ten years, decision theory, conversational computers, and library programs should occupy the same role for the manager as calculus, slide rules, and mathematical tables do for the engineer today. The engineer of Roman times had none of these, but he could make perfectly good bridges. However, he could not compete today even in bridge building, let alone astro-engineering. Management is today at the stage of Roman engineering. Needless to say, managers will still use specialists, just as engineers use heat transfer experts.[2]

Newman's time schedule has proved to be overly optimistic. However, there has been a steadily growing conviction in the management community that decision analysis should and will play a very important role in executive decision making.

As a systematic approach to decision making, decision analysis is particularly useful in making choices among actions with complex and uncertain future effects. Thus, decision analysis has been applied to a wide range of business problems, such as product development, packaging design, pricing, production, facility expansion, and investment. In addition, there have been many applications of decision analysis in the areas of engineering, government, and medicine. To illustrate practical applications of decision analysis, selected real-world examples are presented below.

The Radio Corporation of America has successfully applied decision analysis to competitive bidding. As reported by Franz Edelman,[3] the work began in 1963 with a general business model, which was primarily concerned with competitive pricing. In April 1964, this model was adapted to competitive bidding. Subsequently, the competitive bidding model, which was based on a decision analysis approach, was applied to seven actual bidding situations involving a variety of products. In all seven test situations, the use of the decision model resulted in a definite improvement of the bid price.

The outcomes of the seven tests are shown in Table 22.4. All these tests were concerned with bids in which the award went to the lowest bidder. Column (1) of this table lists the seven tests. Columns (2) and (3) contain the bids prepared without and with the use of the model. The lowest competitive bid is shown in column (4). The bids without and with the model relative to the lowest com-

---

[2]Rex V. Brown, "Do Managers Find Decision Theory Useful?" *Harvard Business Review*, May–June 1970, pp. 78–89.

[3]Franz Edelman, "Art and Science of Competitive Bidding," *Harvard Business Review*, July–August 1965.

Table 22.4 Performance of RCA's Competitive Bidding Model
(Measured under Seven Live Tests)

(1)	*(2)*	*(3)*	*(4)*	*(5)* Bid without Model:	*(6)*
Test	*Bid without Model*	*Bid with Model*	*Lowest Competitive Bid*	*Percent under (over) Lowest Competitive Bid*	*Bid with Model: Percent under Lowest Competitive Bid*
1	$44.53	$46.00	$46,49	4.2	1.1
2	47.36	42.68	42.93	(10.3)	0.6
3	62.73	59.04	60.76	(3.2)	2.8
4	47.72	51.05	53.38	10.6	4.4
5	50.18	42.80	44.16	(13.7)	3.1
6	60.39	54.61	55.10	(9.6)	0.9
7	39.73	39.73	40.47	1.8	1.8

petitive bid are shown in columns (5) and (6), respectively. These two columns indicate that in each of the test cases, the bid determined by the model was superior to the bid made in the traditional manner, in the sense of making greater profit contribution. The bids prepared through the use of the model were on the average only 2% below the lowest competitive price, with a range of 0.6 to 4.4%.

Joseph Newman[4] reports a case in which Maxwell House used decision analysis to consider a major packaging change for its ground coffee. Prior to 1963, the packaging of coffee in the United States had undergone no major changes since the late 1920s, when a key-opening can that had been developed for shortening products was adapted for coffee. New activity in packaging became apparent in October 1962, when Folger's began the test marketing of a keyless can made by the American Can Company. The no-key can was taller, narrower, and less expensive than the traditional key-opening can. It was made to be opened with a regular can opener and employed a polyethylene lid for reclosure. After examining the results of market studies, Maxwell House decided in July 1963 to convert its plants to the keyless can. National conversion was achieved in October 1963.

In November 1963, Maxwell House was notified by the American Can Company that developmental work on a container design based on the tearstrip opening principle was about to be completed and that a supply of new cans soon could be made available. Maxwell House executives considered the "quick-strip" can to be superior to both the keyless and the traditional key cans, combining their advantages. However, there were many other factors to be considered, such as cost of the quick-strip can, cost to convert the plants to the new can, possible effects of the new can on coffee sales, and major competitors' reactions.

As a result of this new design, the executives of Maxwell House were not certain if they should change the container again during that year. In fact, they wondered whether an immediate decision should be made to adopt or reject the quick-strip can, or whether the decision should be delayed to obtain

---

[4]Joseph W. Newman, *Management Applications of Decision Theory* (New York: Harper & Row, 1971).

evidence concerning its probable effect on demand. Figure 22.8 displays the four major alternatives that were under consideration. After an extensive analysis of each of these alternatives, it was determined that the optimal action was to convert to the quick-strip can as soon as possible with a price increase of 2 cents per pound.

Keeney and Raiffa[5] discuss an application of decision analysis to a large-scale public decision problem involving the selection of a strategy for developing the major airport facilities of the Mexico City metropolitan area. Rapid growth in the demand for air travel, combined with increasingly difficult operating conditions at the existing airport facilities, compelled the Mexican government to ask: How should the airport facilities of Mexico City be developed to assure adequate service for the region during the period from now to the year 2000? This question was examined by the decision analysis team in 1971.

Two previous studies for developing the airport facilities of Mexico City had recommended very different alternatives. One concluded that the current airport, 5 miles away from the city center, should be greatly expanded, whereas the other suggested moving all aircraft operations to Zumpango, 25 miles north of the city. In light of this discrepancy, the decision analysis team was asked to evaluate the various alternatives and to recommend the most effective program for airport development.

The following six objectives were selected to evaluate the alternatives:

1. Minimize total construction and maintenance costs.
2. Provide adequate capacity to meet the air traffic demands.
3. Minimize the access time to the airport.
4. Maximize the safety of the system.
5. Minimize social disruption caused by the provision of new airport facilities.
6. Minimize the effects of noise pollution due to air traffic.

Using these objectives, the decision analysis of the airport development problem showed that the best strategy was a phased development involving a gradual shift to Zumpango. This strategy was different from either of the

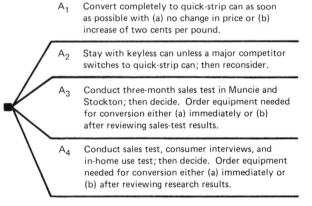

A_1 — Convert completely to quick-strip can as soon as possible with (a) no change in price or (b) increase of two cents per pound.

A_2 — Stay with keyless can unless a major competitor switches to quick-strip can; then reconsider.

A_3 — Conduct three-month sales test in Muncie and Stockton; then decide. Order equipment needed for conversion either (a) immediately or (b) after reviewing sales-test results.

A_4 — Conduct sales test, consumer interviews, and in-home use test; then decide. Order equipment needed for conversion either (a) immediately or (b) after reviewing research results.

Figure 22.8   Decision Tree for Coffee-Packaging Problem

[5]Ralph L. Keeney and Howard Raiffa, *Decisions with Multiple Objectives: Preferences and Value Tradeoffs* (New York: John Wiley & Sons, Inc., 1976).

recommendations of the two previous studies. It is significant to note that an analysis undertaken for advocacy purposes (i.e., to justify going all-out to Zumpango) turned out to convince the sponsors of the analysis that perhaps a more flexible stance was really in the best interest of Mexico.

PROBLEMS

22.1 Suppose that you have a sum of money which you wish to invest for a 1-year period. You have narrowed down your choices to three alternatives:

a_1: Invest in a construction firm

a_2: Deposit the money in a savings and loan association

a_3: Invest in an industrial consulting firm

You are concerned with three possible states of nature which might affect the profit you would realize on your investment:

θ_1: Housing starts will increase next year

θ_2: Housing starts will remain at the same level

θ_3: Housing starts will decline next year

You have determined the probabilities of the possible states of nature and the possible profits (in thousands of dollars) associated with various action–state pairs as shown in the following payoff table:

θ_i	$P(\theta_i)$	a_1	a_2	a_3
θ_1	.2	20	12	16
θ_2	.5	14	12	15
θ_3	.3	6	12	10

(a) Draw a decision tree (i.e., decision diagram) representing your investment problem described above.

(b) Analyze the decision tree in part (a) to determine the optimal course of action that will maximize the expected profit.

22.2 Bob Bond, a gift department buyer for the Greengrass Department Store, has located a wholesaler of crystal bunnies, which he feels would be a good item for the Easter season. These bunnies can be purchased at a unit cost of $20 and Bob plans to price them at $45. He feels sure that any bunnies remaining in stock after Easter can be sold at a reduced price of $10. Bob estimates the following probability distribution of pre-Easter demand for the bunnies:

Demand	Probability
10	.10
11	.15
12	.30
13	.25
14	.20

(a)   Prepare a payoff table for Bob Bond's decision problem and analyze the table to determine the optimal number of bunnies for Bob to buy.

(b)   Draw a decision tree representing Bob Bond's decision problem, and analyze the tree to determine the optimal number of bunnies for Bob to buy.

(c)   Do the analyses in parts (a) and (b) always lead to the same optimal decision? Explain.

22.3   On the basis of past sales records, a news dealer has derived the following probability distribution of monthly demand for *Harpy's Bazaar*, a fashion magazine for matrons and dowagers.

Demand	Probability
20 copies	.20
21 copies	.30
22 copies	.40
23 copies	.10

Each copy of this magazine costs the news dealer 60 cents and sells for $1.00. Unsold copies are nonreturnable. The news dealer wishes to determine how many copies she should stock each month.

(a)   Draw a decision tree representing the news dealer's stocking problem.

(b)   Analyze the decision tree in part (a) to determine the optimal number of copies the news dealer should stock to maximize her expected profit.

22.4   Refer to Problem 22.3 in answering the following questions:

(a)   Suppose that the publisher of *Harpy's Bazaar* offers to sell the news dealer an option of consignment, whereby the news dealer can return all unsold copies each month and pay only for the copies sold. The publisher charges $5.00 a year for this option. Draw a decision tree for evaluating the consignment option for the news dealer.

(b)   Analyze the decision tree to determine if the news dealer should accept the consignment option.

22.5   Tom Tinker holds some municipal bonds which are due to mature within a few days in an amount of $10,000. Tom is anxious to reinvest this sum immediately, and he has narrowed his alternatives to two different oil stocks. He plans to sell the stock after holding it for 1 year. As a result of a scheduled visit to Washington by the Sheik of Araby, which will occur in 6 weeks, Tom is uncertain about which of the two stocks to buy. If the Sheik agrees to sign a proposed trade pact during his visit, Tom estimates that the value of stock *A* will increase by 25% in a year's time, but that the value of stock *B* will decrease by 10%. However, if the Sheik declines to sign the pact, Tom estimates that the value of stock *A* will decrease by 25% and the value of stock *B* will increase by 20%. On the basis of his research, Tom estimates a .60 probability that the Sheik will sign the pact.

(a)   Draw a decision tree representing Tom Tinker's investment problem.

(b)   Analyze the decision tree in part (a) to determine which stock Tom should buy if he wishes to maximize the expected profit on his investment.

22.6   Refer to Problem 22.5 in answering the following questions:

(a)   While casually contemplating the All-Seeing Eye one evening, the Sheik's Grand Chamberlain becomes aware of Tom's quandary. The Grand Chamberlain contacts Tom by telephone and offers to sell him guaranteed "inside information" as to whether or not the Sheik will sign the contract. The Grand Chamberlain asks $1,500 for this information. Draw a decision tree for evaluating the option to buy the information from the Grand Chamberlain.

(b)   Analyze the decision tree to determine if Tom Tinker should buy the Grand Chamberlain's information.

Decision Analysis: Basic Concepts and Procedures

22.7 The Delta Company specializes in manufacturing canned tuna fish. The company has just completed a production run of 10,000 cans of tuna. Just as the production manager is about to ship this batch of cans to the Gamma Supermarket chain, he learns from the quality control manager that due to the malfunction of some of the equipment in the inspection process, the mercury content of the tuna cans may exceed the limit set by the Food and Drug Administration (FDA). If the batch is shipped to Gamma and is found to violate the FDA standard, the Delta Company will be required to supply another batch to replace the bad one. Furthermore, the company will have to reimburse Gamma for any losses incurred, such as consumers' claims and FDA fines. The quality control manager indicates that rather than deciding immediately whether to ship or to dump this batch he can ask his staff to conduct a test by drawing a random sample of 100 cans and measuring the mercury content of the cans in the sample. Based on the sample result, he will give either a "favorable" or "unfavorable" indication regarding the quality of the batch. He emphasizes, however, that neither indication can be interpreted as definite assurance of the batch's true quality. To help the production manager decide what to do with the batch, the quality control manager offers the diagram shown below, with the following explanation: "The diagram represents the possible sequences of events that could occur. The batch is either good (low mercury content) or bad (high mercury content) as soon as it has been produced; testing cannot change its quality. Naturally, the test is not infallible, so we cannot be perfectly certain whether or not we should ship the batch, regardless of the outcome of the test." Does the quality control manager's diagram correctly represent the logical structure of the decision problem faced by the production manager? If not, pinpoint the errors and draw a correct diagram. In your diagram, be sure to use ■ and ● to distinguish between a decision node and a chance node.

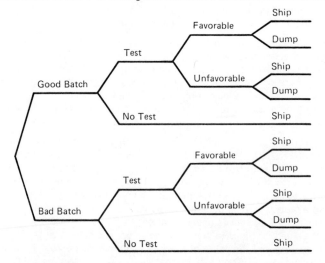

22.8 You have $10,000 in your savings account, which earns simple interest at an annual rate of 6%. You have received an offer to engage in a speculative real estate venture for an investment of $6,000, but you must decide within two weeks. Specifically, the investment is to purchase a parcel of land that is on one of the only two possible routes for a proposed highway. The highway department will announce its selection of route 6 months from today. If the land under consideration is selected for the proposed highway, you can sell the land immediately for $17,000, in which case you will make a profit of $11,000. Otherwise, you can sell it for only $4,000, in which case you will suffer an out-of-pocket loss of $2,000. After some analysis of the available information, you estimate that there is a .40 probability that the land will be selected for the highway. Thus, if

θ_1: The land will be used for the proposed highway
θ_2: The land will not be used for the proposed highway

then $P(\theta_1) = .40$ and $P(\theta_2) = 1 - .40 = .60$. At this point, you are faced with the decision of choosing one of the two alternative acts:

a_1: Continue to keep your money in the savings account

a_2: Invest in the real estate venture

(a) Draw a decision tree representing your investment problem and analyze the tree to determine your optimal course of action.

(b) Determine the EVPI. How do you interpret this figure?

22.9 Refer to Problem 22.8. Reluctant to make your decision hastily, you consider the possibility of purchasing additional information from an expert in the real estate business. At a price, this expert is willing to conduct a study of the situation, and then predict whether the land will be used for the highway. Unfortunately, this expert is not perfectly reliable. His record of similar predictions shows that, of the the parcels that were eventually used for highways, he was able to predict this fact 90% of the time and was wrong 10% of the time. On those parcels that were not used for highways, he was able to predict correctly 80% of the time and was wrong 20% of the time. Adopt the following notation:

o_1: The expert predicts that the land will be selected for the highway

o_2: The expert predicts that the land will not be selected for the highway

Then,

$$P(o_1|\theta_1) = .90 \qquad P(o_2|\theta_1) = .10 \qquad P(o_2|\theta_2) = .80 \qquad P(o_1|\theta_2) = .20$$

(a) Draw a decision tree for evaluating the desirability of purchasing additional information from the real estate expert.

(b) Compute the probabilities needed for analyzing the decision tree in part (a).

(c) Complete the analysis of the decision tree in part (a) to determine the maximum amount that you should be willing to pay the expert for his imperfect prediction.

22.10 Suppose that the real estate expert discussed in Problem 22.9 will charge $500 for his service. Draw a decision tree representing your entire decision problem as described in Problems 22.8 and 22.9. (*Hint*: Make use of the two decision trees that you have worked out for these problems.)

22.11 Mrs. Rona Rich has an opportunity to purchase an apartment building. The total price of the building is $250,000. However, she has to pay only $75,000 in cash, and the seller agrees to accept the balance in the form of a mortgage. Mrs. Rich plans to hold the building for 2 years. The profitability of this investment depends largely on a proposed rent control ordinance that is under consideration by the city council. If the council passes the ordinance, the price appreciation of the property in 2 years will be negligible. In that case, owing to the various expenses involved in buying and selling the property, Mrs. Rich will suffer a total loss of $20,000. If, however, the council fails to pass the ordinance, the value of the property will appreciate substantially so that she will make a net profit of $60,000 on this investment. Based on her preliminary analysis of various newspaper articles regarding the rent control issue, she concludes that the odds are 50:50 that the council will pass the ordinance.

(a) Draw a decision tree and analyze the tree to determine if Mrs. Rich should (1) open a certificate account for her money with an annual interest rate of 10%, or (2) purchase the apartment building.

(b) Mr. Bob Buck, a successful real estate broker, has offered to perform a study of the attitude of each council member toward the proposed rent control ordinance. Based on this study, Mr. Buck will prepare a report for Mrs. Rich, which will predict whether or not the council will pass the ordinance. Because some council members may wish to conceal their judgment until the formal voting, or may change their minds between the time of the study and the time of formal voting, Mr. Buck's prediction cannot be perfect. He indicates, however, that his prediction will be 80% accurate. Draw a decision tree for Mrs. Rich's evaluation of the desirability of purchasing the imperfect prediction from Mr. Buck. Analyze the tree to determine the maximum amount that Mrs. Rich should be willing to pay for this imperfect prediction.

22.12 The R&D department of the New Gadget Manufacturing Company has just completed the development of a new type of scouring pad that is exceptionally durable and efficient. Because of its chemical composition, it is believed the scouring pad will be difficult for the competition to duplicate. Bill Adams, vice-president of marketing, thinks that Kitchen Giant would be a nice name for this new product. His assignment now is to determine whether or not to actually introduce this product into the market.

To begin his analysis of this decision problem, Bill estimates the following probabilities, which take into account the highly competitive nature of the scouring pad market.

Demand Level	$P(\theta_i)$
θ_1: high	.20
θ_2: moderate	.50
θ_3: low	.30

Bill also estimates that the present value of profits from Kitchen Giant for the next 5 years will be $500,000 if demand is high and $200,000 if demand is moderate. However, if demand is low, he estimates that the present value of the loss during the next 5 years will be $600,000.

At this point in the analysis of the decision problem, Bill is faced with the following decision alternatives:

a_1: Introduce Kitchen Giant into the market

a_2: Do not introduce Kitchen Giant into the market

(a) Draw a decision tree for Bill's marketing problem, and analyze the tree to determine which action he should take.

(b) At this point, what is the EVPI of Bill's decision? What does this figure mean?

22.13 Refer to Problem 22.12. Bill Adams considers requesting his market research group to conduct a sample survey of potential demand for Kitchen Giant. The budget for this survey is set at $40,000. The group's report will consist of a prediction of the demand for Kitchen Giant in one of the following categories:

o_1: Demand will be high

o_2: Demand will be moderate

o_3: Demand will be low

To obtain probabilities that reflect the reliability of the research group's survey methods, Bill prepares the following table, which is based on his analysis of the group's past performance:

If Actual Demand Is:	Probability That Survey Prediction Will Be:		
	High	Moderate	Low
High	.70	.20	.10
Moderate	.10	.80	.10
Low	.20	.20	.60

(a) Revise the diagram in Problem 22.12 to include the option of conducting a market survey.

(b) Analyze the revised decision tree in part (a) to determine if the survey should be conducted.

22.14 Jill Willis, marketing manager of Stratford Cosmetics Company, is considering whether or not to introduce the firm's newly developed Cheshire Kitten vanishing cream into a particular marketing area. On the basis of the sales of other of the firm's products in this market, Jill estimates the following probabilities of demand during the first 6 months:

Demand Level	Probability
θ_1: high	.30
θ_2: moderate	.50
θ_3: low	.20

Jill estimates that sales of this product will result in a $60,000 profit if sales are high, and in a $20,000 profit if sales are moderate. However, if sales are low, she estimates a $70,000 loss.

At this point, Jill is faced with the decision of choosing one of the two alternative acts:

a_1: Introduce Cheshire Kitten into the market

a_2: Do not introduce Cheshire Kitten into the market

Reluctant to make her decision hastily, Jill considers the possibility of requesting her research group to conduct a survey in the proposed target area. The survey will cost $1,500. The group's report would consist essentially of one of the following predictions of the demand for Cheshire Kitten:

o_1: Demand will be high

o_2: Demand will be moderate

o_3: Demand will be low

From past performance of the research group, Jill prepares the following table of conditional probabilities, which reflect the reliability of the survey procedure.

If Actual Demand Is:	Probability That Survey Prediction Will Be:		
	High	Moderate	Low
High	.60	.20	.20
Moderate	.10	.80	.10
Low	.10	.20	.70

(a) Draw a decision tree representing Jill Willis' entire decision problem. Be sure to include the possibility of conducting a market survey.

(b) Analyze the decision tree to determine Jill Willis' optimal course of action.

22.15 The Ample Money Credit Card Company (AMCCC) issues general-purpose credit cards. Mr. Eagle, credit manager for AMCCC, must accept or reject each credit card application. He may make his decision either (1) on the basis of his subjective evaluation of the information contained in the application, or (2) on the basis of his subjective evaluation plus a credit rating that he can purchase from the Better Credit Rating Center (BCRC) at a price of $30 per application. To investigate the reliability of BCRC reports, Mr. Eagle selected and examined those applicants' files containing a BCRC report. He found 70% of cases that proved to be good risks had been reported as "favorable" and 90% of cases that proved to be bad risks had been reported as "unfavorable."

Mr. Eagle has just received a credit application from Tammy White. After his usual evaluation procedure, Mr. Eagle assigns a prior probability of 0.6 that Tammy is a good risk. From past experience, the credit manager estimates that a good credit risk will produce a profit of $500, whereas a bad credit will result in a loss of $190.

(a) Draw a decision tree representing Mr. Eagle's decision problem regarding Tammy White's credit application. Be sure to include the possibility of purchasing a credit rating from BCRC.

(b) Analyze the decision tree to determine Mr. Eagle's optimal course of action.

22.16 Refer to Problem 22.15 in answering the following questions.

(a) What is the maximum amount that Mr. Eagle should be willing to pay BCRC for its service?

(b) Suppose that another credit-rating agency, called Sigma, can provide perfect prediction concerning Tammy. That is, Sigma can foretell for sure whether or not Tammy is a good risk. What is the maximum amount that Mr. Eagle should be willing to pay Sigma for its service?

22.17 Assume that you are the president of a large engineering research and development firm that is nearing completion of a major project and you must decide what the company's next project will be. You have been considering two speculative ventures:

a_1: Design a revolutionary atomic power-generating system

a_2: Design a rotary engine for buses and trucks

In addition to these speculative projects, you have a third alternative:

a_3: Accept an offer to design a tunnel under the Mississippi River

In considering your alternatives, you have been particularly concerned with the eventual fate of two environmental control bills—the Mossback Bill and the Goodheart Bill. The provisions of these two bills are such that passage of either would preclude passage of the other. Thus, you are concerned with three possibilities:

θ_1: The Mossback Bill will be passed

θ_2: The Goodheart Bill will be passed

θ_3: Neither bill will be passed

On the basis of the information that is currently available, you estimate the probabilities of these possible states of nature as follows:

$$P(\theta_1) = .30 \qquad P(\theta_2) = .50 \qquad P(\theta_3) = .20$$

By proceeding with the atomic power project, you estimate that you would lose $7 million if the Mossback Bill passes, make a profit of $4 million if the Goodheart Bill passes, and make a profit of $8 million if neither bill passes. By undertaking the rotary engine project, you figure that you would make a profit of $6 million if the Mossback Bill passes, suffer a loss of $3 million if the Goodheart Bill passes, and make a profit of $5 million if neither bill passes. Regardless of the fate of either bill, undertaking the tunnel project would yield a sure profit of $2 million.

(a) Draw a decision tree representing your decision problem and analyze the tree to determine your optimal course of action.

(b) Because of the impact of your decision, you feel that you would like to obtain additional information regarding the possible states of nature before you commit yourself. You therefore consider the possibility of seeking the consulting services of Dr. Stanley Livingstone, an eminent political scientist and ecologist. If you should enlist Dr. Livingstone's services, you would ask him to fly to Washington, interview key Congress members and administration officials, and report his conclusions to you. His report would be one of the following:

o_1: Passage of the Mossback Bill appears likely

o_2: Passage of the Goodheart Bill appears likely

o_3: Most likely neither bill will pass

Since Dr. Livingstone has provided his services to your company many times during the past 20 years, you have a reasonable background of experience on which to evaluate his predictions. You therefore estimate the following conditional probabilities of receiving each possible report given each possible state of nature:

| | State of Nature | | |
Report	θ_1	θ_2	θ_3
O_1	.7	.1	.2
O_2	.1	.7	.2
O_3	.2	.2	.6

Draw a decision tree for evaluating the desirability of enlisting Dr. Livingstone's services and analyze the tree to determine the maximum amount that you should be willing to pay him for his services.

22.18 The use of decision analysis in oil-drilling problems represents one of the earliest applications of decision analysis to real-world problems. To illustrate this type of application, consider the following simplified version of an oil-drilling problem. The Gumble Oil Company has an opportunity to purchase a tract of land for drilling. The price of the land is $200,000, and the cost of drilling is $50,000. If oil is found after drilling, the company will make a net profit of $450,000, which is obtained by deducting the costs of the land and drilling from the gross profit of $700,000. If no oil is found after drilling, the company can sell the land for other usage at half price (i.e., $100,000). At a cost of $10,000, the Gumble Oil Company can conduct a seismic test on the land before deciding whether or not to purchase it. The test will indicate either "limestone," "shale," or "granite." The probability of the test indicating limestone is .4; of shale, .4; of granite, .2. If the test predicts limestone, the probability of oil being present is .5; if the test predicts shale, the probability of oil being present is .1; and if the test predicts granite, the probability of oil being present is 0.

  (a) Draw a decision tree representing the decision problem faced by the Gumble Oil Company.

  (b) Analyze the decision tree to answer the following questions:

   (i) Should the company conduct the seismic test? If not, what action should the company take regarding the purchase of the land?

   (ii) If the test should be conducted, what is the optimal course of action to take conditional on each possible outcome of the test? What is the maximum amount that the company should be willing to pay for the seismic test?

  (c) The Omega Research Institute claims that their newly developed geological test can provide perfect prediction regarding the presence of oil. What is the maximum amount that the Gumble Oil Company should be willing to pay the Institute for its geological test?

23

Decision Analysis:
Use of Utility Functions

In Chapter 22 we formulated and analyzed Andy Adams' decision problem to illustrate the basic procedure of the decision analysis approach. In that illustration, the EMV criterion was used to analyze Andy's problem of deciding whether to open a certificate account with a savings institution or to purchase the stock of Carter Engineering Company. The EMV criterion implicitly assumes that the *value* of money is a *linear* function of the *amount* of money in the sense that the value of money to a decision maker is directly proportional to the amount of money. However, the value of money to a decision maker is not necessarily a linear function of the amount of money being considered. As pointed out in Section 22.5, when the value of money is not linear, the monetary amounts will not accurately reflect the relative values that the decision maker attaches to various monetary consequences. This difficulty can be resolved by replacing the monetary values by utility measures. The present chapter discusses the decision analysis approach using utility measures.

23.1 THE DECISION MAKER'S ATTITUDE TOWARD RISK

To demonstrate why the EMV criterion may not be a valid guide for some decision making, let us consider several examples.

As a first example, consider an individual who has to make a choice between the two alternatives:

1. Receive a $2 million gift for certain
2. A 50:50 chance of receiving either $6 million or nothing

The EMV of alternative (2) is

$$(\$6,000,000)\left(\frac{1}{2}\right) + (\$0)\left(\frac{1}{2}\right) = \$3,000,000$$

Clearly, the EMV of act (2) is greater than the payoff of act (1). In spite of this fact, most people would choose act (1). One might argue that he would like to have the $2 million for certain to enjoy a quite comfortable life rather than to play a game in which, on the flip of a fair coin, he might receive nothing at all. It would be even nicer, of course, to have $6 million, but one might feel that $6 million is not so much more preferable to $2 million that it is worth a risk of winding up with nothing. In other words, he might feel that $6 million is not worth three times as much as $2 million.

As a second example, consider the case of two management consultants, Jennie Jones and Kent Kemp, who have agreed to prepare a prospectus for the organizers of a new company. When the prospectus is completed, each of the two consultants will receive an amount of $9,000 in the form of either cash or stock at his or her own choice. This choice, however, has to be made before they start to work. In view of the potential products and the key personnel of the company, Jennie and Kent estimate that the odds are 2:1 that the company will operate successfully. The price of the stock will be doubled if the company succeeds, but the price will drop to 30% of its initial value otherwise. Thus, the $9,000 in stock will be worth either ($9,000 × 200%) = $18,000 or ($9,000 × 30%) = $2,700, depending on whether or not the company succeeds. Consequently, the EMV of the stock is

$$(\$18,000)\left(\frac{2}{3}\right) + (\$2,700)\left(\frac{1}{3}\right) = \$12,900$$

Now, Jennie and Kent start arguing with each other about the choice between the cash and the stock.

Jennie: Look! The EMV of the stock is substantially higher than the cash amount. Of course, I prefer the stock.

Kent: Be careful! This is a one-time decision. If you choose the stock, your consulting fee will be either $18,000 or $2,700, but not the EMV of $12,900. Obviously, the sure amount of $9,000 is preferable to a risky stock.

Jennie: I know the EMV is not the actual amount. However, think about the great chance of receiving that large amount of $18,000. I personally believe that you are overly cautious. Have you thought hard enough about what you could do with that amount?

Kent: Certainly, I have. The trouble is that you have not taken the whole thing seriously enough. How can you even consider giving up a sure amount of $9,000 for such a wild gamble?

Jennie: The worst thing that could happen is to receive $2,700. After all, it isn't too bad.

Kent: What do you mean by that? It drops from $9,000 to $2,700. That is bad enough for me. I have just decided to take the cash. I hope you will too.

Jennie: In spite of your decision, I am going to take the stock. I hope you will change your mind.

Kent: I will never change my mind. But I wish you good luck.

Clearly, Jennie and Kent have come to opposite decisions even though they both had the same alternatives and the same information available to them. However, these two decision makers had different attitudes toward the same risk, and each of them based his decision on his own attitude toward risk.

A decision maker's attitude toward risk may depend on a combination of factors such as his or her financial condition, propensity for gambling, and temperamental predisposition. Consequently, not only may two decision makers have different attitudes toward risk, but each of them also may have different attitudes toward risk at different points in time.

To illustrate this point, let us consider a third example. An architectural and engineering (A&E) firm has been asked by a client to conduct a feasibility study for a construction project. The study is to determine whether or not it is economically feasible to build a new manufacturing plant in a specific industrial area. The client will pay a nominal fee of $1,000, although it will cost the A&E firm $11,000 to conduct the study. However, should the study convince the client that the plant construction is feasible, the client will award the firm a design contract for preparing all the construction documents. The A&E firm estimates that this design contract, which is on a "cost plus" basis, will yield a profit of $30,000. Consequently, the firm would make a net profit of ($1,000 − $11,000) + ($30,000) = $20,000 if the plant construction is feasible, and would suffer a loss of ($11,000 − $1,000) = $10,000 otherwise. The firm further estimates that the odds are 3:2 that the plant construction will be feasible. Therefore, the EMV of agreeing to undertake the feasibility study is ($20,000)($\frac{3}{5}$) + (−$10,000)($\frac{2}{5}$) = $8,000, and the corresponding figure of declining the offer obviously is zero. According to the EMV criterion, the A&E firm clearly should accept the client's offer. Since this firm engages in many feasibility studies and building designs for clients, the use of the EMV criterion for selecting various offers would lead the firm to the achievement of maximum average profit in the long run. Thus, the EMV criterion is used by this firm under normal circumstances. However, the A&E firm now has inadequate working capital and is extremely hard pressed for cash. The manager figures that should the loss of $10,000 be incurred, his firm would undergo even more serious financial difficulties. As a result, the manager has decided to decline the client's offer. Clearly, the manager is more averse to risk at this time than he usually is.

Finally, let us consider an example in which the EMVs of the alternatives are negative. Specifically, take the case of a manufacturer who must decide whether to insure his $10 million plant against fire for an annual premium of $2,000. The manufacturer believes the chance that his plant will be destroyed by fire during the next year is 1 in 10,000. Thus, the EMV of the act of not buying the insurance is

$$(-\$10,000,000)\left(\frac{1}{10,000}\right) + (\$0)\left(\frac{9,999}{10,000}\right) = -\$1,000$$

In other words, the expected loss is $1,000. However, the manufacturer realizes that should the plant burn, the *actual* loss would be $10,000,000 rather than the theoretical expected loss of $1,000. Such a disastrous occurrence would force the manufacturer to go out of business. Consequently, he is willing to pay an insurance premium of $2,000, which is higher than the expected loss, to insure the plant against fire. This phenomenon is fairly common among many firms and individuals. Since the insurance company must pay its expenses and make a profit in addition to covering the risk, the insurance premium should be higher than the expected loss. From the insured's viewpoint, the expected monetary value of the benefit is smaller than the payment of the insurance premium.

However, many firms and individuals are willing to pay such an insurance premium to guard against a possible heavy loss (disastrous occurrence), even though the chance of a disaster's occurring is quite small.

23.2 UTILITY FUNCTIONS

The examples in the preceding section illustrate various types of situations in which a decision maker would shy away from the EMV criterion. The fundamental reason for the inadequacy of the EMV criterion in such situations is that the calculation of EMV implicitly assumes that the *value* of money is a *linear function* of the *amount* of money. If the assumption of linearity is not satisfied, then the monetary amounts will not accurately reflect the relative values that the decision maker attaches to various monetary consequences. As a result, the EMVs that are computed from such monetary consequences will fail to represent the relative desirability among the alternative courses of action. One way of resolving this difficulty is to adopt the utility approach developed by von Neumann and Morgenstern.[1] The basic idea of the von Neumann–Morgenstern approach is to express the possible consequences of the alternative acts in terms of utility rather than monetary amount. For this purpose, utility measures are obtained in such a way that they reflect the relative preferences of the various possible consequences to the decision maker.

To apply the von Neumann–Morgenstern approach, it is necessary to obtain a utility corresponding to each of the possible monetary consequences involved in the decision problem. One way of doing this is to ask the decision maker to indicate the utility measure that he would assign to each of these monetary consequences. However, experience has shown that this direct assignment of utilities is often difficult and tedious, particularly if a decision problem involves many monetary consequences. Therefore, it is generally more practical to establish a *utility function* for the decision maker.

The procedure used to establish the utility function for a specific decision maker involves several steps. To illustrate these procedural steps, consider again the A&E firm example. Recall that this firm was considering a contract to conduct a feasibility study for a client. For this proposed contract there was a .60 probability of making a net profit of $20,000 and a .40 probability of suffering a loss of $10,000.

The *first* step for constructing a utility function is to select two monetary values that are sufficiently wide apart that they encompass all the possible monetary consequences associated with the decision problem concerned. Specifically, one monetary value denoted as x_b, is selected so that it is at least as large as the best possible monetary consequence in the decision problem. The other monetary value, denoted as x_w, is selected so that it is at most equal to the worst possible monetary consequence. For our example, x_b should be equal to or greater than $20,000 and x_w should be equal to or less than $-$10,000. Suppose that the A&E firm selects $x_b = $20,000 and $x_w = -$10,000.

The *second* step is to assign two arbitrary real numbers: one to x_b and one to x_w such that the number assigned to x_b exceeds that assigned to x_w. These two

---

[1] J. von Neumann and O. Morgenstern, *Theory of Games and Economic Behavior* (Princeton, N.J.: Princeton University Press, 1944).

numbers are the utilities of the two reference monetary consequences. Suppose
that the A&E firm assigns

$$u(\$20,000) = 1$$
$$u(-\$10,000) = 0$$

where the symbol u denotes "utility." For instance, $u(\$20,000) = 1$ is read as
"the utility of \$20,000 is equal to 1." It is important to bear in mind that the
assignment of the numbers 1 and 0 is arbitrary. Any other numbers could have
been assigned, just so the utility assigned to the most desirable monetary consequence is greater than that assigned to the least desirable monetary consequence.

The *third* step is to determine the utilities corresponding to several selected
monetary amounts between x_b and x_w. This is accomplished by obtaining
responses from the decision maker in a series of simple, imaginary situations.
In each of these situations, the decision maker is asked to imagine that he is
committed to a contract and does not know for sure what its consequence will
be. If the decision maker regards the contract as undesirable to him, he is asked
to specify the maximum amount that he would be willing to pay in order to
be released from the contract. However, if he regards the contract as desirable,
he is asked to determine the minimum amount for which he would be willing
to sell the contract. In either case, the amount specified by the decision maker is
called the *certainty equivalent* of the contract.

To make the decision maker's judgment task as easy as possible, each
imaginary contract that is presented to him has precisely two possible consequences. In describing a contract to the decision maker, both the specific monetary amount and the probability of each of these consequences are specified.
Such an imaginary contract is called a *reference contract*. The probabilities
assigned to the two monetary consequences of a reference contract can be
arbitrarily selected, although it is common practice to assign each consequence
a probability of 1/2.

In using a reference contract to obtain the utility of a monetary amount,
it is necessary that the monetary amounts of the two consequences specified
in the contract have known utilities. In step 2, the utilities of x_b and x_w were
specified, and at the outset of step 3 these are the only two monetary amounts
whose utilities have been established. Consequently, we must begin the series
of imaginary situations with a reference contract that has x_b and x_w as its two
monetary consequences. Thus, following this procedure, the A&E firm is asked
to imagine that it is committed to a contract that has a 1/2 probability of a
\$20,000 profit and a 1/2 probability of incurring a \$10,000 loss. In responding
to this imaginary situation, the firm indicates that, in its current financial condition, a loss of \$10,000 would be disastrous, and a contract that has a 50%
chance of incurring such a loss would therefore be undesirable. Under such
conditions, management makes the subjective estimate that it would be willing
to pay up to \$4,000 in order to be released from this contract. However, it would
keep the contract rather than pay a sum in excess of \$4,000. In other words,
this firm is *indifferent* between the contract and an immediate payment of
\$4,000. This is equivalent to saying that the utility of $-\$4,000$ is equal to the
utility of the contract. Since the utilities of the two possible monetary consequences already have been specified, the utility of the reference contract may
be computed as follows:

$$[u(\$20,000)]\frac{1}{2} + [u(-\$10,000)]\frac{1}{2} = (1)\frac{1}{2} + (0)\frac{1}{2} = .50$$

Hence, the certainty equivalent of the contract is $-\$4,000$ and the utility of this amount is .50.

Now, since the utility of $-\$4,000$ has been determined, this monetary value may be used as one of the consequences of a new reference contract, together with either x_b or x_w as the other consequence. Thus we now are able to ask the A&E firm to imagine another reference contract with a 1/2 probability of incurring a $4,000 loss and a 1/2 probability of making a $20,000 profit. Through questioning, it is determined that the A&E firm would regard such a contract as somewhat desirable, but would be willing to sell it if they could obtain a price of at least $2,600. This implies that the utility of $2,600 is equal to the utility of the contract. Hence, we obtain

$$u(\$2,600) = [u(-\$4,000)]\frac{1}{2} + [u(\$20,000)]\frac{1}{2}$$

$$= (.50)\frac{1}{2} + (1)\frac{1}{2} = .75$$

Thus, the utility attached to $2,600 is .75.

In a similar manner, the A&E firm is asked to consider a third reference contract with a 1/2 probability at $-\$4,000$ and a 1/2 probability at $-\$10,000$. For such an undesirable contract, the A&E firm figures that it would be willing to pay up to $7,500 in order to be released from this contract. This indicates that the utility of $-\$7,500$ is equal to the utility of the contract. That is,

$$u(-\$7,500) = [u(-\$4,000)]\frac{1}{2} + [u(-\$10,000)]\frac{1}{2}$$

$$= \frac{1}{2}(.50) + \frac{1}{2}(0) = .25$$

Hence, the utility for $-\$7,500$ is .25.

Thus far, the A&E firm has determined five money–utility pairs. These pairs are displayed in Table 23.1. If the firm wishes, it may follow the same

Table 23.1 A&E Firm's Utilities for Selected Monetary Consequences

Monetary Consequence	Utility
−$10,000	.00
−7,500	.25
−4,000	.50
2,600	.75
20,000	1.00

procedure to determine the utilities for other monetary consequences—that is, specify a reference contract that has two possible monetary consequences, x_1 and x_2, each of which has a known utility and a 1/2 probability of occurring.

Then, ask the decision maker to specify his certainty equivalent for the contract. Using x_0 to denote the certainty equivalent, the utility for x_0 is obtained from the equation

$$u(x_0) = u(x_1)\frac{1}{2} + u(x_2)\frac{1}{2} \qquad (23.1)$$

In Formula (23.1), the decision maker's response, x_0 depends on his attitude toward risk. This attitude, in turn, depends on such factors as his asset position and his propensity for risk taking. Thus, it is imperative that the decision maker's asset position remain constant during the construction of his utility function. This requirement is implicit in Formula (23.1). If we denote the decision maker's present asset position as m_0, then the corresponding *explicit* formula[2] is

$$u(m_0 + x_0) = u(m_0 + x_1)\frac{1}{2} + u(m_0 + x_2)\frac{1}{2} \qquad (23.2)$$

The *fourth* step is to plot all the assessed money–utility pairs on a graph, with the horizontal axis denoting the monetary consequence and the vertical axis showing the utility. It is a common practice to assess only a limited number of pairs, and then use these pairs to approximate the entire utility function by drawing a smooth curve. The utility function for the A&E firm shown in Figure 23.1 is obtained by smoothing the points represented by the money–utility pairs in Table 23.1. Once this utility curve is established, the utility for any monetary consequence on the horizontal axis may be obtained by reading the height of the curve at that point. For instance, the utility for $0 is equal to .67.

The *final* step is to check for consistency, using several new reference contracts. As an illustration, suppose that the A&E firm considers the reference contract with a 50:50 chance of $2,600, or −$7,500. The firm determines that it would be indifferent between a payment of $4,000 and this undersirable contract. This means the utility of −$4,000 is equal to the utility of the contract:

$$u(-\$4,000) = [u(\$2,600)]\frac{1}{2} + [u(-\$7,500)]\frac{1}{2}$$
$$= (.75)\frac{1}{2} + (.25)\frac{1}{2} = .50$$

Thus, the utility of −$4,000 is .50. Since this is identical to that obtained previously, no inconsistency is revealed. If inconsistencies are found, appropriate revisions should be made so that the decision maker is confident that the function properly expresses his utilities for monetary consequences.

---

[2]For a brief but clear discussion of the significance of a decision maker's asset position and the explicit formula, see Chi-Yuan Lin and Paul D. Berger, "On the Selling Price and Buying Price of a Lottery," *The American Statistician*, December 1969. For a detailed and technical discussion of this subject, see John Pratt, "Risk Aversion in the Small and in the Large," *Econometrica*, Vol. 32, No. 1–2 (January–April 1964).

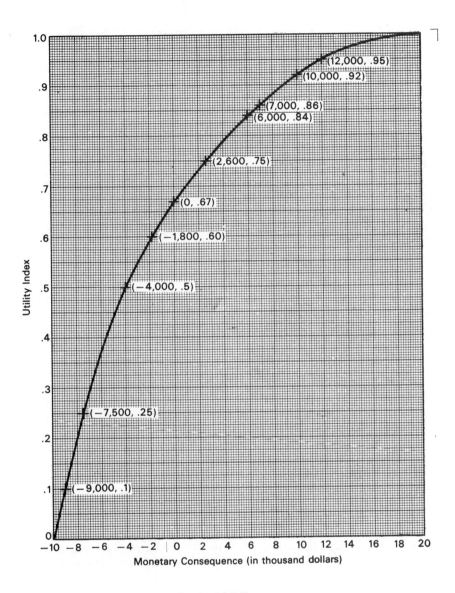

Figure 23.1 Utility Function for the A&E Firm

23.3 EXPECTED UTILITY CRITERION

Once the utility function of a decision maker has been established, the monetary consequences of a decision problem may be reexpressed in terms of utilities rather than monetary values. This makes it possible to replace the EMV criterion with the *Expected Utility* (EU) criterion. Application of the EU criterion involves (1) computing the expected utility of each of the alternative acts, and (2) selecting that act that has the maximum expected utility. The computation of the EU of an act is identical to that of the EMV of an act, except that the original monetary values are replaced by the corresponding utilities.

As a simple illustration, let us return to the A&E firm's problem of deciding whether or not to accept the offer to perform a feasibility study. Recall that, if the offer is accepted, the firm has a .60 probability of making an eventual profit of $20,000 and a .40 probability of suffering a $10,000 loss. Thus, the EMV for the act of accepting the offer is $8,000, whereas the EMV for the act of declining the offer is $0. Hence, according to the EMV criterion, the firm should accept the offer. However, as we have seen, the firm has decided to decline the offer in defiance of the EMV criterion.

Let us now see whether the A&E firm's decision to decline the offer can be justified by the EU criterion. From the firm's utility function in Figure 23.1, we see that the utilities corresponding to $20,000 and $-\$10,000$ are 1 and 0, respectively. Therefore, we obtain the expected utility for the act of accepting the offer as follows:

$$1(.60) + 0(.40) = .60$$

For the alternative act of refusing the offer, which has a monetary value of $0, Figure 23.1 yields a corresponding utility of .67. Since the EU of declining the offer (.67) is greater than the EU of accepting the offer (.60), the preferable act under the EU criterion is to decline the offer. Hence, the A&E firm's decision is justified by the EU criterion.

It should be pointed out that once the expected utility of an act is computed, the certainty equivalent of the act may readily be obtained from the utility function. For example, to obtain the A&E firm's certainty equivalent for the act of accepting the feasibility study, we first note that the expected utility of this is .60. From Figure 23.1, it may be seen that this utility has a corresponding monetary value of $-\$1,800$. This amount of $-\$1,800$ is the certainty equivalent of that act.

In evaluating alternative acts, a utility function is particularly useful if each alternative involves several possible monetary consequences. To illustrate this point, suppose that the A&E firm has been offered two contracts, A and B, by different clients. Because of its limited resources (particularly technical personnel), the firm can accept only one of these contracts, even though both of them seem profitable. The A&E firm has estimated the monetary consequences and the probabilities associated with each of these contracts as shown in Figure 23.2.

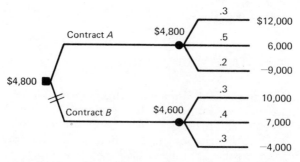

Figure 23.2 Structure and Analysis of the A&E Firm's Decision Problem Using the EMV Criterion

The reader can verify that the EMV of contract A is \$4,800, whereas the EMV of contract B is \$4,600. According to the EMV criterion, the A&E firm should choose contract A. This criterion, however, fails to consider the firm's *present attitude toward risk* as reflected in the utility function shown in Figure 23.1. To consider its attitude toward risk in evaluating the contracts, the firm first reads off the utility for each of the six monetary consequences associated with these contracts. These utilities, together with the initial estimates of probabilities and monetary consequences, are shown in Figure 23.3. Using the information given above, the expected utility of contract A is computed as follows:

$$\text{EU(contract } A) = (.3)(.95) + (.5)(.84) + (.2)(.10) = .725$$

Similarly, the expected utility of contract B is computed as follows:

$$\text{EU(contract } B) = (.3)(.92) + (.4)(.86) + (.3)(.50) = .770$$

According to the EU criterion, the A&E firm should choose contract B since it has the higher expected utility. It is interesting that the expected utility of either contract is greater than .67, which is the utility of \$0. Thus, without the resources constraint, the acceptance of either contract would be preferable to doing nothing.

As pointed out in the preceding example, once the expected utilities are computed, the certainty equivalents can be obtained from the utility function. As the reader may verify from Figure 23.1, the certainty equivalent of contract A (which has an EU of .725) is \$1,700. Similarly, the certainty equivalent of contract B (which has an EU of .770) is \$3,200. Thus, contract B is preferable to contract A, since contract B has the higher certainty equivalent. This is the same act that was selected by maximizing the expected utility. This is not a mere coincidence. Rather, it is always true that the act that has the maximum EU will also have the maximum certainty equivalent.

It should be emphasized that a utility function established for a given decision situation reflects the decision maker's attitude toward risk *at the time when such a function is established*. Thus, in using the utility function to evaluate alternatives associated with subsequent decision problems as illustrated above, extreme caution should be exercised to make certain that the decision maker's attitude

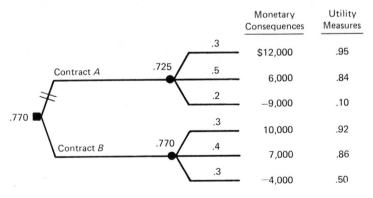

Figure 23.3 Structure and Analysis of the A&E Firm's Decision Problem Using the EU Criterion

toward risk has not changed significantly. Otherwise, such evaluations of alternatives might be in error. If a significant change has occurred, a new utility function must be constructed.

23.4 THREE BASIC SHAPES OF UTILITY FUNCTIONS

The A&E firm's utility function depicted in Figure 23.1 represents only one of numerous possible shapes of utility functions. Three basic shapes of utility functions, however, are of particular interest. To illustrate these three basic shapes, consider three different decision makers—Abe, Bob, and Chuck—whose utility functions are shown in Figure 23.4.

The utility functions shown in Figures 23.4 and 23.1 have a common characteristic in that each has a positive slope over its range. In other words, each utility function is an increasing function of money. Stated in a less technical manner, each curve rises consistently from the lower-left to the upper-right side of the graph. This simply means that all of these decision makers attach greater utility to a larger amount of money than to a smaller amount. This phenomenon, which often is referred to as "positive marginal utility for money," holds for all but a very few mystical decision makers.

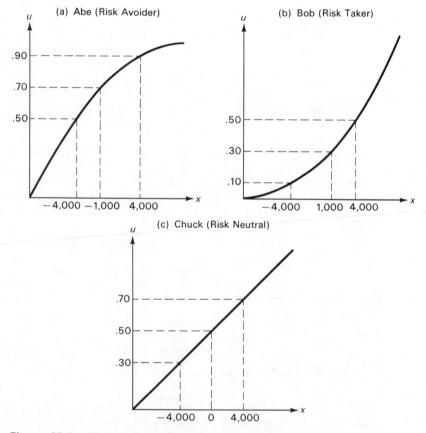

Figure 23.4   Three Basic Shapes of Utility Functions

The utility function for Abe, shown in Figure 23.4a is similar to that shown in Figure 23.1. The concave downward shape of the utility curve indicates that the decision maker's utility for money increases at a decreasing rate. In other words, he has a *diminishing marginal utility for money*. A decision maker with this shape of utility function is averse to risk or he is a risk avoider. In other words, he prefers a *sure* monetary amount to the same amount of *expected* monetary value. As an illustration, suppose that Abe has to decide whether or not to accept a contract with a 50:50 chance of $4,000 or −$4,000. The EMV of this contract clearly is zero. As shown in Figure 23.4a the utilities for these two possible monetary consequences are .90 and .50, respectively. Thus, the expected utility of the contract is $(.90)(1/2) + (.50)(1/2) = .70$. As depicted in the graph, the certainty equivalent of the contract, which is the monetary value corresponding to the utility of .70, is equal to −$1,000. This means that the decision maker is willing to pay up to $1,000 to be released from the contract. Consequently, Abe prefers doing nothing rather than accepting the contract. In the vernacular, this example shows that this kind of decision maker prefers one bird in the hand to a 50:50 chance of two birds in the bush.

The utility function shown in Figure 23.4b is convex in shape, indicating that Bob has an *increasing marginal utility* for money. That is, Bob's utility for money increases at an increasing rate. A decision maker with this shape of utility function is *not* risk averse. Indeed, he is a risk lover or risk taker. He prefers to take a risk with a given expected payoff rather than accept an equal amount for certain. Suppose that Bob considers the same contract presented to Abe. For Bob, the EU of this contract is $.50(1/2) + .10(1/2) = .30$. Thus, as indicated in Figure 23.4b the certainty equivalent of the contract for Bob is $1,000, since this is the amount corresponding to the utility of .30. Clearly, this shows that he prefers this risk alternative rather than doing nothing. This is because he is much more interested in the possibility of receiving $4,000 than he is concerned with the possibility of losing $4,000. The reader may wonder if such decision makers exist. In fact, they do. For example, Grayson[3] has shown that some oil wildcatters are not willing to sell their rights to a venture for a price equal to its EMV, especially if some of the possible, but not very probable, monetary consequences hold out the promise of a "new way of life."

The utility function shown in Figure 23.4c is a linear function, indicating that Chuck has a *constant marginal utility* for money. That is, Chuck's utility for money increases at a constant rate. A decision maker with this type of utility function is neutral to risk. He is indifferent between a sure amount and an alternative for which the EMV is equal to the sure amount. Suppose that Chuck considers the same contract presented to Abe and Bob. For Chuck, the EU of this contract is $.70(1/2) + .30(1/2) = .50$. Thus, as indicated in Figure 23.4c, the certainty equivalent of the contract for Chuck is $0, which is the amount corresponding to the utility of .50. Clearly, this shows that he is indifferent between the contract and doing nothing.

It is important to note that, when a utility function is linear, the certainty equivalent of a risky alternative is *always* equal to the expected monetary value of the same alternative. Consequently, if a decision maker's utility function is

[3]C. J. Grayson, Jr., *Decision under Uncertainty: Drilling Decisions by Oil and Gas Operators*, Division of Research, Graduate School of Business Administration, Harvard University, Boston, 1965.

linear, the optimal act obtained by maximizing the certainty equivalent is always identical to that obtained by maximizing the EMV. Stated in a different way, the criterion of maximizing expected utility is identical to the criterion of maximizing the expected monetary value whenever the decision maker has a linear utility function.

PROBLEMS

23.1 Lance Buck, the famous industrialist and jetset playboy, has retained the noted psychologist, Dr. Sigmund Wise, as a member of his personal staff. To gain insight into Buck's decision-making behavior, Dr. Wise asks him to respond to a series of reference contracts. Buck agrees readily, and the following dialogue ensues:

Wise Imagine that you are committed to a contract that gives you a 50% chance of a $100,000 profit and a 50% chance of a $20,000 loss. Would this contract be desirable to you?

Buck: Of course!

Wise: If you had a chance to sell the contract, what is the least amount you would accept for it?

Buck: Hmm . . . I suppose I'd be willing to let it go for about $70,000.

Wise: Now suppose that you are committed to another contract with a 50% chance of losing $20,000 and a 50% chance of making $70,000. How do you like this one?

Buck: Sounds good to me.

Wise: What is the lowest price you would accept for this one?

Buck: Well, since it's not as good a deal as the first contract, I guess I'd take $40,000 for it.

Wise: I see. Let's try one more. Suppose you hold a contract that has a 50% chance of yielding a $100,000 profit and a 50% chance of a $70,000 profit. I assume that this contract is not entirely abhorrent to you?

Buck: I can live with it comfortably.

Wise: If you were to sell, how much would you ask?

Buck: I'd have to get at least $90,000 for that one.

At this point the dialogue is interrupted by a transatlantic telephone call from Buck's broker in London.

(a) On the basis of Buck's responses to the reference contracts, prepare a graph of his utility function for money. Assume a utility of 0 for $20,000 and a utility of 1 for $100,000.

(b) From the graph, what utility measure would be assigned to a monetary amount of $80,000?

(c) Is Buck a risk taker or a risk avoider? Explain.

23.2 Assume that you hold a reference contract that gives you a .50 probability of winning $5,000 and a .50 probability of winning $1,000.

(a) What is the minimum price you would accept if you had an opportunity to sell this contract?

(b) On the basis of your response to part (a), present yourself with a new reference contract. Continue doing this until you have responded to several contracts. Then prepare a graph of your personal utility function for money.

23.3 Suppose that the A&E firm discussed in this chapter has been asked by another client to conduct a study under circumstances quite similar to those described in the text. The client will pay a nominal fee of $2,500 for the preparation of a feasibility study for the construction of a proposed facility. It will cost A&E $10,000 to conduct the study. However, the client will award the construction contract to the A&E firm if the study convinces the client that construction of the new facility is desirable. A&E estimates that if they are fortunate enough to obtain the construction contract for the new facility, their profit should be $25,000. A&E's best guess of the probability that they will obtain the contract to build the new facility is .75.

(a) Assuming that the utility function shown in Figure 23.1 is pertinent to this new contract situation, determine the expected utility for the act of accepting the feasibility study.

(b) Should A&E accept the study?

23.4 Mrs. Green's utility function for money is

$$u(x) = 10 + 8x \quad \text{for } -\$100 \le x \le \$1,000$$

Mrs. Green holds a contract that has a .60 probability of making a profit of $500 and a .40 probability of suffering a loss of $100.

(a) Determine the certainty equivalent of the contract for Mrs. Green.

(b) Compute the expected monetary value of Mrs. Green's contract.

(c) Is the expected monetary value in part (b) equal to the certainty equivalent in part (a)? If they are equal, explain why. If they are not equal, which of the two represents the minimum amount for which Mrs. Green should be willing to sell the contract? Explain.

23.5 Mr. Strait's utility function for money may be expressed mathematically as a function for x (in dollars):

$$u(x) = -200 + .1x \quad \text{for } -10,000 \le x \le 10,000$$

(a) Graph Mr. Strait's utility function. How would you classify the shape of his utility function?

(b) Is Mr. Strait averse to risk, neutral to risk, or a risk taker? Why?

23.6 Referring to Problem 23.5, suppose that Mr. Strait has an opportunity to undertake a project which has a .60 probability of making a profit of $3,500 and a .40 probability of losing $2,000.

(a) Calculate the expected monetary value of the project under consideration. According to the EMV criterion, should Mr. Strait undertake the project?

(b) Compute the expected utility of the project. According to the EU criterion, should Mr. Strait undertake the project?

(c) Determine the certainty equivalent of the project. If Mr. Strait would make his decision based on certainty equivalent, should he undertake the project?

(d) Is the optimal decision found in part (c) the same as that found in part (a)? Is this a general phenomenon or a mere coincidence?

23.7 Ms. Ray's utility function for money may be expressed by the following function:

$$u(x) = \sqrt{x + 150} \quad \text{for } -100 \le x \le 10,000$$

Ms. Ray holds a contract that has a .80 probability of making a profit of $9,850 and a .20 probability of incurring a loss of $50.

(a) Determine the certainty equivalent of Ms. Ray's contract.

(b) Compute the expected monetary value of Ms. Ray's contract.

(c) Is the expected monetary value in part (b) equal to the certainty equivalent in part (a)? If not, which of the two represents the minimum amount for which Ms. Ray would be willing to sell the contract?

23.8 Mr. Ryder's utility function for money is

$$u(x) = \begin{cases} +\sqrt{x} & \text{if } x > \$1 \\ x & \text{if } x \le \$1 \end{cases}$$

Decision Analysis: Use of Utility Functions

He is committed to a contract for which he has a .70 probability of making a profit of $10,000 and a .30 probability of losing $500. Is this contract desirable to him? If not, what is the maximum amount that he should be willing to pay in order to be released from the contract?

23.9 As a talented decision analyst, you have helped Mr. S. Q. Root assess his utility function for money. Because of your mathematical insight, you have discovered that Mr. Root's utility function can be accurately represented by a mathematical function. Specifically, if x is used to denote monetary value in dollars, then the utility of money, which will be designated as $u(x)$, may be expressed by the following function:

$$u(x) = \begin{cases} +\sqrt{x} & \text{if } x > 1 \\ x & \text{if } x \leq 1 \end{cases}$$

Mr. Root wishes to compare the following two alternative courses of action:

(a) Compute the EMV of each of the two alternative acts. According to the EMV criterion, which is the optimal act? Should Mr. Root adopt the EMV criterion for decision making? Why?

(b) Calculate the EU of each of the two alternative acts. According to the EU criterion, which should Mr. Root choose?

(c) Find the certainty equivalent for each of the two alternative acts. By comparing the certainty equivalents, which should Mr. Root choose?

(d) Is the optimal decision found in part (c) the same as that obtained in part (b)? Is this a general phenomenon or a mere coincidence?

(e) Is Mr. Root risk averse, risk taking, or risk neutral? Explain.

23.10 Mr. Square's utility function for money may be expressed mathematically as

$$u(x) = x^2 \quad \text{for } 0 \leq x \leq 10,000$$

He holds a contract for which he estimates that there is a .25 probability of making $2,000 and a .75 probability of breaking even.

(a) Determine the certainty equivalent of the contract for Mr. Square.

(b) Compute the expected monetary value of the contract.

(c) Is the expected monetary value in part (b) equal to the certainty equivalent in part (a)? If not, which of the two represents the minimum amount for which Mr. Square should be willing to sell the contract? Explain.

23.11 Elsie White has established her utility function for money over the interval $0 \leq x \leq \$400$. Her utility function can be accurately represented by the following mathematical function:

$$u(x) = 400x - .5x^2 \quad \text{for } 0 \leq x \leq 400$$

Miss White must choose between the following two alternatives:

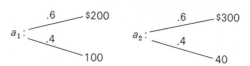

(a) If Elsie White were to adopt the EMV criterion, which alternative would she choose?

(b) Using the EU criterion, which alternative should Elsie White choose?

23.12 Referring to Problem 23.11, continue the analysis of Miss White's problem as follows:

(a) Using the CE criterion, which alternative should Miss White choose?

(b) Discuss the relationship among the EMV, EU, and CE criteria for decision making.

(c) What is Elsie White's attitude toward risk?

23.13 A decision maker must make a choice between two alternative acts, A and B. The expected monetary value, expected utility, and certainty equivalent of each of these two alternative acts have been determined.

(a) If it is known that act A has the higher expected utility but act B has the higher expected monetary value, then which of the following is the correct answer?

(i) He must find out the certainty equivalents of the two acts before he can make his decision.

(ii) He can be sure that either expected utilities or expected monetary values are in error.

(iii) He should choose act A.

(iv) He should choose act B.

(b) If it is known that act A has the higher certainty equivalent but that act B has the higher expected monetary value, which of the following is the correct answer?

(i) He must find out the expected utilities of the two acts before he can make his decision.

(ii) He can be sure that either certainty equivalents or expected monetary values are in error.

(iii) He should choose act A.

(iv) He should choose act B.

(c) If it is known that act A has a higher expected utility than an alternative act B, but act B has a higher certainty equivalent, which of the following is correct?

(i) The decision maker must find out the expected monetary values of the two acts before he can make his decision.

(ii) The decision maker can be sure that either expected utilities or certainty equivalents are in error.

(iii) The decision maker should choose act A.

(iv) The decision maker should choose act B.

23.14 A decision maker has determined the possible utilities associated with the four action–state pairs for a particular decision problem as shown in the following table:

State of Nature	Utility	
	a_1	a_2
θ_1	.5	.9
θ_2	.8	.2

He feels, however, that it is extremely difficult to specify the probability for θ_1. Naturally, if $P(\theta_1)$ is specified, then $P(\theta_2)$ is $1 - P(\theta_1)$. Because of the difficulty, he is interested in knowing the minimum value of $P(\theta_1)$ for which he would prefer a_2 over a_1. Find this minimum value.

23.15 The conditional payoffs for Mr. Quade's decision problem are as follows:

State of Nature	Conditional Payoffs	
	a_1	a_2
θ_1	$144	256
θ_2	289	121

Mr. Quade's utility function for x (dollars) is:

$$u(x) = +\sqrt{x} \qquad \text{for } x \geq 1$$

Although Mr. Quade has established his utility function, he still has difficulty in deciding which of the two alternatives to choose. This difficulty is due to his lack of information concerning the probability of the occurrence of θ_1 or θ_2.

(a) Rather than quantify his subjective probabilities, Mr. Quade wishes to determine the minimum probability of θ_1 for which he would prefer a_2 over a_1. Find this minimum probability for him.

(b) If $P(\theta_1)$ is such that Mr. Quade is indifferent between the two alternatives, what is the certainty equivalent of his decision?

23.16 The holding company of Diversified Plutocrats (DP) has an opportunity to purchase either or both of two other firms during the next 2 years. If the first purchase is highly successful in producing a sufficient cash flow, the second purchase might be possible at a later date unless the firm is sold elsewhere in the meantime. The resulting decision problem is a typical example of the way a current decision may affect future options.

The first firm, Amalgamated Carborundum (AC), will generate one more year of cash revenues before advancing technologies put it out of business. Its selling price is $40,000 cash, and if not bought now, there is a .20 probability it will still be on the market next year. The second firm, Digital Circuitry (DC), is good for one more year's revenues before being closed by advancing creditors. Its price is $50,000 and there is a .50 chance that it will still be available next year. The respective single year cash revenues (in thousands of dollars) for each firm and their probabilities of occurrence are:

AC		DC	
Cash Revenues	Probability	Cash Revenues	Probability
$60	.2	$100	.5
$40	.6	$ 40	.3
$20	.2	-$ 20	.2

The potential parent company, DP, has current net liquid assets of $50,000 and is already so extended that no new borrowing will be possible for the next 2 years.

(a) Construct the decision diagram for this problem, showing all relevant acts and events, probabilities, and partial and total cash flows.

(b) Despite their highly leveraged position, management of DP claims to be risk neutral. If this is so, analyze the diagram of part (a) to determine their optimal strategy.

(c) Since EMV is used as the criterion here, what role (if any) do net liquid assets have in this problem? Would the same optimal strategy result if the problem were analyzed with the terminal values of net liquid assets instead of total cash flows?

Appendix I

Summary of
Basic Integral Calculus

The operation of summation is possible only if the values to be summed are a discrete set—that is, only if it is possible to list the specific values to be summed. When the set of values to be summed is continuous rather than discrete, the values in the set cannot be listed, and the operation of summation is replaced by the operation of integration. Indeed, the integral sign $\int$ is simply an old-fashioned elongated S standing for "summation."

I.1 BASIC RULES

Although the subject of integral calculus includes a large number of rules, many of which are very complicated, this book requires only the simplest and most elementary of those rules. You can easily handle the examples and problems in this book by mastering the four basic rules given below.

Rule 1: Integral of a constant

$$\int k \, dx = kx + c$$

where k is a specified constant and c is an unspecified constant.

Examples:

$$\int 3 \, dx = 3x + c$$

$$\int 5 \, dy = 5y + c$$

$$\int 7 \, dz = 7z + c$$

Rule 2: Integral of x^n

$$\int x^n \, dx = \frac{x^{n+1}}{n+1} + c$$

where n is a specified constant. This rule is valid for any value of n except $n = -1$.

Examples:

$$\int x^3\, dx = \frac{x^4}{4} + c$$

$$\int y^5\, dy = \frac{y^6}{6} + c$$

Rule 3: Integral of kx^n

$$\int kx^n\, dx = k \int x^n\, dx$$

where k is a specified constant.

Examples:

$$\int 5x^2\, dx = 5 \int x^2\, dx = 5\left(\frac{x^3}{3}\right) + c = \frac{5x^3}{3} + c$$

$$\int 12y^5\, dy = 12 \int y^5\, dy = 12\left(\frac{y^6}{6}\right) + c = 2y^6 + c$$

$$\int 4z^3\, dz = 4 \int z^3\, dz = 4\left(\frac{z^4}{4}\right) + c = z^4 + c$$

Rule 4: Integration of sums and differences

$$\int (u + v - w)\, dx = \int u\, dx + \int v\, dx - \int w\, dx$$

where u, v, and w are functions of x.

Example 1:

$$\int (5x + 2x^2)\, dx = \int 5x\, dx + \int 2x^2\, dx$$

$$= 5 \int x\, dx + 2 \int x^2\, dx$$

$$= 5\left(\frac{x^2}{2}\right) + 2\left(\frac{x^3}{3}\right) + c$$

$$= \frac{5x^2}{2} + \frac{2x^3}{3} + c$$

Example 2:

$$\int (y^2 - 5y + 3)\, dy = \int y^2\, dy - \int 5y\, dy + \int 3\, dy$$

$$= \frac{y^3}{3} - \frac{5y^2}{2} + 3y + c$$

I.2 DEFINITE INTEGRALS

The definite integral is denoted by

$$\int_a^b f(x)\, dx$$

where a and b (the lower and upper limits of integration) are any specified values such that $a < b$. A definite integral is evaluated as follows:

1. Determine the indefinite integral of the function. That is, perform the integration $\int f(x)\, dx$.
2. Substitute the value of the upper limit b into the result of (1).
3. Substitute the value of the lower limit a into the result of (1).
4. Subtract the result of (3) from the result of (2).

Example 1:

$$\int_1^4 x^2\, dx = \left[\frac{x^3}{3} + c\right]_1^4$$

$$= \left[\frac{4^3}{3} + c\right] - \left[\frac{1^3}{3} + c\right]$$

$$= \frac{4^3}{3} - \frac{1^3}{3}$$

$$= 21$$

In performing definite integration, the constant c is customarily ignored, because it vanishes during the subtraction process.

Example 2:

$$\int_1^3 (5x - 4)\, dx = \left[\frac{5x^2}{2} - 4x\right]_1^3$$

$$= \left[\frac{5(3)^2}{2} - 4(3)\right] - \left[\frac{5(1)^2}{2} - 4(1)\right]$$

$$= \left[\frac{5(9)}{2} - 12\right] - \left[\frac{5(1)}{2} - 4\right]$$

$$= 10.5 - (-1.5) = 12.0$$

Example 3:

$$\int_1^2 x(4x - 1)\, dx = \int_1^2 (4x^2 - x)\, dx = \left[\frac{4x^3}{3} - \frac{x^2}{2}\right]_1^2$$

$$= \left[\frac{4(2)^3}{3} - \frac{2^2}{2}\right] - \left[\frac{4(1)^3}{3} - \frac{1^2}{2}\right]$$

$$= 8\tfrac{2}{3} - \tfrac{5}{6} = 7\tfrac{5}{6}$$

EXERCISES

1. Determine the following integrals:

   (a) $\int 2\, dx$ (b) $\int 4\, dq$ (c) $\int 8\, dt$

2. Determine the following integrals:

   (a) $\int x^6\, dx$ (b) $\int r^7\, dr$ (c) $\int w^9\, dw$

3. Determine the following integrals:

   (a) $\int 3x\, dx$ (b) $\int 2y^4\, dy$ (c) $\int 3z^2\, dz$

   (d) $\int 5q^4\, dq$ (e) $\int 2r^5\, dr$ (f) $\int 10w^4\, dw$

4. Integrate each of the following functions:
   (a) $f(x) = x^3 + 2$
   (b) $f(y) = 2y^2 - 1$
   (c) $f(z) = 3z^2 - 2z + 4$

5. Evaluate the following definite integrals:

(a) $\int_1^2 x^3 \, dx$

(b) $\int_0^3 y^2 \, dy$

(c) $\int_2^4 (x^2 - 1) \, dx$

(d) $\int_1^2 (r^2 + 3) \, dr$

(e) $\int_1^2 (2x - 3) \, dx$

(f) $\int_0^1 x(x - 1) \, dx$

(g) $\int_1^2 x(5x + 2) \, dx$

(h) $\int_1^2 x^2(2x + 3) \, dx$

(i) $\int_2^4 x^2(x^2 - x) \, dx$

Answers

1. (a) $2x + c$ (b) $4q + c$ (c) $8t + c$

2. (a) $\dfrac{x^7}{7} + c$ (b) $\dfrac{r^8}{8} + c$ (c) $\dfrac{w^{10}}{10} + c$

3. (a) $\dfrac{3x^2}{2} + c$ (b) $\dfrac{2y^5}{5} + c$ (c) $z^3 + c$

   (d) $q^5 + c$ (e) $\dfrac{r^6}{3} + c$ (f) $2w^5 + c$

4. (a) $\dfrac{x^4}{4} + 2x + c$ (b) $\dfrac{2y^3}{3} - y + c$ (c) $z^3 - z^2 + 4z + c$

5. (a) 3.75   (b) 9.00   (c) 16.67
   (d) 5.33   (e) 0   (f) −0.17
   (g) 14.67   (h) 0.50   (i) 138.4

Appendix II

Tables

Table A Factorial Values

$n! = c(10^x)$: where c is tabulated in the second column and x is tabulated in the third column. In other words, $n!$ is obtained by selecting the corresponding c and moving the decimal point x places to the right.

Example: $9! = 3.6288(10^5) = 362,880$

n	c	x	n	c	x	n	c	x	n	c	x
1	1.0000	0	26	4.0329	26	51	1.5511	66	76	1.8855	111
2	2.0000	0	27	1.0889	28	52	8.0658	67	77	1.4518	113
3	6.0000	0	28	3.0489	29	53	4.2749	69	78	1.1324	115
4	2.4000	1	29	8.8418	30	54	2.3084	71	79	8.9462	116
5	1.2000	2	30	2.6525	32	55	1.2696	73	80	7.1569	118
6	7.2000	2	31	8.2228	33	56	7.1100	74	81	5.7971	120
7	5.0400	3	32	2.6313	35	57	4.0527	76	82	4.7536	122
8	4.0320	4	33	8.6833	36	58	2.3506	78	83	3.9455	124
9	3.6288	5	34	2.9523	38	59	1.3868	80	84	3.3142	126
10	3.6288	6	35	1.0333	40	60	8.3210	81	85	2.8171	128
11	3.9917	7	36	3.7199	41	61	5.0758	83	86	2.4227	130
12	4.7900	8	37	1.3764	43	62	3.1470	85	87	2.1078	132
13	6.2270	9	38	5.2302	44	63	1.9826	87	88	1.8548	134
14	8.7178	10	39	2.0398	46	64	1.2689	89	89	1.6508	136
15	1.3077	12	40	8.1592	47	65	8.2477	90	90	1.4857	138
16	2.0923	13	41	3.3453	49	66	5.4434	92	91	1.3520	140
17	3.5569	14	42	1.4050	51	67	3.6471	94	92	1.2438	142
18	6.4024	15	43	6.0415	52	68	2.4800	96	93	1.1568	144
19	1.2165	17	44	2.6583	54	69	1.7112	98	94	1.0874	146
20	2.4329	18	45	1.1962	56	70	1.1979	100	95	1.0330	148
21	5.1091	19	46	5.5026	57	71	8.5048	101	96	9.9168	149
22	1.1240	21	47	2.5862	59	72	6.1234	103	97	9.6193	151
23	2.5852	22	48	1.2414	61	73	4.4701	105	98	9.4269	153
24	6.2045	23	49	6.0828	62	74	3.3079	107	99	9.3326	155
25	1.5511	25	50	3.0414	64	75	2.4809	109	100	9.3326	157

Table B   Binomial Coefficients—Combinations of n Objects Taken r at a Time

$$\binom{n}{r} = \binom{n}{n-r} = \frac{n!}{r!\,(n-r)!}$$

Examples: $\binom{18}{6} = 18{,}564$ $\binom{18}{12} = \binom{18}{18-12} = 18{,}564$

r → n ↓	0	1	2	3	4	5	6	7	8	9	10
1	1	1									
2	1	2	1								
3	1	3	3	1							
4	1	4	6	4	1						
5	1	5	10	10	5	1					
6	1	6	15	20	15	6	1				
7	1	7	21	35	35	21	7	1			
8	1	8	28	56	70	56	28	8	1		
9	1	9	36	84	126	126	84	36	9	1	
10	1	10	45	120	210	252	210	120	45	10	1
11	1	11	55	165	330	462	462	330	165	55	11
12	1	12	66	220	495	792	924	792	495	220	66
13	1	13	78	286	715	1287	1716	1716	1287	715	286
14	1	14	91	364	1001	2002	3003	3432	3003	2002	1001
15	1	15	105	455	1365	3003	5005	6435	6435	5005	3003
16	1	16	120	560	1820	4368	8008	11440	12870	11440	8008
17	1	17	136	680	2380	6188	12376	19448	24310	24310	19448
18	1	18	153	816	3060	8568	18564	31824	43758	48620	43758
19	1	19	171	969	3876	11628	27132	50388	75582	92378	92378
20	1	20	190	1140	4845	15504	38760	77520	125970	167960	184756

Table C   Random Digits

70926	14068	90617	51352	05865	25126	21435	69981	06479	54942
38294	02507	86133	46888	21711	98619	05872	54301	87716	26002
51447	00598	36601	60566	32418	06444	18754	79000	29678	33535
33733	65492	09115	87007	43944	90683	36936	70086	26343	44499
98578	16717	53459	98243	68053	14785	94556	24145	73756	02966
98045	35229	65436	97032	90692	92839	48741	46015	60649	78986
11030	27678	40435	23421	30446	68355	41264	56845	25972	24239
06398	01268	40461	42165	76730	80605	64851	45178	40698	45023
66982	99502	99638	32288	81444	22186	99057	35949	63798	62111
49990	41133	65203	58173	33477	09119	34541	41143	46943	46256
22975	87537	49981	83262	55604	56229	84786	38692	16164	86948
56363	46172	55878	38017	28757	23228	36018	72170	51051	75235
25239	51964	68059	75456	39179	09456	92300	65626	48879	31402
59897	48512	00334	45937	19369	41725	17979	02825	84411	90936
07445	43199	11331	84333	24530	07944	18773	94012	01441	40655
52821	36525	86483	01485	27152	22479	34278	29029	82444	32543
04483	39213	14609	02255	65310	22945	48013	36887	71101	33008
85207	37425	35526	59376	85614	97070	30842	27193	62451	28179
36385	78567	05346	74610	26141	87177	19154	53851	05824	59090
55407	39812	30331	60144	17516	98353	69388	48352	58137	77898
46331	84545	74655	37810	71052	47561	38516	00995	29132	67466
04897	76974	58825	06219	35829	94137	86723	33959	58960	78467
66731	13895	78598	34046	33819	31321	28214	15552	79956	93786
43230	46708	41391	27181	83392	83917	50354	06317	82244	64964
66454	90538	67155	16330	47634	26177	91044	95720	98046	97875
15390	36462	55477	37908	88709	79835	02268	34899	43576	94090
46247	72875	26162	79014	84536	95251	08529	38081	20459	00237
55637	15060	33992	51861	89417	48441	81158	34236	95130	56722
02487	37297	82484	66076	52244	52682	24153	95903	16598	18839
42610	30603	43360	37782	74207	42717	30680	04798	49349	80247
76181	27103	98753	17717	75804	70789	38568	18708	96245	97479
24240	59688	23292	40949	74821	74395	15182	28469	39961	16523
81005	08991	34680	03514	44197	25382	59596	78425	98515	94769
56871	37208	97581	82371	26370	49617	59215	38569	14739	48414
33208	81662	43605	20558	79985	90844	17530	99091	10285	21540
43803	95466	93094	97246	31204	85156	37718	08525	91170	63419
39723	01384	22765	93642	60124	99086	45153	32542	47145	48575
62515	76499	84234	06259	51069	60919	55124	78419	58554	94540
45055	24644	30258	39939	53071	26932	18676	19285	62417	63764
69681	82442	84755	30753	38850	46942	61530	59202	11087	18121
83385	60015	99787	68177	43030	09512	56402	52055	69511	95801
04458	50325	13625	59771	52638	03817	31659	90880	61424	19064
35754	46420	40662	91784	10383	86003	18461	37487	07663	29044
10162	66613	00105	17031	85743	46022	84098	43084	05707	94180
89831	87771	78854	87869	25562	86955	25525	10040	73737	96766
55684	77321	42361	69034	44115	03720	97262	71890	16199	59265
52365	07152	28678	69439	55376	06525	59029	29933	27542	74515
33636	30300	46185	47790	80994	17002	12405	42203	99491	54380
38313	14021	53007	04659	93128	86269	29475	28220	71108	33211
12929	16404	65222	46174	52721	30713	10441	13115	06313	78985

Table C Random Digits (continued)

11767	41715	96921	39440	91713	01252	95477	90091	74570	47814
10209	39469	04395	96949	68306	59930	43058	74922	84796	25716
88035	86619	10325	12403	59223	80176	03721	42071	86811	58308
01488	22623	75963	52672	08033	94360	23673	80897	68904	98109
85453	72323	32385	04738	68076	97592	19285	41760	42244	51078
94870	60073	79608	75998	05122	18855	98943	26426	84879	74388
92793	48899	87556	46924	20939	72246	53768	14024	09495	40912
02048	90603	58746	02696	73115	25929	51870	61184	65085	78295
99402	91657	18017	77315	39059	24381	21328	36197	89852	69923
52804	36184	32274	65204	35397	44192	06055	60314	10940	34627
74967	53533	93594	69969	16216	97183	95154	37719	90074	06928
15360	86221	06240	68606	05993	28257	80451	90422	20624	31777
53092	10820	71341	56926	48072	70936	33884	63004	81011	90241
78293	43707	65260	46559	21593	61172	05802	48592	96801	88425
24698	22898	26339	77971	47433	41759	74193	54506	04385	71026
36341	31972	45946	23649	94999	27633	01609	19345	83854	65117
70032	05924	91583	26358	42395	85283	36548	48571	90295	65056
58505	19927	12491	29716	88554	84748	75150	20811	92332	52934
73594	99247	47006	04316	15214	68184	50502	00906	58323	81340
76445	56970	29913	49346	49418	89565	90371	02911	18781	49995
25906	22504	11638	73444	50364	29434	37229	81270	17091	08384
30906	29090	62259	64926	45247	63145	97190	79048	25472	63993
65174	27188	78410	88819	89691	71654	85623	76958	93888	34121
95707	46159	04585	08264	31148	55333	66354	20732	83733	71859
86800	89098	64605	45971	11658	89650	14679	29076	11295	26756
27050	19535	80967	86429	53087	24524	45176	58099	21062	93277
10321	30484	20157	44523	17221	52332	02171	69984	24729	45615
81688	67931	83947	92274	47572	05921	73696	13267	12007	36060
87754	63269	20414	97007	85234	02765	25037	08013	58209	32893
61003	95084	61292	17324	93461	48671	92398	73811	32577	03895
92634	41808	82881	62269	33586	15206	06382	92818	07525	18506
43023	46101	12756	91289	97832	03007	11112	83193	38078	10928
56571	76602	83541	73035	54212	82112	39610	98224	02571	03610
02277	75958	49212	59055	91260	88372	70664	91292	17350	78812
26333	27670	05556	64366	57386	17327	60852	92021	15754	55988
58163	45678	12771	96906	76195	16623	54681	38763	44930	12599
24866	01275	00882	31104	25970	06468	59772	11493	25244	57906
86997	96175	69773	38015	23916	94438	43706	85667	87188	72475
64237	20191	40654	96516	81157	18779	32641	89064	70199	22278
50601	68108	35854	45951	96090	18262	21094	13284	03783	47529
76183	41550	85252	38048	61986	96431	58408	90223	36116	13558
59038	73354	29214	64984	42285	99793	79106	35548	59039	40442
08430	83898	82979	99138	72201	37238	62822	29049	66756	80217
28493	94724	84455	17948	67633	89500	41013	08398	42274	57451
00322	75838	71501	37001	36824	74950	60632	11372	43392	66804
99942	82603	23184	26296	50994	21524	46967	28332	19674	32822
97872	36870	47178	69926	36075	93302	04530	10172	04809	96867
64219	06580	26192	82666	74607	31539	77593	73076	41422	56992
58098	55623	26057	28619	79776	69449	97532	09986	68865	92882
89624	83227	06730	16023	23771	51774	40547	13335	80053	88160

Extracted with permission from the RAND Corporation, *A Million Random Digits* (New York: The Free Press, 1955).

Table D Hypergeometric Distribution—Individual and Cumulative Terms for *N* = 20

Note: This table gives $f(r)$ and $F(r)$ for $D \leq n$. If $D > n$, these probabilities may be read directly from the table by interchanging D and n. Entries for $D > 8$ are omitted.

n	D	r	f(r)	F(r)	n	D	r	f(r)	F(r)
1	1	0	.9500	.9500	5	5	1	.4402	.6339
1	1	1	.0500	1.0000	5	5	2	.2935	.9274
2	1	0	.9000	.9000	5	5	3	.0677	.9951
2	1	1	.1000	1.0000	5	5	4	.0048	.9999
2	2	0	.8053	.8053	5	5	5	.0001	1.0000
2	2	1	.1895	.9947	6	1	0	.7000	.7000
2	2	2	.0053	1.0000	6	1	1	.3000	1.0000
3	1	0	.8500	.8500	6	2	0	.4789	.4789
3	1	1	.1500	1.0000	6	2	1	.4421	.9211
3	2	0	.7158	.7158	6	2	2	.0789	1.0000
3	2	1	.2684	.9842	6	3	0	.3193	.3193
3	2	2	.0158	1.0000	6	3	1	.4789	.7982
3	3	0	.5965	.5965	6	3	2	.1842	.9825
3	3	1	.3579	.9544	6	3	3	.0175	1.0000
3	3	2	.0447	.9991	6	4	0	.2066	.2066
3	3	3	.0009	1.0000	6	4	1	.4508	.6574
4	1	0	.8000	.8000	6	4	2	.2817	.9391
4	1	1	.2000	1.0000	6	4	3	.0578	.9969
4	2	0	.6316	.6316	6	4	4	.0031	1.0000
4	2	1	.3368	.9684	6	5	0	.1291	.1291
4	2	2	.0316	1.0000	6	5	1	.3874	.5165
4	3	0	.4912	.4912	6	5	2	.3522	.8687
4	3	1	.4211	.9123	6	5	3	.1174	.9861
4	3	2	.0842	.9965	6	5	4	.0135	.9996
4	3	3	.0035	1.0000	6	5	5	.0004	1.0000
4	4	0	.3756	.3756	6	6	0	.0775	.0775
4	4	1	.4623	.8380	6	6	1	.3099	.3874
4	4	2	.1487	.9866	6	6	2	.3874	.7748
4	4	3	.0132	.9998	6	6	3	.1878	.9626
4	4	4	.0002	1.0000	6	6	4	.0352	.9978
5	1	0	.7500	.7500	6	6	5	.0022	1.0000
5	1	1	.2500	1.0000	6	6	6	.0000	1.0000
5	2	0	.5526	.5526	7	1	0	.6500	.6500
5	2	1	.3947	.9474	7	1	1	.3500	1.0000
5	2	2	.0526	1.0000	7	2	0	.4105	.4105
5	3	0	.3991	.3991	7	2	1	.4789	.8895
5	3	1	.4605	.8596	7	2	2	.1105	1.0000
5	3	2	.1316	.9912	7	3	0	.2509	.2509
5	3	3	.0088	1.0000	7	3	1	.4789	.7298
5	4	0	.2817	.2817	7	3	2	.2395	.9693
5	4	1	.4696	.7513	7	3	3	.0307	1.0000
5	4	2	.2167	.9680	7	4	0	.1476	.1476
5	4	3	.0310	.9990	7	4	1	.4132	.5608
5	4	4	.0010	1.0000	7	4	2	.3381	.8989
5	5	0	.1937	.1937	7	4	3	.0939	.9928

n	D	r	f(r)	F(r)	n	D	r	f(r)	F(r)
7	4	4	.0072	1.0000	8	7	1	.0954	.1056
7	5	0	.0830	.0830	8	7	2	.2861	.3916
7	5	1	.3228	.4058	8	7	3	.3576	.7492
7	5	2	.3874	.7932	8	7	4	.1987	.9479
7	5	3	.1761	.9693	8	7	5	.0477	.9956
7	5	4	.0293	.9986	8	7	6	.0043	.9999
7	5	5	.0014	1.0000	8	7	7	.0001	1.0000
7	6	0	.0443	.0443	8	8	0	.0039	.0039
7	6	1	.2324	.2767	8	8	1	.0503	.0542
7	6	2	.3874	.6641	8	8	2	.2054	.2596
7	6	3	.2583	.9223	8	8	3	.3521	.6117
7	6	4	.0704	.9928	8	8	4	.2751	.8868
7	6	5	.0070	.9998	8	8	5	.0978	.9846
7	6	6	.0002	1.0000	8	8	6	.0147	.9992
7	7	0	.0221	.0221	8	8	7	.0008	1.0000
7	7	1	.1550	.1771	8	8	8	.0000	1.0000
7	7	2	.3486	.5257	9	1	0	.5500	.5500
7	7	3	.3228	.8486	9	1	1	.4500	1.0000
7	7	4	.1291	.9777	9	2	0	.2895	.2895
7	7	5	.0211	.9988	9	2	1	.5211	.8105
7	7	6	.0012	1.0000	9	2	2	.1895	1.0000
7	7	7	.0000	1.0000	9	3	0	.1447	.1447
8	1	0	.6000	.6000	9	3	1	.4342	.5789
8	1	1	.4000	1.0000	9	3	2	.3474	.9263
8	2	0	.3474	.3474	9	3	3	.0737	1.0000
8	2	1	.5053	.8526	9	4	0	.0681	.0681
8	2	2	.1474	1.0000	9	4	1	.3065	.3746
8	3	0	.1930	.1930	9	4	2	.4087	.7833
8	3	1	.4632	.6561	9	4	3	.1907	.9740
8	3	2	.2947	.9509	9	4	4	.0260	1.0000
8	3	3	.0491	1.0000	9	5	0	.0298	.0298
8	4	0	.1022	.1022	9	5	1	.1916	.2214
8	4	1	.3633	.4654	9	5	2	.3831	.6045
8	4	2	.3814	.8469	9	5	3	.2980	.9025
8	4	3	.1387	.9856	9	5	4	.0894	.9919
8	4	4	.0144	1.0000	9	5	5	.0081	1.0000
8	5	0	.0511	.0511	9	6	0	.0119	.0119
8	5	1	.2554	.3065	9	6	1	.1073	.1192
8	5	2	.3973	.7038	9	6	2	.3065	.4257
8	5	3	.2384	.9422	9	6	3	.3576	.7833
8	5	4	.0542	.9964	9	6	4	.1788	.9621
8	5	5	.0036	1.0000	9	6	5	.0358	.9978
8	6	0	.0238	.0238	9	6	6	.0022	1.0000
8	6	1	.1635	.1873	9	7	0	.0043	.0043
8	6	2	.3576	.5449	9	7	1	.0536	.0579
8	6	3	.3179	.8627	9	7	2	.2146	.2724
8	6	4	.1192	.9819	9	7	3	.3576	.6300
8	6	5	.0173	.9993	9	7	4	.2682	.8982
8	6	6	.0007	1.0000	9	7	5	.0894	.9876
8	7	0	.0102	.0102	9	7	6	.0119	.9995

Table D   Hypergeometric Distribution (continued)

n	D	r	f(r)	F(r)	n	D	r	f(r)	F(r)
9	7	7	.0005	1.0000	10	8	5	.2401	.9151
9	8	0	.0013	.0013	10	8	6	.0750	.9901
9	8	1	.0236	.0249	10	8	7	.0095	.9996
9	8	2	.1320	.1569	10	8	8	.0004	1.0000
9	8	3	.3081	.4650	11	1	0	.4500	.4500
9	8	4	.3301	.7951	11	1	1	.5500	1.0000
9	8	5	.1650	.9601	11	2	0	.1895	.1895
9	8	6	.0367	.9968	11	2	1	.5211	.7105
9	8	7	.0031	.9999	11	2	2	.2895	1.0000
9	8	8	.0001	1.0000	11	3	0	.0737	.0737
10	1	0	.5000	.5000	11	3	1	.3474	.4211
10	1	1	.5000	1.0000	11	3	2	.4342	.8553
10	2	0	.2368	.2368	11	3	3	.1447	1.0000
10	2	1	.5263	.7632	11	4	0	.0260	.0260
10	2	2	.2368	1.0000	11	4	1	.1907	.2167
10	3	0	.1053	.1053	11	4	2	.4087	.6254
10	3	1	.3947	.5000	11	4	3	.3065	.9319
10	3	2	.3947	.8947	11	4	4	.0681	1.0000
10	3	3	.1053	1.0000	11	5	0	.0081	.0081
10	4	0	.0433	.0433	11	5	1	.0894	.0975
10	4	1	.2477	.2910	11	5	2	.2980	.3955
10	4	2	.4180	.7090	11	5	3	.3831	.7786
10	4	3	.2477	.9567	11	5	4	.1916	.9702
10	4	4	.0433	1.0000	11	5	5	.0298	1.0000
10	5	0	.0163	.0163	11	6	0	.0022	.0022
10	5	1	.1354	.1517	11	6	1	.0358	.0379
10	5	2	.3483	.5000	11	6	2	.1788	.2167
10	5	3	.3483	.8483	11	6	3	.3576	.5743
10	5	4	.1354	.9837	11	6	4	.3065	.8808
10	5	5	.0163	1.0000	11	6	5	.1073	.9881
10	6	0	.0054	.0054	11	6	6	.0119	1.0000
10	6	1	.0650	.0704	11	7	0	.0005	.0005
10	6	2	.2438	.3142	11	7	1	.0119	.0124
10	6	3	.3715	.6858	11	7	2	.0894	.1018
10	6	4	.2438	.9296	11	7	3	.2682	.3700
10	6	5	.0650	.9946	11	7	4	.3576	.7276
10	6	6	.0054	1.0000	11	7	5	.2146	.9421
10	7	0	.0015	.0015	11	7	6	.0536	.9957
10	7	1	.0271	.0286	11	7	7	.0043	1.0000
10	7	2	.1463	.1749	11	8	0	.0001	.0001
10	7	3	.3251	.5000	11	8	1	.0031	.0032
10	7	4	.3251	.8251	11	8	2	.0367	.0399
10	7	5	.1463	.9714	11	8	3	.1650	.2049
10	7	6	.0271	.9985	11	8	4	.3301	.5350
10	7	7	.0015	1.0000	11	8	5	.3081	.8431
10	8	0	.0004	.0004	11	8	6	.1320	.9751
10	8	1	.0095	.0099	11	8	7	.0236	.9987
10	8	2	.0750	.0849	11	8	8	.0013	1.0000
10	8	3	.2401	.3250	12	1	0	.4000	.4000
10	8	4	.3501	.6750	12	1	1	.6000	1.0000

Table D   Hypergeometric Distribution (continued)

n	D	r	f(r)	F(r)	n	D	r	f(r)	F(r)
12	2	0	.1474	.1474	13	3	3	.2509	1.0000
12	2	1	.5053	.6526	13	4	0	.0072	.0072
12	2	2	.3474	1.0000	13	4	1	.0939	.1011
12	3	0	.0491	.0491	13	4	2	.3381	.4392
12	3	1	.2947	.3439	13	4	3	.4132	.8524
12	3	2	.4632	.8070	13	4	4	.1476	1.0000
12	3	3	.1930	1.0000	13	5	0	.0014	.0014
12	4	0	.0144	.0144	13	5	1	.0293	.0307
12	4	1	.1387	.1531	13	5	2	.1761	.2068
12	4	2	.3814	.5346	13	5	3	.3874	.5942
12	4	3	.3633	.8978	13	5	4	.3228	.9170
12	4	4	.1022	1.0000	13	5	5	.0830	1.0000
12	5	0	.0036	.0036	13	6	0	.0002	.0002
12	5	1	.0542	.0578	13	6	1	.0070	.0072
12	5	2	.2384	.2962	13	6	2	.0704	.0777
12	5	3	.3973	.6935	13	6	3	.2583	.3359
12	5	4	.2554	.9489	13	6	4	.3874	.7233
12	5	5	.0511	1.0000	13	6	5	.2324	.9557
12	6	0	.0007	.0007	13	6	6	.0443	1.0000
12	6	1	.0173	.0181	13	7	0	.0000	.0000
12	6	2	.1192	.1373	13	7	1	.0012	.0012
12	6	3	.3179	.4551	13	7	2	.0211	.0223
12	6	4	.3576	.8127	13	7	3	.1291	.1514
12	6	5	.1635	.9762	13	7	4	.3228	.4743
12	6	6	.0238	1.0000	13	7	5	.3486	.8229
12	7	0	.0001	.0001	13	7	6	.1550	.9779
12	7	1	.0043	.0044	13	7	7	.0221	1.0000
12	7	2	.0477	.0521	13	8	1	.0001	.0001
12	7	3	.1987	.2508	13	8	2	.0043	.0044
12	7	4	.3576	.6084	13	8	3	.0477	.0521
12	7	5	.2861	.8944	13	8	4	.1987	.2508
12	7	6	.0954	.9898	13	8	5	.3576	.6084
12	7	7	.0102	1.0000	13	8	6	.2861	.8944
12	8	0	.0000	.0000	13	8	7	.0954	.9898
12	8	1	.0008	.0008	13	8	8	.0102	1.0000
12	8	2	.0147	.0154	14	1	0	.3000	.3000
12	8	3	.0978	.1132	14	1	1	.7000	1.0000
12	8	4	.2751	.3883	14	2	0	.0789	.0789
12	8	5	.3521	.7404	14	2	1	.4421	.5211
12	8	6	.2054	.9458	14	2	2	.4789	1.0000
12	8	7	.0503	.9961	14	3	0	.0175	.0175
12	8	8	.0039	1.0000	14	3	1	.1842	.2018
13	1	0	.3500	.3500	14	3	2	.4789	.6807
13	1	1	.6500	1.0000	14	3	3	.3193	1.0000
13	2	0	.1105	.1105	14	4	0	.0031	.0031
13	2	1	.4789	.5895	14	4	1	.0578	.0609
13	2	2	.4105	1.0000	14	4	2	.2817	.3426
13	3	0	.0307	.0307	14	4	3	.4508	.7934
13	3	1	.2395	.2702	14	4	4	.2066	1.0000
13	3	2	.4789	.7491	14	5	0	.0004	.0004

Table D Hypergeometric Distribution (continued)

n	D	r	f(r)	F(r)	n	D	r	f(r)	F(r)
14	5	1	.0135	.0139	15	6	5	.3874	.8709
14	5	2	.1174	.1313	15	6	6	.1291	1.0000
14	5	3	.3522	.4835	15	7	2	.0014	.0014
14	5	4	.3874	.8709	15	7	3	.0293	.0307
14	5	5	.1291	1.0000	15	7	4	.1761	.2068
14	6	0	.0000	.0000	15	7	5	.3874	.5942
14	6	1	.0022	.0022	15	7	6	.3228	.9170
14	6	2	.0352	.0374	15	7 ·	7	.0830	1.0000
14	6	3	.1878	.2252	15	8	3	.0036	.0036
14	6	4	.3874	.6126	15	8	4	.0542	.0578
14	6	5	.3099	.9225	15	8	5	.2384	.2962
14	6	6	.0775	1.0000	15	8	6	.3973	.6935
14	7	1	.0002	.0002	15	8	7	.2554	.9489
14	7	2	.0070	.0072	15	8	8	.0511	1.0000
14	7	3	.0704	.0777	16	1	0	.2000	.2000
14	7	4	.2583	.3359	16	1	1	.8000	1.0000
14	7	5	.3874	.7233	16	2	0	.0316	.0316
14	7	6	.2324	.9557	16	2	1	.3368	.3684
14	7	7	.0443	1.0000	16	2	2	.6316	1.0000
14	8	2	.0007	.0007	16	3	0	.0035	.0035
14	8	3	.0173	.0181	16	3	1	.0842	.0877
14	8	4	.1192	.1373	16	3	2	.4211	.5088
14	8	5	.3179	.4551	16	3	3	.4912	1.0000
14	8	6	.3576	.8127	16	4	0	.0002	.0002
14	8	7	.1635	.9762	16	4	1	.0132	.0134
14	8	8	.0238	1.0000	16	4	2	.1486	.1620
15	1	0	.2500	.2500	16	4	3	.4623	.6244
15	1	1	.7500	1.0000	16	4	4	.3756	1.0000
15	2	0	.0526	.0526	16	5	1	.0010	.0010
15	2	1	.3947	.4474	16	5	2	.0310	.0320
15	2	2	.5526	1.0000	16	5	3	.2167	.2487
15	3	0	.0088	.0088	16	5	4	.4696	.7183
15	3	1	.1316	.1404	16	5	5	.2817	1.0000
15	3	2	.4605	.6009	16	6	2	.0031	.0031
15	3	3	.3991	1.0000	16	6	3	.0578	.0609
15	4	0	.0010	.0010	16	6	4	.2817	.3426
15	4	1	.0310	.0320	16	6	5	.4508	.7934
15	4	2	.2167	.2487	16	6	6	.2066	1.0000
15	4	3	.4696	.7183	16	7	3	.0072	.0072
15	4	4	.2817	1.0000	16	7	4	.0939	.1011
15	5	0	.0001	.0001	16	7	5	.3381	.4392
15	5	1	.0048	.0049	16	7	6	.4132	.8524
15	5	2	.0677	.0726	16	7	7	.1476	1.0000
15	5	3	.2935	.3661	16	8	4	.0144	.0144
15	5	4	.4402	.8063	16	8	5	.1387	.1531
15	5	5	.1937	1.0000	16	8	6	.3814	.5346
15	6	1	.0004	.0004	16	8	7	.3633	.8978
15	6	2	.0135	.0139	16	8	8	.1022	1.0000
15	6	3	.1174	.1313	17	1	0	.1500	.1500
15	6	4	.3522	.4835	17	1	1	.8500	1.0000

Table D Hypergeometric Distribution (continued)

n	D	r	f(r)	F(r)	n	D	r	f(r)	F(r)
17	2	0	.0158	.0158	18	4	2	.0316	.0316
17	2	1	.2684	.2842	18	4	3	.3368	.3684
17	2	2	.7158	1.0000	18	4	4	.6316	1.0000
17	3	0	.0009	.0009	18	5	3	.0526	.0526
17	3	1	.0447	.0456	18	5	4	.3948	.4474
17	3	2	.3579	.4035	18	5	5	.5526	1.0000
17	3	3	.5965	1.0000	18	6	4	.0790	.0789
17	4	1	.0035	.0035	18	6	5	.4421	.5211
17	4	2	.0842	.0877	18	6	6	.4789	1.0000
17	4	3	.4211	.5088	18	7	5	.1105	.1105
17	4	4	.4912	1.0000	18	7	6	.4789	.5895
17	5	2	.0088	.0088	18	7	7	.4105	1.0000
17	5	3	.1316	.1404	18	8	6	.1474	.1474
17	5	4	.4605	.6009	18	8	7	.5053	.6526
17	5	5	.3991	1.0000	18	8	8	.3474	1.0000
17	6	3	.0175	.0175	19	1	0	.0500	.0500
17	6	4	.1842	.2018	19	1	1	.9500	1.0000
17	6	5	.4789	.6807	19	2	1	.1000	.1000
17	6	6	.3193	1.0000	19	2	2	.9000	1.0000
17	7	4	.0307	.0307	19	3	2	.1500	.1500
17	7	5	.2395	.2702	19	3	3	.8500	1.0000
17	7	6	.4789	.7491	19	4	3	.2000	.2000
17	7	7	.2509	1.0000	19	4	4	.8000	1.0000
17	8	5	.0491	.0491	19	5	4	.2500	.2500
17	8	6	.2947	.3439	19	5	5	.7500	1.0000
17	8	7	.4632	.8070	19	6	5	.3000	.3000
17	8	8	.1930	1.0000	19	6	6	.7000	1.0000
18	1	0	.1000	.1000	19	7	6	.3500	.3500
18	1	1	.9000	1.0000	19	7	7	.6500	1.0000
18	2	0	.0053	.0053	19	8	7	.4000	.4000
18	2	1	.1895	.1948	19	8	8	.6000	1.0000
18	2	2	.8053	1.0000					
18	3	1	.0158	.0158					
18	3	2	.2684	.2842					
18	3	3	.7158	1.0000					

Reprinted from *Tables of the Hypergeometric Probability Distribution* by Gerald J. Lieberman and Donald B. Owen, with the permission of the publishers, Stanford University Press. © 1961 by the Board of Trustees of the Leland Stanford Junior University.

Table E Binomial Distribution—Individual Terms

$$f_b(r|n,\pi) = \binom{n}{r}\pi^r(1-\pi)^{n-r}$$

n	r	π=.001	.005	.01	.02	.03	.04	.05	.10	.15	.20	.25	.30	1/3	.40	.50	r
2	0	.9980	.9900	.9801	.9604	.9409	.9216	.9025	.8100	.7225	.6400	.5625	.4900	.4444	.3600	.2500	2
	1	.0020	.0099	.0198	.0392	.0582	.0768	.0950	.1800	.2550	.3200	.3750	.4200	.4444	.4800	.5000	1
	2	.0000	.0000	.0001	.0004	.0009	.0016	.0025	.0100	.0225	.0400	.0625	.0900	.1111	.1600	.2500	0
3	0	.9970	.9851	.9703	.9412	.9127	.8847	.8574	.7290	.6141	.5120	.4219	.3430	.2963	.2160	.1250	3
	1	.0030	.0149	.0294	.0576	.0847	.1106	.1354	.2430	.3251	.3840	.4219	.4410	.4444	.4320	.3750	2
	2	.0000	.0001	.0003	.0012	.0026	.0046	.0071	.0270	.0574	.0960	.1406	.1890	.2222	.2880	.3750	1
	3	.0000	.0000	.0000	.0000	.0000	.0001	.0001	.0010	.0034	.0080	.0156	.0270	.0370	.0640	.1250	0
4	0	.9960	.9801	.9606	.9224	.8853	.8493	.8145	.6561	.5220	.4096	.3164	.2401	.1975	.1296	.0625	4
	1	.0040	.0197	.0388	.0753	.1095	.1416	.1715	.2916	.3685	.4096	.4219	.4116	.3951	.3456	.2500	3
	2	.0000	.0001	.0006	.0023	.0051	.0088	.0135	.0486	.0975	.1536	.2109	.2646	.2963	.3456	.3750	2
	3	.0000	.0000	.0000	.0000	.0001	.0002	.0005	.0036	.0115	.0256	.0469	.0756	.0988	.1536	.2500	1
	4	.0000	.0000	.0000	.0000	.0000	.0000	.0000	.0001	.0005	.0016	.0039	.0081	.0123	.0256	.0625	0
5	0	.9950	.9752	.9510	.9039	.8587	.8154	.7738	.5905	.4437	.3277	.2373	.1681	.1317	.0778	.0313	5
	1	.0050	.0245	.0480	.0922	.1328	.1699	.2036	.3280	.3915	.4096	.3955	.3601	.3292	.2592	.1563	4
	2	.0000	.0002	.0010	.0038	.0082	.0142	.0214	.0729	.1382	.2048	.2637	.3087	.3292	.3456	.3125	3
	3	.0000	.0000	.0000	.0001	.0003	.0006	.0011	.0081	.0244	.0512	.0879	.1323	.1646	.2304	.3125	2
	4	.0000	.0000	.0000	.0000	.0000	.0000	.0000	.0004	.0022	.0064	.0146	.0283	.0412	.0768	.1563	1
	5	.0000	.0000	.0000	.0000	.0000	.0000	.0000	.0000	.0001	.0003	.0010	.0024	.0041	.0102	.0313	0
6	0	.9940	.9704	.9415	.8858	.8330	.7828	.7351	.5314	.3771	.2621	.1780	.1176	.0878	.0467	.0156	6
	1	.0060	.0293	.0571	.1085	.1546	.1957	.2321	.3543	.3993	.3932	.3560	.3025	.2634	.1866	.0938	5
	2	.0000	.0004	.0014	.0055	.0120	.0204	.0305	.0984	.1762	.2458	.2966	.3241	.3292	.3110	.2344	4
	3	.0000	.0000	.0000	.0002	.0005	.0011	.0021	.0146	.0415	.0819	.1318	.1852	.2195	.2765	.3125	3
	4	.0000	.0000	.0000	.0000	.0000	.0000	.0001	.0012	.0055	.0154	.0330	.0595	.0823	.1382	.2344	2
	5	.0000	.0000	.0000	.0000	.0000	.0000	.0000	.0001	.0004	.0015	.0044	.0102	.0165	.0369	.0938	1
		π=.999	.995	.99	.98	.97	.96	.95	.90	.85	.80	.75	.70	2/3	.60	.50	r

Table E Binomial Distribution—Individual Terms (continued)

n	r	π = .001	.005	.01	.02	.03	.04	.05	.10	.15	.20	.25	.30	1/3	.40	.50	r
6	6	.0000	.0000	.0000	.0000	.0000	.0000	.0000	.0000	.0000	.0001	.0002	.0007	.0014	.0041	.0156	0
7	0	.9930	.9655	.9321	.8681	.8080	.7514	.6983	.4783	.3206	.2097	.1335	.0824	.0585	.0280	.0078	7
	1	.0070	.0340	.0659	.1240	.1749	.2192	.2573	.3720	.3960	.3670	.3115	.2471	.2048	.1306	.0547	6
	2	.0000	.0005	.0020	.0076	.0162	.0274	.0406	.1240	.2097	.2753	.3115	.3177	.3073	.2613	.1641	5
	3	.0000	.0000	.0000	.0003	.0008	.0019	.0036	.0230	.0617	.1147	.1730	.2269	.2561	.2903	.2734	4
	4	.0000	.0000	.0000	.0000	.0000	.0001	.0002	.0026	.0109	.0287	.0577	.0972	.1280	.1935	.2734	3
	5	.0000	.0000	.0000	.0000	.0000	.0000	.0000	.0002	.0012	.0043	.0115	.0250	.0384	.0774	.1641	2
	6	.0000	.0000	.0000	.0000	.0000	.0000	.0000	.0000	.0001	.0004	.0013	.0036	.0064	.0172	.0547	1
	7	.0000	.0000	.0000	.0000	.0000	.0000	.0000	.0000	.0000	.0000	.0001	.0002	.0005	.0016	.0078	0
8	0	.9920	.9607	.9227	.8508	.7837	.7214	.6634	.4305	.2725	.1678	.1001	.0576	.0390	.0168	.0039	8
	1	.0079	.0386	.0746	.1389	.1939	.2405	.2793	.3826	.3847	.3355	.2670	.1977	.1561	.0896	.0313	7
	2	.0000	.0007	.0026	.0099	.0210	.0351	.0515	.1488	.2376	.2936	.3115	.2965	.2731	.2090	.1094	6
	3	.0000	.0000	.0001	.0004	.0013	.0029	.0054	.0331	.0839	.1468	.2076	.2541	.2731	.2787	.2188	5
	4	.0000	.0000	.0000	.0000	.0001	.0002	.0004	.0046	.0185	.0459	.0865	.1361	.1707	.2322	.2734	4
	5	.0000	.0000	.0000	.0000	.0000	.0000	.0000	.0004	.0026	.0092	.0231	.0467	.0683	.1239	.2188	3
	6	.0000	.0000	.0000	.0000	.0000	.0000	.0000	.0000	.0002	.0011	.0038	.0100	.0171	.0413	.1094	2
	7	.0000	.0000	.0000	.0000	.0000	.0000	.0000	.0000	.0000	.0001	.0004	.0012	.0024	.0079	.0313	1
	8	.0000	.0000	.0000	.0000	.0000	.0000	.0000	.0000	.0000	.0000	.0000	.0001	.0002	.0007	.0039	0
9	0	.9910	.9559	.9135	.8337	.7602	.6925	.6302	.3874	.2316	.1342	.0751	.0404	.0260	.0101	.0020	9
	1	.0089	.0432	.0830	.1531	.2116	.2597	.2985	.3874	.3679	.3020	.2253	.1556	.1171	.0605	.0176	8
	2	.0000	.0009	.0034	.0125	.0262	.0433	.0629	.1722	.2597	.3020	.3003	.2668	.2341	.1612	.0703	7
	3	.0000	.0000	.0001	.0006	.0019	.0042	.0077	.0446	.1069	.1762	.2336	.2668	.2731	.2508	.1641	6
	4	.0000	.0000	.0000	.0000	.0001	.0003	.0006	.0074	.0283	.0661	.1168	.1715	.2048	.2508	.2461	5
	5	.0000	.0000	.0000	.0000	.0000	.0000	.0000	.0008	.0050	.0165	.0389	.0735	.1024	.1672	.2461	4
	6	.0000	.0000	.0000	.0000	.0000	.0000	.0000	.0001	.0006	.0028	.0087	.0210	.0341	.0743	.1641	3
	7	.0000	.0000	.0000	.0000	.0000	.0000	.0000	.0000	.0000	.0003	.0012	.0039	.0073	.0212	.0703	2
	8	.0000	.0000	.0000	.0000	.0000	.0000	.0000	.0000	.0000	.0000	.0001	.0004	.0009	.0035	.0176	1
	9	.0000	.0000	.0000	.0000	.0000	.0000	.0000	.0000	.0000	.0000	.0000	.0000	.0001	.0003	.0020	0
		π = .999	.995	.99	.98	.97	.96	.95	.90	.85	.80	.75	.70	2/3	.60	.50	r

Table E Binomial Distribution—Individual Terms (continued)

n	r	π = .001	.005	.01	.02	.03	.04	.05	.10	.15	.20	.25	.30	1/3	.40	.50	r
10	0	.9900	.9511	.9044	.8171	.7374	.6648	.5987	.3487	.1969	.1074	.0563	.0282	.0173	.0060	.0010	10
	1	.0099	.0478	.0914	.1667	.2281	.2770	.3151	.3874	.3474	.2684	.1877	.1211	.0867	.0403	.0098	9
	2	.0000	.0011	.0042	.0153	.0317	.0519	.0746	.1937	.2759	.3020	.2816	.2335	.1951	.1209	.0439	8
	3	.0000	.0000	.0001	.0008	.0026	.0058	.0105	.0574	.1298	.2013	.2503	.2668	.2601	.2150	.1172	7
	4	.0000	.0000	.0000	.0000	.0001	.0004	.0010	.0112	.0401	.0881	.1460	.2001	.2276	.2508	.2051	6
	5	.0000	.0000	.0000	.0000	.0000	.0000	.0001	.0015	.0085	.0264	.0584	.1029	.1366	.2007	.2461	5
	6	.0000	.0000	.0000	.0000	.0000	.0000	.0000	.0001	.0012	.0055	.0162	.0368	.0569	.1115	.2051	4
	7	.0000	.0000	.0000	.0000	.0000	.0000	.0000	.0000	.0001	.0008	.0031	.0090	.0163	.0425	.1172	3
	8	.0000	.0000	.0000	.0000	.0000	.0000	.0000	.0000	.0000	.0001	.0004	.0014	.0030	.0106	.0439	2
	9	.0000	.0000	.0000	.0000	.0000	.0000	.0000	.0000	.0000	.0000	.0000	.0001	.0003	.0016	.0098	1
	10	.0000	.0000	.0000	.0000	.0000	.0000	.0000	.0000	.0000	.0000	.0000	.0000	.0000	.0001	.0010	0
11	0	.9891	.9464	.8953	.8007	.7153	.6382	.5688	.3138	.1673	.0859	.0422	.0198	.0116	.0036	.0005	11
	1	.0109	.0523	.0995	.1798	.2433	.2925	.3293	.3835	.3248	.2362	.1549	.0932	.0636	.0266	.0054	10
	2	.0001	.0013	.0050	.0183	.0376	.0609	.0867	.2131	.2866	.2953	.2581	.1998	.1590	.0887	.0269	9
	3	.0000	.0000	.0002	.0011	.0035	.0076	.0137	.0710	.1517	.2215	.2581	.2568	.2384	.1774	.0806	8
	4	.0000	.0000	.0000	.0000	.0002	.0006	.0014	.0158	.0536	.1107	.1721	.2201	.2384	.2365	.1611	7
	5	.0000	.0000	.0000	.0000	.0000	.0000	.0001	.0025	.0132	.0388	.0803	.1321	.1669	.2207	.2256	6
	6	.0000	.0000	.0000	.0000	.0000	.0000	.0000	.0003	.0023	.0097	.0268	.0566	.0835	.1471	.2256	5
	7	.0000	.0000	.0000	.0000	.0000	.0000	.0000	.0000	.0003	.0017	.0064	.0173	.0298	.0701	.1611	4
	8	.0000	.0000	.0000	.0000	.0000	.0000	.0000	.0000	.0000	.0002	.0011	.0037	.0075	.0234	.0806	3
	9	.0000	.0000	.0000	.0000	.0000	.0000	.0000	.0000	.0000	.0000	.0001	.0005	.0012	.0052	.0269	2
	10	.0000	.0000	.0000	.0000	.0000	.0000	.0000	.0000	.0000	.0000	.0000	.0000	.0001	.0007	.0054	1
	11	.0000	.0000	.0000	.0000	.0000	.0000	.0000	.0000	.0000	.0000	.0000	.0000	.0000	.0000	.0005	0
12	0	.9881	.9416	.8864	.7847	.6938	.6127	.5404	.2824	.1422	.0687	.0317	.0138	.0077	.0022	.0002	12
	1	.0119	.0568	.1074	.1922	.2575	.3064	.3413	.3766	.3012	.2062	.1267	.0712	.0462	.0174	.0029	11
	2	.0001	.0016	.0060	.0216	.0438	.0702	.0988	.2301	.2924	.2835	.2323	.1678	.1272	.0639	.0161	10
	3	.0000	.0000	.0002	.0015	.0045	.0098	.0173	.0852	.1720	.2362	.2581	.2397	.2120	.1419	.0537	9
	4	.0000	.0000	.0000	.0001	.0003	.0009	.0021	.0213	.0683	.1329	.1936	.2311	.2384	.2128	.1208	8
		π = .999	.995	.99	.98	.97	.96	.95	.90	.85	.80	.75	.70	2/3	.60	.50	r

Table E Binomial Distribution—Individual Terms (continued)

n	r	π = .001	.005	.01	.02	.03	.04	.05	.10	.15	.20	.25	.30	1/3	.40	.50	r
12	5	.0000	.0000	.0000	.0000	.0000	.0001	.0002	.0038	.0193	.0532	.1032	.1585	.1908	.2270	.1934	7
	6	.0000	.0000	.0000	.0000	.0000	.0000	.0000	.0005	.0040	.0155	.0401	.0792	.1113	.1766	.2256	6
	7	.0000	.0000	.0000	.0000	.0000	.0000	.0000	.0000	.0006	.0033	.0115	.0291	.0477	.1009	.1934	5
	8	.0000	.0000	.0000	.0000	.0000	.0000	.0000	.0000	.0001	.0005	.0024	.0078	.0149	.0420	.1208	4
	9	.0000	.0000	.0000	.0000	.0000	.0000	.0000	.0000	.0000	.0001	.0004	.0015	.0033	.0125	.0537	3
	10	.0000	.0000	.0000	.0000	.0000	.0000	.0000	.0000	.0000	.0000	.0000	.0002	.0005	.0025	.0161	2
	11	.0000	.0000	.0000	.0000	.0000	.0000	.0000	.0000	.0000	.0000	.0000	.0000	.0000	.0003	.0029	1
	12	.0000	.0000	.0000	.0000	.0000	.0000	.0000	.0000	.0000	.0000	.0000	.0000	.0000	.0000	.0002	0
13	0	.9871	.9369	.8775	.7690	.6730	.5882	.5133	.2542	.1209	.0550	.0238	.0097	.0051	.0013	.0001	13
	1	.0128	.0612	.1152	.2040	.2706	.3186	.3512	.3672	.2774	.1787	.1029	.0540	.0334	.0113	.0016	12
	2	.0001	.0018	.0070	.0250	.0502	.0797	.1109	.2448	.2937	.2680	.2059	.1388	.1002	.0453	.0095	11
	3	.0000	.0000	.0003	.0019	.0057	.0122	.0214	.0997	.1900	.2457	.2517	.2181	.1837	.1107	.0349	10
	4	.0000	.0000	.0000	.0001	.0004	.0013	.0028	.0277	.0838	.1535	.2097	.2337	.2296	.1845	.0873	9
	5	.0000	.0000	.0000	.0000	.0000	.0001	.0003	.0055	.0266	.0691	.1258	.1803	.2067	.2214	.1571	8
	6	.0000	.0000	.0000	.0000	.0000	.0000	.0000	.0008	.0063	.0230	.0559	.1030	.1378	.1968	.2095	7
	7	.0000	.0000	.0000	.0000	.0000	.0000	.0000	.0001	.0011	.0058	.0186	.0442	.0689	.1312	.2095	6
	8	.0000	.0000	.0000	.0000	.0000	.0000	.0000	.0000	.0001	.0011	.0047	.0142	.0258	.0656	.1571	5
	9	.0000	.0000	.0000	.0000	.0000	.0000	.0000	.0000	.0000	.0001	.0009	.0034	.0072	.0243	.0873	4
	10	.0000	.0000	.0000	.0000	.0000	.0000	.0000	.0000	.0000	.0000	.0001	.0006	.0014	.0065	.0349	3
	11	.0000	.0000	.0000	.0000	.0000	.0000	.0000	.0000	.0000	.0000	.0000	.0001	.0002	.0012	.0095	2
	12	.0000	.0000	.0000	.0000	.0000	.0000	.0000	.0000	.0000	.0000	.0000	.0000	.0000	.0001	.0016	1
	13	.0000	.0000	.0000	.0000	.0000	.0000	.0000	.0000	.0000	.0000	.0000	.0000	.0000	.0000	.0001	0
14	0	.9861	.9322	.8687	.7536	.6528	.5647	.4877	.2288	.1028	.0440	.0178	.0068	.0034	.0008	.0001	14
	1	.0138	.0656	.1229	.2153	.2827	.3294	.3593	.3559	.2539	.1539	.0832	.0407	.0240	.0073	.0009	13
	2	.0001	.0021	.0081	.0286	.0568	.0892	.1229	.2570	.2912	.2501	.1802	.1134	.0779	.0317	.0056	12
	3	.0000	.0000	.0003	.0023	.0070	.0149	.0259	.1142	.2056	.2501	.2402	.1943	.1559	.0845	.0222	11
	4	.0000	.0000	.0000	.0001	.0006	.0017	.0037	.0349	.0998	.1720	.2202	.2290	.2143	.1549	.0611	10
	r	π = .999	.995	.99	.98	.97	.96	.95	.90	.85	.80	.75	.70	2/3	.60	.50	r

Table E Binomial Distribution—Individual Terms (continued)

n	r	π = .001	.005	.01	.02	.03	.04	.05	.10	.15	.20	.25	.30	1/3	.40	.50	r
14	5	.0000	.0000	.0000	.0000	.0000	.0001	.0004	.0078	.0352	.0860	.1468	.1963	.2143	.2066	.1222	9
	6	.0000	.0000	.0000	.0000	.0000	.0000	.0000	.0013	.0093	.0322	.0734	.1262	.1607	.2066	.1833	8
	7	.0000	.0000	.0000	.0000	.0000	.0000	.0000	.0002	.0019	.0092	.0280	.0618	.0918	.1574	.2095	7
	8	.0000	.0000	.0000	.0000	.0000	.0000	.0000	.0000	.0003	.0020	.0082	.0232	.0402	.0918	.1833	6
	9	.0000	.0000	.0000	.0000	.0000	.0000	.0000	.0000	.0000	.0003	.0018	.0066	.0134	.0408	.1222	5
	10	.0000	.0000	.0000	.0000	.0000	.0000	.0000	.0000	.0000	.0000	.0003	.0014	.0033	.0136	.0611	4
	11	.0000	.0000	.0000	.0000	.0000	.0000	.0000	.0000	.0000	.0000	.0000	.0002	.0006	.0033	.0222	3
	12	.0000	.0000	.0000	.0000	.0000	.0000	.0000	.0000	.0000	.0000	.0000	.0000	.0001	.0005	.0056	2
	13	.0000	.0000	.0000	.0000	.0000	.0000	.0000	.0000	.0000	.0000	.0000	.0000	.0000	.0001	.0009	1
	14	.0000	.0000	.0000	.0000	.0000	.0000	.0000	.0000	.0000	.0000	.0000	.0000	.0000	.0000	.0001	0
15	0	.9851	.9276	.8601	.7386	.6333	.5421	.4633	.2059	.0874	.0352	.0134	.0047	.0023	.0005	.0000	15
	1	.0148	.0699	.1303	.2261	.2938	.3388	.3658	.3432	.2312	.1319	.0668	.0305	.0171	.0047	.0005	14
	2	.0001	.0025	.0092	.0323	.0636	.0988	.1348	.2669	.2856	.2309	.1559	.0916	.0599	.0219	.0032	13
	3	.0000	.0001	.0004	.0029	.0085	.0178	.0307	.1285	.2184	.2501	.2252	.1700	.1299	.0634	.0139	12
	4	.0000	.0000	.0000	.0002	.0008	.0022	.0049	.0428	.1156	.1876	.2252	.2186	.1948	.1268	.0417	11
	5	.0000	.0000	.0000	.0000	.0001	.0002	.0006	.0105	.0449	.1032	.1651	.2061	.2143	.1859	.0916	10
	6	.0000	.0000	.0000	.0000	.0000	.0000	.0000	.0019	.0132	.0430	.0917	.1472	.1786	.2066	.1527	9
	7	.0000	.0000	.0000	.0000	.0000	.0000	.0000	.0003	.0030	.0138	.0393	.0811	.1148	.1771	.1964	8
	8	.0000	.0000	.0000	.0000	.0000	.0000	.0000	.0000	.0005	.0035	.0131	.0348	.0574	.1181	.1964	7
	9	.0000	.0000	.0000	.0000	.0000	.0000	.0000	.0000	.0001	.0007	.0034	.0116	.0223	.0612	.1527	6
	10	.0000	.0000	.0000	.0000	.0000	.0000	.0000	.0000	.0000	.0001	.0007	.0030	.0067	.0245	.0916	5
	11	.0000	.0000	.0000	.0000	.0000	.0000	.0000	.0000	.0000	.0000	.0001	.0006	.0015	.0074	.0417	4
	12	.0000	.0000	.0000	.0000	.0000	.0000	.0000	.0000	.0000	.0000	.0000	.0001	.0003	.0016	.0139	3
	13	.0000	.0000	.0000	.0000	.0000	.0000	.0000	.0000	.0000	.0000	.0000	.0000	.0000	.0003	.0032	2
	14	.0000	.0000	.0000	.0000	.0000	.0000	.0000	.0000	.0000	.0000	.0000	.0000	.0000	.0000	.0005	1
16	0	.9841	.9229	.8515	.7238	.6143	.5204	.4401	.1853	.0743	.0281	.0100	.0033	.0015	.0003	.0000	16
	1	.0158	.0742	.1376	.2363	.3040	.3469	.3706	.3294	.2096	.1126	.0535	.0228	.0122	.0030	.0002	15
	2	.0001	.0028	.0104	.0362	.0705	.1084	.1463	.2745	.2775	.2111	.1336	.0732	.0457	.0150	.0018	14
	3	.0000	.0001	.0005	.0034	.0102	.0211	.0359	.1423	.2285	.2463	.2079	.1465	.1066	.0468	.0085	13
		π = .999	.995	.99	.98	.97	.96	.95	.90	.85	.80	.75	.70	2/3	.60	.50	r

Table E Binomial Distribution—Individual Terms (continued)

n	r	$\pi = .001$	.005	.01	.02	.03	.04	.05	.10	.15	.20	.25	.30	1/3	.40	.50	r
16	4	.0000	.0000	.0000	.0002	.0010	.0029	.0061	.0514	.1311	.2001	.2252	.2040	.1732	.1014	.0278	12
	5	.0000	.0000	.0000	.0000	.0001	.0003	.0008	.0137	.0555	.1201	.1802	.2099	.2078	.1623	.0667	11
	6	.0000	.0000	.0000	.0000	.0000	.0000	.0001	.0028	.0180	.0550	.1101	.1649	.1905	.1983	.1222	10
	7	.0000	.0000	.0000	.0000	.0000	.0000	.0000	.0004	.0045	.0197	.0524	.1010	.1361	.1889	.1746	9
	8	.0000	.0000	.0000	.0000	.0000	.0000	.0000	.0001	.0009	.0055	.0197	.0487	.0765	.1417	.1964	8
	9	.0000	.0000	.0000	.0000	.0000	.0000	.0000	.0000	.0001	.0012	.0058	.0185	.0340	.0840	.1746	7
	10	.0000	.0000	.0000	.0000	.0000	.0000	.0000	.0000	.0000	.0002	.0014	.0056	.0119	.0392	.1222	6
	11	.0000	.0000	.0000	.0000	.0000	.0000	.0000	.0000	.0000	.0000	.0002	.0013	.0032	.0142	.0667	5
	12	.0000	.0000	.0000	.0000	.0000	.0000	.0000	.0000	.0000	.0000	.0000	.0002	.0007	.0040	.0278	4
	13	.0000	.0000	.0000	.0000	.0000	.0000	.0000	.0000	.0000	.0000	.0000	.0000	.0001	.0008	.0085	3
	14	.0000	.0000	.0000	.0000	.0000	.0000	.0000	.0000	.0000	.0000	.0000	.0000	.0000	.0001	.0018	2
	15	.0000	.0000	.0000	.0000	.0000	.0000	.0000	.0000	.0000	.0000	.0000	.0000	.0000	.0000	.0002	1
17	0	.9831	.9183	.8429	.7093	.5958	.4996	.4181	.1668	.0631	.0225	.0075	.0023	.0010	.0002	.0000	17
	1	.0167	.0784	.1447	.2461	.3133	.3539	.3741	.3150	.1893	.0957	.0426	.0169	.0086	.0019	.0001	16
	2	.0001	.0032	.0117	.0402	.0775	.1180	.1575	.2800	.2673	.1914	.1136	.0581	.0345	.0102	.0010	15
	3	.0000	.0001	.0006	.0041	.0120	.0246	.0415	.1556	.2359	.2393	.1893	.1245	.0863	.0341	.0052	14
	4	.0000	.0000	.0000	.0003	.0013	.0036	.0076	.0605	.1457	.2093	.2209	.1868	.1510	.0796	.0182	13
	5	.0000	.0000	.0000	.0000	.0001	.0004	.0010	.0175	.0668	.1361	.1914	.2081	.1963	.1379	.0472	12
	6	.0000	.0000	.0000	.0000	.0000	.0000	.0001	.0039	.0236	.0680	.1276	.1784	.1963	.1839	.0944	11
	7	.0000	.0000	.0000	.0000	.0000	.0000	.0000	.0007	.0065	.0267	.0668	.1201	.1542	.1927	.1484	10
	8	.0000	.0000	.0000	.0000	.0000	.0000	.0000	.0001	.0014	.0084	.0279	.0644	.0964	.1606	.1855	9
	9	.0000	.0000	.0000	.0000	.0000	.0000	.0000	.0000	.0003	.0021	.0093	.0276	.0482	.1070	.1855	8
	10	.0000	.0000	.0000	.0000	.0000	.0000	.0000	.0000	.0000	.0004	.0025	.0095	.0193	.0571	.1484	7
	11	.0000	.0000	.0000	.0000	.0000	.0000	.0000	.0000	.0000	.0001	.0005	.0026	.0061	.0242	.0944	6
	12	.0000	.0000	.0000	.0000	.0000	.0000	.0000	.0000	.0000	.0000	.0001	.0006	.0015	.0081	.0472	5
	13	.0000	.0000	.0000	.0000	.0000	.0000	.0000	.0000	.0000	.0000	.0000	.0001	.0003	.0021	.0182	4
	14	.0000	.0000	.0000	.0000	.0000	.0000	.0000	.0000	.0000	.0000	.0000	.0000	.0000	.0004	.0052	3
		$\pi = .999$	.995	.99	.98	.97	.96	.95	.90	.85	.80	.75	.70	2/3	.60	.50	r

Table E Binomial Distribution—Individual Terms (continued)

n	r	π=.001	.005	.01	.02	.03	.04	.05	.10	.15	.20	.25	.30	1/3	.40	.50	r
17	15	.0000	.0000	.0000	.0000	.0000	.0000	.0000	.0000	.0000	.0000	.0000	.0000	.0000	.0001	.0010	2
	16	.0000	.0000	.0000	.0000	.0000	.0000	.0000	.0000	.0000	.0000	.0000	.0000	.0000	.0000	.0001	1
18	0	.9822	.9137	.8345	.6951	.5780	.4796	.3972	.1501	.0536	.0180	.0056	.0016	.0007	.0001	.0000	18
	1	.0177	.0826	.1517	.2554	.3217	.3597	.3763	.3002	.1704	.0811	.0338	.0126	.0061	.0012	.0001	17
	2	.0002	.0035	.0130	.0443	.0846	.1274	.1683	.2835	.2556	.1723	.0958	.0458	.0259	.0069	.0006	16
	3	.0000	.0001	.0007	.0048	.0140	.0283	.0473	.1680	.2406	.2297	.1704	.1046	.0690	.0246	.0031	15
	4	.0000	.0000	.0000	.0004	.0016	.0044	.0093	.0700	.1592	.2153	.2130	.1681	.1294	.0614	.0117	14
	5	.0000	.0000	.0000	.0000	.0001	.0005	.0014	.0218	.0787	.1507	.1988	.2017	.1812	.1146	.0327	13
	6	.0000	.0000	.0000	.0000	.0000	.0000	.0002	.0052	.0301	.0816	.1436	.1873	.1963	.1655	.0708	12
	7	.0000	.0000	.0000	.0000	.0000	.0000	.0000	.0010	.0091	.0350	.0820	.1376	.1682	.1892	.1214	11
	8	.0000	.0000	.0000	.0000	.0000	.0000	.0000	.0002	.0022	.0120	.0376	.0811	.1157	.1734	.1669	10
	9	.0000	.0000	.0000	.0000	.0000	.0000	.0000	.0000	.0004	.0033	.0139	.0386	.0643	.1284	.1855	9
	10	.0000	.0000	.0000	.0000	.0000	.0000	.0000	.0000	.0001	.0008	.0042	.0149	.0289	.0771	.1669	8
	11	.0000	.0000	.0000	.0000	.0000	.0000	.0000	.0000	.0000	.0001	.0010	.0046	.0105	.0374	.1214	7
	12	.0000	.0000	.0000	.0000	.0000	.0000	.0000	.0000	.0000	.0000	.0002	.0012	.0031	.0145	.0708	6
	13	.0000	.0000	.0000	.0000	.0000	.0000	.0000	.0000	.0000	.0000	.0000	.0002	.0007	.0045	.0327	5
	14	.0000	.0000	.0000	.0000	.0000	.0000	.0000	.0000	.0000	.0000	.0000	.0000	.0001	.0011	.0117	4
	15	.0000	.0000	.0000	.0000	.0000	.0000	.0000	.0000	.0000	.0000	.0000	.0000	.0000	.0002	.0031	3
	16	.0000	.0000	.0000	.0000	.0000	.0000	.0000	.0000	.0000	.0000	.0000	.0000	.0000	.0000	.0006	2
	17	.0000	.0000	.0000	.0000	.0000	.0000	.0000	.0000	.0000	.0000	.0000	.0000	.0000	.0000	.0001	1
19	0	.9812	.9092	.8262	.6812	.5606	.4604	.3774	.1351	.0456	.0144	.0042	.0011	.0005	.0001	.0000	19
	1	.0187	.0868	.1586	.2642	.3294	.3645	.3774	.2852	.1529	.0685	.0268	.0093	.0043	.0008	.0000	18
	2	.0002	.0039	.0144	.0485	.0917	.1367	.1787	.2852	.2428	.1540	.0803	.0358	.0193	.0046	.0003	17
	3	.0000	.0001	.0008	.0056	.0161	.0323	.0533	.1796	.2428	.2182	.1517	.0869	.0546	.0175	.0018	16
	4	.0000	.0000	.0000	.0005	.0020	.0054	.0112	.0798	.1714	.2182	.2023	.1491	.1093	.0467	.0074	15
	5	.0000	.0000	.0000	.0000	.0002	.0007	.0018	.0266	.0907	.1636	.2023	.1916	.1639	.0933	.0222	14
	6	.0000	.0000	.0000	.0000	.0000	.0001	.0002	.0069	.0374	.0955	.1574	.1916	.1912	.1451	.0518	13
	π = .999	.995	.99	.98	.97	.96	.95	.90	.85	.80	.75	.70	2/3	.60	.50	r

Table E Binomial Distribution—Individual Terms (continued)

n	r (π=)	.001	.005	.01	.02	.03	.04	.05	.10	.15	.20	.25	.30	1/3	.40	.50	r
19	7	.0000	.0000	.0000	.0000	.0000	.0000	.0000	.0014	.0122	.0443	.0974	.1525	.1776	.1797	.0961	12
	8	.0000	.0000	.0000	.0000	.0000	.0000	.0000	.0002	.0032	.0166	.0487	.0981	.1332	.1797	.1442	11
	9	.0000	.0000	.0000	.0000	.0000	.0000	.0000	.0000	.0007	.0051	.0198	.0514	.0814	.1464	.1762	10
	10	.0000	.0000	.0000	.0000	.0000	.0000	.0000	.0000	.0001	.0013	.0066	.0220	.0407	.0976	.1762	9
	11	.0000	.0000	.0000	.0000	.0000	.0000	.0000	.0000	.0000	.0003	.0018	.0077	.0166	.0532	.1442	8
	12	.0000	.0000	.0000	.0000	.0000	.0000	.0000	.0000	.0000	.0000	.0004	.0022	.0055	.0237	.0961	7
	13	.0000	.0000	.0000	.0000	.0000	.0000	.0000	.0000	.0000	.0000	.0001	.0005	.0015	.0085	.0518	6
	14	.0000	.0000	.0000	.0000	.0000	.0000	.0000	.0000	.0000	.0000	.0000	.0001	.0003	.0024	.0222	5
	15	.0000	.0000	.0000	.0000	.0000	.0000	.0000	.0000	.0000	.0000	.0000	.0000	.0001	.0005	.0074	4
	16	.0000	.0000	.0000	.0000	.0000	.0000	.0000	.0000	.0000	.0000	.0000	.0000	.0000	.0001	.0018	3
	17	.0000	.0000	.0000	.0000	.0000	.0000	.0000	.0000	.0000	.0000	.0000	.0000	.0000	.0000	.0003	2
20	0	.9802	.9046	.8179	.6676	.5438	.4420	.3585	.1216	.0388	.0115	.0032	.0008	.0003	.0000	.0000	20
	1	.0196	.0909	.1652	.2725	.3364	.3683	.3774	.2702	.1368	.0576	.0211	.0068	.0030	.0005	.0000	19
	2	.0002	.0043	.0159	.0528	.0988	.1458	.1887	.2852	.2293	.1369	.0669	.0278	.0143	.0031	.0002	18
	3	.0000	.0001	.0010	.0065	.0183	.0364	.0596	.1901	.2428	.2054	.1339	.0716	.0429	.0123	.0011	17
	4	.0000	.0000	.0000	.0006	.0024	.0065	.0133	.0898	.1821	.2182	.1897	.1304	.0911	.0350	.0046	16
	5	.0000	.0000	.0000	.0000	.0002	.0009	.0022	.0319	.1028	.1746	.2023	.1789	.1457	.0746	.0148	15
	6	.0000	.0000	.0000	.0000	.0000	.0001	.0003	.0089	.0454	.1091	.1686	.1916	.1821	.1244	.0370	14
	7	.0000	.0000	.0000	.0000	.0000	.0000	.0000	.0020	.0160	.0545	.1124	.1643	.1821	.1659	.0739	13
	8	.0000	.0000	.0000	.0000	.0000	.0000	.0000	.0004	.0046	.0222	.0609	.1144	.1480	.1797	.1201	12
	9	.0000	.0000	.0000	.0000	.0000	.0000	.0000	.0001	.0011	.0074	.0271	.0654	.0987	.1597	.1602	11
	10	.0000	.0000	.0000	.0000	.0000	.0000	.0000	.0000	.0002	.0020	.0099	.0308	.0543	.1171	.1762	10
	11	.0000	.0000	.0000	.0000	.0000	.0000	.0000	.0000	.0000	.0005	.0030	.0120	.0247	.0710	.1602	9
	12	.0000	.0000	.0000	.0000	.0000	.0000	.0000	.0000	.0000	.0001	.0008	.0039	.0092	.0355	.1201	8
	13	.0000	.0000	.0000	.0000	.0000	.0000	.0000	.0000	.0000	.0000	.0002	.0010	.0028	.0146	.0739	7
	14	.0000	.0000	.0000	.0000	.0000	.0000	.0000	.0000	.0000	.0000	.0000	.0002	.0007	.0049	.0370	6
	15	.0000	.0000	.0000	.0000	.0000	.0000	.0000	.0000	.0000	.0000	.0000	.0000	.0001	.0013	.0148	5
	π =	.999	.995	.99	.98	.97	.96	.95	.90	.85	.80	.75	.70	2/3	.60	.50	r

Table E Binomial Distribution—Individual Terms (continued)

n	r	π = .001	.005	.01	.02	.03	.04	.05	.10	.15	.20	.25	.30	1/3	.40	.50	r
20	16	.0000	.0000	.0000	.0000	.0000	.0000	.0000	.0000	.0000	.0000	.0000	.0000	.0000	.0003	.0046	4
	17	.0000	.0000	.0000	.0000	.0000	.0000	.0000	.0000	.0000	.0000	.0000	.0000	.0000	.0000	.0011	3
	18	.0000	.0000	.0000	.0000	.0000	.0000	.0000	.0000	.0000	.0000	.0000	.0000	.0000	.0000	.0002	2
25	0	.9753	.8822	.7778	.6035	.4670	.3604	.2774	.0718	.0172	.0038	.0008	.0001	.0000	.0000	.0000	25
	1	.0244	.1108	.1964	.3079	.3611	.3754	.3650	.1994	.0759	.0236	.0063	.0014	.0005	.0000	.0000	24
	2	.0003	.0067	.0238	.0754	.1340	.1877	.2305	.2659	.1607	.0708	.0251	.0074	.0030	.0004	.0000	23
	3	.0000	.0003	.0018	.0118	.0318	.0600	.0930	.2265	.2174	.1358	.0641	.0243	.0114	.0019	.0001	22
	4	.0000	.0000	.0001	.0013	.0054	.0137	.0269	.1384	.2110	.1867	.1175	.0572	.0313	.0071	.0004	21
	5	.0000	.0000	.0000	.0001	.0007	.0024	.0060	.0646	.1564	.1960	.1645	.1030	.0658	.0199	.0016	20
	6	.0000	.0000	.0000	.0000	.0001	.0003	.0010	.0239	.0920	.1633	.1828	.1472	.1096	.0442	.0053	19
	7	.0000	.0000	.0000	.0000	.0000	.0000	.0001	.0072	.0441	.1108	.1654	.1712	.1487	.0800	.0143	18
	8	.0000	.0000	.0000	.0000	.0000	.0000	.0000	.0018	.0175	.0623	.1241	.1651	.1673	.1200	.0322	17
	9	.0000	.0000	.0000	.0000	.0000	.0000	.0000	.0004	.0058	.0294	.0781	.1336	.1580	.1511	.0609	16
	10	.0000	.0000	.0000	.0000	.0000	.0000	.0000	.0001	.0016	.0118	.0417	.0916	.1264	.1612	.0974	15
	11	.0000	.0000	.0000	.0000	.0000	.0000	.0000	.0000	.0004	.0040	.0189	.0536	.0862	.1465	.1328	14
	12	.0000	.0000	.0000	.0000	.0000	.0000	.0000	.0000	.0001	.0012	.0074	.0268	.0503	.1139	.1550	13
	13	.0000	.0000	.0000	.0000	.0000	.0000	.0000	.0000	.0000	.0003	.0025	.0115	.0251	.0760	.1550	12
	14	.0000	.0000	.0000	.0000	.0000	.0000	.0000	.0000	.0000	.0001	.0007	.0042	.0108	.0434	.1328	11
	15	.0000	.0000	.0000	.0000	.0000	.0000	.0000	.0000	.0000	.0000	.0002	.0013	.0040	.0212	.0974	10
	16	.0000	.0000	.0000	.0000	.0000	.0000	.0000	.0000	.0000	.0000	.0000	.0004	.0012	.0088	.0609	9
	17	.0000	.0000	.0000	.0000	.0000	.0000	.0000	.0000	.0000	.0000	.0000	.0001	.0003	.0031	.0322	8
	18	.0000	.0000	.0000	.0000	.0000	.0000	.0000	.0000	.0000	.0000	.0000	.0000	.0001	.0009	.0143	7
	19	.0000	.0000	.0000	.0000	.0000	.0000	.0000	.0000	.0000	.0000	.0000	.0000	.0000	.0002	.0053	6
	20	.0000	.0000	.0000	.0000	.0000	.0000	.0000	.0000	.0000	.0000	.0000	.0000	.0000	.0000	.0016	5
	21	.0000	.0000	.0000	.0000	.0000	.0000	.0000	.0000	.0000	.0000	.0000	.0000	.0000	.0000	.0004	4
	22	.0000	.0000	.0000	.0000	.0000	.0000	.0000	.0000	.0000	.0000	.0000	.0000	.0000	.0000	.0001	3
50	0	.9512	.7783	.6050	.3642	.2181	.1299	.0769	.0052	.0003	.0000	.0000	.0000	.0000	.0000	.0000	50
	1	.0476	.1956	.3056	.3716	.3372	.2706	.2025	.0286	.0026	.0002	.0000	.0000	.0000	.0000	.0000	49
	π = .999	.995	.99	.98	.97	.96	.95	.90	.85	.80	.75	.70	2/3	.60	.50	r

538

Table E Binomial Distribution—Individual Terms (continued)

n	r	π = .001	.005	.01	.02	.03	.04	.05	.10	.15	.20	.25	.30	1/3	.40	.50	r
50	2	.0012	.0241	.0756	.1858	.2555	.2762	.2611	.0779	.0113	.0011	.0001	.0000	.0000	.0000	.0000	48
	3	.0000	.0019	.0122	.0607	.1264	.1842	.2199	.1386	.0319	.0044	.0004	.0000	.0000	.0000	.0000	47
	4	.0000	.0001	.0015	.0145	.0459	.0902	.1360	.1809	.0661	.0128	.0016	.0001	.0000	.0000	.0000	46
	5	.0000	.0000	.0001	.0027	.0131	.0346	.0658	.1849	.1072	.0295	.0049	.0006	.0001	.0000	.0000	45
	6	.0000	.0000	.0000	.0004	.0030	.0108	.0260	.1541	.1419	.0554	.0123	.0018	.0004	.0000	.0000	44
	7	.0000	.0000	.0000	.0001	.0006	.0028	.0086	.1076	.1575	.0870	.0259	.0048	.0012	.0000	.0000	43
	8	.0000	.0000	.0000	.0000	.0001	.0006	.0024	.0643	.1493	.1169	.0463	.0110	.0033	.0002	.0000	42
	9	.0000	.0000	.0000	.0000	.0000	.0001	.0006	.0333	.1230	.1364	.0721	.0220	.0077	.0005	.0000	41
	10	.0000	.0000	.0000	.0000	.0000	.0000	.0001	.0152	.0890	.1398	.0985	.0386	.0157	.0014	.0000	40
	11	.0000	.0000	.0000	.0000	.0000	.0000	.0000	.0061	.0571	.1271	.1194	.0602	.0286	.0035	.0000	39
	12	.0000	.0000	.0000	.0000	.0000	.0000	.0000	.0022	.0328	.1033	.1294	.0838	.0465	.0076	.0001	38
	13	.0000	.0000	.0000	.0000	.0000	.0000	.0000	.0007	.0169	.0755	.1261	.1050	.0679	.0147	.0003	37
	14	.0000	.0000	.0000	.0000	.0000	.0000	.0000	.0002	.0079	.0499	.1110	.1189	.0898	.0260	.0008	36
	15	.0000	.0000	.0000	.0000	.0000	.0000	.0000	.0001	.0033	.0299	.0888	.1223	.1077	.0415	.0020	35
	16	.0000	.0000	.0000	.0000	.0000	.0000	.0000	.0000	.0013	.0164	.0648	.1147	.1178	.0606	.0044	34
	17	.0000	.0000	.0000	.0000	.0000	.0000	.0000	.0000	.0005	.0082	.0432	.0983	.1178	.0808	.0087	33
	18	.0000	.0000	.0000	.0000	.0000	.0000	.0000	.0000	.0001	.0037	.0264	.0772	.1080	.0987	.0160	32
	19	.0000	.0000	.0000	.0000	.0000	.0000	.0000	.0000	.0000	.0016	.0148	.0558	.0910	.1109	.0270	31
	20	.0000	.0000	.0000	.0000	.0000	.0000	.0000	.0000	.0000	.0006	.0077	.0370	.0705	.1146	.0419	30
	21	.0000	.0000	.0000	.0000	.0000	.0000	.0000	.0000	.0000	.0002	.0036	.0227	.0503	.1091	.0598	29
	22	.0000	.0000	.0000	.0000	.0000	.0000	.0000	.0000	.0000	.0001	.0016	.0128	.0332	.0959	.0788	28
	23	.0000	.0000	.0000	.0000	.0000	.0000	.0000	.0000	.0000	.0000	.0006	.0067	.0202	.0778	.0960	27
	24	.0000	.0000	.0000	.0000	.0000	.0000	.0000	.0000	.0000	.0000	.0002	.0032	.0114	.0584	.1080	26
	25	.0000	.0000	.0000	.0000	.0000	.0000	.0000	.0000	.0000	.0000	.0001	.0014	.0059	.0405	.1123	25
	26	.0000	.0000	.0000	.0000	.0000	.0000	.0000	.0000	.0000	.0000	.0000	.0006	.0028	.0259	.1080	24
	27	.0000	.0000	.0000	.0000	.0000	.0000	.0000	.0000	.0000	.0000	.0000	.0002	.0013	.0154	.0960	23
	28	.0000	.0000	.0000	.0000	.0000	.0000	.0000	.0000	.0000	.0000	.0000	.0001	.0005	.0084	.0788	22
	29	.0000	.0000	.0000	.0000	.0000	.0000	.0000	.0000	.0000	.0000	.0000	.0000	.0002	.0043	.0598	21
		π = .999	.995	.99	.98	.97	.96	.95	.90	.85	.80	.75	.70	2/3	.60	.50	r

Table E Binomial Distribution—Individual Terms (continued)

n	r	π = .001	.005	.01	.02	.03	.04	.05	.10	.15	.20	.25	.30	1/3	.40	.50	r
50	30	.0000	.0000	.0000	.0000	.0000	.0000	.0000	.0000	.0000	.0000	.0000	.0000	.0001	.0020	.0419	20
	31	.0000	.0000	.0000	.0000	.0000	.0000	.0000	.0000	.0000	.0000	.0000	.0000	.0000	.0009	.0270	19
	32	.0000	.0000	.0000	.0000	.0000	.0000	.0000	.0000	.0000	.0000	.0000	.0000	.0000	.0003	.0160	18
	33	.0000	.0000	.0000	.0000	.0000	.0000	.0000	.0000	.0000	.0000	.0000	.0000	.0000	.0001	.0087	17
	34	.0000	.0000	.0000	.0000	.0000	.0000	.0000	.0000	.0000	.0000	.0000	.0000	.0000	.0000	.0044	16
	35	.0000	.0000	.0000	.0000	.0000	.0000	.0000	.0000	.0000	.0000	.0000	.0000	.0000	.0000	.0020	15
	36	.0000	.0000	.0000	.0000	.0000	.0000	.0000	.0000	.0000	.0000	.0000	.0000	.0000	.0000	.0008	14
	37	.0000	.0000	.0000	.0000	.0000	.0000	.0000	.0000	.0000	.0000	.0000	.0000	.0000	.0000	.0003	13
	38	.0000	.0000	.0000	.0000	.0000	.0000	.0000	.0000	.0000	.0000	.0000	.0000	.0000	.0000	.0001	12
75	0	.9277	.6866	.4706	.2198	.1018	.0468	.0213	.0004	.0000	.0000	.0000	.0000	.0000	.0000	.0000	75
	1	.0696	.2588	.3565	.3364	.2362	.1463	.0843	.0031	.0001	.0000	.0000	.0000	.0000	.0000	.0000	74
	2	.0026	.0481	.1332	.2540	.2703	.2255	.1641	.0127	.0004	.0000	.0000	.0000	.0000	.0000	.0000	73
	3	.0001	.0059	.0327	.1261	.2034	.2287	.2101	.0343	.0019	.0001	.0000	.0000	.0000	.0000	.0000	72
	4	.0000	.0005	.0060	.0463	.1132	.1715	.1991	.0685	.0060	.0003	.0000	.0000	.0000	.0000	.0000	71
	5	.0000	.0000	.0009	.0134	.0497	.1015	.1488	.1081	.0150	.0009	.0000	.0000	.0000	.0000	.0000	70
	6	.0000	.0000	.0001	.0032	.0179	.0493	.0914	.1402	.0309	.0027	.0001	.0000	.0000	.0000	.0000	69
	7	.0000	.0000	.0000	.0006	.0055	.0203	.0474	.1535	.0538	.0065	.0004	.0000	.0000	.0000	.0000	68
	8	.0000	.0000	.0000	.0001	.0014	.0072	.0212	.1450	.0807	.0139	.0011	.0000	.0000	.0000	.0000	67
	9	.0000	.0000	.0000	.0000	.0003	.0022	.0083	.1199	.1060	.0258	.0027	.0001	.0000	.0000	.0000	66
	10	.0000	.0000	.0000	.0000	.0001	.0006	.0029	.0880	.1235	.0426	.0060	.0004	.0001	.0000	.0000	65
	11	.0000	.0000	.0000	.0000	.0000	.0002	.0009	.0578	.1288	.0630	.0118	.0011	.0001	.0000	.0000	64
	12	.0000	.0000	.0000	.0000	.0000	.0000	.0003	.0342	.1212	.0840	.0209	.0024	.0004	.0000	.0000	63
	13	.0000	.0000	.0000	.0000	.0000	.0000	.0001	.0184	.1037	.1017	.0338	.0050	.0010	.0000	.0000	62
	14	.0000	.0000	.0000	.0000	.0000	.0000	.0000	.0091	.0810	.1126	.0500	.0095	.0021	.0000	.0000	61
	15	.0000	.0000	.0000	.0000	.0000	.0000	.0000	.0041	.0581	.1145	.0677	.0166	.0043	.0001	.0000	60
	16	.0000	.0000	.0000	.0000	.0000	.0000	.0000	.0017	.0385	.1073	.0846	.0267	.0081	.0003	.0000	59
	17	.0000	.0000	.0000	.0000	.0000	.0000	.0000	.0007	.0236	.0931	.0979	.0397	.0141	.0007	.0000	58
	18	.0000	.0000	.0000	.0000	.0000	.0000	.0000	.0002	.0134	.0750	.1052	.0549	.0227	.0015	.0000	57
		π = .999	.995	.99	.98	.97	.96	.95	.90	.85	.80	.75	.70	2/3	.60	.50	r

Table E Binomial Distribution—Individual Terms (continued)

n	r	π = .001	.005	.01	.02	.03	.04	.05	.10	.15	.20	.25	.30	1/3	.40	.50	r
75	19	.0000	.0000	.0000	.0000	.0000	.0000	.0000	.0001	.0071	.0563	.1052	.0705	.0340	.0030	.0000	56
	20	.0000	.0000	.0000	.0000	.0000	.0000	.0000	.0000	.0035	.0394	.0982	.0846	.0476	.0056	.0000	55
	21	.0000	.0000	.0000	.0000	.0000	.0000	.0000	.0000	.0016	.0258	.0857	.0950	.0623	.0097	.0001	54
	22	.0000	.0000	.0000	.0000	.0000	.0000	.0000	.0000	.0007	.0158	.0701	.0999	.0765	.0159	.0001	53
	23	.0000	.0000	.0000	.0000	.0000	.0000	.0000	.0000	.0003	.0091	.0539	.0987	.0881	.0244	.0003	52
	24	.0000	.0000	.0000	.0000	.0000	.0000	.0000	.0000	.0001	.0049	.0389	.0917	.0954	.0352	.0007	51
	25	.0000	.0000	.0000	.0000	.0000	.0000	.0000	.0000	.0000	.0025	.0265	.0801	.0973	.0479	.0014	50
	26	.0000	.0000	.0000	.0000	.0000	.0000	.0000	.0000	.0000	.0012	.0170	.0660	.0936	.0614	.0027	49
	27	.0000	.0000	.0000	.0000	.0000	.0000	.0000	.0000	.0000	.0005	.0103	.0514	.0849	.0742	.0049	48
	28	.0000	.0000	.0000	.0000	.0000	.0000	.0000	.0000	.0000	.0002	.0059	.0377	.0728	.0848	.0083	47
	29	.0000	.0000	.0000	.0000	.0000	.0000	.0000	.0000	.0000	.0001	.0032	.0262	.0590	.0917	.0135	46
	30	.0000	.0000	.0000	.0000	.0000	.0000	.0000	.0000	.0000	.0000	.0016	.0172	.0452	.0937	.0207	45
	31	.0000	.0000	.0000	.0000	.0000	.0000	.0000	.0000	.0000	.0000	.0008	.0107	.0328	.0907	.0300	44
	32	.0000	.0000	.0000	.0000	.0000	.0000	.0000	.0000	.0000	.0000	.0004	.0063	.0226	.0831	.0413	43
	33	.0000	.0000	.0000	.0000	.0000	.0000	.0000	.0000	.0000	.0000	.0002	.0035	.0147	.0722	.0538	42
	34	.0000	.0000	.0000	.0000	.0000	.0000	.0000	.0000	.0000	.0000	.0001	.0019	.0091	.0595	.0665	41
	35	.0000	.0000	.0000	.0000	.0000	.0000	.0000	.0000	.0000	.0000	.0000	.0009	.0053	.0464	.0779	40
	36	.0000	.0000	.0000	.0000	.0000	.0000	.0000	.0000	.0000	.0000	.0000	.0004	.0030	.0344	.0865	39
	37	.0000	.0000	.0000	.0000	.0000	.0000	.0000	.0000	.0000	.0000	.0000	.0002	.0016	.0242	.0912	38
	38	.0000	.0000	.0000	.0000	.0000	.0000	.0000	.0000	.0000	.0000	.0000	.0001	.0008	.0161	.0912	37
	39	.0000	.0000	.0000	.0000	.0000	.0000	.0000	.0000	.0000	.0000	.0000	.0000	.0004	.0102	.0865	36
	40	.0000	.0000	.0000	.0000	.0000	.0000	.0000	.0000	.0000	.0000	.0000	.0000	.0002	.0061	.0779	35
	41	.0000	.0000	.0000	.0000	.0000	.0000	.0000	.0000	.0000	.0000	.0000	.0000	.0001	.0035	.0665	34
	42	.0000	.0000	.0000	.0000	.0000	.0000	.0000	.0000	.0000	.0000	.0000	.0000	.0000	.0019	.0538	33
	43	.0000	.0000	.0000	.0000	.0000	.0000	.0000	.0000	.0000	.0000	.0000	.0000	.0000	.0010	.0413	32
	44	.0000	.0000	.0000	.0000	.0000	.0000	.0000	.0000	.0000	.0000	.0000	.0000	.0000	.0005	.0300	31
	45	.0000	.0000	.0000	.0000	.0000	.0000	.0000	.0000	.0000	.0000	.0000	.0000	.0000	.0002	.0207	30
		π = .999	.995	.99	.98	.97	.96	.95	.90	.85	.80	.75	.70	2/3	.60	.50	r

Table E Binomial Distribution—Individual Terms (continued)

n	r	.50	.40	1/3	.30	.25	.20	.15	.10	.05	.04	.03	.02	.01	.005	π = .001	r
75	46	.0135	.0001	.0000	.0000	.0000	.0000	.0000	.0000	.0000	.0000	.0000	.0000	.0000	.0000	.0000	29
	47	.0083	.0000	.0000	.0000	.0000	.0000	.0000	.0000	.0000	.0000	.0000	.0000	.0000	.0000	.0000	28
	48	.0049	.0000	.0000	.0000	.0000	.0000	.0000	.0000	.0000	.0000	.0000	.0000	.0000	.0000	.0000	27
	49	.0027	.0000	.0000	.0000	.0000	.0000	.0000	.0000	.0000	.0000	.0000	.0000	.0000	.0000	.0000	26
	50	.0014	.0000	.0000	.0000	.0000	.0000	.0000	.0000	.0000	.0000	.0000	.0000	.0000	.0000	.0000	25
	51	.0007	.0000	.0000	.0000	.0000	.0000	.0000	.0000	.0000	.0000	.0000	.0000	.0000	.0000	.0000	24
	52	.0003	.0000	.0000	.0000	.0000	.0000	.0000	.0000	.0000	.0000	.0000	.0000	.0000	.0000	.0000	23
	53	.0001	.0000	.0000	.0000	.0000	.0000	.0000	.0000	.0000	.0000	.0000	.0000	.0000	.0000	.0000	22
	54	.0001	.0000	.0000	.0000	.0000	.0000	.0000	.0000	.0000	.0000	.0000	.0000	.0000	.0000	.0000	21
100	0	.0000	.0000	.0000	.0000	.0000	.0000	.0000	.0000	.0059	.0169	.0476	.1326	.3660	.6058	.9048	100
	1	.0000	.0000	.0000	.0000	.0000	.0000	.0000	.0003	.0312	.0703	.1471	.2707	.3697	.3044	.0906	99
	2	.0000	.0000	.0000	.0000	.0000	.0000	.0000	.0016	.0812	.1450	.2252	.2734	.1849	.0757	.0045	98
	3	.0000	.0000	.0000	.0000	.0000	.0000	.0001	.0059	.1396	.1973	.2275	.1823	.0610	.0124	.0001	97
	4	.0000	.0000	.0000	.0000	.0000	.0000	.0003	.0159	.1781	.1994	.1706	.0902	.0149	.0015	.0000	96
	5	.0000	.0000	.0000	.0000	.0000	.0000	.0011	.0339	.1800	.1595	.1013	.0353	.0029	.0001	.0000	95
	6	.0000	.0000	.0000	.0000	.0000	.0001	.0031	.0596	.1500	.1052	.0496	.0114	.0005	.0000	.0000	94
	7	.0000	.0000	.0000	.0000	.0000	.0002	.0075	.0889	.1060	.0589	.0206	.0031	.0001	.0000	.0000	93
	8	.0000	.0000	.0000	.0000	.0000	.0006	.0153	.1148	.0649	.0285	.0074	.0007	.0000	.0000	.0000	92
	9	.0000	.0000	.0000	.0000	.0000	.0015	.0276	.1304	.0349	.0121	.0023	.0002	.0000	.0000	.0000	91
	10	.0000	.0000	.0000	.0000	.0001	.0034	.0444	.1319	.0167	.0046	.0007	.0000	.0000	.0000	.0000	90
	11	.0000	.0000	.0000	.0000	.0003	.0069	.0640	.1199	.0072	.0016	.0002	.0000	.0000	.0000	.0000	89
	12	.0000	.0000	.0000	.0000	.0006	.0128	.0838	.0988	.0028	.0005	.0000	.0000	.0000	.0000	.0000	88
	13	.0000	.0000	.0000	.0000	.0014	.0216	.1001	.0743	.0010	.0001	.0000	.0000	.0000	.0000	.0000	87
	14	.0000	.0000	.0000	.0001	.0030	.0335	.1098	.0513	.0003	.0000	.0000	.0000	.0000	.0000	.0000	86
	15	.0000	.0000	.0000	.0002	.0057	.0481	.1111	.0327	.0001	.0000	.0000	.0000	.0000	.0000	.0000	85
	16	.0000	.0000	.0001	.0006	.0100	.0638	.1041	.0193	.0000	.0000	.0000	.0000	.0000	.0000	.0000	84
	17	.0000	.0000	.0001	.0012	.0165	.0789	.0908	.0106	.0000	.0000	.0000	.0000	.0000	.0000	.0000	83
		.50	.60	2/3	.70	.75	.80	.85	.90	.95	.96	.97	.98	.99	.995	π = .999	r

Table E Binomial Distribution—Individual Terms (continued)

n	r	π = .001	.005	.01	.02	.03	.04	.05	.10	.15	.20	.25	.30	1/3	.40	.50	r
100	18	.0000	.0000	.0000	.0000	.0000	.0000	.0000	.0054	.0739	.0909	.0254	.0024	.0003	.0000	.0000	82
	19	.0000	.0000	.0000	.0000	.0000	.0000	.0000	.0026	.0563	.0981	.0365	.0044	.0006	.0000	.0000	81
	20	.0000	.0000	.0000	.0000	.0000	.0000	.0000	.0012	.0402	.0993	.0493	.0076	.0013	.0000	.0000	80
	21	.0000	.0000	.0000	.0000	.0000	.0000	.0000	.0005	.0270	.0946	.0626	.0124	.0024	.0001	.0000	79
	22	.0000	.0000	.0000	.0000	.0000	.0000	.0000	.0002	.0171	.0849	.0749	.0190	.0043	.0001	.0000	78
	23	.0000	.0000	.0000	.0000	.0000	.0000	.0000	.0001	.0103	.0720	.0847	.0277	.0073	.0001	.0000	77
	24	.0000	.0000	.0000	.0000	.0000	.0000	.0000	.0000	.0058	.0577	.0906	.0380	.0117	.0003	.0000	76
	25	.0000	.0000	.0000	.0000	.0000	.0000	.0000	.0000	.0031	.0439	.0918	.0496	.0178	.0006	.0000	75
	26	.0000	.0000	.0000	.0000	.0000	.0000	.0000	.0000	.0016	.0316	.0883	.0613	.0256	.0012	.0000	74
	27	.0000	.0000	.0000	.0000	.0000	.0000	.0000	.0000	.0008	.0217	.0806	.0720	.0351	.0022	.0000	73
	28	.0000	.0000	.0000	.0000	.0000	.0000	.0000	.0000	.0004	.0141	.0701	.0804	.0458	.0038	.0000	72
	29	.0000	.0000	.0000	.0000	.0000	.0000	.0000	.0000	.0002	.0088	.0580	.0856	.0569	.0063	.0000	71
	30	.0000	.0000	.0000	.0000	.0000	.0000	.0000	.0000	.0001	.0052	.0458	.0868	.0673	.0100	.0000	70
	31	.0000	.0000	.0000	.0000	.0000	.0000	.0000	.0000	.0000	.0029	.0344	.0840	.0760	.0151	.0001	69
	32	.0000	.0000	.0000	.0000	.0000	.0000	.0000	.0000	.0000	.0016	.0248	.0776	.0819	.0217	.0001	68
	33	.0000	.0000	.0000	.0000	.0000	.0000	.0000	.0000	.0000	.0008	.0170	.0685	.0844	.0297	.0002	67
	34	.0000	.0000	.0000	.0000	.0000	.0000	.0000	.0000	.0000	.0004	.0112	.0579	.0831	.0391	.0005	66
	35	.0000	.0000	.0000	.0000	.0000	.0000	.0000	.0000	.0000	.0002	.0070	.0468	.0784	.0491	.0009	65
	36	.0000	.0000	.0000	.0000	.0000	.0000	.0000	.0000	.0000	.0001	.0042	.0362	.0708	.0591	.0016	64
	37	.0000	.0000	.0000	.0000	.0000	.0000	.0000	.0000	.0000	.0000	.0024	.0268	.0612	.0682	.0027	63
	38	.0000	.0000	.0000	.0000	.0000	.0000	.0000	.0000	.0000	.0000	.0013	.0191	.0507	.0754	.0045	62
	39	.0000	.0000	.0000	.0000	.0000	.0000	.0000	.0000	.0000	.0000	.0007	.0130	.0403	.0799	.0071	61
	40	.0000	.0000	.0000	.0000	.0000	.0000	.0000	.0000	.0000	.0000	.0004	.0085	.0308	.0812	.0108	60
	41	.0000	.0000	.0000	.0000	.0000	.0000	.0000	.0000	.0000	.0000	.0002	.0053	.0225	.0792	.0159	59
	42	.0000	.0000	.0000	.0000	.0000	.0000	.0000	.0000	.0000	.0000	.0001	.0032	.0158	.0742	.0223	58
	43	.0000	.0000	.0000	.0000	.0000	.0000	.0000	.0000	.0000	.0000	.0000	.0019	.0107	.0667	.0301	57
	44	.0000	.0000	.0000	.0000	.0000	.0000	.0000	.0000	.0000	.0000	.0000	.0010	.0069	.0576	.0390	56
		π = .999	.995	.99	.98	.97	.96	.95	.90	.85	.80	.75	.70	2/3	.60	.50	r

Table E Binomial Distribution—Individual Terms (continued)

n	r	π = .001	.005	.01	.02	.03	.04	.05	.10	.15	.20	.25	.30	1/3	.40	.50	r
100	45	.0000	.0000	.0000	.0000	.0000	.0000	.0000	.0000	.0000	.0000	.0000	.0005	.0043	.0478	.0485	55
	46	.0000	.0000	.0000	.0000	.0000	.0000	.0000	.0000	.0000	.0000	.0000	.0003	.0026	.0381	.0580	54
	47	.0000	.0000	.0000	.0000	.0000	.0000	.0000	.0000	.0000	.0000	.0000	.0001	.0015	.0292	.0666	53
	48	.0000	.0000	.0000	.0000	.0000	.0000	.0000	.0000	.0000	.0000	.0000	.0001	.0008	.0215	.0735	52
	49	.0000	.0000	.0000	.0000	.0000	.0000	.0000	.0000	.0000	.0000	.0000	.0000	.0004	.0152	.0780	51
	50	.0000	.0000	.0000	.0000	.0000	.0000	.0000	.0000	.0000	.0000	.0000	.0000	.0002	.0103	.0796	50
	51	.0000	.0000	.0000	.0000	.0000	.0000	.0000	.0000	.0000	.0000	.0000	.0000	.0001	.0068	.0780	49
	52	.0000	.0000	.0000	.0000	.0000	.0000	.0000	.0000	.0000	.0000	.0000	.0000	.0001	.0042	.0735	48
	53	.0000	.0000	.0000	.0000	.0000	.0000	.0000	.0000	.0000	.0000	.0000	.0000	.0000	.0026	.0666	47
	54	.0000	.0000	.0000	.0000	.0000	.0000	.0000	.0000	.0000	.0000	.0000	.0000	.0000	.0015	.0580	46
	55	.0000	.0000	.0000	.0000	.0000	.0000	.0000	.0000	.0000	.0000	.0000	.0000	.0000	.0008	.0485	45
	56	.0000	.0000	.0000	.0000	.0000	.0000	.0000	.0000	.0000	.0000	.0000	.0000	.0000	.0004	.0390	44
	57	.0000	.0000	.0000	.0000	.0000	.0000	.0000	.0000	.0000	.0000	.0000	.0000	.0000	.0002	.0301	43
	58	.0000	.0000	.0000	.0000	.0000	.0000	.0000	.0000	.0000	.0000	.0000	.0000	.0000	.0001	.0223	42
	59	.0000	.0000	.0000	.0000	.0000	.0000	.0000	.0000	.0000	.0000	.0000	.0000	.0000	.0001	.0159	41
	60	.0000	.0000	.0000	.0000	.0000	.0000	.0000	.0000	.0000	.0000	.0000	.0000	.0000	.0000	.0108	40
	61	.0000	.0000	.0000	.0000	.0000	.0000	.0000	.0000	.0000	.0000	.0000	.0000	.0000	.0000	.0071	39
	62	.0000	.0000	.0000	.0000	.0000	.0000	.0000	.0000	.0000	.0000	.0000	.0000	.0000	.0000	.0045	38
	63	.0000	.0000	.0000	.0000	.0000	.0000	.0000	.0000	.0000	.0000	.0000	.0000	.0000	.0000	.0027	37
	64	.0000	.0000	.0000	.0000	.0000	.0000	.0000	.0000	.0000	.0000	.0000	.0000	.0000	.0000	.0016	36
	65	.0000	.0000	.0000	.0000	.0000	.0000	.0000	.0000	.0000	.0000	.0000	.0000	.0000	.0000	.0009	35
	66	.0000	.0000	.0000	.0000	.0000	.0000	.0000	.0000	.0000	.0000	.0000	.0000	.0000	.0000	.0005	34
	67	.0000	.0000	.0000	.0000	.0000	.0000	.0000	.0000	.0000	.0000	.0000	.0000	.0000	.0000	.0002	33
	68	.0000	.0000	.0000	.0000	.0000	.0000	.0000	.0000	.0000	.0000	.0000	.0000	.0000	.0000	.0001	32
	69	.0000	.0000	.0000	.0000	.0000	.0000	.0000	.0000	.0000	.0000	.0000	.0000	.0000	.0000	.0001	31
		π = .999	.995	.99	.98	.97	.96	.95	.90	.85	.80	.75	.70	2/3	.60	.50	r

Table F Binomial Distribution—Cumulative Terms

$$F_b(r|n, \pi) = \sum_{t=0}^{r} \binom{n}{t} \pi^t (1 - \pi)^{n-t}$$

n	r	π=.001	.01	.03	.05	.10	.20	.25	.50	.60	.65	.70	.75	.80	.90	.95	r
2	0	.9980	.9801	.9409	.9025	.8100	.6400	.5625	.2500	.1600	.1225	.0900	.0625	.0400	.0100	.0025	0
	1	1.0000	.9999	.9991	.9975	.9900	.9600	.9375	.7500	.6400	.5775	.5100	.4375	.3600	.1900	.0975	1
3	0	.9970	.9703	.9127	.8574	.7290	.5120	.4219	.1250	.0640	.0429	.0270	.0156	.0080	.0010	.0001	0
	1	1.0000	.9997	.9974	.9927	.9720	.8960	.8438	.5000	.3520	.2817	.2160	.1563	.1040	.0280	.0072	1
	2	1.0000	1.0000	1.0000	.9999	.9990	.9920	.9844	.8750	.7840	.7254	.6570	.5781	.4880	.2710	.1426	2
4	0	.9960	.9606	.8853	.8145	.6561	.4096	.3164	.0625	.0256	.0150	.0081	.0039	.0016	.0001	.0000	0
	1	1.0000	.9994	.9948	.9860	.9477	.8192	.7383	.3125	.1792	.1265	.0837	.0508	.0272	.0037	.0005	1
	2	1.0000	1.0000	.9999	.9995	.9963	.9728	.9492	.6875	.5248	.4370	.3483	.2617	.1808	.0523	.0140	2
	3	1.0000	1.0000	1.0000	1.0000	.9999	.9984	.9961	.9375	.8704	.8215	.7599	.6836	.5904	.3439	.1855	3
5	0	.9950	.9510	.8587	.7738	.5905	.3277	.2373	.0313	.0102	.0053	.0024	.0010	.0003	.0000	.0000	0
	1	1.0000	.9990	.9915	.9774	.9185	.7373	.6328	.1875	.0870	.0540	.0308	.0156	.0067	.0005	.0000	1
	2	1.0000	1.0000	.9997	.9988	.9914	.9421	.8965	.5000	.3174	.2352	.1631	.1035	.0579	.0086	.0012	2
	3	1.0000	1.0000	1.0000	1.0000	.9995	.9933	.9844	.8125	.6630	.5716	.4718	.3672	.2627	.0815	.0226	3
	4	1.0000	1.0000	1.0000	1.0000	1.0000	.9997	.9990	.9688	.9222	.8840	.8319	.7627	.6723	.4095	.2262	4
6	0	.9940	.9415	.8330	.7351	.5314	.2621	.1780	.0156	.0041	.0018	.0007	.0002	.0001	.0000	.0000	0
	1	1.0000	.9985	.9875	.9672	.8857	.6554	.5339	.1094	.0410	.0223	.0109	.0046	.0016	.0001	.0000	1
	2	1.0000	1.0000	.9995	.9978	.9841	.9011	.8306	.3438	.1792	.1174	.0705	.0370	.0170	.0013	.0001	2
	3	1.0000	1.0000	1.0000	.9999	.9987	.9830	.9624	.6563	.4557	.3529	.2557	.1694	.0989	.0158	.0022	3
	4	1.0000	1.0000	1.0000	1.0000	.9999	.9984	.9954	.8906	.7667	.6809	.5798	.4661	.3440	.1143	.0328	4
	5	1.0000	1.0000	1.0000	1.0000	1.0000	.9999	.9998	.9844	.9533	.9246	.8824	.8220	.7379	.4686	.2649	5
7	0	.9930	.9321	.8080	.6983	.4783	.2097	.1335	.0078	.0016	.0006	.0002	.0001	.0000	.0000	.0000	0
	1	1.0000	.9980	.9829	.9556	.8503	.5767	.4449	.0625	.0188	.0090	.0038	.0013	.0004	.0000	.0000	1
	2	1.0000	1.0000	.9991	.9962	.9743	.8520	.7564	.2266	.0963	.0556	.0288	.0129	.0047	.0002	.0000	2
	3	1.0000	1.0000	1.0000	.9998	.9973	.9667	.9294	.5000	.2898	.1998	.1260	.0706	.0333	.0027	.0002	3
	4	1.0000	1.0000	1.0000	1.0000	.9998	.9953	.9871	.7734	.5801	.4677	.3529	.2436	.1480	.0257	.0038	4
n	r	π=.001	.01	.03	.05	.10	.20	.25	.50	.60	.65	.70	.75	.80	.90	.95	r

Table F Binomial Distribution—Cumulative Terms (continued)

n	r	π = .001	.01	.03	.05	.10	.20	.25	.50	.60	.65	.70	.75	.80	.90	.95	r
7	5	1.0000	1.0000	1.0000	1.0000	1.0000	.9996	.9987	.9375	.8414	.7662	.6706	.5551	.4233	.1497	.0444	5
	6	1.0000	1.0000	1.0000	1.0000	1.0000	1.0000	.9999	.9922	.9720	.9510	.9176	.8665	.7903	.5217	.3017	6
8	0	.9920	.9227	.7837	.6634	.4305	.1678	.1001	.0039	.0007	.0002	.0001	.0000	.0000	.0000	.0000	0
	1	1.0000	.9973	.9777	.9428	.8131	.5033	.3671	.0352	.0085	.0036	.0013	.0004	.0001	.0000	.0000	1
	2	1.0000	.9999	.9986	.9942	.9619	.7969	.6785	.1445	.0498	.0253	.0113	.0042	.0012	.0004	.0000	2
	3	1.0000	1.0000	.9999	.9996	.9950	.9437	.8862	.3633	.1737	.1061	.0580	.0273	.0104	.0004	.0000	3
	4	1.0000	1.0000	1.0000	1.0000	.9996	.9896	.9727	.6367	.4059	.2936	.1941	.1138	.0563	.0050	.0004	4
	5	1.0000	1.0000	1.0000	1.0000	1.0000	.9988	.9958	.8555	.6846	.5722	.4482	.3215	.2031	.0381	.0058	5
	6	1.0000	1.0000	1.0000	1.0000	1.0000	.9999	.9996	.9648	.8936	.8309	.7447	.6329	.4967	.1869	.0572	6
	7	1.0000	1.0000	1.0000	1.0000	1.0000	1.0000	1.0000	.9961	.9832	.9681	.9424	.8999	.8322	.5695	.3366	7
9	0	.9910	.9135	.7602	.6302	.3874	.1342	.0751	.0020	.0003	.0001	.0000	.0000	.0000	.0000	.0000	0
	1	1.0000	.9966	.9718	.9288	.7748	.4362	.3003	.0195	.0038	.0014	.0004	.0001	.0000	.0000	.0000	1
	2	1.0000	.9999	.9980	.9916	.9470	.7382	.6007	.0898	.0250	.0112	.0043	.0013	.0003	.0000	.0000	2
	3	1.0000	1.0000	.9999	.9994	.9917	.9144	.8343	.2539	.0994	.0536	.0253	.0100	.0031	.0001	.0000	3
	4	1.0000	1.0000	1.0000	1.0000	.9991	.9804	.9511	.5000	.2666	.1717	.0988	.0489	.0196	.0009	.0000	4
	5	1.0000	1.0000	1.0000	1.0000	.9999	.9969	.9900	.7461	.5174	.3911	.2703	.1657	.0856	.0083	.0006	5
	6	1.0000	1.0000	1.0000	1.0000	1.0000	.9997	.9987	.9102	.7682	.6627	.5372	.3993	.2618	.0530	.0084	6
	7	1.0000	1.0000	1.0000	1.0000	1.0000	1.0000	.9999	.9805	.9295	.8789	.8040	.6997	.5638	.2252	.0712	7
	8	1.0000	1.0000	1.0000	1.0000	1.0000	1.0000	1.0000	.9980	.9899	.9793	.9596	.9249	.8658	.6126	.3698	8
10	0	.9900	.9044	.7374	.5987	.3487	.1074	.0563	.0010	.0001	.0000	.0000	.0000	.0000	.0000	.0000	0
	1	1.0000	.9957	.9655	.9139	.7361	.3758	.2440	.0107	.0017	.0005	.0001	.0000	.0000	.0000	.0000	1
	2	1.0000	.9999	.9972	.9885	.9298	.6778	.5256	.0547	.0123	.0048	.0016	.0004	.0001	.0000	.0000	2
	3	1.0000	1.0000	.9999	.9990	.9872	.8791	.7759	.1719	.0548	.0260	.0106	.0035	.0009	.0000	.0000	3
	4	1.0000	1.0000	1.0000	.9999	.9984	.9672	.9219	.3770	.1662	.0949	.0473	.0197	.0064	.0001	.0000	4
	5	1.0000	1.0000	1.0000	1.0000	.9999	.9936	.9803	.6230	.3669	.2485	.1503	.0781	.0328	.0016	.0001	5
	6	1.0000	1.0000	1.0000	1.0000	1.0000	.9991	.9965	.8281	.6177	.4862	.3504	.2241	.1209	.0128	.0010	6
	7	1.0000	1.0000	1.0000	1.0000	1.0000	.9999	.9996	.9453	.8327	.7384	.6172	.4744	.3222	.0702	.0115	7
n	r	π = .001	.01	.03	.05	.10	.20	.25	.50	.60	.65	.70	.75	.80	.90	.95	r

Table F Binomial Distribution—Cumulative Terms (continued)

n	r	π = .001	.01	.03	.05	.10	.20	.25	.50	.60	.65	.70	.75	.80	.90	.95	r
10	8	1.0000	1.0000	1.0000	1.0000	1.0000	1.0000	1.0000	.9893	.9536	.9140	.8507	.7560	.6242	.2639	.0861	8
	9	1.0000	1.0000	1.0000	1.0000	1.0000	1.0000	1.0000	.9990	.9940	.9865	.9718	.9437	.8926	.6513	.4013	9
11	0	.9891	.8953	.7153	.5688	.3138	.0859	.0422	.0005	.0000	.0000	.0000	.0000	.0000	.0000	.0000	0
	1	.9999	.9948	.9587	.8981	.6974	.3221	.1971	.0059	.0007	.0002	.0000	.0000	.0000	.0000	.0000	1
	2	1.0000	.9998	.9963	.9848	.9104	.6174	.4552	.0327	.0059	.0020	.0006	.0001	.0000	.0000	.0000	2
	3	1.0000	1.0000	.9998	.9984	.9815	.8389	.7133	.1133	.0293	.0122	.0043	.0012	.0002	.0000	.0000	3
	4	1.0000	1.0000	1.0000	.9999	.9972	.9496	.8854	.2744	.0994	.0501	.0216	.0076	.0020	.0000	.0000	4
	5	1.0000	1.0000	1.0000	1.0000	.9997	.9883	.9657	.5000	.2465	.1487	.0782	.0343	.0117	.0003	.0000	5
	6	1.0000	1.0000	1.0000	1.0000	1.0000	.9980	.9924	.7256	.4672	.3317	.2103	.1146	.0504	.0028	.0001	6
	7	1.0000	1.0000	1.0000	1.0000	1.0000	.9998	.9988	.8867	.7037	.5744	.4304	.2867	.1611	.0185	.0016	7
	8	1.0000	1.0000	1.0000	1.0000	1.0000	1.0000	.9999	.9673	.8811	.7999	.6873	.5448	.3826	.0896	.0152	8
	9	1.0000	1.0000	1.0000	1.0000	1.0000	1.0000	1.0000	.9941	.9698	.9394	.8870	.8029	.6779	.3026	.1019	9
	10	1.0000	1.0000	1.0000	1.0000	1.0000	1.0000	1.0000	.9995	.9964	.9912	.9802	.9578	.9141	.6862	.4312	10
12	0	.9881	.8864	.6938	.5404	.2824	.0687	.0317	.0002	.0000	.0000	.0000	.0000	.0000	.0000	.0000	0
	1	.9999	.9938	.9514	.8816	.6590	.2749	.1584	.0032	.0003	.0001	.0000	.0000	.0000	.0000	.0000	1
	2	1.0000	.9998	.9952	.9804	.8891	.5583	.3907	.0193	.0028	.0008	.0002	.0000	.0000	.0000	.0000	2
	3	1.0000	1.0000	.9997	.9978	.9744	.7946	.6488	.0730	.0153	.0056	.0017	.0004	.0001	.0000	.0000	3
	4	1.0000	1.0000	1.0000	.9998	.9957	.9274	.8424	.1938	.0573	.0255	.0095	.0028	.0006	.0000	.0000	4
	5	1.0000	1.0000	1.0000	1.0000	.9995	.9806	.9456	.3872	.1582	.0846	.0386	.0143	.0039	.0001	.0000	5
	6	1.0000	1.0000	1.0000	1.0000	.9999	.9961	.9857	.6128	.3348	.2127	.1178	.0544	.0194	.0005	.0000	6
	7	1.0000	1.0000	1.0000	1.0000	1.0000	.9994	.9972	.8062	.5618	.4167	.2763	.1576	.0726	.0043	.0002	7
	8	1.0000	1.0000	1.0000	1.0000	1.0000	.9999	.9996	.9270	.7747	.6533	.5075	.3512	.2054	.0256	.0022	8
	9	1.0000	1.0000	1.0000	1.0000	1.0000	1.0000	1.0000	.9807	.9166	.8487	.7472	.6093	.4417	.1109	.0196	9
	10	1.0000	1.0000	1.0000	1.0000	1.0000	1.0000	1.0000	.9968	.9804	.9576	.9150	.8416	.7251	.3410	.1184	10
	11	1.0000	1.0000	1.0000	1.0000	1.0000	1.0000	1.0000	.9998	.9978	.9943	.9862	.9683	.9313	.7176	.4596	11
13	0	.9871	.8775	.6730	.5133	.2542	.0550	.0238	.0001	.0000	.0000	.0000	.0000	.0000	.0000	.0000	0
n	r	π = .001	.01	.03	.05	.10	.20	.25	.50	.60	.65	.70	.75	.80	.90	.95	r

Table F Binomial Distribution—Cumulative Terms (continued)

n	r	π = .001	.01	.03	.05	.10	.20	.25	.50	.60	.65	.70	.75	.80	.90	.95	r
13	1	.9999	.9928	.9436	.8646	.6211	.2336	.1267	.0017	.0001	.0000	.0000	.0000	.0000	.0000	.0000	1
	2	1.0000	.9997	.9938	.9755	.8661	.5017	.3326	.0112	.0013	.0003	.0001	.0000	.0000	.0000	.0000	2
	3	1.0000	1.0000	.9995	.9969	.9658	.7473	.5843	.0461	.0078	.0025	.0007	.0001	.0000	.0000	.0000	3
	4	1.0000	1.0000	1.0000	.9997	.9935	.9009	.7940	.1334	.0321	.0126	.0040	.0010	.0002	.0000	.0000	4
	5	1.0000	1.0000	1.0000	1.0000	.9991	.9700	.9198	.2905	.0977	.0462	.0182	.0056	.0012	.0000	.0000	5
	6	1.0000	1.0000	1.0000	1.0000	.9999	.9930	.9757	.5000	.2288	.1295	.0624	.0243	.0070	.0001	.0000	6
	7	1.0000	1.0000	1.0000	1.0000	1.0000	.9988	.9944	.7095	.4256	.2841	.1654	.0802	.0300	.0009	.0000	7
	8	1.0000	1.0000	1.0000	1.0000	1.0000	.9998	.9990	.8666	.6470	.4995	.3457	.2060	.0991	.0065	.0003	8
	9	1.0000	1.0000	1.0000	1.0000	1.0000	1.0000	.9999	.9539	.8314	.7217	.5794	.4157	.2527	.0342	.0031	9
	10	1.0000	1.0000	1.0000	1.0000	1.0000	1.0000	1.0000	.9888	.9421	.8868	.7975	.6674	.4983	.1339	.0245	10
	11	1.0000	1.0000	1.0000	1.0000	1.0000	1.0000	1.0000	.9983	.9874	.9704	.9363	.8733	.7664	.3787	.1354	11
	12	1.0000	1.0000	1.0000	1.0000	1.0000	1.0000	1.0000	.9999	.9987	.9963	.9903	.9762	.9450	.7458	.4867	12
14	0	.9861	.8687	.6528	.4877	.2288	.0440	.0178	.0001	.0000	.0000	.0000	.0000	.0000	.0000	.0000	0
	1	.9999	.9916	.9355	.8470	.5846	.1979	.1010	.0009	.0001	.0000	.0000	.0000	.0000	.0000	.0000	1
	2	1.0000	.9997	.9923	.9699	.8416	.4481	.2811	.0065	.0006	.0001	.0000	.0000	.0000	.0000	.0000	2
	3	1.0000	1.0000	.9994	.9958	.9559	.6982	.5213	.0287	.0039	.0011	.0002	.0000	.0000	.0000	.0000	3
	4	1.0000	1.0000	1.0000	.9996	.9908	.8702	.7415	.0898	.0175	.0060	.0017	.0003	.0000	.0000	.0000	4
	5	1.0000	1.0000	1.0000	1.0000	.9985	.9561	.8883	.2120	.0583	.0243	.0083	.0022	.0004	.0000	.0000	5
	6	1.0000	1.0000	1.0000	1.0000	.9998	.9884	.9617	.3953	.1501	.0753	.0315	.0103	.0024	.0000	.0000	6
	7	1.0000	1.0000	1.0000	1.0000	1.0000	.9976	.9897	.6047	.3075	.1836	.0933	.0383	.0116	.0002	.0000	7
	8	1.0000	1.0000	1.0000	1.0000	1.0000	.9996	.9978	.7880	.5141	.3595	.2195	.1117	.0439	.0015	.0000	8
	9	1.0000	1.0000	1.0000	1.0000	1.0000	1.0000	.9997	.9102	.7207	.5773	.4158	.2585	.1298	.0092	.0004	9
	10	1.0000	1.0000	1.0000	1.0000	1.0000	1.0000	1.0000	.9713	.8757	.7795	.6448	.4787	.3018	.0441	.0042	10
	11	1.0000	1.0000	1.0000	1.0000	1.0000	1.0000	1.0000	.9935	.9602	.9161	.8392	.7189	.5519	.1584	.0301	11
	12	1.0000	1.0000	1.0000	1.0000	1.0000	1.0000	1.0000	.9991	.9919	.9795	.9525	.8990	.8021	.4154	.1530	12
	13	1.0000	1.0000	1.0000	1.0000	1.0000	1.0000	1.0000	.9999	.9992	.9976	.9932	.9822	.9560	.7712	.5123	13
15	0	.9851	.8601	.6333	.4633	.2059	.0352	.0134	.0000	.0000	.0000	.0000	.0000	.0000	.0000	.0000	0
n	r	π = .001	.01	.03	.05	.10	.20	.25	.50	.60	.65	.70	.75	.80	.90	.95	r

Table F Binomial Distribution—Cumulative Terms (continued)

n	r	π = .001	.01	.03	.05	.10	.20	.25	.50	.60	.65	.70	.75	.80	.90	.95	r
15	1	.9999	.9904	.9270	.8290	.5490	.1671	.0802	.0005	.0000	.0000	.0000	.0000	.0000	.0000	.0000	1
	2	1.0000	.9996	.9906	.9638	.8159	.3980	.2361	.0037	.0003	.0001	.0000	.0000	.0000	.0000	.0000	2
	3	1.0000	1.0000	.9992	.9945	.9444	.6482	.4613	.0176	.0019	.0005	.0001	.0000	.0000	.0000	.0000	3
	4	1.0000	1.0000	.9999	.9994	.9873	.8358	.6865	.0592	.0093	.0028	.0007	.0001	.0000	.0000	.0000	4
	5	1.0000	1.0000	1.0000	.9999	.9977	.9389	.8516	.1509	.0338	.0124	.0037	.0008	.0001	.0000	.0000	5
	6	1.0000	1.0000	1.0000	1.0000	.9997	.9819	.9434	.3036	.0950	.0422	.0152	.0042	.0008	.0000	.0000	6
	7	1.0000	1.0000	1.0000	1.0000	1.0000	.9958	.9827	.5000	.2131	.1132	.0500	.0173	.0042	.0000	.0000	7
	8	1.0000	1.0000	1.0000	1.0000	1.0000	.9992	.9958	.6964	.3902	.2452	.1311	.0566	.0181	.0003	.0000	8
	9	1.0000	1.0000	1.0000	1.0000	1.0000	.9999	.9992	.8491	.5968	.4357	.2784	.1484	.0611	.0022	.0001	9
	10	1.0000	1.0000	1.0000	1.0000	1.0000	1.0000	.9999	.9408	.7827	.6481	.4845	.3135	.1642	.0127	.0006	10
	11	1.0000	1.0000	1.0000	1.0000	1.0000	1.0000	1.0000	.9824	.9095	.8273	.7031	.5387	.3518	.0556	.0055	11
	12	1.0000	1.0000	1.0000	1.0000	1.0000	1.0000	1.0000	.9963	.9729	.9383	.8732	.7639	.6020	.1841	.0362	12
	13	1.0000	1.0000	1.0000	1.0000	1.0000	1.0000	1.0000	.9995	.9948	.9858	.9647	.9198	.8329	.4510	.1710	13
	14	1.0000	1.0000	1.0000	1.0000	1.0000	1.0000	1.0000	1.0000	.9995	.9984	.9953	.9866	.9648	.7941	.5367	14
16	0	.9841	.8515	.6143	.4401	.1853	.0281	.0100	.0000	.0000	.0000	.0000	.0000	.0000	.0000	.0000	0
	1	.9999	.9891	.9182	.8108	.5147	.1407	.0635	.0003	.0000	.0000	.0000	.0000	.0000	.0000	.0000	1
	2	1.0000	.9995	.9887	.9571	.7892	.3518	.1971	.0021	.0001	.0000	.0000	.0000	.0000	.0000	.0000	2
	3	1.0000	1.0000	.9989	.9930	.9316	.5981	.4050	.0106	.0009	.0002	.0000	.0000	.0000	.0000	.0000	3
	4	1.0000	1.0000	.9999	.9991	.9830	.7982	.6302	.0384	.0049	.0013	.0003	.0000	.0000	.0000	.0000	4
	5	1.0000	1.0000	1.0000	.9999	.9967	.9183	.8103	.1051	.0191	.0062	.0016	.0003	.0000	.0000	.0000	5
	6	1.0000	1.0000	1.0000	1.0000	.9995	.9733	.9204	.2272	.0583	.0229	.0071	.0016	.0002	.0000	.0000	6
	7	1.0000	1.0000	1.0000	1.0000	.9999	.9930	.9729	.4018	.1423	.0671	.0257	.0075	.0015	.0000	.0000	7
	8	1.0000	1.0000	1.0000	1.0000	1.0000	.9985	.9925	.5982	.2839	.1594	.0744	.0271	.0070	.0001	.0000	8
	9	1.0000	1.0000	1.0000	1.0000	1.0000	.9998	.9984	.7728	.4728	.3119	.1753	.0796	.0267	.0005	.0000	9
	10	1.0000	1.0000	1.0000	1.0000	1.0000	1.0000	.9997	.8949	.6712	.5100	.3402	.1897	.0817	.0033	.0001	10
	11	1.0000	1.0000	1.0000	1.0000	1.0000	1.0000	1.0000	.9616	.8334	.7108	.5501	.3698	.2018	.0170	.0009	11
	12	1.0000	1.0000	1.0000	1.0000	1.0000	1.0000	1.0000	.9894	.9349	.8661	.7541	.5950	.4019	.0684	.0070	12
	13	1.0000	1.0000	1.0000	1.0000	1.0000	1.0000	1.0000	.9979	.9817	.9549	.9006	.8029	.6482	.2108	.0429	13
n	r	π = .001	.01	.03	.05	.10	.20	.25	.50	.60	.65	.70	.75	.80	.90	.95	r

Table F Binomial Distribution—Cumulative Terms (continued)

n	r	π = .001	.01	.03	.05	.10	.20	.25	.50	.60	.65	.70	.75	.80	.90	.95	r
16	14	1.0000	1.0000	1.0000	1.0000	1.0000	1.0000	1.0000	.9997	.9967	.9902	.9739	.9365	.8593	.4853	.1822	14
	15	1.0000	1.0000	1.0000	1.0000	1.0000	1.0000	1.0000	1.0000	.9997	.9990	.9967	.9900	.9719	.8147	.5599	15
17	0	.9831	.8429	.5958	.4181	.1668	.0225	.0075	.0000	.0000	.0000	.0000	.0000	.0000	.0000	.0000	0
	1	.9999	.9877	.9091	.7922	.4818	.1182	.0501	.0001	.0000	.0000	.0000	.0000	.0000	.0000	.0000	1
	2	1.0000	.9994	.9866	.9497	.7618	.3096	.1637	.0012	.0001	.0000	.0000	.0000	.0000	.0000	.0000	2
	3	1.0000	1.0000	.9986	.9912	.9174	.5489	.3530	.0064	.0005	.0001	.0000	.0000	.0000	.0000	.0000	3
	4	1.0000	1.0000	.9999	.9988	.9779	.7582	.5739	.0245	.0025	.0006	.0001	.0000	.0000	.0000	.0000	4
	5	1.0000	1.0000	1.0000	.9999	.9953	.8943	.7653	.0717	.0106	.0030	.0007	.0001	.0000	.0000	.0000	5
	6	1.0000	1.0000	1.0000	1.0000	.9992	.9623	.8929	.1662	.0348	.0120	.0032	.0006	.0001	.0000	.0000	6
	7	1.0000	1.0000	1.0000	1.0000	.9999	.9891	.9598	.3145	.0919	.0383	.0127	.0031	.0005	.0000	.0000	7
	8	1.0000	1.0000	1.0000	1.0000	1.0000	.9974	.9876	.5000	.1989	.0994	.0403	.0124	.0026	.0000	.0000	8
	9	1.0000	1.0000	1.0000	1.0000	1.0000	.9995	.9969	.6855	.3595	.2128	.1046	.0402	.0109	.0001	.0000	9
	10	1.0000	1.0000	1.0000	1.0000	1.0000	1.0000	.9994	.8338	.5522	.3812	.2248	.1071	.0377	.0008	.0000	10
	11	1.0000	1.0000	1.0000	1.0000	1.0000	1.0000	.9999	.9283	.7361	.5803	.4032	.2347	.1057	.0047	.0001	11
	12	1.0000	1.0000	1.0000	1.0000	1.0000	1.0000	1.0000	.9755	.8740	.7652	.6113	.4261	.2418	.0221	.0012	12
	13	1.0000	1.0000	1.0000	1.0000	1.0000	1.0000	1.0000	.9936	.9536	.8972	.7981	.6470	.4511	.0826	.0088	13
	14	1.0000	1.0000	1.0000	1.0000	1.0000	1.0000	1.0000	.9988	.9877	.9673	.9226	.8363	.6904	.2382	.0503	14
	15	1.0000	1.0000	1.0000	1.0000	1.0000	1.0000	1.0000	.9999	.9979	.9933	.9807	.9499	.8818	.5182	.2078	15
	16	1.0000	1.0000	1.0000	1.0000	1.0000	1.0000	1.0000	1.0000	.9998	.9993	.9977	.9925	.9775	.8332	.5819	16
18	0	.9822	.8345	.5780	.3972	.1501	.0180	.0056	.0000	.0000	.0000	.0000	.0000	.0000	.0000	.0000	0
	1	.9998	.9862	.8997	.7735	.4503	.0991	.0395	.0001	.0000	.0000	.0000	.0000	.0000	.0000	.0000	1
	2	1.0000	.9993	.9843	.9419	.7338	.2713	.1353	.0007	.0000	.0000	.0000	.0000	.0000	.0000	.0000	2
	3	1.0000	1.0000	.9982	.9891	.9018	.5010	.3057	.0038	.0002	.0000	.0000	.0000	.0000	.0000	.0000	3
	4	1.0000	1.0000	.9998	.9985	.9718	.7164	.5187	.0154	.0013	.0003	.0000	.0000	.0000	.0000	.0000	4
	5	1.0000	1.0000	1.0000	.9998	.9936	.8671	.7175	.0481	.0058	.0014	.0003	.0000	.0000	.0000	.0000	5
	6	1.0000	1.0000	1.0000	1.0000	.9988	.9487	.8610	.1187	.0203	.0062	.0014	.0002	.0000	.0000	.0000	6
	7	1.0000	1.0000	1.0000	1.0000	.9998	.9837	.9431	.2403	.0576	.0212	.0061	.0012	.0002	.0000	.0000	7

Table F Binomial Distribution—Cumulative Terms (continued)

n	r	π = .001	.01	.03	.05	.10	.20	.25	.50	.60	.65	.70	.75	.80	.90	.95	r
18	8	1.0000	1.0000	1.0000	1.0000	1.0000	.9957	.9807	.4073	.1347	.0597	.0210	.0054	.0009	.0000	.0000	8
	9	1.0000	1.0000	1.0000	1.0000	1.0000	.9991	.9946	.5927	.2632	.1391	.0596	.0193	.0043	.0000	.0000	9
	10	1.0000	1.0000	1.0000	1.0000	1.0000	.9998	.9988	.7597	.4366	.2717	.1407	.0569	.0163	.0002	.0000	10
	11	1.0000	1.0000	1.0000	1.0000	1.0000	1.0000	.9998	.8811	.6257	.4509	.2783	.1390	.0513	.0012	.0000	11
	12	1.0000	1.0000	1.0000	1.0000	1.0000	1.0000	1.0000	.9519	.7912	.6450	.4656	.2825	.1329	.0064	.0002	12
	13	1.0000	1.0000	1.0000	1.0000	1.0000	1.0000	1.0000	.9846	.9058	.8114	.6673	.4813	.2836	.0282	.0015	13
	14	1.0000	1.0000	1.0000	1.0000	1.0000	1.0000	1.0000	.9962	.9672	.9217	.8354	.6943	.4990	.0982	.0109	14
	15	1.0000	1.0000	1.0000	1.0000	1.0000	1.0000	1.0000	.9993	.9918	.9764	.9400	.8647	.7287	.2662	.0581	15
	16	1.0000	1.0000	1.0000	1.0000	1.0000	1.0000	1.0000	.9999	.9987	.9954	.9858	.9605	.9009	.5497	.2265	16
	17	1.0000	1.0000	1.0000	1.0000	1.0000	1.0000	1.0000	1.0000	.9999	.9996	.9984	.9944	.9820	.8499	.6028	17
19	0	.9812	.8262	.5606	.3774	.1351	.0144	.0042	.0000	.0000	.0000	.0000	.0000	.0000	.0000	.0000	0
	1	.9998	.9847	.8900	.7547	.4203	.0829	.0310	.0000	.0000	.0000	.0000	.0000	.0000	.0000	.0000	1
	2	1.0000	.9991	.9817	.9335	.7054	.2369	.1113	.0004	.0000	.0000	.0000	.0000	.0000	.0000	.0000	2
	3	1.0000	1.0000	.9978	.9868	.8850	.4551	.2631	.0022	.0001	.0000	.0000	.0000	.0000	.0000	.0000	3
	4	1.0000	1.0000	.9998	.9980	.9648	.6733	.4654	.0096	.0006	.0001	.0000	.0000	.0000	.0000	.0000	4
	5	1.0000	1.0000	1.0000	.9998	.9914	.8369	.6678	.0318	.0031	.0007	.0001	.0000	.0000	.0000	.0000	5
	6	1.0000	1.0000	1.0000	1.0000	.9983	.9324	.8251	.0835	.0116	.0031	.0006	.0001	.0000	.0000	.0000	6
	7	1.0000	1.0000	1.0000	1.0000	.9997	.9767	.9225	.1796	.0352	.0114	.0028	.0005	.0000	.0000	.0000	7
	8	1.0000	1.0000	1.0000	1.0000	1.0000	.9933	.9713	.3238	.0885	.0347	.0105	.0023	.0003	.0000	.0000	8
	9	1.0000	1.0000	1.0000	1.0000	1.0000	.9984	.9911	.5000	.1861	.0875	.0326	.0089	.0016	.0000	.0000	9
	10	1.0000	1.0000	1.0000	1.0000	1.0000	.9997	.9977	.6762	.3325	.1855	.0839	.0287	.0067	.0000	.0000	10
	11	1.0000	1.0000	1.0000	1.0000	1.0000	.9999	.9995	.8204	.5122	.3344	.1820	.0775	.0233	.0003	.0000	11
	12	1.0000	1.0000	1.0000	1.0000	1.0000	1.0000	.9999	.9165	.6919	.5188	.3345	.1749	.0676	.0017	.0000	12
	13	1.0000	1.0000	1.0000	1.0000	1.0000	1.0000	1.0000	.9682	.8371	.7032	.5261	.3322	.1631	.0086	.0002	13
	14	1.0000	1.0000	1.0000	1.0000	1.0000	1.0000	1.0000	.9904	.9304	.8500	.7178	.5346	.3267	.0352	.0020	14
	15	1.0000	1.0000	1.0000	1.0000	1.0000	1.0000	1.0000	.9978	.9770	.9409	.8668	.7369	.5449	.1150	.0132	15
	16	1.0000	1.0000	1.0000	1.0000	1.0000	1.0000	1.0000	.9996	.9945	.9830	.9538	.8887	.7631	.2946	.0665	16
n		π = .001	.01	.03	.05	.10	.20	.25	.50	.60	.65	.70	.75	.80	.90	.95	r

Table F Binomial Distribution—Cumulative Terms (continued)

n	r	π = .001	.01	.03	.05	.10	.20	.25	.50	.60	.65	.70	.75	.80	.90	.95	r
19	17	1.0000	1.0000	1.0000	1.0000	1.0000	1.0000	1.0000	1.0000	.9992	.9969	.9896	.9690	.9171	.5797	.2453	17
	18	1.0000	1.0000	1.0000	1.0000	1.0000	1.0000	1.0000	1.0000	.9999	.9997	.9989	.9958	.9856	.8649	.6226	18
20	0	.9802	.8179	.5438	.3585	.1216	.0115	.0032	.0000	.0000	.0000	.0000	.0000	.0000	.0000	.0000	0
	1	.9998	.9831	.8802	.7358	.3917	.0692	.0243	.0000	.0000	.0000	.0000	.0000	.0000	.0000	.0000	1
	2	1.0000	.9990	.9790	.9245	.6769	.2061	.0913	.0002	.0000	.0000	.0000	.0000	.0000	.0000	.0000	2
	3	1.0000	1.0000	.9973	.9841	.8670	.4114	.2252	.0013	.0000	.0000	.0000	.0000	.0000	.0000	.0000	3
	4	1.0000	1.0000	.9997	.9974	.9568	.6296	.4148	.0059	.0003	.0000	.0000	.0000	.0000	.0000	.0000	4
	5	1.0000	1.0000	1.0000	.9997	.9887	.8042	.6172	.0207	.0016	.0003	.0000	.0000	.0000	.0000	.0000	5
	6	1.0000	1.0000	1.0000	1.0000	.9976	.9133	.7858	.0577	.0065	.0015	.0003	.0000	.0000	.0000	.0000	6
	7	1.0000	1.0000	1.0000	1.0000	.9996	.9679	.8982	.1316	.0210	.0060	.0013	.0002	.0001	.0000	.0000	7
	8	1.0000	1.0000	1.0000	1.0000	.9999	.9900	.9591	.2517	.0565	.0196	.0051	.0009	.0006	.0000	.0000	8
	9	1.0000	1.0000	1.0000	1.0000	1.0000	.9974	.9861	.4119	.1275	.0532	.0171	.0039	.0006	.0000	.0000	9
	10	1.0000	1.0000	1.0000	1.0000	1.0000	.9994	.9961	.5881	.2447	.1218	.0480	.0139	.0026	.0000	.0000	10
	11	1.0000	1.0000	1.0000	1.0000	1.0000	.9999	.9991	.7483	.4044	.2376	.1133	.0409	.0100	.0001	.0000	11
	12	1.0000	1.0000	1.0000	1.0000	1.0000	1.0000	.9998	.8684	.5841	.3990	.2277	.1018	.0321	.0004	.0000	12
	13	1.0000	1.0000	1.0000	1.0000	1.0000	1.0000	1.0000	.9423	.7500	.5834	.3920	.2142	.0867	.0024	.0000	13
	14	1.0000	1.0000	1.0000	1.0000	1.0000	1.0000	1.0000	.9793	.8744	.7546	.5836	.3828	.1958	.0113	.0003	14
	15	1.0000	1.0000	1.0000	1.0000	1.0000	1.0000	1.0000	.9941	.9490	.8818	.7625	.5852	.3704	.0432	.0026	15
	16	1.0000	1.0000	1.0000	1.0000	1.0000	1.0000	1.0000	.9987	.9840	.9556	.8929	.7748	.5886	.1330	.0159	16
	17	1.0000	1.0000	1.0000	1.0000	1.0000	1.0000	1.0000	.9998	.9964	.9879	.9645	.9087	.7939	.3231	.0755	17
	18	1.0000	1.0000	1.0000	1.0000	1.0000	1.0000	1.0000	1.0000	.9995	.9979	.9924	.9757	.9308	.6083	.2642	18
	19	1.0000	1.0000	1.0000	1.0000	1.0000	1.0000	1.0000	1.0000	1.0000	.9998	.9992	.9968	.9885	.8784	.6415	19
25	0	.9753	.7778	.4670	.2774	.0718	.0038	.0008	.0000	.0000	.0000	.0000	.0000	.0000	.0000	.0000	0
	1	.9997	.9742	.8280	.6424	.2712	.0274	.0070	.0000	.0000	.0000	.0000	.0000	.0000	.0000	.0000	1
	2	1.0000	.9980	.9620	.8729	.5371	.0982	.0321	.0000	.0000	.0000	.0000	.0000	.0000	.0000	.0000	2
	3	1.0000	.9999	.9938	.9659	.7636	.2340	.0962	.0001	.0000	.0000	.0000	.0000	.0000	.0000	.0000	3
	4	1.0000	1.0000	.9992	.9928	.9020	.4207	.2137	.0005	.0000	.0000	.0000	.0000	.0000	.0000	.0000	4
n	r	π = .001	.01	.03	.05	.10	.20	.25	.50	.60	.65	.70	.75	.80	.90	.95	r

Table F Binomial Distribution—Cumulative Terms (continued)

n	r	π = .001	.01	.03	.05	.10	.20	.25	.50	.60	.65	.70	.75	.80	.90	.95	r
25	5	1.0000	1.0000	.9999	.9988	.9666	.6167	.3783	.0020	.0001	.0000	.0000	.0000	.0000	.0000	.0000	5
	6	1.0000	1.0000	1.0000	.9998	.9905	.7800	.5611	.0073	.0003	.0000	.0000	.0000	.0000	.0000	.0000	6
	7	1.0000	1.0000	1.0000	1.0000	.9977	.8909	.7265	.0216	.0012	.0002	.0000	.0000	.0000	.0000	.0000	7
	8	1.0000	1.0000	1.0000	1.0000	.9995	.9532	.8506	.0539	.0043	.0008	.0001	.0000	.0000	.0000	.0000	8
	9	1.0000	1.0000	1.0000	1.0000	.9999	.9827	.9287	.1148	.0132	.0029	.0005	.0000	.0000	.0000	.0000	9
	10	1.0000	1.0000	1.0000	1.0000	1.0000	.9944	.9703	.2122	.0344	.0093	.0018	.0002	.0000	.0000	.0000	10
	11	1.0000	1.0000	1.0000	1.0000	1.0000	.9985	.9893	.3450	.0778	.0255	.0060	.0009	.0001	.0000	.0000	11
	12	1.0000	1.0000	1.0000	1.0000	1.0000	.9996	.9966	.5000	.1538	.0604	.0175	.0038	.0004	.0000	.0000	12
	13	1.0000	1.0000	1.0000	1.0000	1.0000	.9999	.9991	.6550	.2677	.1254	.0442	.0107	.0015	.0000	.0000	13
	14	1.0000	1.0000	1.0000	1.0000	1.0000	1.0000	.9998	.7878	.4142	.2288	.0978	.0297	.0056	.0000	.0000	14
	15	1.0000	1.0000	1.0000	1.0000	1.0000	1.0000	1.0000	.8852	.5754	.3697	.1894	.0713	.0173	.0001	.0000	15
	16	1.0000	1.0000	1.0000	1.0000	1.0000	1.0000	1.0000	.9461	.7265	.5332	.3231	.1494	.0468	.0005	.0000	16
	17	1.0000	1.0000	1.0000	1.0000	1.0000	1.0000	1.0000	.9784	.8464	.6939	.4882	.2735	.1091	.0023	.0000	17
	18	1.0000	1.0000	1.0000	1.0000	1.0000	1.0000	1.0000	.9927	.9264	.8266	.6593	.4389	.2200	.0095	.0002	18
	19	1.0000	1.0000	1.0000	1.0000	1.0000	1.0000	1.0000	.9980	.9706	.9174	.8065	.6217	.3833	.0334	.0012	19
	20	1.0000	1.0000	1.0000	1.0000	1.0000	1.0000	1.0000	.9995	.9905	.9680	.9095	.7863	.5793	.0980	.0072	20
	21	1.0000	1.0000	1.0000	1.0000	1.0000	1.0000	1.0000	.9999	.9976	.9903	.9668	.9038	.7660	.2364	.0341	21
	22	1.0000	1.0000	1.0000	1.0000	1.0000	1.0000	1.0000	1.0000	.9996	.9979	.9910	.9679	.9018	.4629	.1271	22
	23	1.0000	1.0000	1.0000	1.0000	1.0000	1.0000	1.0000	1.0000	.9999	.9997	.9984	.9930	.9726	.7288	.3576	23
	24	1.0000	1.0000	1.0000	1.0000	1.0000	1.0000	1.0000	1.0000	1.0000	1.0000	.9999	.9992	.9962	.9282	.7226	24
50	0	.9512	.6050	.2181	.0769	.0052	.0000	.0000	.0000	.0000	.0000	.0000	.0000	.0000	.0000	.0000	0
	1	.9988	.9106	.5553	.2794	.0338	.0000	.0000	.0000	.0000	.0000	.0000	.0000	.0000	.0000	.0000	1
	2	1.0000	.9862	.8108	.5405	.1117	.0013	.0001	.0000	.0000	.0000	.0000	.0000	.0000	.0000	.0000	2
	3	1.0000	.9984	.9372	.7604	.2503	.0057	.0005	.0000	.0000	.0000	.0000	.0000	.0000	.0000	.0000	3
	4	1.0000	.9999	.9832	.8964	.4312	.0185	.0021	.0000	.0000	.0000	.0000	.0000	.0000	.0000	.0000	4
	5	1.0000	1.0000	.9963	.9622	.6161	.0480	.0070	.0000	.0000	.0000	.0000	.0000	.0000	.0000	.0000	5
	6	1.0000	1.0000	.9993	.9882	.7702	.1034	.0194	.0000	.0000	.0000	.0000	.0000	.0000	.0000	.0000	6
n	r	π = .001	.01	.03	.05	.10	.20	.25	.50	.60	.65	.70	.75	.80	.90	.95	r

Table F Binomial Distribution—Cumulative Terms (continued)

n	r	π = .001	.01	.03	.05	.10	.20	.25	.50	.60	.65	.70	.75	.80	.90	.95
50	7	1.0000	1.0000	.9999	.9968	.8779	.1904	.0453	.0000	.0000	.0000	.0000	.0000	.0000	.0000	.0000
	8	1.0000	1.0000	1.0000	.9992	.9421	.3073	.0916	.0000	.0000	.0000	.0000	.0000	.0000	.0000	.0000
	9	1.0000	1.0000	1.0000	.9998	.9755	.4437	.1637	.0000	.0000	.0000	.0000	.0000	.0000	.0000	.0000
	10	1.0000	1.0000	1.0000	1.0000	.9906	.5836	.2622	.0000	.0000	.0000	.0000	.0000	.0000	.0000	.0000
	11	1.0000	1.0000	1.0000	1.0000	.9968	.7107	.3816	.0000	.0000	.0000	.0000	.0000	.0000	.0000	.0000
	12	1.0000	1.0000	1.0000	1.0000	.9990	.8139	.5110	.0002	.0000	.0000	.0000	.0000	.0000	.0000	.0000
	13	1.0000	1.0000	1.0000	1.0000	.9997	.8894	.6370	.0005	.0000	.0000	.0000	.0000	.0000	.0000	.0000
	14	1.0000	1.0000	1.0000	1.0000	.9999	.9393	.7481	.0013	.0000	.0000	.0000	.0000	.0000	.0000	.0000
	15	1.0000	1.0000	1.0000	1.0000	1.0000	.9692	.8369	.0033	.0000	.0000	.0000	.0000	.0000	.0000	.0000
	16	1.0000	1.0000	1.0000	1.0000	1.0000	.9856	.9017	.0077	.0001	.0000	.0000	.0000	.0000	.0000	.0000
	17	1.0000	1.0000	1.0000	1.0000	1.0000	.9937	.9449	.0164	.0002	.0000	.0000	.0000	.0000	.0000	.0000
	18	1.0000	1.0000	1.0000	1.0000	1.0000	.9975	.9713	.0325	.0005	.0000	.0000	.0000	.0000	.0000	.0000
	19	1.0000	1.0000	1.0000	1.0000	1.0000	.9991	.9861	.0595	.0014	.0001	.0000	.0000	.0000	.0000	.0000
	20	1.0000	1.0000	1.0000	1.0000	1.0000	.9997	.9937	.1013	.0034	.0003	.0000	.0000	.0000	.0000	.0000
	21	1.0000	1.0000	1.0000	1.0000	1.0000	.9999	.9974	.1611	.0076	.0007	.0000	.0000	.0000	.0000	.0000
	22	1.0000	1.0000	1.0000	1.0000	1.0000	1.0000	.9990	.2399	.0160	.0019	.0001	.0000	.0000	.0000	.0000
	23	1.0000	1.0000	1.0000	1.0000	1.0000	1.0000	.9996	.3359	.0314	.0045	.0003	.0000	.0000	.0000	.0000
	24	1.0000	1.0000	1.0000	1.0000	1.0000	1.0000	.9999	.4439	.0573	.0100	.0009	.0000	.0000	.0000	.0000
	25	1.0000	1.0000	1.0000	1.0000	1.0000	1.0000	1.0000	.5561	.0978	.0207	.0024	.0001	.0000	.0000	.0000
	26	1.0000	1.0000	1.0000	1.0000	1.0000	1.0000	1.0000	.6641	.1562	.0396	.0056	.0004	.0000	.0000	.0000
	27	1.0000	1.0000	1.0000	1.0000	1.0000	1.0000	1.0000	.7601	.2340	.0710	.0123	.0010	.0000	.0000	.0000
	28	1.0000	1.0000	1.0000	1.0000	1.0000	1.0000	1.0000	.8389	.3299	.1187	.0251	.0026	.0001	.0000	.0000
	29	1.0000	1.0000	1.0000	1.0000	1.0000	1.0000	1.0000	.8987	.4390	.1861	.0478	.0063	.0003	.0000	.0000
	30	1.0000	1.0000	1.0000	1.0000	1.0000	1.0000	1.0000	.9405	.5535	.2736	.0848	.0139	.0009	.0000	.0000
	31	1.0000	1.0000	1.0000	1.0000	1.0000	1.0000	1.0000	.9675	.6644	.3784	.1406	.0287	.0025	.0000	.0000
	32	1.0000	1.0000	1.0000	1.0000	1.0000	1.0000	1.0000	.9836	.7631	.4940	.2178	.0551	.0063	.0000	.0000
	33	1.0000	1.0000	1.0000	1.0000	1.0000	1.0000	1.0000	.9923	.8439	.6111	.3161	.0983	.0144	.0000	.0000
	34	1.0000	1.0000	1.0000	1.0000	1.0000	1.0000	1.0000	.9967	.9045	.7199	.4308	.1631	.0308	.0000	.0000
n	r	π = .001	.01	.03	.05	.10	.20	.25	.50	.60	.65	.70	.75	.80	.90	.95

Table F Binomial Distribution—Cumulative Terms (continued)

n	r	π = .001	.01	.03	.05	.10	.20	.25	.50	.60	.65	.70	.75	.80	.90	.95	r
50	35	1.0000	1.0000	1.0000	1.0000	1.0000	1.0000	1.0000	.9987	.9460	.8122	.5532	.2519	.0607	.0001	.0000	35
	36	1.0000	1.0000	1.0000	1.0000	1.0000	1.0000	1.0000	.9995	.9720	.8837	.6721	.3630	.1106	.0003	.0000	36
	37	1.0000	1.0000	1.0000	1.0000	1.0000	1.0000	1.0000	.9998	.9867	.9339	.7771	.4890	.1861	.0010	.0000	37
	38	1.0000	1.0000	1.0000	1.0000	1.0000	1.0000	1.0000	1.0000	.9943	.9658	.8610	.6184	.2893	.0032	.0000	38
	39	1.0000	1.0000	1.0000	1.0000	1.0000	1.0000	1.0000	1.0000	.9978	.9840	.9211	.7378	.4164	.0094	.0000	39
	40	1.0000	1.0000	1.0000	1.0000	1.0000	1.0000	1.0000	1.0000	.9992	.9933	.9598	.8363	.5563	.0245	.0002	40
	41	1.0000	1.0000	1.0000	1.0000	1.0000	1.0000	1.0000	1.0000	.9998	.9975	.9817	.9084	.6927	.0579	.0008	41
	42	1.0000	1.0000	1.0000	1.0000	1.0000	1.0000	1.0000	1.0000	.9999	.9992	.9927	.9547	.8096	.1221	.0032	42
	43	1.0000	1.0000	1.0000	1.0000	1.0000	1.0000	1.0000	1.0000	1.0000	.9998	.9975	.9806	.8966	.2298	.0118	43
	44	1.0000	1.0000	1.0000	1.0000	1.0000	1.0000	1.0000	1.0000	1.0000	.9999	.9993	.9930	.9520	.3839	.0378	44
	45	1.0000	1.0000	1.0000	1.0000	1.0000	1.0000	1.0000	1.0000	1.0000	1.0000	.9998	.9979	.9815	.5688	.1036	45
	46	1.0000	1.0000	1.0000	1.0000	1.0000	1.0000	1.0000	1.0000	1.0000	1.0000	1.0000	.9995	.9943	.7497	.2396	46
	47	1.0000	1.0000	1.0000	1.0000	1.0000	1.0000	1.0000	1.0000	1.0000	1.0000	1.0000	.9999	.9987	.8883	.4595	47
	48	1.0000	1.0000	1.0000	1.0000	1.0000	1.0000	1.0000	1.0000	1.0000	1.0000	1.0000	1.0000	.9998	.9662	.7206	48
	49	1.0000	1.0000	1.0000	1.0000	1.0000	1.0000	1.0000	1.0000	1.0000	1.0000	1.0000	1.0000	1.0000	.9948	.9231	49
75	0	.9277	.4706	.1018	.0213	.0004	.0000	.0000	.0000	.0000	.0000	.0000	.0000	.0000	.0000	.0000	0
	1	.9974	.8271	.3380	.1056	.0035	.0000	.0000	.0000	.0000	.0000	.0000	.0000	.0000	.0000	.0000	1
	2	.9999	.9603	.6083	.2697	.0161	.0000	.0000	.0000	.0000	.0000	.0000	.0000	.0000	.0000	.0000	2
	3	1.0000	.9931	.8118	.4798	.0504	.0001	.0000	.0000	.0000	.0000	.0000	.0000	.0000	.0000	.0000	3
	4	1.0000	.9990	.9250	.6789	.1189	.0003	.0000	.0000	.0000	.0000	.0000	.0000	.0000	.0000	.0000	4
	5	1.0000	.9999	.9747	.8276	.2271	.0012	.0000	.0000	.0000	.0000	.0000	.0000	.0000	.0000	.0000	5
	6	1.0000	1.0000	.9927	.9190	.3673	.0039	.0002	.0000	.0000	.0000	.0000	.0000	.0000	.0000	.0000	6
	7	1.0000	1.0000	.9981	.9664	.5208	.0104	.0005	.0000	.0000	.0000	.0000	.0000	.0000	.0000	.0000	7
	8	1.0000	1.0000	.9996	.9876	.6658	.0243	.0016	.0000	.0000	.0000	.0000	.0000	.0000	.0000	.0000	8
	9	1.0000	1.0000	.9999	.9959	.7858	.0501	.0044	.0000	.0000	.0000	.0000	.0000	.0000	.0000	.0000	9
	10	1.0000	1.0000	1.0000	.9988	.8737	.0928	.0103	.0000	.0000	.0000	.0000	.0000	.0000	.0000	.0000	10
	11	1.0000	1.0000	1.0000	.9997	.9315	.1557	.0221	.0000	.0000	.0000	.0000	.0000	.0000	.0000	.0000	11
	12	1.0000	1.0000	1.0000	.9999	.9657	.2397	.0431	.0000	.0000	.0000	.0000	.0000	.0000	.0000	.0000	12
n	r	π = .001	.01	.03	.05	.10	.20	.25	.50	.60	.65	.70	.75	.80	.90	.95	r

Table F Binomial Distribution—Cumulative Terms (continued)

n	r	π = .001	.01	.03	.05	.10	.20	.25	.50	.60	.65	.70	.75	.80	.90	.95	r
75	13	1.0000	1.0000	1.0000	1.0000	.9841	.3414	.0769	.0000	.0000	.0000	.0000	.0000	.0000	.0000	.0000	13
	14	1.0000	1.0000	1.0000	1.0000	.9932	.4540	.1269	.0000	.0000	.0000	.0000	.0000	.0000	.0000	.0000	14
	15	1.0000	1.0000	1.0000	1.0000	.9973	.5685	.1946	.0000	.0000	.0000	.0000	.0000	.0000	.0000	.0000	15
	16	1.0000	1.0000	1.0000	1.0000	.9990	.6759	.2792	.0000	.0000	.0000	.0000	.0000	.0000	.0000	.0000	16
	17	1.0000	1.0000	1.0000	1.0000	.9996	.7690	.3772	.0000	.0000	.0000	.0000	.0000	.0000	.0000	.0000	17
	18	1.0000	1.0000	1.0000	1.0000	.9999	.8440	.4823	.0000	.0000	.0000	.0000	.0000	.0000	.0000	.0000	18
	19	1.0000	1.0000	1.0000	1.0000	1.0000	.9003	.5875	.0000	.0000	.0000	.0000	.0000	.0000	.0000	.0000	19
	20	1.0000	1.0000	1.0000	1.0000	1.0000	.9397	.6857	.0000	.0000	.0000	.0000	.0000	.0000	.0000	.0000	20
	21	1.0000	1.0000	1.0000	1.0000	1.0000	.9654	.7714	.0001	.0000	.0000	.0000	.0000	.0000	.0000	.0000	21
	22	1.0000	1.0000	1.0000	1.0000	1.0000	.9813	.8415	.0002	.0000	.0000	.0000	.0000	.0000	.0000	.0000	22
	23	1.0000	1.0000	1.0000	1.0000	1.0000	.9904	.8954	.0005	.0000	.0000	.0000	.0000	.0000	.0000	.0000	23
	24	1.0000	1.0000	1.0000	1.0000	1.0000	.9953	.9343	.0012	.0000	.0000	.0000	.0000	.0000	.0000	.0000	24
	25	1.0000	1.0000	1.0000	1.0000	1.0000	.9978	.9607	.0026	.0000	.0000	.0000	.0000	.0000	.0000	.0000	25
	26	1.0000	1.0000	1.0000	1.0000	1.0000	.9991	.9777	.0053	.0000	.0000	.0000	.0000	.0000	.0000	.0000	26
	27	1.0000	1.0000	1.0000	1.0000	1.0000	.9996	.9879	.0101	.0000	.0000	.0000	.0000	.0000	.0000	.0000	27
	28	1.0000	1.0000	1.0000	1.0000	1.0000	.9998	.9938	.0185	.0001	.0000	.0000	.0000	.0000	.0000	.0000	28
	29	1.0000	1.0000	1.0000	1.0000	1.0000	.9999	.9970	.0320	.0002	.0000	.0000	.0000	.0000	.0000	.0000	29
	30	1.0000	1.0000	1.0000	1.0000	1.0000	1.0000	.9986	.0527	.0004	.0000	.0000	.0000	.0000	.0000	.0000	30
	31	1.0000	1.0000	1.0000	1.0000	1.0000	1.0000	.9994	.0827	.0008	.0000	.0000	.0000	.0000	.0000	.0000	31
	32	1.0000	1.0000	1.0000	1.0000	1.0000	1.0000	.9997	.1240	.0018	.0001	.0000	.0000	.0000	.0000	.0000	32
	33	1.0000	1.0000	1.0000	1.0000	1.0000	1.0000	.9999	.1778	.0037	.0002	.0000	.0000	.0000	.0000	.0000	33
	34	1.0000	1.0000	1.0000	1.0000	1.0000	1.0000	1.0000	.2443	.0072	.0004	.0000	.0000	.0000	.0000	.0000	34
	35	1.0000	1.0000	1.0000	1.0000	1.0000	1.0000	1.0000	.3222	.0133	.0009	.0000	.0000	.0000	.0000	.0000	35
	36	1.0000	1.0000	1.0000	1.0000	1.0000	1.0000	1.0000	.4088	.0235	.0019	.0001	.0000	.0000	.0000	.0000	36
	37	1.0000	1.0000	1.0000	1.0000	1.0000	1.0000	1.0000	.5000	.0396	.0038	.0001	.0000	.0000	.0000	.0000	37
	38	1.0000	1.0000	1.0000	1.0000	1.0000	1.0000	1.0000	.5912	.0637	.0074	.0003	.0000	.0000	.0000	.0000	38
	39	1.0000	1.0000	1.0000	1.0000	1.0000	1.0000	1.0000	.6778	.0981	.0138	.0008	.0000	.0000	.0000	.0000	39
n	r	π = .001	.01	.03	.05	.10	.20	.25	.50	.60	.65	.70	.75	.80	.90	.95	r

Table F Binomial Distribution—Cumulative Terms (continued)

n	r	π = .001	.01	.03	.05	.10	.20	.25	.50	.60	.65	.70	.75	.80	.90	.95	r
75	40	1.0000	1.0000	1.0000	1.0000	1.0000	1.0000	1.0000	.7557	.1446	.0245	.0017	.0000	.0000	.0000	.0000	40
	41	1.0000	1.0000	1.0000	1.0000	1.0000	1.0000	1.0000	.8221	.2041	.0414	.0036	.0001	.0000	.0000	.0000	41
	42	1.0000	1.0000	1.0000	1.0000	1.0000	1.0000	1.0000	.8760	.2763	.0668	.0071	.0003	.0000	.0000	.0000	42
	43	1.0000	1.0000	1.0000	1.0000	1.0000	1.0000	1.0000	.9173	.3594	.1030	.0134	.0006	.0000	.0000	.0000	43
	44	1.0000	1.0000	1.0000	1.0000	1.0000	1.0000	1.0000	.9473	.4501	.1519	.0242	.0014	.0000	.0000	.0000	44
	45	1.0000	1.0000	1.0000	1.0000	1.0000	1.0000	1.0000	.9680	.5438	.2144	.0414	.0030	.0001	.0000	.0000	45
	46	1.0000	1.0000	1.0000	1.0000	1.0000	1.0000	1.0000	.9815	.6354	.2902	.0676	.0062	.0002	.0000	.0000	46
	47	1.0000	1.0000	1.0000	1.0000	1.0000	1.0000	1.0000	.9898	.7203	.3770	.1053	.0120	.0004	.0000	.0000	47
	48	1.0000	1.0000	1.0000	1.0000	1.0000	1.0000	1.0000	.9947	.7945	.4711	.1567	.0223	.0009	.0000	.0000	48
	49	1.0000	1.0000	1.0000	1.0000	1.0000	1.0000	1.0000	.9974	.8558	.5673	.2227	.0393	.0021	.0000	.0000	49
	50	1.0000	1.0000	1.0000	1.0000	1.0000	1.0000	1.0000	.9988	.9037	.6603	.3029	.0657	.0047	.0000	.0000	50
	51	1.0000	1.0000	1.0000	1.0000	1.0000	1.0000	1.0000	.9995	.9389	.7449	.3945	.1046	.0096	.0000	.0000	51
	52	1.0000	1.0000	1.0000	1.0000	1.0000	1.0000	1.0000	.9998	.9633	.8174	.4932	.1585	.0187	.0000	.0000	52
	53	1.0000	1.0000	1.0000	1.0000	1.0000	1.0000	1.0000	.9999	.9791	.8759	.5932	.2286	.0345	.0000	.0000	53
	54	1.0000	1.0000	1.0000	1.0000	1.0000	1.0000	1.0000	1.0000	.9888	.9201	.6882	.3143	.0603	.0000	.0000	54
	55	1.0000	1.0000	1.0000	1.0000	1.0000	1.0000	1.0000	1.0000	.9944	.9515	.7729	.4125	.0997	.0000	.0000	55
	56	1.0000	1.0000	1.0000	1.0000	1.0000	1.0000	1.0000	1.0000	.9973	.9723	.8434	.5176	.1560	.0001	.0000	56
	57	1.0000	1.0000	1.0000	1.0000	1.0000	1.0000	1.0000	1.0000	.9988	.9851	.8983	.6228	.2310	.0003	.0000	57
	58	1.0000	1.0000	1.0000	1.0000	1.0000	1.0000	1.0000	1.0000	.9995	.9926	.9380	.7208	.3241	.0010	.0000	58
	59	1.0000	1.0000	1.0000	1.0000	1.0000	1.0000	1.0000	1.0000	.9998	.9965	.9647	.8054	.4315	.0027	.0000	59
	60	1.0000	1.0000	1.0000	1.0000	1.0000	1.0000	1.0000	1.0000	.9999	.9985	.9813	.8731	.5460	.0068	.0000	60
	61	1.0000	1.0000	1.0000	1.0000	1.0000	1.0000	1.0000	1.0000	1.0000	.9994	.9909	.9231	.6586	.0159	.0000	61
	62	1.0000	1.0000	1.0000	1.0000	1.0000	1.0000	1.0000	1.0000	1.0000	.9998	.9959	.9569	.7603	.0343	.0000	62
	63	1.0000	1.0000	1.0000	1.0000	1.0000	1.0000	1.0000	1.0000	1.0000	.9999	.9983	.9779	.8443	.0685	.0001	63
	64	1.0000	1.0000	1.0000	1.0000	1.0000	1.0000	1.0000	1.0000	1.0000	1.0000	.9994	.9897	.9072	.1263	.0003	64
	65	1.0000	1.0000	1.0000	1.0000	1.0000	1.0000	1.0000	1.0000	1.0000	1.0000	.9998	.9956	.9499	.2142	.0041	65
	66	1.0000	1.0000	1.0000	1.0000	1.0000	1.0000	1.0000	1.0000	1.0000	1.0000	.9999	.9984	.9757	.3342	.0124	66
	67	1.0000	1.0000	1.0000	1.0000	1.0000	1.0000	1.0000	1.0000	1.0000	1.0000	1.0000	.9995	.9896	.4792	.0336	67
n	r	π = .001	.01	.03	.05	.10	.20	.25	.50	.60	.65	.70	.75	.80	.90	.95	r

Table F   Binomial Distribution—Cumulative Terms   (continued)

n	r	π=.001	.01	.03	.05	.10	.20	.25	.50	.60	.65	.70	.75	.80	.90	.95	r
75	68	1.0000	1.0000	1.0000	1.0000	1.0000	1.0000	1.0000	1.0000	1.0000	1.0000	1.0000	.9998	.9961	.6327	.0810	68
	69	1.0000	1.0000	1.0000	1.0000	1.0000	1.0000	1.0000	1.0000	1.0000	1.0000	1.0000	1.0000	.9988	.7729	.1724	69
	70	1.0000	1.0000	1.0000	1.0000	1.0000	1.0000	1.0000	1.0000	1.0000	1.0000	1.0000	1.0000	.9997	.8811	.3212	70
	71	1.0000	1.0000	1.0000	1.0000	1.0000	1.0000	1.0000	1.0000	1.0000	1.0000	1.0000	1.0000	.9999	.9496	.5202	71
	72	1.0000	1.0000	1.0000	1.0000	1.0000	1.0000	1.0000	1.0000	1.0000	1.0000	1.0000	1.0000	1.0000	.9839	.7303	72
	73	1.0000	1.0000	1.0000	1.0000	1.0000	1.0000	1.0000	1.0000	1.0000	1.0000	1.0000	1.0000	1.0000	.9965	.8944	73
	74	1.0000	1.0000	1.0000	1.0000	1.0000	1.0000	1.0000	1.0000	1.0000	1.0000	1.0000	1.0000	1.0000	.9996	.9787	74
100	0	.9048	.3660	.0476	.0059	.0000	.0000	.0000	.0000	.0000	.0000	.0000	.0000	.0000	.0000	.0000	0
	1	.9954	.7358	.1946	.0371	.0003	.0000	.0000	.0000	.0000	.0000	.0000	.0000	.0000	.0000	.0000	1
	2	.9998	.9206	.4198	.1183	.0019	.0000	.0000	.0000	.0000	.0000	.0000	.0000	.0000	.0000	.0000	2
	3	1.0000	.9816	.6472	.2578	.0078	.0000	.0000	.0000	.0000	.0000	.0000	.0000	.0000	.0000	.0000	3
	4	1.0000	.9966	.8179	.4360	.0237	.0000	.0000	.0000	.0000	.0000	.0000	.0000	.0000	.0000	.0000	4
	5	1.0000	.9995	.9192	.6160	.0576	.0000	.0000	.0000	.0000	.0000	.0000	.0000	.0000	.0000	.0000	5
	6	1.0000	.9999	.9688	.7660	.1172	.0001	.0000	.0000	.0000	.0000	.0000	.0000	.0000	.0000	.0000	6
	7	1.0000	1.0000	.9894	.8720	.2060	.0003	.0000	.0000	.0000	.0000	.0000	.0000	.0000	.0000	.0000	7
	8	1.0000	1.0000	.9968	.9369	.3209	.0009	.0000	.0000	.0000	.0000	.0000	.0000	.0000	.0000	.0000	8
	9	1.0000	1.0000	.9991	.9718	.4513	.0023	.0000	.0000	.0000	.0000	.0000	.0000	.0000	.0000	.0000	9
	10	1.0000	1.0000	.9998	.9885	.5832	.0057	.0001	.0000	.0000	.0000	.0000	.0000	.0000	.0000	.0000	10
	11	1.0000	1.0000	1.0000	.9957	.7030	.0126	.0004	.0000	.0000	.0000	.0000	.0000	.0000	.0000	.0000	11
	12	1.0000	1.0000	1.0000	.9985	.8018	.0253	.0010	.0000	.0000	.0000	.0000	.0000	.0000	.0000	.0000	12
	13	1.0000	1.0000	1.0000	.9995	.8761	.0469	.0025	.0000	.0000	.0000	.0000	.0000	.0000	.0000	.0000	13
	14	1.0000	1.0000	1.0000	.9999	.9274	.0804	.0054	.0000	.0000	.0000	.0000	.0000	.0000	.0000	.0000	14
	15	1.0000	1.0000	1.0000	1.0000	.9601	.1285	.0111	.0000	.0000	.0000	.0000	.0000	.0000	.0000	.0000	15
	16	1.0000	1.0000	1.0000	1.0000	.9794	.1923	.0211	.0000	.0000	.0000	.0000	.0000	.0000	.0000	.0000	16
	17	1.0000	1.0000	1.0000	1.0000	.9900	.2712	.0376	.0000	.0000	.0000	.0000	.0000	.0000	.0000	.0000	17
	18	1.0000	1.0000	1.0000	1.0000	.9954	.3621	.0630	.0000	.0000	.0000	.0000	.0000	.0000	.0000	.0000	18
	19	1.0000	1.0000	1.0000	1.0000	.9980	.4602	.0995	.0000	.0000	.0000	.0000	.0000	.0000	.0000	.0000	19
n	r	π=.001	.01	.03	.05	.10	.20	.25	.50	.60	.65	.70	.75	.80	.90	.95	r

Table F Binomial Distribution—Cumulative Terms (continued)

n	r	π = .001	.01	.03	.05	.10	.20	.25	.50	.60	.65	.70	.75	.80	.90	.95	r
100	20	1.0000	1.0000	1.0000	1.0000	.9992	.5595	.1488	.0000	.0000	.0000	.0000	.0000	.0000	.0000	.0000	20
	21	1.0000	1.0000	1.0000	1.0000	.9997	.6540	.2114	.0000	.0000	.0000	.0000	.0000	.0000	.0000	.0000	21
	22	1.0000	1.0000	1.0000	1.0000	.9999	.7389	.2864	.0000	.0000	.0000	.0000	.0000	.0000	.0000	.0000	22
	23	1.0000	1.0000	1.0000	1.0000	1.0000	.8109	.3711	.0000	.0000	.0000	.0000	.0000	.0000	.0000	.0000	23
	24	1.0000	1.0000	1.0000	1.0000	1.0000	.8686	.4617	.0000	.0000	.0000	.0000	.0000	.0000	.0000	.0000	24
	25	1.0000	1.0000	1.0000	1.0000	1.0000	.9125	.5535	.0000	.0000	.0000	.0000	.0000	.0000	.0000	.0000	25
	26	1.0000	1.0000	1.0000	1.0000	1.0000	.9442	.6417	.0000	.0000	.0000	.0000	.0000	.0000	.0000	.0000	26
	27	1.0000	1.0000	1.0000	1.0000	1.0000	.9658	.7224	.0000	.0000	.0000	.0000	.0000	.0000	.0000	.0000	27
	28	1.0000	1.0000	1.0000	1.0000	1.0000	.9800	.7925	.0000	.0000	.0000	.0000	.0000	.0000	.0000	.0000	28
	29	1.0000	1.0000	1.0000	1.0000	1.0000	.9887	.8505	.0000	.0000	.0000	.0000	.0000	.0000	.0000	.0000	29
	30	1.0000	1.0000	1.0000	1.0000	1.0000	.9939	.8962	.0000	.0000	.0000	.0000	.0000	.0000	.0000	.0000	30
	31	1.0000	1.0000	1.0000	1.0000	1.0000	.9969	.9306	.0001	.0000	.0000	.0000	.0000	.0000	.0000	.0000	31
	32	1.0000	1.0000	1.0000	1.0000	1.0000	.9984	.9554	.0002	.0000	.0000	.0000	.0000	.0000	.0000	.0000	32
	33	1.0000	1.0000	1.0000	1.0000	1.0000	.9993	.9724	.0004	.0000	.0000	.0000	.0000	.0000	.0000	.0000	33
	34	1.0000	1.0000	1.0000	1.0000	1.0000	.9997	.9836	.0009	.0000	.0000	.0000	.0000	.0000	.0000	.0000	34
	35	1.0000	1.0000	1.0000	1.0000	1.0000	.9998	.9906	.0018	.0000	.0000	.0000	.0000	.0000	.0000	.0000	35
	36	1.0000	1.0000	1.0000	1.0000	1.0000	.9999	.9948	.0033	.0000	.0000	.0000	.0000	.0000	.0000	.0000	36
	37	1.0000	1.0000	1.0000	1.0000	1.0000	1.0000	.9972	.0060	.0000	.0000	.0000	.0000	.0000	.0000	.0000	37
	38	1.0000	1.0000	1.0000	1.0000	1.0000	1.0000	.9985	.0105	.0000	.0000	.0000	.0000	.0000	.0000	.0000	38
	39	1.0000	1.0000	1.0000	1.0000	1.0000	1.0000	.9993	.0176	.0000	.0000	.0000	.0000	.0000	.0000	.0000	39
	40	1.0000	1.0000	1.0000	1.0000	1.0000	1.0000	.9997	.0284	.0000	.0000	.0000	.0000	.0000	.0000	.0000	40
	41	1.0000	1.0000	1.0000	1.0000	1.0000	1.0000	.9998	.0443	.0001	.0000	.0000	.0000	.0000	.0000	.0000	41
	42	1.0000	1.0000	1.0000	1.0000	1.0000	1.0000	.9999	.0666	.0002	.0000	.0000	.0000	.0000	.0000	.0000	42
	43	1.0000	1.0000	1.0000	1.0000	1.0000	1.0000	1.0000	.0967	.0004	.0000	.0000	.0000	.0000	.0000	.0000	43
	44	1.0000	1.0000	1.0000	1.0000	1.0000	1.0000	1.0000	.1356	.0009	.0000	.0000	.0000	.0000	.0000	.0000	44
	45	1.0000	1.0000	1.0000	1.0000	1.0000	1.0000	1.0000	.1841	.0017	.0000	.0000	.0000	.0000	.0000	.0000	45
	46	1.0000	1.0000	1.0000	1.0000	1.0000	1.0000	1.0000	.2421	.0032	.0001	.0000	.0000	.0000	.0000	.0000	46
n	r	π = .001	.01	.03	.05	.10	.20	.25	.50	.60	.65	.70	.75	.80	.90	.95	r

Table F Binomial Distribution—Cumulative Terms (continued)

n	r	π = .001	.01	.03	.05	.10	.20	.25	.50	.60	.65	.70	.75	.80	.90	.95	r
100	47	1.0000	1.0000	1.0000	1.0000	1.0000	1.0000	1.0000	.3086	.0058	.0002	.0000	.0000	.0000	.0000	.0000	47
	48	1.0000	1.0000	1.0000	1.0000	1.0000	1.0000	1.0000	.3822	.0100	.0004	.0000	.0000	.0000	.0000	.0000	48
	49	1.0000	1.0000	1.0000	1.0000	1.0000	1.0000	1.0000	.4602	.0168	.0007	.0000	.0000	.0000	.0000	.0000	49
	50	1.0000	1.0000	1.0000	1.0000	1.0000	1.0000	1.0000	.5398	.0271	.0015	.0000	.0000	.0000	.0000	.0000	50
	51	1.0000	1.0000	1.0000	1.0000	1.0000	1.0000	1.0000	.6178	.0423	.0027	.0001	.0000	.0000	.0000	.0000	51
	52	1.0000	1.0000	1.0000	1.0000	1.0000	1.0000	1.0000	.6913	.0638	.0050	.0001	.0000	.0000	.0000	.0000	52
	53	1.0000	1.0000	1.0000	1.0000	1.0000	1.0000	1.0000	.7579	.0930	.0088	.0003	.0000	.0000	.0000	.0000	53
	54	1.0000	1.0000	1.0000	1.0000	1.0000	1.0000	1.0000	.8159	.1311	.0150	.0005	.0000	.0000	.0000	.0000	54
	55	1.0000	1.0000	1.0000	1.0000	1.0000	1.0000	1.0000	.8644	.1789	.0246	.0011	.0000	.0000	.0000	.0000	55
	56	1.0000	1.0000	1.0000	1.0000	1.0000	1.0000	1.0000	.9033	.2365	.0389	.0021	.0000	.0000	.0000	.0000	56
	57	1.0000	1.0000	1.0000	1.0000	1.0000	1.0000	1.0000	.9334	.3033	.0594	.0040	.0001	.0000	.0000	.0000	57
	58	1.0000	1.0000	1.0000	1.0000	1.0000	1.0000	1.0000	.9557	.3775	.0877	.0072	.0001	.0000	.0000	.0000	58
	59	1.0000	1.0000	1.0000	1.0000	1.0000	1.0000	1.0000	.9715	.4567	.1250	.0125	.0003	.0000	.0000	.0000	59
	60	1.0000	1.0000	1.0000	1.0000	1.0000	1.0000	1.0000	.9824	.5379	.1724	.0210	.0007	.0000	.0000	.0000	60
	61	1.0000	1.0000	1.0000	1.0000	1.0000	1.0000	1.0000	.9895	.6178	.2301	.0340	.0014	.0000	.0000	.0000	61
	62	1.0000	1.0000	1.0000	1.0000	1.0000	1.0000	1.0000	.9940	.6932	.2975	.0530	.0027	.0000	.0000	.0000	62
	63	1.0000	1.0000	1.0000	1.0000	1.0000	1.0000	1.0000	.9967	.7614	.3731	.0799	.0052	.0001	.0000	.0000	63
	64	1.0000	1.0000	1.0000	1.0000	1.0000	1.0000	1.0000	.9982	.8205	.4542	.1161	.0094	.0001	.0000	.0000	64
	65	1.0000	1.0000	1.0000	1.0000	1.0000	1.0000	1.0000	.9991	.8697	.5376	.1629	.0164	.0003	.0000	.0000	65
	66	1.0000	1.0000	1.0000	1.0000	1.0000	1.0000	1.0000	.9996	.9087	.6197	.2207	.0276	.0007	.0000	.0000	66
	67	1.0000	1.0000	1.0000	1.0000	1.0000	1.0000	1.0000	.9998	.9385	.6971	.2893	.0446	.0016	.0000	.0000	67
	68	1.0000	1.0000	1.0000	1.0000	1.0000	1.0000	1.0000	.9999	.9601	.7669	.3669	.0693	.0031	.0000	.0000	68
	69	1.0000	1.0000	1.0000	1.0000	1.0000	1.0000	1.0000	1.0000	.9752	.8270	.4500	.1038	.0061	.0000	.0000	69
	70	1.0000	1.0000	1.0000	1.0000	1.0000	1.0000	1.0000	1.0000	.9852	.8764	.5377	.1495	.0112	.0000	.0000	70
	71	1.0000	1.0000	1.0000	1.0000	1.0000	1.0000	1.0000	1.0000	.9916	.9152	.6232	.2075	.0200	.0000	.0000	71
	72	1.0000	1.0000	1.0000	1.0000	1.0000	1.0000	1.0000	1.0000	.9954	.9442	.7036	.2776	.0342	.0000	.0000	72
	73	1.0000	1.0000	1.0000	1.0000	1.0000	1.0000	1.0000	1.0000	.9976	.9648	.7758	.3583	.0558	.0000	.0000	73
n	r	π = .001	.01	.03	.05	.10	.20	.25	.50	.60	.65	.70	.75	.80	.90	.95	r

Table F   Binomial Distribution—Cumulative Terms (continued)

n	r	π = .001	.01	.03	.05	.10	.20	.25	.50	.60	.65	.70	.75	.80	.90	.95	r
100	74	1.0000	1.0000	1.0000	1.0000	1.0000	1.0000	1.0000	1.0000	.9988	.9788	.8369	.4465	.0875	.0000	.0000	74
	75	1.0000	1.0000	1.0000	1.0000	1.0000	1.0000	1.0000	1.0000	.9994	.9879	.8864	.5383	.1314	.0000	.0000	75
	76	1.0000	1.0000	1.0000	1.0000	1.0000	1.0000	1.0000	1.0000	.9997	.9934	.9246	.6286	.1891	.0000	.0000	76
	77	1.0000	1.0000	1.0000	1.0000	1.0000	1.0000	1.0000	1.0000	.9999	.9966	.9521	.7136	.2611	.0001	.0000	77
	78	1.0000	1.0000	1.0000	1.0000	1.0000	1.0000	1.0000	1.0000	.9999	.9983	.9712	.7886	.3460	.0003	.0000	78
	79	1.0000	1.0000	1.0000	1.0000	1.0000	1.0000	1.0000	1.0000	1.0000	.9992	.9835	.8512	.4405	.0008	.0000	79
	80	1.0000	1.0000	1.0000	1.0000	1.0000	1.0000	1.0000	1.0000	1.0000	.9996	.9911	.9005	.5398	.0020	.0000	80
	81	1.0000	1.0000	1.0000	1.0000	1.0000	1.0000	1.0000	1.0000	1.0000	.9998	.9955	.9370	.6379	.0046	.0000	81
	82	1.0000	1.0000	1.0000	1.0000	1.0000	1.0000	1.0000	1.0000	1.0000	.9999	.9978	.9624	.7288	.0100	.0000	82
	83	1.0000	1.0000	1.0000	1.0000	1.0000	1.0000	1.0000	1.0000	1.0000	1.0000	.9990	.9789	.8077	.0206	.0000	83
	84	1.0000	1.0000	1.0000	1.0000	1.0000	1.0000	1.0000	1.0000	1.0000	1.0000	.9996	.9889	.8715	.0399	.0000	84
	85	1.0000	1.0000	1.0000	1.0000	1.0000	1.0000	1.0000	1.0000	1.0000	1.0000	.9998	.9946	.9195	.0726	.0001	85
	86	1.0000	1.0000	1.0000	1.0000	1.0000	1.0000	1.0000	1.0000	1.0000	1.0000	.9999	.9975	.9531	.1239	.0005	86
	87	1.0000	1.0000	1.0000	1.0000	1.0000	1.0000	1.0000	1.0000	1.0000	1.0000	1.0000	.9990	.9747	.1982	.0015	87
	88	1.0000	1.0000	1.0000	1.0000	1.0000	1.0000	1.0000	1.0000	1.0000	1.0000	1.0000	.9996	.9874	.2070	.0043	88
	89	1.0000	1.0000	1.0000	1.0000	1.0000	1.0000	1.0000	1.0000	1.0000	1.0000	1.0000	.9999	.9943	.4168	.0115	89
	90	1.0000	1.0000	1.0000	1.0000	1.0000	1.0000	1.0000	1.0000	1.0000	1.0000	1.0000	.9999	.9977	.5487	.0282	90
	91	1.0000	1.0000	1.0000	1.0000	1.0000	1.0000	1.0000	1.0000	1.0000	1.0000	1.0000	1.0000	.9991	.6791	.0631	91
	92	1.0000	1.0000	1.0000	1.0000	1.0000	1.0000	1.0000	1.0000	1.0000	1.0000	1.0000	1.0000	.9997	.7939	.1280	92
	93	1.0000	1.0000	1.0000	1.0000	1.0000	1.0000	1.0000	1.0000	1.0000	1.0000	1.0000	1.0000	.9999	.8828	.2340	93
	94	1.0000	1.0000	1.0000	1.0000	1.0000	1.0000	1.0000	1.0000	1.0000	1.0000	1.0000	1.0000	1.0000	.9424	.3840	94
	95	1.0000	1.0000	1.0000	1.0000	1.0000	1.0000	1.0000	1.0000	1.0000	1.0000	1.0000	1.0000	1.0000	.9763	.5640	95
	96	1.0000	1.0000	1.0000	1.0000	1.0000	1.0000	1.0000	1.0000	1.0000	1.0000	1.0000	1.0000	1.0000	.9922	.7422	96
	97	1.0000	1.0000	1.0000	1.0000	1.0000	1.0000	1.0000	1.0000	1.0000	1.0000	1.0000	1.0000	1.0000	.9980	.8817	97
	98	1.0000	1.0000	1.0000	1.0000	1.0000	1.0000	1.0000	1.0000	1.0000	1.0000	1.0000	1.0000	1.0000	.9997	.9629	98
	99	1.0000	1.0000	1.0000	1.0000	1.0000	1.0000	1.0000	1.0000	1.0000	1.0000	1.0000	1.0000	1.0000	1.0000	.9941	99
n	r	π = .001	.01	.03	.05	.10	.20	.25	.50	.60	.65	.70	.75	.80	.90	.95	r

Table G Poisson Distribution—Individual Terms

$$f_P\,(r\,|\,\lambda,\,t) = \frac{(\lambda t)^r e^{-\lambda t}}{r!}$$

r	.001	.002	.003	.004	.005	.006	.007	.008	.009	0.010	r
0	.9990	.9980	.9970	.9960	.9950	.9940	.9930	.9920	.9910	.9900	0
1	.0010	.0020	.0030	.0040	.0050	.0060	.0070	.0079	.0089	.0099	1
2	.0000	.0000	.0000	.0000	.0000	.0000	.0000	.0000	.0000	.0000	2

r	.010	.020	.030	.040	.050	.060	.070	.080	.090	0.100	r
0	.9900	.9802	.9704	.9608	.9512	.9418	.9324	.9231	.9139	.9048	0
1	.0099	.0196	.0291	.0384	.0476	.0565	.0653	.0738	.0823	.0905	1
2	.0000	.0002	.0004	.0008	.0012	.0017	.0023	.0030	.0037	.0045	2
3	.0000	.0000	.0000	.0000	.0000	.0000	.0001	.0001	.0001	.0002	3
4	.0000	.0000	.0000	.0000	.0000	.0000	.0000	.0000	.0000	.0000	4

r	0.10	0.20	0.30	0.40	0.50	0.60	0.70	0.80	0.90	1.00	r
0	.9048	.8187	.7408	.6703	.6065	.5488	.4966	.4493	.4066	.3679	0
1	.0905	.1637	.2222	.2681	.3033	.3293	.3476	.3595	.3659	.3679	1
2	.0045	.0164	.0333	.0536	.0758	.0988	.1217	.1438	.1647	.1839	2
3	.0002	.0011	.0033	.0072	.0126	.0198	.0284	.0383	.0494	.0613	3
4	.0000	.0001	.0003	.0007	.0016	.0030	.0050	.0077	.0111	.0153	4
5	.0000	.0000	.0000	.0001	.0002	.0004	.0007	.0012	.0020	.0031	5
6	.0000	.0000	.0000	.0000	.0000	.0000	.0001	.0002	.0003	.0005	6
7	.0000	.0000	.0000	.0000	.0000	.0000	.0000	.0000	.0000	.0001	7
8	.0000	.0000	.0000	.0000	.0000	.0000	.0000	.0000	.0000	.0000	8

r	1.10	1.20	1.30	1.40	1.50	1.60	1.70	1.80	1.90	2.00	r
0	.3329	.3012	.2725	.2466	.2231	.2019	.1827	.1663	.1496	.1353	0
1	.3662	.3614	.3543	.3452	.3347	.3230	.3106	.2975	.2842	.2707	1
2	.2014	.2169	.2303	.2417	.2510	.2584	.2640	.2678	.2700	.2707	2
3	.0738	.0867	.0998	.1128	.1255	.1378	.1496	.1607	.1710	.1804	3
4	.0203	.0260	.0324	.0395	.0471	.0551	.0636	.0723	.0812	.0902	4
5	.0045	.0062	.0084	.0111	.0141	.0176	.0216	.0260	.0309	.0361	5
6	.0008	.0012	.0018	.0026	.0035	.0047	.0061	.0078	.0098	.0120	6
7	.0001	.0002	.0003	.0005	.0008	.0011	.0015	.0020	.0027	.0034	7
8	.0000	.0000	.0001	.0001	.0001	.0002	.0003	.0005	.0006	.0009	8
9	.0000	.0000	.0000	.0000	.0000	.0000	.0001	.0001	.0001	.0002	9
10	.0000	.0000	.0000	.0000	.0000	.0000	.0000	.0000	.0000	.0000	10

r	2.10	2.20	2.30	2.40	2.50	2.60	2.70	2.80	2.90	3.00	r
0	.1225	.1108	.1003	.0907	.0821	.0743	.0672	.0608	.0550	.0498	0
1	.2572	.2438	.2306	.2177	.2052	.1931	.1815	.1703	.1596	.1494	1
2	.2700	.2681	.2652	.2613	.2565	.2510	.2450	.2384	.2314	.2240	2
3	.1890	.1966	.2033	.2090	.2138	.2176	.2205	.2225	.2237	.2240	3
4	.0992	.1082	.1169	.1254	.1336	.1414	.1488	.1557	.1622	.1680	4

Table G   Poisson Distribution—Individual Terms (continued)

r	2.10	2.20	2.30	2.40	2.50	2.60	2.70	2.80	2.90	3.00	r
5	.0417	.0476	.0538	.0602	.0668	.0735	.0804	.0872	.0940	.1008	5
6	.0146	.0174	.0206	.0241	.0278	.0319	.0362	.0407	.0455	.0504	6
7	.0044	.0055	.0068	.0083	.0099	.0118	.0139	.0163	.0188	.0216	7
8	.0011	.0015	.0019	.0025	.0031	.0038	.0047	.0057	.0068	.0081	8
9	.0003	.0004	.0005	.0007	.0009	.0011	.0014	.0018	.0022	.0027	9
10	.0001	.0001	.0001	.0002	.0002	.0003	.0004	.0005	.0006	.0008	10
11	.0000	.0000	.0000	.0000	.0000	.0001	.0001	.0001	.0002	.0002	11
12	.0000	.0000	.0000	.0000	.0000	.0000	.0000	.0000	.0000	.0001	12
13	.0000	.0000	.0000	.0000	.0000	.0000	.0000	.0000	.0000	.0000	13

r	3.10	3.20	3.30	3.40	3.50	3.60	3.70	3.80	3.90	4.00	r
0	.0450	.0408	.0369	.0334	.0302	.0273	.0247	.0224	.0202	.0183	0
1	.1397	.1304	.1217	.1135	.1057	.0984	.0915	.0850	.0789	.0733	1
2	.2165	.2087	.2008	.1929	.1850	.1771	.1692	.1615	.1539	.1465	2
3	.2237	.2226	.2209	.2186	.2158	.2125	.2087	.2046	.2001	.1954	3
4	.1733	.1781	.1823	.1858	.1888	.1912	.1931	.1944	.1951	.1954	4
5	.1075	.1140	.1203	.1264	.1322	.1377	.1429	.1477	.1522	.1563	5
6	.0555	.0608	.0662	.0716	.0771	.0826	.0881	.0936	.0989	.1042	6
7	.0246	.0278	.0312	.0348	.0385	.0425	.0466	.0508	.0551	.0595	7
8	.0095	.0111	.0129	.0148	.0169	.0191	.0215	.0241	.0269	.0298	8
9	.0033	.0040	.0047	.0056	.0066	.0076	.0089	.0102	.0116	.0132	9
10	.0010	.0013	.0016	.0019	.0023	.0028	.0033	.0039	.0045	.0053	10
11	.0003	.0004	.0005	.0006	.0007	.0009	.0011	.0013	.0016	.0019	11
12	.0001	.0001	.0001	.0002	.0002	.0003	.0003	.0004	.0005	.0006	12
13	.0000	.0000	.0000	.0000	.0001	.0001	.0001	.0001	.0002	.0002	13
14	.0000	.0000	.0000	.0000	.0000	.0000	.0000	.0000	.0000	.0001	14
15	.0000	.0000	.0000	.0000	.0000	.0000	.0000	.0000	.0000	.0000	15

r	4.10	4.20	4.30	4.40	4.50	4.60	4.70	4.80	4.90	5.00	r
0	.0166	.0150	.0136	.0123	.0111	.0101	.0091	.0082	.0074	.0067	0
1	.0679	.0630	.0583	.0540	.0500	.0462	.0427	.0395	.0365	.0337	1
2	.1393	.1323	.1254	.1188	.1125	.1063	.1005	.0948	.0894	.0842	2
3	.1904	.1852	.1798	.1743	.1687	.1631	.1574	.1517	.1460	.1404	3
4	.1951	.1944	.1933	.1917	.1898	.1875	.1849	.1820	.1789	.1755	4
5	.1600	.1633	.1662	.1687	.1708	.1725	.1738	.1747	.1753	.1755	5
6	.1093	.1143	.1191	.1237	.1281	.1323	.1362	.1398	.1432	.1462	6
7	.0640	.0686	.0732	.0778	.0824	.0869	.0914	.0959	.1002	.1044	7
8	.0328	.0360	.0393	.0428	.0463	.0500	.0537	.0575	.0614	.0653	8
9	.0150	.0168	.0188	.0209	.0232	.0255	.0281	.0307	.0334	.0363	9
10	.0061	.0071	.0081	.0092	.0104	.0118	.0132	.0147	.0164	.0181	10
11	.0023	.0027	.0032	.0037	.0043	.0049	.0056	.0064	.0073	.0082	11
12	.0008	.0009	.0011	.0013	.0016	.0019	.0022	.0026	.0030	.0034	12
13	.0002	.0003	.0004	.0005	.0006	.0007	.0008	.0009	.0011	.0013	13
14	.0001	.0001	.0001	.0001	.0002	.0002	.0003	.0003	.0004	.0005	14
15	.0000	.0000	.0000	.0000	.0001	.0001	.0001	.0001	.0001	.0002	15
16	.0000	.0000	.0000	.0000	.0000	.0000	.0000	.0000	.0000	.0000	16

r	5.10	5.20	5.30	5.40	5.50	5.60	5.70	5.80	5.90	6.00	r
0	.0061	.0055	.0050	.0045	.0041	.0037	.0033	.0030	.0027	.0025	0
1	.0311	.0287	.0265	.0244	.0225	.0207	.0191	.0176	.0162	.0149	1
2	.0793	.0746	.0701	.0659	.0618	.0580	.0544	.0509	.0477	.0446	2
3	.1348	.1293	.1239	.1185	.1133	.1082	.1033	.0938	.0938	.0892	3
4	.1719	.1681	.1641	.1600	.1558	.1515	.1472	.1428	.1383	.1339	4
5	.1753	.1748	.1740	.1728	.1714	.1697	.1678	.1656	.1632	.1606	5
6	.1490	.1515	.1537	.1555	.1571	.1584	.1594	.1601	.1605	.1606	6
7	.1086	.1125	.1163	.1200	.1234	.1267	.1298	.1326	.1353	.1377	7
8	.0692	.0731	.0771	.0810	.0849	.0887	.0925	.0962	.0998	.1033	8
9	.0392	.0423	.0454	.0486	.0519	.0552	.0586	.0620	.0654	.0688	9
10	.0200	.0220	.0241	.0262	.0285	.0309	.0334	.0359	.0386	.0413	10
11	.0093	.0104	.0116	.0129	.0143	.0157	.0173	.0190	.0207	.0225	11
12	.0039	.0045	.0051	.0058	.0065	.0073	.0082	.0092	.0102	.0113	12
13	.0015	.0018	.0021	.0024	.0028	.0032	.0036	.0041	.0046	.0052	13
14	.0006	.0007	.0008	.0009	.0011	.0013	.0015	.0017	.0019	.0022	14
15	.0002	.0002	.0003	.0003	.0004	.0005	.0006	.0007	.0008	.0009	15
16	.0001	.0001	.0001	.0001	.0001	.0002	.0002	.0002	.0003	.0003	16
17	.0000	.0000	.0000	.0000	.0000	.0001	.0001	.0001	.0001	.0001	17
18	.0000	.0000	.0000	.0000	.0000	.0000	.0000	.0000	.0000	.0000	18

r	6.10	6.20	6.30	6.40	6.50	6.60	6.70	6.80	6.90	7.00	r
0	.0022	.0020	.0018	.0017	.0015	.0014	.0012	.0011	.0010	.0009	0
1	.0137	.0126	.0116	.0106	.0098	.0090	.0082	.0076	.0070	.0064	1
2	.0417	.0390	.0364	.0340	.0318	.0296	.0276	.0258	.0240	.0223	2
3	.0848	.0806	.0765	.0726	.0688	.0652	.0617	.0584	.0552	.0521	3
4	.1294	.1249	.1205	.1162	.1118	.1076	.1034	.0992	.0952	.0912	4
5	.1579	.1549	.1519	.1487	.1454	.1420	.1385	.1349	.1314	.1277	5
6	.1605	.1601	.1595	.1586	.1575	.1562	.1546	.1529	.1511	.1490	6
7	.1399	.1418	.1435	.1450	.1462	.1472	.1480	.1486	.1489	.1490	7
8	.1066	.1099	.1130	.1160	.1188	.1215	.1240	.1263	.1284	.1304	8
9	.0723	.0757	.0791	.0825	.0858	.0891	.0923	.0954	.0985	.1014	9
10	.0441	.0469	.0498	.0528	.0558	.0588	.0618	.0649	.0679	.0710	10
11	.0244	.0265	.0285	.0307	.0330	.0353	.0377	.0401	.0426	.0452	11
12	.0124	.0137	.0150	.0164	.0179	.0194	.0210	.0227	.0245	.0263	12
13	.0058	.0065	.0073	.0081	.0089	.0099	.0108	.0119	.0130	.0142	13
14	.0025	.0029	.0033	.0037	.0041	.0046	.0052	.0058	.0064	.0071	14
15	.0010	.0012	.0014	.0016	.0018	.0020	.0023	.0026	.0029	.0033	15
16	.0004	.0005	.0005	.0006	.0007	.0008	.0010	.0011	.0013	.0014	16
17	.0001	.0002	.0002	.0002	.0003	.0003	.0004	.0004	.0005	.0006	17
18	.0000	.0001	.0001	.0001	.0001	.0001	.0001	.0002	.0002	.0002	18
19	.0000	.0000	.0000	.0000	.0000	.0000	.0001	.0001	.0001	.0001	19
20	.0000	.0000	.0000	.0000	.0000	.0000	.0000	.0000	.0000	.0000	20

r	7.10	7.20	7.30	7.40	7.50	7.60	7.70	7.80	7.90	8.00	r
0	.0008	.0007	.0007	.0006	.0006	.0005	.0005	.0004	.0004	.0003	0
1	.0059	.0054	.0049	.0045	.0041	.0038	.0035	.0032	.0029	.0027	1
2	.0208	.0194	.0180	.0167	.0156	.0145	.0134	.0125	.0116	.0107	2
3	.0492	.0464	.0438	.0413	.0389	.0366	.0345	.0324	.0305	.0286	3
4	.0874	.0836	.0799	.0764	.0729	.0696	.0663	.0632	.0602	.0573	4

Table G Poisson Distribution—Individual Terms (continued)

r	7.10	7.20	7.30	7.40	7.50	7.60	7.70	7.80	7.90	8.00	r
5	.1241	.1204	.1167	.1130	.1094	.1057	.1021	.0986	.0951	.0916	5
6	.1468	.1445	.1420	.1394	.1367	.1339	.1311	.1282	.1252	.1221	6
7	.1489	.1486	.1481	.1474	.1465	.1454	.1442	.1428	.1413	.1396	7
8	.1321	.1337	.1351	.1363	.1373	.1381	.1388	.1392	.1395	.1396	8
9	.1042	.1070	.1096	.1121	.1144	.1167	.1187	.1207	.1224	.1241	9
10	.0740	.0770	.0800	.0829	.0858	.0887	.0914	.0941	.0967	.0993	10
11	.0478	.0504	.0531	.0558	.0585	.0613	.0640	.0667	.0695	.0722	11
12	.0283	.0303	.0323	.0344	.0366	.0388	.0411	.0434	.0457	.0481	12
13	.0154	.0168	.0181	.0196	.0211	.0227	.0243	.0260	.0278	.0296	13
14	.0078	.0086	.0095	.0104	.0113	.0123	.0134	.0145	.0157	.0169	14
15	.0037	.0041	.0046	.0051	.0057	.0062	.0069	.0075	.0083	.0090	15
16	.0016	.0019	.0021	.0024	.0026	.0030	.0033	.0037	.0041	.0045	16
17	.0007	.0008	.0009	.0010	.0012	.0013	.0015	.0017	.0019	.0021	17
18	.0003	.0003	.0004	.0004	.0005	.0006	.0006	.0007	.0008	.0009	18
19	.0001	.0001	.0001	.0002	.0002	.0002	.0003	.0003	.0003	.0004	19
20	.0000	.0000	.0001	.0001	.0001	.0001	.0001	.0001	.0001	.0002	20
21	.0000	.0000	.0000	.0000	.0000	.0000	.0000	.0000	.0001	.0001	21
22	.0000	.0000	.0000	.0000	.0000	.0000	.0000	.0000	.0000	.0000	22

r	8.10	8.20	8.30	8.40	8.50	8.60	8.70	8.80	8.90	9.00	r
0	.0003	.0003	.0002	.0002	.0002	.0002	.0002	.0002	.0001	.0001	0
1	.0025	.0023	.0021	.0019	.0017	.0016	.0014	.0013	.0012	.0011	1
2	.0100	.0092	.0086	.0079	.0074	.0068	.0063	.0058	.0054	.0050	2
3	.0269	.0252	.0237	.0222	.0208	.0195	.0183	.0171	.0160	.0150	3
4	.0544	.0517	.0491	.0466	.0443	.0420	.0398	.0377	.0357	.0337	4
5	.0882	.0849	.0816	.0784	.0752	.0722	.0692	.0663	.0635	.0607	5
6	.1191	.1160	.1128	.1097	.1066	.1034	.1003	.0972	.0941	.0911	6
7	.1378	.1358	.1338	.1317	.1294	.1271	.1247	.1222	.1197	.1171	7
8	.1395	.1392	.1388	.1382	.1375	.1366	.1356	.1344	.1332	.1318	8
9	.1256	.1269	.1280	.1290	.1299	.1306	.1311	.1315	.1317	.1318	9
10	.1017	.1040	.1063	.1084	.1104	.1123	.1140	.1157	.1172	.1186	10
11	.0749	.0776	.0802	.0828	.0853	.0878	.0902	.0925	.0948	.0970	11
12	.0505	.0530	.0555	.0579	.0604	.0629	.0654	.0679	.0703	.0728	12
13	.0315	.0334	.0354	.0374	.0395	.0416	.0438	.0459	.0481	.0504	13
14	.0182	.0196	.0210	.0225	.0240	.0256	.0272	.0289	.0306	.0324	14
15	.0098	.0107	.0116	.0126	.0136	.0147	.0158	.0169	.0182	.0194	15
16	.0050	.0055	.0060	.0066	.0072	.0079	.0086	.0093	.0101	.0109	16
17	.0024	.0026	.0029	.0033	.0036	.0040	.0044	.0048	.0053	.0058	17
18	.0011	.0012	.0014	.0015	.0017	.0019	.0021	.0024	.0026	.0029	18
19	.0005	.0005	.0006	.0007	.0008	.0009	.0010	.0011	.0012	.0014	19
20	.0002	.0002	.0002	.0003	.0003	.0004	.0004	.0005	.0005	.0006	20
21	.0001	.0001	.0001	.0001	.0001	.0002	.0002	.0002	.0002	.0003	21
22	.0000	.0000	.0000	.0000	.0001	.0001	.0001	.0001	.0001	.0001	22
23	.0000	.0000	.0000	.0000	.0000	.0000	.0000	.0000	.0000	.0000	23

r	9.10	9.20	9.30	9.40	9.50	9.60	9.70	9.80	9.90	10.00	r
0	.0001	.0001	.0001	.0001	.0001	.0001	.0001	.0001	.0001	.0000	0
1	.0010	.0009	.0009	.0008	.0007	.0007	.0006	.0005	.0005	.0005	1
2	.0046	.0043	.0040	.0037	.0034	.0031	.0029	.0027	.0025	.0023	2
3	.0140	.0131	.0123	.0115	.0107	.0100	.0093	.0087	.0081	.0076	3
4	.0319	.0302	.0285	.0269	.0254	.0240	.0226	.0213	.0201	.0189	4

Table G Poisson Distribution—Individual Terms (continued)

r	9.10	9.20	9.30	9.40	9.50	9.60	9.70	9.80	9.90	10.00	r
5	.0581	.0555	.0530	.0506	.0483	.0460	.0439	.0418	.0398	.0378	5
6	.0881	.0851	.0822	.0793	.0764	.0736	.0709	.0682	.0656	.0631	6
7	.1145	.1118	.1091	.1064	.1037	.1010	.0982	.0955	.0928	.0901	7
8	.1302	.1286	.1269	.1251	.1232	.1212	.1191	.1170	.1148	.1126	8
9	.1317	.1315	.1311	.1306	.1300	.1293	.1284	.1274	.1263	.1251	9
10	.1198	.1210	.1219	.1228	.1235	.1241	.1245	.1249	.1250	.1251	10
11	.0994	.1012	.1031	.1049	.1067	.1083	.1098	.1112	.1125	.1137	11
12	.0752	.0776	.0799	.0822	.0844	.0866	.0888	.0908	.0928	.0948	12
13	.0526	.0549	.0572	.0594	.0617	.0640	.0662	.0685	.0707	.0729	13
14	.0342	.0361	.0380	.0399	.0419	.0439	.0459	.0479	.0500	.0521	14
15	.0208	.0221	.0235	.0250	.0265	.0281	.0297	.0313	.0330	.0347	15
16	.0118	.0127	.0137	.0147	.0157	.0168	.0180	.0192	.0204	.0217	16
17	.0063	.0069	.0075	.0081	.0088	.0095	.0103	.0111	.0119	.0128	17
18	.0032	.0035	.0039	.0042	.0046	.0051	.0055	.0060	.0065	.0071	18
19	.0015	.0017	.0019	.0021	.0023	.0026	.0028	.0031	.0034	.0037	19
20	.0007	.0008	.0009	.0010	.0011	.0012	.0014	.0015	.0017	.0019	20
21	.0003	.0003	.0004	.0004	.0005	.0006	.0006	.0007	.0008	.0009	21
22	.0001	.0001	.0002	.0002	.0002	.0002	.0003	.0003	.0004	.0004	22
23	.0000	.0001	.0001	.0001	.0001	.0001	.0001	.0001	.0002	.0002	23
24	.0000	.0000	.0000	.0000	.0000	.0000	.0000	.0001	.0001	.0001	24
25	.0000	.0000	.0000	.0000	.0000	.0000	.0000	.0000	.0000	.0000	25

r	11.00	12.00	13.00	14.00	15.00	16.00	17.00	18.00	19.00	20.00	r
0	.0000	.0000	.0000	.0000	.0000	.0000	.0000	.0000	.0000	.0000	0
1	.0002	.0001	.0000	.0000	.0000	.0000	.0000	.0000	.0000	.0000	1
2	.0010	.0004	.0002	.0001	.0000	.0000	.0000	.0000	.0000	.0000	2
3	.0037	.0018	.0008	.0004	.0002	.0001	.0000	.0000	.0000	.0000	3
4	.0102	.0053	.0027	.0013	.0006	.0003	.0001	.0001	.0000	.0000	4
5	.0224	.0127	.0070	.0037	.0019	.0010	.0005	.0002	.0001	.0001	5
6	.0411	.0255	.0152	.0087	.0048	.0026	.0014	.0007	.0004	.0002	6
7	.0646	.0437	.0281	.0174	.0104	.0060	.0034	.0019	.0010	.0005	7
8	.0888	.0655	.0457	.0304	.0194	.0120	.0072	.0042	.0024	.0013	8
9	.1085	.0874	.0661	.0473	.0324	.0213	.0135	.0083	.0050	.0029	9
10	.1194	.1048	.0859	.0663	.0486	.0341	.0230	.0150	.0095	.0058	10
11	.1194	.1144	.1015	.0844	.0663	.0496	.0355	.0245	.0164	.0106	11
12	.1094	.1144	.1099	.0984	.0829	.0661	.0504	.0368	.0259	.0176	12
13	.0926	.1056	.1099	.1060	.0956	.0814	.0658	.0509	.0378	.0271	13
14	.0728	.0905	.1021	.1060	.1024	.0930	.0800	.0655	.0514	.0387	14
15	.0534	.0724	.0885	.0989	.1024	.0992	.0906	.0786	.0650	.0516	15
16	.0367	.0543	.0719	.0866	.0960	.0992	.0963	.0884	.0772	.0646	16
17	.0237	.0383	.0550	.0713	.0847	.0934	.0963	.0936	.0863	.0760	17
18	.0145	.0255	.0397	.0554	.0706	.0830	.0909	.0936	.0911	.0844	18
19	.0084	.0161	.0272	.0409	.0557	.0699	.0814	.0887	.0911	.0888	19
20	.0046	.0097	.0177	.0286	.0418	.0559	.0692	.0798	.0866	.0888	20
21	.0024	.0055	.0109	.0191	.0299	.0426	.0560	.0684	.0783	.0846	21
22	.0012	.0030	.0065	.0121	.0204	.0310	.0433	.0560	.0676	.0769	22
23	.0006	.0016	.0037	.0074	.0133	.0216	.0320	.0438	.0559	.0669	23
24	.0003	.0008	.0020	.0043	.0083	.0144	.0226	.0328	.0442	.0557	24
25	.0001	.0004	.0010	.0024	.0050	.0092	.0154	.0237	.0336	.0446	25
26	.0000	.0002	.0005	.0013	.0029	.0057	.0101	.0164	.0246	.0343	26
27	.0000	.0001	.0002	.0007	.0016	.0034	.0063	.0109	.0173	.0254	27

Table G Poisson Distribution—Individual Terms (continued)

	λt										
r	*11.00*	*12.00*	*13.00*	*14.00*	*15.00*	*16.00*	*17.00*	*18.00*	*19.00*	*20.00*	*r*
28	.0000	.0000	.0001	.0003	.0009	.0019	.0038	.0070	.0117	.0181	28
29	.0000	.0000	.0001	.0002	.0004	.0011	.0023	.0044	.0077	.0125	29
30	.0000	.0000	.0000	.0001	.0002	.0006	.0013	.0026	.0049	.0083	30
31	.0000	.0000	.0000	.0000	.0001	.0003	.0007	.0015	.0030	.0054	31
32	.0000	.0000	.0000	.0000	.0001	.0001	.0004	.0009	.0018	.0034	32
33	.0000	.0000	.0000	.0000	.0000	.0001	.0002	.0005	.0010	.0020	33
34	.0000	.0000	.0000	.0000	.0000	.0000	.0001	.0002	.0006	.0012	34
35	.0000	.0000	.0000	.0000	.0000	.0000	.0000	.0001	.0003	.0007	35
36	.0000	.0000	.0000	.0000	.0000	.0000	.0000	.0001	.0002	.0004	36
37	.0000	.0000	.0000	.0000	.0000	.0000	.0000	.0000	.0001	.0002	37
38	.0000	.0000	.0000	.0000	.0000	.0000	.0000	.0000	.0000	.0001	38
39	.0000	.0000	.0000	.0000	.0000	.0000	.0000	.0000	.0000	.0001	39

Table H   Poisson Distribution—Cumulative Terms

$$F_P(r \mid \lambda, t) = \sum_{y=0}^{r} \frac{(\lambda t)^y e^{-\lambda t}}{y!}$$

r	.001	.002	.003	.004	.005	.006	.007	.008	.009	0.010	r
0	.9990	.9980	.9970	.9960	.9950	.9940	.9930	.9920	.9910	.9900	0
1	1.0000	1.0000	1.0000	1.0000	1.0000	1.0000	1.0000	1.0000	1.0000	1.0000	1

r	.010	.020	.030	.040	.050	.060	.070	.080	.090	0.100	r
0	.9900	.9802	.9704	.9608	.9512	.9418	.9324	.9231	.9139	.9048	0
1	1.0000	.9998	.9996	.9992	.9988	.9983	.9977	.9970	.9962	.9953	1
2	1.0000	1.0000	1.0000	1.0000	1.0000	1.0000	.9999	.9999	.9999	.9998	2
3	1.0000	1.0000	1.0000	1.0000	1.0000	1.0000	1.0000	1.0000	1.0000	1.0000	3

r	0.10	0.20	0.30	0.40	0.50	0.60	0.70	0.80	0.90	1.00	r
0	.9048	.8187	.7408	.6703	.6065	.5488	.4966	.4493	.4066	.3679	0
1	.9953	.9825	.9631	.9384	.9098	.8781	.8442	.8088	.7725	.7358	1
2	.9998	.9989	.9964	.9921	.9856	.9769	.9659	.9526	.9371	.9197	2
3	1.0000	.9999	.9997	.9992	.9982	.9966	.9942	.9909	.9865	.9810	3
4	1.0000	1.0000	1.0000	.9999	.9998	.9996	.9992	.9986	.9977	.9963	4
5	1.0000	1.0000	1.0000	1.0000	1.0000	1.0000	.9999	.9998	.9997	.9994	5
6	1.0000	1.0000	1.0000	1.0000	1.0000	1.0000	1.0000	1.0000	1.0000	.9999	6
7	1.0000	1.0000	1.0000	1.0000	1.0000	1.0000	1.0000	1.0000	1.0000	1.0000	7

r	1.10	1.20	1.30	1.40	1.50	1.60	1.70	1.80	1.90	2.00	r
0	.3329	.3012	.2725	.2466	.2231	.2019	.1827	.1653	.1496	.1353	0
1	.6990	.6626	.6268	.5918	.5578	.5249	.4932	.4628	.4337	.4060	1
2	.9004	.8795	.8571	.8335	.8088	.7834	.7572	.7306	.7037	.6767	2
3	.9743	.9662	.9569	.9463	.9344	.9212	.9068	.8913	.8747	.8571	3
4	.9946	.9923	.9893	.9857	.9814	.9763	.9704	.9636	.9559	.9473	4
5	.9990	.9985	.9978	.9968	.9955	.9940	.9920	.9896	.9868	.9834	5
6	.9999	.9997	.9996	.9994	.9991	.9987	.9981	.9974	.9966	.9955	6
7	1.0000	1.0000	.9999	.9999	.9998	.9997	.9996	.9994	.9992	.9989	7
8	1.0000	1.0000	1.0000	1.0000	1.0000	1.0000	.9999	.9999	.9998	.9998	8
9	1.0000	1.0000	1.0000	1.0000	1.0000	1.0000	1.0000	1.0000	1.0000	1.0000	9

r	2.10	2.20	2.30	2.40	2.50	2.60	2.70	2.80	2.90	3.00	r
0	.1225	.1108	.1003	.0907	.0821	.0743	.0672	.0608	.0550	.0498	0
1	.3796	.3546	.3309	.3084	.2873	.2674	.2487	.2311	.2146	.1991	1
2	.6496	.6227	.5960	.5697	.5438	.5184	.4936	.4695	.4460	.4232	2
3	.8386	.8194	.7993	.7787	.7576	.7360	.7141	.6919	.6696	.6472	3
4	.9379	.9275	.9162	.9041	.8912	.8774	.8629	.8477	.8318	.8153	4
5	.9796	.9751	.9700	.9643	.9580	.9510	.9433	.9349	.9258	.9161	5
6	.9941	.9925	.9906	.9884	.9858	.9828	.9794	.9756	.9713	.9665	6
7	.9985	.9980	.9974	.9967	.9958	.9947	.9934	.9919	.9901	.9881	7
8	.9997	.9995	.9994	.9991	.9989	.9985	.9981	.9976	.9969	.9962	8
9	.9999	.9999	.9999	.9998	.9997	.9996	.9995	.9993	.9991	.9989	9
10	1.0000	1.0000	1.0000	1.0000	.9999	.9999	.9999	.9998	.9998	.9997	10
11	1.0000	1.0000	1.0000	1.0000	1.0000	1.0000	1.0000	1.0000	.9999	.9999	11
12	1.0000	1.0000	1.0000	1.0000	1.0000	1.0000	1.0000	1.0000	1.0000	1.0000	12

Table H   Poisson Distribution—Cumulative Terms (continued)

r	3.10	3.20	3.30	3.40	3.50	3.60	3.70	3.80	3.90	4.00	r
0	.0450	.0408	.0369	.0334	.0302	.0273	.0247	.0224	.0202	.0183	0
1	.1847	.1712	.1586	.1468	.1359	.1257	.1162	.1074	.0992	.0916	1
2	.4012	.3799	.3594	.3397	.3208	.3027	.2854	.2689	.2531	.2381	2
3	.6248	.6025	.5803	.5584	.5366	.5152	.4942	.4735	.4532	.4335	3
4	.7982	.7806	.7626	.7442	.7254	.7064	.6872	.6678	.6484	.6288	4
5	.9057	.8946	.8829	.8705	.8576	.8441	.8301	.8156	.8006	.7851	5
6	.9612	.9554	.9490	.9421	.9347	.9267	.9182	.9091	.8995	.8893	6
7	.9858	.9832	.9802	.9769	.9733	.9692	.9648	.9599	.9546	.9489	7
8	.9953	.9943	.9931	.9917	.9901	.9883	.9863	.9840	.9815	.9786	8
9	.9986	.9982	.9978	.9973	.9967	.9960	.9952	.9942	.9931	.9919	9
10	.9996	.9995	.9994	.9992	.9990	.9987	.9984	.9981	.9977	.9972	10
11	.9999	.9999	.9998	.9998	.9997	.9996	.9995	.9994	.9993	.9991	11
12	1.0000	1.0000	1.0000	.9999	.9999	.9999	.9999	.9998	.9998	.9997	12
13	1.0000	1.0000	1.0000	1.0000	1.0000	1.0000	1.0000	1.0000	.9999	.9999	13
14	1.0000	1.0000	1.0000	1.0000	1.0000	1.0000	1.0000	1.0000	1.0000	1.0000	14

r	4.10	4.20	4.30	4.40	4.50	4.60	4.70	4.80	4.90	5.00	r
0	.0166	.0150	.0136	.0123	.0111	.0101	.0091	.0082	.0074	.0067	0
1	.0845	.0780	.0719	.0663	.0611	.0563	.0518	.0477	.0439	.0404	1
2	.2238	.2102	.1974	.1851	.1736	.1626	.1523	.1425	.1333	.1247	2
3	.4142	.3954	.3772	.3594	.3423	.3257	.3097	.2942	.2793	.2650	3
4	.6093	.5898	.5704	.5512	.5321	.5132	.4946	.4763	.4582	.4405	4
5	.7693	.7531	.7367	.7199	.7029	.6858	.6684	.6510	.6335	.6160	5
6	.8786	.8675	.8558	.8436	.8311	.8180	.8046	.7908	.7767	.7622	6
7	.9427	.9361	.9290	.9214	.9134	.9049	.8960	.8867	.8769	.8666	7
8	.9755	.9721	.9683	.9642	.9597	.9549	.9497	.9442	.9382	.9319	8
9	.9905	.9889	.9871	.9851	.9829	.9805	.9778	.9749	.9717	.9682	9
10	.9966	.9959	.9952	.9943	.9933	.9922	.9910	.9896	.9880	.9863	10
11	.9989	.9986	.9983	.9980	.9976	.9971	.9966	.9960	.9953	.9945	11
12	.9997	.9996	.9995	.9993	.9992	.9990	.9988	.9986	.9983	.9980	12
13	.9999	.9999	.9998	.9998	.9997	.9997	.9996	.9995	.9994	.9993	13
14	1.0000	1.0000	1.0000	.9999	.9999	.9999	.9999	.9999	.9998	.9998	14
15	1.0000	1.0000	1.0000	1.0000	1.0000	1.0000	1.0000	1.0000	.9999	.9999	15
16	1.0000	1.0000	1.0000	1.0000	1.0000	1.0000	1.0000	1.0000	1.0000	1.0000	16

r	5.10	5.20	5.30	5.40	5.50	5.60	5.70	5.80	5.90	6.00	r
0	.0061	.0055	.0050	.0045	.0041	.0037	.0033	.0030	.0027	.0025	0
1	.0372	.0342	.0314	.0289	.0266	.0244	.0224	.0206	.0189	.0174	1
2	.1165	.1088	.1016	.0948	.0884	.0824	.0768	.0715	.0666	.0626	2
3	.2513	.2381	.2254	.2133	.2017	.1906	.1800	.1700	.1604	.1512	3
4	.4231	.4061	.3895	.3733	.3575	.3422	.3272	.3127	.2987	.2851	4
5	.5984	.5809	.5635	.5461	.5289	.5119	.4950	.4783	.4619	.4457	5
6	.7474	.7324	.7171	.7017	.6860	.6703	.6544	.6384	.6224	.6063	6
7	.8560	.8449	.8335	.8217	.8095	.7970	.7841	.7710	.7576	.7440	7
8	.9252	.9181	.9106	.9027	.8944	.8857	.8766	.8672	.8574	.8472	8
9	.9644	.9603	.9559	.9512	.9462	.9409	.9352	.9292	.9228	.9161	9
10	.9844	.9823	.9800	.9775	.9747	.9718	.9686	.9651	.9614	.9574	10
11	.9937	.9927	.9916	.9904	.9890	.9875	.9859	.9841	.9821	.9799	11
12	.9976	.9972	.9967	.9962	.9955	.9949	.9941	.9932	.9922	.9912	12
13	.9992	.9990	.9988	.9986	.9983	.9980	.9977	.9973	.9969	.9964	13
14	.9997	.9997	.9996	.9995	.9994	.9993	.9991	.9990	.9988	.9986	14

Table H   Poisson Distribution—Cumulative Terms (continued)

r	5.10	5.20	5.30	5.40	5.50	5.60	5.70	5.80	5.90	6.00	r
15	.9999	.9999	.9999	.9998	.9998	.9998	.9997	.9996	.9996	.9995	15
16	1.0000	1.0000	1.0000	.9999	.9999	.9999	.9999	.9999	.9999	.9998	16
17	1.0000	1.0000	1.0000	1.0000	1.0000	1.0000	1.0000	1.0000	1.0000	.9999	17
18	1.0000	1.0000	1.0000	1.0000	1.0000	1.0000	1.0000	1.0000	1.0000	1.0000	18

r	6.10	6.20	6.30	6.40	6.50	6.60	6.70	6.80	6.90	7.00	r
0	.0022	.0020	.0018	.0017	.0015	.0014	.0012	.0011	.0010	.0009	0
1	.0159	.0146	.0134	.0123	.0113	.0103	.0095	.0087	.0080	.0073	1
2	.0577	.0536	.0498	.0463	.0430	.0400	.0371	.0344	.0320	.0296	2
3	.1425	.1342	.1264	.1189	.1118	.1052	.0988	.0928	.0871	.0818	3
4	.2719	.2592	.2469	.2351	.2237	.2127	.2022	.1920	.1823	.1730	4
5	.4298	.4141	.3988	.3837	.3690	.3547	.3406	.3270	.3137	.3007	5
6	.5902	.5742	.5582	.5423	.5265	.5108	.4953	.4799	.4647	.4497	6
7	.7301	.7160	.7017	.6873	.6728	.6581	.6433	.6285	.6136	.5987	7
8	.8367	.8259	.8148	.8033	.7916	.7796	.7673	.7548	.7420	.7291	8
9	.9090	.9016	.8939	.8858	.8774	.8686	.8596	.8502	.8405	.8305	9
10	.9531	.9486	.9437	.9386	.9332	.9274	.9214	.9151	.9084	.9015	10
11	.9776	.9750	.9723	.9693	.9661	.9627	.9591	.9552	.9510	.9467	11
12	.9900	.9887	.9873	.9857	.9840	.9821	.9801	.9779	.9755	.9730	12
13	.9958	.9952	.9945	.9937	.9929	.9920	.9909	.9898	.9885	.9872	13
14	.9984	.9981	.9978	.9974	.9970	.9966	.9961	.9956	.9950	.9943	14
15	.9994	.9993	.9992	.9990	.9988	.9986	.9984	.9982	.9979	.9976	15
16	.9998	.9997	.9997	.9996	.9996	.9995	.9994	.9993	.9992	.9990	16
17	.9999	.9999	.9999	.9999	.9998	.9998	.9998	.9997	.9997	.9996	17
18	1.0000	1.0000	1.0000	1.0000	.9999	.9999	.9999	.9999	.9999	.9999	18
19	1.0000	1.0000	1.0000	1.0000	1.0000	1.0000	1.0000	1.0000	1.0000	1.0000	19

r	7.10	7.20	7.30	7.40	7.50	7.60	7.70	7.80	7.90	8.00	r
0	.0008	.0007	.0007	.0006	.0006	.0005	.0005	.0004	.0004	.0003	0
1	.0067	.0061	.0056	.0051	.0047	.0043	.0039	.0036	.0033	.0030	1
2	.0275	.0255	.0236	.0219	.0203	.0188	.0174	.0161	.0149	.0138	2
3	.0767	.0719	.0674	.0632	.0591	.0554	.0518	.0485	.0453	.0424	3
4	.1641	.1555	.1473	.1395	.1321	.1249	.1181	.1117	.1055	.0996	4
5	.2881	.2759	.2640	.2526	.2414	.2307	.2203	.2103	.2006	.1912	5
6	.4349	.4204	.4060	.3920	.3782	.3646	.3514	.3384	.3257	.3134	6
7	.5838	.5689	.5541	.5393	.5246	.5100	.4956	.4812	.4670	.4530	7
8	.7160	.7027	.6892	.6757	.6620	.6482	.6343	.6204	.6065	.5925	8
9	.8202	.8097	.7988	.7877	.7764	.7649	.7531	.7411	.7290	.7166	9
10	.8942	.8867	.8788	.8707	.8622	.8535	.8445	.8352	.8257	.8159	10
11	.9420	.9371	.9319	.9265	.9208	.9148	.9085	.9020	.8952	.8881	11
12	.9703	.9673	.9642	.9609	.9673	.9536	.9496	.9454	.9409	.9362	12
13	.9857	.9841	.9824	.9805	.9784	.9762	.9739	.9714	.9687	.9658	13
14	.9935	.9927	.9918	.9908	.9897	.9886	.9873	.9859	.9844	.9827	14
15	.9972	.9969	.9964	.9959	.9954	.9948	.9941	.9934	.9926	.9918	15
16	.9989	.9987	.9985	.9983	.9980	.9978	.9974	.9971	.9967	.9963	16
17	.9996	.9995	.9994	.9993	.9992	.9991	.9989	.9988	.9986	.9984	17
18	.9998	.9998	.9998	.9997	.9997	.9996	.9996	.9995	.9994	.9993	18
19	.9999	.9999	.9999	.9999	.9999	.9999	.9998	.9998	.9998	.9997	19
20	1.0000	1.0000	1.0000	1.0000	1.0000	1.0000	.9999	.9999	.9999	.9999	20
21	1.0000	1.0000	1.0000	1.0000	1.0000	1.0000	1.0000	1.0000	1.0000	1.0000	21

					λt						
r	8.10	8.20	8.30	8.40	8.50	8.60	8.70	8.80	8.90	9.00	r
0	.0003	.0003	.0002	.0002	.0002	.0002	.0002	.0002	.0001	.0001	0
1	.0028	.0025	.0023	.0021	.0019	.0018	.0016	.0015	.0014	.0012	1
2	.0127	.0118	.0109	.0100	.0093	.0086	.0079	.0073	.0068	.0062	2
3	.0396	.0370	.0346	.0323	.0301	.0281	.0262	.0244	.0228	.0212	3
4	.0940	.0887	.0837	.0789	.0744	.0701	.0660	.0621	.0584	.0550	4
5	.1822	.1736	.1653	.1573	.1496	.1422	.1352	.1284	.1219	.1157	5
6	.3013	.2896	.2781	.2670	.2562	.2457	.2355	.2256	.2160	.2068	6
7	.4391	.4254	.4119	.3987	.3856	.3728	.3602	.3478	.3357	.3239	7
8	.5786	.5647	.5507	.5369	.5231	.5094	.4958	.4823	.4689	.4557	8
9	.7041	.6915	.6788	.6659	.6530	.6400	.6269	.6137	.6006	.5874	9
10	.8058	.7956	.7850	.7743	.7634	.7522	.7409	.7294	.7178	.7060	10
11	.8807	.8731	.8652	.8571	.8487	.8400	.8311	.8220	.8126	.8030	11
12	.9313	.9261	.9207	.9150	.9091	.9029	.8965	.8898	.8829	.8758	12
13	.9628	.9595	.9561	.9524	.9486	.9445	.9403	.9358	.9311	.9261	13
14	.9810	.9791	.9771	.9749	.9726	.9701	.9675	.9647	.9617	.9585	14
15	.9908	.9898	.9887	.9875	.9862	.9848	.9832	.9816	.9798	.9780	15
16	.9958	.9953	.9947	.9941	.9934	.9926	.9918	.9909	.9899	.9889	16
17	.9982	.9979	.9977	.9973	.9970	.9966	.9962	.9957	.9952	.9947	17
18	.9992	.9991	.9990	.9989	.9987	.9985	.9983	.9981	.9978	.9976	18
19	.9997	.9997	.9996	.9995	.9995	.9994	.9993	.9992	.9991	.9989	19
20	.9999	.9999	.9998	.9998	.9998	.9998	.9997	.9997	.9996	.9996	20
21	1.0000	1.0000	.9999	.9999	.9999	.9999	.9999	.9999	.9999	.9998	21
22	1.0000	1.0000	1.0000	1.0000	1.0000	1.0000	1.0000	1.0000	.9999	.9999	22
23	1.0000	1.0000	1.0000	1.0000	1.0000	1.0000	1.0000	1.0000	1.0000	1.0000	23

					λt						
r	9.10	9.20	9.30	9.40	9.50	9.60	9.70	9.80	9.90	10.00	r
0	.0001	.0001	.0001	.0001	.0001	.0001	.0001	.0001	.0001	.0000	0
1	.0011	.0010	.0009	.0009	.0008	.0007	.0007	.0006	.0005	.0005	1
2	.0058	.0053	.0049	.0045	.0042	.0038	.0035	.0033	.0030	.0028	2
3	.0198	.0184	.0172	.0160	.0149	.0138	.0129	.0120	.0111	.0103	3
4	.0517	.0486	.0456	.0429	.0403	.0378	.0355	.0333	.0312	.0293	4
5	.1098	.1041	.0986	.0935	.0885	.0838	.0793	.0750	.0710	.0671	5
6	.1978	.1897	.1808	.1727	.1649	.1574	.1502	.1433	.1366	.1301	6
7	.3123	.3010	.2900	.2792	.2687	.2584	.2485	.2388	.2294	.2202	7
8	.4426	.4296	.4168	.4042	.3918	.3796	.3676	.3558	.3442	.3328	8
9	.5742	.5611	.5479	.5349	.5218	.5089	.4960	.4832	.4706	.4579	9
10	.6941	.6820	.6699	.6576	.6453	.6329	.6205	.6080	.5955	.5830	10
11	.7932	.7832	.7730	.7626	.7520	.7412	.7303	.7193	.7081	.6968	11
12	.8684	.8607	.8529	.8448	.8364	.8279	.8191	.8101	.8009	.7916	12
13	.9210	.9156	.9100	.9042	.8981	.8919	.8853	.8786	.8716	.8645	13
14	.9552	.9517	.9480	.9441	.9400	.9357	.9312	.9265	.9216	.9165	14
15	.9760	.9738	.9715	.9691	.9665	.9638	.9609	.9579	.9546	.9513	15
16	.9878	.9865	.9852	.9838	.9823	.9806	.9789	.9770	.9751	.9730	16
17	.9941	.9934	.9927	.9919	.9911	.9902	.9892	.9881	.9870	.9857	17
18	.9973	.9969	.9966	.9962	.9957	.9952	.9947	.9941	.9935	.9928	18
19	.9988	.9986	.9985	.9983	.9980	.9978	.9975	.9972	.9969	.9965	19
20	.9995	.9994	.9993	.9992	.9991	.9990	.9989	.9987	.9986	.9984	20
21	.9998	.9998	.9997	.9997	.9996	.9996	.9995	.9995	.9994	.9993	21
22	.9999	.9999	.9999	.9999	.9999	.9998	.9998	.9998	.9997	.9997	22
23	1.0000	1.0000	1.0000	1.0000	.9999	.9999	.9999	.9999	.9999	.9999	23
24	1.0000	1.0000	1.0000	1.0000	1.0000	1.0000	1.0000	1.0000	1.0000	1.0000	24

Table H Poisson Distribution—Cumulative Terms (continued)

r	11.00	12.00	13.00	14.00	15.00	16.00	17.00	18.00	19.00	20.00	r
0	.0000	.0000	.0000	.0000	.0000	.0000	.0000	.0000	.0000	.0000	0
1	.0002	.0001	.0000	.0000	.0000	.0000	.0000	.0000	.0000	.0000	1
2	.0012	.0005	.0002	.0001	.0000	.0000	.0000	.0000	.0000	.0000	2
3	.0049	.0023	.0011	.0005	.0002	.0001	.0000	.0000	.0000	.0000	3
4	.0151	.0076	.0037	.0018	.0009	.0004	.0002	.0001	.0000	.0000	4
5	.0375	.0203	.0107	.0055	.0028	.0014	.0007	.0003	.0002	.0001	5
6	.0786	.0458	.0259	.0142	.0076	.0040	.0021	.0010	.0005	.0003	6
7	.1432	.0895	.0540	.0316	.0180	.0100	.0054	.0029	.0015	.0008	7
8	.2320	.1550	.0998	.0621	.0374	.0220	.0126	.0071	.0039	.0021	8
9	.3405	.2424	.1658	.1094	.0699	.0433	.0261	.0154	.0089	.0050	9
10	.4599	.3472	.2517	.1757	.1185	.0774	.0491	.0304	.0183	.0108	10
11	.5793	.4616	.3532	.2600	.1848	.1270	.0847	.0549	.0347	.0214	11
12	.6887	.5760	.4631	.3585	.2676	.1931	.1350	.0917	.0606	.0390	12
13	.7813	.6815	.5730	.4644	.3632	.2745	.2009	.1426	.0984	.0661	13
14	.8540	.7720	.6751	.5704	.4657	.3675	.2808	.2081	.1497	.1049	14
15	.9074	.8444	.7636	.6694	.5681	.4667	.3715	.2867	.2148	.1565	15
16	.9441	.8987	.8355	.7559	.6641	.5660	.4677	.3751	.2920	.2211	16
17	.9678	.9370	.8905	.8272	.7489	.6593	.5640	.4686	.3784	.2970	17
18	.9823	.9626	.9302	.8826	.8195	.7423	.6550	.5622	.4695	.3814	18
19	.9907	.9787	.9573	.9235	.8752	.8122	.7363	.6509	.5606	.4703	19
20	.9953	.9884	.9750	.9521	.9170	.8682	.8055	.7307	.6472	.5591	20
21	.9977	.9939	.9859	.9712	.9469	.9108	.8615	.7991	.7255	.6437	21
22	.9990	.9970	.9924	.9833	.9673	.9418	.9047	.8551	.7931	.7206	22
23	.9995	.9985	.9960	.9907	.9805	.9633	.9367	.8989	.8490	.7875	23
24	.9998	.9993	.9980	.9950	.9888	.9777	.9594	.9317	.8933	.8432	24
25	.9999	.9997	.9990	.9974	.9938	.9869	.9748	.9554	.9269	.8878	25
26	1.0000	.9999	.9995	.9987	.9967	.9925	.9848	.9718	.9514	.9221	26
27	1.0000	.9999	.9998	.9994	.9983	.9959	.9912	.9827	.9687	.9475	27
28	1.0000	1.0000	.9999	.9997	.9991	.9978	.9950	.9897	.9805	.9657	28
29	1.0000	1.0000	1.0000	.9999	.9996	.9989	.9973	.9941	.9882	.9787	29
30	1.0000	1.0000	1.0000	.9999	.9998	.9994	.9986	.9967	.9930	.9865	30
31	1.0000	1.0000	1.0000	1.0000	.9999	.9997	.9993	.9982	.9960	.9919	31
32	1.0000	1.0000	1.0000	1.0000	1.0000	.9999	.9996	.9990	.9978	.9953	32
33	1.0000	1.0000	1.0000	1.0000	1.0000	.9999	.9998	.9995	.9988	.9973	33
34	1.0000	1.0000	1.0000	1.0000	1.0000	1.0000	.9999	.9998	.9994	.9985	34
35	1.0000	1.0000	1.0000	1.0000	1.0000	1.0000	1.0000	.9999	.9997	.9992	35
36	1.0000	1.0000	1.0000	1.0000	1.0000	1.0000	1.0000	.9999	.9998	.9996	36
37	1.0000	1.0000	1.0000	1.0000	1.0000	1.0000	1.0000	1.0000	.9999	.9998	37
38	1.0000	1.0000	1.0000	1.0000	1.0000	1.0000	1.0000	1.0000	1.0000	.9999	38
39	1.0000	1.0000	1.0000	1.0000	1.0000	1.0000	1.0000	1.0000	1.0000	.9999	39
40	1.0000	1.0000	1.0000	1.0000	1.0000	1.0000	1.0000	1.0000	1.0000	1.0000	40

Table I Standard Normal Integral

$$F_N(z) = \int_{-\infty}^{z} \frac{1}{\sqrt{2\pi}} e^{-t^2/2} \, dt \text{ for } z \leq 0$$

z	−.09	−.08	−.07	−.06	−.05	−.04	−.03	−.02	−.01	.00	z
−3.8	.0001	.0001	.0001	.0001	.0001	.0001	.0001	.0001	.0001	.0001	−3.8
−3.7	.0001	.0001	.0001	.0001	.0001	.0001	.0001	.0001	.0001	.0001	−3.7
−3.6	.0001	.0001	.0001	.0001	.0001	.0001	.0001	.0001	.0002	.0002	−3.6
−3.5	.0002	.0002	.0002	.0002	.0002	.0002	.0002	.0002	.0002	.0002	−3.5
−3.4	.0002	.0003	.0003	.0003	.0003	.0003	.0003	.0003	.0003	.0003	−3.4
−3.3	.0003	.0004	.0004	.0004	.0004	.0004	.0004	.0005	.0005	.0005	−3.3
−3.2	.0005	.0005	.0005	.0006	.0006	.0006	.0006	.0006	.0007	.0007	−3.2
−3.1	.0007	.0007	.0008	.0008	.0008	.0008	.0009	.0009	.0009	.0010	−3.1
−3.0	.0010	.0010	.0011	.0011	.0011	.0012	.0012	.0013	.0013	.0014	−3.0
−2.9	.0014	.0014	.0015	.0015	.0016	.0016	.0017	.0018	.0018	.0019	−2.9
−2.8	.0019	.0020	.0021	.0021	.0022	.0023	.0023	.0024	.0025	.0026	−2.8
−2.7	.0026	.0027	.0028	.0029	.0030	.0031	.0032	.0033	.0034	.0035	−2.7
−2.6	.0036	.0037	.0038	.0039	.0040	.0041	.0043	.0044	.0045	.0047	−2.6
−2.5	.0048	.0049	.9951	.0052	.0054	.0055	.0057	.0059	.0060	.0062	−2.5
−2.4	.0064	.0066	.0068	.0069	.0071	.0073	.0076	.0078	.0080	.0082	−2.4
−2.3	.0084	.0087	.0089	.0091	.0094	.0096	.0099	.0102	.0104	.0107	−2.3
−2.2	.0110	.0113	.0116	.0119	.0122	.0125	.0129	.0132	.0136	.0139	−2.2
−2.1	.0143	.0146	.0150	.0154	.0158	.0162	.0166	.0170	.0174	.0179	−2.1
−2.0	.0183	.0188	.0192	.0197	.0202	.0207	.0212	.0217	.0222	.0228	−2.0
−1.9	.0233	.0239	.0244	.0250	.0256	.0262	.0268	.0274	.0281	.0287	−1.9
−1.8	.0294	.0301	.0307	.0314	.0322	.0329	.0336	.0344	.0352	.0359	−1.8
−1.7	.0367	.0375	.0384	.0392	.0401	.0409	.0418	.0427	.0436	.0446	−1.7
−1.6	.0455	.0465	.0475	.0485	.0495	.0505	.0516	.0526	.0537	.0548	−1.6
−1.5	.0559	.0571	.0582	.0594	.0606	.0618	.0630	.0643	.0655	.0668	−1.5
−1.4	.0681	.0694	.0708	.0721	.0735	.0749	.0764	.0778	.0793	.0808	−1.4
−1.3	.0823	.0838	.0853	.0869	.0885	.0901	.0918	.0934	.0951	.0968	−1.3
−1.2	.0985	.1003	.1020	.1038	.1057	.1075	.1094	.1112	.1131	.1151	−1.2
−1.1	.1170	.1190	.1210	.1230	.1251	.1271	.1292	.1314	.1335	.1357	−1.1
−1.0	.1379	.1401	.1423	.1446	.1469	.1492	.1515	.1539	.1562	.1587	−1.0
−0.9	.1611	.1635	.1660	.1685	.1711	.1736	.1762	.1788	.1814	.1841	−0.9
−0.8	.1867	.1894	.1922	.1949	.1977	.2005	.2033	.2061	.2090	.2119	−0.8
−0.7	.2148	.2177	.2206	.2236	.2266	.2296	.2327	.2358	.2389	.2420	−0.7
−0.6	.2451	.2483	.2514	.2546	.2578	.2611	.2643	.2676	.2709	.2743	−0.6
−0.5	.2776	.2810	.2843	.2877	.2912	.2946	.2981	.3015	.3050	.3085	−0.5
−0.4	.3121	.3156	.3192	.3228	.3264	.3300	.3336	.3372	.3409	.3446	−0.4
−0.3	.3483	.3520	.3557	.3594	.3632	.3669	.3707	.3745	.3783	.3821	−0.3
−0.2	.3859	.3897	.3936	.3974	.4013	.4052	.4090	.4129	.4168	.4207	−0.2
−0.1	.4247	.4286	.4325	.4364	.4404	.4443	.4483	.4522	.4562	.4602	−0.1
0.0	.4641	.4681	.4721	.4761	.4801	.4840	.4880	.4920	.4960	.5000	0.0

Table I   Standard Normal Integral (continued)

$$F_N(z) = \int_{-\infty}^{z} \frac{1}{\sqrt{2\pi}} e^{-t^2/2} \, dt \text{ for } z \geq 0$$

z	.00	.01	.02	.03	.04	.05	.06	.07	.08	.09	z
0.0	.5000	.5040	.5080	.5120	.5160	.5199	.5239	.5279	.5319	.5359	**0.0**
0.1	.5398	.5438	.5478	.5517	.5557	.5596	.5636	.5675	.5714	.5753	**0.1**
0.2	.5793	.5832	.5871	.5910	.5948	.5987	.6026	.6064	.6103	.6141	**0.2**
0.3	.6179	.6217	.6255	.6293	.6331	.6368	.6406	.6443	.6480	.6517	**0.3**
0.4	.6554	.6591	.6628	.6664	.6700	.6736	.6772	.6808	.6844	.6879	**0.4**
0.5	.6915	.6950	.6985	.7019	.7054	.7088	.7123	.7157	.7190	.7224	**0.5**
0.6	.7257	.7291	.7324	.7357	.7389	.7422	.7454	.7486	.7517	.7549	**0.6**
0.7	.7580	.7651	.7642	.7673	.7704	.7734	.7764	.7794	.7823	.7852	**0.7**
0.8	.7881	.7900	.7939	.7967	.7995	.8023	.8051	.8078	.8106	.8133	**0.8**
0.9	.8159	.8186	.8212	.8238	.8264	.8289	.8315	.8340	.8365	.8389	**0.9**
1.0	.8413	.8438	.8461	.8485	.8508	.8531	.8554	.8577	.8599	.8621	**1.0**
1.1	.8643	.8665	.8686	.8708	.8729	.8749	.8770	.8790	.8810	.8830	**1.1**
1.2	.8849	.8869	.8888	.8906	.8925	.8943	.8962	.8980	.8997	.9015	**1.2**
1.3	.9032	.9049	.9066	.9082	.9099	.9115	.9131	.9147	.9162	.9177	**1.3**
1.4	.9192	.9207	.9222	.9236	.9251	.9265	.9279	.9292	.9306	.9319	**1.4**
1.5	.9332	.9345	.9357	.9370	.9382	.9394	.9406	.9418	.9429	.9441	**1.5**
1.6	.9452	.9463	.9474	.9484	.9495	.9505	.9515	.9525	.9535	.9545	**1.6**
1.7	.9554	.9564	.9573	.9582	.9591	.9599	.9608	.9616	.9625	.9633	**1.7**
1.8	.9641	.9648	.9656	.9664	.9671	.9678	.9686	.9693	.9699	.9706	**1.8**
1.9	.9713	.9719	.9726	.9732	.9738	.9744	.9750	.9756	.9761	.9767	**1.9**
2.0	.9772	.9778	.9783	.9788	.9793	.9798	.9803	.9808	.9812	.9812	**2.0**
2.1	.9821	.9826	.9830	.9834	.9838	.9842	.9846	.9850	.9854	.9857	**2.1**
2.2	.9861	.9864	.9868	.9871	.9875	.9878	.9881	.9884	.9887	.9890	**2.2**
2.3	.9893	.9896	.9898	.9901	.9904	.9906	.9909	.9911	.9913	.9916	**2.3**
2.4	.9918	.9920	.9922	.9924	.9927	.9929	.9931	.9932	.9934	.9936	**2.4**
2.5	.9938	.9940	.9941	.9943	.9945	.9946	.9948	.9949	.9951	.9952	**2.5**
2.6	.9953	.9955	.9956	.9957	.9959	.9960	.9961	.9962	.9963	.9964	**2.6**
2.7	.9965	.9966	.9967	.9968	.9969	.9970	.9971	.9972	.9973	.9974	**2.7**
2.8	.9974	.9975	.9976	.9977	.9977	.9978	.9979	.9979	.9980	.9981	**2.8**
2.9	.9981	.9982	.9982	.9983	.9984	.9984	.9985	.9985	.9986	.9986	**2.9**
3.0	.9986	.9987	.9987	.9988	.9988	.9989	.9989	.9989	.9990	.9990	**3.0**
3.1	.9990	.9991	.9991	.9991	.9992	.9992	.9992	.9992	.9993	.9993	**3.1**
3.2	.9993	.9993	.9994	.9994	.9994	.9994	.9994	.9995	.9995	.9995	**3.2**
3.3	.9995	.9995	.9995	.9996	.9996	.9996	.9996	.9996	.9996	.9997	**3.3**
3.4	.9997	.9997	.9997	.9997	.9997	.9997	.9997	.9997	.9997	.9998	**3.4**
3.5	.9998	.9998	.9998	.9998	.9998	.9998	.9998	.9998	.9998	.9998	**3.5**
3.6	.9998	.9998	.9999	.9999	.9999	.9999	.9999	.9999	.9999	.9999	**3.6**
3.7	.9999	.9999	.9999	.9999	.9999	.9999	.9999	.9999	.9999	.9999	**3.7**
3.8	.9999	.9999	.9999	.9999	.9999	.9999	.9999	.9999	.9999	.9999	**3.8**

Table J   Fractiles of the Standard Normal
Distribution

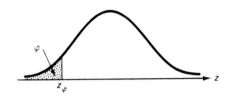

φ	z_φ	φ	z_φ
.0005	−3.291	.50	.000
.0010	−3.090	.55	.126
.0025	−2.807	.60	.253
.005	−2.576	.65	.385
.010	−2.326	.70	.524
.020	−2.054	.75	.675
.025	−1.960	.80	.842
.03	−1.881	.85	1.036
.04	−1.751	.90	1.282
.05	−1.645	.91	1.341
.06	−1.555	.92	1.405
.07	−1.476	.93	1.476
.08	−1.405	.94	1.555
.09	−1.341	.95	1.645
.10	−1.282	.96	1.751
.15	−1.036	.97	1.881
.20	− .842	.975	1.960
.25	− .675	.980	2.054
.30	− .524	.990	2.326
.35	− .385	.995	2.576
.40	− .253	.9975	2.807
.45	− .126	.9990	3.090
.50	.000	.9995	3.291

Table K   Fractiles of the χ^2 Distribution

Entries are values of $\chi^2_{\nu;\varphi}$ where $P(X^2_\nu \le \chi^2_{\nu;\varphi}) = \varphi$

ν \ φ	.005	.01	.025	.05	.10	.90	.95	.975	.99	.995
1	.000039	.00016	.00098	.0039	.016	2.71	3.84	5.02	6.63	7.88
2	.010	.020	.051	.10	.21	4.61	5.99	7.38	9.21	10.60
3	.072	.12	.22	.35	.58	6.25	7.81	9.35	11.34	12.84
4	.21	.30	.48	.71	1.06	7.78	9.49	11.14	13.28	14.86
5	.41	.55	.83	1.15	1.61	9.24	11.07	12.83	15.09	16.75
6	.68	.87	1.24	1.64	2.20	10.64	12.59	14.45	16.81	18.55
7	.99	1.24	1.69	2.17	2.83	12.02	14.07	16.01	18.48	20.28
8	1.34	1.65	2.18	2.73	3.49	13.36	15.51	17.53	20.09	21.96
9	1.73	2.09	2.70	3.33	4.17	14.68	16.92	19.02	21.67	23.59
10	2.16	2.56	3.25	3.94	4.87	15.99	18.31	20.48	23.21	25.19
11	2.60	3.05	3.82	4.57	5.58	17.28	19.68	21.92	24.73	26.76
12	3.07	3.57	4.40	5.23	6.30	18.55	21.03	23.34	26.22	28.30
13	3.57	4.11	5.01	5.89	7.04	19.81	22.36	24.74	27.69	29.82

Table K Fractiles of the χ^2 Distribution (continued)

ν \ φ	.005	.01	.025	.05	.10	.90	.95	.975	.99	.995
14	4.07	4.66	5.63	6.57	7.79	21.06	23.68	26.12	29.14	31.32
15	4.60	5.23	6.26	7.26	8.55	22.31	25.00	27.49	30.58	32.80
16	5.14	5.81	6.91	7.96	9.31	23.54	26.30	28.85	32.00	34.27
17	5.70	6.41	7.56	8.67	10.09	24.77	27.59	30.19	33.41	35.72
18	6.26	7.01	8.23	9.39	10.86	25.99	28.87	31.53	34.81	37.16
19	6.84	7.63	8.91	10.12	11.65	27.20	30.14	32.85	36.19	38.58
20	7.43	8.26	9.59	10.85	12.44	28.41	31.41	34.17	37.57	40.00
21	8.03	8.90	10.28	11.59	13.24	29.62	32.67	35.48	38.93	41.40
22	8.64	9.54	10.98	12.34	14.04	30.81	33.92	36.78	40.29	42.80
23	9.26	10.20	11.69	13.09	14.85	32.01	35.17	38.08	41.64	44.18
24	9.89	10.86	12.40	13.85	15.66	33.20	36.42	39.36	42.98	45.56
25	10.52	11.52	13.12	14.61	16.47	34.38	37.65	40.65	44.31	46.93
26	11.16	12.20	13.84	15.38	17.29	35.56	38.89	41.92	45.64	48.29
27	11.81	12.88	14.57	16.15	18.11	36.74	40.11	43.19	46.96	49.64
28	12.46	13.56	15.31	16.93	18.94	37.92	41.34	44.46	48.28	50.99
29	13.12	14.26	16.05	17.71	19.77	39.09	42.55	45.72	49.59	52.34
30	13.79	14.95	16.79	18.49	20.60	40.26	43.77	46.98	50.89	53.67
40	20.71	22.16	24.43	26.51	29.05	51.80	55.76	59.34	63.69	66.77
50	27.99	29.71	32.36	34.76	37.69	63.17	67.50	71.42	76.15	79.49
60	35.53	37.48	40.48	43.19	46.46	74.40	79.08	83.30	88.38	91.95
70	43.28	45.44	48.76	51.74	55.33	85.53	90.53	95.02	100.43	104.22
80	51.17	53.54	57.15	60.39	64.28	96.58	101.88	106.63	112.33	116.32
90	59.20	61.75	65.65	69.13	73.29	107.57	113.15	118.14	124.12	128.30
100	67.33	70.06	74.22	77.93	82.36	118.50	124.34	129.56	135.81	140.17

Extracted with permission from H. L. Harter, "A New Table of Percentage Points of the Chi-Square Distribution." *Biometrika*, June 1964.

Table L Fractiles of Student's *t* Distribution

Entries are values of $t_{\nu;\,\phi}$ where $P(t_\nu \leq t_{\nu;\,\varphi}) = \varphi$

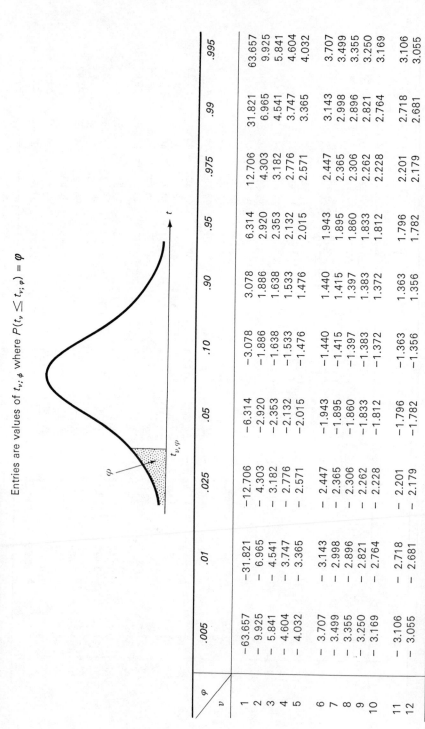

ν \ φ	.005	.01	.025	.05	.10	.90	.95	.975	.99	.995
1	−63.657	−31.821	−12.706	−6.314	−3.078	3.078	6.314	12.706	31.821	63.657
2	− 9.925	− 6.965	− 4.303	−2.920	−1.886	1.886	2.920	4.303	6.965	9.925
3	− 5.841	− 4.541	− 3.182	−2.353	−1.638	1.638	2.353	3.182	4.541	5.841
4	− 4.604	− 3.747	− 2.776	−2.132	−1.533	1.533	2.132	2.776	3.747	4.604
5	− 4.032	− 3.365	− 2.571	−2.015	−1.476	1.476	2.015	2.571	3.365	4.032
6	− 3.707	− 3.143	− 2.447	−1.943	−1.440	1.440	1.943	2.447	3.143	3.707
7	− 3.499	− 2.998	− 2.365	−1.895	−1.415	1.415	1.895	2.365	2.998	3.499
8	− 3.355	− 2.896	− 2.306	−1.860	−1.397	1.397	1.860	2.306	2.896	3.355
9	− 3.250	− 2.821	− 2.262	−1.833	−1.383	1.383	1.833	2.262	2.821	3.250
10	− 3.169	− 2.764	− 2.228	−1.812	−1.372	1.372	1.812	2.228	2.764	3.169
11	− 3.106	− 2.718	− 2.201	−1.796	−1.363	1.363	1.796	2.201	2.718	3.106
12	− 3.055	− 2.681	− 2.179	−1.782	−1.356	1.356	1.782	2.179	2.681	3.055

Table L Fractiles of Student's *t* Distribution (continued)

v \ φ	.005	.01	.025	.05	.10	.90	.95	.975	.99	.995
13	− 3.012	− 2.650	− 2.160	−1.771	−1.350	1.350	1.771	2.160	2.650	3.012
14	− 2.977	− 2.624	− 2.145	−1.761	−1.345	1.345	1.761	2.145	2.624	2.977
15	− 2.947	− 2.602	− 2.131	−1.753	−1.341	1.341	1.753	2.131	2.602	2.947
16	− 2.921	− 2.583	− 2.120	−1.746	−1.337	1.337	1.746	2.120	2.583	2.921
17	− 2.898	− 2.567	− 2.110	−1.740	−1.333	1.333	1.740	2.110	2.567	2.898
18	− 2.878	− 2.552	− 2.101	−1.734	−1.330	1.330	1.734	2.101	2.552	2.878
19	− 2.861	− 2.539	− 2.093	−1.729	−1.328	1.328	1.729	2.093	2.539	2.861
20	− 2.845	− 2.528	− 2.086	−1.725	−1.325	1.325	1.725	2.086	2.528	2.845
21	− 2.831	− 2.518	− 2.080	−1.721	−1.323	1.323	1.721	2.080	2.518	2.831
22	− 2.819	− 2.508	− 2.074	−1.717	−1.321	1.321	1.717	2.074	2.508	2.819
23	− 2.807	− 2.500	− 2.069	−1.714	−1.319	1.319	1.714	2.069	2.500	2.807
24	− 2.797	− 2.492	− 2.064	−1.711	−1.318	1.318	1.711	2.064	2.492	2.797
25	− 2.787	− 2.485	− 2.060	−1.708	−1.316	1.316	1.708	2.060	2.485	2.787
26	− 2.779	− 2.479	− 2.056	−1.706	−1.315	1.315	1.706	2.056	2.479	2.779
27	− 2.771	− 2.473	− 2.052	−1.703	−1.314	1.314	1.703	2.052	2.473	2.771
28	− 2.763	− 2.467	− 2.048	−1.701	−1.313	1.313	1.701	2.048	2.467	2.763
29	− 2.756	− 2.462	− 2.045	−1.699	−1.311	1.311	1.699	2.045	2.462	2.756
30	− 2.750	− 2.457	− 2.042	−1.697	−1.310	1.310	1.697	2.042	2.457	2.750
40	− 2.704	− 2.423	− 2.021	−1.684	−1.303	1.303	1.684	2.021	2.423	2.704
60	− 2.660	− 2.390	− 2.000	−1.671	−1.296	1.296	1.671	2.000	2.390	2.660
120	− 2.617	− 2.358	− 1.980	−1.658	−1.289	1.289	1.658	1.980	2.358	2.617
∞	− 2.576	− 2.326	− 1.960	−1.645	−1.282	1.282	1.645	1.960	2.326	2.576

Taken from Table III of Fisher and Yates, *Statistical Tables for Biological, Agricultural and Medical Research*, published by Longman Group Ltd., London (previously published by Oliver & Boyd, Edinburgh) and by permission of the authors and publishers.

Table M Fractiles of the F Distribution

$$F_{\nu_1, \nu_2;\,.025}$$

$\nu_2 \backslash \nu_1$	1	2	3	4	5	6	7	8	9	10	12	15	20	24	30	40	60	120	∞
1	$.0^2 25$	.026	.057	.082	.100	.113	.124	.132	.139	.144	.153	.161	.170	.175	.180	.184	.189	.194	.199
2	$.0^2 13$	.026	.062	.094	.119	.138	.153	.165	.175	.183	.196	.210	.224	.232	.239	.247	.255	.263	.271
3	$.0^2 12$	.026	.065	.100	.129	.152	.170	.185	.197	.207	.224	.241	.259	.269	.279	.289	.299	.310	.321
4	$.0^2 11$	.026	.066	.104	.135	.161	.181	.198	.212	.224	.243	.263	.284	.296	.308	.320	.332	.346	.359
5	$.0^2 11$	.025	.067	.107	.140	.167	.189	.208	.223	.236	.257	.280	.304	.317	.330	.344	.359	.374	.390
6	$.0^2 11$	.025	.068	.109	.143	.172	.195	.215	.231	.246	.268	.293	.320	.334	.349	.364	.381	.398	.415
7	$.0^2 10$	.025	.068	.110	.146	.176	.200	.221	.238	.253	.277	.304	.333	.348	.364	.381	.399	.418	.437
8	$.0^2 10$	.025	.069	.111	.148	.179	.204	.226	.244	.259	.285	.313	.343	.360	.377	.395	.415	.435	.456
9	$.0^2 10$	.025	.069	.112	.150	.181	.207	.230	.248	.265	.291	.320	.352	.370	.388	.408	.428	.450	.473
10	$.0^2 10$	.025	.069	.113	.151	.183	.210	.233	.252	.269	.296	.327	.360	.379	.398	.419	.441	.464	.488
11	$.0^2 10$	.025	.069	.114	.152	.185	.212	.236	.256	.273	.301	.332	.368	.386	.407	.429	.450	.476	.503
12	$.0^2 10$	.025	.070	.114	.153	.186	.214	.238	.259	.276	.305	.337	.374	.394	.416	.437	.461	.487	.514
13	$.0^2 10$	.025	.070	.115	.154	.187	.216	.240	.261	.279	.308	.342	.378	.399	.421	.444	.469	.497	.525
14	$.0^2 10$	.025	.070	.115	.155	.189	.217	.242	.263	.281	.311	.346	.384	.404	.427	.451	.477	.506	.536
15	$.0^2 10$	.025	.070	.116	.156	.190	.219	.244	.265	.284	.315	.349	.389	.410	.433	.458	.485	.514	.546
16	$.0^2 10$	.025	.070	.116	.156	.190	.220	.245	.267	.286	.317	.352	.392	.414	.437	.463	.491	.522	.553
17	$.0^2 10$	.025	.070	.116	.156	.191	.221	.246	.268	.287	.319	.355	.396	.417	.441	.468	.497	.529	.563
18	$.0^2 10$	.025	.070	.116	.157	.192	.222	.248	.270	.289	.321	.357	.399	.421	.446	.473	.503	.535	.569
19	$.0^2 10$	.025	.070	.117	.157	.192	.223	.249	.271	.291	.323	.360	.403	.425	.450	.478	.509	.542	.577
20	$.0^2 10$	.025	.071	.117	.158	.193	.224	.250	.273	.292	.325	.363	.406	.430	.456	.484	.514	.548	.585
21	$.0^2 10$	.025	.071	.117	.158	.194	.224	.251	.274	.293	.327	.364	.409	.432	.458	.487	.519	.554	.591
22	$.0^2 10$	.025	.071	.117	.159	.194	.225	.252	.275	.295	.328	.366	.411	.435	.461	.490	.524	.559	.597
23	$.0^2 10$	.025	.071	.117	.159	.195	.226	.252	.276	.296	.330	.368	.413	.438	.464	.494	.528	.563	.603
24	$.0^2 10$	.025	.071	.117	.159	.195	.227	.253	.277	.297	.331	.370	.415	.441	.468	.498	.531	.568	.610
25	$.0^2 10$	.025	.071	.118	.159	.196	.227	.254	.278	.298	.332	.372	.417	.442	.470	.500	.535	.572	.614
26	$.0^2 10$	.025	.071	.118	.160	.196	.227	.254	.278	.299	.333	.373	.418	.444	.472	.503	.538	.576	.619

Table M Fractiles of the F Distribution (continued)

$F_{\nu_1,\nu_2;\,.025}$

ν_2 \ ν_1	1	2	3	4	5	6	7	8	9	10	12	15	20	24	30	40	60	120	∞
27	$.0^{2}10$	.025	.071	.118	.160	.196	.228	.255	.279	.299	.334	.375	.420	.475	.446	.506	.541	.580	.623
28	$.0^{2}10$	.025	.071	.118	.160	.197	.228	.256	.279	.300	.336	.376	.422	.448	.478	.509	.543	.584	.628
29	$.0^{2}10$	.025	.071	.118	.160	.197	.229	.256	.280	.301	.337	.377	.424	.450	.480	.512	.546	.588	.632
30	$.0^{2}10$	.025	.071	.118	.161	.197	.229	.257	.281	.302	.337	.378	.426	.453	.482	.515	.551	.592	.639
40	$.0^{3}99$	.025	.071	.119	.162	.199	.232	.260	.285	.307	.344	.387	.437	.466	.498	.533	.573	.620	.674
60	$.0^{3}99$	.025	.071	.120	.163	.204	.235	.264	.290	.313	.351	.396	.450	.481	.515	.555	.600	.654	.720
120	$.0^{3}99$	.025	.072	.120	.165	.204	.238	.268	.295	.318	.359	.406	.464	.498	.536	.580	.633	.698	.789
∞	$.0^{3}98$	.025	.072	.121	.166	.206	.241	.272	.300	.325	.367	.418	.480	.517	.560	.611	.675	.763	1.000

$F_{\nu_1,\nu_2;\,.05}$

ν_2 \ ν_1	1	2	3	4	5	6	7	8	9	10	12	15	20	24	30	40	60	120	∞
1	$.0^{2}62$	.054	.099	.130	.151	.167	.179	.188	.195	.201	.211	.220	.230	.235	.240	.245	.250	.255	.261
2	$.0^{2}50$	.053	.105	.144	.173	.194	.211	.224	.235	.244	.257	.272	.286	.294	.302	.309	.317	.326	.334
3	$.0^{2}46$	.052	.108	.152	.185	.210	.230	.246	.259	.270	.287	.304	.323	.332	.342	.352	.363	.373	.384
4	$.0^{2}44$	.052	.110	.157	.193	.221	.243	.261	.275	.288	.307	.327	.349	.360	.372	.384	.396	.409	.422
5	$.0^{2}43$	.052	.111	.160	.198	.228	.252	.271	.287	.301	.322	.345	.369	.382	.395	.408	.422	.437	.452
6	$.0^{2}43$	.052	.112	.162	.202	.233	.259	.279	.296	.311	.334	.358	.385	.399	.413	.428	.444	.460	.476
7	$.0^{2}42$	.052	.113	.164	.205	.238	.264	.286	.304	.319	.343	.369	.398	.413	.428	.445	.461	.479	.498
8	$.0^{2}42$	.052	.113	.166	.208	.241	.268	.291	.310	.326	.351	.379	.409	.425	.441	.459	.477	.496	.516
9	$.0^{2}40$	.052	.113	.167	.210	.244	.272	.296	.315	.331	.358	.386	.418	.435	.452	.471	.490	.510	.532
10	$.0^{2}41$	.052	.114	.168	.211	.246	.275	.299	.319	.336	.363	.393	.426	.444	.462	.481	.502	.523	.546
11	$.0^{2}41$	.052	.114	.168	.212	.248	.278	.302	.323	.340	.368	.398	.433	.452	.469	.490	.513	.535	.559
12	$.0^{2}41$	.052	.114	.169	.214	.250	.280	.305	.325	.343	.372	.404	.439	.458	.478	.499	.522	.545	.571

Table M Fractiles of the F Distribution (continued)

$$F_{\nu_1, \nu_2; .05}$$

$\nu_2 \backslash \nu_1$	1	2	3	4	5	6	7	8	9	10	12	15	20	24	30	40	60	120	∞
13	$.0^2 41$	.052	.115	.170	.215	.251	.282	.307	.328	.346	.375	.408	.444	.464	.485	.507	.528	.555	.580
14	$.0^2 41$	.051	.115	.170	.216	.253	.283	.309	.330	.348	.378	.412	.449	.469	.491	.514	.536	.563	.589
15	$.0^2 41$	.051	.115	.170	.216	.254	.285	.311	.333	.351	.382	.416	.454	.474	.496	.519	.545	.571	.600
16	$.0^2 41$	.051	.115	.171	.217	.255	.286	.312	.334	.353	.384	.419	.458	.478	.502	.525	.549	.577	.606
17	$.0^2 41$	.051	.115	.171	.218	.256	.287	.313	.335	.355	.386	.422	.461	.481	.506	.530	.554	.583	.613
18	$.0^2 41$	.051	.115	.172	.218	.257	.288	.315	.337	.357	.389	.424	.465	.485	.510	.534	.560	.590	.621
19	$.0^2 40$	.051	.115	.172	.219	.257	.290	.316	.339	.359	.391	.427	.468	.489	.514	.539	.566	.596	.629
20	$.0^2 40$	.051	.115	.172	.219	.258	.290	.318	.340	.360	.393	.430	.471	.493	.518	.544	.572	.603	.637
21	$.0^2 40$	.051	.116	.173	.220	.259	.291	.318	.341	.362	.395	.431	.474	.496	.521	.547	.576	.607	.642
22	$.0^2 40$	.051	.116	.173	.220	.259	.292	.319	.342	.363	.396	.433	.476	.499	.524	.551	.580	.612	.647
23	$.0^2 40$	.051	.116	.173	.220	.260	.293	.320	.344	.364	.397	.435	.478	.502	.526	.555	.584	.616	.653
24	$.0^2 40$	.051	.116	.173	.221	.260	.293	.321	.345	.365	.399	.437	.480	.504	.530	.558	.588	.622	.659
25	$.0^2 40$	.051	.116	.173	.221	.261	.294	.321	.346	.366	.399	.438	.482	.507	.531	.561	.591	.625	.662
26	$.0^2 40$	.051	.116	.174	.221	.261	.294	.322	.346	.367	.401	.439	.484	.508	.534	.564	.594	.629	.667
27	$.0^2 40$	.051	.116	.174	.221	.261	.295	.323	.347	.368	.402	.441	.485	.510	.536	.567	.597	.633	.671
28	$.0^2 40$	.051	.116	.174	.222	.262	.295	.323	.348	.369	.403	.442	.487	.512	.539	.569	.600	.637	.676
29	$.0^2 40$	.051	.116	.174	.222	.262	.295	.324	.349	.369	.404	.443	.489	.514	.541	.572	.603	.641	.680
30	$.0^2 40$	.051	.116	.174	.222	.263	.296	.325	.349	.370	.406	.445	.490	.516	.543	.573	.606	.644	.685
40	$.0^2 40$	.051	.116	.175	.224	.265	.299	.329	.354	.376	.412	.454	.502	.529	.558	.591	.627	.669	.717
60	$.0^2 40$	.051	.116	.176	.226	.267	.303	.333	.359	.382	.419	.463	.514	.543	.575	.611	.652	.700	.759
120	$.0^2 39$	.051	.117	.177	.227	.270	.306	.337	.364	.388	.427	.473	.527	.559	.594	.634	.682	.727	.819
∞	$.0^2 39$	.051	.117	.178	.229	.273	.310	.342	.369	.394	.436	.484	.543	.577	.617	.663	.720	.781	1.000

Table M   Fractiles of the F Distribution (continued)

$$F_{\nu_1, \nu_2;\ .95}$$

ν_2 \ ν_1	1	2	3	4	5	6	7	8	9	10	12	15	20	24	30	40	60	120	∞
1	161.4	199.5	215.7	224.6	230.2	234.0	236.8	238.9	240.5	241.9	243.9	245.9	248.0	249.1	250.1	251.1	252.2	253.3	254.3
2	18.51	19.00	19.16	19.25	19.30	19.33	19.35	19.37	19.38	19.40	19.41	19.43	19.45	19.45	19.46	19.47	19.48	19.49	19.50
3	10.13	9.55	9.28	9.12	9.01	8.94	8.89	8.85	8.81	8.79	8.74	8.70	8.66	8.64	8.62	8.59	8.57	8.55	8.53
4	7.71	6.94	6.59	6.39	6.26	6.16	6.09	6.04	6.00	5.96	5.91	5.86	5.80	5.77	5.75	5.72	5.69	5.66	5.63
5	6.61	5.79	5.41	5.19	5.05	4.95	4.88	4.82	4.77	4.74	4.68	4.62	4.56	4.53	4.50	4.46	4.43	4.40	4.36
6	5.99	5.14	4.76	4.53	4.39	4.28	4.21	4.15	4.10	4.06	4.00	3.94	3.87	3.84	3.81	3.77	3.74	3.70	3.67
7	5.59	4.74	4.35	4.12	3.97	3.87	3.79	3.73	3.68	3.64	3.57	3.51	3.44	3.41	3.38	3.34	3.30	3.27	3.23
8	5.32	4.46	4.07	3.84	3.69	3.58	3.50	3.44	3.39	3.35	3.28	3.22	3.15	3.12	3.08	3.04	3.01	2.97	2.93
9	5.12	4.26	3.86	3.63	3.48	3.37	3.29	3.23	3.18	3.14	3.07	3.01	2.94	2.90	2.86	2.83	2.79	2.75	2.71
10	4.96	4.10	3.71	3.48	3.33	3.22	3.14	3.07	3.02	2.98	2.91	2.85	2.77	2.74	2.70	2.66	2.62	2.58	2.54
11	4.84	3.98	3.59	3.36	3.20	3.09	3.01	2.95	2.90	2.85	2.79	2.72	2.65	2.61	2.57	2.53	2.49	2.45	2.40
12	4.75	3.89	3.49	3.26	3.11	3.00	2.91	2.85	2.80	2.75	2.69	2.62	2.54	2.51	2.47	2.43	2.38	2.34	2.30
13	4.67	3.81	3.41	3.18	3.03	2.92	2.83	2.77	2.71	2.67	2.60	2.53	2.46	2.42	2.38	2.34	2.30	2.25	2.21
14	4.60	3.74	3.34	3.11	2.96	2.85	2.76	2.70	2.65	2.60	2.53	2.46	2.39	2.35	2.31	2.27	2.22	2.18	2.13
15	4.54	3.68	3.29	3.06	2.90	2.79	2.71	2.64	2.59	2.54	2.48	2.40	2.33	2.29	2.25	2.20	2.16	2.11	2.07
16	4.49	3.63	3.24	3.01	2.85	2.74	2.66	2.59	2.54	2.49	2.42	2.35	2.28	2.24	2.19	2.15	2.11	2.06	2.01
17	4.45	3.59	3.20	2.96	2.81	2.70	2.61	2.55	2.49	2.45	2.38	2.31	2.23	2.19	2.15	2.10	2.06	2.01	1.96
18	4.41	3.55	3.16	2.93	2.77	2.66	2.58	2.51	2.46	2.41	2.34	2.27	2.19	2.15	2.11	2.06	2.02	1.97	1.92
19	4.38	3.52	3.13	2.90	2.71	2.63	2.54	2.48	2.42	2.38	2.31	2.23	2.16	2.11	2.07	2.03	1.98	1.93	1.88
20	4.35	3.49	3.10	2.87	2.71	2.60	2.51	2.45	2.39	2.35	2.28	2.20	2.12	2.08	2.04	1.99	1.95	1.90	1.84
21	4.32	3.47	3.07	2.84	2.68	2.57	2.49	2.42	2.37	2.32	2.25	2.18	2.10	2.05	2.01	1.96	1.92	1.87	1.81
22	4.30	3.44	3.05	2.82	2.66	2.55	2.46	2.40	2.34	2.30	2.23	2.15	2.07	2.03	1.98	1.94	1.89	1.84	1.78
23	4.28	3.42	3.03	2.80	2.64	2.53	2.44	2.37	2.32	2.27	2.20	2.13	2.05	2.01	1.96	1.91	1.86	1.81	1.76
24	4.26	3.40	3.01	2.78	2.62	2.51	2.42	2.36	2.30	2.25	2.18	2.11	2.03	1.98	1.94	1.89	1.84	1.79	1.73

$F_{\nu_1, \nu_2; .95}$

ν_1 / ν_2	1	2	3	4	5	6	7	8	9	10	12	15	20	24	30	40	60	120	∞
25	4.24	3.39	2.99	2.76	2.60	2.49	2.40	2.34	2.28	2.24	2.16	2.09	2.01	1.96	1.92	1.87	1.82	1.77	1.71
26	4.23	3.37	2.98	2.74	2.59	2.47	2.39	2.32	2.27	2.22	2.15	2.07	1.99	1.95	1.90	1.85	1.80	1.75	1.69
27	4.21	3.35	2.96	2.73	2.57	2.46	2.37	2.31	2.25	2.20	2.13	2.06	1.97	1.93	1.88	1.84	1.79	1.73	1.67
28	4.20	3.34	2.95	2.71	2.56	2.45	2.36	2.29	2.24	2.19	2.12	2.04	1.96	1.91	1.87	1.82	1.77	1.71	1.65
29	4.18	3.33	2.93	2.70	2.55	2.43	2.35	2.28	2.22	2.18	2.10	2.03	1.94	1.90	1.85	1.81	1.75	1.70	1.64
30	4.17	3.32	2.92	2.69	2.53	2.42	2.33	2.27	2.21	2.16	2.09	2.01	1.93	1.89	1.84	1.79	1.74	1.68	1.62
40	4.08	3.23	2.84	2.61	2.45	2.34	2.25	2.18	2.12	2.08	2.00	1.92	1.84	1.79	1.74	1.69	1.64	1.58	1.51
60	4.00	3.15	2.76	2.53	2.37	2.25	2.17	2.10	2.04	1.99	1.92	1.84	1.75	1.70	1.65	1.59	1.53	1.47	1.39
120	3.92	3.07	2.68	2.45	2.29	2.17	2.09	2.02	1.96	1.91	1.83	1.75	1.66	1.61	1.55	1.50	1.43	1.35	1.25
∞	3.84	3.00	2.60	2.37	2.21	2.10	2.01	1.94	1.88	1.83	1.75	1.67	1.57	1.52	1.46	1.39	1.32	1.22	1.00

$F_{\nu_1, \nu_2; .975}$

ν_1 / ν_2	1	2	3	4	5	6	7	8	9	10	12	15	20	24	30	40	60	120	∞
1	647.8	799.5	864.2	899.6	921.8	937.1	948.2	956.7	963.3	968.6	976.7	984.9	993.1	997.2	1001	1006	1010	1014	1018
2	38.51	39.00	39.17	39.25	39.30	39.33	39.36	39.37	39.39	39.40	39.41	39.43	39.45	39.46	39.46	39.47	39.48	39.49	39.50
3	17.44	16.04	15.44	15.10	14.88	14.73	14.62	14.54	14.47	14.42	14.34	14.25	14.17	14.12	14.08	14.04	13.99	13.95	13.90
4	12.22	10.65	9.98	9.60	9.36	9.20	9.07	8.98	8.90	8.84	8.75	8.66	8.56	8.51	8.46	8.41	8.36	8.31	8.26
5	10.01	8.43	7.76	7.39	7.15	6.98	6.85	6.76	6.68	6.62	6.52	6.43	6.33	6.28	6.23	6.18	6.12	6.07	6.02
6	8.81	7.26	6.60	6.23	5.99	5.82	5.70	5.60	5.52	5.46	5.37	5.27	5.17	5.12	5.07	5.01	4.96	4.90	4.85
7	8.07	6.54	5.89	5.52	5.29	5.12	4.99	4.90	4.82	4.76	4.67	4.57	4.47	4.42	4.36	4.31	4.25	4.20	4.14
8	7.57	6.06	5.42	5.05	4.82	4.65	4.53	4.43	4.36	4.30	4.20	4.10	4.00	3.95	3.89	3.84	3.78	3.73	3.67
9	7.21	5.71	5.08	4.72	4.48	4.32	4.20	4.10	4.03	3.96	3.87	3.77	3.67	3.61	3.56	3.51	3.45	3.39	3.33

$$F_{\nu_1, \nu_2;\,.975}$$

ν_2 \\ ν_1	1	2	3	4	5	6	7	8	9	10	12	15	20	24	30	40	60	120	∞
10	6.94	5.46	4.83	4.47	4.24	4.07	3.95	3.85	3.78	3.72	3.62	3.52	3.42	3.37	3.31	3.26	3.20	3.14	3.08
11	6.72	5.26	4.63	4.28	4.04	3.88	3.76	3.66	3.59	3.53	3.43	3.33	3.23	3.17	3.12	3.06	3.00	2.94	2.88
12	6.55	5.10	4.47	4.12	3.89	3.73	3.61	3.51	3.44	3.37	3.28	3.18	3.07	3.02	2.96	2.91	2.85	2.79	2.72
13	6.41	4.97	4.35	4.00	3.77	3.60	3.48	3.39	3.31	3.25	3.15	3.05	2.95	2.89	2.84	2.78	2.72	2.66	2.60
14	6.30	4.86	4.24	3.89	3.66	3.50	3.38	3.29	3.21	3.15	3.05	2.95	2.84	2.79	2.73	2.67	2.61	2.55	2.49
15	6.20	4.77	4.15	3.80	3.58	3.41	3.29	3.20	3.12	3.06	2.96	2.86	2.76	2.70	2.64	2.59	2.52	2.46	2.40
16	6.12	4.69	4.08	3.73	3.50	3.34	3.22	3.12	3.05	2.99	2.89	2.79	2.68	2.63	2.57	2.51	2.45	2.38	2.32
17	6.04	4.62	4.01	3.66	3.44	3.28	3.16	3.06	2.98	2.92	2.82	2.72	2.62	2.56	2.50	2.44	2.38	2.32	2.25
18	5.98	4.56	3.95	3.61	3.38	3.22	3.10	3.01	2.93	2.87	2.77	2.67	2.56	2.50	2.44	2.38	2.32	2.26	2.19
19	5.92	4.51	3.90	3.56	3.33	3.17	3.05	2.96	2.88	2.82	2.72	2.62	2.51	2.45	2.39	2.33	2.27	2.20	2.13
20	5.87	4.46	3.86	3.51	3.29	3.13	3.01	2.91	2.84	2.77	2.68	2.57	2.46	2.41	2.35	2.29	2.22	2.16	2.09
21	5.83	4.42	3.82	3.48	3.25	3.09	2.97	2.87	2.80	2.73	2.64	2.53	2.42	2.37	2.31	2.25	2.18	2.11	2.04
22	5.79	4.38	3.78	3.44	3.22	3.05	2.93	2.84	2.76	2.70	2.60	2.50	2.39	2.33	2.27	2.21	2.14	2.08	2.00
23	5.75	4.35	3.75	3.41	3.18	3.02	2.90	2.81	2.73	2.67	2.57	2.47	2.36	2.30	2.24	2.18	2.11	2.04	1.97
24	5.72	4.32	3.72	3.38	3.15	2.99	2.87	2.78	2.70	2.64	2.54	2.44	2.33	2.27	2.21	2.15	2.08	2.01	1.94
25	5.69	4.29	3.69	3.35	3.13	2.97	2.85	2.75	2.68	2.61	2.51	2.41	2.30	2.24	2.18	2.12	2.05	1.98	1.91
26	5.66	4.27	3.67	3.33	3.10	2.94	2.82	2.73	2.65	2.59	2.49	2.39	2.28	2.22	2.16	2.09	2.03	1.95	1.88
27	5.63	4.24	3.65	3.31	3.08	2.92	2.80	2.71	2.63	2.57	2.47	2.36	2.25	2.19	2.13	2.07	2.00	1.93	1.85
28	5.61	4.22	3.63	3.29	3.06	2.90	2.78	2.69	2.61	2.55	2.45	2.34	2.23	2.17	2.11	2.05	1.98	1.91	1.83
29	5.59	4.20	3.61	3.27	3.04	2.88	2.76	2.67	2.59	2.53	2.43	2.32	2.21	2.15	2.09	2.03	1.96	1.89	1.81
30	5.57	4.18	3.59	3.25	3.03	2.87	2.75	2.65	2.57	2.51	2.41	2.31	2.20	2.14	2.07	2.01	1.94	1.87	1.79
40	5.42	4.05	3.46	3.13	2.90	2.74	2.62	2.53	2.45	2.39	2.29	2.18	2.07	2.01	1.94	1.88	1.80	1.72	1.64
60	5.29	3.93	3.34	3.01	2.79	2.63	2.51	2.41	2.33	2.27	2.17	2.06	1.94	1.88	1.82	1.74	1.67	1.58	1.48
120	5.15	3.80	3.23	2.89	2.67	2.52	2.39	2.30	2.22	2.16	2.05	1.94	1.82	1.76	1.69	1.61	1.53	1.43	1.31
∞	5.02	3.69	3.12	2.79	2.57	2.41	2.29	2.19	2.11	2.05	1.94	1.83	1.71	1.64	1.57	1.48	1.39	1.27	1.00

Table M Fractiles of the F Distribution (continued)

$$F_{v_1, v_2; .99}$$

v_2 \ v_1	1	2	3	4	5	6	7	8	9	10	12	15	20	24	30	40	60	120	∞
1	4052	4999.5	5403	5625	5764	5859	5928	5982	6022	6056	6106	6157	6209	6235	6261	6287	6313	6339	6366
2	98.50	99.00	99.17	99.25	99.30	99.33	99.36	99.37	99.39	99.40	99.42	99.43	99.45	99.46	99.47	99.47	99.48	99.49	99.50
3	34.12	30.82	29.46	28.71	28.24	27.91	27.67	27.49	27.35	27.23	27.05	26.87	26.69	26.60	26.50	26.41	26.32	26.22	26.13
4	21.00	18.00	16.69	15.98	15.52	15.21	14.98	14.80	14.66	14.55	14.37	14.20	14.02	13.93	13.84	13.75	13.65	13.56	13.46
5	16.26	13.27	12.06	11.39	10.97	10.67	10.46	10.29	10.16	10.05	9.89	9.72	9.55	9.47	9.38	9.29	9.20	9.11	9.02
6	13.75	10.92	9.78	9.15	8.75	8.47	8.26	8.10	7.98	7.87	7.72	7.56	7.40	7.31	7.23	7.14	7.06	6.97	6.88
7	12.25	9.55	8.45	7.85	7.46	7.19	6.99	6.84	6.72	6.62	6.47	6.31	6.16	6.07	5.99	5.91	5.82	5.74	5.65
8	11.26	8.65	7.59	7.01	6.63	6.37	6.18	6.03	5.91	5.81	5.67	5.52	5.36	5.28	5.20	5.12	5.03	4.95	4.86
9	10.56	8.02	6.99	6.42	6.06	5.80	5.61	5.47	5.35	5.26	5.11	4.96	4.81	4.73	4.65	4.57	4.48	4.40	4.31
10	10.04	7.56	6.55	5.99	5.64	5.39	5.20	5.06	4.94	4.85	4.71	4.56	4.41	4.33	4.25	4.17	4.08	4.00	3.91
11	9.65	7.21	6.22	5.67	5.32	5.07	4.89	4.74	4.63	4.54	4.40	4.25	4.10	4.02	3.94	3.86	3.78	3.69	3.60
12	9.33	6.93	5.95	5.41	5.06	4.82	4.64	4.50	4.39	4.30	4.16	4.01	3.86	3.78	3.70	3.62	3.54	3.45	3.36
13	9.07	6.70	5.74	5.21	4.86	4.62	4.44	4.30	4.19	4.10	3.96	3.82	3.66	3.59	3.51	3.43	3.34	3.25	3.17
14	8.86	6.51	5.56	5.04	4.69	4.46	4.28	4.14	4.03	3.94	3.80	3.66	3.51	3.43	3.35	3.27	3.18	3.09	3.00
15	8.68	6.36	5.42	4.89	4.56	4.32	4.14	4.00	3.89	3.80	3.67	3.52	3.37	3.29	3.21	3.13	3.05	2.96	2.87
16	8.53	6.23	5.29	4.77	4.44	4.20	4.03	3.89	3.78	3.69	3.55	3.41	3.26	3.18	3.10	3.02	2.93	2.84	2.75
17	8.40	6.11	5.18	4.67	4.34	4.10	3.93	3.79	3.68	3.59	3.46	3.31	3.16	3.08	3.00	2.92	2.83	2.75	2.65
18	8.29	6.01	5.09	4.58	4.25	4.01	3.84	3.71	3.60	3.51	3.37	3.23	3.08	3.00	2.92	2.84	2.75	2.66	2.57
19	8.18	5.93	5.01	4.50	4.17	3.94	3.77	3.63	3.52	3.43	3.30	3.15	3.00	2.92	2.84	2.76	2.67	2.58	2.49
20	8.10	5.85	4.94	4.43	4.10	3.87	3.70	3.56	3.46	3.37	3.23	3.09	2.94	2.86	2.78	2.69	2.61	2.52	2.42
21	8.02	5.78	4.87	4.37	4.04	3.81	3.64	3.51	3.40	3.31	3.17	3.03	2.88	2.80	2.72	2.64	2.55	2.46	2.36
22	7.95	5.72	4.82	4.31	3.99	3.76	3.59	3.45	3.35	3.26	3.12	2.98	2.83	2.75	2.67	2.58	2.50	2.40	2.31
23	7.88	5.66	4.76	4.26	3.94	3.71	3.54	3.41	3.30	3.21	3.07	2.93	2.78	2.70	2.62	2.54	2.45	2.35	2.26
24	7.82	5.61	4.72	4.22	3.90	3.67	3.50	3.36	3.26	3.17	3.03	2.89	2.74	2.66	2.58	2.49	2.40	2.31	2.21

Table M Fractiles of the F Distribution (continued)

$$F_{v_1, v_2;\,.99}$$

v_2 \ v_1	1	2	3	4	5	6	7	8	9	10	12	15	20	24	30	40	60	120	∞
25	7.77	5.57	4.68	4.18	3.85	3.63	3.46	3.32	3.22	3.13	2.99	2.85	2.70	2.62	2.54	2.45	2.36	2.27	2.17
26	7.72	5.53	4.64	4.14	3.82	3.59	3.42	3.29	3.18	3.09	2.96	2.81	2.66	2.58	2.50	2.42	2.33	2.23	2.13
27	7.68	5.49	4.60	4.11	3.78	3.56	3.39	3.26	3.15	3.06	2.93	2.78	2.63	2.55	2.47	2.38	2.29	2.20	2.10
28	7.64	5.45	4.57	4.07	3.75	3.53	3.36	3.23	3.12	3.03	2.90	2.75	2.60	2.52	2.44	2.35	2.26	2.17	2.06
29	7.60	5.42	4.54	4.04	3.73	3.50	3.33	3.20	3.09	3.00	2.87	2.73	2.57	2.49	2.41	2.33	2.23	2.14	2.03
30	7.56	5.39	4.51	4.02	3.70	3.47	3.30	3.17	3.07	2.98	2.84	2.70	2.55	2.47	2.39	2.30	2.21	2.11	2.01
40	7.31	5.18	4.31	3.83	3.51	3.29	3.12	2.99	2.89	2.80	2.66	2.52	2.37	2.29	2.20	2.11	2.02	1.92	1.80
60	7.08	4.98	4.13	3.65	3.34	3.12	2.95	2.82	2.72	2.63	2.50	2.35	2.20	2.12	2.03	1.94	1.84	1.73	1.60
120	6.85	4.79	3.95	3.48	3.17	2.96	2.79	2.66	2.56	2.47	2.34	2.19	2.03	1.95	1.86	1.76	1.66	1.53	1.38
∞	6.63	4.61	3.78	3.32	3.02	2.80	2.64	2.51	2.41	2.32	2.18	2.04	1.88	1.79	1.70	1.59	1.47	1.32	1.00

Table N   Bias Correction Factors for Estimating σ
When Population Is Normal

Sample Size, n	Correction Factor, c
2	1.253
3	1.128
4	1.085
5	1.064
6	1.051
7	1.042
8	1.036
9	1.032
10	1.028

Note: For $n > 10$, a satisfactory approximation, accurate to three decimal places, may be obtained from the formula

$$c \approx 1 + \frac{1}{4(n-1)}$$

A technical explanation of this factor is given by A. Hald, *Statistical Theory with Applications* (New York: John Wiley & Sons, Inc., 1952), pp. 299–300.

Table O   Conversion of a Pearson *r* into a Corresponding
Fisher's *Z*-Coefficient

r	Z_r	*r*	Z_r	*r*	Z_r
.20	.203	.50	.549	.80	1.099
.21	.213	.51	.563	.81	1.127
.22	.224	.52	.576	.82	1.157
.23	.234	.53	.590	.83	1.188
.24	.245	.54	.604	.84	1.221
.25	.255	.55	.618	.85	1.256
.26	.266	.56	.633	.86	1.293
.27	.277	.57	.648	.87	1.333
.28	.288	.58	.662	.88	1.376
.29	.299	.59	.678	.89	1.422
.30	.310	.60	.693	.900	1.472
.31	.321	.61	.709	.905	1.499
.32	.332	.62	.725	.910	1.528
.33	.343	.63	.741	.915	1.557
.34	.354	.64	.758	.920	1.589
.35	.365	.65	.775	.925	1.623
.36	.377	.66	.793	.930	1.658
.37	.388	.67	.811	.935	1.697
.38	.400	.68	.829	.940	1.738
.39	.412	.69	.848	.945	1.783
.40	.424	.70	.867	.950	1.832
.41	.436	.71	.887	.955	1.886
.42	.448	.72	.908	.960	1.946
.43	.460	.73	.929	.965	2.014
.44	.472	.74	.950	.970	2.092
.45	.485	.75	.973	.975	2.185
.46	.497	.76	.996	.980	2.298
.47	.510	.77	1.020	.985	2.443
.48	.523	.78	1.045	.990	2.647
.49	.536	.79	1.071	.995	2.994

Table P   Fractiles of the Distribution of the Kolmogorov-Smirnov Statistic (Parameters Specified)

φ \ n	.90	.95	.975	.995
1	.900	.950	.975	.995
2	.684	.776	.842	.929
3	.565	.642	.708	.829
4	.494	.564	.624	.734
5	.446	.510	.563	.669
6	.410	.470	.521	.618
7	.381	.438	.486	.577
8	.358	.411	.457	.543
9	.339	.388	.432	.514
10	.322	.368	.409	.486
11	.307	.352	.391	.468
12	.295	.338	.375	.450
13	.284	.325	.361	.433
14	.274	.314	.349	.418
15	.266	.304	.338	.404
16	.258	.295	.328	.391
17	.250	.286	.318	.380
18	.244	.278	.309	.370
19	.237	.272	.301	.361
20	.231	.264	.294	.352
25	.21	.24	.264	.32
30	.19	.22	.242	.29
35	.18	.21	.23	.27
40			.21	.25
50			.19	.23
60			.17	.21
70			.16	.19
80			.15	.18
90			.14	
100			.14	

Adapted with permission from Table 1 in L. H. Miller, "Table of Percentage Points of Kolmogorov Statistics," *Journal of the American Statistical Association,* 51 (1956), 111–21.

Table Q Fractiles of the Distribution of the Kolmogorov-Smirnov Statistic for a Normality Test (μ and σ Estimated)

n \\ φ	.80	.90	.95	.99
4	.300	.352	.381	.417
5	.285	.315	.337	.405
6	.265	.294	.319	.364
7	.247	.276	.300	.348
8	.233	.261	.285	.331
9	.223	.249	.271	.294
10	.215	.239	.258	.284
11	.206	.230	.249	.275
12	.199	.223	.242	.268
13	.190	.214	.234	.261
14	.183	.207	.227	.257
15	.177	.201	.220	.250
16	.173	.195	.213	.245
17	.169	.189	.206	.239
18	.166	.184	.200	.235
19	.163	.179	.195	.231
20	.160	.174	.190	.200
25	.142	.158	.173	.187
30	.131	.144	.161	
Over 30	$\dfrac{.736}{\sqrt{n}}$	$\dfrac{.805}{\sqrt{n}}$	$\dfrac{.886}{\sqrt{n}}$	$\dfrac{1.031}{\sqrt{n}}$

Adapted with permission from Table 1 of H. W. Lilliefors, "On the Kolmogorov-Smirnov Test for Normality with Mean and Variance Unknown," *Journal of the American Statistical Association,* 62 (1967), 399–402, as corrected on advice of Carl B. Bates in *Journal of the American Statistical Association,* 64 (1969), 1702.

Table R Fractiles of the Distribution of R for the Sign Test

n	α .005	.025	.05	.125	n	α .005	.025	.05	.125	n	α .005	.025	.05	.125
1	—	—	—	—	31	7	9	10	11	61	20	22	23	25
2	—	—	—	—	32	8	9	10	12	62	20	22	24	25
3	—	—	—	0	33	8	10	11	12	63	20	23	24	26
4	—	—	—	0	34	9	10	11	13	64	21	23	24	26
5	—	—	0	0	35	9	11	12	13	65	21	24	25	27
6	—	0	0	1	36	9	11	12	14	66	22	24	25	27
7	—	0	0	1	37	10	12	13	14	67	22	25	26	28
8	0	0	1	1	38	10	12	13	14	68	22	25	26	28
9	0	1	1	2	39	11	12	13	15	69	23	25	27	29
10	0	1	1	2	40	11	13	14	15	70	23	26	27	29
11	0	1	2	3	41	11	13	14	16	71	24	26	28	30
12	1	2	2	3	42	12	14	15	16	72	24	27	28	30
13	1	2	3	3	43	12	14	15	17	73	25	27	28	31
14	1	2	3	4	44	13	15	16	17	74	25	28	29	31
15	2	3	3	4	45	13	15	16	18	75	25	28	29	32
16	2	3	4	5	46	13	15	16	18	76	26	28	30	32
17	2	4	4	5	47	14	16	17	19	77	26	29	30	32
18	3	4	5	6	48	14	16	17	19	78	27	29	31	33
19	3	4	5	6	49	15	17	18	19	79	27	30	31	33
20	3	5	5	6	50	15	17	18	20	80	28	30	32	34
21	4	5	6	7	51	15	18	19	20	81	28	31	32	34
22	4	5	6	7	52	16	18	19	21	82	28	31	33	35
23	4	6	7	8	53	16	18	20	21	83	29	32	33	35
24	5	6	7	8	54	17	19	20	22	84	29	32	33	36
25	5	7	7	9	55	17	19	20	22	85	30	32	34	36
26	6	7	8	9	56	17	20	21	23	86	30	33	34	37
27	6	7	8	10	57	18	20	21	23	87	31	33	35	37
28	6	8	9	10	58	18	21	22	24	88	31	34	35	38
29	7	8	9	10	59	19	21	22	24	89	31	34	36	38
30	7	9	10	11	60	19	21	23	25	90	32	35	36	39

Adapted with permission from Table 1 in W. J. Mockinnon, "Table for Both the Sign Test and Distribution-Free Confidence Intervals of the Median for Sizes to 1,000," *Journal of the American Statistical Association,* 59 (1964), 935–56.

Table S Fractiles of the Distribution of *W* for the
Wilcoxon Signed-Ranks Test

φ n	.025	.01	.005
6	0	—	—
7	2	0	—
8	4	2	0
9	6	3	2
10	8	5	3
11	11	7	5
12	14	10	7
13	17	13	10
14	21	16	13
15	25	20	16
16	30	24	20
17	35	28	23
18	40	33	28
19	46	38	32
20	52	43	38
21	59	49	43
22	66	56	49
23	73	62	55
24	81	69	61
25	89	77	68

Note: For large *n*, the value of $W_{n;\alpha}$ is approximately

$$\frac{n(n+1)}{4} - z_{1-\alpha}\sqrt{\frac{n(n+1)(2n+1)}{24}}$$

where $z_{1-\alpha}$ is the $(1-\alpha)$ fractile of the standard normal distribution.

Adapted with permission from Table II in F. Wilcoxon, S. K. Katti, and Roberta A. Wilcox, *Critical Values and Probability Levels for the Wilcoxon Rank Sum Test and the Wilcoxon Signed Rank Test,* American Cyanamid Company (Lederle Laboratories Division, Pearl River, N.Y.) and the Florida State University (Department of Statistics, Tallahassee, Fla.), August 1963.

Table T   Fractiles of the Distribution of T for the Mann–Whitney–Wilcoxon Test

n_b	φ	1	2	3	4	5	6	7	8	9	10	11	12	13	14	15	16
															n_a (Smaller Sample)		
3	.10		3	7													
	.05			6													
	.025																
	.005																
4	.10		3	7	13												
	.05			6	11												
	.025				10												
	.005																
5	.10		4	8	14	20											
	.05		3	7	12	19											
	.025			6	11	17											
	.005				15												
6	.10		4	9	15	22	30										
	.05		3	8	13	20	28										
	.025			7	12	18	26										
	.005				10	16	23										
7	.10		4	10	16	23	32	41									
	.05		3	8	14	21	29	39									
	.025			7	13	20	27	36									
	.005				10	16	24	32									
8	.10		5	11	17	25	34	44	55								
	.05		4	9	15	23	31	41	51								
	.025		3	8	14	21	29	38	49								
	.005				11	17	25	34	43								
9	.10	1	5	11	19	27	36	46	58	70							
	.05		4	10	16	24	33	43	54	66							
	.025		3	8	14	22	31	40	51	62							
	.005			6	11	18	26	35	45	56							
10	.10	1	6	12	20	28	38	49	60	73	87						
	.05		4	10	17	26	35	45	56	69	82						
	.025		3	9	15	23	32	42	53	65	78						
	.005			6	12	19	27	37	47	58	71						
11	.10	1	6	13	21	30	40	51	63	76	91	106					
	.05		4	11	18	27	37	47	59	72	86	100					
	.025		3	9	16	24	34	44	55	68	81	96					
	.005			6	12	20	28	38	49	61	73	87					
12	.10	1	7	14	22	32	42	54	66	80	94	110	127				
	.05		5	11	19	28	38	49	62	75	89	104	120				
	.025		4	10	17	26	35	46	58	71	84	99	115				
	.005			7	13	21	30	40	51	63	76	90	105				
13	.10	1	7	15	23	33	44	56	69	83	98	114	131	149			
	.05		5	12	20	30	40	52	64	78	92	108	125	142			
	.025		4	10	18	27	37	48	60	73	88	103	119	136			
	.005			7	13	22	31	41	53	65	79	93	109	125			

Table T   Fractiles of the Distribution of T for the Mann–Whitney–Wilcoxon Test
(continued)

| n_b | φ | \multicolumn{16}{c}{n_a (Smaller Sample)} |
		1	2	3	4	5	6	7	8	9	10	11	12	13	14	15	16
14	.10	1	8	16	25	35	46	59	72	86	102	118	136	154	174		
	.05		6	13	21	31	42	54	67	81	96	112	129	147	166		
	.025		4	11	19	28	38	50	62	76	91	106	123	141	160		
	.005			7	14	22	32	43	54	67	81	96	112	129	147		
15	.10	1	8	16	26	37	48	61	75	90	106	123	141	159	179	200	
	.05		6	13	22	33	44	56	69	84	99	116	133	152	171	192	
	.025		4	11	20	29	40	52	65	79	94	110	127	145	164	184	
	.005			8	15	23	33	44	56	69	84	99	115	133	151	171	
16	.10	1	8	17	27	38	50	64	78	93	109	127	145	165	185	206	229
	.05		6	14	24	34	46	58	72	87	103	120	138	156	176	197	219
	.025		4	12	21	30	42	54	67	82	97	113	131	150	169	190	211
	.005			8	15	24	34	46	58	72	86	102	119	136	155	175	196

Adapted with permission from D. B. Owen, *Handbook of Statistical Tables* (Reading, Mass.:
Addison-Wesley, 1962), pp. 355–61.

Answers to Selected Problems

CHAPTER 1

1.1 Since a statistical inference is drawn from limited evidence obtained from a sample rather than from the entire population, it is possible for the inference to be incorrect and lead to a wrong decision.

1.3 Used in the singular, statistics refers to a branch of scientific methodology dealing with the collection and analysis of numerical evidence. Used in the plural, statistics may refer to either (1) a tabulation of numerical facts, or (2) two or more numerical quantities derived from the outcome of a sampling study.

1.5 (a) Statistic (b) Population (c) Parameter
(d) Sample (e) Statistic

CHAPTER 2

2.1 (a) The statement of the problem should clearly identify: (i) each of the available alternative actions, (ii) the population of concern, (iii) the decision parameter, and (iv) the possible consequences of each of the alternative actions.

(b) So that the decision maker can determine whether uncertainty exists and, if so, exactly what data is required to reduce the uncertainty.

2.3 (a) A nominal scale is a naming device by which numbers are assigned to individual observations simply to identify the attribute categories to which they belong. An ordinal scale is one on which there is an ordered relationship among numbers on the scale.

(b) An ordinal scale is one on which there is an ordered relationship among the numbers on the scale, but the intervals between successive values on the scale are not necessarily equal. An interval scale is one on which equal differences anywhere along the scale represent equal amounts of difference in the characteristic being measured.

(c) An interval scale is one on which equal differences anywhere along the scale represent equal amounts of difference in the characteristic being measured, but the zero point is arbitrary. A ratio scale is an interval scale which has an absolute zero point in the sense that the numeral "0" represents complete absence of the characteristic being measured.

2.5

Element of Observation	Variable	Unit of Measurement
(a) Housewife	Amount Spent	Dollars
(b) Floodlamp	Burning Life	Minutes
(c) Box	Net Contents	Ounces
(d) Car	Speed	Miles per hour

2.7 (a) $\dfrac{90}{80} = 1.125$

(b) Allen: $.80(90) + 50 = 122$
Barker: $.80(80) + 50 = 114$

(c) $\dfrac{122}{114} = 1.070$

(d) Psychological measurements such as the mental ability test score and IQ are not on ratio scales. Therefore, the ratios have no meaning.

2.9 (a) No. of males: 8,000
No. of females: 4,000

Both of these numbers are parameters, i.e., quantitative properties of the population.

(b) Males: $\dfrac{8,000}{12,000} \times 100 = 66.67\%$

Females: $\dfrac{4,000}{12,000} \times 100 = 33.33\%$

Both of these percentages are parameters.

(c) Division I: $\dfrac{4,000}{12,000} \times 100 = 33.33\%$

Division II: $\dfrac{5,000}{12,000} \times 100 = 41.67\%$

Division III: $\dfrac{3,000}{12,000} \times 100 = 25.00\%$

All of these percentages are parameters.

2.13 The chart should be identical to Figure 2.4 except that the vertical axis should be a cumulative *relative* frequency scale rather than a cumulative frequency scale.

2.15

Class Limits	Frequency	Class Boundaries	Midpoint	Cumulative Frequency
55-59	10	54.5-59.5	57	10
60-64	19	59.5-64.5	62	29
65-69	19	64.5-69.5	67	48
70-74	26	69.5-74.5	72	74
75-79	11	74.5-79.5	77	85
80-84	18	79.5-84.5	82	103
85-89	7	84.5-89.5	87	110
90-94	6	89.5-94.5	92	116
95-99	3	94.5-99.5	97	119

Class Limits	Frequency	Relative Frequency	Cumulative Frequency	Cumulative Relative Frequency
75.00-79.99	3	.06	3	.06
80.00-84.99	4	.08	7	.14
85.00-89.99	5	.10	12	.24
90.00-94.99	4	.08	16	.32
95.00-99.99	8	.16	24	.48
100.00-104.99	8	.16	32	.64
105.00-109.99	9	.18	41	.82
110.00-114.99	5	.10	46	.92
115.00-119.99	2	.04	48	.96
120.00-124.99	2	.04	50	1.00

CHAPTER 3

3.1 (a) No. Data are nominal.

    (b) Same as (a) above.

    (c) Mean and median are meaningful.

3.3 $\mu = 110$; $\sigma^2 = 13.33$; $\sigma = 3.65$

3.5 $\sigma^2 = 84.214$; $\sigma = 9.18$

3.7 (a) .30 (b) .2583 (c) .11 (d) .33

3.9 (a) 41.5 (b) 41 (c) 32 (d) 44

3.11

Apollo	Bacchus	Ceres
13.00	13.00	13.00
13.00	13.00	14.00
1.15	3.46	2.94

3.13 (a) 33; 32.52; 26.09; 5.11

    (b) 32.625; 33.0; 31.714

    (c) 32.52

CHAPTER 4

4.1 Casino probabilities are theoretical; insurance probabilities are empirical.

4.3 (a) 1/13 (b) 3/13 (c) 1/52

    (d) 1/4 (e) 1/2 (f) 1

    (g) 9/13 (h) 3/52 (i) 1/2

4.5 .00013

4.7 .75

4.9 $P(A) = .5$; $P(B) = .3$; $P(C) = .2$

4.11 6

4.13 24

4.15 720

4.17 1,663,200

4.19 1,287

4.21 .21795 × 10^{12}

4.23 (a) 144   (b) 50,400

4.25 (a) 729   (b) 60

4.27 15,504

4.29 3.718 × 10^9

4.31 635 billions

4.33 (a) 109,824   (b) 624   (c) 3,744   (d) 54,912

CHAPTER 5

5.1 $S_1 = \{$January, February, March, April$\}$
$S_2 = \{$Prince Albert, Prince Phillip$\}$
$S_3 = \{$New York, Chicago, Los Angeles$\}$
$S_4 = \{0, 1, 2, \ldots\}$

5.3 (a) A is discrete and uses listing; B is continuous and uses describing.
(b) $A = \{a|a$ is positive integer between 2 and 4 inclusive$\}$
(c) Because B is a continuous set.

5.5 (a) 252   (b) 1,024

5.7 $H = \{5, 6, 7\}$ $K = \{3, 4, 5, 6, 7, 8, 9\}$
$I = \{3, 4, 5, 6, 7\}$ $L = \{l|3 \leq l \leq 7\}$
$J = \{j|5 < j < 7\}$ $M = \{m|3 \leq m \leq 9\}$

5.9 (a) and (d)

5.11 .25

5.13 .24

5.15 (a) $P(M' \cap T)$; $P(M' \cap T')$; $P(M|T')$; $P(T'|M)$; $P(M'|T')$
(b) .05; .35; .53; .67; .47

5.17 (a) .50   (b) .167   (c) .90

5.19 $P(X) = .40$; $P(Y) = .40$; $P(Z) = .20$

5.21 .80

5.23 .42

5.27 (a) .32   (b) .48   (c) .08   (d) .12
(e) .80   (f) .80   (g) .20   (h) .20

5.29 (a) .80   (b) No

5.31 (a) .18   (b) .30   (c) .12   (d) .30
(e) .72   (f) .82   (g) .88   (h) .58

5.33 (a) Not all three firms will survive the first year.
(c) Statement (iv) is correct.
(e) .30
(g) .925

5.35 .9656

5.37 .15

5.39 P(High) = .36; P(Low) = .10; P(Average) = .54

5.41 2/3

CHAPTER 6

6.1 $y = f(x) = x/.24$

6.3 (a) $f(1) = 1,010; f(5) = 1,050; f(10) = 1,100$
(b) Domain: $\{1, 2, \ldots, 50\}$
Range: $\{1010, 1020, 1030, \ldots, 1100\}$
(c) y is dependent and x is independent

6.5 (a) $T = 20 + 5H$
(b) $P = 50 - T; P = 30 - 5H$

6.7 (a)

x	$f(x)$		(c)	x	$F(x)$
1	.12			1	.12
2	.16			2	.28
3	.20			3	.48
4	.24			4	.72
5	.28			5	1.00

6.9 (a)

x	$f(x)$		(c)	x	$F(x)$
2	.06			2	.06
3	.08			3	.14
4	.10			4	.24
5	.12			5	.36
6	.14			6	.50
7	.20			7	.70
8	.15			8	.85
9	.10			9	.95
10	.05			10	1.00

6.11 (a) .16 (b) .18 (c) .34
(d) 1.00 (e) .60

6.13 (a) .324 (b) .324 (c) .324 (d) .324

6.15 (a) .4096 (b) .9728

6.17 (a) $k = .10$ (b) .33

6.19 (a) p.m.f.
(c) .50; .25; .125; .0625; .75; .875; .25; .125; .4375; .375

6.21 (d) .216; .512
(e) .216; .512

6.23 (a) $F(x) = (x - 2)/6$
(b) 1/2; 1/6

6.25 (d) .30; .49; .21

6.27 (d) .125; .875; .32; .84

6.29 (b) 1/4; 3/16; 5/16; 15/16; 5/12

(c) No

CHAPTER 7

7.1 (a) 2   (b) 5   (c) 6

    (d) 7   (e) 8   (f) 9.

7.3 1; 2.80; 3; 4

7.5 $5.00

7.7 5; 5

7.9 1.58

7.11 (a) .30; .55   (b) $172.50

7.13 (a) 5 units   (b) $27,000

7.15 (a) 6 2/3 hours   (b) $5.33 hundreds   (c) .25

7.17 $\sigma^2 = 1.64$; $\sigma = 1.28$

7.19 $\sigma^2 = 4.66$; $\sigma = 2.16$

7.21 $\sigma^2 = 2/9$; $\sigma = .471$

7.23 $\sigma^2 = .05$; $\sigma = .224$

7.25 (b) 8/3   (c) $\sigma^2 = 8/9$; $\sigma = .9428$ (d) 5/16

7.27 150,000

CHAPTER 8

8.5 (a) .60   (b) .30   (c) .10

8.7 (a) 41   (b) 62   (c) 64   (d) 87

8.13 (a) 14.2   (b) .1148   (c) .1148   (d) .3388

8.15 (a) .44   (b) 1; 3; 4   (c) 16   (d) 2.56; 3.34; 1.83

    (e) 15.28; 80.71; 8.98

CHAPTER 9

9.1 (c) .357; .536; .107

    (f) Because you are sampling without replacement from a finite dichotomy.

9.3 (a) .9692   (b) .9537

9.5 (a) .043   (b) .103   (d) $\mu = .40$; $\sigma^2 = .338$

9.7 (a) .0115   (b) .0702   (c) .3222   (d) .4744

9.11 (a) .0035   (c) $\mu = 2.5$; $\sigma = 1.37$

9.13 (a) .2707 (b) .5940 (c) .4060 (d) .3233 (e) .6767

9.15 (a) .1681 (b) .4061 (c) .7619 (d) No

9.17 (a) .1255 (b) .9964 (c) .6577 (d) 3

9.19 (a) .80 (b) .0819 (c) .0989

CHAPTER 10

10.1 (a) Action space consists of the two alternatives:

a_1: Offer home delivery service

a_2: Do not offer home delivery service

State space consists of the set of all possible proportions of families having at least one child under the age of 16:

$\{\pi \mid 0 \leq \pi \leq 1\}$

(b) $\{\pi \mid 0 \leq \pi \leq .25\}$ and $\{\pi \mid .25 < \pi \leq 1\}$

(c) H_0: $\pi \leq .25$

H_1: $\pi > .25$

(d) The test statistic is R, the number of households in the sample who have at least one child under the age of 16.

(e) Binomial distribution

(f) $\{r \mid r = 0, 1, 2, \ldots, 50\}$

(g) $P(R \geq c \mid n = 50, \pi = .25) \leq .05$

$F_b(c - 1 \mid n = 50, \pi = .25) \geq .95$

$c - 1 = 18$, so $c = 19$

Acceptance region: $\{r \mid r = 0, 1, 2, \ldots, 18\}$

Rejection region: $\{r \mid r = 19, 20, \ldots, 50\}$

(h) If $R \geq 19$, reject H_0 and accordingly offer service; otherwise accept H_0 and do not offer home delivery.

10.3 (a) Action space consists of the two alternatives:

a_1: Offer a new stock purchase plan

a_2: Do not offer a new stock purchase plan

State space consists of the set of all possible proportions of employees who would participate in the plan:

$\{\pi \mid 0 \leq \pi \leq 1\}$

(b) $\{\pi \mid 0 \leq \pi \leq 0.50\}$ and $\{\pi \mid .50 < \pi \leq 1\}$

(c) H_0: $\pi \leq .50$

H_1: $\pi > .50$

(d) R, the number of employees in the sample who would participate in the plan if it were offered.

(e) Binomial distribution

(f) $\{r \mid r = 0, 1, 2, \ldots, 100\}$

(g) $P(R \geq c \mid n = 100, \pi = .50) \leq .01$

$1 - F_b(c - 1 \mid n = 100 \ \pi = .50) \leq .01$

$F_b(c - 1 \mid n = 100, \pi = .50) \geq .99$

$c - 1 = 62, c = 63$

Acceptance region: $\{r \mid r = 0, 1, 2, \ldots, 62\}$

Rejection region: $\{r \mid r = 63, 64, \ldots, 100\}$

(h) If $R \geq 63$, reject H_0 and offer new plan; otherwise, accept H_0 and do not offer the plan.

10.5 H_0: $\pi \geq .25$
H_1: $\pi < .25$
$P(Y \leq c | n = 50, \pi = .25) \leq .10$
Thus, $c = 8$

If $R \leq 8$, reject null hypothesis and do not purchase radio time; otherwise, accept null hypothesis and purchase radio time.

10.7 (a) Action space consists of the two alternatives:
a_1: Allow process to continue
a_2: Shut down process for adjustment
State space consists of the set of all possible proportions of defective parts being produced by the automatic production process:
$\{\pi | 0 \leq \pi \leq 1\}$
(b) $\{\pi | 0 \leq \pi \leq .10\}$ and $\{\pi | .10 < \pi \leq 1\}$
(c) H_0: $\pi \leq .10$
H_1: $\pi > .10$

10.9 (a)

π	$\beta = P(R \leq 4 | n = 20, \pi)$
.20	.6296
.25	.4148
.50	.0059
.60	.0003

CHAPTER 11

11.1 (a) Action space consists of the two alternatives:
a_1: Accept the lot
a_2: Reject the lot
State space consists of the set of all possible numbers of defectives in the lot:
$\{D | D = 0, 1, 2, \ldots, 20\}$
(b) $H_0 = D \leq 3$
$H_1 = D > 3$
(c) Hypergeometric because you are sampling without replacement from a finite, dichotomous population.
(d) $P(R \leq c - 1 | N = 20, n = 5, D = 3) \geq .85$
From Table D, $F_h(0) = .3991$, $F_h(1) = .8596$
$c - 1 = 1$, so $c = 2$
If $R \geq 2$, reject H_0 and, accordingly, reject the lot.
If $R < 2$, accept H_0 and, accordingly, accept the lot.

11.3 (a) Action space consists of the two alternatives:
a_1: Accept the lot
a_2: Reject the lot
State space consists of the set of all possible numbers of defectives in the lot:
$\{D | D = 0, 1, 2, \ldots, 20\}$
(b) H_0: $D \leq 4$
H_1: $D > 4$
(c) Hypergeometric because you are sampling without replacement from a finite, dichotomous population.

(d) $P(R \leq c - 1 | N = 20, n = 8, D = 4) \geq .80$
From Table D, $F_h(1) = .4654$, $F_h(2) = .8469$
$c - 1 = 2$, so $c = 3$
If $R \geq 3$, reject H_0 and, accordingly, reject the lot; otherwise accept H_0 and, accordingly, accept the lot.

11.5 $P(R \leq c - 1 | N = 20, n = 5, D = 3) \geq .80$
From Table D, $F_h(0) = .3991$, $F_h(1) = .8596$
$c - 1 = 1$, so $c = 2$
If $R \geq 2$, reject H_0 and, accordingly, reject the lot; otherwise, accept H_0 and, accordingly, accept the lot. Thus, the decision rule remains the same as that in Problem 11.1

11.7 $P(R \leq c - 1 | N = 20, n = 6, D = 5) \geq .80$
From Table D, $F_h(1) = .5165$, $F_h(2) = .8687$
$c - 1 = 2$, so $c = 3$
If $R \geq 3$, reject H_0 and, accordingly, reject the lot; otherwise, accept H_0 and, accordingly, accept the lot.

11.9 $F_b(c - 1 | n = 75, \pi = .60) \geq .95$
$c - 1 = 52$, so $c = 53$
If $R \geq 53$, reject H_0 and adopt the new process; otherwise, accept H_0 and don't adopt the new process.

11.11 (a) $H_0: \pi \geq .10$
$H_1: \pi < .10$
$F_b(c | n = 75, \pi = .1) \leq .15$
From Table F, $F_b(4) = .1189$, $F_b(5) = .2271$ so $c = 4$
If $R \leq 4$, reject H_0 and do not accept the offer; otherwise, accept H_0 and accept the offer.
(b) $1 - F_b(4 | n = 75, \pi = .05) = 1 - .6789 = .3211$
(c) $F_b(4 | n = 75, \pi = .20) = .0003$

11.13 (a) Action space consists of the two alternatives:
a_1: Purchase spot commercial time
a_2: Don't purchase spot commercial time
State space consists of the set of all possible proportions of households who regularly listen to the show:
$\{\pi | 0 \leq \pi \leq 1\}$
(b) $H_0: \pi \geq .25$
$H_1: \pi < .25$
(c) Binomial because you are sampling from an effectively infinite, dichotomous population.
(d) $F_b(c | n = 100, \pi = .25) \leq .10$
$c = 19$
If $R \leq 19$, reject H_0 and don't purchase spot commercial time; otherwise, accept H_0 and purchase spot commercial time.

11.15 $H_0: \lambda \leq .05$
$H_1: \lambda > .05$
$F_p(3 | \lambda t = 1.5) = .9344$
$c - 1 = 3$, so $c = 4$
Reject H_0 if total errors are equal to or greater than 4.
(a) Not acceptable
(b) 3

11.17

λ	λt	$\beta \lambda = F_p \ (R \le 15 \vert \lambda)$
6.0	10	.9513
7.2	12	.8444
8.4	14	.6694
9.6	16	.4667
10.8	18	.2867
12.0	20	.1565

11.19 (a) Action space consists of the two alternatives:

a_1: Use the new process

a_2: No change in the process

State space consists of the set of all possible values of the defect rate:

$\{\lambda \vert 0 \le \lambda < \infty\}$

(b) H_0: $\lambda \ge .20$

H_1: $\lambda < .20$

(c) $F_p \ (R \le c \vert \lambda = .20, \ t = 50) \le .10$

$c = 5$

If $R \le 5$, reject H_0 and use the new process; otherwise accept H_0 and don't change the process.

CHAPTER 12

12.1 (a) $E(X) = 3.40$; $V(X) = 1.84$

(b) $E(\overline{X}) = 3.40$; $V(\overline{X}) = .092$

12.3 (a)

$$f(\overline{x}) = \begin{cases} .24 & \text{if } \overline{x} = 1 \\ .32 & \text{if } \overline{x} = 1.5 \\ .29 & \text{if } \overline{x} = 2 \\ .13 & \text{if } \overline{x} = 2.5 \\ .03 & \text{if } \overline{x} = 3 \end{cases}$$

(b) $E(\overline{X}) = 1.7$; $V(\overline{X}) = .31$

12.5 (a) $E(X) = 2.2$; $V(X) = .56$

(c) $E(\overline{X}) = 2.2$; $V(\overline{X}) = .1867$

12.7 (a) .2743   (b) .0197   (c) .2547

(d) .4133   (e) .0388   (f) .95

12.9 (a) .2877   (b) .0749

12.11 .5631

12.13 .8399

12.15 20.41%

12.17 (a) 16.2   (b) 23.8

12.19 (a) .1151   (b) .0548   (c) .0082

(d) .0007

12.21 (a) .0668   (b) .0122   (c) .9210

12.23 .2743

CHAPTER 13

13.1 (a) H_0: $\mu \leq 10.6$ (b) H_0: $\mu \geq 200$
           H_1: $\mu > 10.6$ H_1: $\mu < 200$

      (c) H_0: $\mu \leq 100$ (d) H_0: $\mu = 14.2$
           H_1: $\mu > 100$ H_1: $\mu \neq 14.2$

13.3 (a)

μ	α_μ
13.6	.1000
13.4	.0373
13.2	.0113
13.0	.0027

      (b)

μ	β_μ
14.0	.6110
14.4	.2364
14.8	.0427
15.2	.0030
15.6	.0001

13.5 (a) Action space consists of the two alternatives:
        a_1: Take action
        a_2: Don't take action
      State space consists of the set of all possible values of the process mean active ingredient:
        $\{\mu \mid 0 \leq \mu < \infty\}$

      (b) H_0: $\mu \geq 500$
          H_1: $\mu < 500$

      (d) $c = 500 - 1.645(12/\sqrt{100}) = 498.026$
         Acceptance region: $\{\bar{x} \mid \bar{x} > 498.026\}$
         Rejection region: $\{\bar{x} \mid \bar{x} \leq 498.026\}$

      (e) If $\bar{X} \leq 498.026$, reject H_0 and accordingly take action; otherwise, accept H_0 and do not take action.

13.7 (a) $\alpha_{500 \cdot 6} = .0160$ (b) $\beta_{498 \cdot 2} = .5577$
      (c) $\beta_{497 \cdot 6} = .3613$ (d) $1 - \beta_{497 \cdot 6} = .6387$

13.9

μ	β_μ
11.5	.0012
11.7	.1492
11.9	.8300
12.1	.8300
12.3	.1492
12.5	.0012

13.11 If $\bar{X} \leq 39.075$, reject H_0 and take action; otherwise, accept H_0 and do not take action.

13.13 (a) Action space consists of the two alternatives:
        a_1: Reduce tax rate
        a_2: Do not reduce tax rate
      State space consists of all possible values of mean home market value in the country:
        $\{\mu \mid 0 \leq \mu < \infty\}$

      (b) H_0: $\mu \leq 55,000$
          H_1: $\mu > 55,000$

(c)   The sampling distribution of $\overline{X}$ is approximately normal with $E(\overline{X}) = 55,000$ and $\sigma_{\overline{x}} = 600$.

(d)   If $\overline{X} > 56,395.60$, reject H_0 and reduce tax rate; otherwise, accept H_0 and do not reduce tax rate.

13.15 (a) H_0: $\mu \geq 30$
$\qquad\qquad$ H_1: $\mu < 30$

(b)   The executive committee is willing to take no more than a 5% risk of accepting the proposal if, in fact, $\mu \geq 30$.

(c)   The sampling distribution of $\overline{X}$ is approximately normal with $E(\overline{X}) = 30$ and $\sigma_{\overline{x}} = .20$.

(d)   If $\overline{X} \leq 29.671$, reject H_0 and accept the proposal; otherwise, accept H_0 and do not accept the proposal.

(e)   Reject the offer.

13.17 (a) $\alpha_{6.0} = .05$

(b) $\beta_{5.6} = .36$

(c) $\beta_{5.8} = .74$

(d) $1 - \beta_{5.7} = 1 - .56 = .44$

13.19 (a)   Action space consists of the two alternatives:
$\qquad\qquad$ a_1: Continue the training program
$\qquad\qquad$ a_2: Drop the training program

(b) H_0: $\delta \leq 2,000$
$\qquad\qquad$ H_1: $\delta > 2,000$

(c)   If $D \geq 2567.50$, reject H_0 and continue the training program; otherwise, accept H_0 and drop the program.

(d)   Reject H_0 and continue the program.

CHAPTER 14

14.1 (a) .1746 $\qquad$ (b) .2174 $\qquad$ (c) .1230
$\qquad$ (d) .2669 $\qquad$ (e) .8092 $\qquad$ (f) .8159

14.3 (a)   Hypergeometric
(b)   If $R \geq 33$ reject H_0 and adopt the book; otherwise accept H_0 and don't adopt the book.

14.5 $\quad$ If $R \geq 4$ reject H_0 and reject the lot; otherwise accept H_0 and accept the lot.

14.7 $\quad$ If $R \geq 4$ reject H_0 and reject the lot; otherwise accept H_0 and accept the lot.

14.9 (a) .0030 $\qquad$ (b) .2384 $\qquad$ (c) .0013
$\qquad$ (d) .0361 $\qquad$ (e) .9881 $\qquad$ (f) .7908

14.11 (a) .0218 $\qquad$ (b) .0884 $\qquad$ (c) .0108 $\qquad$ (d) .7829

14.13 $\quad$ If 4 or fewer persons in the sample have undesirable side effects, reject H_0 and announce the new vaccine; otherwise accept H_0 and don't announce the vaccine.

14.15 (a) .0558 $\qquad$ (b) .0237 $\qquad$ (c) .0430
$\qquad$ (d) .7123 $\qquad$ (e) .2327

14.17 .0409

14.19 (a) H_0: $\pi \leq .20$
$\qquad\qquad$ H_1: $\pi > .20$

(b) If $R \geq 28$ reject H_0 and buy the time; otherwise accept H_0 and don't buy the time.

(c) Same as (b)

14.21 If $\overline{X} \geq 19.9108$ reject H_0 and purchase inventory; otherwise accept H_0 and don't purchase inventory.

14.23 If $\overline{X} \geq 14.8818$ reject H_0 and install a second crib; otherwise accept H_0 and don't install a second crib.

CHAPTER 15

15.1 (1902, 2098)

15.3 (a) .0062   (b) .0099   (c) .0456

15.5 (a) \$42,096   (b) (\$37,909.20, \$46,282.20)

15.7 (a) (9.541, 14.523)   (b) (\$34,623, \$44,569)

15.9 (a) (157.8618, 162.1328)
(b) Same as (a)
(c) (157.66, 162.34)
(d) (157.862, 162.138)

15.11 (13.952, 55.218)

15.13 (.17368, .22632)

15.15 241

15.17 2,017

CHAPTER 16

16.1 Reject H_0 if $|t| \geq 2.131$; $t = -3.055$; therefore reject H_0.

16.3 (a) $H_0: \mu \geq 7$ vs. $H_1: \mu < 7$
(b) The distribution of the TRIs of the population of all filters produced by this process will be essentially normal.
(c) Student's t
(d) Reject H_0 if $t \leq -2.306$.
(e) $t = -1.488$; accept H_0

16.5 Reject H_0 if $x^2 \geq 22.31$; $x^2 = 20.625$; accept H_0.

16.7 Reject H_0 if $t \geq 3.365$; $t = 4.49$; reject H_0.

16.9 Reject H_0 if $F \leq .211$ or if $F \geq 3.333$; $F = .25$; accept H_0.

16.11 Reject H_0 if $x^2 \leq 1.753$; $x^2 = 12.67$; accept H_0.

16.13 Reject H_0 if $t \geq 1.753$; $t = 3.87$; reject H_0 and buy from Iris.

16.15 Reject H_0 if $t \geq 1.345$; $t = -.591$; accept H_0; evidence is insufficient to justify replacement.

16.17 (a)

Source	SS	DF	MS	F
Between	360	3	120	6.00
Within	800	40	20	

(b)   Reject H_0 if $F \geq 2.84$; reject H_0 and conclude that not all processes are the same with respect to mean tensile strength.

16.19

Source	SS	DF	MS	F
Between	45.6	2	22.8	.36
Within	760.0	12	63.3	
Total	805.6	14		

Reject H_0 if $F \geq 6.93$. Accept H_0; data are insufficient to conclude that any differences exist.

16.21 (a) $t = 12.72$; reject H_0

(b) $z = -6.325$; reject H_0

(c) $z = -2.75$; reject H_0

(d) $z = -2.44$; reject H_0

16.23 $z = 2.132$; reject H_0

16.25 $z = -8.87$; reject H_0

CHAPTER 17

17.1 (a)   1,200

(b) $\rho^2 = .694$

(c)   69.4% of total variance of GRE scores is explained by the linear relationship with GMAT scores.

(d) $\rho = .833$

17.3 (a)   62.01 thousands of Ozbills

(b)   81.59 thousands of Ozbills

(c)   The expected error will be smaller using the Wizard's estimate, since he is using the actual population equation.

17.5 $\overline{y}|x = .757 + .035x$

17.7 (b) $\overline{y}|x = .561 + 1.012x$

(c)   2.9898 hundreds of thousands

17.9 (a)   SSR = 1609.98

(b)   SSE = 7337.76

(c)   SST = 8947.73

(d) $r^2 = .180$

(e) $r = .424$

17.11 (a)   36.8%

(b) $r = .50$

(c)   Reject H_0 if $|t| \geq 2.021$; $t = 3.65$; therefore, reject H_0.

17.13 (a)   (3.24, 4.96) in hundreds of thousands

(b)   (.263, 7.937) in hundreds of thousands

17.15   Reject H_0 if $t \geq 1.860$; $t = .028$; therefore, accept H_0.

17.17

Source	SS	DF	MS	F
Regression	60.9962	1	60.9962	37.59
Error	12.9798	8	1.6225	
Total	73.9760	9		

Reject H_0 if $F \geq 5.32$; $F = 37.59$; therefore reject H_0 and conclude that a relationship exists.

17.19 (.66, .98)

17.21 Reject H_0 if $Z \geq 1.645$; $z = .817$; therefore evidence is not sufficient.

17.23 Reject H_0 if $Z \leq -1.645$; $z = -2.212$; therefore reject H_0.

17.25 Reject H_0 if $|Z| \geq 1.645$; $z = 1.45$; therefore accept H_0.

17.27 (a) $\bar{y}|x = 51.6521 + .4815x$

(b) 75.7271

(c) Yes, since obtained F of 14.9479 exceeds critical F of 4.08.

(d) 27.2%

CHAPTER 18

18.1 (a) $\bar{y}|x = -3688.0482 + 1.4193x_1 - 0.1461x_2 + 8483.8731x_3$

(b) 7044.298 tons

(c) X_1 and X_2

18.3 (a) 107.958

(b) 101.912

18.5 (a) $\bar{y}|x = 8.0804 - 0.9777x_1 + 0.0104x_2 + 0.4367x_3 - 0.0182x_4$

(b) 11.8714

18.7 (a) $\bar{y}|x = -2.66863 + 0.24117x_1 + 0.09430x_2 - 0.12223x_3 + 0.29044x_4$

(b) 40.978% of the variation in salaries is explained by the relationship with the set of independent variables.

(c) Since obtained F of 3.4714 exceeds the critical F of 2.87, conclude that a relationship exists.

(d) $\hat{y} = 14.44648$

18.9 (a) $r^2 = .9217$; thus 92.17% of the variation in average daily output is explained by the linear relationship with score on Dixie Dexterity Test.

(b) Reject H_0 if $|t| \geq 2.101$; $t = 14.56$; therefore, a significant relationship exists.

(c) 234.185

18.13 See Section 18.4.1

CHAPTER 19

19.1 .67

19.3 Reject H_0 if $\chi^2 \geq 6.63$; $\chi^2 = .985$; accept H_0.

19.5 Reject H_0 if $\chi^2 \geq 7.78$; $\chi^2 = 13.43$; yes, reject H_0.

19.7 Reject H_0 if $\chi^2 \geq 3.84$; $\chi^2 = 16.67$; reject H_0.

19.9 Reject H_0 if $\chi^2 \geq 9.49$; $\chi^2 = 2.131$; accept H_0.

19.11 (a) Reject H_0 if $\chi^2 \geq 9.21$; $\chi^2 = 3.21$; accept H_0.
(b) Expected frequency for "at least \$30" would be too small; combine this category with "less than \$30."

19.13 Reject H_0 if $\chi^2 \geq 11.14$; $\chi^2 = 193.36$; reject H_0.

19.15 Reject H_0 if $\chi^2 \geq 9.49$; $\chi^2 = 46.25$; reject H_0.

19.17 Reject H_0 if $D \geq .432$; $D = .319$; accept H_0.

19.19 Reject H_0 if $D \geq .304$; $D = .327$; reject H_0.

19.21 Reject H_0 if $D \geq .20$; $D = .1057$; accept H_0.

CHAPTER 20

20.1 Reject H_0 if $R \leq 2$; $R = 3$; accept H_0.

20.3 (a) Reject H_0 if $R \leq 2$; $R = 3$; accept H_0.
(b) Reject H_0 if $W \leq 21$; $W = 12.5$; reject H_0.
(c) Disagree; signed-ranks test is more powerful if symmetry assumption is warranted.

20.5 Reject H_0 if $T \leq 115$; $T = 140.5$; accept H_0.

20.7 Reject H_0 if $T \leq 60$; $T = 48.5$; reject H_0.

20.9 Reject H_0 if $W \leq 14$; $W = 10.5$; reject H_0.

20.11 Reject H_0 if $W \leq 16$; $W = 13$; reject H_0.

CHAPTER 21

21.1 (a) a_2 (b) a_1 (c) a_3 (d) a_3

21.3 (a) No (b) Yes (c) No (d) Build

21.5 (a)

	a_1	a_2	a_3	a_4
θ_1	2	-3	-8	-13
θ_2	2	4	-1	-6
θ_3	2	4	6	1
θ_4	2	4	6	8

(b) 2 (c) 3 (d) 2 (e) 3

21.7 (a)

	a_1	a_2
θ_1	100	-10
θ_2	-20	90

(b) Snow shoes

(c)

	a_1	a_2
θ_1	0	110
θ_2	110	0

(d) Snow shoes

(e) Yes

21.9 (a) 25 (b) 30 (c) 30 (d) 28 or 29

  (e) 27 (f) 27 (g) 27 (h) 29

  (i) 28 (j) 28

21.11 .60

21.13 (a) a_1 (b) $P(\theta_1) = .2, P(\theta_2) = .8$ (c) a_1 (d) $78

  (e)

	a_1	a_2
θ_1	70	90
θ_2	80	30

21.15 (a) $14 (b) $2

  (c)

	a_5	a_6	a_7	a_8
θ_1	0	3	6	9
θ_2	2	0	3	6
θ_3	4	2	0	3
θ_4	6	4	2	0
EOL	4	2.5	2	3

  STOCK 7

  (d) Always the same

21.17 (a) $4.20 (b) $.65

21.19 27

21.21 24

21.23 892

21.25 (a) 220 (b) 20

21.27 1,026

21.29 (a) .125 (b) 10:00 A.M.

CHAPTER 22

22.1 (b) a_3

22.3 (b) 21 copies

22.5 (b) Stock A

22.9 (b) $P(\theta_1 | o_1) = .75; P(\theta_2 | o_1) = .25; P(\theta_1 | o_2) = .08; P(\theta_2 | o_2) = .92$

  (c) $613.60

22.11 (b) $9,875

22.13 (b) Conduct survey; EMV = $68,000

22.15 (b) Do not purchase credit rating; EMV = $224

22.17 (a) Select tunnel project

  (b) $1.782 millions

CHAPTER 23

23.1 (b) $u($80,000) = .60$ (c) Risk taker

23.3 (a) .809 (b) Yes

23.5 (a) Linear   (b) Neutral

23.7 (a) $6,574   (b) $7,870

(c) Not equal; $6,574

23.9 (a) EMV(a_1) = $1,175; EMV($a_2$) = $1,825; a_2; no, since his preference function is not linear.

(b) EU(a_1) = 5; EU(a_2) = −12.5; choose a_1.

(c) CE(a_1) = $25; CE($a_2$) = −$12.50; choose a_1.

(d) Yes, this is general.

(e) Risk averse

23.11 (a) a_2 (b) a_2

23.13 (a) iii   (b) iii   (c) ii

23.15 (a) .60   (b) $196

Index

Acceptance region, 187, 196
Acceptance sampling, 200-205
Ackoff, R., 302
Action space, 183, 195
Aggregate, 37
Alpha error (*see* Type I error)
Alternative courses of action, 2, 183, 195
Alternative hypothesis, 184, 195
Analysis of variance:
  in multiple regression analysis, 391-93
  in simple regression analysis, 374-75
  test for equality of several means,
    338-44
Anderson, T. W., 278
ANOVA (*see* Analysis of variance)
Approximations:
  binomial approximation to
    hypergeometric, 275-78
  normal approximation to binomial,
    280-89
  normal approximation to discrete
    sampling distribution of the mean,
    289-95
  Poisson approximation to binomial,
    278-80
Arithmetic mean (*see* Mean)
Array, 33
Attribute, 12
Averages (*see also* Expected value, Mean,
    Median, Mode):
  of a finite population, 35-39
  of a probability function, 123-31
  of a sample, 151

Bartlett's test for homogeneity, 339
Bayes, Thomas, 85
Bayes' theorem, 84-87, 482
Berger, Paul, 504
Bernoulli, Jacques, 6, 66, 167
Bernoulli process, 167-68, 173
Beta error (*see* Type II error)
Bias in estimation, 300
Binomial coefficients:
  defined, 170
  table, 521
Binomial distribution, 167-73:
  approximated by normal (*see*
    Approximations)
  approximated by Poisson (*see*
    Approximations)
  as approximation to hypergeometric (*see*
    Approximations)
  cumulative mass function, 170-71
  hypothesis testing with, 206-11
  mass function, 168-70
  mean of, 172-73
  shape, effect of parameters on, 281-82
  table, cumulative terms, 545-61
  table, individual terms, 530-44
  tables, use of, 171-72
  variance of, 172-73
Bivariate normal distribution, 357
Bivariate population, 357
Boundaries:
  of a class, 23
  of numbers, 15
Bradley, James V., 239

Brown, **Rex** 487
Brunk, H. D., 275

Calculus (*see* Integral calculus)
Census, 5
Central limit theorem, 239-41
Central tendency (*see* Averages)
Centroid, 38
Certainty (*see* Decision conditions)
Certainty equivalent, 502
Chance experiment (*see* Random process)
Chebyshev's inequality, 136-38
Chernoff, H., 301
Chi-square:
  test concerning a variance, 325-26
  test of goodness of fit to a normal
    distribution with parameters
    estimated, 420-22
  test of goodness of fit to a normal
    distribution with parameters specified,
    411-20
  test of goodness of fit to Poisson
    distribution with parameter
    estimated, 416-18
  test of goodness of fit to Poisson
    distribution with parameter specified,
    414-16
  test of homogeneity, 411-13
  test of independence, 407-11
  used to obtain confidence interval for a
    variance, 313-14
Chi-square distribution:
  described, 312-13
  table, 576-77
Chunk sampling, 143
Class, 17:
  boundaries of, 23
  interval, 21-22
  limits, 22
  midpoint, 25
  modal, 35
Cluster sampling, 148
Cochran's test for homogeneity, 339
Coefficient of correlation (*see* Correlation
  coefficient)
Coefficient of determination, 360, 365-67,
  387
COL (Conditional opportunity loss), 450
Collectively exhaustive events, 72
Combinations:
  defined, 60
  related to permutations, 61
Complementary event, 70
Complementary set, 68
Compound event, 69

Conditional:
  distribution, 357-58
  opportunity loss (*see* Opportunity loss)
  payoff table (*see* Payoff table)
  probability, 76-79, 84-86
Confidence interval:
  for a conditional mean, 368-69
  for an individual prediction, 370
  for a mean, 304-12
  for a proportion, 314-15
  for a simple correlation coefficient,
    370-72
  for a variance, 312-14
  interpretation of, 306-308
Conflict (*see* Decision conditions)
Contingency table, 407
Continuous:
  probability function (*see* Cumulative
    density function, Probability density
    function)
  random variable, 100, 109-14
  scale, 15
  variable, 15
Convenience sampling, 143
Corrrelation analysis:
  multiple, 387, 392-93, 394-95
  simple, 356, 365-68, 370-72, 376-79
Correlation coefficient:
  multiple, 387-92
  simple, 360, 367, 370-72, 376-78
Correlation matrix, 389
Counting, 55-62:
  combinations (*see* Combinations)
  fundamental principle of, 56
  permutations (*see* Permutations)
Cowden, D. J., 301
Criteria for decision making (*see* Decision
  criteria)
Critical value, 186
Cumulative density function, 110-14
Cumulative frequency distribution, 20, 32
Cumulative mass function, 106-109
Cumulative relative frequencies, 20, 32

Data:
  defined, 4
  primary, 9-10
  secondary, 9
  sources of, 9-10
Decision analysis:
  based on prior information, 477-79
  criteria for (*see* Decision criteria)
  cycle, 485-87
  defined, 444
  practical applications of, 487-90

Measures:
of central tendency (*see* Expected values, Mean, Median, Mode)
of variability (*see* Variability)
Median:
of continuous probability distribution, 125
of discrete probability distribution, 124-25
of finite population, 35
of a sample, 152
tests of hypotheses concerning (*see* Hypothesis testing)
Midpoint, 25
Minimax regret criterion, 453-54
Modal class, 35
Mode:
of a population, 35
of a probability distribution, 123-24
Model construction, 394-97
Morgenstern, O., 501
Moses, L. E., 301
Multicollinearity, 394-95
Multiple correlation (*see* Correlation analysis)
Multiple regression (*see* Regression analysis)
Mutually exclusive events:
compared to independent events, 83
definition, 71
unions of, 71, 79-80

Neter, J., 397
Newman, J. W., 488
Newman, R., 487
Node, 477
Nominal scale of measurement, 13
Nonparameteric statistics, 405-41
Normal distribution:
as approximation to binomial (*see* Approximations)
as approximation to discrete sampling distribution of the mean (*see* Approximations)
bivariate, 357
characteristics of, 228-30
fractiles of, 234
ogive, 230
standard, 230-33
table, 573-74
tests concerning, 418-26
use of tables, 230-34
Normal equations, 363
Null hypothesis, 184, 195
Numbers:
approximate, 15, 23

boundaries of, 15, 23
exact, 15
significant digits in, 15

Observation, 10
Odds, 54-55
Ogive, 25, 230
Operating characteristic curve, 192
Opportunity loss:
conditional, 450
expected (*see* EOL)
Ordinal scale of measurement, 13
Owen, D. B., 165, 275

Paired observations tests, 334-38, 438-41
Parameter:
compared to statistic, 149-53
of a population, 3, 31
space, 183
Partial regression coefficient, 387
Partition, 72-73, 184, 187, 195
Pascal, Blaise, 6, 66
Payoff table, 446
Percentiles, 34
Permutations, 57-59:
defined, 57
involving indistinguishable objects, 58
of n distinguishable objects, 57
of r objects selected from n objects, 59
related to combinations, 61
Pessimism-optimism coefficient, 452
Point estimation, 299-302:
of a coefficient of determination, 365-67
of a mean, 299-302
of a multiple correlation coefficient, 392-93
of a multiple regression equation, 388-91
of a proportion, 303-304
of a simple correlation coefficient, 367
of a simple regression equation, 361-65
of a standard deviation, 302-303
of a variance, 302-303
Point estimator:
defined, 299
properties of, 300-302
Poisson, S. D., 174
Poisson distribution, 173-78:
as approximation to binomial (*see* Approximations)
cumulative mass function, 177
hypothesis testing with, 211-14
mass function, 175-77
mean of, 178
table, cumulative terms, 568-72
table, individual terms, 562-67